D0908837

SISTERS IN THE SKY
VOLUME I —THE WAFS

SISTERS IN THE SKY

VOLUME I—THE WAFS

ADELA RIEK SCHARR

FOREWORD BY
SENATOR BARRY GOLDWATER

THE PATRICE PRESS
ST. LOUIS, MISSOURI

THE PATRICE PRESS
ST. LOUIS, MISSOURI

Second Printing, May 1987

**Library of Congress
Cataloging In Publication Data**

Scharr, Adela Riek, 1907-
    Sisters in the sky.
    Contents: v. 1. The WAFS.
    1. Scharr, Adela Riek, 1907-   . 2. World War,
1939-1945 — Aerial operations, American.
3. World War, 1939-1945 — Personal narratives,
American. 4. Women Airforce Service Pilots (U.S.)
— Biography. 5. Women air pilots — United States
— Biography. I. Title.
D790.S334A3 1986   940.54'4973   86-25321
ISBN 0-935284-46-X (v.1)

Printed in the United States of America

Published by
The Patrice Press
1701 South Eighth Street
St. Louis, Missouri 63104

DEDICATION

I DEDICATE BOTH VOLUMES OF *Sisters in the Sky* to my late husband, Harold Nathan Scharr. Without his understanding and cooperation the stories of the WAFS and the WASP could never have been written so accurately.

In my first letter to Harold after I arrived at NCAAB, I asked him to save every one of them, which he did faithfully. I wrote at least every other day, and sometimes on a mission, postcards besides. I was in the Ferrying Division of Air Transport Command, AAF, from the beginning to the end of utilization of women pilots by a military service in World War II and related to Harold my experiences and all that I observed.

As a reservist, Harold served his country in naval aviation from 1930 to 1946. Unselfishly, he placed the nation's need for military pilots and my duty to serve in that capacity as more important than his own wishes. He was the most mature person I have ever known.

CONTENTS

FOREWORD

IT BECAME MY PLEASURE not only to check some of these women out in high powered fighter aircraft, such as the P-47, but to have added to that pleasure that of flying with them.

I remember one delivery we made of P-47s from Farmingdale, Long Island, to Oakland, California, and the woman whose wing I flew asked if she could fly under the hood the entire distance. She did just that and I acted as a ground controller, flying on her wing and talking to her, simulating the way the controller on the ground would act. At about fifty feet above the ground, I would tell her to come out and make a normal landing, which she did. I think that was a very remarkable thing for a woman to do — fly clear across the United States, with five different stops for fuel and not see where she was going all the way.

These women also flew B-17s, B-24s, and P-38s. In fact, eventually they flew every aircraft we had in the inventory or those we were asked to deliver to different places in the United States and overseas. They did a truly remarkable job. Not only did they keep combat pilots away from the necessity of ferrying, but they showed men they were just as capable behind the stick and throttle as the men are. I do not know a man in the outfit who did not leave it with a great and deep respect for women pilots.

We graduate them today from our flying schools. They fly in the regular Air Force. The Women Auxiliary Ferrying Squadron in World War II was the start of women really becoming active in our Air Force.

— Barry Goldwater
Chairman, Committee on Armed Services
United States Senate

ACKNOWLEDGEMENTS

I AM GRATEFUL to Major General Barry Goldwater, USAFR, the United States Senator from Arizona, for the Foreword to *Sisters in the Sky*. He knew first hand who the WAFS were, for he, too was a ferry pilot stationed at NCAAB, Wilmington, Delaware.

Dr. Dora Dougherty Strother steered me to authentic historical details by lending me her copy of Lettice Curtis's book, *The Forgotten Pilots*. This treasure of information about the British RAF's Air Transport Auxiliary (ATA) backs its factual account with statistics in the appendixes which differ greatly at times with Jacqueline Cochran's, *The Stars at Noon,* her version of her life in the ATA. Without dates from beginning to end, Cochran's book has little value as a historical document, but it does serve to give insight about the author's personality.

I needed Top Secret clearance to research the papers pertaining to the WAFS/WASP twice in the 1950s, while on active reserve duty at Air University, Montgomery, Alabama. (I saw no need for this secrecy.) The material was not organized and when I questioned an employee, she implied that parts were missing because the files had been subjected to tampering.

The inaccurate document that ensued was later rectified by Captain Walter J. Marx, the FERD historical officer, who wrote 175 pages on *Women Pilots in the Air Transport Command.* Meticulously, his report aims at being fair to everyone. His footnotes are invaluable guides to the authentic documents and where to find them. Again I thank Dora Strother for making this material available to me.

I coordinated with my personal correspondence all such necessary documentation as my log books, military bulletins, orders, flight missions, change of station, attendance at schools, technical orders, the set of continental United States aeronautical charts, instrument flight and radio range data, the Pilot's Information File, and other correspondence with WAFS, friends, and persons I had met in the service.

It pleases me that the individual WAFs named with their photographs cooperated to add greatly to the interest in this story. Many assisted by either verifying the information I already had or by adding further details. At times they related other incidents I had not witnessed nor heard of before. Especially generous in this regard were Betty Gillies, Teresa James, Gertrude Meserve Tubbs, and Katherine Rawls Thompson.

A clever logo introducing each chapter was the contribution of Laura Franzwa. Laura Sellinger's proofreading was of genius quality. I also wish to thank Vivian Gilbert, Marjorie Keklikian, and editor Dr. Betty Burnett for their critical assistance. Last, but not least, I appreciate the interest and guidance given to me by the publisher, Gregory M. Franzwa, of The Patrice Press.

SISTERS IN THE SKY
VOLUME I —THE WAFS

INTRODUCTION

AMERICA'S PRESENT-DAY female military pilots were not the first. They are breaking new ground, it is true, but we, the WAFS (Women's Auxiliary Ferrying Squadron) were the first women who flew aircraft on military missions as part of a United States military organization. Our small band never numbered more than twenty-seven, and it took almost four months to attain that number.

Later, as other women were trained to serve as military pilots in the WASP (Women's Airforce Service Pilots), their larger organization swallowed us, and we seemed to disappear. This book will keep us from disappearing altogether. We were pioneers and our story deserves to be remembered.

On Labor Day 1942, the Air Transport Command of the United States Army Air Corps asked eighty-nine experienced women pilots to volunteer for ferrying duty. Secretary of War Henry L. Stimson made the invitation public on September 10. I was one of the handful who responded at once.

Even at that time American flying women were not unique. Russian women were reported as military pilots. And the British Royal Air Force (RAF) employed women pilots from November 1939 until war's end in 1945.

The story of British women pilots (and the American women who joined them) has been documented by Lettice Curtis in her remarkable book, *The Forgotten Pilots.* Curtis showed in her fact-crammed study that the British government was not as male chauvinistic as the United States Congress. It forgot *all* its volunteer pilots, both male and female. In this country, only we women pilots were discriminated against by being overlooked.

With the declaration of war on September 3, 1939, civilian flying in Great Britain ceased. The RAF carried on its own military duties until November, when it found it needed pilots to ferry large planes to air bases. It had begun to take in male civilian pilots for ferrying, but soon realized that it needed many more.

At the same time, Pauline Gower, an experienced pilot of excellent social standing, appealed to the Director-General of Civil Aviation (DGCA) to be allowed to help. The DGCA told her to find eight of the best women pilot/flight instructors from the old civilian flying clubs. She was chosen to lead them. She wanted equal pay with men doing the same work, but "the Treasury invariably insisted on a percentage reduction in the basic salaries paid to women for the same jobs as men." Women pilots were to get eighty pounds less per annum than men in a similar grade — in American dollars, about $800 less per year.

When Gower was hired in December 1939, the British press was highly indignant and readers wrote in saying that women, hungry for publicity, were taking on men's jobs using the war as an excuse. Meanwhile, with or without publicity, the women who passed the RAF flight tests had to agree to the terms laid out for them. Women could not eat with the men. They had to arrange for all their own accommodations without subsidy or assistance from the RAF's Air Transport Auxiliary (ATA). Female patriotism paid its price.

In May 1940, the war in Europe turned hot. Norway fell to the Germans. Then came the Nazi invasion of the low countries, Belgium and Holland. In France, German troops and tanks bypassed the Maginot Line and closed in on Paris. It was a terrifying time. The heartstopping evacuation at Dunkirk and the Battle of Britain, when German bombers darkened English skies, showed the desperate condition of the Allies.

Great Britain was unable to manufacture enough airplanes to continue to fight. The attrition rates of both airplanes in combat and pilots who manned them was very high. At that time ten women were already hopping Tiger Moths about the island, from factories to flight schools. Their number increased to twenty-eight on July 10.

Lord Beaverbrook, Minister of Aircraft Production, used his considerable influence to initiate the purchase of American airplanes. In this way, he became acquainted with Floyd Odlum, the personal financial advisor to President Franklin D. Roosevelt. Odlum's second wife was a hairdresser whom he had helped establish a cosmetics firm. She flew airplanes, and by winning a Bendix transcontinental air race several years earlier, had won much publicity. Her name was Jacqueline Cochran.

Some critics of President Roosevelt thought that he was itching to join the conflict on the side of the British; others thought he was holding the country back from entering the war with Hitler because it was not politically expedient. Roosevelt devised a way to help the British without the United States losing its neutrality in the eyes of international law. He instituted a Lend-Lease program, offering American materiel without requiring payment. He said it was like lending your neighbor your garden hose when his house was on fire.

And Britain's homes were burning indeed, as Nazi incendiary bombs shrilled from the sky. A worried Lord Beaverbrook, ill, asthmatic, afraid to displease the American government, emphatically hoped that the United States would turn over to him at least 3,000 airplanes per month instead of the 300 that moved monthly via Canada. Both the trickle of Canadian planes and the fighter aircraft from the United States were pickled to protect them from salt spray and placed on convoyed merchant vessels with the hope that they would reach a British port. German submarines were a menace to that hope.

Treacherous weather over the North Atlantic was also a menace to aviation, but the Royal Canadian Air Force (RCAF) flew anyway. Bombers and transports made frequent trips via Gander (in Newfoundland), Greenland, and Iceland to Scotland.

Robert M. Love, president of Boston's Intercity Airlines, bid for and won a contract to fly American-made airplanes to the Canadian border. His wife, like he, was an experienced pilot. Nancy Harkness Love had begun flying at the age of sixteen. She had started selling airplanes in Boston in the mid-thirties and had married Love, a business competitor.

In relating her 1940 ferrying experiences, Nancy Love said, "I landed at an airport right at the boundary of the United States. I taxied the plane to the border, cut the switch, and climbed out. Then some Canadians pulled and shoved the airplane across the border. I turned around and brought back another one." She was America's first, unofficial woman ferry pilot moving military airplanes.

Wanting to be more helpful, Love wrote to Lt. Col. Robert Olds,

Nancy Harkness Love, head of the WAFS.

head of the Plans Division of the Office of Chief, Army Air Corps, in May 1940. (The AAC was then commanded by General Henry H. "Hap" Arnold.) She informed Colonel Olds that she knew of forty-nine qualified women pilots who could ferry airplanes. And at least fifteen more might be eligible for service.

The idea appealed to Colonel Olds. Love was offering an array of eligible ferry pilots and there was a shortage. The male pilots qualified for such work had already found employment as test pilots with airplane manufacturers or as flight instructors with schools under government contracts. If Olds could employ as many as one hundred women as copilots in transport squadrons or as pilots ferrying single-engine airplanes, he could release the same number of male pilots in the Air Corps Ferry Command (ACFC), transferring them to the General Headquarters Air Force (GHQAF). Then General Arnold could use the men for defense. With capable pilots in such short supply, the move would be most helpful.

The Army Air Corps (AAC) could give the women a quick orientation course and then commission them as second lieutenants in the Air Corps reserve. At the same time, the U.S. Navy was pushing for a bill (H.R. 10030) which would authorize women pilots in the navy and Marine Corps. Alas! Even a moron untutored in the politics of the time could have guessed what would happen to that bill in the Congress of the United States.

Nothing happened in the AAC either. Brigadier General Arnold emphatically rejected the plan that Colonel Olds showed him. He wanted men. The men he considered fit for ferrying military aircraft were airline copilots. Let women pilots replace them, he said. But tradition stood in the way. Airline passengers, everyone believed, would refuse to fly with a woman pilot.

Nevertheless, more women were getting up in the air. One means was through a government-subsidized program. As war spread in 1939, the military brass knew that many more men with aviation knowledge and training would be needed. Military flying schools did not accept candidates with fewer than two years of college credits. During the Great Depression, not many young people attended college, and those who did often worked to pay some of their expenses. They could not afford to learn to fly.

To meet the need, the government instituted flight training in each interested college or university under the Civil Aeronautics Authority (CAA). The plan was to offer classes to ten students every three months at no expense to the students or to the school. The schools were to contract with an independent, fixed-base operator at a local airport, who would supply all textbooks, airplanes, flight instructors and ground school training necessary for each student to attain at least a private license to fly. The CAA supervised the program, laid out the courses and textbooks and tested the instruction. Operators were paid quite well. For most of them, it was the first reliable steady income they had seen as pilots.

From these Civilian Pilot Training Programs (CPTP) came not only instructors, but students who became ferry pilots for the United States. Some of them were women. In order for the CPTP to appear innocent of military purposes, the quota of women students allowed in was in the same proportion as licensed women civilian pilots to licensed men civilian pilots. The ratio was one in ten. Therefore, every class of ten flight students had one female member.

As U.S. involvement in the war seemed more likely, women — who already wanted to fly badly enough to pay for instruction — saw that it might bring them opportunities for employment in the air and for service to their country. The CPTP began to hire them as flight and ground instructors.

During the Great Depression, before the development of the CPTP program, the Betsy Ross Corps in Florida bought a training plane which its members could use to keep their skills current and active. A charter member of the Ninety-Nines, the Park Avenue socialite Opal Kuntz, headed this group of licensed women pilots and offered their services on December 7, 1941, to the Army Air Corps. General Arnold turned them down.

In the January 1941 issue of the National Aeronautical Association's magazine, Betty Huyler Gillies wrote an entreaty to all the Ninety-Nines, the international organization of licensed women pilots, to sharpen their flying skills and to gain more flight experience and higher ratings in order to be prepared. Gillies, a charter member of the Ninety-Nines and a former president of the organization, had been flying since 1928.

The woman who was to succeed Betty Gillies as president of the Ninety-Nines, Jacqueline Cochran, published an article in the June 1941 issue of *Flying*. She advocated governmental development of a 1,000-member corps of women to be used in instructing ground and flying schools, in ferrying bombers, fighters, supply, ambulance and courier airplanes — every task except combat.

She mentioned the use of women by foreign governments. Hannah Reitsch trained hundreds of glider pilots in Germany after World War I. (The victors refused Germany the privilege of a powered air force, so they glided instead to learn what they needed to know.) Amy Johnson ferried for Great Britain until she crashed into the Thames. Russian women were combat pilots in the war with Finland.

Cochran points out in her article, ''the first fifty hours of solo constitute but the bare beginning. It is only after about two hundred hours that a pilot finds out how much there is still to learn in order to do the job well.''

She continued to work for women pilots. She states in her autobiography, *The Stars at Noon,* that in the summer of 1941, she and her husband were dinner guests at the Roosevelt family home at Hyde Park, New York. There she told President and Eleanor Roosevelt that there were 1,500 to 2,000 American women pilots already trained to fly. Wasn't it possible to organize them for pilot duties in order to release men for combat duty?

The president's interest was aroused. Cochran volunteered to obtain the exact information for him. According to her, the president wrote a note for her to give to the assistant secretary of war for air. (The note has disappeared.) She then approached Secretary of War Stimson with her plan for a huge organized army of women pilots.

Despite her obviously useful political weapons — the friendship with the president of the United States, the influence of her shrewd, industry-wise and wealthy husband, and her own expensively-won notoriety — Cochran was given the runaround. The secretary of war received her in his office, but he had more to do than to cater to a female. She should know that military life was a masculine occupation. Stimson got rid of her shortly by passing her downward to Gen. Henry H. Arnold, whose new title was Chief of the Army Air Forces. General Arnold passed her on to the office of the recently-promoted Col. Robert Olds, now commanding officer of the newly established Ferrying Command (ACFC), and the man approached by Nancy Love a year earlier.

To Colonel Olds, Cochran emphasized that great numbers of women were available. He decided to call her bluff. He asked her to find out exactly how many women were qualified and available to serve as ferry pilots. She went then to the CAA, where records of the 300,000 civilian licenses were kept. To find in those files the names of women who were still living and flying was an impossible task, even for a woman who flew through life with the throttle bent forward. She hired seven researchers to do the job. Working as rapidly as possible, they found that only 3,000 women in the U.S. had been licensed to fly — or at least had had current physical examinations which would allow them to be licensed.

Unfortunately for Cochran's dream, only about 131 of these had more than 200 solo hours, the minimum requirement for a commercial license. Of these, only fifty would pass the other qualifications necessary for a ferrying job.

Cochran did not concede defeat. Instead, on her own, she sent questionnaires to the women pilots. From the returns, she learned that only thirty women had more than 1,000 flying hours. Twenty had between 500 and 1000. Twenty-eight more could possibly qualify for the Ferrying Command with 350 to 500 hours. Only seventy-eight women in all!

Ah, but there were fifty-three with 200 to 350 hours who might be eligible if given a short course in a training school. Perhaps she could scrape up 131 women as a total. But no matter — reality was a sad comedown from the pipe dream she had presented to President Roosevelt.

Nonetheless, on she went. She wrote a letter to Colonel Olds on July 21, 1941, telling him that she needed 200 women to start with, based upon a projected ferrying of 850 trainers per month. She presumed that what she wanted was agreeable to him. She was also letting people know that she was working with Colonel Olds as a "tactical consultant." (Whether or not he was aware of her impertinence is unknown.)

With regularity, she sent letters to Olds. In her July 21 letter, she stated that she was "against a group of women pilots hired primarily for their ability and doing pretty much as they please while not in actual ferry work." What she proposed was "a group of women selected from the standpoint of background and personal qualities as well as flying ability . . . under strict routine and regulations at all times. . . ."

At the time her letter was written, General Arnold expected to take male cadet graduates who would later be assigned to General Headquarters and place them as ferry pilots. While they ferried, they would also become more competent and seasoned in cross-country flying in the very combat airplanes they would fly after being assigned to GHQ. Arnold's plan had merit. He would use the Ferrying Command not only for ferrying airplanes but also to train the pilots who ferried them.

Cochran's plan did not have much value in Arnold's opinion. He refused to consider her recommendation on August 25, 1941. At this point she spelled out another detail — a ninety-day test period, such as the Ferrying Division (now called FERD) instituted. If successful at the end of that period, "her women" would be commissioned in the Air Corps Specialist Reserve in grades of second lieutenant to captain. She would be rated as Chief of Women Pilots Division.

General Arnold said no. He gave as his reasons that the country had adequate manpower in aviation and that ferry experience should be necessary training for military reserve duty for men. He thought that "the use of women pilots presents a difficult situation as to housing and messing of personnel at Air Corps Stations." (Messing refers to providing food and a place for women to dine.) He went on to state that the records of the CAA indicated that 12,429 men and only 154 women were presently holding commercial licenses.

Despite Arnold's lack of enthusiasm, Colonel Olds decided that it would be wise to have on hand a list of qualified women and to update it periodically, just in case. On November 5, 1941, he turned that list over to Fiorello H. LaGuardia, the head of the Civilian Defense Agency. From then on, the War Department handed all communications about women pilots to LaGuardia.

On the British scene, women pilots had ferried 3,900 aircraft since January 1940. One plane had been demolished and fourteen were slightly bent. The ATA now had fifty women pilots and 450 men. By September 1941, twenty women had become eligible to fly Hurricanes and Spitfires, so-called "hot" combat planes.

By her own admission, Cochran had been spending most of her time since the war began in Europe nurturing her young cosmetics business and knitting afghans for the RAF. She looked longingly at Great Britain where the action was. In *The Stars at Noon,* she tells how, at the Collier Trophy luncheon, she met Clayton Knight who headed American recruiting for the British ATA. That contact led her to the British authorities stationed in Washington, D.C., who set up an interview for her in Montreal. But the wily Canadians saw her request to fly a bomber across the Atlantic as another publicity stunt. Nothing came of it.

Next, Cochran cabled Lord Beaverbrook, who was in a position to help. He wired an order to the RCAF that she be allowed to fly a bomber from Canada to England. She then pushed the Canadian office of ATA for permission to be checked out in a bomber.

As a single-engine rated pilot, Miss Cochran stood a good chance of being failed. So beforehand she talked officials at Northeast Airlines into selling her some multi-engine check time. Northeast already flew to Iceland by way of Newfoundland and Greenland. Their problems were similar to those of the RCAF and ATA.

Cochran passed the test in Montreal, but afterward was restricted by the proviso that she not be allowed to handle such large equipment (a bomber) alone. All hell broke loose among the pilots. The Canadian and U.S. ferry pilots resented her intrusion. They said she was getting into line ahead of them. They held mass meetings in protest. Still, she went to England. Capt. Grafton Carlisle accompanied her. He took off and landed and set the course. She was allowed to take over the controls in the air.

Only one hop was made with Cochran in the airplane, but the resulting publicity led Margaret Truman to write in her biography of her father, President Harry S. Truman, that Jacqueline Cochran spent all of the war years ferrying bombers from Canada to England.

When Cochran arrived in England, she spoke with Lord Beaverbrook and Pauline Gower. The upshot was that the British asked her to bring 200 women pilots to the ATA. She was wily; she knew it was impossible. Instead, they agreed to a trial of twenty-five women to begin with. With that decided upon, Cochran went home to get recruitment organized.

On Sunday, December 7, 1941, all debate about whether or not the United States should enter the war ended. In a surprise attack, Japanese planes bombed Pearl Harbor near Honolulu, Hawaii.

American aircraft factories had already begun shaping up their production to supply Great Britain, and they had hired some of the country's best test pilots. The RCAF had under contract a number of American male pilots, whom they paid well. As for flight instructors, the CAA's CPTP had taken its share of men, as well as had civilian schools in war-training programs (WTP). And there was no immediate way to find out how many male pilots had withheld their services from the draft by taking a safer haven in a defense plant.

To make sure that he could get all the pilots he would need, Colonel Olds submitted another plan to General Arnold. He proposed hiring individual women, as civilians, at a salary of $300 per month. As soon as Jacqueline Cochran discovered the plan to use women right away, she wrote to Arnold. In her letter of January 1942, she gave three reasons against the plan. She said she wouldn't be able to recruit women pilots for ATA if the American plan were realized, because English living conditions and pay were poorer than at home. She stated that individual women without organization would "bring disrepute on the service before very long and injure the interests of the women themselves. Here, just as in England, a woman in charge of women is essential. . . . In addition, it would wash me out of the supervision of women flyers here rather than the contrary. . . ." She concluded that Olds' plan "should be put on ice for a least six months or my program for England should be stopped." General Arnold concurred. On January 19, 1942, he told Colonel Olds via memo not to hire women until Jacqueline Cochran completed her agreement with British authorities and returned to the States. (Jackie got her program going in

England in the nick of time. Winston Churchill replaced Odlum's friend, Lord Beaverbrook, in February because of the old man's health. Churchill had no reason to think highly of her.)

On January 24, 1942, I saw an article in the *St. Louis Star-Times* stating that Cochran was recruiting women to fly for Great Britain. About a month later I was not surprised to receive a two-page telegram from her asking me to journey to Montreal for a flight test. I turned down the chance because I felt no loyalty to England, and I felt certain that I could never leave my husband and home.

How did Cochran's British program fare? Readers of her autobiography receive an erroneous impression. She claims that twenty-five American women arrived in England in the spring of 1942. In fact, only four arrived in April and three in May. None came in June; two arrived in July. A close look at the record shows that Jacqueline Cochran-Odlum, Hon. Flight Captain, joined the ATA January 24, 1942 and left July 7, 1942. Only nine American women recruited by her were flying in ATA during her time there. Twelve more joined in 1942 after she left. It is unlikely that Cochran recruited any of those who signed up after she was no longer associated with the program.

Of Cochran's service to ATA as head of the seven American women who arrived before July 1942, Curtis writes in *The Forgotten Pilots,* "When the American women pilots arrived in England, the ATA had been running for over two years, during which it evolved standard procedures and training for everyone who joined, regardless of previous flying experience or rank. Each had to pass a medical, had to check out in light aircraft and do a course in cross-country flight.

"They also had to complete the various technical courses and generally work their way through the ATA school routine. Jackie, however, immediately set about short-circuiting these procedures. As a race, the British are — or were in those days — perhaps averse to anyone who set out to bypass the 'system' and ATA did its best to enforce its own rules.

"But Jackie and her husband, besides being immensely wealthy, moved in the highest political and military circles in the United States and at the time, with the United States only newly entered into the war, it was of the utmost importance to Britain that good relations were maintained. . . ."

In this respect, Miss Cochran agreed with her, for she wrote, "I spent more time on the ground fighting administrative battles than I did in piloting planes in the air."

Curtis continues, "But, as head of the American 'gals,' she was given the rank of Flight Captain (honorary and not on the payroll), a fact bitterly resented by some of her own pilots because in the time she was here, she had little time for flying. Our main memories of her are of someone who lived at the Savoy Hotel, wore a lush fur coat and arrived at White Waltham (the air base where the pool of women pilots was stationed) in a Rolls Royce, both noticeable because by now we had clothes as well as petrol and food rationing.''

From two of Jackie's recruits I learned that she became so unpopular in the early summer of 1942 that the ATA pilots were set to strike unless she disappeared from the scene. Cochran herself said that she was released from ATA because the 8th Air Force needed her advice on their military matters. At any rate, she remained in England for a while, fraternizing with the nobility.

Questions surface in my mind. Why weren't the AAF generals aware of the situation in ATA? When freed of her ''duties'' on July 2, 1942, why wasn't Cochran informed that General George, head of the Air Transport Command, had written to headquarters staff on June 11, 1942, ''It is desired to use commissioned officers of the Women's Auxiliary Army Corps (WAAC) for ferrying of airplanes under this command, to replace and supplement male pilots insofar as qualified women may be available.''

I didn't question Cochran's statement that she held only an honorary captain's position and wasn't on ATA's payroll because she wanted to leave at any time to take over the American program when called upon to do so. But according to FAA figures, she wasn't on ATA's payroll because she couldn't be. She was not qualified.

In 1942 the Air Corps Ferrying Command (ACFC) grew so large it was redesignated the Air Transport Command (ATC). The ever increasing production of American-made airplanes was divided between those needed in the States and those which went overseas. The domestic wing of ATC was now known as the Ferrying Division (FERD), but pilots usually called it the Ferry Command. From June 20, 1942, to June 20, 1944, FERD's personnel was multiplied thirteen times.

Immediately after Pearl Harbor was attacked, all civilian flying was stopped along the coasts of this country. Coastal flying schools went inland at least 150 miles. In Boston, Bob and Nancy Love's aviation business came to a standstill. With their previous ferrying experience, both found berths in FERD immediately. Bob was commissioned as a major and became the administrative executive to Col. William Tunner. (His title was later changed to Deputy Chief of Staff.) Nancy took a job in operations in a civilian capacity. There she learned a great deal about the inner workings of the administrative system in dealing with airplanes and pilots.

Nancy Harkness Love was then twenty-eight years old, quiet, intelligent, beautiful, efficient, and knowledgeable about flying. It wasn't any wonder that she was popular with everyone of importance in ATC. Nancy had instigated the idea of women ferrying airplanes for military purposes in 1940. Now she approached the subject again. This time she conferred with Colonel Tunner, the CO of FERD, who had learned from Major Love that his wife commuted by air between Washington and Baltimore daily — and she was the pilot.

Tunner and Nancy Love planned what the qualifications of women ferry pilots should be. They'd need to show credentials of their flight experience. On passing a flight check, their names would be reported to Col. Oveta Culp Hobby, the head of the WAAC, who would then commission them. The women pilots would be assigned as second lieutenants at the Second Ferrying Group, Newcastle Army Base, Wilmington, Delaware. (Newcastle was chosen because it was close to the operations office of the Northeast Sector, ATC, in Baltimore.)

General Olds approved the plan and sent it on to General George, who forwarded it to Gen. Arnold. Then followed quick conferences and visits until something halted the wheels of progress toward commissioning women pilots through the WAAC. The "something" was that there was no authority to grant women the flight pay that men received.

An amendment was suggested to the bill then being considered by Congress for making the WAAC a true part of the U.S. Army and changing its name to WAC. The WAC bill appeared likely to pass eventually because legislators could see a need for women replacing men at desks and typewriters or doing other civilian-type jobs for the army, freeing men for combat duty. The army could also control the WAC more closely than if they were merely civilians and WAACs. Moreover, one must satisfy one's constituents, and WAACs could muster many votes at the polls come re-election time. As for women pilots, Congress was as stuffy about commissioning them as officers as it had been with the navy's earlier request.

By June 22, 1942, Colonel Tunner was able to show General George that at Newcastle Army Air Base, a seventy-four-man barracks would soon be ready to accommodate as many as fifty women pilots. They could eat with the officers in a mess hall next door. The AAF orientation course could include women in its classes, as well as men. The women were to be paid $250 per month and $6 per diem while on missions away from home base. Funds were available to install venetian blinds at the windows (male barracks had no shades), to change the plumbing and to provide each room with a small chest of drawers with a mirror above it. Nancy Love was to be director of women pilots.

General George sent the plan along with his own memo to General Arnold. He proposed that the women be hired as Civil Service employees at first, just as civilian men were. Their requirements would be: proof of citizenship, of high school graduation, of 500 hours of flying time, of which some must be in the 200-h.p. category. (At the time, CAA airplane classification for 80-360 h.p. was "2-S.") And they must present two letters of recommendation.

In another memo, George pointed out to Arnold that if Congress delayed in commissioning the Women's Auxiliary Ferrying Troop (WAFT), as he called it, the formation of the group would be delayed indefinitely. Arnold replied by memo that George should speak to the CAA and Major Johnson of Civil Air Patrol (CAP) in order to try to get every possible qualified male pilot from them. He would consider women pilots only if they were needed after the supply of male pilots was exhausted.

Nonetheless, on September 3, 1942, General George let General Arnold know that "plans for the WAFT were sufficiently organized to permit the starting of activities within 24 hours." He advised that some type of uniform be designated after the group was formed.

On Saturday, September 5, Gen. Arnold capitulated and directed that immediate action be taken. The recruiting of women pilots began twenty-four hours later.

I received my telegram on Monday, Labor Day. Thus I entered the picture, not knowing anything at all about the people and the events that had occurred beforehand.

A GATHERING OF BIRDS

To UNKNOT THE TANGLES that our lives become, especially when love and duty oppose each other, we must force ourselves to act in order to make new orderly patterns. Unraveling the intricacies of our problems takes all the patience and resolute persistence at our command. Once successful, we feel at peace . . . until the next time, when something again disrupts our redesigned patterns. And so it goes —

The sun was halfway up from the eastern horizon on Friday, September 11, 1942, when I decided to eat breakfast. The dining car was two coaches and a Pullman behind me. I was still apprehensive about the course I was taking. That apprehension added to the weariness from travel and sleeplessness that I had struggled with before I left home, putting me on edge.

Yesterday morning I had boarded the daily B&O passenger train, long, monstrous and black, minutes before it bustled out of Union Station in St. Louis. It was bound for Washington, D.C. Pacing Eads Bridge with cautious dignity, it crossed the Mississippi slowly. Then, traversing Illinois, the train traveled increasingly faster, hurrying toward the edge of the Mason-Dixon line.

The swing of the pistons slapping back and forth made a steady, monotonous rhythm. The wheels clacked over and over again my maiden name — Adela Riek, Adela Riek, Adela Riek — on and on, through the day and night. The train slowed gradually to pick up mail pouches from station hooks or snatch them up from platforms, but did not stop. At road crossings, it gave out a mournful whistle to warn unwary pedestrians and motorists off the track. Sometimes it waited on a siding to allow a train with greater priority to take the right of way, perhaps a freight train laden with military materiel or a coach bursting with military personnel. It stopped only for water or to let passengers on and off. Boarding passengers crowded the narrow aisle, shoving their luggage ahead, trying not to lose their balance as the car swayed and bounced. They searched with hopeful eyes for an empty seat.

All America was on the go. Reservations for a Pullman on this train had been filled weeks before. The best accommodations available were in day coaches with reclining seats. I had rested poorly on mine during the night.

I should have hopped a twenty-three passenger DC-3, that airplane ubiquitous to every airline. But buying a ticket was no longer an assurance that an airline passenger would reach a destination. I had seen stranded travelers in Lambert Field at St. Louis, worrying about getting on the next flight. A passenger with a government priority could ''bump'' an ordinary passenger, no matter if a ticket had already been paid for. I couldn't take that chance. I took the train.

America's highways on the other hand were almost desolate. Automobile gasoline was being severely rationed so that it could be piped to military use, and the manufacture of automobiles had all but halted in favor of the production of jeeps and tanks. The country had been coping with shortages since Pearl Harbor had been attacked ten months earlier and it looked as if we would be doing so for a long time.

I felt an empathy with the mindless train I rode, rushing to its destiny. Like me, it couldn't know where it was going nor what awaited it there. Unfortunately for me, when I don't know what I'm about, I make mistakes. The conductor did not inform me that I should have gotten off at Baltimore to make connections to Wilmington, Delaware, until we arrived in Washington. I had to backtrack and I wasted several precious hours doing so.

At last, after several shudders during which I almost lost my balance in the narrow aisle near the end of the coach, the northward bound train halted at Wilmington. I had finally arrived! I looked at my wristwatch. Almost two in the afternoon, Friday, September 11. It didn't seem to be a good time to begin anything, but I was committed.

I waited for the passengers to clear the platform below before I touched the metal handhold and descended the high steps. The conductor, waiting below, offered me his hand. Once down, I picked up my large suitcase and looked about, uncertain and curious about the place.

The station was old. Years of trains blowing soot had darkened the walls and the wooden trim. Although fairly clean, the building appeared untidy and as worn with use as the crowded coach car I'd just left. I followed the passengers disappearing into the nearby door. Inside, the waiting room was drab and cheerless.

I went directly to the stationmaster's cage and waited in line impatiently, knowing I must not waste any more time. At last my turn came.

"Could you tell me where I could get a streetcar or a bus to Newcastle Army Air Base?" I asked.

"Ain't no streetcar here in Wilmington," he answered brusquely. "None of the buses go to the air base from here."

"Is the base very far? Can I walk it?"

He peered at me over his glasses and replied with annoyance, "Lady, you can't get to Newcastle Army Air Base from here unless you take a cab. Ain't no other way." His answer was final. He looked past me to the next person in line.

I picked up my suitcase and walked to the door facing the town. Through the heavy plate glass, I spotted a taxicab parked at the curb about fifty feet away. I wasn't familiar with cabs; I only knew they were an extravagance, a luxury. I looked at my heavy suitcase. It would be a tiresome burden if I had to walk very far at the base. I mused, "And if they don't want me or I don't like any part of it, I'll turn right around and go back home on the train."

I walked back to where the stationmaster, now alone, was penciling on a paper. To get his attention, I said, "Excuse me." He looked up.

"Is there a place where I can check this suitcase?"

He pointed to a row of lockers on the station wall. "All you need is a quarter and the key is yours."

I carried my suitcase to the end locker, that being an easy one to remember, set it down and fished for a coin from the tiny purse in my handbag. I hoisted the suitcase, put the quarter in the slot, shoved in my burden, closed the door, and turned the key. It came out easily. I put it into my bag. Then, misgivings put behind, I shoved the heavy door aside and strode to the taxicab.

The driver nodded when I gave my destination. I tried to ignore a tightening ring in my chest that pained my heart. To disregard the hurt, which I had felt off and on since last weekend, I looked at Wilmington as we passed through it.

Downtown, the city resembled the older parts of St. Louis. The frame houses were built at the edge of the sidewalks and some showed their age by settling slightly off the perpendicular. The homes were not as imposing as the two-story, rich red-brick St. Louis buildings, with their French mansard roofs or Germanic arched windows.

The driver took us over a high viaduct. Beneath was an extensive dump. Scattered among the piles of trash were discarded odds and ends of furniture. I turned away. How obscene, I thought, to expose to public view the remains of outworn loves, hopes and cherished dreams.

A gliding hawk caught my eye. Above it, a high, gray overcast was spreading into the pale blue sky. I wondered how different the weather is here. At home I would have named the clouds as altostratus, following a thin high cirrus layer, a sign of rain to follow in the warm front moving in. Here, I wasn't so sure of myself, although the air was warm and humid. I regretted wearing my woolen suit. It was too hot and the pleats in the skirt had lost some of their sharpness. The hawk stopped wheeling. Flapping its large wings, it disappeared among a stand of trees.

The possibility of not passing the flight check fleetingly entered my mind before my self-assurance dispatched it. But I hoped I wouldn't be required to fly immediately. Twenty-eight hours sitting up in a coach had left me feeling fuzzyheaded. And before that, I had spent three sleepless nights trying to make up my mind to come. NO. My vanity refused to allow for failure. I must avoid a flight check today.

On the left, the cab was moving past a high metal fence. Now it slowed to a halt at a gate guarded by an armed soldier who came forward saying, "State your business." I pulled the telegram from my purse. The sentry took it, read it, went to his sentry box, lifted a telephone and began to talk. Shortly afterward, he came back and returned my telegram.

"Okay," he said to the driver. "Here's a pass only as far as headquarters. It's right up the hill. You can't miss it."

The driver positioned the pass on his windshield and drove through the opened gate, up a winding road to a cluster of buildings. He stopped near a dull drab-green barracks. A limp American flag drooped on its staff in front. I got out.

Two civilian women — there were as yet no other kind — were leaving the building as I reached the steps. One I recognized at once, Alice Hammond from Grosse Pointe, Michigan.

"Hi! Are you volunteering, too?" I asked Alice and her friend.

Alice blinked her eyes nervously. She replied, "I want to, but I know I can't. There was a possibility I could and that's why I came." Her expressive brown eyes showed the stress that she was undergoing. She continued, "I can't leave my children. No amount of patriotism can take me away from them so much of the time. They need me more than Uncle Sam does."

A few words more and the two left. I entered the building. Inside, a narrow passageway led down the middle of the entire length of it. I had gone only a few steps when a stout young woman appeared before me. She greeted me with, "Good afternoon. I'm Miss Cohee, Mrs. Love's secretary. I'll show you to the office waiting room."

Miss Cohee led me down the hall, paused at the second door on the right, turned, and gestured for me to enter. "Please have a seat," she said before she disappeared through a doorless passage leading to an inner office.

At the far side of the small reception room were two bentwood chairs. I chose the one in front of an open window. Miss Cohee reappeared momentarily saying, "Mrs. Love will be with you shortly."

To while away the time, I looked about. The walls of the room were painted a light gray. Gray steel filing cabinets lined the partition that defined the inner office. A bookcase with four shelves directly opposite me was stacked with sheaves of pamphlets and military aviation books. I hungered to read them, but dared not. The impersonal gray surrounding me showed no cheer, mercy, nor warmth. It was, it seemed, a forecast of a stark future purged of all civilian color and freedom. I sighed, and wondered if I dared take off my suit jacket.

Before I did so, however, a woman came from the inner room. I could see that she was younger than I, but her wavy light blonde hair was mixed with gray. It framed a face as serene as an Anglo-Saxon cherub into whose life no earthly problems nor torments had ever entered. She was slightly taller than the average woman. Her figure indicated soft femininity, roundness without bulk. I was embarrassed that I stared at her so, for she was a most beautiful woman, with great blue eyes.

"I'm Nancy Love," she stated graciously. I sensed a calculated wariness, although there was no undertone of antagonism. As yet, her name held no meaning to me.

"I'm Del Scharr," I replied. "I received a telegram."

"Two telegrams," corrected Mrs. Love firmly. "We sent a third one yesterday and Western Union informed us they had good reason to believe that Mrs. Scharr was on her way."

As she spoke, I knew she was measuring me. How gauche and pro-

Nancy Love being congratulated by Maj. Gen. Harold L. George, chief of the Army Transport Command.

vincial I felt — too tall, too muscular and thin, my eyes, skin and hair all shades of brown, no sign of cosmetics or nail polish, my woolen suit bringing perspiration to my upper lip.

"Did you bring along your log books and all your transcripts and recommendations?" she asked.

"They're right here," I answered, as I took them from my handbag.

"I'll look them over," said Mrs. Love, taking the piles of credentials. "Just wait out here." She turned and took the materials into the inner office.

I sat and waited. Now and then I'd look out the window. No breeze stirred. The air became muggier. Nature hadn't provided me with much cushion to sit on, so I squirmed and shifted my weight by crossing and recrossing my legs. I knew that for me the time passed more slowly than usual, for such inactivity was foreign to my habits. I still felt too timid to take a military manual to read.

A dapper young blond lieutenant wearing a flying suit came through the room and walked into the inner sanctum without knocking. He was, I later found out, Lt. Joseph Tracy, the man who gave the flight tests. Soon he and Mrs. Love came out into the reception room.

He was saying, "Lieutenant Sacchio is out with Mrs. Slocum now. We had to get a summer flying suit for her."

"Will you be able to take Mrs. Clark, sweetie?" she asked him, with a distinct sibilance to the letter "s."

"Right away. Is she around?"

"She'll be back . . . here she is now." Then, addressing the young woman who entered, she said, "Helen Mary, this is Lieutenant Tracy. If you are ready, he's waiting to give you your flight check now."

The newcomer turned her head to one side and blushed. Then her blue eyes looked straight into Nancy's, expectant and hesitant at the same time.

To me, Helen Mary Clark's shyness was appealing. She appeared a patrician, with delicate hands and feet. She was slender, with a proudly straight bearing. She held her pointed chin high, displaying an enviable throatline. Unlike Nancy Love's soft features, hers were clearly chiseled in a slender, oval face. Her strawberry blonde hair, styled in a short page boy, curled only at her cheeks. Her fair skin had a rosy cast.

"Let's get going," urged Lieutenant Tracy. He nodded to Mrs. Love. To Helen Mary he said, "Come — we'll fly a BT-13A."

Mrs. Love returned to her office, taking no notice of me. I found my thoughts wandering back and forth, from home to Newcastle Army Air Base and back home again. Surely I was out of my mind to have spent all that money and time to come here. I was only a poor policeman's daughter who had followed a crazy dream. How could I fit in with these beautiful women?

My tormented thinking stopped with the entrance of a doll-like woman in slacks. She glanced toward the inner office as she approached me. She had a distinct air of assurance and a familiarity with our surroundings. As soon as she hit the other chair, she struck up a conversation.

"I'm Pat Rhonie," she introduced herself. "My name is Aline, but I like to be called Pat."

"I'm Del Scharr," was my answer. "My name is Adela, but nobody spells it or pronounces it correctly, so call me Del."

I thought to myself, Good Heavens! They all look like movie stars!

"Are you volunteering for the Ferry Command?" Pat asked.

"Yeah," I replied.

"I've been accepted already," she said smugly and continued, "Where are you from?"

"St. Louis."

"I'm from New York. Long Island." Pat spoke as if that were a much better place to be from. Then, interrogating further, she asked, "Do you have all your qualifications?"

I shrank from her inquisitiveness. "Mrs. Love has my credentials," I answered evasively.

Pat had been looking me over from head to toe, so I reciprocated. In contrast to my height, Pat was petite, looking not much taller than a child. Dark curls and bobbed hair framed her pale oval face in which dark, melancholy eyes brooded, giving her a wistful look.

"Do you own your own airplane?" Pat continued questioning me.

"No," I said regretfully. "I never could afford one."

That wasn't exactly true. I could have owned a second-hand plane once, years ago. But an uncommon sense held me back from investing in anything so risky — I had seen too many similar investments cracked up by little errors in judgment. Instead, I had taken the $2,500 I had saved from my school teacher's salary and made a down payment on a fairly new two-family brick flat.

Pat was still not satisfied. "How many hours do you have now?" she asked.

"Almost fifteen hundred."

Her face showed satisfaction. "I have 2,627," she said. "I have more than Nancy Love or Betty Gillies or any of the others so far."

She must have been a pretty good pilot, I thought. She also must have had money from family or a sponsor, someone that my flight instructor Spike Saladin called a "sugar daddy." In truth, she needed good luck and excellent flying skills to have accumulated that much time in the air. Before Piper introduced the Cub with its reliable Franklin engine, flying was so dangerous that instructors drummed into their students the importance of knowing at all times where the plane could be safely landed if the engine quit. To keep that from happening to me, I helped Spike tear into the Kinner engines after each twenty hours of flying. We checked the valves and the trueness of the rods, lifting them inside the rocker arm boxes. Even so, I had a forced landing once because a valve dropped into one of the five cylinders of that radial engine.

Pat had been talking and I hadn't been listening. I must be tired, I thought, as I concentrated on her words.

"I had my own airplane for years and years," she was saying, "until the government confiscated it. They took all the heavier ones like mine first. Since war had begun in Europe, I went to France to be an ambulance driver." She paused. "Have you been to France?"

"No."

She prated on. "My husband had his own airplane, too. I was married to Peter Brooks," she said, as if everyone knew who he was. I didn't, nor did I care that he was the nephew of industrialist Charles M. Schwab.

"We're divorced," said Pat. And then, perhaps because to be divorced in 1942 still carried a stigma, a sign of personal fault and failure, she explained. "He was inconsiderate. On our honeymoon, can you guess what he did? He wrote postcards to all his friends everywhere we went. That's how I spent my honeymoon — with a man writing postcards."

I tried to mask my amusement by changing the subject. "It must have been nice to have money to own an airplane. Two airplanes! He must have been very rich."

Pat was affronted. "Yes, he was. But *my* family owned Singer Sewing Machines."

So, she was an heiress. I wondered about the others.

"What about Nancy Love?"

"Oh, her husband Bob had his own aircraft sales and service company in Boston. When the war started, he got on the staff of Air Transport Command. That's how *she* got in with the Ferry Command, through him." Pat spoke regretfully, as if Nancy had surprised her with a hidden trump, and all the while she had more flying hours than anyone.

"How about Betty Gillies?" I asked. "Could she afford her own airplane, too?"

Pat stared condescendingly. "You know Huyler candies?"

I shook my head no.

"It's about the biggest and best candy company in New York. Betty's family owns Huyler Candy Company. Do you know Betty?"

"No, but I admire her and I'd like to meet her. I'm a Ninety-Nine."

"So am I," Pat interrupted.

I jumped back in. "Remember when Betty fought the CAA over their regulation that a pregnant women must not pilot a plane?"

Pat's face veiled any emotion. She replied, "Well, she lost."

"But she was right. That's a regulation that should be changed. Suppose a woman became pregnant and couldn't fly the required ten hours in six months because she couldn't pass the CAA physical exam. She'd lose her license and have to take her commercial test all over again after the baby was born. It's not fair."

We said no more while Nancy Love, a brown beanie perched on her head, left her office, walked across the reception room without looking

The Morris Code *of Morris Field, Charlotte, N.C., ran this picture of the cadre of five WAFS pilots who arrived there in November 1942. In rear, from left, Barbara Towne, Helen Richards and Barbara Jane Erickson. In front, Teresa James and Betty Gillies.*

at us, and turned into the hall. Pat resumed her recital.

"The Gillies belong to the Aviation Country Club on Long Island. When Betty was pregnant, she could always fly with her husband Bud as her safety pilot. He was a navy pilot and has been working for Grumman."

Pat was off on a story, I could tell. And I was curious about these people whose lives I would soon touch.

"They now have a twin-engine Grumman amphibian," she was saying. "Betty used to have a Waco. Oh, Long Island has always had lots of flying going on, even before Lindbergh . . . Roosevelt Field, Mitchel Field, Farmingdale. . . .

"I remember once that Betty lent Jackie Cochran her Waco and when Jackie came down, she said the airplane was no good for acrobatics. Everybody was going over to Aviation Country Club to eat lunch, so someone — I don't remember who, now — begged Betty to let him fly the airplane over there while the rest drove. He waited until he was sure they'd be at the Club and could see him. Then he came across the field pretty low and gave a remarkable demonstration of slow rolls, snap rolls, Cuban eights, and everything, one right after another before he landed. Jackie never touched that Waco again."

"Do you know Jacqueline Cochran, too?"

"Yes. But she hasn't flown as long or as much as we have. She'd never have gotten anywhere except for Floyd Odlum. Especially on ground school. And that's how she got into racing hot planes. You know she hates to have a woman beat her. She fought until they opened the Bendix trophy race to her, and she raced until she beat the men."

"I got a telegram from her about six months ago," I said. "She wanted me to go to Montreal for a flight check and to England to fly for ATA."

"Yes, I know," said Pat unhappily. "After my ambulance work in France, I went to England. I laid the groundwork with Pauline Gower so we could have an American women's auxiliary flying unit to help the women pilots of the United Kingdom. Then along came Jackie, and she pulled strings with Lord Beaverbrook. Floyd knew him through government connections. Well, Jackie took over."

"She's not in this at Wilmington, is she?"

"I hear she tried to get it. Of course she wasn't the only one who thought about it. Did you ever hear of the Betsy Ross?"

"No, never," I replied.

"They wanted to be aviatrix minutemen. General Arnold ignored that group, too."

"So they took off like a lead balloon," I offered.

Pat paid no attention to my comment. "I know Jimmie Doolittle personally," she said. "When I was in England, he gave me a letter recommending me as head of a unit over here, but —" Her voice trailed off and we both sank into our own thoughts. Being from Missouri, I thought that no matter how thin you sliced it, it was still baloney. I needed proof.

I surmised that Pat felt a bitterness she couldn't express without being criticized. She must have considered herself as top rank, for she had beauty, brains, money, perhaps social position, and all those hours of solo time in an airplane. She was undoubtedly as much Junior League as Amelia Earhart. Yet here she was, summoned like me, as a volunteer, to be subjected to the approval of Nancy Love. And in Britain, an unschooled hairdresser superseded her. It was as if she had banked a fortune, only to discover it had been diverted surreptitiously into someone else's account.

Pat stood suddenly and announced she was going down the hall for a drink of water. Even with her gossip, time dragged. I stood and stretched, yawned and looked out the window. I noticed it was grayer outside now. In a few minutes Pat returned.

"Your turn is coming up next," she said. "Why don't you put on your slacks?"

"I can't. They're in my grip at the depot."

She looked me over. "I'll lend you mine," she offered.

I could see that Pat's slacks would be much too short for me. And I'd probably strain the seams while flying. "Thanks," I said, "but I'd better not. Maybe they've got something for me to wear here."

Pat returned to her chair. "Lindbergh was from St. Louis, wasn't he?"

"Well, he worked for Robertson, flying the mail from St. Louis to Chicago. He was originally from Minnesota."

"After Lindbergh came back from Paris, I painted the mural inside the hangar at Roosevelt Field. If you ever get there, try to see it." Pat was proudly letting me know she not only had other talents, but that she had been in aviation during its Golden Age, in the late twenties.

She asked, "Did you ever meet Lindbergh?"

"No," I answered. "I just saw him, that's all."

"He was an odd ball. Not a bit sociable, really. He never drank, you know."

"He looked like a nice young man." I defended him.

"Once we were at a party. Charles wasn't entering into the conversation. After a while, he dipped his fingers into his glass and began to flick water at Ann. She just glanced at him and then ignored what he was trying to signal her. She had on a pale blue silk dress. He kept it up, flicking water on her dress, and you know how silk waterspots. Finally she went over to him and poured the water from her glass all over him. She was little, but he couldn't bluff her."

I was delighted to find a human touch in the hero of my college days. Lindbergh must have been like Harold, who never enjoyed the way a loud drunk might try to dominate a party with exaggerated hangar flying.

Pat looked at her wristwatch. She had evidently made all the impressions on me that she could manage in that space of time. "I'll be going now," she said. "Good luck!"

"Thanks," was all I managed to reply.

Not long after she left, Nancy Love returned and disappeared again into her office. Soon Lieutenant Tracy and Helen Mary Clark entered. He went directly to the inner sanctum, while she waited in the room with me. Then both Tracy and Nancy Love came out.

"Congratulations," said Mrs. Love softly.

A faint smile appeared on Helen Mary's face. "Thank you," she answered.

Lieutenant Tracy glanced at me nervously. He looked at Mrs. Love and whispered to her in a confidential tone, "I'll be right back." He disappeared down the hall.

Helen Mary drew a silver cigarette case and matches from her shoulder bag. She chose a cigarette. With a facile gesture she tapped the cigarette on the case she had snapped shut. Then gracefully she lifted the cigarette to her lips, struck a match, and through half-closed eyes watched it until the flame took hold. She inhaled, withdrew the cigarette, closed her lips, and placed her left forefinger on the side of her left nostril, closing that air passage. Then she lifted the still burning match to about four inches from her right nostril. The puff of smoke that she exhaled extinguished the flame. She looked about and carefully placed the spent match in the tin can on top of the bookcase.

Nancy had gone into her office and came out again, also holding a lighted cigarette.

She said, "I didn't have a chance to ask you how Gerry and the boys are."

"They're just fine. I talked it over with them and they agreed that I should come down here to find out what is happening."

"How old are the boys now?"

"Eleven and thirteen." Helen Mary was not a chatterer. She looked expectantly at Nancy Love.

"We already have Betty Gillies, you know. I called her to come immediately and she did. She has gone back home to make arrangements. I think this Ferry Command project will be a good thing for Betty. You know she lost her youngest to leukemia this past year."

Helen Mary nodded.

"And we have two others. Cornelia Fort. She's from Nashville. You read about the girl flight instructor out with a student near Pearl Harbor when the Japanese bombed Hawaii?"

Helen Mary's "yes" was barely audible.

"That was Cornelia. Great girl. And we also have Pat Rhonie." Nancy stared at Helen Mary as a momentary pout hinted at her sentiments.

Helen Mary raised her eyebrows. "Oh?" was her only comment, but she blushed.

Abruptly Nancy Love realized that I wasn't part of the furnishings in the room.

"Let's go into my office, Sweetie," she said to Helen Mary, "and I'll finish looking at your credentials. I've been so busy. We'll probably have a board meeting on candidates this afternoon, if we can get all the officers together."

The two women disappeared into the doorway. Murmurs drifted out the reception room, but the words were indistinguishable. In a few minutes Lt. Tracy re-entered, and looked into the inner office as he leaned against the doorjamb. He announced, "Mrs. Slocum passed. She'll be here as soon as they finish on the flight line." Then he looked at me.

"Do you have flying clothes with you?"

"No."

Lt. Tracy frowned as he looked at his wristwatch. He said, "Supply has already closed for the day. I can't draw anything out for you." He seemed very serious. "I really don't think we have time for a complete flight check anyway. It looks like it's going to rain pretty soon."

I had gotten to my feet and stood, waiting his pleasure.

He gave it. "Come back Monday morning and we'll take you the first thing."

I was glad not to have to take the flight test. I was very tired by then. But where should I go until Monday? I asked him if he could tell me the name of a good hotel.

"There's the Hotel Dupont and the Hotel Darling. The Darling is nice enough and it's not so expensive," he replied.

Lt. Tracy pointed me toward a telephone so I could call a cab. As I walked down the hall, a wave of utter loneliness engulfed me. The perfunctory and cool politeness of the few people I'd met stung me. How could the Ferry Command wire me to come, to leave all that was dear and familiar to me, and then not even care if I had a place to lay my head? Was the angelic-looking Nancy Love really thoughtless? Well, I'd take that flight test and I'd see.

I went into the women's room. Inside, a very young woman, perhaps a clerk or a stenographer, looked at me in the mirror and, turning around, asked, "You're one of the lady pilots?"

I vowed that I was. At last, recognition of my true worth! — although in a most unlikely place.

She said happily, "My mother always wants to know what's going on here. Me on a base with all these men, and I can't ever tell her anything. Did you see the announcement about you girls in the morning paper?"

"Yes," I answered, edging to a stall, "on the train coming in."

"Oh, I'm so proud of you," she said. "And my mother won't feel so uneasy now that she'll know there will be women flying, too, and I'll have things I can tell her."

Well, I thought as she departed, somebody is going to appreciate my coming after all.

GETTING MY BEARINGS

I LOCKED THE DOOR. The well-worn furnishings in the Hotel Darling were unimportant compared to the need for resting my aching body. Even so, before lying limp upon the bed, I removed my suit, hanging it up carefully, and slipped off my shoes. Then, oblivion.

Later, hunger pangs urged me from that state of nothingness. Half-past seven by my wristwatch. If I wanted anything to eat, I'd better make tracks, I thought. I jumped up, dressed, washed my face and combed my hair, then went in search of the dining room.

Eating alone was something I had had no practice in. It embarrassed me. I chose roast beef because, as Mama said, it couldn't be ruined too much. But the hour was late and the meat was tough and cold. Covering it and the mashed potatoes was a gluey gravy. I ate it all, for in my family we learned never to leave food on a plate.

Afterwards, from the lobby I saw rain sprinkling the sidewalk outside. I had been right about the clouds. From habit I touched the tip of my right index finger to my tongue and made an invisible tally on an invisible wall in the air before me. Chalk one up for me, I thought. Then, back to bed.

Rain pelting the window pane awakened me. Too early for the dining room. I bathed and chose fresh clothing from the suitcase. Then I washed and hung up over the tub the underwear and the blouse I had worn the two previous days. At last to breakfast.

The options of exploring a wet Wilmington or sitting alone in the hotel lobby were both distasteful. I went back to my room and reviewed the reasons why I was here.

Seventh grade history as taught by acerbic Miss Teresa Debatin of room 2, Arlington School in St. Louis gave me an ideal. His name was Nathan Hale, a schoolteacher turned spy for the Continental Army and caught by the British during the American Revolution. His famous last words were, "I only regret that I have but one life to lose for my country." I was a serious and impressionable child who hoped that I might also be as heroic. What lay ahead for me was serving mankind as a public school teacher. My parents and I had held that goal for me from the time I was in kindergarten.

There were few jobs open to women when I was young. In the professions, one could choose between nursing and teaching. In business, one could clerk, wrap bundles, cashier, or type letters. Unskilled, one could work in a factory, wait on tables, or do housework for rich people. Or, one could marry and expect a man to provide the financial support. A new job, brought about by bobbed hair and the marcel iron, was hairdressing. But my destiny was in the classroom.

Still, I had fantasies and desires that I was reluctant to express for fear of ridicule. My three brothers and even my sister had more freedom than I, who was needed to help about the home. If only I had been a boy, I thought, I'd be a sailor and roam the earth until it was as familiar to me as a thin dime. During my days at Harris Teachers College, Col. Charles Lindbergh caught my fancy. A notion struck me that wouldn't go away, even though it was far- fetched: I, like he, could fly. I knew flying was expensive and for women, not pragmatic.

Then came some bad luck. On the first payday of the school year, October 1933, a pain in my right side put me into DePaul Hospital where Dr. Arthur Gundlach took out a pus-laden appendix. He also discovered that I had anemia. That winter my social activity was curtailed, for I needed all my endurance to teach and thus to earn a living. Alone, with newspapers to read and books to study for an up- coming Masters of Arts degree from the University of Missouri at Columbia, my only diversion in the evenings was listening to my newly-purchased Philco radio.

Adolph Hitler was then emerging into German politics. I read about his phenomenal rise, wondering, like everyone else, how this Austrian dared to push his way into the news. Where they came from I do not know, but I sensed the words: "There is going to be a war in Europe and the United States will be drawn into it." My response was, "And I'm getting into it, too."

Ridiculous! How? What could I do? There was some precedent for women helping in a war. Telephone operators, nurses, and factory workers participated in World War I. None of those jobs were for me. Save my money, buy a boat, and learn navigation? No. Learn photography? I envisioned myself alone, taking pictures, and then developing them alone. No. I had had enough of loneliness. How about flying? That tantalizing idea beckoned again and again, but my common sense and thrifty habits warned me that it was too costly. At that time, news of every aircraft accident that occurred made the front page. Flying was a dangerous occupation and that intrigued me. If a gunner didn't hit a bullseye, all he lost was a bullet and some pride. If an aviator made a mistake, there was a lot more at stake — his life. Say I became a flyer, what could I lose? All that lay ahead of me then was my "fate" to be an old-maid public servant.

I gave myself a loophole. If, after I graduated from Mizzou with a Master's degree, I could pass the physical examination for a pilot's license, I would do it. I'd had enough of inside work, chained to my desk during summers, weekends, and evenings, marking papers and preparing lessons. I yearned for the sun and the space outside. In the hope of seeking wider horizons, I banked as much of my meager salary as I could.

As soon as I completed my degree, I presented myself to Dr. Maurice Green for a pilot's physical exam. He marked my student pilot permit "eligible for transport." I bought a pair of jodhpurs, a helmet and goggles, and thus my new career began. Through years of no encouragement, only stubborn tenacity and an inner faith kept me flying — weather permitting — a half hour a week, year after year.

Unable to afford more than that, it took me five years to earn a commercial license, but I kept at it. There was no job in aviation for a woman in St. Louis at the time; only stubborness kept me hanging in there.

During those Sundays at Lambert Field, I made friends and had numerous acquaintances up and down the apron. Self-consciousness at being the only woman who wouldn't quit gradually became a realization that most of the men considered me as one of them. I was free and happy there as I never had been before. Although I would not date anyone at Lambert because I was there for the sole purpose of learning to fly, three men and I often attended ice hockey games on Sunday nights — Spike Saladin, Milton Richards, and Harold Scharr. It was several years before Harold and I both realized that we had come to love each other. The inevitable was, of course, marriage.

At that time, the instruction department of the St. Louis Board of Education forced all women employees to resign or be fired when they married. Married women teachers were denied employment. But I had obtained five ground school ratings by then, so after we were married I taught ground school at St. Louis University under contract with Brayton Flying Service for the Civilian Pilot Training Program (CPTP) three hours per evening, five evenings per week. Twice a week I taught a psychology class at Jefferson College. I hopped passengers on joyrides on weekends, kept house, and kept on learning. Soon I had a flight instructor's rating. Then, as civilian aviation boomed prior to our entry into the war, I had my own evening ground school in the administration building at Lambert Field, and my flight students were booking me for weeks ahead. I even soloed Harold and put him through a private license.

The CPTP fixed-base operators would not hire me because I was a woman, but private owners of airplanes wanted lessons and hired me. They allowed me to use their airplanes for instruction and, as a freelance operator, I earned as much as the men under contracts. The cost of flying matched the low salary scales of those Depression days. I was paid $2 per hour flying time.

And then came Pearl Harbor. For months ground school went on as before, then draft boards started calling away the men. One of my students was a young woman named Tess, who also enjoyed speed skating, rowing and skiing. With as much vigor as she used to change the attitude and direction of a scull by forcing an oar through the water, she shoved stick and rudders in compliance with her will. No amount of insistence on my part that she use a gentle touch could break Tess of her habits.

Tess joined the group of students who met informally at our flat once a week, on Friday evenings. Usually one of the boys gave Tess a ride home. Then, all the boys were gone, drafted or enlisted, so Harold took her home. I had noticed that Harold and Tess spent time together while I was in the air with a student, but had not thought much of it. Then on the Friday before Labor Day 1942, instead of returning in the usual twenty minutes it took to drive Tess home, Harold did not come back for almost two hours.

Did she sit in the car, making small talk to prolong their time together? Was there more to it than that? I went to bed hurt, aloof, and afraid to say anything for fear it would come out wrong. Harold would

Spike Saladin, shown with a Kinner Fleet. He is the author of the sage remark, "Nobody will fly with a woman!"

have to explain, but he never broached the subject.

I flew with students that weekend. Harold, who was in the Naval Reserve, had the watch on Sunday, which meant that he was on duty from Sunday morning until Monday evening. Usually our relationship was warm and loving. Now, I was cool and didn't even kiss him good-bye. If he wants Tess instead of me, I thought, I won't stand in his way.

Another complication surfaced that weekend. I'd had a student for several weeks named John Henry Overall, who was desperately trying to get into marine aviation. He was handsome, intelligent and very wealthy. He was also a good student.

On the Sunday before Labor Day, I was sitting in the shade of a wing on the grass at the airport with a former student of mine, Jane Champlin. We had a deep regard for each other. She, because I had been her instructor. I, because I thought she was so good a pilot I soloed her in five hours, although CAA regulations stated that a student must have at least eight. As we talked, her face showed how much she loved flying. She was asking my advice about a maneuver she had been practicing, when along came John Henry.

I guess that Jane was stricken by his good looks, for she began to prattle instead of continuing the intelligent conversation we had been having. John Henry announced that he would be leaving for Quantico Air Base next week.

Jane said, "All the little chicks are flying away. See them go up into the wild blue yonder? Only the Mama bird can't go. She has to stay behind in the nest on the ground." Jane smiled and I returned her smile, but her words hurt.

It was true. Some of my students were already in the service. Some had been picked up by airlines to replace the captains lost to the Army Air Corps. (Jane herself would volunteer for WFTD, the Women's Flying Training Detachment, and be killed in a freak accident.) After Jane had gone, John Henry asked if he could take Harold and me to the Cheshire Inn for dinner to celebrate his successful solo. I demurred, saying that Harold was on watch.

"Is there any good reason why I can't take you?" he asked.

I couldn't think of one, so he did. It was a fascinating evening. I scarcely savored what I ate, for I enjoyed his conversation so much. He gave me a view of a life-style that I had never experienced or even dreamed about, and his attention salved my wounded vanity.

I was still feeling cool toward Harold when he returned home from his watch on Labor Day evening. As we drove up to the house we could see a telegram hanging from our front doorknob. It was addressed to

Harold N. Scharr, in front of a ''Yellow Peril'' — the N2S.

me. I opened it at once. It read:

AFATC S938 PERIOD FERRYING DIVISION AIR TRANSPORT COM-
MAND IS ESTABLISHING GROUP OF WOMEN PILOTS FOR
DOMESTIC FERRYING STOP NECESSARY QUALIFICATIONS ARE
HIGH SCHOOL EDUCATION AGE BETWEEN TWENTY ONE AND
THIRTY FIVE COMMERCIAL LICENSE FIVE HUNDRED HOURS
COMMANDING OFFICER SECOND FERRYING GROUP FERRYING
DIVISION AIR TRANSPORT COMMAND NEWCASTLE COUNTY
AIRPORT WILMINGTON DELAWARE IF YOU ARE IMMEDIATELY
AVAILABLE AND CAN REPORT AT ONCE AT WILMINGTON AT
YOUR OWN EXPENSE FOR INTERVIEW AND FLIGHT CHECK STOP
BRING TWO LETTERS RECOMMENDATION PROOF OF EDUCA-
TION AND FLYING TIME STOP BAKER END GEORGE ARNOLD
COMMANDING GENERAL ARMY AIR FORCE WASHINGTON

We were both dumbfounded. Inarticulate, we went to bed. Harold
was soon asleep, but ideas chasing through my mind kept me awake.
Sorting them out and evaluating them wasn't easy. What was I to do?

We knew that Harold would soon be shipping out with the navy.
Once he left, there was no reason for me to remain at home. By nibbles
here and there, the government had been biting into civilian flying.
First the airplanes began to disappear — Bert Lambert's Gullwing
Stinson, for one. Then the Civil Air Patrol took over the four-place
cabin planes for patrolling the coasts.

Instead of civilian planes in the airfield's traffic pattern were more
and more navy SNJ's, which were then used in navy instruction, even
for formation flying, from takeoffs to landings. No longer were civilian
student solo flights allowed from the municipal airport. Our planes
were based at Lambert, but we were forced to fly our students to outly-
ing airports for instructions. Most of my students had transferred to the
small triangular field of the Private Flyers of America, north of the city
of St. Charles.

Personnel were also disappearing into the services or into defense
plants. Oliver Parks, head of Parks Air College across the river in Illinois, contracted to instruct flight students for the army. He put many
local flight instructors on his payroll at Cahokia, Illinois, and at
Malden and Sikeston, Missouri. Some pilots drifted down to where
Brayton Flying Service established its operation at Cuero, Texas. By
Labor Day 1942 only older men and those with physical defects remained. And I, because I was a woman.

I could clearly see the trend toward the slackening off of civilian flying. Before the war, I had been flying a hundred hours per month. The
past week, even including the three-day holiday, I instructed only sixteen hours. My solo students were still flying, but few new students
were signing up. And I depended on getting new students.

Tuesday morning Harold left for work without me. I could judge by

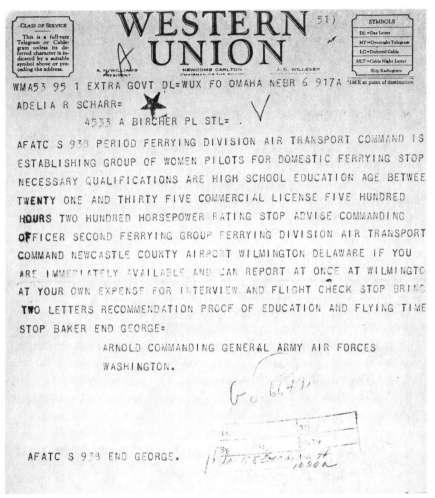

CLASS OF SERVICE		SYMBOLS	
This is a full-rate Telegram or Cablegram unless its deferred character is indicated by a suitable symbol above or preceding the address.		DL = Day Letter	
		NT = Overnight Telegram	
		LC = Deferred Cable	
		NLT = Cable Night Letter	
		Ship Radiogram	

A. N. WILLIAMS PRESIDENT   NEWCOMB CARLTON CHAIRMAN OF THE BOARD   J. C. WILLEVER

WMA53 95 1 EXTRA GOVT DL=WUX FO OMAHA NEBR 6 917A

ADELIA R SCHARR=

4533 A BIRCHER PL STL=

AFATC S 938 PERIOD FERRYING DIVISION AIR TRANSPORT COMMAND IS ESTABLISHING GROUP OF WOMEN PILOTS FOR DOMESTIC FERRYING STOP NECESSARY QUALIFICATIONS ARE HIGH SCHOOL EDUCATION AGE BETWEE TWENTY ONE AND THIRTY FIVE COMMERCIAL LICENSE FIVE HUNDRED HOURS TWO HUNDRED HORSEPOWER RATING STOP ADVISE COMMANDING OFFICER SECOND FERRYING GROUP FERRYING DIVISION AIR TRANSPORT COMMAND NEWCASTLE COUNTY AIRPORT WILMINGTON DELAWARE IF YOU ARE IMMEDIATELY AVAILABLE AND CAN REPORT AT ONCE AT WILMINGTO AT YOUR OWN EXPENSE FOR INTERVIEW AND FLIGHT CHECK STOP BRING TWO LETTERS RECOMMENDATION PROOF OF EDUCATION AND FLYING TIME STOP BAKER END GEORGE=

ARNOLD COMMANDING GENERAL ARMY AIR FORCES WASHINGTON.

AFATC S 938 END GEORGE.

The telegram which lured Adela Scharr into the WAFS.

the trees in the backyard that the wind was already more than twenty miles per hour. It would pick up and it was too windy to fly students in Cubs. I stayed home.

Later in the morning, the telephone rang. I answered it in our tiny central hallway that had space for only a small telephone stand. It was John Henry.

"I couldn't leave for the wars without telling you good-bye," he said.

"You know what?" I asked. "I might go East, too. The Army Air Corps sent me a telegram last night asking me to come to Wilmington,

Delaware, to fly in the Ferry Command.''

"You're going, aren't you?"

"I don't know yet."

"I'm calling from Union Station. Just say the word that you'll go with me and I'll put my foot down as a brake. I'll hold this train 'til you get here."

I thought I probably would if I weren't married. But I told him, "Let's not be rash."

"The trip will be so boring without you. Come along."

"I can't."

"I'm going to Washington first and then to Quantico. When you come East, you must come to see me. Say that you will."

"I'll try," I answered. "Yes, it's been great knowing you, too. Good-bye."

Wretched as I was, John Henry's call cheered me a bit. I began to consider seriously my call to duty. Wasn't this why I started flying in the first place? It was for this call that I had waited for so long, and now that the opportunity was here, what would I do with it?

I called three people: Oscar Parks, manager of Lambert Field, Rev. William Lampe of West Presbyterian Church, and Duke Trowbridge at Brayton Flying Service. The first two promised a letter of recommendation that I could pick up on Wednesday. Duke gave his word that he'd meet me early the next morning at Lambert. All promised to tell no one of my requests. If I failed, it would be alone, without either jeers or comfort.

Duke Trowbridge was a pilot's pilot, of barnstorming vintage, who came to Lambert Field in 1937. He became renowned for disobeying the CAA warning that if an engine quits on taking off from a field, one should land straight ahead. Instead of obeying — for the administration building, the parking lot, wires and Long Road were ahead of him — Duke shoved the plane's nose down to keep his speed and made a safe turn back into the field. He was also the first male pilot instructor who championed women students. He said that their air work was better than the men's, that they really could fly; and he lent a compassionate ear to women's aviation problems.

And that is why, after Duke and I tied down the Waco on the apron in front of Brayton's, I told him about Tess and John Henry. About Tess, Duke declared, "If Harold pays any attention to her, he's a damn fool. But I don't think you have anything to worry about now or when you're gone."

When I told him about John Henry's quick wit and the giddiness I felt, Duke studied my face before answering.

John L. ("Duke") Trowbridge, who avowed the flying ability of women. This photo accompanied newspaper accounts of his death, killed while testing experimental aircraft on May 10, 1943.

"There's some professions you have to look out for," he said. "One is aviation and the other is show business. The ordinary housewife doesn't meet many men outside her husband. The butcher, the grocer, the mailman. And if they belong to a little group that plays cards regularly, she looks at the other husbands and catches on to their defects. She's satisfied that she's married to her own husband and wouldn't want to change. But in aviation, you meet a whole lot of men."

I nodded in agreement.

"Now, I don't believe there's just one lid can fit a pot. You can be happy married to someone else. If you meet a lot of people, sooner or later, one comes along you could have gotten married to instead. If you fall hard enough, your marriage breaks up. That's the danger. You've got to look out for it in flying. So watch it."

"Okay," I said, my eyes looking down at the scuffed toes of my shoes. But I didn't know then what one must watch out for.

That had been on Wednesday. Now it was Saturday and I was stuck in a musty hotel room in Wilmington, Delaware, with nothing to do until Monday. I hadn't the patience to remain there. John Henry came to mind. I had said I'd try to see him and there was all day tomorrow. Visiting John Henry as a friend was plausible, even a kind and generous act, I thought. Besides, anything was better than being holed up alone. I found the telephone book in the bedside table, picked up the telephone and asked the operator to dial a number. Soon I was asking, "What train would take me to Quantico?" I wrote notes on an envelope I found in the drawer.

At the Quantico compound the next afternoon, I waited only a few minutes while someone found John Henry. Then, there he was. At first I didn't recognize the stranger standing, smiling, before me. All that was left of the dark blond mop of hair he'd had was a short crewcut. Gone was the sun-bleached tousle; what was left was much darker than I remembered. He wore an olive green uniform with no evidence of rank. Was this man really John Henry?

"Come on in," he invited, smiling as if he was delighted to see me. "We'll find a place to sit down."

We walked toward a small park just off the entrance gate and headed for an unoccupied bench. "You did it!" he exclaimed as we both sat down. "When did you leave?"

"Thursday. How have you been?"

"It's not too bad yet. The marines like to toughen you up, but, of course, I've always played tennis. It's not the same as if I had sat at a desk all day without any exercise."

I told him about waiting for my flight check. And then both of us strained to keep conversation going. Outside of a student/teacher relationship, what did we have?

A mosquito lit on my bare, browned leg. I swatted it. Another landed and then another. I could think of nothing to say. John Henry dug into the heavy silence. "How did the brassy blonde in the airport office react to your leaving?"

"I didn't tell her," I admitted.

"You'll be the best pilot in the Ferry Command," he said. "And before long, you'll be sporting a lieutenant's bars."

I thought that was insanity. "Please don't kid me!" I replied.

"Of course you will. They'll have to make you an officer," John Henry answered firmly.

Then, silence. Without the chit-chat I had heard other women indulge in, I felt stupid. I was unable to run off at the mouth unless there was a good reason for it. Another mosquito took my mind off my predicament.

John Henry offered some diversion by offering to drive us over to an unusual airport in Virginia that he had discovered. It was located in a valley and a barn served as the hangar. I didn't feel I had time to take the trip before I caught my train back to Wilmington.

We left the bench and strolled about for a while until I said, "I'd better find out when the next train goes to Washington. And you must be having things to do, too."

He seemed a bit relieved. He waited with me until I boarded the train. As we bid each other farewell, he bent down and lightly kissed the tip of my nose.

"That's with my puppy love," he said softly.

The train ride back to Wilmington was a burden on my senses. The coach rode uneasily, lurching forward when least expected. And it was crowded, filthy, and noisy.

I thought about the magic that briefly had been in John Henry when we had had dinner together in St. Louis. It was gone; it would never come back. I was relieved that it had disappeared so quickly. Still in all, I was glad that it had happened. As Duke said, I now knew what to watch out for.

I felt lucky, being married to Harold. I knew that he didn't protest about my going East because he really wanted me to have my wish, and he wouldn't stand in the way. And I had left him because I didn't want to stand in his way in making his own choice about Tess.

What was I to do about all the men I was bound to meet in the Ferry Command? I would be distant, and if it looked like trouble ahead, I'd turn around and run like hell!

The same Friday that I arrived at Newcastle Air Base, the generals in the War Department were busy trying to get an upper hand in the life-and-death struggle with Japan and Germany. Suddenly into their problems was thrust a new one — Jacqueline Cochran, newly arrived from England and hopping mad. She had just found out that women pilots were gathering at Wilmington with the purpose of ferrying for ATC. She had neither been informed about the move nor chosen to lead them. And who had been favored instead? Someone who had been working in Colonel Olds' office at the same time she and her research assistants were searching out qualified women pilots like little needles in the vast haystack of the CAA records.

Who did General Arnold think Nancy Love was, compared to Jackie Cochran?

Arnold listened as Jackie reminded him that he "had promised" her the assignment early in the year. He apparently told her that Nancy Love had been doing an efficient job in ATC operations and knew the entire ferrying business well, including the flying, and that she was popular with everyone at headquarters. She was also well- educated, attractive, and an accomplished pilot with many hours. Therefore, he had no intention of removing her from her assignment.

It has been reputed that General Arnold's heart was easily swayed by ladies in distress. Jackie, claiming extra-sensory perception, must have felt some power over the general in her earlier encounters with him. She had been able to influence men in the past. But the general himself must have sensed that his gallantry could be his undoing if he refereed a contest between two strong women. He slid out by passing the buck.

Before Jackie got to Arnold's office, he had already spoken with Gen. Bart Yount, the head of Training Command. He warned Yount not to forget the priority of his command, nor to lose sight of it: the combat training of male pilots in order to win the war. He told Yount to listen to Jackie's arguments, but he didn't have to agree to them. He was ordered to keep *all* his command's airfields, *all* the airplanes, and *all* the instructors working at the missions they were busy with and not to siphon off any of them to suit Cochran's requirements. He was to be pleasant to her without catering to her demands.

Col. William H. Tunner, chief of ATC's Ferrying Division, had stated several months earlier that his command needed no more than fifty qualified women pilots; one hundred at the most. Tunner wanted the women pilots to be almost twice as experienced as the civilian men the command was accepting, for the theory still existed that women could not equal men in the man's world of aviation.

As Cochran had discovered, there were in the then forty-eight states enough women with more than 200 flying hours to justify a government-sponsored school which could offer the training needed to qualify them for the Ferry Command. At least Jackie could command such a school. But Tunner knew that when he got the women pilots he needed, that would end the project and Jacqueline Cochran would be finished.

Notwithstanding the fact that the projected plans did not coincide with her ideas, Jackie refused to give up the possibility of commanding thousands of women pilots. She conceded that Nancy Love, secure in the position Jackie had hoped for, was an accomplished pilot. Her own job of heading the training of a few women to augment Nancy Love's "troops" wasn't what she thought was her due. For the time being, however, she took the crust, adding it to the crust she already had.

Since delegating responsibility is the quickest method of unburdening the boss, General Yount turned Jackie over to the officer in charge of individual training, Col. Luke Smith. Training pilots was part of his

Col. (later Brig. Gen.) William H. Tunner. He was named head of the Ferry Command in June 1941; later headed the Air Transport Command.

authority. Smith must have had outstanding qualifications to have obtained his rank. And he was tough.

On the other hand, what qualifications did Jackie have for commanding a flight training school? The truth was that Jackie had never taught flying nor was she qualified by the CAA to do so. She held no ground school rating. Any and all knowledge she had in aviation had been gained through special instruction and tutoring, the best that money could buy.

No one in the WAFTs (we were still going by General George's name for us, Women's Auxiliary Ferrying Troop) realized that Jacqueline Cochran was not qualified to be one of us — except some knew that she was over age and lacked a formal education. But a few were aware that, like the brass at the War Department, she could be tough.

While I was waiting in Wilmington, developing calluses on my seat, Jackie was in Washington, refusing to be stymied by the position in which the generals had placed her.

Colonel Olds had been promoted and transferred from ATC. In his place was General George. Chances were he'd be nicer to Jackie than was Olds, whose plans she had ruined in January. Reconnoitering, she found George an agreeable sort, as long as what she proposed did not interfere with the smooth running of his command. Willingly he sent off a memo to the Chief of Staff, Maj. Gen. G.H. Stratemeyer.

"It is my belief that the utilization of women pilots should be divided into two classifications:

1. Enlistment and Training
2. Subsequent employment in ferrying operations.

It is recommended that the program of pilot training not at this time be part of the functions of ATC."

General Arnold, as the link in the chain of command to General Stratemeyer, added that Cochran should "pick out any 500 of the best women fliers she can find in the United States." He also stated that some highly experienced women could go to ATC directly. He thought that a time would come when some women with a great many flying hours would progress to flying advanced trainers. He concluded that Cochran could worry about a training program until the pilots were ready for the WAFS and "the Transport Command can worry about them from that time on."

After seeing General George, Jackie turned to Col. Luke Smith, in charge of individual training. Unlike George, Smith did not make her happy. He said he had no airfields to give her except Sikeston, in rural Missouri. It wasn't an attractive setup. She refused it.

Smith had no airplanes for her, nor any instructors, nor any maintenance personnel. But Jackie did not surrender to him. Instead, she began a busy weekend. By the time she left Washington she was a "dollar-a-year man.*" She was in.

At 8:00 A. M. Monday, September 14, dressed in slacks, shirt, and sneakers, I deposited my suitcase in Nancy Love's reception room. Miss Cohee, hearing the thud, came out to see what was going on. Before I could open my mouth, she said, "I'll call the flight line," and disappeared.

Soon she stuck her head out the doorway. "Lieutenant Tracy is coming right up." Back she went.

In a few minutes, Tracy breezed into the office jauntily, saying, "Hi! Ready?" and started down the hall to the left.

As he opened the front door of the headquarters building for me to

---

*Dollar-a-year men were not under the rules nor on the payroll of Civil Service. Neither were they elected nor appointed. Because they had access to governmental plans before the general public did and knew about contracts before they were let, they were subject to the temptation of discussing the terms of such contracts for the enrichment of their friends or associates. They had a ringside seat where the action was. The question is: Did the government get what it paid for?

precede him, he said, "We'll get something to put on to keep you clean. That's our jeep ahead."

Lieutenant Tracy hopped into the front seat next to the enlisted driver. I climbed into the back seat and off we went. The sun shone warmly through the lifting mist. The rush of cool air was welcome, slapping me into a state of readiness for my ordeal. And then we were on top of the hill on the airport side of an oversized hangar with gigantic bombers inside and in front. I was face to face with pilot's heaven.

As I stared about in awe, Tracy said, "Wait here," and soon returned with what I needed — a summer flying suit, a helmet, and goggles. I quickly put them on.

As I raced after Tracy going down the flight line, my eyes moistened and little bumps stood up on my arms. My breath and heart held for an instant as I thought, "Hey! This is great!"

He stopped at a silver airplane that looked exactly like the black and orange Fairchilds that CAA inspectors flew about the country to meet their exam appointments. In my mind I saw CAA inspector Cooper strutting away from one as if it were the ultimate in aerodynamics and far above my poor powers to handle.

"This is a PT-19A," Lieutenant Tracy was telling me, "with a Ranger 165 horsepower inline engine."

The tail bore the number 33652. I'd have to remember that and put it in my log book when I got back. We pre-flighted the airplane. That done, I trotted after Tracy again, back to a barracks office he called flight operations, where he filled the blanks of a clearance sheet. In an adjoining office we checked weather conditions and the forecast. Then we returned to operations. He picked up a parachute from the floor and motioned for me to take the one lying beside it.

He had to wait while I turned the chute over, unsnapped its little packet, and saw that it had been recently packed. It would open without fail. Then, out the door he went, heading for the airplane with me at his heels.

The trailing edge of the left wing root, low as it was, was an easy step up. Tracy climbed it with his parachute buckled on. I, from force of habit with Piper Cubs, instead lifted my parachute by its straps and climbed up to arrange it on the metal bucket seat in the rear cockpit. I had to step first on it and then on the floorboards before lowering myself onto the parachute. I fastened the straps around my chest and each thigh. The safety belt wasn't like any I had seen before; it was wide and substantial, and its buckle was more secure than those I had known.

Tracy waited until I was settled. He glanced over his left shoulder and said, "Put on the earphones. There — on the left. I have a speaking tube here. You won't be able to talk back to me."

The earphones needed adjustment. I squashed the bar connecting them, for my head wasn't as large as the last wearer's. Meanwhile, an enlisted man in fatigues had come up on the left wing alongside me with a crank in his hand. At the engine cowling he engaged the crank. Another enlistee stood near the right wing tip with a huge red fire extinguisher upright at his feet.

"I'll show you how to start this thing," said Tracy.

But everything went too fast for me to grasp. As the crank moved faster, the inertia starter zinged to a higher and higher whine. Meanwhile, Tracy was telling me to watch the wobble pump. What was that? It must be the knob I saw moving forward and backward which was now going fast enough to show three or four pounds of pressure on an indicator on the instrument panel. The propeller, starting with a slow whirling, began turning faster and faster until suddenly the engine kicked over. I learned later that Tracy turned the ignition switch onto the left magneto and then on both. The propeller now whirred without assistance. The crank was disengaged and stowed in the fuselage.

Tracy waved for the wheel chocks to be pulled away. Then the PT-19A rolled away from the apron and down the taxi strip. We were facing incoming traffic near the takeoff position. Tracy ran the engine up to 1,900 rpm, pulled the carburetor heat momentarily for a drop in rpm, and then shoved the button in as power resurged. He tested each magneto for no more than a 100 rpm drop in power. Then he positioned the plane for takeoff, got the green light from the tower, and off we went. As I watched him, I was not a spectator; in my mind I was flying right along with him.

My stomach jumped up and down a little as I chuckled to myself. The traffic pattern Tracy took as we left the field area was exactly the one I had been teaching my students. It was also the one that the CAA demanded that everyone use.

Tracy leveled the plane at 1,300 feet altitude, headed northwest of Newcastle and west of Wilmington. Then he spoke. "We're going to DuPont Airport where we practice takeoffs and landings. We do aerobatics near there. I'll show you. Take it, and keep this heading. Make forty-five degree turns until we climb to 3,000 feet."

I shook the control stick to indicate that I had it. First I did what I always did in a strange airplane. I made several coordination exercises, looking out at the plane's wingtips and nose relative to the horizon. Even planes of the same model are not always rigged alike, and I had to feel what control pressures were necessary in order to fly with precision. Then I began the climbing turns.

"Let's see your power-off stalls," ordered Tracy.

In reply I nodded my head, although he couldn't see me. Instead of being the instructor, I was relegated to the back seat, where a student sat. After a left turn of ninety degrees, with my head swiveling to see what might be in the air behind, above, and below us, I took the same turn to the right. Satisfied that we wouldn't lock props with anyone, I leveled off and pulled out the carburetor heat control button. My left hand smoothly pulled back the throttle as my right hand pulled back on the stick to raise the nose to a higher-than-normal climbing angle. *Wait, keep it level,* I thought. Suddenly the nose fell abruptly forward. I relaxed the stick and allowed it to move forward on its own. As the airplane picked up flying speed, I brought the stick back to where I felt pressure. The nose began to move toward the horizon, so my left hand automatically pushed the throttle smoothly forward to its previous setting and we were back to flying straight out and level. In went the carburetor heat control.

"How about a power stall?" asked Tracy.

The flight test went on to chandelles. After learning that maneuver in Duke's Luscombe two years before, I hadn't found another airplane to duplicate its speed and life until the PT-19A. After chandelles came lazy eights, to prove that my coordination was good enough for the varying degrees of banks and speeds through climbing and diving. That maneuver ended the high work.

Tracy asked me to lose altitude through gliding turns, until we reached 800 feet. He said, "The army doesn't take a chance with glides at idling speed. If you have power available, never cut it off."

As soon as we were at the required altitude Tracy ordered, "Give me some pylon eights."

I was worried about finding in this strange terrain two pylons at right angles to the wind direction which also had a field for me to get into, in case Tracy gave me a forced landing, simulated, of course. I didn't want to play around and waste time, either.

Pylon eights was a maneuver my old flight instructor Spike Saladin loved to make me do in the Kinner Fleet. I had no problems with it. As a flight instructor I had evolved my own way of helping students to avoid slipping and skidding all over the sky. It was a simple matter of keeping proper coordination between rudder, aileron, and throttle to maintain a constant altitude around the lopsided cone. The "cone" was steep on the windward side and became shallow downwind. One couldn't miss if one sat facing straight forward, upright and not leaning. The trick was to look at the pylon and keep going around it, looking directly across one's shoulder at a true right angle. If the pylon appeared to creep back from one's gaze, banking steeper would keep it in place. If the pylon seemed to be moving ahead, the bank should be lessened. The technique also worked well in cutting a neat traffic pattern around an airport and especially in making accurate spot landings.

After a couple of S turns along a road, we approached DuPont Airport, where Tracy made the first traffic pattern and landing. I made the second. Keeping power on in a glide made landing accuracy easy. It was like shooting fish in a basket.

Tracy said, "Take off without flaps. Try landing with half flaps."

When I slowed the airplane to a glide, he warned, "Never try to put on flaps over ninety miles per hour. The best normal gliding speed is eighty."

Flying back to Newcastle, Tracy showed me the effect on the airplane of putting the flaps down full on an approach and taking them off in a hurry. After we landed, he taxied to a taxi strip and stopped to tell me, "You take it now and do a go-around."

I had noticed that Tracy taxied a lot faster than I did, in fact, much faster than was comfortable for me. I didn't realize then how many hours he had had in the PT-19A or that he could see much better than I, since he was sitting higher and farther forward. I decided to imitate him, trying to go as fast as he did. Immediately I felt the throttle being pulled back and the toe brakes applied. The plane stopped. Tracy turned his head to look me in the eye and he rebuked me emphatically and sternly:

"Never, never taxi fast like that! If you ground loop or damage an airplane, you can be court-martialed and you will have to pay the damages."

I was chagrined. I had tried something against my better judgment — and during a test, too. He had frightened me. How could I, poor as I was, pay for damages? With compunction and a sense of Victorian dignity, I carefully snaked the airplane down the taxi strip, looking ahead on the left as the right rudder swung the nose to the right, and vice versa, hoping all the time that I would be forgiven.

The landing I made was perfect — a three point "navy carrier landing." Tracy was mollified. He said, "Let's go in." The test was over. We'd been gone forty minutes.

Back at headquarters Nancy Love had a little time for me. She left her inner office long enough to say, "Although you have passed the flight test and your qualifications are acceptable, the examining board won't be able to meet until later today, so you are not accepted officially — yet. It's possible the officers will question your lack of cross-country flying.''

The announcement both relieved and depressed me. Nancy Love, I was beginning to learn, had a way of putting a person in her place. Yet she managed not to rub the spot hard enough to evoke bitterness. How does one acquire that art, I wondered.

She added, ''I am sorry that you cannot be with those already accepted. *Life* magazine and Pathe newsreel photographers are taking pictures this morning at ten o'clock.''

Now I did hurt. I regretted not having taken the flight test on Friday. Imagine how exciting to be seen in a national magazine and in the movies! And here I was, really in, but not in enough to count.

Two more women had arrived while Tracy and I were flying — Teresa James from Pittsburgh and Esther Nelson from Ontario, California. We stood together out of the way, behind the photographers, as Nancy Love, now dressed in a gray-green pants suit, came in from a side entrance and stood on the stoop, waiting. Then in single file, walking toward the cameras, came the women pilots who had been accepted. They were dressed in skirt suits and each carried a suitcase. They walked in the order in which they had been accepted into the Ferry Command.

Each woman mounted the three steps to the stoop, was greeted by Love, and disappeared into the building. Ah, I learned a bit more. This wasn't the way their moments of glory had happened at all. The whole ceremony was staged, so it could be flashed on movie screens throughout the country the following week. I admit now that I was envious and felt cheated, if only for a moment.

The first woman was Betty Gillies. Her photograph had been in the National Aeronautics Association monthly magazine in January 1941 when she had written an article asking Ninety-Nines to sharpen their flying skills in preparation for war. The next woman, as tall as I, must be Cornelia Fort. Then came Aline (Pat) Rhonie and Helen Mary Clark. Bringing up the rear was another tall woman who gave the cameras a bright, wide smile, showing her beautiful white teeth. She had to be Catherine Slocum. Almost my height of 5'9", she was a good thirty pounds heavier.

Matronly, I thought. The guess was correct. Mrs. Slocum had four children. I was to learn by bits and pieces that she lived in Bryn Mawr and her husband, Richard Slocum, was the publisher/editor of a Philadelphia newspaper.

Some of the first women pilots to report to Nancy H. Love, left, were Cornelia Fort, Helen Mary Clark, Aline Rhonie, and Betty Gillies.

Helen Mary was married to Gerould Clark, the son of a "robber baron" who dabbled in expensive real estate. Her childhood home was next door to that of Ambassador Dwight Morrow. His daughter Anne married Charles Lindbergh. The term "elite" aptly fit the first volunteers.

During the hours that dragged until the examining board met, my thoughts often turned homeward. I missed Harold and longed for the sheltered, loving relationship we had had until last week. Yet I was loathe to quit Newcastle Army Air Base. The drama unfolding about me was too exciting to miss. Disquieted, I hoped to speak alone with Nancy Love.

Finally I was called into the inner office and told that I had been accepted. "Do you know when the program is to begin?" I asked.

Nancy answered, "We are not sure. We want to begin with twenty-five women in the squadron."

Twenty-five? There were only nine now, counting Love and the two who had just arrived. How could I afford the hotel bills until everyone got here?

I said, "I want to return to St. Louis until the program is really under way."

What was happening within the military establishment was unknown to me. I didn't realize that at that point Nancy Love needed every woman she could muster.

She answered, "You can't do that."

I was chary of speech about my personal affairs, but in this instance I knew I would have to tell her. My excuse was, "I have a mortgage coming due in November. It has to be refinanced and I think I should be there personally for that."

"Once the indoctrination and orientation are over in school here and you have made a delivery or two, there'll be ample time for you to return home for your business," she stated.

I couldn't deny that her solution sounded plausible, and she'd made a promise that I'd get back home. However, if the program had to wait until twenty-five women were assembled as a squadron, the indoctrination might not begin until January. What then was to keep me in?

OUTBRASSING THE BRASS

THAT SAME DAY, Col. Robert Baker conferred with Love about the success of the eighty-nine telegrams that they had sent out a week before. The results weren't promising, and Colonel Baker wanted results.

Nancy told us later that she ventured this reply, "It's possible that some of the women are instructing in CPTP and must finish their contracts before they are free to join us."

He answered, "Now, Nancy, be careful. Don't get panicky about building up your numbers and think you have to grab everyone who walks in the door. We've made our mistakes like that in the past."

Nancy assured him, "The examining board will screen all the applicants carefully. They'll keep out the unsuitable ones."

"If anyone doesn't work out, we'll give them ninety days. Then they go, the same as the men."

Later during the day Colonel Tunner told Colonel Baker via telephone that a meeting with Jacqueline Cochran was scheduled the following day at the War Department concerning the course of study and the flying required for women "almost qualified" for the Ferrying

Division. Tunner decided not to attend, no doubt not considering Cochran's project of sufficient scope to warrant his time and effort.

Instead he sent Capt. James I. Teague, a capable officer, to represent the Ferrying Division, which was demanding that all graduates from Cochran's school meet all the basic requirements of the WAFS now entering the command. Tunner stated, "Air Transport Command is not interested in large numbers of female pilots, only in securing pilots of either sex who meet its standards. The Command does not want numbers but those with high skills."

The conference began in the War Department on Tuesday, September 15. The military conferees were taken by surprise. Since Cochran had been blocked by Colonel Smith, she made an end run he did not expect. Besides Smith, Teague, and a Lieutenant Colonel Kelly, she had invited some CAA personnel conversant with the CPTP. Military aviation conferees certainly could not disparage the accomplishments of that civilian attempt to develop pilots for the military. When it became apparent that the Air Training Command would not cooperate in running Cochran's school, it was decided that the CPTP would.

After that decision, it was comparatively easy to decide that 180 hours of ground school subjects, patterned after the course of study required for CPTP graduates, would be sufficient. Any indoctrination courses that ATC required for its own command would not be included. These would be the responsibility of ATC.

The discussion became heated during the question of required flying hours. Captain Teague began with Colonel Tunner's statement, which Tunner had also sent to his boss, General George, reiterating FERD's requirements of 500 hours.

Jackie wanted her students to fly 100 hours, of which twenty-five would be in sixty-five horsepower aircraft. The next twenty-five hours would be in ninety h.p. airplanes, and the final fifty hours in 200 h.p. airplanes. The women Jackie wanted to recruit possessed a commercial license, which meant that some of them might have no more than 200 hours of flying time. With the 100 hours provided through her program, some might be entering the Ferrying Command with considerably fewer than 500 flying hours. They could not meet Tunner's standards. Besides, he claimed he needed only fifty women.

General George was asked to decide what the flight requirements should be. He said that ATC would accept all graduates from the course. ATC had set a precedent by taking in male cadet graduates with fewer than 300 hours. Perhaps his sense of fairness caused him to demand no more of women cadets than he did of men. Or had Cochran

charmed him on her visit the Friday before the meeting? At any rate,
he let Tunner down.

What is more, on the strength of General Arnold's estimate of the
number of women candidates needed to obtain a total of 100 women
flyers, the conferees declared that "training would be laid out for 500
women, if that number can be selected with proper qualifications."
After that, Cochran's usefulness would end.

For the benefit of the Ferrying Division, Captain Teague fought
Cochran on the quality of more advanced training in aircraft to no
avail. In his report to Tunner, Teague wrote, "This is the only argument I lost . . . Miss Cochran stated flatly and emphatically that this
would almost automatically preclude her securing the services of more
than a very few pilots. In lieu of this, we got Link time and hood time
in the training program."

Graduates were to complete fifteen hours in a Link trainer, a
classroom device which presented varying flying conditions to a pilot
seated inside a closed cockpit. An operator outside the module supervised the changes inside. The student peered at the dimly lit instruments of the cockpit, worked the controls, consulted a chart depicting the chosen radio station and its four ranges, and listened to changes
of signal strength. Morse code signals told her of her whereabouts in
relation to the airport where she hoped to land.

On a table outside the trainer, a larger version of an identical chart
was spread on top of a large table. A stylus inked in the path the student pilot was covering as she worked at her problem. At the end of the
lesson period, the operator opened the hood, allowing the student to
see on the big chart what mistakes may have been made along the way
and whether or not the plane arrived at the correct destination.

The "hood" time to which Captain Teague referred was also instrument flying, but was more expensive. This time the pilot really was in
an airplane; a hood prevented her from seeing the horizon, earth, and
sky. She had to rely solely on instruments. A safety pilot rode along to
keep the student from running into things. If the student placed the
airplane in an unusual attitude and needed a "seeing eye" to bring it
back to normal, the safety pilot took over.

In the FERD central files is a memo written by Captain Teague concerning the September 15 meeting. He wrote, "Miss Cochran stated
quite positively that our demands, even after we had lowered them
[from 500 to 300 hours], were ridiculous. She felt she could take a
woman pilot with 50 or 75 hours and a private license, and give them
50 hours or more and put them in a P-40 or a similar hot plane, and she
insisted that she had trained women with only that much experience to

fly Spitfires and Hurricanes. . . .''

However, in the Curtis account of the ATA pilots in England, she states that the first eight women hired for ferrying in England flew for about two years before they were allowed to fly Hurricanes and Spitfires. All pilots joining ATA in Britain had to have 350 flying hours as a minimum. It was later in the war that some women with 100 to 200 hours were schooled in order to qualify them as ferry pilots. Neither Curtis nor Cochran ever mentioned that the latter worked as a flight instructor in England, much less as an honest-to-goodness ferry pilot. Yet no one in that War Department conference asked Miss Cochran for specifics or proof of her statement. Why didn't they call her bluff?

On September 15, 1942, the Women's Flying Training Detachment (WFTD) was officially begun with Jacqueline Cochran as its director. The successful applicants to the school were to be paid $150 per month during a training course projected to last four months.

Cochran could hardly avoid Col. Luke Smith. He, as director of individual training, was in charge of pilot instruction. He was stationed in Fort Worth, Texas, and this is where she also would be.

There were several areas of antagonism between those two. Besides not having been generous to Jackie about facilities for a school, Colonel Smith had hired a young woman, Lillian Connors, to work in his office. Jackie calls this woman ''his protege'' — with implications — in her autobiography. She suspected that Smith wanted his Miss Connors to run the training school instead of herself. His ploy, according to Cochran, was to give orders that she could not approach him on flying matters except with Lillian Connors as an intermediary.

This picayune delayed Jackie from getting what she was after. Movement through the chain of command could be stymied for weeks at any one of the links. If Jackie wanted to communicate with Maj. Gen. George H. Stratemeyer, for instance, the memo or letter she sent him had to go through the proper channels first — the desks of Smith, Yount, and Arnold — before reaching its destination. Each of those men might, if he wished, add to it a memo of his own. Whoever shortcutted the chain of command would be ruled out of order and subject to military discipline and reprimand.

In spite of their initial differences, by September 16 Colonel Smith brought an unusual proposal to a planning staff meeting of AAF Command representatives in the War Department. (Lower echelon personnel nicknamed that group ''the crystal ball department.'') The gist of what Smith said was that when flight training schools ask for more , they often must wait six weeks before the Ferry Command them. Meanwhile the Flying Training Command (FTC) didn't have as many airplanes as students and instructors could use. There had to be a more efficient way to bring aircraft from the factories to the schools.

The AAF placed most of the training bases in the south because the weather was milder there. Colonel Smith suggested that an exception to the regular Ferry Command practices be made for the WAFS. He wanted them to be stationed in Fort Worth, where they would be close to the air fields where deliveries would be made. Then, when factories reported to ATC that certain aircraft were completed, the women could go directly to the factories, deliver the planes, and return to their base at Fort Worth. This plan would save time and the cost of transportation back to Wilmington.

Gen. D. E. Gates, who was chief of air staff in charge of management control, agreed that the suggestion made better use of materiel and personnel. But Colonel Tunner took the suggestion as an attack upon the principles on which his command was instituted. Tunner pointed out to Gates that the WAFS had already begun indoctrination at Wilmington. To change their station at this point would mean a longer interval before they were eligible to deliver the sorely needed airplanes to FTC. He realized that the plan seemed simple and direct, but the group should not resort to snap judgments. He asked for several days in which to reply. His request was granted.

Thus ended the first session — or perhaps, round one. In contrast to the fast moves in Washington, at Wilmington events moved slowly.

Teresa James got off the southbound train at Wilmington on Sunday evening, September 13. Seeing two other young women, a slender strawberry blonde with a short pageboy haircut and a petite brunette with a brooding expression, she guessed that they, too, were bound for Newcastle Army Air Base.

Teresa approached them and said, "I'll bet you came to fly for the army."

The brunette looked at her with suspicious eyes, taking in Teresa from head to toe. The other woman calmly and gently answered, "Yes, we did."

Teresa said, "I want to get there first thing tomorrow morning. I guess you do, too. That's why I came tonight, to get an early start. Say, I wonder where there's a hotel around here."

The blonde, who was Helen Mary Clark, said, "We are taking a taxi to the DuPont. If you wish, you may ride along with us."

The other, who was Aline (Pat) Rhonie, looked down her long, aristocratic nose, her chin tilted upward in a hostile position, and said nothing.

"Gee, thanks," replied Teresa. "I'll just trot along with you then and we can all go out together in the morning."

So they spent the night at the DuPont.

Teresa, still unaware that the other two had already been in Wilmington, joined the other two at breakfast in the coffee shop the next morning. The only conversation was between Teresa and Helen Mary. As Pat Rhonie led the way into a taxi after breakfast, Teresa overheard the tail end of a remark she was making about "black, topsy curls." Teresa didn't like it.

That Monday morning, while I was taking my flight check with Lieutenant Tracy, Nancy Love was checking details of the program with Colonel Baker. When she asked when the WAFs indoctrination was to begin, he answered, "The Civil Service pay period begins on the first and the sixteenth of the month. We must wait until the beginning of a pay period or the bookkeeping will be messed up."

Nancy asked him to consider starting on Wednesday. The girls had come at their own expense, and the cost for patriotism would be much too high if they had to pay for hotel rooms, meals off base, and transportation to and from without getting any income.

Baker asked about Nancy's program. She showed him her portfolio. All the ground instructors, subjects, and classrooms were assigned for specific dates. All flight instructors, airplanes, and flight checks were arranged for. The colonel approved.

Our barracks, BOQ 14, was still not ready for us. This left Nancy with eight women on her hands. Where could we stay as a unit? She was rooming at the Kent Manor Inn, a large old mansion that had been converted into an inn on the highway from Wilmington to the air base. She telephoned the proprietor and got permission for the WAFs to sleep there until our permanent home was ready. Most of us were happy to move to the Inn, except for Pat Rhonie, who stayed at the DuPont, and Catherine Slocum, who returned home each evening.

Also during my flight check Teresa James had bounced into headquarters, dressed in a man's khaki shirt and pants, ready to fly. When I met her she was happy and enthusiastic about flying. Her bright black eyes flashed and she grinned as she spoke in what I guessed was a New Jersey accent. She moved like quicksilver, the curls of her thick, black hair bouncing about her shoulders. Later we learned that Pat Rhonie had already told Nancy that Teresa's hair was "unthinkable." But, curls or no curls, Teresa could really fly. She stayed.

The other new arrival, Esther Nelson, was nervous about the outcome of her test. She had very few more flying hours than the minimum required, but she said she simply had to belong, for her husband already had joined the Ferry Command and was stationed at Love Field in Dallas, Texas. After her flight check, she said, "I was worried, but Lieutenant Tracy was such a doll." So she, too, was in.

Another young woman arrived very late in the afternoon to see Nancy. There was no time to check her credentials, but it appeared that she wouldn't be fully qualified. Nonetheless, Nancy gave Barbara Poole the option of staying with the group at Kent Manor that night, and Barbara accepted.

Our suitcases had been piled into an alcove at headquarters. At the end of the day we each found ours and went to the inn. There the gracious landlady assigned us to rooms on the second floor, which led to a mutually shared rear hallway, a chummy arrangement.

After climbing the stairs and before we separated to freshen up for dinner, Betty said to the group, "I always have a drink before dinner. We have a little sitting room here, and you may join me if you wish."

I was assigned a bedroom with twin beds, two dressers, and a tiny washbasin with a mirror above. The bathroom was down the hall. From the corner of my eye, I sized up the roommate, Esther Nelson, who was seated on the bed she chose. She was taking clothing of excellent quality and California design from her suitcase.

"I'll wash my face first," I said, thinking to save time, for Esther had started to hang up her clothes.

Esther's voice shrilled. "I'll die when those officers see my logbook! Can you smell my perfume from over there?"

"Yeah. I sure can."

Esther complained, "It was in my suitcase and leaked out over everything. It soaked my logbook and smeared the ink."

I thought that was sort of stupid, but I replied in my instructor's voice, "Well, you see, at higher altitudes the air pressures are lower. The air in your bottle tried to equalize with the air pressure outside, so it needed more room and spilled out of the bottle."

"I thought the airlines pressurized their cabins."

"The suitcase wasn't in the cabin, was it?"

"I didn't think of that!" Esther's lips were mobile and loose as she spoke.

Even so, and although her unsymmetrical features were large, she was a passably good-looking woman. The nondescript dull brown of her hair held evidence of its childhood blondeness. Her pale gray-blue eyes were set a bit too close to the bridge of her nose. I wondered about Esther, with her voluptuous body and her need to carry perfume with her to a test qualifying her to enter a completely masculine world. Was she pampering herself? Would she succeed?

I was itching to be sociable as I waited for Esther to apply fresh makeup. At last she finished and we went down the hall to the first room near the stairs where Betty and Nancy sat, each with a drink in her hand. Each woman who entered the room brought her own glass, already filled. I was amazed. They must have all brought their bottles from home. How did they know that was the thing to do? What am I getting into, I wondered.

Esther possessed more aplomb in sophisticated society than I did. She looked about and said, "I'll buy some bourbon tomorrow and pay you back if somebody will stand me to a drink tonight."

Teresa hopped up quickly. "Okay. Where's your glass?" she asked, taking her own with her.

They returned just as Betty was saying, "Even when I had my gall bladder out, Bud would visit me and we'd have our little drink together. The nurses were incensed and reported us to the doctor. He simply laughed and said, 'Think nothing of it. They always have a rum and coke before dinner.'"

Someone asked Nancy to explain what kind of flying the government wanted us to do. It didn't seem to bother Nancy that Catherine Slocum and Pat Rhonie were not present. We soon learned that was Nancy's way — if you weren't around, you didn't find out, except second or third hand. The choicest news was often told when the persons in attendance sat with drinks in their hands.

Nancy said, "We'll go to the factories for training planes. Only the small ones made in this region, which will be the Piper Cubs and Fairchild PT-19s. By the way, Cubs are known as L-4Bs in the army. We'll deliver them to the airfields where cadet training is going on, mostly in the South."

She paused to sip. We waited eagerly for her to continue.

"Our men pilots have been stuck with this job. We've taken in as many of the airline pilots as we could get and other civilian men with radio experience and instrument flight cards. The Ferry Command has put them into multi-engines as soon as possible. But we need many more to fly the oceans and the Hump."

"The Hump?" Esther broke in.

"The Himalayan Mountains over the India-Burma-China Road." Nancy paused to sip again before continuing.

"The domestic ferrying division has five other groups besides this one. A number of men ferrying trainers right now should be in transition school learning to fly bombers, fighters, and cargo, and getting radio and instrument experience. We are to take their places to allow them to do that.''

''Jeez!'' breathed Teresa. ''Just let me get my hands on one of those bombers.''

Nancy's face turned cold. Her left hand strayed to her hip and her left shoulder moved forward just a trifle. ''We are here to help the war effort by flying training planes. No more.'' She looked directly at Teresa. ''In fact, we were lucky to get this assignment at Newcastle.''

The maid appeared to announce that dinner was ready. Self- consciously, not knowing what protocol to follow, we trailed Nancy, who chose her place at the dining table. Betty sat next to her, and the others scattered about the table. The food was both appetizing and adequate, and the service was leisurely paced, which allowed us an opportunity for small talk about ourselves and about flying.

After dinner everyone retired to the second floor. Restless after a long day of comparative inactivity, the women visited in each other's rooms. I sat for a while writing to Harold. I told him that I had passed the flight test and urged him to go out to parties and movies while I was gone. I didn't want him to become a hermit. And I said, ''This place is like the building of Oklahoma — a mushroom growth — with dust and mud and rough-boarded interiors and activity galore. I feel a part of a large pioneering scene. All my life I've wanted something like this — with spirit and hope and with hardships, too, that we can't foresee — a real life, vigorous and lusty.''

After a while the sound of voices drifted down the hall to my room. I discovered that all the others had gathered in Betty's sitting room where hangar flying was in session.

Barbara Poole steered the conversation on a new tack. ''Anyone heard from Jackie?''

At first, silence. Barbara offered, ''I guess she's still in England.''

Nancy with studied carefulness replied, ''No, I'm sure she has returned.'' She decided she might as well let some of the cat hang out of the bag. ''She found out the WAFs are being organized.''

And I — fool that I was — in all innocence exclaimed, ''Oh, she's come back to join us!''

''I doubt it.'' Nancy's face showed no emotion.

''It's likely that she lacks the educational prerequisites,'' added Betty Gillies.

''Do you think she is too old?'' asked Cornelia Fort.

''I believe that is so,'' Nancy told her.

''Why is the upper age limit thirty-five years?'' I asked. ''If the squadron needed pilots, you're cutting out some famous Ninety-Nines. Their experience would help a lot.''

Nancy was glad to explain. "The Army Air Forces medical staff determined the upper age limit. The flight surgeons have no way of knowing how long the war will last. They don't want to be bothered with middle-aged women with menopause problems. The Ferry Command doesn't want to be responsible for the welfare and morals of minors. So that set the lower age limit at twenty-one. They take in male cadets at nineteen, however, and men up to the age of forty-five."

"Did any of you go to Montreal?" asked Barbara, dabbing her nose. She had an awful head cold.

No one replied. She continued, "Sis Bernheim and I were up there. We took a test in an AT-6. We washed out."

Teresa remarked, "I had some correspondence with Miss Cochran about that British deal, but I passed it up."

I said, "She sent me a telegram and it was two pages long. But I wouldn't leave Harold or my home to fly for Britain. I'm not loyal to the British. But here, this is different."

An undercurrent of dread passed from one person to another in the room. I sensed it in the women's eyes, in the set of their lips, and how they tightened up when Jackie Cochran's name was mentioned. That excited my curiosity. I wanted to be fair and not act how a child does with new-found friends, making their enemies her enemies. By getting bits and information here and there, someday I hoped to develop an unprejudiced picture of what the woman was really like.

All that I knew was that the woman owned the Jacqueline Cochran cosmetic firm. She had plenty of money, which permitted her to buy and fly expensive, fast aircraft in Bendix races. These began on the West Coast and ended on Labor Day at the Cleveland Air Races. After she won the Bendix trophy at last, she continued flying to the East Coast and set a new coast-to-coast flying record.

Harold told me he saw her at Lambert Field one day. She had long, golden curls in the Mary Pickford fashion that many young women affected in the late thirties, before the back-upsweep was combined with a pompadour.

I left off daydreaming to hear Nancy telling us goodnight. Dismissed, we went to our bedrooms.

Later Esther and I looked up to see a visitor, Barbara Poole, who had wandered in, hoping for companionship. I had just finished addressing my letter. Esther rose in welcome.

Our room was well out of earshot of Nancy's. Perhaps that is why Barbara spoke so freely. "Why does the weather have to be so cold and windy here?" she began.

No answer was forthcoming. Whatever the weather is, it is, and who can do anything about it?

"You'd think I'd get a break once in a while," she continued. "I have a miserable cold." She blew her nose and her moist eyes looked over her handkerchief mournfully.

I thought, why gripe about it? and hoped we'd hear no more. But we did.

"I don't see why I have to get any more 2-S time [the CAA classification for aircraft heavier than light trainers which use engines up to 200 horsepower]. I know they'll go over my log books and say I haven't enough recent time to suit them. For crying out loud, a person has to go 150 miles inland just to find an airfield open and hope to get an airplane to fly."

"I thought that's what the telegram said we'd need," replied Esther.

Barbara ignored that remark. "Here I am, and yet she won't allow me to take a flight test."

"Of course. You have a bad cold," I said.

"I'd take it anyway, cold or no cold. She says I haven't enough flying time for this year. Some of what I do have dates pretty far back," Barbara grumbled, looking to us for sympathy. We made no comment.

Then Barbara made her premise clearer. "If they'd only give me a flight test and I passed, I wouldn't mind spending all that money. I want to be sure it is for something. I want to be sure," she reiterated.

Esther answered, "They want to be sure, too, you know."

Soon Barbara drifted away to perhaps more compassionate ears. When she had gone, Esther whispered, "She knew what was in the telegram. The qualifications were as plain as a mud hen."

"Yeah," I agreed. "She should have played it fair and gotten her flying time first and then showed up to see if she'd be accepted — just as we did."

The next morning, Tuesday, we were all at the air base by eight o'clock.

"I can't wait to get started," vowed Teresa. I agreed, for I also wasn't used to wasting time. I felt hemmed in by the shilly- shally organizational snafus that kept us from work. The examining board met and passed both Esther and Teresa. Esther's scented logbook was returned with no comment. She said, "I'd have given anything to have seen their faces when they looked at it." Me, too.

As Barbara Poole surmised, her flight experience was within the proper categories, but she hadn't had enough recent time in large aircraft. She begged Nancy to allow her to take a flight test. Nancy was adamant: Barbara must have more hours in 2-S airplanes. But Barbara did win a point. If and when she reappeared at the base, and if she passed the flight test, she would be considered as having joined immediately after Teresa James. This satisfied her. She knew that an officer with the earliest service date would be the senior officer, in case promotions or benefits were passed out.

The irksome tedium of waiting for things to happen was relieved by the arrival of Helen Richards, a Californian who had been instructing in a CPTP at Boise, Idaho. Although she was only twenty-one, she already had 841 hours in the air. She was a lissome tomboy, as slender hipped and as tall as Amelia Earhart had been. Helen had a Nordic look, with long, naturally light blonde hair, fair skin, and clear blue, intelligent and innocent eyes.

At noon Nancy gathered her small brood around her. We walked down the main road toward the officers mess. As we passed BOQ 14, our future domicile, on sudden impulse Nancy halted. Everyone else did, too.

"I want to see what progress has been made," she said. "If you want to, you may come in with me."

We all jumped the ditch at the side of the road, walked up the dirt path, ascended the steps, and went in. Nancy was in front, looking confident and knowing. The rest of us were hesitant and awed. It's doubtful that any of us had been in a men's barracks before.

Although this was a two story building, the arrangement of rooms was similar to the headquarters building, with a long, narrow hall down the middle. Wooden partitions separated the sleeping rooms from the hall.

As we tiptoed along, we peeked in where the doors were open. Black tarpaper predominated on the walls. Each room was furnished with a narrow metal cot and a shoddy bureau painted to resemble hardwood. Nancy paused at the drinking fountain in the middle of the hall. She turned the faucet and the water ran. A sign above the fixture read NOT POTABLE. Nancy read it aloud without an explanation. I wondered what it meant, but would not ask for fear of being considered stupid. Later in the day I found a dictionary at headquarters. The sign meant the water was not fit to drink.

Toward the end of the hall, Nancy entered a room to the right where all the water hookups were located. Facing them at the left was what would be "our laundry facilities," she said. Along the inner wall were strange, white porcelain something-or-others. Beneath them was a drain, level with the floor. I couldn't imagine what these were.

The group then turned its attention to a small room to the right of the hall entrance. On the hall side were two shower stalls minus curtains. Don't tell me we'll take showers out in front of God and everybody, I thought. Even more shocking was the fact that the commode stalls had no privacy doors.

Nancy could see from the expressions on our faces that we agreed with her own feelings about personal privacy. She declared, "This has to be changed. I'm asking for doors and curtains right away."

That's all we had time for. We left the way we had come in, with Nancy leading. Somewhat soberly we proceeded to the officers club next door where we ate our lunch thoughtfully. What we had just seen was to be our new home — crude, rough, austere, and not unlike a barn. It certainly didn't look like home.

That evening after dinner, Nancy looked about the sitting room and everyone quieted down.

"You are probably wondering about our barracks," she began. "The building isn't quite ready yet, although I have kept right with it. Some masculine plumbing must be torn out. We're to use the larger room as soon as tubs and faucets are installed. Every room is to have venetian blinds on the window. You see, the men's barracks on a base don't have shades. This is a concession to our being female."

There were titters.

"Another thing," Nancy added. "Colonel Baker says the next military pay period starts tomorrow, so we begin our indoctrination tomorrow."

"Then we are in for keeps?" Teresa asked.

"Only for three months, just like the men civilian pilots. Then we will be renewed for three months until we are militarized. If anyone steps out of line, that person will be dismissed from the service."

There was a bit of tete-a-tete going on throughout the room, but we all stopped to listen as Nancy told Helen Richards, "Pearl Harbor caught us terribly short of pilots. What makes it so difficult for the Ferry Command is that some of our best pilots cannot be used for ferrying duty per se. The transition school uses them to train others with less experience."

Then in reply to a question from Cornelia, Nancy said, "The British coined the word 'ferry' to mean transporting an aircraft by air from one place to another."

A bit more conversation and then, as the hour was getting late, everyone dispersed to her room, each with her own emotions about the morrow.

On Wednesday, September 16, at the same time that Colonel Smith was trying to station the WAFS at Fort Worth, members of the examining board and Colonel Baker assembled us in the headquarters of the Third Ferrying Group for a series of ceremonies. In the first, Nancy Harkness Love swore an oath identical to that given to all officers accepting a commission. Afterward Baker declared, ''I now officially appoint Mrs. Nancy Love as the commanding officer of the Women's Auxiliary Ferrying Squadron.''

Following Nancy, in the order of our seniority, we eight volunteers who had already been accepted, were similarly sworn in. We each signed an official document. Then Nancy led us to the building where ground school classes were to be held during the mornings. Morning fogs could disrupt a flying schedule, so flying was to be arranged for later in the day.

Quietly we entered the first classroom. The instructor was introduced and soon we were studying the AAF forms that someday the army would require us to fill out. Nancy remained with us, sitting in the rear and monitoring the class. After an hour of this new tedium, Nancy led us to another classroom where we reviewed civil air regulations, just to keep a friendly peace with the CAA. During this session a secretary came to the door and motioned to Nancy. ''Colonel Baker wants you in his office right away,'' she whispered, and Nancy left.

We learned after dinner that Colonel Tunner had called Colonel Baker to tell him of a new development and Baker wanted to discuss it with Nancy right away.

When I entered the sitting room at the Kent Manor that evening, Nancy was saying, ''I didn't realize she would try to put me down so soon.''

With no show of emotion, Betty Gillies replied, ''You know she's noted for speed.''

Nancy said carefully, as if to reinforce her position to herself, ''What I proposed was so simple. It would only include the women pilots who are already capable of ferrying, so that more men may be able to fly overseas. That is the need.''

''It's no longer that simple,'' replied Betty.

''I bet Colonel Baker that Fort Worth was suggested because that's where she must have her office. I was right.''

Betty fluffed out her upper lip thoughtfully and drew on her cigarette. She said, ''Lord knows who she'll bring into the organization.''

''I came as fast as I could to help win the war as soon as possible,'' cried Cornelia.

''Me, too,'' I declared. Echoes of that sentiment were heard about the room.

''How is Bill Tunner taking it?'' asked Betty.

''Bill realizes he is at a disadvantage. She has the ear of the higher echelons, even up to the White House."

"He'll find a way to block this move," soothed Betty.

Nancy looked glumly at the floor, studying it, and answered slowly, "But even if he does this time, it leaves us with a never-ending problem. How can we anticipate what to do when we don't know beforehand the moves she will make?" She lifted her eyes to Betty's. "I'll be uncomfortable, off balance and on guard."

Betty answered, "Too bad the militarization wasn't set up without question while she was in the United Kingdom. She could never have gotten in then."

Looking at the problems that Jackie Cochran was making for the Ferry Command and knowing what hurdles we had passed in order to volunteer for military service, those few of us at Newcastle Army Air Base felt drawn together, rallying around what we felt Nancy stood for. She made sense; her reasoning was orthodox.

Later, after we had moved to BOQ 14, there were many other evening sessions of question-and-answers interspersed with gossip. The name of Jackie Cochran came up again and again. As I listened, although I wholeheartedly supported our leader, Nancy Love, misgivings about people's judgment of the character and behavior of others crept into my mind. I was given to remembering small bits and pieces of news and tying them together into a mental bundle.

There was no dayroom or lounge in BOQ 14, so the first bedroom on the left was used for this. Someone put up a dart board at which we unleashed our aggression now and then. In that room one evening during a conversational lull, someone said, "I just got a letter from one of the girls in England. She's hot about Jackie. When Jackie got over there she declared that she was the greatest woman pilot in America. The ATA girls were furious, although they thought what she said was hilarious."

"What nerve!" another commented.

Someone who had had contact with Jackie's flying added her opinion. "I don't think she really can fly all that well."

I answered, "But how can you say that? Didn't she win the Bendix?"

"Yes, but not every race she was in. If she ever had to drop out along the way, she blamed it on the airplane."

"You should have seen her on Long Island," said one of our group. "I never saw her fly unless she had a man with her. They'd make a landing and then the plane stopped at the other end of the field for a long time. The fellows in the tower used their binoculars and they saw her changing seats so she could come up to the ramp in the left seat, as if she had made the landing.''

"Oh, that sounds ridiculous. She didn't have a man with her on the Bendix.'' This from Cornelia.

''No, but before the race, they covered the course to be run by flying over the length of it until she knew it. You know nobody in racing can afford to do all that. They don't have that kind of money. All she can do is take off, bend the throttle full forward, and land — and have the luck not to crash.''

To me at the time it seemed unkind and unsportsmanlike to criticize another pilot. On the other hand, I believed that Amelia Earhart was not as great as her publicity made her appear. But I held my tongue about Amelia's failings, not only because it held no value to give my opinion, but I had already learned that among these friends of Amelia's, she could do no wrong.

"All these men around here," said Teresa, "Do they need the same qualifications we do?''

Nancy, with an expressionless face, weighed her answer. She replied, "That depends. Last January, it was 300 hours, three years of high school, and a man could be as old as forty-five. The Ferry Command was in a bind and by May the age level went from twenty-one to nineteen with only 200 solo hours required.''

"Good heavens!" Esther Nelson was aghast. "That's nothing at all! I know what I was like at 200 hours. I wasn't good enough to ferry airplanes. I've got more than 500 now and I'm still leery.''

Most of us were afraid to look at each other. So! The army made the rules of the game and changed those rules to suit itself.

Another applicant for the WAFS came soon after Helen Richards. She was Barbara Towne from the Watsonville, California, area. She was not a product of the government subsidized CPTP. Instead, drawn toward flying she had taken money from her allowance to pay for flying lessons after school hours. When her father discovered what she was doing, he sent her to Ryan School of Aeronautics at San Diego. There she learned as much as she could about airplanes as she worked alongside the mechanics in the shop. Then her father bought her an airplane.

Barbara said she had been a fashion model. I thought she must have made a good one. Her shoulders were wide and square, her delicate lithe and supple body enhanced any garment she wore, for her hips and bustline did not obtrude to detract from the garment itself. Her arms were just a trifle long, yet the total effect was very stylish.

Barbara was more sociable than Helen and very observant. She tried to get to know us as soon as possible. She soon told me she was married to a serviceman named Bob Dixon, but she would keep her maiden name in the WAFS.

Again and again as we all talked, the subject of Jackie came up. The WAFS touched upon her much as the sufferer of a gum chancre, who feels it with her tongue, hoping that it will go away. But Jackie didn't.

Once someone exclaimed with pique, "Just who does she think she is?"

"All she used to be was Mrs. Floyd Odlum's hairdresser."

"No!"

"Yes. She nabbed him after he divorced his wife."

"For her? Is that true?"

"Yes," replied Pat. "Just guess what he gave the first Mrs. Odlum in the divorce settlement?"

"Tell me — what?" asked Esther.

With a Mona Lisa smile, Pat replied, "Bonwit Teller."

My knowledge of New York City was limited, but I had read that Bonwit Teller was a store selling high-priced merchandise in the latest vogue. I sighed and said, "What a lovely going away present!" which caused a few smiles.

But I had serious thoughts about this information. If possible, I must check it out to find if it were true. It struck me that the great differences between Amelia Earhart, whom everyone admired and championed, and Jackie Cochran, who was apparently friendless, were not so great after all.

Both had cracked up airplanes upon landing them. Both had raced and lost. Both had been highly publicized. Both were physically attractive, although Amelia was naturally so and Jackie got some of her charm from cosmetics.

Amelia was chosen to be the first woman to cross the Atlantic. George Putnam, a book publisher, made the choice when a wealthy woman sponsor asked him to find an aviatrix. The flight was successful and began Amelia's climb to fame. She had been a house guest of the Putnams, just as Jackie had been a guest at the Odlums. Subsequently, George divorced his wife and married Amelia.

The marriage contract that Amelia and George drew up outlined a business arrangement without the "until death do us part" vow. Putnam provided himself with notoriety and a chance to take part in Amelia's exciting life. She got the opportunity to be published and to continue flying more and more expensive airplanes on longer and longer flights. Gossip was that he provided Purdue University with a DC-3 to be used as a flying laboratory for Amelia, who spent time there advising coeds about aviation.

Yet no one criticized Amelia. So what was the difference between her and Jackie Cochran?

Amelia, although not wealthy, had a college education. Her father was a professional man. She had the social status necessary to be eligible for the Junior League. In contrast, Jackie gave herself her own name. She said that she didn't know her origins, but was raised by a woman in a poor mill town in the South. After only a year or two of formal schooling, she went to work in a cotton mill, left that and got a job in a beauty shop where she learned her skills by apprenticeship. Always ambitious, she landed in a salon in New York City, met the Odlums, and with Floyd's help, started her own cosmetics company. She jumped the barriers to high society.

After Amelia disappeared on the Pacific leg of her around-the- world flight, Jackie tried to make herself Amelia's successor. She got some publicity, but did not win the admiration of aviation society or the attention of the press, such as Amelia had done.

We WAFS also discussed at length the question of becoming military officers. The first plan was to make us WAACs under the command of Col. Oveta Culp Hobby, the wife of a Houston, Texas, publisher. Militarization of the WAACs would take "auxiliary" out of their name and they would be known as WACs.

As things stood in September 1942, we could decide to stay in the WAFS or leave after a three month probationary period, just as civilian male pilots could. If we were militarized, we were in for the duration.

Pat Rhonie asked one night about becoming part of the WAACs. "Won't Jackie get her fingers in those plans, too?"

Betty frowned and turned to Nancy. She said, "I don't want to be militarized if there's a possibility of Jackie becoming the head of the women pilots."

Pat said, "If she does, she could transfer you wherever she wanted and you'd have to go, regardless."

Betty said, "The way we are now, if we never are militarized, I can stay here close to Bud and the children. I can see how the family is doing. They'll be able to run down to visit me between missions."

Nancy smiled, saying, "I can just imagine what she'd do to me because the WAFS began without her knowledge."

"Isn't there any other way we can fly for our country?" asked Helen Richards, squirming with tension.

"Any suggestions?" Nancy asked as she looked about the room.

Only Betty had one. "What about the navy?"

No one spoke. Then Betty promised, "I'll ask Bud to look into it for us."

Nancy said, "If you want to approach the navy, you have my blessing, Betty. But I am determined to stick with this.''

But the U. S. Navy had considered using women pilots in the spring of 1942 and had already turned down the idea.

Meanwhile the proposal for shipping the WAFS off to Fort Worth had also been turned down. Colonel Tunner told the next meeting of the AAF brass, ''In the past, General Arnold has been rigid about any conflict of command objectives. He opposed the Air Transport Command setting up a formal flight training program within the Ferrying Division for the upgrading of our pilots. General Arnold said then, 'Formal flight training is the duty of the Training Command.'

''Now, we have needed some form of transitional training so that pilots might transfer from training planes to ferrying cargo, bomber, and pursuit type planes for combat purposes. The war effort needs those planes as soon as they roll out of the assembly lines, and we haven't the men to fly them . . . To our purpose in being, when a pilot is on base awaiting orders, he must attend informal training. We have available Link trainers, Morse code equipment, some films, and instrument flight ground school classes he might catch between missions. We try to upgrade by *seniority* methods, so a pilot gets copilot time in ferrying and can get checked out in multi-engine and on instruments at the base.

''Mainly, ferrying is training that is valuable to give a pilot more experience in delivering aircraft safely. It allows him to make judgments and is a necessary step for domestic and foreign ferry operations in military aircraft. The WAFS have been instituted in the Ferrying Division simply to make it possible for men to make the transition to heavier aircraft.

''Ferrying is the function of ATC alone, as training is the function of Training Command alone. Now, if the Training Command takes the WAFS out of ATC, it can also commandeer the men. They will be taking over the domain of the Ferrying Division, which would be against Gen. Arnold's ruling on conflict of command objectives.''

The WAFS remained at Newcastle Army Air Base. Bill Tunner had won; Nancy prevailed. We WAFS, figuratively, spit on our hands, rubbed them in glee, and were ready to take on any hurdles that the Ferry Command and its men would raise before us.

PLAYING BY THE RULES

On FRIDAY, SEPTEMBER 18, we moved on base. The ditch at BOQ 14 still had no bridge, so we helped each other across. Nancy, as usual, led the way and turned to watch us as we followed. Most of us were strong or agile enough to carry our suitcases as we jumped, but I teamed with Esther because she was a bit fearful. She handed me her suitcase and I had my hand ready to catch her should she fall, but she made it all right. Then, carrying our luggage, we followed Nancy along the long north wall of the building to the back stairs.

She warned us, "If you come back late at night from a mission, you must take this way if your room is upstairs so your tramping along the first floor hall won't disturb the girls living downstairs." There was no front stair, but at the front of the building was a vertical ladder which could serve as a fire escape.

When we had all entered the barracks, Nancy again stressed seniority. She said, "You are to choose your room in the order in which you were accepted."

As we followed her up the wooden stairs, I wondered who would dare to sleep downstairs by herself. The farther we were from the outside, the safer I would feel — as far as possible from the strange men

BOQ 14, home of the WAFS at New Castle Army Air Base.

living on the base.

Upstairs, Nancy headed toward the front of the building, closely followed by Betty Gillies. Pat Rhonie, Helen Mary Clark, and Cornelia Fort almost made a trio catching up with them. It appeared that the easterners preferred the east rooms. But Catherine Slocum had a mind of her own and knew a good thing when she saw it. She turned toward a corner room with two windows which faced the northwest.

My turn. I'd made some quick calculations. No west or north exposures for me, winter or summer. There'd be more summer breeze from the south and fewer cold drafts in the winter. I usually slept fitfully in cold weather, for I never seemed to get warm until it was time to get out of bed. So I chose a room closest to the southwest corner.

With a "whoops!" Esther Nelson ran to the room I had rejected, as if afraid someone might take it away before she could claim it. Teresa James, no doubt thinking of the convenience, went to the south room opposite the entrance to the john, as she called the lavatory facilities. The two youngest and latest arrivals, Helen Richards and Barbara Towne, went eastward, possibly for the comfort and reassurance of being near Nancy.

As we unpacked, Betty came around to tell us that Nancy had gone to headquarters and we were to join her there in a quarter hour. We were about to take our third step into military life. Nancy sent us to the sub-depot for GI flight equipment and told us Betty would be in charge of that operation.

Betty was first. The clerks had a difficult time getting a good fit for her and for the other small WAFS. They had to turn up a deep hem in the pant leg of Betty's wool summer flying suit (which was like a coverall) and even the narrowest man's size was too wide for her. But she looked very attractive in her new outfit.

I had no problem, since I was as tall as the average male. My new goatskin jacket was a size 38. We also received helmets, goggles and parachutes. Unused to receiving gifts, I felt as if I were favored by fate.

But there were strings to our gifts. We were warned that we had to return them someday. We must be sure to hold onto our copies of the memorandum receipts of the supplies we were given. When we turned in our equipment, we'd get another copy of that transaction, which we must not lose. If we had no proof of returning the goods, we would be forced to pay Uncle Sam for them.

The truck driver took us with our stacks of new GI equipment and delivered us to the parachute loft. We left our chutes for the enlisted men to stencil with the appropriate name. We'd have to return later to be fitted. Then we returned to BOQ 14.

We hadn't all jumped the ditch yet when Betty Gillies squatted and rubbed her new, shiny goatskin jacket in the dust. I was too shocked to say anything. She looked about at us when she stood up, displaying her handiwork, and said, "No old pilot would ever wear a shiny new jacket. The only people who wear new looking stuff are people who haven't soloed yet."

Helen Richards and several others followed Betty's example. My guess was that they wanted to do the "in" thing. But to me, who had never had such a jacket before and who would try to keep it looking new as long as possible, the act was a sacrilege.

Since we had been assigned different times for going back to the parachute loft, I took my new equipment to room 42. I hung up the flying suit and the jacket and put the helmet and goggles in the top drawer of the chest. Then I looked about at what I had exchanged for my humble home in St. Louis.

Two-by-four framing stood out from the black tarpaper on the walls. A high shelf about two feet deep and three feet wide had been built into the northwest corner of the room. It could be used to hold books and charts or anything a person wouldn't mind inspectors seeing. Below the shelf and attached to it was a bar for hanging clothes, since there was no closet. On the west wall was a cheap, maple-finished chest with

Helen Mary Clark dons her flight suit in her room at BOQ 14.

five drawers. (The furniture trade termed this kind of merchandise "borax.") A couple of nails next to it supported my towel and washcloth. I had placed a bar of soap, toothpaste, and toothbrush on the horizontal framing. A cheap mirror hung on a nail directly above the chest of drawers.

To the south was the venetian-blind shaded window and to its left was the bed. The army did not provide us anything to sit upon except the bed, so it was not only a resting place, but also a chair. That bed — where had it been before I lay on it?

Nancy had told us that the narrow metal cots were left over from a Civilian Conservation Corps (CCC) encampment. They had been stored somewhere on the East Coast, gathering rust until they were brought out for the benefit of civilian pilots living in BOQ 14.

I lay down and sank as if in a hammock. In getting up and out of the cot, I hit my arms and knees on the metal side frames. An inspection showed the mattress to be made of wadded cotton about two inches thick. Below it was a sagging flatlink spring, lifeless from the years of weight that it had borne. I felt hopeless.

Esther, who also had to wait her turn at the parachute loft, came in and asked, "What do you think of the beds?"

"Terrible," I answered.

"We've got to do something," she mused. "There are forty-four rooms and only a few of us. Why don't we go downstairs and find a better bed and make an exchange?"

That seemed to me a good idea. We could manage a switch by working as a team. So we sneaked downstairs and toured the rooms, only to discover that all the cots were in as bad a condition as the ones upstairs. Esther suggested that we swipe another mattress to put on top of ours, so we wouldn't hit the iron bedstead every time we turned in our sleep.

We whisked away two mattresses and placed them under the ones already on our beds. I tried out the arrangement. The hollow I lay in wasn't as deep as it had been, but the iron sides were still up there, waiting to hit me when I turned.

"I'm going down and borrow a khaki blanket from a bed," I whispered to Esther, and did so.

With the woolen blanket rolled and placed lengthwise down the middle of the cot beneath both mattresses, a little more slack was taken from the middle. I still was not completely safe from bruises, but was a wee bit more comfortable than before.

Later I wrote to Harold, "You know how I love to sleep, one leg curled up like a stork. I must learn some new habits, trying to be a Japanese lady or a mummy in its case. In fact, I wish I could sleep like that because every morning I've torn the narrow sheets from their moorings and the bed apart and must remake the whole thing. It would be so simple to slip out as from a cocoon instead."

We had to learn to make the beds the army way, just as if we were enlisted personnel. Betty Gillies, who had had nurses' training as well as some polishing at Ogoontz finishing school, went about the rooms to make sure we were doing it right. She bounced a quarter off the top blanket to test the tightness of our finished product.

It must have been about 1630 the same afternoon when Teresa appeared at my door.

"My Gawd!" Teresa whispered, her dark eyes open wide. "Did you ever think we'd be with such classy dames?"

I laid my homework on my pillow, patted the cot beside me, and Teresa sat down.

"You know who just came in to interview Nancy?"

I shook my head negatively.

"Alma Heflin! You know who Alma Heflin is?"

"Sure," I replied. "A test pilot for Piper Aircraft."

With awe Teresa whispered, "She writes books."

"Yeah, pretty interesting books. About her adventures while flying in Cubs."

"I wonder sometimes what I'm doing here," Teresa complained. "Those babies are so much competition." She paused. "I might not even last." Then she looked me squarely in the eye, more like her usual self.

I thought Teresa was only shooting the breeze. Before she came to Wilmington, she had been instructing in a CPTP secondary program in Pennsylvania, flying much heavier, faster, and more dangerous aircraft than Cubs.

I laughed, "You've got nothing to worry about. Don't you see what a hard time they're having getting anybody? We're not in any danger of flunking."

Before any of the other women saw Alma, she was gone. She went, just as Barbara Poole had, to find an aviation school with 2-S airplanes to fly to bring her flying hours up to the minimum. When she returned the following week, she passed her initial flight test.

When I saw her for the first time as she entered the barracks, I could understand immediately why Piper had chosen her to fly and to write for them. She was a mere wisp of a woman, much too thin to be attractive physically, for the slenderness of her face caused her nose to look too prominent. But I knew that tiny Alma had flown a Cub over Canadian and Alaskan terrain that was harsh and desolate. She had a genuine talent for telling her adventures. Piper was smart to hire her, I thought.

During the few days that Alma remained at Newcastle, all of us were inspired by her fame. She, on the other hand, wore an air of pathetic isolation. Hoping to draw her out, I said to her, "I want you to know how much I enjoyed reading your books, especially the one about your flight to Alaska. That trip took a lot of guts."

In another encounter, Alma confided in me what was uppermost in her heart. "I just got married," she said. "I should call myself McCormick, but I'm not used to it yet." She paused and I read pain and fear in her eyes. "He's an RAF pilot and on his way to England."

She didn't have to tell *me* how dreadfully she missed him.

Alma's monetary sacrifice in buying flying time was for naught. She disappeared. The flight instructors told a few of us, "She really can't fly anything but a Cub" and "she flew Cubs too long, so that's the only plane she can fly."

"What do you think, kid?" Teresa asked me.

"She probably didn't have any chances to fly anything else," I replied, "if all the flying she got at Piper was to test certain specifics of the Cub."

"Yeah, she wouldn't be wise to what different pressures each kind take on the controls."

I agreed, nodding my head. "Right, and they vary even in the same model if the rigging is off. You can't fly well except by the seat of your pants."

"Those Cubs sure forgive a lot of student mistakes," Teresa explained as if to herself. "Hey! Maybe nobody at Piper ever gave her a recheck."

"Recheck a test pilot? That's humiliating," I replied.

"Well," retorted Teresa, "it's plenty humiliating to wash out of this."

"Not nearly as bad as what could have happened if they let her go on and break her neck."

"Your cooking on the front burner there, sister," mused Teresa. She must have read my mind about what such a tragedy would have done to the rest of us.

Teresa was called in for an interview with Nancy Love early in our program. Nancy decided that something had to be done about Teresa's hair. Pat Rhonie had called it to her attention several times and the irritation Nancy felt was mainly from Rhonie's attempts to make the decisions. Still, those long black curls didn't look military. So she telephoned the barracks and asked Teresa to come to her office immediately.

After Miss Cohee discreetly left the office, Teresa sat down in the chair facing Nancy's desk. On edge, she waited, mystified by the sudden call.

Nancy's face showed no emotion as she spoke. "You realize, Teresa, that we are at a military establishment and that we must conform to the standards set for the men. None of us, although feminine, must flaunt it. We have to blend into the scheme of things as they are here."

"Mrs. Love, have I done anything out of line?" Teresa asked.

"Not really," answered Nancy. "But I must tell you that you simply must have your hair cut. It is outrageously long. It shouldn't be below your collar in length. Curling it will put it closer to your ears, which is acceptable. I realize that you must be proud of your hair, Teresa, but long hair just emphasizes that we are females and besides, it becomes too untidy when blasted by prop wash and the high winds we encounter while flying. It is necessary for the WAFS to be neat at all times. You understand that everyone of us has to give up something in order for us to make a success of this venture."

Teresa, like the rest of us, had already learned that an officer's expressed wish was really a command. But she was stunned and her jaw dropped as she realized what Nancy had said. She thought, I'll bet that blasted Rhonie put a bug in her ear. Aloud she replied, "Yes, Mrs. Love, I understand."

Nancy turned to some papers on her desk, thus closing the interview.

Seething, Teresa returned to the barracks. She kicked at a clod of dirt, hurting her toe, and gave forth with a "damn!" She looked to be certain that no one had heard a WAFS use an expletive. Then she relieved her feelings again. "Damn! She didn't have to be so cold about it."

The interview with Nancy prompted Teresa to a hasty haircut, which she hated. But, as she told me later, she would have hated even more to have been dismissed from the WAFS. She decided to conform and to try to avoid another dressing down from Nancy.

However, another one came. Teresa had written home, asking for some "comforts" to use in making her barracks room more pleasant. Her sister Betty decided to bring them herself and came to Wilmington for a weekend in late September. When she arrived, Teresa remembered all the right things to do. No civilians were allowed to stay on base, so Teresa got Betty a room at the Hotel DuPont. Since there was no good (or official) reason for Teresa to remain on the base Saturday night, she joined her there.

The two sisters chatted away the hours. They were so engrossed in their conversation that they were unaware of who else was dining in the hotel's restaurant. A four-piece combo plunked out the latest songs from "Your Hit Parade." There was a small dance floor, and whenever one of their favorite tunes was played, the two sisters danced together joyfully and energetically.

On Monday morning, Teresa was given a message to report to Mrs. Love's office. Now what? she thought.

Nancy was in a quandry. Teresa was a good pilot and Nancy needed her badly. On the other hand, she had not learned the formalities of a finishing school. Nancy did not want to teach military protocol or proper etiquette. Yet the implications of what Teresa had done were serious enough to dismiss her. No wonder she sat as rigid as a judge when Teresa arrived!

Nancy began, "You were in Wilmington over the weekend."

"Oh, yes!" said Teresa happily. "My sister Betty came down to see me and she brought me some things I need. I made sure I wouldn't miss out on any flying or anything or I wouldn't have gone."

"So that's who she was. You two were seen dancing together," added Nancy, a bit mollified and relieved. "Didn't you know that girls never dance together? It just isn't done."

Teresa felt a belligerent gorge welling up in her chest and she had difficulty repressing it. Carefully she replied, "Oh, I didn't know it wasn't done here. Up in Pittsburgh we do it all the time. And nobody thinks nothing about it."

"Perhaps it might be done while learning a step or in one's own small social circle, but never in public. It isn't the thing to do and I expect you to remember not to do it in the future." Another thought occurred to Nancy. "And warn the other girls not to dance together in public, either."

I saw Teresa's troubled look as she slowly climbed the back stairs of the barracks. I wondered what was paining her. Soon she came into my room, but not before looking about the hall to see if anyone was around. She closed the door behind her.

"What do you think?" she asked. "I dance with my sister Saturday night and somebody snitches and Nancy bawls me out. She acts like women don't dance together. Well, they do in Pittsburgh!"

"They do in St. Louis, too," I said, soothingly. "Why should we deprive ourselves of enjoyment when the music is going on just because some fellows are too clumsy or lazy or bashful to dance with us?"

"She seems to think you have to sit and wait until some guy condescends to ask you."

"That might be all right if your papa is giving the party and invites more men than girls and the fellows know they're supposed to dance with the girls or they don't get invited again. But my papa never ever gave me a party, and I say, what can be wrong with two women dancing together if they want to?"

"It beats me," said Teresa, shaking her head. "I don't get why it's so wrong."

"I guess I'll have to watch myself from now on," I said. "I'm pretty much a tomboy. Out at Lambert Field, the fellows and I would play leapfrog over the fireplugs and hop the fence or even get up and tap-dance to a tune in the jukebox in the restaurant. This army sure puts a crimp in my style."

Later I mulled over our conversation and thought about when I had attended Harris Teachers College. It was an all-girl school. Since I was tall and thin, I was always assigned a boy's part at the Harvest and May festivals. On one occasion I was in a sword dance where *all* the parts were masculine. During our short noon recesses, we girls often taught each other new dances — the Charleston, the Camel Walk, the Black Bottom, and others. I saw nothing "bad" about it.

Because we were women and in spite of the fact that many of us had been of voting age for some time and were wives and mothers, it was thought necessary for us to have a chaperone. Perhaps the decision was Colonel Baker's, who was a southern gentleman. Or maybe he wished to forestall any criticism by Cochran, who evidently did not trust women to live and work freely without supervision.

One Monday a quiet lady made her appearance at BOQ 14 and remained at Wilmington as our house mother as long as women pilots served there. She was Mrs. Anderson, who forthwith was nicknamed Andy.

We "westerners" of the barracks had an uncomfortable meeting with Andy that week. We were afraid an inspection team might arrive at any time and our rooms weren't as clean as the army demanded. I had found a broom in a tiny closet near the lavatory and was using it to sweep my floor. Andy must have heard the swish. All of a sudden, a frail, elderly lady was glaring at me with faded blue eyes from behind steel-rimmed spectacles.

Fretfully she exclaimed, "It isn't necessary for you to do that!"

I had never talked back to my elders and I had no idea as yet that Mrs. Anderson had official business in our BOQ. Well, humor her, I thought. She waited while I put the broom back where I had found it.

Then she floated off to the east.

"Who's she?" I whispered to Nelson, who had come out of her room next door, hiding a dustcloth behind her back.

"She's supposed to be our housekeeper," she whispered back.

"If she's so sore, why doesn't *she* clean up this place?" I asked, looking after Andy's trim little figure retreating down the hall.

Teresa James had heard the encounter and came out of her room to scowl at the intruder disappearing into a room. I put my forefinger to my lips, tiptoed into the john, and came back with the broom. We all swept without swishing after that just to keep the peace.

In explaining the presence of Mrs. Anderson a few days later, Nancy said, "Colonel Baker ordered a housemother for the barracks. She is not to be at your beck and call to help you with your clothing, but she will see that the house is kept clean and will serve as a chaperone." (The barracks was off-limits to all male personnel except officers making an inspection.)

Withal, Mrs. Anderson was pleasant, and it comforted us later when we got back at all hours from our missions to know that someone would be in the barracks when we returned.

The presence of a chaperone didn't take away our military or social responsibilities, however. One evening Betty gathered us together so that Nancy could speak to us. She began with, "Let it be understood that under no circumstances are you to date enlisted personnel."

Nancy knew that I was married to an enlisted man. I felt that her implication was that my husband was inferior to me. I refused to consider this true. Was I lower in her eyes because of my marriage?

Teresa had questions, too. She said to me privately, "I wonder if Nancy or somebody saw Slocum and me talking to some enlisted men in the base exchange and decided because we were laughing at something that we were getting too chummy? It looks like I always get off on the wrong foot."

I answered, "I wonder if Colonel Baker and all the officers keep apart from the troops as if they aren't fighting on the same side. It's not like fraternizing with the enemy! What does she expect me to do — divorce Harold until after the war?"

Eventually Nancy made her position more explicit. One night she told us, "We must conduct ourselves so that no one will get the notion that we are like camp followers."

We understood what she meant and did not want that designation either. We decided to keep as aloof as we could and to appear as demure as possible to any visitors on base and to the officers' wives who would see us at dances or at a Sunday evening buffet.

The majority of us were married and happily so. Of the others, Pat Rhonie was not interested in any second lieutenant a dozen or so years younger than she. Her sights were set much higher. Cornelia Fort was enjoying the company of other distinguished women pilots. She didn't appeal to young men her own age, fresh out of cadet training. She looked older than her years and was tall, which was a handicap to romance in those days. She had a look of austere bookishness and her long, handsome face did not correspond to the pretty-pretty face so beloved by moviegoers of that era. So Cornelia was ignored by the young men on the base.

Helen Richards, tall, tomboyish, aloof and shy, may have excited the interest of the lieutenants, but she seemed blind to any attempt on their part to become acquainted. Teresa James wouldn't call attention to herself by mixing with the boys at the club. Even Gertrude Meserve, who moved into our barracks after our first week on the base and who was as attractive as Helen, was too quiet and shy to draw men.

There were times when Nancy remained at the officers' club after dinner. We did, too, and if we didn't join her, we at least kept her in view so that when she left the building we followed. Our concerted action showed our solidarity.

Nancy usually sat on a couch in the lounge. On either side of her and on the floor at her feet would be a gaggle of immobilized young men, feasting their eyes upon her beauty and thrilled to be near a celebrity. Nancy captivated her audience. It was never the same group, because officers might remain on the base for only one evening before orders sent them on another mission.

One evening we learned from Nancy that the Ferry Command staff frowned on our having flight contacts with men ferry pilots on our missions.

She said, "When operations places you on an order to deliver an airplane, none of you will be on the same flight plan with any men. In going cross-country, even though their flight is going your way, avoid them. Operations will make a point of not having the WAFS mission start out at the same time a male flight does when they go to the same factory or deliver at the same place."

"Why is that?" asked Cornelia.

"All the cadets have had flight training in close formation. They may be tempted to fly on your wing and horse around. It's against Civil Air Regulations, but they get by with it when they can. We haven't had the training, and as civilians we must not get closer to any other airplane than 500 feet.

"Above all, never get into the same airplane with the men."

"Oh," I said, "what's wrong with that?" I had the unique idea that men were just people like us.

Nancy turned and looked steadily into my eyes, which was enough to make an upstart like me keep her mouth closed for the time being.

She replied, "People will gossip and we are not giving them a chance to do so. If they saw a woman copilot leave an airplane with the pilot and the flight engineer, they'd think that there'd been some playing house in the sky in government property."

"The inference could not be disproved," added Betty.

She was right. Although men might invite us for a ride, we couldn't accept it.

"We're too much in the public eye," said Nancy. "Any adverse publicity would harm not only us, but all of the women pilots in this country. You are forbidden to solicit a ride just to get experience in flying heavier military aircraft."

It was a hard rule to follow, especially for the pretty young WAFS that the men hoped to impress. Because of that, the message needed repetition. One late afternoon in October we gathered again to listen to Nancy on the subject.

She began, "One of the WAFS came into headquarters today smoking. Colonel Baker has said that we are forbidden to smoke in that building and he means it. Never do it again.

"And another thing — about joy riding." Nancy looked coolly about the room. "I overheard one of you saying that a lieutenant invited you to ride along with him while he is taking transition. No matter how great the temptation, you cannot accept rides.

"Colonel Baker wrote these orders, and I quote," said Nancy, reading from a piece of paper. "'Under no circumstances are the WAFS to solicit rides in bomber-type aircraft whether for local flying or for cross-country without the specific authority from the group commander' — meaning himself."

"I didn't ask him to take me," said Evelyn Sharp. Her big brown eyes widened further, while the corners of her mouth turned down. She was one of the new WAFS. No doubt she felt herself accused of wrongdoing when, in fact, she had done nothing beyond being the attractive young female that she was.

"I didn't say that you did," replied Nancy. "But the boys like to show off. It isn't their flight time and airplanes to give. Transition is serious business. It isn't easy to come by; it must not be used for play. If he gives you a chance to fly with him, the opportunity is being taken away from someone else who should get that air experience. An officer who misuses his transition may find he'll be deprived of it. He may even lose a promotion.''

Betty added her bit. ''Girls, the general public does not understand that a mixed crew may work as a flight team. They are suspicious and people aren't ready for mixed crews just yet.''

Nancy concluded the session with, ''We don't want any girl here to feel obligated to be especially nice to any man who would let her handle the controls of an airplane during the joyride. I'm sure you understand me.''

We started away from the room, but Nancy stopped us. ''There should be no breath of scandal about us. The order protects all of us. Besides, we want everyone to be treated fairly and not having this policy could lead to problems. If Colonel Baker didn't pursue this policy, some of you girls might vie for the favors of young men who would allow them to sit in the right hand seat of a bomber or a transport and you would get ahead of the rest. Jealousy and bickering could break apart the *esprit de corps* we now have. So watch it.''

At only one time when I was at Wilmington was there a chance for me to disobey Colonel Baker's order. In November I was about to return to St. Louis to renew the mortgage on our flat and to put it in both our names. In operations I met a pilot who knew me from Lambert Field. As we chatted he told me he was to deliver a Martin B-26 out West and expected to make a stop at Lambert or Scott Airfield across the river from St. Louis on the way.

Most pilots feared, or pretended to fear, the B-26. This one said, ''You should see what a B-26 is like coming in for a landing. You glide about 165 miles per hour. Once you get used to it, it isn't bad. Why don't you come along with me? You're going to St. Louis anyway. I could save you the air fare.''

I turned him down regretfully. I wasn't as afraid of gossip or of the airplane as I was of the wrath of Nancy Love and Colonel Baker, whose nickname was ''Black Bob.'' The name came not only from his black hair and moustache, but also for his mood when he was crossed. It never occurred to me to ask him if he would make an exception and give me permission to go.

ROUGHING IT IN BOQ 14

ON OUR FIRST SATURDAY TOGETHER we congregated at 1700 in the dayroom. Nancy was wearing a dinner dress, for she was dining at the officers' club with some of the DuPonts and their friends. As she came into the room, she draped the uniform she had worn for the first newsreel cameras over a chair.

She said, "Before you arrived on base, I went to Carlson's, the tailor in Wilmington who tailors the men's uniforms. I wanted to arrange for the uniforms we'll be required to wear for identification on military bases. Uniforms are as necessary for us as for the men. Officers provide their own uniforms . . . ''

Betty broke in, "They get a clothing allowance."

"Yes," agreed Nancy. "We won't receive an allowance until we are officially militarized." She continued with her explanation. "There wasn't enough wool cloth for twenty-five uniforms which could match the color and materials used for officers' uniforms. All Carlson had in any quantity was this gray-green wool serge. I took what I could get.

"They measured me and when I had my first fitting, you should have seen it! I don't think Carlson knew what a woman's figure looked like. The outer parts of the pants in the thighs were cut something like jodhpurs. They were awful. So, we had other fittings. It was possible for me to wear this,'' she pointed to the uniform, ''for the newsreel and then I took it back again.''

''The clothes that Carlson makes for the men look just great,'' reassured Betty on seeing the anxiety on our faces.

''Maybe they got their ideas from pictures of women pilots when we all wore jodhpurs because there was nothing else we could wear,'' I said.

Nancy replied, ''That may be. I imagine we had better get started on your uniforms so that you'll be wearing them on your first mission.''

''How much is it going to cost?'' asked Barbara Towne.

''Approximately seventy-five dollars per suit. That includes the skirt, the trousers, and the blouse.''

With that I caught on that ''blouse'' meant the jacket.

Nancy continued, ''Manhattan makes a woman's khaki cotton shirt that goes well with the uniform, especially at the neckline. You'll also have to buy a white silk shirt for dress wear, but it's impossible to be uniform on that item. The cap is an overseas cap such as American Legionnaires wear.''

''What about shoes?'' asked Pat Rhonie.

''Oh, we'll all wear brown oxfords with a cuban heel. And carry a brown leather purse with a shoulder strap.''

After that came babble as we each talked to our nearest neighbor about our new clothes. When Nancy began to speak again, we stopped, not wanting to miss a thing.

She said, ''I'd advise you to get two uniforms. While one is at the cleaners, you'll be wearing the other. You must look sharp and military at all times, with your shoes shined and trousers creased. No wrinkles! And every button buttoned.''

My heart stopped with dismay. For a moment, her declaration daunted me. I never walked if I could run and I moved from one task to another so rapidly that my favorite expression for years had been, ''Clothes, if you want to come along, hang on!'' Now I would have to slow down, buy shoe polish, worry about my appearance. And every button buttoned? Could I manage or would I forget?

Nancy was explaining, ''The overcoat has an extra inner lining you button in when the weather gets colder. It's of gray wool, like a melton, but harder. The overcoat will cost seventy-five dollars.''

I did some rapid mental arithmetic. The sum was $225 for uniforms. A purse, shoes, socks, shoe polish, two blouses — I mean shirts — and what else? My first month's salary would not pay for all this. And yet I couldn't bring myself to back out. I thought about the other requirements for spit and polish. For my nails? And perhaps powder, lipstick and rouge, and a beauty parlor for my hair.

Nancy was answering another question. She said, "We are unable to duplicate the army khaki because we are neither enlisted nor commissioned."

With that, my stomach cramped. After all this expense, if we were commissioned, we'd get a uniform allowance, but we'd never realize any compensation for our original uniform investment!

We had appointments to visit Carlson's in Wilmington the following week for our measurements and fittings. It was an embarrassing experience for a woman to be measured by a tailor for the first time in her life. The tailor nonchalantly placed the end of the cloth tape up in my crotch and slipped his hand along the tape — and my leg — to the ankle.

Later I said to Esther, "He was getting a little fresh, wasn't he?"

At my first try-on, the uniform pants were droopy-drawered in back. To emphasize how flat I was in the rear: sometimes when I dressed hurriedly and put on a girdle, I could feel something was amiss after walking about for a few minutes. I didn't feel comfortable. There was nothing to do but to take off the girdle and to put it on right.

Teresa was also disappointed with her trousers. With a groan, she exclaimed, "Just look how baggy these pants are! I can tuck my parachute in them and still have inches to spare."

My skirt was just as bad. There were three more inches on each side than I needed for what I considered to be a loose fit. Those who complained the loudest were finally satisfied, and we got our altered uniforms in time before our first official ferry assignment. As a bonus, Carlson gave each of us one substantially constructed suit hangar to go with the uniform. I still have mine.

From the time the WAFS first came to Newcastle, the air was filled with the noise and confusion of men and machines working. A sense of urgency prevailed. One day giant tractors and bulldozers thundered up and down, leveling the the raw earth. The next day a huge mechanized roller relentlessly pressed the strip flat. Then work crews laid down black, cinder-like rock. And before the week was up, a new road was ready for use.

All the while the road was being created, other workmen were excavating earth and teams were pouring concrete which would become the foundations for buildings. In a few days, cinder block walls rose. When roofed and windowed, although the mortar was still setting and damp, these structures served as barracks for men officers. In just weeks, the base was burgeoning with other barracks, as the needs of the war demanded.

It wasn't long before I learned how much the officers appreciated what was being done in their behalf. At the lunch/brunch line the first Sunday we were on base, an officer in the line ahead of me half-turned and glanced at me sideways.

"You're one of the women pilots?" he asked.

"Yeah," I answered.

"You're not too popular with the men around here."

I shifted my weight and rubbed the back of my neck, then opened my eyes wider as they circled the room. Enemies here? I thought.

He continued, "We used your barracks when we were civilian pilots. We got back from a trip one day and had to move out. Do you know where they put us?"

I shook my head. "No."

"In Mosquito Meadows, and it's not the best place in the world, let me tell you!" This in a mordant tone, no doubt meant to inflict burning wounds of guilt.

"Oh, those must be the nice, new concrete barracks they're building on the other side of headquarters —"

"Hmpf! Maybe they look good to you from the road, but I don't like living there. You sink into the mud and you can't keep your shoes clean. Did you see the building they put in the middle? That's where the plumbing is, and it's for all four barracks surrounding the yard."

The line moved forward several feet. This activity relieved some of the tension that this disgruntled man was causing me. But he had more to get off his chest.

"That's where we take our showers and shave. Then we have to go back to our room to put on our clothes because there's no place out there to change. We go out in the cold and the rain in a bathrobe. Listen, if anybody has to go to the bathroom at night and he doesn't feel well or just got back from a trip, it ain't convenient."

"I'm sorry," I apologized.

"And mosquitoes breed in there. When it gets colder, can you imagine what it'll be like to take a shower and have to go out in zero weather to your barracks still wet? We'll be calling it Pneumonia Alley by then."

He had a valid criticism of his living quarters, for I saw later how quaggy the mud paths around the base were, including those around BOQ 14. We kept to the paved roads as much as possible. And we WAFS still had to ford that confounded ditch coming and going from

Cosmopolitan *magazine ran this picture of the first WAFS. From left: Aline Rhonie, Helen Mary Clark, Teresa James, Adela Scharr, Esther Nelson, Cornelia Fort, Catherine Slocum, and Betty Gillies.*

the barracks.

During the WAFS's salad days, we were expected to be good sports and to bear much of the unpleasantness of being female as silently as possible. The concept that we were an inferior sex and one to be blamed for the ills of mankind seemed to be rooted in Eve's persuasion of Adam to bite the apple, which led to their banishment from Paradise. So I didn't inform the complaining officer that in some respects he was luckier than we. As soon as he had arrived on the base he had been placed in the barracks at fifteen dollars per month rent and he was able to eat all meals at the club next door. We bore the costs of hotel lodging, food, and transportation to and from the base — without a salary — as we waited for our program to begin.

One day, while an equatorial sun slanted down on us from a cloudless sky, we met the press. It was a perfect day for taking photographs and doing a routine for the newsreel cameras. The first eight qualified WAFS stood in a line on the concrete apron south of the hangar. From left to right, we were: Betty Gillies, Pat Rhonie, Teresa James, Cornelia Fort, Helen Mary Clark, Adela Scharr, Esther Nelson, and Catherine Slocum. We looked very military, wearing helmets and goggles and khaki flying suits. But if one glanced at our feet the image dissipated. We wore tennis shoes, black-and-white oxfords, or whatever we had. The following Friday we watched the newsreels for our big scene — it flickered by so rapidly that no one could notice our footgear. In fact, we hardly recognized ourselves.

Our performance was planned. At a signal rehearsed beforehand, each of us picked up her parachute from the concrete apron. Firmly holding onto the leg straps, each resolutely swung the straps over her right shoulder so that the parachute hung like a dead weight down her back.

Then as a group we trudged across the concrete. Each stopped at an open cockpit trainer, a Fairchild PT-19A, previously assigned to her. Each climbed onto the trailing edge of the left wing root, placed her chute in the rear cockpit, lowered herself onto its cushion, slid the shoulder harness on, fastening it across her chest, and waited. On being told, "That's it!", each unsnapped her shoulder harness, climbed out, picked up the chute, and jumped off the trailing edge of the wing.

The news photographers thought it was a good take, so we didn't need to go through the routine again. The photographers promised to return at the end of the week to take stills of individuals and small groups. Years later I discovered one of those photographs in a book, *Women with Wings.* It was of Gertrude Meserve, Barbara Towne and me, seated on the concrete next to an airplane. We were concentrating on an unfolded sectional chart as if we were planning a flight.

Because we were women, the press sent their feature writers, nicknamed "sob sisters," to interview us. They reputedly had had experience writing aviation news. But their ignorance was outstanding. For example, one reporter asked Nancy as they looked at an AT-6 parked on the flight line, "What do you mean by 'the hatch'"?

Nancy told her and pointed out the difference between the open cockpit Fairchilds and the closed cockpit AT-6. The enclosure, of course, was the hatch.

"Oh?" replied the expert. "You mean the lid."

Reporters tried their best to find out something sensational about us. They accompanied us to our barracks, but BOQ 14 in all its inelegance did not appeal to them. They scurried about, each trying to find something that the others did not. This caused confusion and I was tired. So I lay down on my bed and started to read a book that Cornelia Fort had lent me. Cornelia was constantly reading, sending and getting books in the mail, and she thought I'd like this one. A reporter snatched the book unceremoniously from my hands, read the title, found it of no interest, and shoved it back at me.

Later, on the way to supper, Teresa told me, "Gee, I was afraid to go to the john. One of those old bags might have stuck her head over

The New York Times *of September 24, 1942, used this picture of the* WAFS *at New Castle, Delaware, passing a row of PT-19s. From left: Teresa James, Cornelia Fort, Esther Nelson, Betty Gillies, Aline Rhonie, Adela Scharr, Nancy Love, and Catherine Slocum. Helen Mary Clark is hidden behind Love.*

the door to see what was happening.''

While the media was agitating the Second Ferrying Group Headquarters for news about the WAFS, politicians, too, were trying to find out information. Congressman Joseph Clark Baldwin, speaking for the American Forum of the Air, invited Nancy Love to appear on radio September 25, with Mildred H. McAfee, commander of the WAVES, and Oveta Culp Hobby, director of the WAACs.

Nancy begged off. She did not enjoy public exposure and had stayed out of the way of photographers and reporters. A Ferrying Division spokesman told Congressman Baldwin that since Mrs. Love had no military status as yet, ''an unprepared discussion of problems which have not yet arisen might provoke criticism all out of proportion to the importance of the actual subject.'' The radio program went on as scheduled, but Nancy Love was not present.

After the second interruption of our training by the media, Air Transport Command placed a lid on all news about us. This restrained factual publicity, but did not hinder magazine writers from fictionalizing episodes about us. We were painted as being sadly overworked and forced to fly in bad weather.

Nancy told us that Colonel Tunner had put the damper on more publicity. "If anyone wants to put you in the news, they must get permission from headquarters," she said. "Don't get into trouble by allowing anyone but the official base photographer to take your picture. He'll do it for identification cards and necessary official business."

We early birds were startled, but heeded the admonition. WAFS who came in one or two months later did not hear such a strong message. As is typical, the oldest child in the family is the best disciplined — there aren't so many of her to contend with at one time.

Because of the length of our classes, we were missing what flying we could do in the afternoon, so our program had to be changed. Flying was shifted to the morning hours and ground school to the afternoons and evenings. One phase of military training we hadn't bargained for abruptly became a part of our lives.

Early one morning, on a fairly level stretch of paved road near headquarters, we lined up for roll call. Nancy Love was facing us, silhouetted against the bright eastern haze that the sun had not yet dispelled. We could see that it was too foggy to fly.

Then Lieutenant Jordan, stepping briskly, left the headquarters building and joined Nancy. Immediately he took charge and began issuing orders. We soon found ourselves in a line arranged according to height. Cornelia Fort and I led. Right behind us were Catherine Slocum and Esther Nelson, followed by Helen Richards and Barbara Towne. Then came Helen Mary Clark and Teresa James. Pat Rhonie and Betty Gillies brought up the rear.

In the days that followed, as new recruits arrived and were accepted, they fitted into the ranks according to their height. But Cornelia and I remained partners until our orientation ended.

Luckily for me, in the three and one-half years I attended Soldan High School in St. Louis, Blanche Higgins had been my gym teacher. We ungainly students under Miss Higgins' stern supervision exercised to a sweat twice a week. Some days Miss Higgins made us march, using changing drill formations to make marvelous patterns that flowed from one to another. At times we girls were eight abreast, wheeling about the gymnasium, accompanied by the strong beat of marches pounded out of a piano.

How I loved it then. Especially the music, for the only music at home came from a dozen or so damaged classical records played on an old Edison phonograph that my father had bought on his beat from someone who was discarding it.

There was no martial music now. Lieutenant Jordan shouted, "One-two-three-four," over and over again. At last he yelled, "Company, halt!" and we stopped, more or less together.

During the first progression, all we had to do was to follow the one in front of us at the correct distance and in step. We learned to pace ourselves evenly, never to break step, and to listen to commands. Some women had had no experience with marching. On the barked instructions, such as "To the rear, march!" or "Right flank, march!" they bolted formation. Upon discovering themselves unaccompanied, they would turn, run, and dart into the positions they had vacated.

No sooner did the group have a semblance of understanding of what was expected of it than Lieutenant Jordan introduced new, more complicated commands. The WAFS never knew what to expect. Each of the WAFS was an independent thinker. She followed her own commands. None of us would have succeeded in aviation if we had not become self-reliant in making important decisions involving life-and-death situations. Yet here everyone subordinated her ego to the group marching effort in order to make the squadron perfect.

We resolved that the WAFS must not fail. All eyes were upon us. We were curiosities, of course, and we easily guessed that inside the nearby administration building onlookers peeked out at us with some amusement, garnering tidbits to relate about our stupidity. The day would come when we would join the men for inspection and parade. They were going to admire us or else!

During the first week after marching drills had begun, one of the newer girls said one evening at the barracks, "I'm not getting that marching at all!"

Betty Gillies responded, "It's not that hard. Of course I find it easy — I always marched a lot at Ogoontz."

"What's an Ogoontz?" Teresa wanted to know.

"A school I attended. It was very strict and had a rigorous discipline."

"It certainly did," broke in Cornelia Fort excitedly. "I didn't know you went to Ogoontz, Betty. I did, too, for a year."

Although their attendance had been separated by a decade or more, the two alumnae smiled at each other over a mutually shared past. Tiny Betty went on pertly, "I was a drill sergeant there, so I know commands. If you girls like, we can practice up and down the hall outside and I'll show you.''

They did. With quick efficiency, Betty eliminated the great majority, who then concerned themselves with writing letters, laundering and pressing clothes, or studying for the next day's classes. Betty's voice was heard for some thirty minutes more before the noise in the hall ceased.

In the days that followed, whenever any of our little band made an obvious mistake, Lieutenant Jordan would call ''Company, halt!'' Then the name of the offender would be announced and she would be removed from our ranks. She had to join Nancy in watching the others do the maneuver that had given her trouble.

All the while we had been practicing, I sensed a wee bit of syncopation between the beat of Cornelia's feet and my own. I knew why. Cornelia was quite knock-kneed. With each step, one of Cornelia's knees rubbed the other as it moved forward, causing her foot to hit the pavement a fraction later than mine. Slocum, behind her, no doubt matched her footfalls with Cornelia's, and the women in that line had trouble hitting the beat just right because what they saw marching in front of them didn't coincide with the commands that they heard.

I couldn't have told Cornelia there was a problem. We two were becoming quite good friends, despite the differences in our ages and backgrounds. After all, weren't we marching buddies?

As we walked up the hill to the barracks after a bowl of oyster stew at McCafferty's Oyster House one night, she said, ''What's so great about this for me is that I'm meeting some of the most wonderful women — Nancy, Betty, and you.''

After that declaration, who could mention a trivial fault like being slightly out of cadence? I quit noticing Cornelia's feet and concentrated on Lieutenant Jordan's count. At the same time, although Cornelia was never publicly reprimanded for being out of sync, something came over her. For some reason, she stopped dragging her feet. The WAFS attained perfection.

Of course the adjutant general of the army had not activated this group of civilians as a military squadron. In fact, he got huffy about us when he found out that's what we were called. Yet on October 3, the WAFS were placed in the inspection and parade at Newcastle. We wore our flying suits, and the woolen gabardine felt quite warm from the exercise, the excitement, and a hot sun approaching its zenith. We stood two rows behind a squadron of men dressed in cotton khaki.

We had been standing at attention for some time, when the the visiting brass slowly walked about us, taking a good look. Suddenly Cornelia crumpled to the ground, just in front of me. I realized that she had fainted. What to do? Every WAF was afraid to move without an order. We worried as much for Cornelia as for ourselves. Her display of nineteenth century femininity might send us all home disgraced. Yet we wanted to help her. At last, with her head level with her body, Cornelia began to recover. With great relief, the squadron heard the order to dismiss. We who were closest to Cornelia helped her to her feet.

Colonel Baker came to the barracks afterwards. The WAFS assembled to hear what he had to say.

"You WAFS did a fine job. I didn't see a single mistake," he beamed paternally. "But what's this I heard about someone fainting?"

We were ashamed, as he could see by our faces.

"Oh," he smiled at our expressions. "Even West Point cadets have been known to faint while standing at parade rest. I think they forget to breathe."

Then everyone felt better and didn't hold the episode against Cornelia. Our motto was rapidly becoming, "If a mere man can do it, we can, too." Cornelia had proved she was equal to a West Point cadet. But we hoped something like this wouldn't happen again.

We never ventured unless bidden to the east end of the second floor of the BOQ 14. There meetings between Betty and Nancy took place. Nancy Love kept a shield between herself and most of the people she worked with. At times she drew this veil aside and entertained her listeners with reminiscences, but most of the time she was careful about her privacy.

Nancy always spoke softly. Her sibilants, more pronounced than usual, gave distinction to her speech. Her mode of speaking was measured and thoughtful, intellectual, and rather formal. What might have appeared stilted in someone less attractive was not objectionable in her. The listener just looked and enjoyed.

At one of our group sessions Nancy announced, "The curriculum has been finally accepted, with some revision by Colonel Baker."

We had thought it was set before we arrived. All eyes focused on Nancy's face.

She said, "The men civilian pilots may work through all their ground school in as little as nine days. Colonel Baker is allowing you four weeks to review all the aeronautical subjects, plus the indoctrination required by the army and the orientation to military flight procedures. This is required of everyone who ferries for ATC."

"Gad! Four weeks!" Teresa James was blunt. "He must think we're some sort of dummies."

Cornelia also spoke up. "We're not going to go through all that again? Why, as flight instructors we know all that. I'm indignant."

Those were my sentiments also, for I had taught ground school for three years.

"You must remember that not all of us have been flight instructors. There can be no such division among us. We shall take all the course as a review together," replied Nancy. Then she dismissed us with, "That will be all at present. Show what you can do."

In those early weeks, we no sooner assimilated one bit of orientation to military life than Nancy gave us another morsel to chew on. Her self-imposed duties included giving us some training in deportment and protocol, the type of training ordinarily done in officer training schools.

One evening she said, "Now that we have the privileges of the officers' club and the officers' mess, we are to pay a stipend for that privilege. And you must pay for your housing on time without fail."

"Is it due now?" Cornelia wanted to know.

'Yes," Nancy answered. "Fifteen dollars per month. You can pay by check. About checks — like all of the officers, no matter where we are, here or on a mission, we are expected never to write a check that bounces nor to owe any money without paying it promptly. So keep your credit good. If you do otherwise, you are subject to immediate dismissal from the service."

"What happens to the men?" asked Towne.

"Their conduct would be unworthy of an officer and a gentleman," replied Nancy. "They would cease to be officers if they aren't gentlemen."

There was some chatting among ourselves before Nancy went on. She said, "You aren't always going to return from missions during daylight hours. Just as the officers do, if you come in at night, you won't have to stand the eight o'clock roll call. You'll be given time to turn in your forms to the finance office and to get your clothing from the cleaners here on the base or to see the flight surgeon if you come back ill. Otherwise, we shall wear summer flying suits for work and stand roll call every day we remain on base.

"But that doesn't mean you will loaf between missions. You'll be on call for a mission at any time operations asks for you. There is a continuing ground school here and when you aren't on orders, you must attend it."

Inwardly we groaned, but outwardly we agreed. Meanwhile, we were trying to turn our new living quarters into a home.

My neighbors Esther Nelson and Catherine Slocum were the first to learn about a wonderful new idea — department stores were staying open on Monday evenings to accommodate shift workers. Nelson and

Slocum went into Wilmington one Monday evening and came back ecstatic, bustling in with huge packages and an air of secrecy. Late the following afternoon found them hammering away. A blessed silence followed, and they called me to come and admire their handiwork.

Framing the venetian blinds at each window in their rooms were gaudy, floral-printed plastic drapes, which looked like kitchen oilcloth, except they were lighter in weight and more flexible. They even had found twin-sized bedspreads to match. My friends were so pleased with their purchases that I held my tongue and tried to fake an admiring stare. Each had talked a green grocer out of an orange crate; in those days they were made of real wood.

"See, we got this cretonne and I'm going to cover my crate and make a dressing table out of it," said Nelson proudly.

It had possibilities. Orange crates were made of thin, unpainted boards. The narrow sides and middle divider were substantially thicker. Turned on its end, a crate could be used as a bedside table with a shelf in the middle.

One morning when Nelson didn't have to fly she took a bus into town and returned with a small wooden barrel.

"You know that dump under the viaduct?" she asked me. "I went down there. I saw this from the bus window. I'm going to cover it and pad the top, so I'll have something to sit on. Why don't you go down and find something? There's oodles of stuff you can make over."

"I don't think I want to right now," I answered. I still felt strange about being in Wilmington and away from Harold. To buy home decorations would somehow make my departure final. I couldn't do that.

Our end of the second floor hall had more life to it than the other. There was no noise there, only an oppressive quiet. At least we had Slocum's hammering to show that someone was living with vim and vigor. We "westerners" often gathered in Teresa James' room, where we usually found something to laugh at. Only one "easterner" ever joined our jollity — Helen Mary Clark.

I remember the first time that she did. She had come from the laundry room and couldn't avoid looking into Teresa's room directly across from it. She met Teresa's eyes as Teresa lay back on her chaise lounge waiting for us to quit laughing so she could go on with her story.

Teresa smiled and Helen Mary paused, as if considering whether she should continue on to her lonely, quiet room. Instead, she chose to take the few steps necessary to put her at the threshold, hesitating still to join us.

"Come on in," Teresa invited. Helen Mary appeared ill at ease at first. She probably missed the activity of her two sons at home. Our gaiety was a magnet that drew her from the other socialites.

We never thought of Slocum as a socialite, for she was one of us from the start. Teresa could call her and the rest of us "you old bag," but she never called Helen Mary anything but her given name.

That evening Teresa said, "Did I ever tell you about the time I was in a dance marathon?"

I couldn't believe her. I had seen a dance marathon during the Great Depression. It was really an endurance contest that went on day and night until all but one couple were eliminated. Sometimes one partner had to support the other and pull him or her along to keep moving. I found the exhibition depressing and I couldn't see Teresa in that role at all.

Teresa was feeling a bit high. She jumped off her chaise, saying, "Do you old bags know how to boogie-woogie?" No response. "Let's go out in the hall and I'll show you how to shag."

She led the way into the hall. We positioned ourselves along the walls. Teresa began humming and doing an intricate step, much too fast for any of us to follow. Richards and I tried again and again to duplicate Teresa's fast footwork. We failed.

Ever since we began living on the base, the WAFS had made a practice of visiting the base exchange. I'd gone with some of them once, but found nothing of interest for me there. It was possible to buy cigarettes cheaper than off base and I suspect that's why the smokers went. One could buy a candy bar, toothpaste, a bottle of Coke, and other things, but most of the counters held dry goods for enlisted men. There was a uniform section to which officers were drawn, and they disappeared into the anteroom for their fittings.

After I heard what was expected of us as to uniforms, I went with Esther and Teresa, saying, "I'll just look around." I really went to buy shoe polish. I didn't want to. To me polishing shoes was unimportant and a waste of time, especially at Newcastle, where one had to keep eternally at it. The dust kicked up from the dirt paths was easy to clean off, but the mud really made a mess.

I stood looking at the assortment of bottles and cans. Teresa was at my right hand, giving advice.

"Kid, you've got to use the solid kind. Esquire is good. What paste stuff gives is a good, hard shine that won't come off."

Esther joined us and said, "I'd get some of the liquid as long as it isn't a dye. Look at the label. If you clean your shoes first, the liquid dries to a shine and you don't have to work so hard buffing them later.''

''I don't want to buff 'em at all,'' I replied. I ended up with a tin of saddle soap and a bottle of brown shoe polish. I thought, I'll try to remember to use it.

We three sauntered from counter to counter until Teresa spied a shelf with insignia displayed in a glass-topped case.

''Hey!'' She called our attention to it with a jerk of her forefinger in its direction. ''We've got to get some of them doodads,'' she said.

We looked at what was on sale. They seemed to be made of silver. One decoration showed the northern hemisphere in white enamel, criss- crossed by the blue grids of longitude and latitude. The tail-end of an airplane going east was imposed upon it and in a quarter circle on the west side were dots and dashes of red and blue. It gave me the feeling of flight.

''We'll need a pair of Ferry Command wings,'' said Esther with authority. ''Art wears a pair. I've seen a lot of the pilots wearing those shoulder buttons. I asked Nancy and she says we need them for our uniforms.''

Of course. The Ferry Command insignia and our uniforms would identify us as bona fide military pilots on a mission. But we weren't through with orientation and couldn't legally purchase the decorations yet.

In my childhood home, ''cleanliness was next to godliness,'' as my mother said. Every morning I'd leave home freshly bathed, teeth brushed, clothes newly laundered and pressed (albeit mended), but I was so active and lacking in a ''feminine'' image that my clothes and I were ready to be washed again upon my return home. All the Riek children had overwhelming energy. My sister and I were tomboys.

But it was more than energy that made me different in appearance from other girls. I always felt that I was not like my playmates. This feeling was reinforced by teasing from my father and two of my brothers. I took their word that I was too thin and homely — and I imagined my nose was as long as a fox's.

That wasn't all. My sister, six years younger than I, was pretty and extremely fair. Her eyes were blue and her hair silvery white. The rest of us were brown-eyed and our hair ranged from dark gold to yellow. My hair just missed being red.

When I was about twelve, my mother made my sister a cotton dress that picked up the blue of her eyes and the pink of her lips and cheeks. After a decent interval during which I waited for my mother to sew a dress for me, I screwed up my courage and approached her. ''Why aren't you making a new dress for me, too?''

My mother, busy peeling potatoes, said brusquely, ''Because a pretty picture deserves a pretty frame.''

I was crushed. And I began to look at what was pretty according to other people's standards. I knew that beauty would never be mine. At the movies shown at the Fairy Theater or at the Mikado, the stars were tiny women like Mary Pickford, the Gish sisters, Helen Hunt Jackson, Pearl White, Theda Bara, Mae Murray, and others who barely reached sixty inches tall. I wept one day when I realized that my mother, who was no more than five feet six or seven, was by far the tallest woman on our long, long city block — and I would be even taller.

To be a woman and tall was to be a freak. My father laughed and said he would put me in a circus. A nasty boy who lived in the hollow of the block called me ''stepladder'' or ''second story,'' and one of my cousins, Johnny Kiesling, continually asked, ''How's the weather up there?'' I hated him. I knew he was jealous that I at sixteen was a bit taller than the average American man.

In my youth, especially during the flapper era, it was fashionable for young ladies to slouch and slink along in a peculiar gliding movement. One could lose inches in appearance that way, but I wouldn't do it. I walked as straight as I could, even though I hated being tall. To do otherwise was to act out a lie. I also became aware of having long, narrow feet and after years of teaching, of walking from desk to desk and to the blackboard, my feet became even longer.

Even as a young girl I had a notion of destiny. Although I did not conform to the current styles in clothing, I made my judgments and did what I thought was right for me. When I turned twelve or thirteen, boys stopped wearing knee-length knickers and black cotton stockings. We girls had always worn long white stockings, but that also began to change. Knee-high socks came into style. I refused to put them on because I didn't want to show my knees.

By the time I was sixteen, girls were cutting off their long curls and braids. I cut mine, too. My hair was almost as fine as a spider web. It grew slowly, and my mother was always snipping off a bit from the ends because she said they were splitting. With bobbed hair, I thought I would look more like everybody else, so I let my mother cut it.

When I was seventeen, skirts, long worn at mid-calf, suddenly drew up to above the knees. I thought most girls' knees were better hidden, especially when seen from behind. The knee was not a pretty joint. Poor nutrition showed up in rickets, knock-knees, and bowlegs.

So my skirts remained right below the knee, for I knew that if I wore them at the stylish length, I'd look as if I had outgrown my clothes. Waistlines lowered to the widest part of the hips, but mine remained where nature had placed it. I found it hard to find ready-made clothes to fit, but I couldn't have afforded them anyway. Fortunately, I was able to design and sew my own clothes. I always made a deep hem, just in case the hemline went down, and I wore my dresses loose in hopes that I might gain a little weight. I was no fashion plate! In fact, I wore clothes only because of modesty and tradition. That we didn't suit each other all the time was of no consequence.

When we got into the Ferry Command, each WAF (as we began to call ourselves singly), except Nancy, found the military jargon as strange to her as the people who used it. Each of us knew the mysteries of civilian aviation language, but this new language had a greatly expanded vocabulary. No wonder the WAFS had to go to ground school to learn how to fit in.

We concentrated on learning the new words and their significance as if our very lives depended upon our getting them right the first time. One who has not flown in the army might find it hard to understand some of these terms. Therefore, an explanation of our orientation is in order.

One of our first courses dealt with the military forms we were required to fill out. Each WAF was handed a large flight envelope. Its contents were prescribed by AAC regulation 15-9 and every form had its own number. Even the envelope had a number! On the outside were printed all the procedures to follow in case of a forced landing. This could be very convenient if the pilot were shaken up and confused — she wouldn't have to rummage through the contents for instructions.

I shuddered inwardly as we touched on all the points the procedure involved. Before I left home I was confident that I would never be killed in an airplane that I piloted. If I were to be killed in a plane, it would be in a commercial airliner in which the pilot, perhaps due to altimeter error, flew into the summit of a high mountain peak.

Quite naturally the instructor began his explanation with form 1. "Each airplane has a metal or wooden pocket," he said, "usually on the right hand side of the pilot's seat, in which form 1's and form 1-A's are carried. They are the records that pilots and mechanics keep of the flights of that aircraft. These forms are never to leave the airplane.

"When you land, you should get into the habit of reaching for form 1, which is on a clipboard, and immediately write on it where you took off, where you landed, and how long it took to get there. That's so we can keep an accurate check in order to service the airplane and to make inspections when they are due.

"Put down any comments about the behavior of the airplane that needs attention. If the left brake is weak, say so. Then when a mechanic looks over the ship, he knows if there is something you found out that he can't see because he doesn't fly the airplane.

"On the other side of form 1 is form 1-A. Read it."

There was a long pause as we read about the flyability of airplanes.

The instructor continued, "If you find a red diagonal marked on this form after the airplane's last flight, something is not right. The red diagonal line tells you that the plane is flyable, but it has a defect. Before you fly it, read what was found to be wrong and inspect the plane yourself to determine if you want to fly it in that condition or not.

"Make sure that you write down anything you find that needs correction, because you don't want to be responsible for anyone else going out in the plane and getting killed.

"If there's a red cross, the defect in the airplane makes it nonflyable. Whatever you do, don't take it up. The fault will be yours if you do. And be sure you find out from the flight engineer who checked its condition what he says about it.

"If there are no red marks, you may feel sure that no one discovered anything was wrong. But you are still responsible for yourself and your airplane. It is up to you to make a ground check all around before you run up the engine."

Sobering thoughts all this!

Next for us to consider was the flight clearance form. A new one had to be filled out for each leg of a mission. We had to list name, home base, the type and serial number of the airplane, the takeoff point, and the expected landing point. Then came the expected length of the flight, the estimated takeoff time, and the estimated time of arrival (ETA). In calculating these figures, I had to know the altitude at which I would fly and the direction and velocity of the wind.

We were expected to check the weather conditions en route ourselves, which all of us were able to do or we wouldn't have been at Wilmington. But our clearance in the AAF operations office would not be valid unless the meteorologist signed the form to indicate that he considered the proposed flight to be safe and that we would have contact flight conditions all the way. For contact flying we needed at least a 1,500-foot ceiling and a three-mile visibility. That was sufficient for piloting Cubs and PT's, which was all we thought we were going to do anyway.

Upon landing at our declared destination, at an alternate airport or wherever, we were instructed to close our flight plan. That meant we made certain that the airport operations officer got the message that we had landed.

The instructor told us, "The Ferry Command doesn't want to waste its manpower or that of the CAP hunting for a WAF when the pilot in question is sleeping peacefully in a hotel somewhere. You'd better close your flight plan or else!" He drew his right index finger across his throat.

Clearances, meteorologist's signature, operations okay, flight plan closing — this seemed like extra work to the many of us who took off from airfields without control towers and who had no contact with anyone except the gas boy upon landing. Well, what must be, must be.

"Another form is the report of weather delay," said our mentor.

We searched our envelopes and waited until everyone had the correct form on her desk.

"Read it."

We did. There were blanks for the date, the station, an explanation for the delay, and for pilot and meteorologist signatures. When all heads were up and eyes on him, the instructor said, "We've had some pilots who wanted to stay longer on some bases than their assignment allowed. Or they landed at a particular field because they had a name in their little black book who lived in a nearby town. So they quit flying and said the weather held them up. After an investigation, we found the weather was good enough for flying.

"That doesn't mean we want you to take chances. You should never fly until an hour after sunup. The time of lowest temperature comes long after the time of greatest cooling, which is midnight. The earth is still radiating heat faster than the early morning sun can build it up, because the slanting rays don't warm the surface very well. You watch the temperature and the dew point. If they are close, and you go up, you might find yourself with a fog building up below and you can't see the ground."

He looked about to see if we had questions. I think all of us knew this already.

Then he continued, "During the coming winter months, you have to be careful about landing before dark. The sun goes down so fast that you'd better find out each day when sundown will occur. The time changes a few minutes every day, and the days get shorter until the latter part of December. Then we gain light as we come toward spring. To be on the safe side, you shouldn't take off any later than what'll put you where you're going by 1600. One hour before sundown is the Ferry Command rule."

One of the WAFS asked, "Why don't you use 4 P.M.?"

"We use an international clock system," he explained. "The first twelve hours of the day count up to twelve. Then, instead of repeating the numbers, you just add twelve and we all make no mistakes.

"Suppose somebody used the civilian clock. He takes off at eleven and expects to land at three. Now, who is to know if he's taking off at eleven at night and landing at three in the morning or is taking off at eleven in the morning and landing at three in the afternoon? If you crash somewhere, the exact time might make a difference in your survival. We need to know when to send rescue teams to find you. You'll find out that messages about takeoffs don't always arrive on time, but we try to keep track of our pilots as accurately as possible."

The next lesson began with the instructor saying, "Let's consider RONs."

Someone asked, "What's a RON?"

"It means 'Remaining Over Night.' The group operations officer here wants to know where each airplane is every night on its way to its destination. Operations isn't particularly interested in *you*, but in the airplane. Look in your envelopes. You'll find a stack of Western Union message forms."

He waited until we pulled them out. Then he said, "As soon as you get into a field where you are staying overnight, the flight leader must find the telegraph office before doing anything else, such as eating dinner or finding a hotel room. The flight leader lets operations know that the RON is for everyone on the mission. Remember: whatever you do, this is a must!"

Then we took up transportation requests. Our instructor eyed us sternly and said sadly, "The men pilots have been taking advantage of this, and they have made it bad for everybody. Transportation by auto won't be honored any longer."

He glanced about the room as if weighing whether he should tell us what came next. Then he said, "Some of the fellows could have asked for transportation into town and back. Motor pools would have done that if there wasn't room in Hotel DeGink.

"But they took taxis to and from the airport and even from one hotel to another for their dinner or to a nightclub. It's too bad a few of those fellows made it hard on the rest of us ferry pilots, but that's the way it is. If you take a taxi, you'll have to pay for it out of your own per diem."

"Won't that be awfully expensive for us?" Esther asked. "With paying for a hotel and taxi and our food? It's not as cheap to eat out as it is on the base."

"Yes, but if there's more than one of you in a flight or someone else is going into town, you can split the fare and it won't be so bad."

That ended the hour. But I worried about what I had heard. In my family the spending of money was something one planned carefully, and we weren't used to transportation such as taxis. They were a luxury. How could I manage all this without going broke simply for the privilege of being patriotic?

I was glad that Nancy decided to review some of the forms with us in the barracks that night. She told us the transportation requests were called T/Rs and added, "The flight leader will make one out for the entire flight under her command and she will give it to the ticket agent as payment for her flight's transportation. You all have T/Rs for future use, but don't ever use them for anything but government business."

"Or you'll land in the hoosegow," warned Betty.

"Will every agent take them?" asked Richards.

"Yes. Buses, trains, and airlines. But your taxi fares and fares for local streetcars and buses you pay yourself, from your per diem.

Nancy had another thought for us. "You'll be using T/Rs most often in returning to the base after making a delivery. Your orders will read that you are to get back the quickest way possible. Now, when you make out your T/R, the clerk might want to see your orders, just to be sure that you are legitimate. You can show the part of it that he must see to determine that, but never show anything about where and what you are ferrying. As to airlines, you'll probably bump a lot of passengers —"

Catherine Slocum interrupted, "What is that?"

Nancy explained, "To bump a passenger means that you take the place of someone who already has a reserved seat on a flight about to take off. You'll leave him stranded. We ferry pilots have a governmental priority next to the president's cabinet."

"You mean we might bump anybody except a cabinet member?" I asked.

"Yes," she replied.

"Boy!" Teresa's face lit up. "We're important."

"I noticed they say per diem instead of an expense account," said Slocum. "Why is that?"

"It's called per diem because it is counted on a day-to-day basis," answered Nancy. "Expense accounts, such as some business firms use, may be unlimited. But the government doesn't do business that way. It used to be more generous, but so many pilots abused the privilege that it was cut down to $7.00 per day for everybody else and $6.00 for us."

"When does it start?" asked Cornelia.

"Not until you take off from this base. If you are on orders to go to a factory to get an airplane and the weather is bad, or if the factory lets us know that the airplane isn't ready yet, you remain here and get no per diem. It stops immediately when you return. You are not to loiter and stop any place unnecessarily in delivering your airplane or in coming back here. The shortest, most direct route is the one you must take.''

''Why do the men get more than we do?'' asked Esther.

''Civilian male pilots get the same as we do until they achieve officer status. That's the difference.''

''Hotels are so expensive, we'll spend most of our per diem just to get some place to sleep,'' reflected Slocum.

I nodded in agreement, as did some others. But Rhonie gave a withering glance in our direction.

Nancy reassured us. ''Most hotels know that we are important to the war effort,'' she said. ''So they have agreed to give a half-price rate to Ferry Command pilots. You'll probably get a $5 hotel room for $2.50. If you use the motor pools for transportation and aren't extravagant, you should be able to remain fairly close to your per diem for expenses.''

Richards had a bright thought. She said, ''The instructor told us there was a Hotel DeGink. Why couldn't we stay on the base and not take a taxi into town?''

Betty and Nancy exchanged glances and smiled. Nancy flicked the ash from her cigarette before she spoke. ''You know how airport hangars are made,'' she said. ''The interior is vaulted and so high that it is possible to use the top as a loft. Many airfields have floored the top of a hangar and converted it into lodgings for itinerant military pilots. Naturally they have all been men, so it is really a male barracks. The men pay only what they would on a base, no more than $1.50 a night. So you see, we can't sleep in any Hotel DeGink.''

Betty added, ''You have quarters assigned to you here. If you are gone a month, you will still have to pay for them, although you might not be using them. Now do you understand the usual military procedure in housing?''

We nodded.

During our next school period, we filled out a practice T/R. As we wrote down the location of takeoff, the starting time, and the destination, we had to use the civilian clock system, which we thought strange. We also had to note what time zone we ended up in. For instance, EWT meant Eastern War Time. In types of travel, C/P stood for commercial plane, C/B was commercial bus, R/R was railroad. There was the possibility we could use G/P (government plane), G/A (government auto), or P/A (private auto). The last type, of course, was forbidden. The G/P and G/A would be possible if another branch of the service demanded a T/R as payment from the AAF for favors done to its members. I never found that demand made during my WAFS and WASP service, but it happened to others.

Then we were given a sample of the type of orders we were to receive.

"You will get a number of these with every mission," said our instructor. "Read it over first."

After we did, he said, "You'll need one to verify that you are authorized to pick up the airplane. You will need another to give the officer in charge at your destination. And make sure you get a receipt for that airplane before you officially give it up!"

He looked about to make certain his admonition took hold before continuing. "You may show the top part of the form to a room clerk to prove you are on orders if you have trouble getting a room or if he tries to charge you too much.

"Two copies of all your orders and amendments to those orders, if any, must be submitted with your claim to the finance officer for your official time away from the base, so you'll get your per diem. You need one to go with your copy of the T/R to keep the bookkeeping straight. The ones you have left you'd better keep for your own records.

"Don't bother the finance office with requests for reimbursement of per diem unless your itinerary totals more than $25 or you have at least four small trips. If it's less than that, the finance office holds up your per diem until the end of the month. If you get on a short shuttle somewhere, you can get a supply of itineraries from the air and rail transportation department in the south hangar or from the finance office."

By this time, we felt that if we didn't understand something on the first run-through, we could get into a jam session with Nancy in the BOQ. So we sat quietly in class without asking questions.

Next we heard, "Take out form 15, invoice. Look it over. When you land at an army installation to get gas or oil, all you have to do is to sign for it and go on your way.

"But you'll be flying Cubs with very short flying range, and you'll find that sometime you'll have to land where there isn't an army field anywhere near. So you'll be landing on civilian fields. That's when you use #15.

"The dealer has to make out this form in quadruplicate. You sign for it, but before you do, check to make sure the invoice is accurate and we don't have to pay for more than you received. You leave the fourth copy with him. The other three you mail immediately to our base supply officer without fail the same day, so the dealer will be assured of payment at the earliest possible moment.

"Transactions at civilian air fields take time and cause delays in ferrying. Try to avoid them. Some ferry pilots have been lax about mailing forms in right away and the operator has had to wait a long time for his money. He may retaliate by giving very slow service. Some of these small airport flight operators are existing on a shoestring to begin with, and we come along and requisition his gas that he needs for his customers. Try to see it his way, too."

Then came the most somber form. We hoped we had to look at it this one time only. Form #17, "damage to property certificate," was to be used to enumerate the estimated damage to an owner or tenant's property. Next was the accident report required by the operations officer. If the pilot was suspected of negligence or of conduct which led to the accident, that could result in a court-martial.

Form 01-1-31 dealt with a restricted technical order to ship parts of damaged or wrecked aircraft. The most sobering thoughts came on reading #95-120. It concerned serious aircraft accidents, ones that involved the services of an undertaker. It reminded us that we were on very dangerous missions.

With a parting admonition from our instructor to have all these forms with us all the time, we left that study for the next.

All of our days had moments of exhilaration. Monday, September 28, was more memorable than most. It was the day the WAFS wept.

First Gertrude Meserve of Boston arrived to break the inert state of WAFS recruitment. Soon after her arrival, other former flight instructors arrived, too, having completed their last quarter of CPTP instruction.

Gert was a blonde, kitten-faced girl in her early twenties with more flying time logged than any of us except Rhonie. I thought, how lucky for the girls on either coast, where midwest prejudices against hiring women did not exist. One couldn't guess what Gert was thinking, for she showed no emotion, never smiling or frowning. We all welcomed her with open arms and, although a New Englander, she took a room opposite the vacant one between Teresa's and mine.

The same day, the base post office began to sell postage stamps to civilians, who couldn't frank letters like the military could. I ran to the post office (only the distance of a city block from BOQ 14) before I went to lunch, hoping the stamps wouldn't be sold out before I got there.

I bought a book and asked the enlisted man who waited on me, "Any mail for me? Scharr?"

He looked and said, "No." Then he said, "Wait a minute. You got a big box here."

My heart leapt. It could only be the things I'd asked Harold to send to me and that I missed so badly. The clerk brought out a footlocker. He looked from it to me and back again. I guess he was weighing the alternatives — to leave his job to help me or to be unchivalrous and let me carry it alone. He might have seen me as an emerging officer. At that time, officers weren't supposed to carry a bundle or even an umbrella.

Finally he said, "Just a minute and I'll take this to the barracks for you."

"Oh, don't bother," I replied. "I can carry it."

But he refused to let me take it and after a few words with the manager, he came from behind the counter and put the footlocker on his shoulder. He carried it all the way. We had trouble getting it over the ditch, but managed to do so without letting it drop. Beyond the back steps of the barracks, he dared not go. So I struggled with it all the way up to my room, lifting first one end to the next higher step and then bringing up the other. And there I left it, as anxious as I was to open it, for if I didn't get to the mess soon, I'd have nothing to eat until dinnertime.

That afternoon we had a course in chemical warfare. It made no difference to the Air Transport Command that the WAFS were expected to ferry airplanes only in the continental United States. We had to take all the same courses that the men did. Men might ferry planes across the Atlantic or Pacific oceans or transport cargo in North Africa or go over the Himalayan Mountains. It was possible that they would need to know survival techniques, for they ran the risk of facing enemy action in a war zone. But it was not likely that we would get close to combat.

At the start of class that day, I knew little of chemical warfare outside of smelling the stink bombs that chemistry students at Soldan High made and used on the rest of the school. Of course, I remembered stories about doughboys being gassed by the Germans as they fought in the trenches of World War I. Gas masks could prevent injuries resulting from gas attacks. At the first whiff of air recognized as being lethal or incapacitating, servicemen could don masks and perhaps save their lives.

Our instructor, a sergeant, introduced himself and his two assistants. Then he announced, "We shall study the fundamental concepts of chemical agents."

To my surprise, I soon found out that a poison "gas" might be a misnomer. Most chemical agents dispersed in the air were either liquid or solid. Some were labeled "harassing." The best known of them caused weeping and was therefore called tear gas. Others were "sternutators," because they made their victims cough or sneeze, get a headache or become nauseated. The "vesicants" were easily absorbed by the human body and both burned and destroyed body tissue. These included mustard gas, which was made from ethylene and sulphur monochloride, and lewisite.

Among the lung irritants were chlorine, phosgene, and chlorpicrin. One dreadful gas was hydrogen cyanide, which directly impeded the circulatory system and stopped heart action. There were also incendiaries. So many variables! The toxic and killing effects of the chemical attack depended upon the concentration of the agent per cubic foot of air, its persistence in the atmosphere, the temperature, and the wind conditions.

There was too much information for the WAFS to assimilate in one class period. With relief we heard the sergeant say, "It will be unnecessary for you to take a test in order to obtain a passing grade in the course." What a pal!

But our "friend" was not above having a go at us. He said, "We are going out into the field next door. We have placed some of each type of poisonous gas out there. Not enough to hurt you, but enough for you to recognize if you ever get a whiff."

We followed him out of the classroom. His assistants were on the far end of the field. They were ready. I wasn't.

The sergeant said, "All you have to do is walk across the field from this side to the other. Everybody got a gas mask?" We did. "Okay," he continued, "when you get to the other side, put on your gas mask and enter that little building. I want you to see how effective a gas mask is, so you won't be too proud to use one if you have to. You'll remain there a few minutes and then you'll leave. Does everybody understand what to do?"

There was no response, so he lined us up along the perimeter of the field. At an order from him, we began to walk slowly forward, obeying the orders he shouted after us. The low weeds appeared hazy or smoky in spots. A light breeze drifted the poisoned air across our path.

I did not want to breathe in a poison gas. Among our family acquaintances were several veterans of World War I whose health and lives had been wrecked by having done so. I walked across that field a coward.

I knew from a test for lung capacity given to all freshmen at Harris Teachers College that mine was fifty percent larger than normal.

Later, I had practiced swimming under water, trying to improve the distance I was able to go without taking a breath. So, gas mask in hand, I took a long, slow breath and exhaled all I could. Then I inhaled as much as I was able. I began walking, holding my breath as long as I could before exhaling slowly. We crossed the field and then I inhaled again.

When we reached the small building, we put on the gas masks under the supervision of the two enlisted men and the sergeant. I was one of the first to enter. As more WAFS came into the empty room, they crowded me farther and farther from the door. We milled about, looking at each other in our masks and seeing strange, hideous creatures impossible to recognize. The sergeant stood in front of the door, the only exit.

Not long after the last WAF entered, he said, "Take off your gas masks before you leave."

He motioned to those closest to the door and helped them remove their masks. They disappeared from view. I didn't take off my mask, thankfully, until I was near the door. I would have liked to have worn it until I was outside, but before me loomed the sergeant, and he grasped it to assist me.

As soon as the mask was gone, my eyes shut involuntarily. I had to force them open to see my way out. When I did, tears welled up in them and they shut fast again. It was torture to force myself to open them in order to escape.

Outside everyone else was suffering, too, and weeping copiously. For what seemed an interminable length of time effects of the gas clung to us. I had enough experience with tear gas in those long minutes to last me all my life.

When I was able to keep my eyes open for a while, I saw that the two enlisted men were enjoying our plight. Our instructor then dismissed us with, "In your career in the army, you may expect to review the effects of chemical warfare again and again. Try to remember what you have learned. It has been a pleasure for me to work with you ladies. Good-bye."

As we walked back to the school building, some of the girls tried to identify the gases they had smelled. I didn't want to know. Tear gas had been enough. To heck with the rest!

WHAT WE CAME FOR

THE DAY WE BEGAN MARCHING was also the day we started flying. We stood assembled in the transition school office, facing an officer and Nancy.

Nancy said to us in a serious voice, "Please pay close attention to what Lieutenant Haines has to tell you."

He began, "I know you are all anxious to start flying the army way. But you're not going to ferry army airplanes until we believe that you justify our faith in you. We have just so many primary trainers and liaison-type airplanes assigned to the school. We use the Fairchild PT-19 with a 165 horsepower Ranger and a Taylorcraft L-2B with a 65 horsepower engine. They will be comparable to what you will deliver to army training schools.

"You have to put time in, in all of these planes. We can't afford to have them idle, so be prompt for your scheduled time to fly. Everybody is going to get the same amount of time in each type. Some will start in PTs, but they'll have to take their L-2B time at the end. We will start flying right away."

The famous Piper Cub, designated by the army as an L-4. This plane could have been one ferried by the WAFS. It is shown at Bougainville in February 1944.

From left, WAFS Claire Callaghan, Margaret McCormick, Adela Scharr, and Gertrude Brown, with Taylorcraft L-2B's.

What he said made sense. No one raised a question. We stood motionless, poised for action, while Lieutenant Sandy Lerner, who had been watching in the background, went to the bulletin board and thumbtacked a piece of paper to it.

As soon as he left, the women moved toward the notice, expectant and hopeful. The shorter ones reached the wall first and we taller women positioned ourselves to the rear, so they could see. We waited for what seemed to be an interminably long time, searching each other's faces for signs of joy or pain. Tiny Betty slipped aside, her cool face discreetly hiding the fact that she would fly a PT-19. But Pat Rhonie turned to gloat, her superiority at last verified, and said, "I get to fly a PT right away."

When at last I could see the schedule, I discovered that my name was not on the first three days of flying. I took the news in silence, uncomfortably disfavored. The choices had nothing to do with seniority. Teresa James, with more 2-S time than I had, and Helen Richards were on the PT list.

Having learned that some of us wouldn't fly that day, we were excused to return to the barracks for study or to practice Morse code. I caught up with Esther Nelson and we walked down the hill together.

She began to fuss in a querulous tone of voice. "They even have Towne on the board before me, and she came in after I did."

"What do you have to kick about?" I asked, "I'm not even on the board. I'm the only one they omitted."

"No!"

"Yeah. But they'll get around to me. What bothers me is that I want to get up in the air."

"Well, I'm not as crazy about flying as you are," Esther replied. "I just want to be treated right."

I kicked a pebble. It flew ten feet ahead and landed on the road in front of us. "I sure miss flying," I said. "At home I flew every day the weather was good. Well, I'm going to practice a little code. I'm slow in that and have to put in some extra time. Want to come with me?"

"Shoot!" Esther was vacillating. Companionship was what she needed in her misery. "Okay, but let's not stay long."

The next day we two were drawn again to the transition office to look at the board, hoping that changes had been made. We overheard an exchange that enlightened us further about what we could expect from Lieutenant Haines, who was talking to Rhonie. We surmised what she had said to him before we were within earshot.

He was saying, "The men civilian pilots who come into transition abide by our rules. And you women, like them, are supposed to have a

Adela Scharr plots her course on an aeronautical chart, prior to a cross-country training flight in October 1942.

minimum number of hours, dual and solo. So even if you feel you don't need an instructor to go with you, those are the rules. You must take your dual if you are to remain in the program.''

A new schedule was posted on Friday. Perhaps to make up for having neglected me, Lieutenant Haines himself took me out in L-2B #42-69 for one hundred fulfilling minutes. He showed me where Du-Pont Airport was in relation to Newcastle Army Base. He demonstrated the traffic pattern for leaving and entering the airport. When he turned the controls over to me, with considerable glee I made three patterns and cut them as precisely as if done with scissors on paper. Heck, it was just like demonstrating the plane for a student.

Lieutenant Haines pointed out an automobile crossing DuPont Field on a road midway across the only long runway in use.

''If there's any ground traffic, it has first priority,'' he told me. ''Go around again. Be sure to watch for anyone driving who might be trying to cross the runway when you are landing or taking off.''

We left DuPont then, with Lieutenant Haines pointing toward the practice area where Lieutenant Tracy and I had flown twelve days earlier. There were fields and farmhouses below.

''Not much traffic over here, but be sure to clear yourself anyway,'' warned my instructor.

It was an unnecessary warning. I never trusted anyone on the ground or in the air. Only the previous month while I had a student up northwest of St. Charles Airport, I spied a dark gray object in the gray sky to the west. It was bearing down on us. I took the controls, slipped the Cub to lose altitude, and watched a B-25 speed past overhead, disappearing in the direction of Lambert Field. I don't think the pilot ever saw me.

I had to show Lieutenant Haines all the maneuvers a pilot makes in order to obtain a commercial license. One thing we did was new — a right hand traffic pattern. Lieutenant Haines said, ''Some army air fields use 'em, so watch when you get near them. Learn 'em; you might need them.'' (The right hand maneuvers were simply a mirror image of the usual traffic pattern.)

As our instruction continued, we found out that our being female caused a predicament we had not anticipated. The medicos ''beat their gums,'' as Teresa would say, and they decided that at least one day each month we should not be allowed to fly. They thought we would endanger ourselves, which in turn would endanger the airplanes we were flying. And airplanes were important. This was the first I had ever heard of not flying while menstruating. Both my licenses were won while flying during such a period. I saw no sense to the ruling. Yet I obeyed it and I did not fly on the proscribed day, which was a Sunday. Nancy had stressed so sternly our compliance with all the regulations, and I knew that if she'd question me, she could tell by my face if I lied. The first day of my period was usually a good day, without any headache or pain. Ordinarily at home, I'd have endured some rough student landings and bumpy taxiing on an uneven rural field.

On Monday morning, Lieutenant Starbuck, another instructor, asked me to show him how I flew a Taylorcraft (L-2B). Our amicable exchange of serious flying talk must have overcome his awareness that I was a female. Or maybe he saw the wedding ring on my finger and decided I wasn't a threat to his bachelor status. At any rate, each time we saw each other after that, he spoke to me as an airport buddy. Sometimes we sat together on a bench, waiting for an airplane to return, and we spoke of many things.

Not so with Lieutenant French, with whom I took dual instruction on Tuesday. He was older than the other transition instructors. His skin had been darkened by long years in the sun. His slender, wiry build and his impatient manner betrayed irritations he did not voice. He was even more laconic than Starbuck was reputed to be; his comments about a student's flying were pared and limited to impatient gestures. It didn't take me long to guess that his wig-wag signals took the place of vocal chords grown tired from shouting commands above the noise of the engine.

On the climb after takeoff, he'd anticipate the altimeter setting at which I had been told to begin a ninety degree turn with a forty degree bank. He'd wave his left hand with the thumb pointing down. Throughout the flight a ballet of hand signals with palm up or down, of flipping hands to right or left took all the initiative out of a student's control over the flight maneuvers. On my first flight with him, I strained to get ahead of him and failed.

When I learned that I'd be with Lieutenant French again the next day, I resolved to show him up. Poor man, I thought, he's been flying so long with students that he's tired of it. He'd rather be flying by himself instead of beating his brains out as an instructor. So when Lieutenant French began to wave his arm for a left turn after takeoff, the plane was already in it. So it went. After fifty minutes, he gave up and allowed me to solo for ten minutes right there on the base.

I began to feel sure I'd catch up with the other WAFS in flying time. Two days of soloing an L-2B gave me three more hours. The following day Lieutenant French gave me a required check ride. I used the same tactics I had used before. We came down in a half hour and he said I didn't need any more dual instruction in that type of aircraft. Another hurdle behind me!

On Thursday, October 1, when I was turning in my clearance sheet, Lieutenant Haines interrupted me. He asked me how the solo in the Fairchild went.

"Just great," I replied.

"I see you have some time to make up," he said. "You can fly solo tomorrow, but you can't have the airplane more than an hour. I think you'll have to get in as much air time as you can on Saturday and Sunday. You come in early Saturday morning and we'll find out how you're doing."

The prospect of flying as much as I could during the weekend heartened me. Two things beside my late scheduling had kept me from getting in my quota of hours — the weather and an officer who usurped the airplane that had been scheduled to me. I didn't complain, however. A lady didn't do such things.

.

In October we were approaching the end of our orientation, we hoped. Nancy Love and Colonel Baker realized that after we started ferrying, we would have no free weekends, so they decided that all the WAFS, even the new arrivals, would be given time off the base that Saturday and Sunday. Immediately I saw where that left me, who wanted nothing more than to get up into the air.

As soon as the gladsome news of a leave was announced, vacation plans were hatched. Esther Nelson brought me the news that Helen Mary Clark had invited her to her home in Englewood, New Jersey. She was agog at the prospect.

Cornelia came into my room that evening, saying in conspiratorial fashion, "Scharr, do you ride?"

"You mean horses?"

"Yes, of course."

"Sure, I've ridden some, but only on a western saddle."

"I have an invitation to go fox hunting in Virginia. I wish you would come along."

Here was a chance for a new experience. By comparison, my promised hours of flying diminished in importance. I hated to say what I had to.

"Thanks, Cornelia, but I can't. I'm behind all of you in my flying. I've got to stay on the base and make up some hours."

Then Catherine Slocum came in and invited me, along with Teresa, to her home in nearby Bryn Mawr. Again I refused. Although I felt chastised by the need for transition, I was grateful that my new friends wanted to include me in their plans.

Wistfully, I bid them farewell on Friday evening. After they left, the barracks was very lonely. For the first time since I had left home I felt alone.

One Fairchild PT-19A, #42-33652, had given me trouble the first time I flew it. The flaps were so stiff at first that I had to take my foot from the left rudder and use it to push down the flap lever while, with my right hand, I tried to release the stiff plunger. When this protruded, it kept the flaps in line with the wings. Meanwhile I had to keep my left hand on the throttle.

During this gymnastic exercise, it was impossible for me to see out, for my head automatically went down as my right arm stretched forward, down, and across. We were not allowed to put the flaps down until we were coming in straight on final approach, so the critical interval of not being able to see the runway or anything else had to be as short as I could possibly make it. I did not want to tell the instructors about this problem, for fear they would think me incompetent or weak, so I memorized my procedure and wham! bang! The flaps were down and I was alert to my approach to a landing. Happily for me, #42-33652 loosened up through constant use and after a while I could forget the procedure I had taught myself.

For those two days, as I gave myself up to the joy of flying solo, the airplane and I were a single entity. I soared and wheeled through the air as if I had wings growing from my body. It made up for being alone in the barracks.

Sunday night the power went off at the base. I had gone to bed early, but during the night I got up to go to the bathroom. I groped in the dark until I got to my doorway. Afraid, I turned back, resolving to buy a flashlight. As the WAFS returned from their holiday, they stumbled about in the blackness. One put her suitcase down in the hall and then was unable to find it. Two WAFS ran into each other and "scared each other half to death."

The next day Nelson reported her impressions of her vacation to me. "I was disappointed in the Clark's house," she said. "It's older than I thought it would be."

"Wasn't it nice?" I asked.

"Yes, it was nice. But I expected something else from people with their money."

"Like what?"

"Modern, like we have in California. Something like a movie star's house."

Teresa had a different story, but she had also been surprised. She said to me, "You know who Catherine Slocum is, don't you?" Her blank face gave me no indication of the answer.

"I really can't guess," I replied as I mulled over how Catherine appeared to me. She was almost as tall as I, but had the wholesome plumpness of a Pennsylvania Dutch housewife. She had a free and easy acceptance of everyone, like a large, happy puppy who hasn't yet learned what it is to be hurt. Her eyes were blue and her fine, rather straight brown hair was cut in a bob just below her ears. She smiled easily and everybody liked her.

Teresa knew how to milk her story, so I had to be patient for the answer. She said, "Wait'll I tell you what happened. We got into this big limousine with a chauffeur and he drives us to Bryn Mawr. We get out in the driveway of this big house, and what I mean, it was really big.

"I had no idea but what she would go in the back way. I wondered what she was doing there. Was she the maid or something? So she goes to the front door and I'm with her and she rings the bell. The butler comes to the door and says, 'Welcome home, Mrs. Slocum.' I like to have died. It was *her* house.''

"You mean she's rich?" I asked with a frown.

"You're darn tootin'," replied Jamesy. "I can tell you, kiddo, she's the Luden cough drop heiress. She's married to a publisher or editor of a big Philadelphia newspaper. And she's got *four* kids!"

Again I frowned. "She left four kids at home?"

"Yeah."

"Who takes care of the children while she's gone?"

"They've got a housekeeper. The youngest kid is three. It looks like the family gets along real well. But the old man didn't want her to leave home. She says she's only a short distance away and they can keep in touch over the phone. She can run over and see 'em almost any time.''

Catherine Slocum wasn't with the first group of WAFS who drew out winter flying clothes later on, but we thought nothing of it. Then word got around that Nelson and Slocum were in danger of washing out. The news made the rest of us very worried.

Catherine discussed her plight with no one. Esther came in my room to tell me what she thought about the challenge facing her. She didn't complain, she merely said, "I'm going to stay in if I can possibly do it. I've been sloppy, I can see that now. But I'll show them I can fly."

The Monday following my lonesome weekend, as usual I awoke before the others and had showered long before anyone stirred to the ringing of her alarm clock. My clock was built in. I always awoke with joy on a day when I expected to fly without students. It would be just me and the airplane making beautiful, smooth patterns together.

When I left the barracks for breakfast at the officers' mess next door, I breathed deeply and looked up to the sky, feeling the cool air of the morning all by myself. As I started down the narrow path leading to the ditch, I danced a little ballet, ending it with a circular leap into the air. By the time I was back and brushing my teeth, the others were scrambling about, getting in each other's way in the bath complex.

That morning it began to rain, so there was no flying. Instead, Lieutenant Guion surprised us with a test in navigation. Afterward, Nancy sent word for us to go to the flight surgeon's office. She greeted us there with, "We have to take form 64 and pass the Schneider or we can't remain in the Ferry Command."

I had already heard of the dreaded Schneider, which was a test of one's heart. The men civilian pilots did not take this test until they had ferried three months and were considered eligible to become officers. Why should we get it now?

The flight surgeon took on the first seven of us; the others were excused. We were each sent to different stations and were rotated as each test was completed. I was weighed, measured, given a chest x-ray, and had my blood pressure taken. Then I was told to run in place while the doctor held a stopwatch. After he told me to quit, I rested a minute before my blood pressure and pulse were taken again. I was very apprehensive, for I knew my blood pressure was not normal.

"Your normal pressure is 106," said the doctor. "After exercise, it jumped all the way up to 110. After a brief rest, it was 106 again. You have just passed the Schneider!"

Each doctor down the line tried to find out if I had flat feet or varicose veins or ingrown toenails. They discovered that my sense of balance was excellent, my hearing was acute, and my eyes could see at twenty feet what the normal person could see at fifteen.

One surgeon said, "I see you still have tonsils. When you get a commission, you might want to have them taken out, since you've had some bad colds that showed up on your chest x-rays."

Then I had to undress and I lay on the table covered with a sheet while a doctor palpitated my abdomen. Next he asked me to turn over on my stomach. How embarrassed I was when, without warning, he pulled my buttocks apart. He chuckled and said, "Congratulations! Only two of you I've examined so far have had no signs of constipation or hemorrhoids." He skipped a pelvic exam. I passed everything. I didn't need a waiver, as some of the others did, in order to be a ferry pilot. One of the waivers went to Helen Mary Clark, who used prescription lenses in her sunglasses and goggles. Any others who needed waivers kept mum.

The completion of the physical exam didn't end the day for us. Nancy Love announced, "You must attend ground school tonight." It was still raining and very dark when we walked up the hill to the school building. Lieutenant Guion went over our navigation exams with us. Two of us, Helen Mary and I, had made 100. The other grades were in the upper eighties and nineties.

We went next to a meteorology class with Lieutenant Fast. We could have skipped it because he told us nothing we didn't already know. On the way back down the hill we walked in the mizzle. Most of the others hurried on into the darkness, headed for the officers' club. Richards, Meserve and I continued on to the barracks. We couldn't see exactly where we were and I jumped the ditch a little too far up the hill, where it was a bit wider. Down I went and came out on the other side a gooey mess.

Nancy had asked Colonel Baker to have a boardwalk placed across our gully, but he had ignored her request, not wanting to make concessions to our femininity, perhaps. I don't know if my sliding into the mud had anything to do with it, but the following day a plank bridged the gap and that evening a porch light appeared at either entrance to BOQ 14.

On October 6 four of us were chosen to be checked on cross- country flying. I was one. Lieutenant Starbuck went with me. He was thorough and monitored my preparations for the flight. Using Washington and New York sectional charts, I drew a line from NCAAB to my destination at Olmstead Field at Middleton, Pennsylvania, on the Susquehanna River. I figured out how long it would take me to fly there by dividing the ground mileage by the ground speed I'd make, after taking the winds into consideration.

I was really worried because Nancy had said I didn't have as much cross-country experience as the others. She told me it was harder to navigate in the East than in the Midwest. Yet I saw on the sectionals a goodly sprinkling of checkpoints that I should be able to use to keep me on course.

I took no chances getting away from NCAAB. I circled it before leaving, taking a tentative course of 310 degrees, aiming halfway between Christiana and Wilmington. At one thousand feet I could accurately sight the next checkpoint coming up. What pleased me most about the flight was that the tiny brown lines depicting an altitude level in the bulging terrain ahead corresponded accurately with the contours of the hills I saw lifting from the valleys. What had I been afraid of?

The only instrument on the panel I could use as a guide was the Carwil compass, which was made in St. Louis. I had flown cross-country at home enough to know that small gusts of air would make the compass needle bobble and swing. A person had to sense almost by clairvoyance where the average of the swings was and make sure that it coincided with the course she was on. One couldn't goof off a second.

Then suddenly there was Olmstead Field, right where it should be, between the Susquehanna and Middletown. The field was camouflaged so that it looked like houses, farmland, and trees. But at eight hundred feet, a pilot could discern the patterns painted on the field to disguise it. While landing I found the patchwork of colors on the runway rather disconcerting and tried not to allow it to interfere with my depth perception.

Training planes were called "tail draggers" at that time; the nose wheel came into vogue only after the war. My favorite stalled landing made in a conventional plane was similar to that of a navy fighter landing on a carrier — the pilot had to get the tail down in a hurry in order to catch the hook. I squeezed the last bit of flying speed I could from the plane. As it skimmed along on the runway, the tail wheel made impact slightly before the landing wheels. The forward roll was the shortest one I could get without using brakes. I was a show-off!

We found a tie down position and secured the L-2B. The other WAFS and instructors landed within minutes of each other. No one got lost. As soon as we all were together, Lieutenant Haines took charge. He said, 'You might want to powder your noses. And there's a cafeteria here. How about seeing what they have to eat?

As we entered the large airport building, Starbuck informed me, "This is an immense military depot and it's a military target. That's the reason for the camouflage. Did you see on your chart it's in the military defense area along the East coast?"

The interior of the building was severely plain and immaculate. Lieutenant Haines led us to the cafeteria. It was after noon, so only doughnuts, rolls, coffee, milk, and soft drinks were available. I needed a cup of coffee to settle the newness of the situation. Including the time spent in circling the field, it had taken only one hour to get to Olmstead Field. We had maintained a ground speed of seventy-one miles per hour. But going back we had a headwind and it took us seventy-five minutes for the return trip. Lieutenant Starbuck said nothing about my navigation. I didn't mind. I didn't need a pat on the back.

By now Barbara Poole had returned to the NCAAB, passed the requirements and her flight test, and was a WAF. She complained about our instructors, ending with, "The one I can't stand is that Starbuck."

"I like him," I answered.

"He's a cold fish," retorted Poole. "He's not a bit friendly."

Some of the others chimed in, agreeing with her, ganging up on poor Starbuck.

My voice rose over the babble. "No, no!" I protested. "He and I talk a lot."

"You can't mean it! He's so distant," was Nelson's opinion.

"He never says anything. He's as dour as they make them," went on Poole.

I explained, "Maybe he doesn't talk much to you. That's the way Vermonters are."

"Hmpf! So he's a Calvin Coolidge type. I didn't like *him* either," answered Poole.

"Maybe he's not very happy here," I retorted. "He has to stay on the base and instruct us in transition." All eyes were on me.

"I'll bet you don't know he got infectious hepatitis somewhere on a ferry trip?" The eyes changed expression. "They still haven't discovered where he got it. And he's not the only one with jaundice in the Ferry Command.''

The eyes showed apprehension. Teresa bolted to a sitting position on her chaise lounge. ''No kidding!'' she exclaimed. Everyone else was as speechless as the accused Starbuck.

I was aware of his illness and continued my defense. ''He hasn't been out of the base hospital very long. Don't you see how thin and sallow he looks? It takes a lot of energy to be sociable, even to instruct flyers, and he hasn't got it. He told me it takes eighteen months to get over hepatitis. The army stuck him in transition school and I know he'd much rather be ferrying.''

There was silence for a while, then someone changed the subject. For a moment we could see that on the airways ahead of us were more dangers than we'd already anticipated. Soon, soberly, we left Jamesy and went back to our rooms and to bed.

One day Pat Rhonie begged a favor of me and I said yes. Not long afterward, Esther Nelson walked determinedly into the lavatory where I was making some last minute changes in my face and hairdo. She scowled at me as she said with a hiss, ''You're not going out with *her!*''

I didn't even turn around. I could see her plainly in the mirror. ''Why not?'' I asked and went on applying lipstick. ''We are only going to eat at Howard Johnson's.''

''What did she have to ask *you* for?''

''She's always wanted a date with Lieutenant Guion and this will be her only chance. Guion won't go with her unless he can drag his buddy Fast along. So they needed someone else to go with them. Lieutenant Fast is a nice country kid and I am sure that nothing will happen to me.''

''Well! I'm surprised at you, Scharr,'' said Nelson as she left in a huff.

Most army personnel ate at either the officers' or the enlisted men's mess. Just to get away from army food and the base was a treat. I had overheard people bragging about eating at the Howard Johnson's on the DuPont Highway. There was, according to the easterners, a string of such restaurants along the east coast of the United States. I was very curious about the place because it had a reputation for being ritzy. When Rhonie pleaded with me to go so she could have her long sought-after date with the dapper, aristocratic Lieutenant Guion, it wasn't the idea of a date that swayed me. It was my curiosity about Howard Johnson's.

I went back to my room. Soon Rhonie came by and we two went down the stairs and out. By the time we had walked to the road, Lieutenant Guion drove up, stopped and let us in the car. We were off.

At the sentry gate, Guion alone returned the guard's salute. After a short drive to the DuPont Highway, we arrived at the famous eating place.

The restaurant was so clean that it shone. Red booths lined the walls. The waitress handed each of us a menu and waited while we chose our food. To me, the prices were a bit high. When the food arrived, it was arranged well, but there was nothing outstanding about its taste. There weren't any other diners in the booth next to ours, so we talked freely.

The men spoke of flying the Atlantic Ocean at night, using celestial navigation because they couldn't contact anyone by radio for fear of giving away their position to the enemy. There was no radio beam for them to follow; the enemy could have used it to find them or could have bombed the transmitter and put it out of commission. When storms were impending, scheduled transoceanic flights were delayed until the weather cleared. Crews stayed on alert, ready to leave at a moment's notice.

Lieutenant Guion told me, "We're on orders now. The first class of WAFS is finished. Somebody else will take the next group in meteorology and navigation."

Ah, I thought, for Rhonie it was now or never. She'd have to hunt elsewhere after tonight.

Lieutenant Fast added, "Now that we're navigating the Atlantic again, we have to practice shooting stars a whole lot more."

Rhonie's eyes were brooding. I'm sure mine lit up. The two officers had allowed each of the WAFS in the class to use their sextants on the sun earlier in the day. My sightings were ridiculously poor. The sun simply would not stay in place in the sky. I was itching for another chance at playing navigator, for I never settled for "poor" in my life.

When we four were again in the automobile, returning to base, Rhonie said, "One of the overseas pilots told me we lost some ferry pilots crossing the Atlantic this year."

I said, "Why? The planes they ferry are new, aren't they?"

She replied, "Some of them were old, from the airlines. And the weather is very treacherous."

The navigators were silent. It wasn't a pleasant subject.

"What kind of planes do you ferry?" I asked Fast.

"We usually take C-47s and usually they are full of cargo."

"That's the DC-3, isn't it?"

"Yes, but earlier, DC-2s made it over."

"Do they put the cargo in the seats?" I asked.

Both men laughed. Fast answered, "They don't come to us with airline seats. There are just metal bucket seats all down either side of the fuselage wall. If we carry personnel, they sit on parachutes that fit into the bucket seats and they face the middle. We strap the cargo into the bays down the middle of the fuselage."

"Do you fly bombers, too?" I asked.

"You bet." Fast sounded uneasy.

"What? B-17s?"

"Usually we get Martin B-26s," said Fast.

"They're the ones you see on the base with the brown and tan markings to look like desert," explained Guion. "They're going to Africa. They aren't popular airplanes."

"What's the matter with them?" asked Rhonie.

"Well," said Guion, and he glanced back at Fast, "they have clipped wings, so they can cruise pretty fast."

"Oh, so they take a long roll on takeoffs and landings?" I asked.

Fast said, "The B-26 has a lot of power and it glides awful hot." He thought a moment and went on. "It's got a nickname I can't tell you."

"Why not? They'll hear it sooner or later. They are called the Baltimore prostitute," said Guion. He paused. "Because they have no visible means of support."

I didn't hear Rhonie laugh either, but the men did. Our arrival at the sentry gate broke the embarrassing silence that followed. When we reached the barracks, the men spoke of what was uppermost in their minds.

"We've enjoyed the evening," Guion said, "but you ladies must excuse us. We're practicing navigation tonight."

My mind ran back to when I taught celestial navigation in Saint Louis University's CPTP. With no sextant and only blackboard diagrams and a nautical almanac, I led my class through homemade problems — ten rapid sightings of three stars from an imaginary location. We then took the average of the sightings on each star. A look in any current almanac gave us the location of each star above the earth's latitude and longitude at each second of a year. Duplicating a Mercator projection, we circled each star at the angle it inclined from our location, for somewhere on that circle was our position. The triangle made by the intersection of the three arcs marked where we had been. From there, we hoped, we could head toward our imaginary destination. "Today at noon I couldn't hold the sextant still," I said. "My hand waved all around. It's not as easy as tracking weather balloons with a theodolite.

Where do you practice?" I was wishing eagerly to be invited to go with them.

"We practice in a vacant open field on the base far from everything," said Guion.

"We don't want lights to interfere and we see the stars better out there," added Fast.

We parted and I never saw the pair again. After they drove off, Rhonie said, "I'm going to the officers' club." I went into the BOQ.

The barracks was quiet, for it was only eight o'clock in the evening. I passed up my own room, going first to the bathroom down the hall. As I went by Gertrude Meserve's room, I glanced in to see that quiet, stone-faced New Englander, clad in pajamas, standing in the middle of the floor. Her shoulders were hunched up and she was giggling soundlessly to herself.

Something is afoot, I thought immediately. I retraced my steps and this time Meserve's door was closed. I never left my own door closed, so I was wary when I saw it was shut.

I pushed the door open and looked up to the top of the doorway, expecting a glass filled with water to tumble down. Nothing happened. Gingerly, I went in to the middle of the room where the string pull of my ceiling light hung. I didn't pull it. By the light from the hall and the skylight above the light bulb, I could see that a water glass stood on one of the two-by-fours.

I took the little barrel that Nelson had retrieved from the dump and given to me for a chair. I mounted it and took down the glass. A dummy string was attached. The real string and light chain were wrapped around the glass. I pulled and the light went on — but ablution was foiled.

The room was not at all as I had left it two hours earlier. My rosy mouthwash had been poured into my drinking glass on top of my dresser. My stockings were knotted and tossed around the room. From the window hung festoons of brassieres and panties for the amusement of passersby outside. Quietly I undid the decorations and put them all back in the dresser.

I found my pajamas under the pillow of the cot. It took me a long time to untie all the knots. Even so, I was amused at all the trouble someone had gone to. I undressed and put on my pajamas, thinking that the bed was probably short-sheeted. Inspection proved my suspicions were unfounded.

"Bunch of amateurs," I muttered as I turned off the light and settled into bed. The cot was never comfortable, but it felt lumpier than ever. I got up, turned on the light, and felt about between the two mattresses. My hands encountered the oranges that I had bought in Wilmington the previous Saturday.

Helen Richards climbing into a PT-19. She was one of the young, unattached WAFS who captivated the base photographers.

Gertrude Meserve shown in October 1942, about to make her first ferrying mission.

With that I could hold back no longer. I never laugh soundlessly as a lady should. My peals of laughter and my exclamations of "Oh, boy!" assured the waiting pranksters that I wasn't angry with them. Indeed, I felt that they must have liked me at least a little bit to have bothered to play such a trick.

All the oranges were back on top of the dresser and I was back in bed when Teresa poked her head in the doorway and then entered on tip-toe.

"What did you go out with her for?" she asked.

"I felt sorry for her. She really wanted a date with Lieutenant Guion and she couldn't get him alone. He and Fast had to practice using their sextants tonight. The only way she could work it was to double date for dinner. The guys left us right afterwards."

"Don't you know she asked everybody else and they all turned her down?"

I doubted that, but I said, "No. Nobody told me."

"We didn't think you'd do it," replied Teresa. "Nobody likes her, especially me. You know when I first got here she complained to Nancy about my hair, and she didn't like the outfit I wore. Geez! A lot she knew about it. All the men instructors in our CPT program wore summer khaki like a uniform and so I did, too. That's what I wore to fly in and I came here to fly. So that's why I dressed like I did. She's a real bitch!"

I answered, "Well, I'm sure it won't happen again. I doubt if she'll ever see Guion again because he's navigating from now on. She won't ask me another time, although I'm no competition like some of the rest would be."

As I lay in bed afterwards and thought over the evening, I came to two conclusions. One was that Nancy must not have liked Teresa's hair either. The other was that Pat Rhonie needed a friend and I was glad that I had done what I'd done.

SETTLING INTO THE ROUTINES

O N OCTOBER 8, we original WAFS heard Betty Gillies call out our names even before she hung up the hall telephone. As soon as we had assembled, she said, "Nancy says she's asked motor pool to send us some transportation and for us to be ready in a jiffy."

"Where are we going?" asked Nelson.

"Back to the subdepot," replied Betty.

A high-topped open automobile that looked as if it had been used in a big-game hunting safari arrived promptly at the barracks. Each woman climbed into the vehicle in her own style. Betty was gracefully composed and sure. Cornelia was large and awkward, but dignified. Helen Mary was a lady of poise and had the bearing befitting a descendant of six generations of Harvard graduates. Pat Rhonie slid in daintily. Helen Richards was the boyish westerner, young, lean of limb and hip, agile as a deer. Teresa James fairly bounced in. Esther Nelson heaved and pushed her weight to its resting place. I leapt to my seat.

This was our second visit to the subdepot, but the clerks were new to us. The two enlisted men on duty were visibly nervous. They must have never waited on women before. Betty was first, as was her prerogative. Uncomfortable, a clerk asked her, "What is you chest size?" Then he hurried into the storeroom to find a winter fur-lined jacket for her.

Each in turn was asked this vital statistic, as well as hip size. Fortunately for me, I fit the first garments handed to me. Poor Nelson! She was bosomy and larger than she wanted anyone to know. She couldn't get into the garments brought to her. "I can't wear this!" she shrilled. The clerk was clever enough to avoid a scene. He brought jacket and pants larger than the ones she couldn't get into and the problem was solved. A true gentleman, he didn't broadcast her size.

Each of us also signed out a fur-lined helmet, a leather face mask, fur-lined gloves, and boots. And then we got a big stack of aeronautical charts and a master chart which showed all the U.S. radio ranges and airways.

"These you won't have to return," said a clerk. "They become torn or obsolete and it's possible to lose one. If necessary, you may obtain duplicates at any air field you fly into or at any of the Ferry Command bases."

What was so wonderful about our booty was that it was all new. No hand-me-downs for us!

After we stowed away our winter flying clothing, I walked double-quick up the hill to fly solo. As I was making out my clearance, Lt. Sandy Lerner asked, "How about giving me a ride over to DuPont? I've got to play ground officer over there and the gas truck isn't going until later."

Lieutenant Haines looked at me from where he stood behind Sandy and nodded his head affirmatively.

"Sure," I replied and put him on my manifest.

Sandy climbed into the front cockpit of PT-19A, #42-33650. I did a quick ground check of the airplane, the line boy cranked, the engine whirred, the chocks were pulled out, and we were off. But before I took off, he turned and yelled to me that he didn't want to get to DuPont too fast. We had a full tank of gas and he knew it. He said, "I want to take the controls when we get out there. I want to play around a little."

Sandy, as a lieutenant, outranked me. Once in the practice area, he shook the stick and I let him have a go at it. He played around in the sky at about 3,000 feet, doing what to him must have served for chandelles, 720s, and lazy eights. When he had had enough, he shook the stick again and I took over. I did several of each. Then Sandy motioned for me to hit the deck and I brought us down with power-glide turns, made the field pattern, and landed.

"Come into the office," he said. "I have something I want to show you."

I followed him. He brought out a Translear radio.

"Richard DuPont has the distributorship on these," he told me. "You know, you girls are the pets of the DuPonts. They think a lot of you. And he'll sell you these radios wholesale."

Sandy showed me how the radio picked up the field control tower at Newcastle on one band and the radio range on another. It also had an AM band so one could get local stations wherever one was. I thought it was nice of DuPont to make such an offer, especially since he was a glider pilot and not an airplane jockey.

"How much is it?" I asked.

"Only forty dollars."

Forty dollars was a fortune to me. The expense of being a military volunteer was proving to be a big burden. The decision about buying a radio would take more thought.

"I'll see," I said. "I'll let you know."

"Before you go, how about a piece of cake?" he asked.

I must have raised my eyebrows, for he added, "My sister is so proud of me being in the service and she wants to do her patriotic bit. She's always making cakes and I've passed them around to the men. I know they appreciate them, but I guess they can eat only so much."

The cake was decorated with colored icing swirls, plainly amateurish, but still not a bad job. Sandy cut off a slice for me and I ate it out of hand. It was a bit coarse, perhaps due to the wartime flour. (In those days there were no packaged cake mixes and baking results varied from time to time and from cook to cook.)

"Thanks, Sandy," I said, licking the icing off my fingers. "Tell your sister I enjoyed it."

That was the wrong thing for me to say, for whenever Sandy saw me thereafter, he wanted to feed me the latest cake. And I never ate many sweets. Sometimes the cake was fair, sometimes it was downright good. But his sister couldn't leave well enough alone. She improvised and covered her cakes with icings of many colors: blue, green, magenta, and some combinations that looked like ptomaine staring one in the face.

Finally, every one of the first batch of WAFS reached the saturation point and no matter how much salesmanship Sandy tried on us, we simply could not accept another bite. I thought it was fortunate that more WAFS were coming in — they would give him a never-ending avenue for his bakery goods.

Everybody liked Sandy Lerner. He kept track of student time and arranged that we got gasoline at the DuPont Airport. He was always pleasant and we were hardly aware that his job was to see that we didn't spend much time on the ground. Transition school wanted as much use of its airplanes as possible.

His family owned the Lerner Shops. One couldn't go into a town of any size in the United States without running into one of them in the shopping district. But there was something that mystified me about Sandy. It hadn't taken me ten minutes with him at the controls to see that he was a sloppy pilot. He had been all over the sky, undisciplined, erratic, and seemingly unaware that the flight patterns he made did not resemble mine.

I had been under the impression that he was an instructor, like Starbuck, Haines, Tracy, and French, although no one had ever mentioned taking a lesson from him. The others were precise in their maneuvers and their work was beautiful to behold.

My guess was that the Ferry Command took Sandy in when it needed pilots desperately or maybe he freaked a good test. Somehow, maybe because he was likeable or had friends higher up, he squeaked through and became an officer. I wondered how many others like him were out there ferrying instead of being protected, as he was.

That evening, seated on my cot, I searched through the aeronautical charts meant to guide us across the airways. My fingers drew out Kansas City. I unfolded the map just so I could look once again at the familiar landmarks of St. Louis and its environs. I was feeling more than a bit homesick and missed Harold. Then out in the hall a guffaw arose among the recurring titters that I had been hearing but ignoring. What was going on out there?

I dropped Kansas City onto my khaki blanket, rose, and in two strides reached the doorway and stepped into the hall. A half dozen WAFS were pressed against the wall near Teresa's door in order to allow her plenty of room. She was marching down to Helen Mary's door. As I watched, she turned and walked back. Then she faced her audience and demanded, "Who was that?"

"Slocum!" exclaimed everyone with one voice as they turned to each other and laughed at their mutual perspicacity.

Teresa returned my questioning gaze with "I'm imitating how everybody marches." She turned to her audience and said, "Now, look at this one."

This time she carried her hands close to her thighs, palms to the rear, with fingers continuously flexing nervously. I had no idea who it was.

"Rhonie," yelled someone. The rest agreed. I felt stupid. But of course Rhonie was at the other end of the drill squad and there were too many women between us for me to have seen what she did with her hands.

As Teresa continued to imitate marchers, I found that I had not been aware of them as individuals. I had been concentrating on the marching. Then Teresa asked, "What about this one?"

She repeated her solo promenade. This time she put one foot directly in front of the other. As the right foot changed position on the floor, it made a hint of a sweep. With each step forward, the opposite hip swayed with a provocative little flip. She came toward me and stared. Everyone was silent. I was on the spot and stumped.

I said, "I can't guess."

"It's you, you old bag," she said, as the others giggled at my discomfort.

I was surprised! I had been curbing the motion of my hips for seven years, since a young man in San Diego informed me that my manner of walking was an invitation to intimacy. After that, I always walked straight ahead with a mental vise on my hips so no one else would ever get similar ideas. Now I found out that I had failed.

The next day after lunch we lined up near headquarters. A truck rolled up and we were herded into it without an instructor to accompany us. As we left, Nancy called, "You're going to ordnance."

On the long ride across the base we passed by several officers shooting at bull's-eye targets in a row somewhat back from the road. Then the truck stopped near a small, one-story building. We jumped off and went inside to find one long room with two rows of tables and chairs. We chose our places like church goers looking for a back seat and sat down.

A good-looking, tall and blond young corporal greeted us. "Good morning, ladies. I'm Corporal Henson, your instructor in ordnance. Shall we begin?"

He picked up a pistol from a table. As he talked about it and explained what ordnance meant, our eyes never left the weapon.

I whispered to Nelson, "I'm going to like this."

She stared at me with disbelief, but Helen Richards on the other side of me whispered, "Me, too."

Corporal Henson placed a pistol in front of each of us. We watched enthralled as he took it apart and put it back together again, naming each of the parts. He asked us, holding the reassembled gun, "Who was the first person to invent a gun with separate parts so that, if one part were damaged, the entire gun didn't have to be discarded?"

I didn't want to sound like a quiz kid, but in a flash I answered, "Eli Whitney?"

The surprised Henson agreed. "Yes," he said, "You're the first person to come in here who knew that."

All eyes turned to me with a "what have we here?" look. I thought, I didn't teach American history for nothing.

Then we played follow the leader. The corporal broke the barrel from the cylinder and watched while each of us did it also. He took six bullets from the cartridge chambers. We did, too.

"Always place your pieces in a certain order and you won't get mixed up when you reverse the process," he said.

By the time we had put the pistols back together again, the hour was over. "Now are we ready to shoot?" I asked.

The corporal ignored my question. Instead he said, "You won't be excused from ordnance until you can take the blindfold test."

Barbara Poole asked in disbelief, "We have to shoot this thing blindfolded?"

"Oh, no!" he replied. "Never. You only take the gun apart and put it back together again blindfolded. You won't get to shoot it at all."

"But there's a rifle range out there and some men were practicing . . .," I said hopefully.

I had the notion that I would show off what a good marksman I was, even though I had had no previous training. I'd had one experience with a gun before, when Hermann, Missouri, held its centennial celebration. Harold and I took my mother to that little Missouri River town near where she and my father had been born and raised. Among the carnival stands set up in the old fairgrounds was a shooting gallery. Harold insisted that I try it and paid for a round of shots.

The proprietor handed me a gun and showed me how to use it. "Line up that little bitty thing sticking up at the end of the barrel so it is in the center of the notch up near where you pull the trigger," he said. "That's all there is to it. Now aim at the center of the target."

I did and pressed the trigger. A bell rang.

To a perplexed me, the man explained, "You hit the center."

I did again what I had done before. Again the bell rang. Fourteen times the bell rang. On the fifteenth and final shot, we were all laughing so hard that I wasn't steady and I missed.

The corporal broke into my reverie. He must have seen a disappointed look on my face, for he said, "Sorry, ladies, but you are civilians. Only men get to use the ranges."

The next day we were back. We spent an hour running our fingers over the Remington pistols. We tried not to peek as we extracted bullets and laid bits and pieces of our firearms on the table directly in front of us. The corporal assisted wherever he could. Everyone was quiet except for an occasional "Rats!" or "Nuts!"

"As soon as you can do this blindfolded, you will be dismissed from ordnance," said our instructor. That statement led us to renewed effort. I wanted to get out as soon as possible; there seemed no point in learning something I'd never get to use.

"May we come over to practice if we're not flying this afternoon?" asked Helen Richards.

"Sure," said Henson. "We're here all day."

That afternoon Richards and I, with no airplanes to fly, hiked to the ordnance building. Without the whole class, we got more attention and we weren't afraid to speak up.

Richards asked, "What is this? A thirty-eight?"

"No, it's forty-four," Henson answered.

"What does that mean?" I asked.

"It's the size of the bore inside each cylinder and it is $^{44}/_{100}$ of an inch," he told me. "The cannon mounted in the airplanes are measured instead in millimeters."

Richards and I took the blindfold test and passed. We'd beat the rest of the class and didn't have to come again. While we were there, a pilot came into the building and began talking to Richards. They went outside and I waited for her inside, thinking he might want to ask her for a date. Corporal Henson got rid of a few other men who'd wandered in and came over to me. He said, "I see you are married."

"Yes," I answered. "My husband is an enlisted man in the naval reserve. He hasn't been called to overseas duty yet, but we expect it any time."

We continued talking about the war, of how it had uprooted us and made the future uncertain. I liked the corporal. When he asked me, "Would you mind going to the movies with me tonight?" I replied yes, but I'd have to meet him there.

He understood. "I'll be in front waiting for you," he said. "See you at seven. We don't want to miss Pathe news."

On the way back Richards didn't notice how quiet I was. She was full of talk about the B-26 the pilot had showed her. She described the airplane to me, "And it glides in at 165 miles per hour. I wonder what that speed feels like."

But I wasn't really listening. I was telling myself that there wasn't anything wrong with sitting next to an enlisted man in the base theater. I was sure I would be surrounded by them on all sides, for the installation was mainly for their use. All officers risked that prospect. The place was not off-limits to any of us.

That evening I put on my woolen suit and looked like a civilian. I wasn't buddy-buddy with any one WAF, so I didn't have to give an excuse for not being with someone. When I got to the front of the theater, the line was still about a dozen feet long. The corporal at the door smiled a greeting and his eyes motioned for me to follow him inside. He already had our tickets. We took seats fairly far back. The lights were just dimming.

"I didn't think you would recognize me," I whispered.

"It was easy," he whispered in return. "Glad you made it."

Pathé news flashed its rooster trademark. One of its lightning quick scenes showed a group of uniformed men carrying their gear and marching up a ramp to board a battlewagon.

"I have a friend back home," I whispered, "who already has two purple hearts. He's been in almost every landing. I just learned from home that he's on his way to —"

"Shhh!" The corporal grasped my wrist to stop me. He was tense and serious. "Don't ever say anything about troop movements or anything like that. You never know who is listening and it might help the enemy."

I felt properly chastised.

The movie was a so-so one with Lana Turner and Clark Gable. Later, the corporal walked me to the board spanning our gulch in front of BOQ 14.

"I enjoyed the show," I thanked him.

"It was a pleasure to have your company," he replied. We said good night and parted.

I never saw Henson again. As I look back, I am glad that, obedient to authority as I was, I had the nerve to defy a rule — fraternizing with enlisted men — that I thought was ridiculous. Harold never would have objected to what I did. And every time I was tempted to speak about something that I shouldn't, I felt the corporal gripping my wrist and I kept my big mouth shut.

Cornelia Fort kept to herself at the other end of the barracks. I guessed that most of the time she was doing what she liked most — reading books or writing to her friends. One Sunday she sought me out. Not finding me in my room, she came into the laundry area where I was pressing a shirt.

Cornelia had a brown package under one arm. She said, "I'm sending these books off and since I'm going to the post office, I wondered if there is anything I can get you."

"No, thanks, Cornelia," I replied. "I bought a book of stamps the last time I was over there. Tell me, isn't it expensive to send books by mail? They really weigh a lot."

She smiled. "You can get a special rate on books or any printed material so long as there's no personal message in the package. I trade books with my friends all the time. The service is speedy and there's never a worry that my package won't get there.

"It'll be better for us," she continued, "when we're commissioned and we can send our mail — letters, at least — franked as the men can."

I turned the collar of my shirt around and started to press the other side. Cornelia started away, but turned and paused at the doorway with an afterthought. She asked, "Would you care to walk yonder to see whether the leaves are turning yet?"

"Yeah, sure," I said. "When you come back I'll be through with this ironing and I'll be glad to get out of here."

The air was crisp and the sky was meant for flying. Cornelia and I walked at a good clip along the road leading to the subdepot on the other side of the base. We cut across a field to look at a cocoon on a milkweed plant and saw several strange plants along the way that we couldn't identify. The glorious show of autumn was just beginning.

I'd heard that Cornelia had been in Hawaii on December 7, 1941, and I wanted to hear about it from her. So I remarked, "Weren't you at Pearl Harbor when the Japs attacked?"

"I was. And it was a Sunday. Do you fly on Sundays?"

"That's the day I fly more than any other," I said. "I was teaching that Sunday. I had been up with students for over three hours straight and was walking to the ad building to get a cup of coffee when a fellow named Charlie Roberts approached me with a big grin on his face. I didn't care much for Roberts anyway, because he acted as if he were superior to other people. I was surprised that he spoke to me. He said, 'The Japs just bombed Pearl Harbor.'

"I thought that was his idea of a joke, and to me it was in poor taste. But in the lobby of the ad building I was shocked to find out it was true. I had another student later that day, but no one was allowed to fly until we could prove that we were natural-born citizens."

Cornelia said, "My mother would never have consented to my flying on a Sunday. I couldn't tell her that my job required me to fly on the day of rest. But I got caught that one time, and she found out that I had not been keeping the Sabbath as I should."

Cornelia was silent as we walked a dozen paces or so, then she went on. "I was instructing in a CPT program in Hawaii, and we flew on any day to catch up. So, on December 7, I was out at about 3,000 feet with a student in a Cub over our acrobatic area.

"We had our own acrobatic area and all the naval cadets had theirs so we wouldn't be endangered by them. My student had made one spin and we were gaining altitude to try another when I saw what looked like a military trainer headed right toward us. I thought, what's he doing, coming into our area? I grabbed the controls and slipped to a lower altitude. As I looked up, I saw the emblem of the rising sun on the plane. It was a Zero.

"I said to the student, 'I'm taking it.' Then I got the Cub down as fast as I could and landed it. We left it right there on the runway after I cut the switch and we ran for cover into a hangar."

"Good Lord!" I exclaimed. "That wasn't a safe move, either."

"We were lucky," replied Cornelia. "Bombs were dropping all over and fires were burning. The Cub was strafed right after we left it. My student called to me as we ran for cover, 'Miss Fort, when are we going to spin again?' I yelled back, 'It'll be a long, long time before you and I fly again.' "

Thoughtfully we walked along. At length Cornelia said, "About my mother. Let me tell you about the day I soloed. Mother knew I had started flying, but flying was a world apart from any of her interests.

"My mother was out in our garden. My home is called Fortland. It is just beautiful. It is a replica of Mount Vernon and it stands on a rise overlooking the Cumberland River at Nashville, just like Mount Vernon is up on a hill overlooking the Potomac.

"My mother was there in the garden, wearing gloves and a big, floppy hat, and she was cutting flowers for the vases in the house. I rushed home after my flight and out to where she was. I was so excited and thrilled. I said, 'Mother! I soloed today.' She didn't miss a snip as she went on cutting some roses that she laid in her basket. She didn't even look up when she answered me. She said, 'That's nice, dear. Now you won't have to do *that* again.' "

I asked, "Didn't she have any idea what flying was all about?"

"No. Mother is in a world of her own. It is set off by how she grew up and what she considers proper."

The woods were beautiful where we were walking. Every so often a car stopped and the driver asked us if we needed a lift, but we always declined. We were enjoying ourselves and didn't want to cut it short. The men must have been mystified that females who flew wouldn't rather ride than walk.

"Aren't those cattails?" asked Cornelia, pointing.

"You bet."

"Let's go over and pick some," Cornelia said.

"They're not roses," I answered as I laughed, remembering her mother.

"Even so, we can put them somewhere as a memento of this jaunt."

The cattails were in a swampy area in a small meadow. Our shoes got coated with mud in reaching them, but that wasn't such a problem to me as cracking the stems low enough to get a decent length. I broke off only three, which was enough.

As we walked back to the BOQ, two enlisted men wearing fatigues came riding along in a jeep. The jeep stopped. The usual question was asked. Cornelia and I looked at each other. We weren't tired yet, but we read each other's mind.

"Thanks, yes, we'll be glad to," she said. We climbed into the back seat and missed the rest of the scenery because we had to squint our eyes against the wind. We took this ride not because we were partial to enlisted men, but because we'd never been in a jeep before. We were deposited right in front of the barracks. We wished that someone had seen us arriving in such style.

I don't recall who asked if we might have a pet as a mascot in the barracks. Nancy gave us the answer. She was as straight as a bristle when she proclaimed, "No animals are allowed in army barracks."

I commented, "Good! I hope all the mice and cockroaches in the neighborhood can read the regulations." That provoked some laughs and seemed to ease the harshness of the ruling. Certainly in some of the homes left behind were family pets that WAFS missed almost as much as family members.

One morning in early October I entered the bathroom before the others and found a half-grown kitten playing on the floor. A shallow cardboard box in the corner held newspapers that had already been used. I found the stench intolerable. Whose chemical warfare was this? I wondered who would have dared to disobey Nancy. Aloud I said, "Where did *that* come from?"

My exclamation brought Teresa from her room across the hall. I looked at her and said, "Whoever brought that cat in here had better get it out before Nancy sees it."

"Any old time, you old bag," replied Teresa. "Nancy herself brought that cat in here last night."

I frowned in amazement. "I thought Nancy said emphatically that there would no pets allowed in the barracks."

Teresa shrugged. She answered, "You know how it is. Mrs. Anderson will have a fit, but she knows who's boss."

"Phew! Then this is going to be a smelly mess around here," I predicted.

However, in a few days the cat and its odor were gone and forgotten. Yet something remained — my first lesson in the disregard some privileged personnel have for regulations. If they have the power, they can bend the law to suit their desires.

I missed "brag night" on the Monday evening that Nelson and I went to shop in Wilmington. I'm sorry I did, although I found in the basement of the department store a Bates bedspread for five dollars that I thought I could use on my cot. And it would be nice on Harold's bed after the war. I also found a gold ring with a row of three topaz stones. Second hand, it cost only ten dollars. I thought it quite elegant.

But while we were gone, the other WAFS held session. Teresa told me about it long afterwards. A sardonic smile was on her face.

"Everybody began to tell what school they went to. Miss Smith's Finishing School figured prominently in the brag session. You know, Miss Smith's is where those wealthy and socially prominent young ladies are made ready for their debuts and a proper entrance in proper society."

Teresa arrested my attention with her choice of words, unlike her usual casual speech.

She continued, "One of the girls had attended Wesleyan. Cornelia went to Ogoontz, like Betty, and then to Radcliffe and ended up at a university near Nashville, her home town. Nancy told us how when she was at Vassar, none of the girls was allowed out of the dormitory or to leave the campus during the school year, and she got to go to the airport where the boys were on the weekends because she had a private license. It made all the other girls jealous and she got a kick out of that."

"I believe it," I said.

Teresa went on with her story. "Meserve was there and she didn't say anything, like she always does, so nobody asked her. But I know for a fact that she didn't attend a fancy school either. I think it was Rhonie who put me on the spot. She asked where *I* went to school.

"I didn't go to college. All I had was high school, but I wasn't going to let them high-hat me. The only name that came to me was Thornhill, so I said it. Everybody looked puzzled and someone asked how you could get into that school. So I said you have to do something outstanding or you can't get into it. Well, nobody asked what I did or I'd have been sunk.

"It's a big joke with Meserve and me. I said to her afterwards, 'You know what Thornhill is? It's a boys' reformatory in Pittsburgh.' "

EXPANSION OF THE RANKS

AS I LOOK BACK NOW, I can see that Nancy's firm hold over the WAFS loosened with the October tide of entries who followed Gertrude Meserve. The great majority of them were in their early twenties, unmarried, attractive, lively, and accustomed to masculine attention. Evidently they saw no reason, as a great number of pioneer women pilots had, to drink alcohol, smoke cigarettes, or listen to vulgarities just to be "one of the boys." And we found that their abstinence in no way interfered with their popularity on the base.

The telephone, which had hitherto been silent, immediately began to ring after 1700 each afternoon. We who were close to it answered it until it became evident that the young WAFS were not moving to answer it so they wouldn't appear eager. Thereafter we let it ring.

The officers' club was the favorite gathering place. There lieutenants, even on their limited salaries, could entertain the girls with a Coke, Ping-Pong or gin rummy in the game room. Mostly they liked to talk, as all pilots do. When the club had a Sunday night buffet, a fellow could treat a girl to dinner. And there was always the base movie theater a short distance away, where all the movies were first run and cost only a quarter. Usually, a group went together.

The telephone rang first for our belle of Odessa, Florene Miller, whose family owned five jewelry stores in that oil-rich area of west Texas. At first glance one thought of Snow White, for Florene was comely and had the traditional fairy tale coloring — creamy pale complexion, thick, naturally curly black hair, and large, clear blue eyes. Men were stricken when they gazed at her, for the alchemy of her beauty rendered them helpless. In time, Nancy called her "flypaper" because she attracted so many flyers.

But Florene had deeper qualities than just physical attractiveness. Her bubbly optimism and easy conversation smoothed the disappointments, hurts, and frustrations we all had from time to time. She soothed our irritations, many of which she endured as well, and we felt relieved simply from being with her.

We enjoyed Florene's southern drawl and her "you-alls." Her gift of gab, akin to that of Henry James' Daisy Miller, allowed any bashful swain with a loss of tongue and wit in her presence to be entertained without the embarrassment of searching for comments of his own. In this, Florene was unlike Richards or Meserve.

This did not mean that Florene's life was without sadness. I recalled reading an account in the Ninety-Nine newsletter of the year past about her family. At a pilot get-together, her father and a brother, in the family Luscombe, had flown into a canyon, hoping, no doubt, to top the rise at the far end. The two must have realized that the engine wasn't powered to accomplish the climb and they turned back. The canyon had narrowed by then and they were unable to escape. The airplane was demolished and both occupants were killed. Florene later told me that, inconsolable, she had been unable to weep at her great loss for a long time. After she was finally able to relieve her grief, she adopted a philosophy of living to enjoy all the moments she had and to make the most of what life brought her without complaint.

Her nature enhanced the good looks she inherited from her mother. From her, too, she must have learned the social graces, for her popular mother had been a deputy Grand Matron of the Order of the Eastern Star of Texas.

The next WAF to appear was Barbara Jane Erickson. She was also about twenty-one years old. Her hair, like Florene's, was naturally curly, thick, and almost coal black. Her skin was light ivory, and her eyes were large, dark, and bold beneath her black brows. She was pretty, too, but shorter than Florene and a bit chunky. She carried that baby fat with her all the war years.

Barbara brought another young lady with her, an admirer named Eleanor who worked in the flying school office where Barbara taught at Walla Walla, Washington. In satellite fashion, Ellie accompanied her idol, hoping to find employment at the air base.

Fortunately for her, a vacancy was about to occur. When I was at headquarters one day, Miss Cohee confided in me, "I think I'll be moving back to Dover."

"Oh, don't do that," I said. "We'll miss you."

"My mother still lives in Dover," she explained, "and they've almost completed a new air base there. I ought to be able to get a transfer without any trouble."

Cohee did, and Love soon placed Ellie in her inner office. But Nancy didn't allow Ellie to reside with us in the barracks. She found a room elsewhere.

One morning, a day or two after Barbara arrived, I was in the bathroom combing my hair, using the middle mirror over the wash basins. I never dawdled, so would have finished in a minute or two. On either side of me were two other WAFS, one washing her face, the other brushing her teeth. Suddenly, Barbara shoved herself between my neighbor and me. She elbowed me, pushed me back, and took over the wash basin. Then she began to brush her teeth vigorously. I didn't remember anyone having been as rude to me. I retreated a step or two. The mirror must have showed the expression of shock I had on my face. After that, I never became friendly with Barbara Erickson and she had no interest in me. I found out several years later that her father was a publisher and her family was socially prominent.

Except for our common marching exercise, the original WAFS were rarely with the newcomers. We were in a different stage of orientation, so we had few daily contacts. And later, if we weren't on the same missions, we didn't really get acquainted. But each WAF left indelible impressions.

Another cutie came from Nebraska — Evelyn Sharp, a slender reed of a girl with dark brown eyes, fair skin, and dark brown hair. She, Barbara, and Florene were our glamour girls until Nancy Batson came up from Birmingham, Alabama, to give them some competition with her blondeness and drawl even slower than Florene's.

From Amarillo, Texas, came Delphine Bohn, who gave the impression of being tall, although she was petite. Her hair was dark blonde and her eyes were hazel green. She differed from the other newcomers in joining the cocktails-before-dinner group, and she smoked. She seemed to prefer to watch others perform, rather than leading the conversation herself.

One day I walked through the lower hall of BOQ 14 instead of chancing the mud along the side. I heard a new voice, loud, deep and as husky as actress Tallulah Bankhead's. There, in a knot in the middle of the hall was a bevy of the most recent arrivals grouped about a tall young woman. As I approached, I wondered how I could squeeze past, but the stranger picked up a piece of luggage and trailing an honest-to-goodness leopard skin coat along the floor behind her, she walked a few steps in the same direction I was going and entered one of the bedrooms, followed by all the others. This was Barbara Donahue.

My first impression was that her listeners were awestruck and had not been aware of my approach. I had no more than a glimpse of this girl, but I saw a tremendous mass of black hair caught up in a pompadour. Her face was quite wide and flat. Her large dark brown, wide-set eyes flashed with excitement and her nose was snubbed. At the time I saw her, her wide mouth was open, displaying two rows of white, wide-arched teeth. It was an arresting face, unusual; in its composition of distinctive features, she could not be classified as pretty.

Another newcomer in that group was Esther Manning, of a wealthy dairy farming family who had a grain and feed business in upstate New York. Also a brunette, she was very photogenic, like Barbara Erickson. In that beauty, men basked and dreamed of marriage.

By October 24, the WAFS numbered twenty. They straggled into Newcastle Army Air Base thereafter during the rest of the year and they were introduced to us one at a time. On November 1, Nancy Love herself brought a slender, petite, pretty girl in her mid-twenties to BOQ 14, and introduced her just as one guides a guest of honor in the cocktail hour before a banquet. This WAF had small features, and what struck me was that her eyes matched exactly the large sapphire ring she wore with her wedding band. One could tell that Nancy was as impressed with her as if she were titled. Most of the WAFS were busy at something when they arrived, so most of the greetings were perfunctory at best. But not mine, for I didn't return Katherine Rawls Thompson's quiet reserve in kind.

I said, "I'm so glad to know you. I've admired you ever since you beat Eleanor Holm."

The episode had happened many years before. The national championship swimming meets were being held in New York. It was a foregone conclusion that Eleanor Holm, the former champion, would win again. News photographers bustled about, snapping shots of her lovely face and voluptuous form, so well displayed by the bathing suit she wore. They wrapped up their stories, paying no attention to a skinny little kid of twelve from Fort Lauderdale, Florida, who had somehow gotten into the competition. When the race was over, there stood the winner, tiny but mighty Katherine Rawls, just where her coach and father intended she would be. He had supervised Katie's and her sisters' swimming since they were toddlers. And he had championship material. It was the biggest sports upset of that year.

Katherine Rawls became world famous as an Olympic medalist in diving and swimming in the 1936 Olympics in Berlin. The United States swimming coach that year was her husband, Ted Thompson. Then they both began flying. Ted was already in the Canadian RAF when Katherine became eligible for the WAFS.

Next appeared Dorothy Fulton. It was rumored that she ran an airport in New Jersey, had her own flight operations and almost 3,000 hours of experience. After she was accepted by the examining board, she and her husband took a little apartment not far from the base. She was of medium build and rather plain with ash blonde hair and light blue eyes. Her most distinguishing feature was the bulk of her nose. It was not large and it went well with her face, but it had a weighty puggishness. As time went on, Dorothy was not really assimilated into any clique, although she yearned to be.

A very pretty blonde with whom I never became well acquainted was Opal (Betsy) Ferguson, who gravitated to the unmarried lovelies. Bernice Batten came from Kansas. She was a tiny woman who looked to be about thirty. Her sad and serious face had hurt written on it. I liked Bernice immediately, maybe because she looked vulnerable and was shy and withdrawn. Then, too, neither of us could have won a beauty contest, so I empathized with her, surrounded as we were by so many gorgeous women. Unlike Donahue's flaunting obtrusiveness, Batten went around hoping, it seemed, that no one would notice her. I also felt that she had had a hard struggle in life. After the war a few of us learned that in order to arrive in Wilmington to apply for the WAFS, she had hitchhiked. She had no other way to get there.

Before we were aware of it, without good-byes, Catherine Slocum was gone. One day I asked Lieutenant Starbuck, "Why did Slocum leave?"

He replied, "It couldn't be helped." He pondered a moment and, trusting me, he tried to explain what seemed like a cruel action on the part of the instructors.

"Slocum didn't make a consistent traffic pattern. She just couldn't fly a rectangular pattern time after time. She wouldn't approach the field at a forty-five degree angle like she was supposed to. She'd take a different angle every time and not always at the right place. We gave her extra time to learn it; she just didn't get it."

Esther Nelson, still a bit loose in technique, displayed the spirit and toughness the instructors wanted to see and she stayed. The day she knew she would stay, she came into my room and sat wearily on the cot. She said simply, "I made it."

"Swell," I said.

"I just wasn't going to take a wash-out. I told Nancy I would fight like mad to stay in, and I forced myself to do exactly what they wanted me to do. I'd never be able to look Art in the eye if I hadn't."

Just then Teresa barged in, saying in sotto voice, "Congratulations! I just heard about it."

"Too bad about Slocum," I said. I was not thinking only of the humiliation, but also of the uniforms she had bought and now would never use.

"Slocum had a little trouble at home," said Teresa. "Her husband wanted her to come back home and Nancy encouraged her to go."

"What? Why?" Esther and I said almost in unison.

"Seems their housekeeper fell and hurt herself and couldn't look after things for a while. So, there wasn't any way to get other domestic help — in wartime who wants to do it? So she resigned and went home. It took her off the hook."

Esther added, "I wonder how she got by the CAA in the first place."

That was a sore spot for me, for personalities did enter into the judging as I knew very well from Lambert Field. I said, "I knew one person at Lambert who always got chummy with the inspector before she was to take a test. Not like the rest of us. She had conferences with him about what maneuvers she was going to fly. She even dated the instructor scheduled to test her the night before her commercial test. She had her own airplane. I know from looking at records that the CAA isn't as tough on pilots who aren't going to be hauling passengers or instructing students. It's the people like me who have nothing and are shooting for making a living that they won't stick their necks out for."

When Slocum was dropped from our roster, Dorothy F. Scott filled the opening. She was a bit taller than average, an Anglo-Saxon blonde with soft features. At about that time, Barbara Poole sent a card to Kathryn Bernheim telling her that there was still room for her if she wanted to come. When "Sis," as Bernheim was nicknamed, met with Love, Nancy told her there was another flyer who had come ahead of her. If she didn't make it, Sis could try, otherwise the ranks were closed at twenty-five.

So Sis went back to Pawling, New York, where she was instructing, feeling bitterly disappointed. The pilot who had applied first was Phyllis Burchfield of Titus, Pennsylvania, who had been working in a

CPTP in Tennessee. There was some talk that Nancy had discouraged Sis because she was Jewish. When she did get into the WAFS, Nancy had left the base to go to Dallas and Betty Gillies was in charge. Betty knew Sis from flying on Long Island.

I never heard Nancy say anything that could have been construed as prejudice. The only possibility that worried her was if a Negro woman pilot with the proper qualifications were to apply. Nancy said, "I don't know what we would do. There are no hotels that I know of that would take a colored person as a guest. And that would rule out her being in the Ferry Command, because she'd have to have a place to sleep while on her missions."

Those of us who were present told Nancy that we didn't know nor had ever heard of a black woman pilot. Nancy wound up the discussion by saying, "Well, then, it appears that we have nothing to worry about."

The examining board accepted Phyllis Burchfield. She was almost dwarfish, but well proportioned. I guessed that in order to pass the minimum height requirement, she must have either raised a lump on her cranium or braided the long hair atop her head.

At the end of three months, when Pat Rhonie's contract was not renewed, Poole sent another card to Bernheim and Sis came back. This time she made it and went into the orientation class with sharp-tongued, blonde Helen McGilvery.

The WAFS squadron was thus complete by January 1943. We were a diverse group, yet shared many similarities. What set us apart from other women? How had we slipped out from the restrictions that inhibited most of our sex?

We appeared like other American women of the same ancestry, social position, and work experience. I think, however, that we had an assurance about us, a purposefulness, that came with our metamorphosis from two- to three-dimensional beings. As soon as we went up in the air, we added a new sphere to the environment in which we moved. That alone made us unusual. And we also had, as a group, superior intelligence, excellent health, and beauty — or at least good looks.

Traditionally in those days, women as the "weaker sex" were expected to dissolve into tears or hysteria under stress. They were forgiven a lack of logic or mathematical sense; any foolishness was excused with the statement, "That's just like a woman!" On the other hand, a woman was expected to be subservient to men and to be grateful for each favor that was bestowed upon her.

Just as a husband was expected to provide financially for his family, a wife was expected to take care of the house. To prepare girls for this work, mothers who could usually taught their daughters cleaning, cooking, washing, ironing, and shopping. My mother was an excellent teacher who taught me also to preserve food, to knit, crochet, quilt, and tailor.

But that was not enough for me. I had no intention of getting married and settling into a household routine. My energies were scattered among many activities beyond teaching — ice skating, swimming, roller skating, hiking, dancing, choral singing, sculpturing in clay, dramatics — I tried them all. I did well, but did not find inner satisfaction until my first short journey into the air.

What made us shift our allegiance from earth and water to the sky? Not hope of financial gain.

Before World War II, there was no way a woman could find employment in aviation as a pilot, unless she owned part interest in an airline or an airplane sales business. (Or was close to an owner.) Helen Ritchie got a job as a copilot in 1933. The job ended abruptly when the Airline Pilots' Association refused to allow her to join them. I once joined a group of men pilots applying to a TWA representative who was recruiting at Lambert Field. The recruiter laughed at me; he considered the other candidates seriously, although my qualifications were as good or better than theirs. Above all, a woman had to be a good sport and take such slights and disappointments in stride.

It wasn't the prospect of a lucrative future that lured us into a career in flying. I recognized what it was for me from the beginning: For once, I felt at home. Something made me belong there. As one lone woman who kept flying through the years while other girls appeared and disappeared, I became "one of the boys," along with students, licensed pilots, redcaps, porters, mechanics, and office workers. They accepted me completely. I found I was more at home with my airport acquaintances and friends than I was with the women teachers I ate lunch with every school day.

Psychologists recently put my feelings into words. Results of personality evaluations showed that men who fly resemble all other men less than they resemble women who fly. On the other hand, women who fly resemble men who fly more than they resemble other women. No one knows why these likenesses exist. Maybe they are in our genes and only become apparent with the experience of flying.

Still, earning a commercial license and an instructor's rating wasn't easy. And it was expensive. Not everyone attempting the shift from earth to sky made the transition. I knew I was on the way to success when the men pilots began to take me aside, leery of being overheard, and gave me the ultimate in praise — "You ain't like any of those

WAFS shown in November 1942 with Colonel Gates at Morris Field, Charlotte, N.C. From left: Barbara Poole, Gates, Esther Manning, Barbara Erickson, Evelyn Sharp, and Barbara Donahue.

other dames. You fly like a man.''

People outside our sphere awarded me accolades, too. Newspapers sent reporters and photographers for interviews. At the airport, people stared at me or asked for my autograph. Civic organizations asked me to speak.

Most of those drawn to flying did little more than solo. They only wanted a taste of it. We WAFS stuck with it. What gave us the courage and the tenacity to do so, made us stay with the Ferry Command, too.

The art of flying was not then a science. Meteorology was inexact. Airplanes were built, licensed, and flown with idiosyncrasies unknown today. Landing gear frequently had wheels so close together that the inattentive pilot could be surprised when a ground loop developed during his landing roll. Inventors sacrificed stability for speed, putting a greater burden of risk on pilots. Instability showed up most often in maneuvers that departed from straight and level flight. The pilot who didn't maintain air speed stalled and, if his controls were in an abnormal position, the plane spun toward the earth. Each aircraft we flew had its own spinning characteristics that we had to learn by putting the airplane into a spin and recovering from it. To qualify for a private or commercial license, the pilot had to demonstrate a pinpoint accuracy in getting out of a two-turn spin, both to the right and to the left.

So I went up to 3,000 feet in a Kinner Fleet, stalled, made a two-turn spin to the left and came out "on the button," exactly at the heading by which I entered it. Then I climbed to 3,000 feet and made a two-turn spin to the right, coming out just as accurately. The inspector observed my skill from a safe distance on the ground. I didn't blame him. At Lindbergh Field in San Diego, I watched a student trying for a private license put the Great Lakes he was flying into a flat spin. He couldn't recover and spun into the water. By the time the navy rescued him, he was sitting up on the tail, which was the only surface of the plane still out of the bay.

Every time a pilot was killed in an accident, the horror of the story and pictures of the crash made front page news. When Wiley Post killed himself and Will Rogers in Alaska, I knew right away that pilot error was to blame. When asked if I'd quit flying because of the accident, I said no. It was up to me never to make a similar mistake.

Even so, in those days pilots risked being disabled, disfigured, or killed by making a mistake and being forced to land on forbidding terrain. At that time pilots told each other, "Any landing is a good landing if you can walk away from it."

When the WAFS converged on Wilmington in the fall of 1942, we were a tiny band, unique among the millions of adult females in the United States. And we knew it. Other people did, too, for we had columns of newspaper publicity to prove it. Some members of the group had been more fortunate than others in the opportunities they had had or in the assistance and guidance they had received from experienced pilots. But we had much in common.

Black grease and dirt had soiled our clothes and hands. Windblown grit flew into our goggled eyes and onto our hair and skin. We took as a matter of course and without complaint the tousling prop wash. We roasted in summer and froze in winter, for no places on earth have the extremes in temperature that airports do. We knew all about the wind chill factor long before it was defined and measured by meteorologists. Weathering toughened our skins, both literally and figuratively, and tested our resolution to continue flying.

We had all flown in airplanes without electric starters, so we had spun the propellers to start the engine — a most risky procedure. Should we have slipped into the propeller's rotation, oops! We had pushed and pulled airplanes in and out of hangars. We had held onto them as a line squall rolled by overhead. We hadn't put on a helpless act nor begged for special consideration. Men lent us a hand as readily as we assisted them.

We continued to fly because we played it safe. When unsure about the condition of a field or whether it was long enough for take off, we'd pace it carefully. We were still alive because we had not taken our machines beyond their limits of endurance.

We had learned many things. For instance, flying taught us about the forces acting upon us in flight — ignorance of these leads to sloppy flying habits and possible accidents. We all flew "by the seat of our pants." That meant that if we were flying in a maneuver other than straight and level, we sat on the cushion as if flying straight and level. And our bodies kept that relationship to the airplane no matter how it related to the horizon.

Our weight was equally distributed on both buttocks. If the pressure was greater on the up or far-out side of a turn, we were skidding; the speed was too much for the bank. If we were banked too steeply for the speed we were using, the inside buttock would feel the weight of the body, which denoted a "slip." We flew without most of the instruments available today. We used the sensations of our own bodies to show us if we were balanced.

We knew more about the engine and the fuselage of the airplanes we flew than most people know about the automobiles they drive. I had helped to take engines apart and put them back together again. We knew all the essential components, why they were necessary, what could go wrong with them, and what resulted when danger signs showed up.

In the decade following Lindbergh's 1927 flight to Paris, many engines were unreliable by today's standards. I often helped Spike Saladin with his twenty-hour check on the Kinner 125-horsepower engine. We changed the oil after every twenty hours of flight, and we felt for babbitt — the metal coating on the internal engine parts — as the oil leaked out of the crankcase. If minute particles were felt in the oil, it meant excessive wear had occurred. We took off the rocker arm boxes, tested the lifters for warp, checked the condition of the valves, and set the valve clearances.

We knew about cotter keys and screwdrivers. Dope had a special meaning to us. It was the smelly, volatile liquid brushed or sprayed on fabric coverings to make a taut, weatherproof surface over the structure of the aircraft.

All of us had patched a small hole with pinked tape and dope after someone had been careless. Others experienced, as I had, helping to cover a wing by ribstitching an envelope fashioned from sea-island or Egyptian cotton fabric. We blanket-stitched the trailing edge before the dope went on. In those days we could look at the ribs of a strange airplane and tell how fast it could fly by how close together the stitching along the rib was. When a captured Messerschmidt sat on exhibition in front of the Lambert terminal in 1942, I knew it was a fighter aircraft without being told.

Of course we had learned more than this. But still, my life up to that moment had not prepared me to become a military pilot. The change was too sudden. Discordant thoughts raced each other about, tumbling through my mind. I was depressed at the same time I was elated by the honor. And awed. I was only a woman, but I was given a mission to perform that had never been given other women — flying in the armed services. Did the ten wise virgins of the New Testament parable feel like that when they were called and found ready?

Certainly not all accomplished and experienced women pilots of that day volunteered for the WAFS. Many of the well-known record breakers were older than allowed. And there were those whose formal education or physical condition did not meet army standards. Family obligations kept many home — Alice Hammond was not alone in putting her children's welfare ahead of love of country. There were also those who lacked a sense of altruism and who considered their own needs first.

For instance, one young woman caused quite a stir when she arrived at headquarters to investigate what the WAFS could offer. She dressed for the occasion in a flashy tailored suit, wore false eyelashes and sported dyed pink hair. She took one look at our tarpaper-lined barracks and another at the "preposterous" airplanes she would be expected to fly and left.

On another occasion, a female CPTP flight instructor at a deep South airport questioned us about our organization after we landed there during a mission. When she found out that we had only showers in our barracks, she proclaimed, "I just couldn't live like that. I have to take a bath in a tub!" I commented to the other WAFS before we hopped off, "We can very well do without anyone who needs a bath."

Helen Stone refused to join us, too, but she was already in war work. She flew a CAP airplane along the coast. It was a bit heavier and faster than the PT-19A Fairchild, and she may have felt that getting down to our level was lowering her status. She returned to New England. It wasn't long thereafter that the CAP decided to keep only men pilots on submarine patrol and Helen no longer had her large airplane to fly. At that point, the only way she could join the Ferry Command was to go through Cochran's cadet training school, which she did, and then was assigned to Wilmington.

In Wilmington I met women with whom I belonged. It had been uncomfortable for me to have so little in common with other women. The things I wanted to talk about they didn't. Now I found myself in the midst of a small group of women whose vocabulary was the same of mine. Like birds of the same species, we descended on the base, chattering with each other in aviation jargon, unintelligible to everyone else save another pilot. We flitted about during the day in our business of becoming military pilots and gathered every evening at sundown in our sanctuary, the refuge we knew as BOQ 14.

We'd talk over the problems of the day or do a bit of hangar flying. The most satisfying aspect of being a member of the WAFS was that we were equals, at least at first. Thus we began welding together a social unit with a common purpose. We wanted to show that, equal among ourselves, we were also equal to men. Anything they could do, we could do, and we would try to do it better. To tell the truth, we had to. Everyone knew that if a woman got a promotion, she had to be twice as good as a man. We vowed we'd make no mistakes. That, like the making of New Year's resolutions, was the first.

WE FLY!

EVERY MOMENT THAT MY MIND WAS FREE of the problems of flying, classes and homework, my thoughts turned toward Harold and I longed for home. I missed him more as the days went by. And I wanted to share with him all of my life in the Ferry Command — the drops of rain, every bit of blue sky, the people I met, and my letters from friends back home.

For instance, I told him that my nails looked decent and were not broken or dirty from motor oil and grease, the way they had been at home. My hair was curled and set, and without the stress of the active life I'd been leading, the fine lines in my face had disappeared. I'd even lost some weight, for I bought a cheap dress in Wilmington that was one size smaller than usual.

By return mail Harold wrote that he had been promoted to aviation chief metalsmith. The news delighted me, for he looked like a chief and he deserved the promotion. With his maturity — for he was thirty-six years old — the white sailor suits and cupcake caps of the navy didn't become him.

I sent him anecdotes about life on the base to give him an idea of how I was living. My letters were a hodgepodge of perceptions and experiences. Some of my news was trivial, but much of it reveals a side of World War II that is not often written about.

As I told Harold, I was in the minority as a milk drinker at NCAAB. Some of the harder drinkers in the WAFS (the one-cocktail- before-dinner crowd) surprised me by beginning to drink milk, too. They had heard whispers that the army was doctoring the coffee with saltpeter as the navy was reputed to do to tone down the sailors during long ocean voyages. I admitted that the idea had its good points and I would continue to drink coffee as usual. Later, when the rumor was declared unfounded, the WAFS switched from milk to coffee with alacrity.

I also told him that several of us saw *Holiday Inn,* starring Bing Crosby. It featured a song called "White Christmas," and when I heard it I cried like a baby.

I was still waiting for the birthday present Harold had not given me in August. I hinted that if he wanted to send me a check for $10 I wouldn't object. Or he could send me perfume — but I didn't want to be more noticeable to the men on base. If nothing else occurred to him, he could reimburse me for the $40 TransLear radio that I had decided to order. Since our planes carried no radios, I thought the TransLear would come in handy while landing at a large airport. With it I could hear the tower communicate with the big planes in the traffic pattern.

My finances were constantly on my mind and I needed to share the details with my husband. My total bill for my stay at the Kent Manor Inn amounted to $17.56 and I'd paid it with the last check in my checkbook.

We'd been paid $100 for our two weeks in September. After that, we received $250 per month. Carlson did not require the first down payment on our uniforms until November 1, which helped. We'd been back again and again for alterations. The latest problem was the overseas cap. It had an exaggerated point fore and aft that made us look like walking cartoons. So back it went. I told Harold that I practically lived in my "monkey suit," for I rarely went out socially and wearing the flying suit helped keep laundry bills down.

Nancy had promised me a leave to take care of my mortgage coming due. I told Harold I wanted to put the flat in both our names, just in case I met with an accident. (It was in my name only at the time, since I had bought it before I was married.) I wanted him to have a home whether I was there or not. After we were commissioned, I could get government insurance. My present insurance was not good if I died while in the service. We needed to be practical — flying was dangerous.

I often asked Harold to send me things from home — we all wanted some of our old comforts. One list I sent him included my rubber over-shoes, a hot plate and cord, a teakettle, an electric iron, a three-speed heating pad, handkerchiefs, a money belt, wool gloves, socks, and most of all, a picture of him.

I began to express my affection more openly to my husband, something that I had felt no need to put into words before. He also felt a need to speak of his emotions and said that he treasured my letters. We both felt our love was solid, a protection against whatever lay before us.

Any tie to St. Louis that I came across stirred strong feelings. I even monitored the St. Louis weather. I knew only one person from St. Louis on the base, Bert Lambert. He was the son of Albert Bond Lambert, the balloonist who took to powered flight and bought an air-port for the city of St. Louis, which, in turn, gave the field his name. Bert rarely said more than hello to me when we met.

One night he appeared at the buffet supper held at the officers' club. He told me he had been through St. Louis three times during the past week or two. He hadn't called anyone the last time he was in town because the time was 2300. He said that Fritz Gundlach and Freddy Koupal, friends of Harold's and mine, were also at Newcastle. The next week I ran into Koupal, who was now a captain. He said he spent most of his time flying bombers eastward. Because he was gone so much, his wife had remained in St. Louis where she wouldn't be so lonely. When I introduced Freddy to Nelson and Richards, they im-mediately liked his midwestern friendly manner. He was no wolf; he was a good flying buddy type.

We WAFS, confident in our skills, were unaware that Colonels Tun-ner and Baker doubted our untried performance as ferry pilots. Not until twenty years after the war did I learn upon reading Capt. Walter Marx's account of us that the colonels thought at first our missions should be short enough for us to be back on home base by nightfall. I wondered why. Was Tunner afraid something might happen to give Jacqueline Cochran reason to criticize him? Did he regret our presence because of the trouble she had already given him? Did Baker think we would get lost or wander into bad weather? Or did they get too many arguments about us from the tradition-bound males on their staffs?

At any rate, the colonels could point to Nancy Love, Betty Gillies, and Pat Rhonie as having flown larger airplanes than the WAFS would; they had much cross-country experience, too. These women expected to be the leaders who would supervise the other WAFS in on-the-job training.

How strange those misgivings appear today! Now major airlines hire women to fly jets on regular passenger routes. Aircraft manufacturers of both single- and multi-engine planes employ women to deliver them to customers, often crossing oceans en route. The Air Force Academy educates women and even trains some in military jet aircraft, and the Air Force uses these graduates in all but combat positions. NASA allows women to compete for crew positions in space travel. Compared to all this, what we did at the beginning was trifling. Yet to us it was new, dramatic, and daring.

The attitudes of the officers at Newcastle Army Air Base varied from cool to warm. Some welcomed us gladly. The hostile sort couldn't very well express their distaste for our presence out of fear of Colonel Baker's ire. But now and then one would needle us. One such fellow was a tall, middle-aged captain with popping gray eyes and the ugliest set of false teeth I ever saw. He stopped me one day on a sidewalk and said with a sly grin, "I was in St. Louis this past weekend." I took it that he wanted me to feel bad because I had not been.

The instructors knew we could fly cross-country in Cubs. They wanted to be sure we would do so in primary trainers. So they made up two flights, again across Pennsylvania. Lieutenant French was to lead Rhonie, Scharr, James, and Richards on October 18 from NCAAB to Scranton Airport at Schultzville and then to the army air base at Middletown and back.

I felt a bit miffed that Lieutenant French chose the other three to lead the legs while I held the position opposite French in the rear of the formation. Didn't anyone trust me? I wondered. Well, I decided, I would fly my course as I'd marked it.

After each hop, French asked me, "What did you think about the flight?"

I pointed out on my chart just where each pilot had wandered a trifle from the course. That was the only way I had of showing him that I knew where I was all the time. All the navigators did well with a pilotage mix of topographical and man-made checkpoints.

On October 21, the operations office alerted Nancy that at least eight Cubs were rolling off the Piper assembly line. WAFS were needed to ferry them. Our first moment of truth was at hand.

Nancy called a session for all the original WAFS who were thought to be capable of going. We crowded into our barracks meeting room where she briefed us. She was full of last minute admonitions. She warned, "Be sure you stay at least 500 feet away from each other and

Courtesy of Dr. Frederick W. Roos

Fairchild's famed PT-19 trainer.

any other thing, like a cloud.''

"Beneath them and to the side," added Betty.

"And high enough over towns that you can land deadstick outside them in case of emergency," said Nancy.

We stirred restlessly in anticipation.

Then Nancy picked up a piece of stationery and a pencil. She said, "The way the men go in a flight, the flight leader decides who will navigate each leg. In that way, he can judge the ability of each one and can tell which are ready to be the next flight leaders. The navigator takes off first.''

She placed a cross at the center of the paper.

"The pilot assigned to the number two position takes off next and moves up to the navigator's right.''

She made a cross to the right and behind the first one.

"The next one, number three, can easily catch up as the navigator makes his left turn in the traffic pattern. He is behind and to the left.''

She put down the crosses in their places.

"The flight leader either takes a wing position at the rear or in a large flight can fly directly behind the lead, but at the rear, for his responsibility is for all members of his flight.

"When the lead plane is about ten miles from the airport destination, the navigator throttles back a little so the flight leader can come forward to lead into the airport. From then on, you move in echelon formation."

"What's that?" I asked.

"Like this," Nancy replied. She turned the paper over and made crosses in a single file, each cross being a bit to the right of the one in front.

"The ones in the rear make a larger traffic pattern," said Betty. "Then they won't catch up to the ones ahead and there's enough time between landings."

"Yes," added Nancy. "The first one can be off the runway before the next girl lands. It's a matter of safety."

"Suppose somebody has a forced landing on the way?" asked Barbara Towne.

Nancy looked at Betty, who returned her glance and said, "Don't you think we should have some signals? If a girl has engine trouble and while she's looking for a place to land, she could dip her nose several times before she goes down."

Nancy said, "That's a good reason for everyone to glance around at the others every so often. The flight leader watches out for everyone else. You look out for the flight leader, too."

"Yes," said Betty. "I don't want to be down in a field somewhere and nobody knowing where to send help."

"What if we know the navigator is off course, should we follow her anyway?" asked Richards.

"The flight leader comes forward and takes over," replied Nancy.

"Why don't we dip our wings to the right if the navigator is heading too far left?" asked Rhonie.

"That's a good suggestion," replied Nancy.

"And lifting the nose could mean we should go to a higher altitude? If we find it too rough where we decided to cruise, we ought to go upstairs," said Teresa.

"We could do that, too, when we might be trying to get a level without as much headwind against us," said Betty.

"Then it's understood, is it?" asked Nancy. "If so, we won't have any problems with formation flying."

I left the meeting anxious to make every flight I would participate in as perfect as possible. But I hadn't had enough cross- country experience yet to stray from the line I made on my charts if the navigator went off course. Continually changing course just to follow her might confuse me and I didn't want to risk getting lost by following anyone else. Secretly I resolved I'd stick to the course I'd laid out and let the navigator come back to it. The possibility of any of these women shooting off into the unknown at too great an angle never occurred to me then.

Finally, after another rainy day, operations cut orders for Aline Rhonie, Cornelia Fort, Helen Mary Clark, Adela Scharr, Betty Gillies, and Teresa James to pick up L4-Bs. Betty was designated the flight leader. We'd get the planes at Lockhaven and deliver them to Mitchel Field on Long Island.

What varying emotions we had! Betty, proud to deliver practically at her own doorstep. Teresa and I, unable to hide our elation, yet agitated, for we only guessed at the proper steps to take in preparing for the flight. We weren't sure what to carry in our B-4 bags. Just getting ready was a thrill.

Usually ferry pilots were sent to Lockhaven by ground transportation. We were not to learn what that entailed until later. Colonel Tunner's cautious attitude and the short break in the weather or his own desire to ease the WAFS into ferrying may have been the basis for Colonel Baker's decision to fly us to the factory.

On the morning of October 22, as soon as we heard there was no danger of fog at our destination, we six climbed the steps of a Boeing twin-engine transport, carrying our parachutes. The interior was not like the usual airliner. A wide space ran down the middle of the fuselage. Strung along either side were bucket seats and on them we placed our parachutes to serve as cushions. Then we went out again, picked up our navigator kits and B-4 bags and toted them up, placing them in the middle of the cargo space. We tried to keep out of the way of the two pilots who were working a slide rule and talking about bays and weights, striving for a balanced load. There really was no problem since the airplane could have carried at least fourteen more passengers.

Helen Mary was smart. She chose a seat where she could peer out a small porthole. She kept out her aeronautical chart and navigated all the way. Betty left her seat during the trip and went into the pilot's compartment to watch what was going on. The rest of us sat quietly, apprehensive because someone else was doing the flying — although I felt that all the men pilots of the base, having been there longer than we, were vastly superior to us.

Soon we began coming in for a landing and hoped for the best. Betty watched it; the rest of us only felt the bounces the pilot made in the landing. It was a real stinker. Then I knew. Colonel Baker was saving T/R expenses by requisitioning a transition school learning period and diverting the plane to deliver us.

When we arrived at the small Piper factory, it was full of helter-skelter activity. But people halted their work to stare at us. We tried to act as if we were old hands at ferrying and paid no attention to them. In the field next to the factory hangar we found the planes with numbers corresponding to our orders. We inspected them thoroughly and decided they were flyable. In checking the amount of fuel in a gasoline tank that I had not watched being filled, I always stuck my finger in — and it had better come out wet. To make absolutely certain it was gas, I smelled it.

The fuel gauge of a Piper Cub was a vertical heavy wire sticking up through the gasoline filler cap, and it was attached to a cork that floated on the surface of the fluid inside. I never trusted it or any other gauge that could stick. Those of us who instructed in them knew the yellow Cubs as J-3s. The ones we picked up were still Cubs with sixty-five horsepower engines, but now they were khaki-colored and called L-4Bs.

Satisfied with our airplanes, we signed for them and took with us the necessary papers. We looked at weather maps and the hourly sequences and waited as Betty made out a clearance for the flight. She decided our first hop would be to Allentown. We scrambled around a big table, getting our flight path penciled in from Cubhaven to Allentown.

Betty said to Rhonie, ''Pat, you are to navigate this time.'' Then she assigned positions for takeoff to the rest of us. When we took off, she was last, like a mother hen following her chicks.

Cubhaven was east of Lockhaven. As soon as we circled the field and headed east, the stream, railroad, and highways fell at an angle to our left. Few specific checkpoints appeared for a while, but the delicate brown gradients of elevation shown on our charts coincided exactly with the curves and elevations of the mountains as we flew over them. This made navigating by pilotage much easier in Pennsylvania than it was in the Missouri Ozarks, where charts showed no gradients.

At Milton we crossed the west branch of the Susquehanna River, and at Danville we crossed the main river. We paralleled it for about five miles to Ringtown. There we crossed a valley with many small cities strung along a chain woven by the railroads and a highway. How narrow seemed the horizons of the people who lived in these valleys, hemmed in by a mountain range on either side. My heart ached for them as I remembered the novel *How Green Was My Valley,* which described a similar setting in Wales.

High in the Alleghenies was a fine lake region not depicted on the chart. If it could have been reached at all on foot, it must have been done on narrow trails. There was much wild country in the area. I thought I would hate to walk through it after a forced landing — if I survived.

Then the earth dropped to elevations of around 500 feet above sea level, except for the ridge to the south of East Penn Airport. We saw cities — Allentown, Northampton, and Bethlehem — strung in Siamese triplet fashion. I felt a thrill as we approached the airport serving the area. All about it were huge steel furnaces and factories belching white clouds of smoke, signaling a welcome to the WAFS. The flight had lasted seventy-five minutes.

While Betty closed our flight plan, each of us watched the gassing of our six Cubs. When she came out of the office, she said to us, "I think we'd better stay here tonight. We can't get to Mitchel before an hour before sundown. I checked when sundown is and we could get into trouble. I telephoned and got rooms for us at the Americus Hotel. Operations is calling taxis for us, and as soon as I sign for the gas, we should be ready to go."

"Who will watch the L-4Bs?" asked Pat.

"They have a night watchman here. You be sure to tie the stick down along with the tail and the wings." So we did. By the time the taxis came, we'd piled our stuff out near the hangar. We went to town in style. Betty's taxi stopped first at the Western Union office so she could send the RON wire. We got to the hotel lobby and waited for her to take charge.

Before dinner Teresa and I went shopping for souvenirs. We discovered that Allentown was a large city. No wonder that the Americus had eleven stories for guests. It towered above the double-tall, arched first floor windows. There appeared to be a lot of money and business here.

That evening I wrote a long letter to Harold. I told him, "It was marvelous to see the world unfold before my eyes, to see cities that before this were only names in geography texts spring into position, full grown, blooming with smoke. The mountains were nice to look at, but not as I had imagined them. The ride across was quite smooth, although the flight to Lockhaven in the Boeing was a bit rough."

"And the places where people live! The valleys of Pennsylvania, hidden from each other by the high ridges ranging diagonally to our course, are more often than not blackened and ugly, with great heaps of dirty slag spewed up along the railroad tracks that tangle in and out from one mining region to another."

The next morning Betty reviewed briefly what we should do to signal each other during flight. She appointed Cornelia Fort as navigator. We could tell that Betty was uneasy. Finally she confided in us, "I talked to

Bud last night. He said flying is grounded along the New York waterfront today because they're doing aerial target practice with the defense gun positions. I think I'd better wire Mitchel Field base operations to let them know we're coming and to tell them to call off the guns for us.'' She went back into the office and we went to look at the weather reports. From the sequences we could guess that weather was closing in on us rapidly from the west. In fact, a drizzle had already begun. The reports from the east were still quite clear except for some smoke.

We trusted Betty. When she said, ''Let's go,'' we stowed our B-4 bags on the shelves behind the rear seat of the Cubs and got in. The line boys swung the props efficiently and off we went behind Cornelia, with Betty trailing and me right in front of her.

It was on this mission that I'm sure Betty found out what I was doing. Our formation was loose, of course, but at times my position was looser than the others, for I flew the straight line I had drawn on my chart. Yet I was mindful of how Cornelia navigated. She wasn't the kind to get lost. She didn't fly a straight course, but edged toward checkpoints on either side as she came toward them, as if mentally touching them for luck. Visibility was poor all along the way, but checkpoints came up every few miles. And we stayed ahead of the weather.

By the time we passed Plainfield, New Jersey, nothing but city stretched ahead. Passing over Elizabeth I thought, Ah! The birthplace of my sewing machine. The enormity of the entire metropolitan complex amazed me. It had been impossible to feel the extent of it when I drove Mom, Pop, and my sister, Ruth, through it in the old Oakland in 1932.

As soon as water appeared below, Betty moved forward, taking over the lead. We moved into an echelon formation. Instead of crossing the narrow stretch between the upper and lower bays, Betty rounded her flight above the lower bay. I, being last, felt like the end of the chain in a game of ''crack the whip.'' It was all I could do to keep the Cub directly in front of me within sight. I pushed the throttle forward and I presume that's what the others must have been doing, for the sight of all that water beneath me made me apprehensive. Wasn't I the one who never allowed students to cross the Missouri River until they had altitude enough to make a forced landing on either shore in case the engine quit? I looked down. Where could I go now if I had to land?

But I was confident that Betty, familiar as she was with the area, knew how to lead us through the maze of restricted areas around New York City. Even as we made an arc across the bay, my thumb moved across the chart in the same direction, just so I'd know where I was.

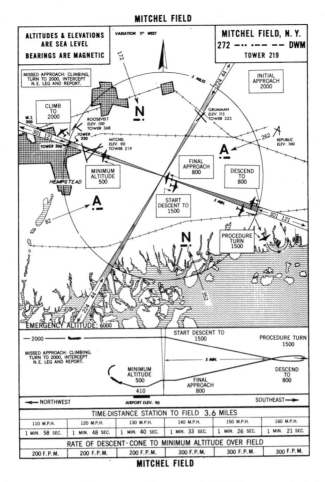

The Mitchel Field radio range, as shown on the 1942 aeronautical charts.

At last we passed over the water and civilization came back into view. The flight slowed back to cruising speed, which in a Cub wasn't much different in velocity from full throttle.

As I looked directly below onto a long, wide stretch of beach, I saw an immense roller coaster and a Ferris wheel. Why, the whole strip was an amusement park! I had never seen it before, but I thought, "Coney Island!" Raising my thumb, I peered at the words my left thumb had hidden. It was, all right. I felt like an explorer who, having read about or heard of wonderful places, was finally seeing them. I flew past like a god. There were the Rockaways!

We flew over south Brooklyn and edged Floyd Bennett Field. Brooklyn amazed me. After flying for miles along the city, there was still more stretching far ahead. Even understanding that one does not whiz by in a Cub, the city was tremendous. Finally it gave way to two neighboring airports, Roosevelt to the north and Mitchel to the south.

We circled Mitchel like Indians around a wagon train, changed to a rectangular pattern, and ended our flight with perfect landings. And why not? We weren't novices, even if the army thought so.

Carefully, proudly, we noted our time (sixty-five minutes) on the Form I's. We gathered our belongings and trouped into the operations office. No smiles greeted us.

Grumbling, the officer behind the counter remarked, "We asked for these two months ago. We don't need them now."

One man went into the hangar and another looked out the door in disbelief at what we had so carefully brought them. I felt rebuffed, but followed Betty's lead as she took out the receipt for him to sign. While he was signing our papers, I said to Teresa, "The camouflage job on this place isn't as good as the one at Middletown, is it?"

She replied, "I'm glad Betty had to lead in. I don't like any of this camouflage myself. It spoils your depth perception with all that paint."

The men began to mellow toward us and one ordered base transportation to take us to the Aviation Country Club where Betty and Pat were members. As we were picking up our B-4 and parachute bags, a telephone message came into the office. It was the telegram Betty had sent hours earlier. The possibility of what might have happened to us over the wide expanse of water made us shudder. If the guns had clobbered us, we would have taken the future for women as pilots for the Army Air Forces with us into the drink. Soberly we left, but not before hearing one officer say *sotto voce* "Let 's fly 'em into the Sound!"

Country clubs were outside my humble sphere. Visiting the Aviation Country Club was a new experience for me. Here was where half of New York society's exclusive Four Hundred came to fly or to be with flyers.

"I'll show you to the ladies' room," said Pat as she led the way. What a crew we were! We carried our B-4 bags into the ladies lounge where we found space to change into our skirts. Several of the club ladies came in as we shed our pants and picked their way around us with questioning glances.

Pat conversed with one beautiful young woman, whom she introduced to us. After she left, Pat said, "She is a former Powers model and she flies, too." I was impressed, having only read of such glamorous creatures.

After we freshened our faces, we took the B-4 bags to the lobby and stowed them alongside the parachute bags. Then we ate lunch. I was not impressed with the food. I thought, rich people don't get much to eat for their money at country clubs.

Betty had good news for us. "While you were changing I called

Nance," she said. "I told her we made a safe delivery. She was in an expansive mood because she said we needn't return immediately to NCAAB. The afternoon would be over by the time we returned, if we left right now."

We looked at each other in wonder.

Betty continued, "I called my mother and I'll go home to see her. She wants to meet Cornelia. I know the train schedules, so if we all meet at Grand Central Station at 6 P.M., we'll catch the train for Wilmington tonight. That gives you some time to run around New York City if you want to."

Helen Mary asked, "Would it be all right if I went on to Englewood?"

"Do that," replied Betty.

The four of us took a taxi to Mineola train station. "I'll make out the T/R," I offered. The agent said our destination was Pennsylvania Station, New York City. Since Teresa wanted to meet some friends who lived in town, she and I went to visit with them until train time, leaving Helen Mary to bear with Pat's "I-I-I-I" idea of good conversation.

At Grand Central we checked our parachute and B-4 bags in the baggage room. Helen Mary went to see her family. Pat said proudly, "I'll take a taxi to Abercrombie & Fitch." That left Teresa and me with our brakes off.

We took a subway ride because I'd never had one. The train wasn't crowded and was it fast! After a short time we got off, climbed the stairs to the street and took a bus to the place where the ball of light falls at midnight each New Year's Eve — Times Square. Small shops, dirty sidewalks, cheap eating places, and pawn brokers made it a very tawdry district without the magic I had expected.

Teresa and I walked along some of the famous streets in Manhattan — Broadway, 42nd Street, Fifth Avenue — and looked into the shop windows of stores advertised in *Vogue* and other high class magazines. In one jewelry store, like any hayseed visitor, I bought a silver souvenir teaspoon. We saw (from the outside) Jack Dempsey's and Lindy's and other night spots mentioned by syndicated gossip columnists.

Teresa was the perfect companion, ready for anything and a speedball. When I suggested we try an automat, she said, "Okay, sister," and beat me in to the bank of dispensers along the wall. We hunted in our purses for change, punched our selections of sandwiches, and deposited the coins. Getting a drink was a disappointment. The small paper cup fell sideways, and the drink splashed all around it. Teresa got a piece of pie, and we sat down for a few minutes to eat at one of the many small tables. The room was large and clean, but the atmosphere was as impersonal as the dispensers.

Next we saw St. Patrick's Cathedral, inside and out. And the sunken pit outside Rockefeller Center where Teresa said that people ice skated during the winter. We rode to the top of Rockefeller Center to the observation roof on the seventieth floor. The speed of the elevator surprised me. It zipped up fifty stories faster than any in St. Louis could do five.

We walked along the rim of the outdoor observation balcony. It was very windy. Through the pay telescopes that were trained on the city below, we could see Manhattan as it would look from the air. We located Central Park and spotted some wonderful pylons where a P-40 could do pylon eights. We saw the Statue of Liberty in the distance. And there were boats, big ships, bridges, and too many buildings to distinguish among them, except for the Chrysler building and the Empire State. To me the city seemed unreal, like a mock-up of a picture postcard. How could hands and minds fashion this creation? I wondered.

We wanted to see the famous Rockettes at Rockefeller Center, but there was no matinee performance that day. Instead we peeked into the equally famous Rainbow Room and I vowed that someday Harold and I would sit in it.

Before we got back to the station, we found Macy's department store and I bought a pint of tincture of green soap for sixty-four cents and a small jar of Brilliantine. My hair would be clean and shining.

The inhabitants of New York City have the reputation for being unfeeling, unfriendly, and always in a hurry. I did not find them so. If anything, they were curious about us. At every street corner where we were stopped by a red light, the others waiting for a signal change stared at us and asked what we were. We had on uniforms, but no identification — no glamour buttons on our shoulder tabs, no wings on our left breasts. (We'd ordered some from the base exchange.) When we replied to one query, "We're ferry pilots," the retort was, "You couldn't handle a boat like that!"

One New Yorker gave us some uncomfortable moments. We were window shopping when we noticed a large burly man with a dark complexion walking toward us. In my imagination he looked Russian. We stopped at another window and looked back. He had turned and was following us. When we stopped at the next window, he stopped, too. This went on until we became worried about our "shadow." Then we began to dawdle so he would walk ahead of us, which he did. Suddenly he wheeled about and came toward us, saying, "Pardon me, I just can't overcome my curiosity. Would you girls tell me who you are?"

So we did.

At train time, Helen Mary's husband, Gerould, and two handsome sons were on hand to bid her farewell. The boys were well behaved. In speaking to her, they addressed her as "Angel." I thought that unusual, for I called my mother nothing but "Mom."

The train was noisy and crowded. Teresa and I were so tired that we hardly opened our mouths all the way to Wilmington. Once there, Pat said, "My car is at the DuPont Hotel. I want to take it to the base. Will somebody ride with me?"

Nobody wanted to. I looked at Teresa, then at the others.

"Will you go with me?" Pat asked me directly.

"Why don't you?" said Betty.

So the two of us took a taxi to the DuPont. In the lobby we met Sandy Lerner, who said, "Tell us about your trip. Everybody else is downstairs having dinner. Come join us."

Pat needed no urging and I had to go along, too, whether I wanted to or not. The three flight instructors made room for us at their table. As we came in, the waiter was putting bibs around their necks. Out came the lobsters. It was the first time I had seen anyone eating lobsters. I watched closely to see what they did, how they cracked the claws and picked out the meat with little forks.

Pat talked about the trip and we all listened. I was too tired to talk, although the Coke that Lieutenant Tracy ordered for me helped to revive me. After the meal there were after-dinner drinks and another Coke for me.

Then Tracy did something that horrified me. He had been drinking creme de menthe, a green drink. He said to me with a smile, "I want another one. Watch this."

He poured water into the cocktail glass, took out his fountain pen, squirted green ink into the glass, stirred it, and called the waitress to the table.

"There's something wrong with this drink," he said. "It doesn't taste right. Can you bring me another?"

She took the glass and several minutes later returned with an identical one. Tracy sipped it. "This is okay," he said. "Thank you very much."

He looked at me and winked. "I won't have to pay for this one," he said.

Finally I got Pat to tear herself away from the masculine company she adored and we returned to the base, at last hitting our cots at about eleven bells.

At roll call the following morning, we learned that we should report to the flight surgeon's office if we came back from a mission with a head cold. We'd be grounded until it cleared up. There was a risk of driving the infection into the eustachian tubes during air travel, especially in cases of too-rapid descents.

After roll call, the first WAFS mission checked its paperwork. We went about the base turning in receipts for each airplane and handing in the per diem requests with the necessary proof.

We continued to go to ground school faithfully while awaiting orders. We practiced code, saw propaganda films, listened to lectures, and, if we were lucky, got some time in transition school. Our laundry was done after working hours.

I met Florene on the way to lunch. She said, "I'm going to try to get a Link trainer lesson. Want to go up there with me after lunch?"

"Link? I didn't know we could have Link time," I replied, puzzled.

"Sure thing," she answered. "We've been sneaking in every hour we can get."

Nancy had never told us we could have Link trainer practice to learn instrument flight. How did these kids get wise to it? I concluded that the lieutenants they were running around with had informed them. The girls had gone without permission. By the time Nancy found out about it, she could say nothing, because Link training was a form of ground school. As it was, I had never caught up with Florene's group, because they'd been practicing every chance they had.

That afternoon rumors breezed about of another cross-country coming up right away to fly some more Cubs. There were so many pilots awaiting orders that straws would be drawn to determine who would remain behind. Like many rumors on base, that one was only idle chatter.

The weather reports indicated that St. Louis had lots of rain and cold weather while we were in New York. The cold front arrived at Wilmington Saturday night. Sunday morning I awoke as a cripple. There was a hellish pain beneath my shoulder blades and my throat hurt.

I knew I'd be grounded. I thought this would be a good time to get my tonsils out. But the tonsil specialist had left for Randolph Field and a bone specialist had taken his place. He prescribed a massage and heat treatment. Some of the WAFS prescribed a shot of whiskey so I bought a fifth of Old Crow for $2.39. As a civilian, I was refused access to hospitalization. Again I wondered, how long would we have to wait to be militarized?

Harold had sent me a hot water bottle. I was very grateful, for I felt helpless without it. Esther Nelson rubbed me with Balm Ben-Gay and I lay in bed listening to my radio. I finally went to sleep after being soothed by "The Contented Hour."

While I was in bed, I worried about Harold. He was not an extrovert and I was concerned he'd be lonely. In my letters I urged him to contact some of the Nixies, the local organization of women pilots. They had sent me a farewell gift of Tailspin cologne and Sirocco cream cologne. They were nice kids and would keep him from being depressed. I felt a bit guilty because I had "deserted" him.

I usually hid my emotions beneath an extrovert exterior. I could not initiate conversations like Florene could, or fling back pungent retorts like Barbara Poole did, but I was able to listen closely to a group conversation and offer repartee to make the others laugh.

On top of being sick, which made me somewhat ashamed anyway, the porcelain cap on a front incisor broke. I wrote to my sister Ruth immediately, telling her where I had stashed the extra one and asking her to send it. In the several days until it arrived, I wouldn't open my mouth any more than necessary even though I had pasted a bit of cotton wool over the gold cap. With a great bit of luck, I found a dentist in Wilmington who cemented the facing. It was almost impossible to get a dental appointment during wartime, but that kind man took me right away.

By October 29 I was better. My back still ached, but I could move about and even went to town to get my uniforms redone. I also went to the subdepot to exchange my winter flying boots for a smaller size. Two days later I was able to go up in a PT-19 for over an hour.

While I was at DuPont Airport shooting the breeze with Sandy Lerner, I watched the mail drop and pickup. Tiny DuPont had a regular schedule of airmail courier service, which was unusual in 1942. I hadn't seen anything like it before and haven't since. The installation necessary for the operation was situated on the eastern side of the field, off to one side of the long runway. It consisted of two goal posts. Shortly before the mail pilot's anticipated arrival, someone brought a small mail sack that was hooked onto a wire stretched between the posts.

The postman arrived in a small cabin airplane about the size of a Stinson Reliant. That day, the pilot approached the field from the south and made a powered glide paralleling the runway. As he passed close to the airport office, he skimmed the ground and shoved off a mail sack. Then he pushed his throttle forward — I could hear the engine rev up — but he didn't climb for altitude. Instead he aimed for a passage just above the posts. It wasn't until his airplane hesitated and then began a climb that I noticed the trailing wire beneath it that had hooked the mail sack. The pilot reeled in his catch and disappeared beyond the tall trees and big brick houses to the north. A small airline company was testing this embryonic provision of airmail service to Appalachian cities where the topography made building airports very costly.

Then Sandy and I watched a PT approach from the north. There was little or no surface wind. The airplane was gliding in too fast, and I was sure it would overshoot the first third of the runway. "Give it the gun and go around," I prayed. But the pilot did neither. She landed much too fast in the last half of the field. When she had not stopped the roll before reaching the edge of the field, she applied the brakes so hard that the PT bowed its head and the whirling propeller struck the ground. The airplane stopped. Who was it? I didn't wait to find out.

The line boy gave me a crank and I started back to NCAAB. I wondered what the accident would do to the experimental position of the squadron. I found out later the pilot was Delphine Bohn. I'm glad I didn't remain on DuPont as a witness, for I would not have excused her mistake. No matter how inexperienced, no student of mine had ever done such a thing.

Delphine remained with the WAFS. A story got around that at the hearing on the accident Nancy reminded the officers that Bohn had landed a L-2B deadstick the week before without mishap. She explained that Delphine came from Amarillo where the pilots are used to very strong winds. WAF Bohn was simply accustomed to gliding fast and letting the wind limit the forward roll in landing. Nancy must have been very convincing. Bohn's accident was of little consequence by the following week.

Another accident occurred that I heard about. Fred Koupal had started toward Great Britain in a B-17 and had to turn back to Newcastle. He landed and in the roll on the runway, the landing gear just "upped." The belly was smashed, the props were bent, and Fred was hopping mad. The accident halted the WAFS flying schedule all afternoon.

Each evening I hoped for a telephone call from home, but one never came. I had written Harold that the phone in our barracks could be reached by getting Newcastle 561, extension 165. The base operator at Newcastle 2941 could also reach me. No doubt Harold believed that long distance telephone calls were used, like Western Union, only for emergencies. Calling long distance cost too much for thrifty people like us.

On Halloween a gala party at the officers' club provided free drinks and buffet. Afterward there was dancing. But I slipped out at ten o'clock and went back to my cot in the barracks. I couldn't enjoy the party without Harold.

Bitching, the typically military form of entertainment which is nothing more than an exchange of gripes and rumors, usually occurs among those whose fate is directed by officials too superior in rank or too distant in space to be confronted and questioned.

We WAFS were fortunate, not only to be pilots, but also to be charged with the FERD mission of delivering aircraft as safely and quickly as possible. Unlike many others, we had options — when we would fly and which routes to follow in order to avoid problems, for instance.

But we were so eager to fly that anything which disrupted our ordered tasks irritated us. The degree of irritation depended on each individual's limits of patience. We all hated to be weathered in. And since low ceilings, poor visibility, high winds, and precipitation were beyond our control, we griped about them.

Each time we returned to base, we hoped for enough time to complete all official matters before we had to go out again. But after the second day on base, when we were obliged to attend ground school or to march in review, the lack of our favorite activity irked us. We complained.

And that was not the extent of our discontent. There was also the War Department. Nancy Love did not dampen our *esprit de corps* unnecessarily, but there were times when we had to be told of the ideas percolating in Washington which concerned the WAFS. In the chain of command, she had three sympathetic informers — her husband, Bob Love, Colonel Baker, and Colonel Tunner. They were able to warn her of and even forestall a disaster in the making. Nancy's confidante in the squadron was Betty Gillies. Sometimes she relayed her vexation to others. Even *she* griped.

Years later I learned that commanders of units much larger than the WAFS had trials, too. Above all, each commander had to act to strengthen his position in the chain of command. In retrospect, the rivalry seemed to hamper the war effort. And the division of duties into commands and forces resulted in some overlapping, which made for dissension among the leaders. Perhaps they bitched, too.

Politics inside the Army Air Forces led to unusual relationships. For instance, when Jacqueline Cochran was introduced into the Flying Training Command (FTC), Generals Barton Yount and Luke Smith were unwilling to accept her. She was given permission to control a temporary and tiny project, that of preparing about fifty experienced women pilots for FERD. The officers assumed that within several months, Cochran would be gone. Since they believed she would be of little value to the command, she got no cooperation. Besides, she was a civilian and a woman. However, more bodies in FTC, such as student flyers, their instructors, and ground personnel, meant more money and equipment for the command. Thereby the leaders would become more important and powerful.

Several sessions of the Army Air Forces staff in the War Department changed the FTC attitude toward Cochran. They saw that she could not be put down and that she had insinuated herself into favor with Gen. Hap Arnold. For example, she almost captured the WAFS from NCAAB in her attempt to transfer them to her office in Fort Worth. She then proceeded to ignore the restrictions which fixed the number of possible applicants to her program and their flying hours. Her strategy was successful. She was broadening the mission of FTC. Early enmity toward her began to dissolve — in FTC at least.

But not so in FERD. Cochran didn't remain inside her own domain. She meddled in WAFS affairs by criticizing our yet unpaid-for uniforms as being too dull and not as resplendent in color and cut as suited her taste. So General Arnold requested that the uniforms be modeled at the War Department before his very eyes. As if the Chiefs of Staff had no more pressing military matters than witnessing a fashion show!

If Nancy decided to confront Cochran personally over this issue, it might appear that her work load was trivial enough to leave it for so inconsequential a matter. So she chose others to model the uniforms — Helen Mary Clark and Helen Richards, who were both beautiful, poised, blonde, and narrow-hipped. For the review, Helen Mary wore the dress skirt and white shirt; Helen wore the pants and tan shirt, which was our workday outfit. Nancy could not have chosen better models.

Cochran's idea for new uniforms was a threat to my pocketbook. To all of us, the uniforms she wanted to substitute for the ones we had, seemed as gaudy as the outfits that pre-war air race contestant Roscoe Turner wore to call attention to himself. We didn't want to stand out; we wanted to fit into ferrying quietly, in a businesslike way. So we were with Nancy all the way.

I saw Clark and Richards as they left for Washington one October morning. They had been primed by Nancy as to proper protocol; they knew what to say. When they returned to the base later that night, they were silent about their ordeal. Several days went by. Then Nancy told us that the general had turned down Cochran's suggestion for new uniforms. He saw no objection to what we were wearing. Jubilation!

The euphoria didn't last long. Jacqueline Cochran began organizing her school, but she didn't leave us alone. FERD had banned reporters and photographers from our area. One day after our first mission, Nancy was approached by Hazel Taylor of the War Department bureau of public relations (WDBPR). She had arrived on base unexpectedly to get news and photographs of the WAFS there. Following Colonel Baker's orders, Nancy refused to allow her to meet the few who were available.

Nancy said to me, "All the cuties like Batson and Miller were off on missions. The only ones left weren't photogenic. I didn't want the WAFS to appear unattractive simply because they didn't take a good picture. I refused to allow it. And I wanted to know the point of why the War Department wanted our publicity. Mrs. Taylor couldn't give me any reason for its importance."

Nancy guessed that Jacqueline Cochran was behind Taylor's visit. I had no ideas at the time. However, ideas came later. In 1954, as an Air Force Reserve major, I attended a two-week seminar at Air University in Montgomery, Alabama. With my orders to attend came a secret clearance for the Air Force archives. All of the WAFS-WASP material from World War II was still being kept secret. My clearance gave me a tool to pry out what information I could about us. Unfortunately the papers were not yet accessioned and so I was unable to get much information.

But I did come across a reply from Cochran to Taylor, who had evidently reported her failure to get any publicity material. She wrote about Nancy Love, "she is a spoiled brat and wants her own way." So Jackie *was* behind that move.

That discovery didn't end my investigation. Some years later I attended the Air University again. This time I chatted with a minor employee of the archives who told me that "Miss Cochran was here and went over what we had about you girls and she added to it." The employee gave me the firm impression that Cochran also knew how to subtract if she found something she considered detrimental to her historical image. I was steered to other sources of information, which had not been tampered with.

Back in 1942, Colonel Tunner sent a letter to the War Department public relations offices on October 31, shortly after Taylor's visit, stating that all publicity about the WAFS should cease because "disproportionate publicity contrasts to the nature, scope, and accomplishments of this squadron until definite and substantial results of the experiment [are] seen."

With this message, Tunner managed to step on the toes of Col. Rex W. D. Smith, the chief of Air Transport Command public relations. He had reached over Smith's link in the chain of command and contacted Smith's superior instead. Smith complained, but Tunner continued to make the same kind of jumps whenever he felt like it.

It wasn't until November 3, 1943, that Hazel Taylor was given the job of clearing and preparing our publicity. Strangely enough, we remained under wraps. But in retrospect it was not so strange. In 1942 publicity about the WAFS would have stimulated more women pilots to enter the school that had not yet begun. By late 1943, there were no reasons to keep us hidden; Jackie no longer needed us.

Meanwhile a controversy was still raging over the number of flying hours necessary to qualify a pilot for the Ferry Command. General George had leaned over backwards in being fair to women. His lack of opposition to Cochran's push had actually led to women being sharply favored over civilian male pilots. In October 1942, he began to side with Tunner, who wanted the maximum number of solo hours possible for pilots. Perhaps George thought of what disastrous accidents were possible if ferry pilots had only 175 hours.

Both men agreed that Cochran could graduate whom she wished. But ATC was not going to welcome every warm body at its gates who wanted to occupy a cockpit in flight. Cochran warily skirted the opposition of George and Tunner as she laid plans and arguments before General Arnold. By now George and Tunner distrusted her. They thought her irrepressible, unpredictable, and scheming and looked for an alternative to dealing with her.

Cochran's own account, from *The Stars at Noon,* states, "The WAC under Colonel Oveta Culp Hobby . . . was having its growing pains at about this time. Many who had joined were using the technical right to resign afforded them by the shift of the Army organization headed by Colonel Hobby from WAAC to WAC and some dramatic move seemed to be indicated to offset this trend. Someone got the bright idea that women pilots should be made a subsidiary part of the WAC. At that time I had more than twenty-five thousand applicants for pilot training. They would be a fine addition to the WAC. Also there were some undercover politics at work. Colonel Smith was fostering the WAC idea but General Arnold was with me in opposition, although not openly. He called me to Washington and asked me to see Colonel Hobby. She opened the conversation by telling me she didn't know one end of a plane from another, but that if the pilots could be brought into the WAC, she would count on my direction of them. I told her that there was just about as much sense putting the women pilots under the WAC as putting the Air Force pilots back in the Army Signal Corps; that I was unalterably opposed to it. . . . I was probably not too diplomatic in my language. . . . However, for some time I kept a suspicious eye on General Smith (by then he had received his star) and some of the others in the Ferry Command, who seemed to me willing to make a trade with Colonel Hobby.''

I have several problems with Cochran's story. She states that she had on hand 25,000 applications for her school, which was just then being organized and was still primarily on paper. How did she receive them when the only people who even knew of such a school were the leaders of the Air Forces commands — a handful of secretive men — concerned with setting it up?

I have already questioned Cochran's recollections of her experiences in ATA in Great Britain. Her memory of chronological events is vague. *The Stars at Noon* contains no specific dates, which keeps it from being a valuable resource, except to indicate her personality.

We first WAFS at Wilmington knew about the unlikely chance that we might become WAACs. Nancy and Betty called a special meeting to tell us of a plan to militarize us and thereby to make us lieutenants. Nancy said that Cochran vehemently opposed the move, which apparently was initiated by the ATC. On the other hand, it seemed the only way for the WAFS to elude Jackie's control. I remained outside the controversy, not knowing much about Cochran nor about the leaders in the Ferry Command. I was just biding my time until all the chips were in. In 1943 Congress militarized the WAAC into the WAC. We should have become militarized at that time, too, and might have, except for the opposition of Cochran and her influence on General Arnold.

That influence did us great harm, because the men pilots of FERD gradually learned a bit more and gossiped about Cochran's power within the AAF. As time went on, they openly criticized General Arnold for allowing himself "to be wrapped around Jackie's finger." I felt the animosity toward her rubbing onto me, because I, too, was a woman.

In November 1942 there was a change in the situation that we WAFS knew nothing about. A letter from the Commanding General of the Army Air Forces to the FTC read,

"Contemplated expansion of the armed forces will tax the nation's manpower. Women must be utilized wherever it is practicable to do so. It is desired that you take immediate and positive action to augment to the maximum possible extent the training of women pilots. The Air Forces objective is to provide at the earliest possible date a sufficient number of women pilots to replace men in every non-combat flying duty in which it is feasible to employ women. [The] course of instruction should be designed to improve the ability of trained pilots as well as training for women with no previous flying experience.''

No longer would Cochran's school be tailored to suit what the Ferry

Command needed. On the other hand, ATC needn't worry about quarreling again and again about graduates who had too few hours for ferrying. General George found himself faced with a projected manpower expansion in 1943. He had to revise his forecast from 100 to 750 women needed in the next year and for 1,000 more in 1944. But he reiterated his minimum flight requirements, just in case.

In 1942 all Air Forces command generals had to decide soon how many pilots they should move from safe, stateside posts to more dangerous ones overseas. And Tunner was told that he would be faced in a month or so with problems of where to put the graduates of Cochran's school in his Ferry Command.

And where was this controversial school that was causing so much ill feeling and confusion in November of 1942? Nowhere.

More than a month after being officially ordered into existence, it had not yet materialized. And if Cochran had in hand 25,000 applications, why did she hire Ethel Sheehy, vice president of the Ninety-Nines, to go about the country recruiting women? Cochran herself, as its new president, visited many monthly Ninety-Nine chapter meetings to attempt to influence licensed pilots.

In Washington, D.C., that November, Cochran honored that city's chapter of Ninety-Nines with her presence. At the 1980 WASP reunion, Jane Straughn of the first WFTD class told me about her visit.

"We went to the Ninety-Nine meeting in November and Jackie was there. After a few drinks she said, 'Would you girls like to fly like the girls are doing in England?'

"Well, sure! We always want to fly, so we said, 'Yes, yes, yes!' It was a week after that we got a telegram one Sunday morning to report to Houston at our own expense in ten days time. And nobody knew what it was — we couldn't find out anything. Mary Lou Colbert and some others said they were going.

"I said I wasn't. And Cochran got wind of it, that I wasn't going because I didn't want to pay my way down. She offered to lend me the money, which was very magnanimous I'm sure, but I would never have lived it down if I had borrowed from her. It wasn't that I needed the money. I didn't. But I thought it was a strange way for the government to send you some place and tell you to pay your own way to get there!"

I agreed. The government had done that to the WAFS, too.

"Finally, at the last minute — three days before classes began — I decided to go down to Houston to see what it was. We were told to go to the Rice Hotel. Cochran was there. We stayed there the first night and then we found rooms in which to stay. One place happened to be Oveta Culp Hobby's old homestead that now took in boarders. Mary

Lou lived there and we lived across the street.

"The next thing we knew we were told to wear our own slacks — purple, blue, green, anything we had. We went out to the airport. Civilian instructors conducted the classes."

"What kind of airplanes?" I asked.

"Junk! Just old civilian airplanes."

They were no doubt requisitioned or found at civilian airports. Jane thought that Aviation Enterprises was the contractor. But who set them up? Who furnished the money for the planes, the rentals of hangars, the salaries for instructors and service personnel, and so forth? I had no answers. I questioned Jane because I wanted to know for certain whether or not Jacqueline Cochran tried to use the flight school as one of her financial investments. What was her purpose in trying to build the strength of that slight enterprise?

Jane continued her story. "After a while we got some PTs and later we got BTs and a while after that, we got AT-6s."

"By that time," I said, "the Army Air Force Training Command must have come into the financial picture. I heard you had some twin-engine stuff, too, before you got out."

"Oh, sure," Jane replied. "We got some sort of twin-engine. I think it was a UC-78, the wooden Cessna."

I asked Jane about the flying requirement for that first class.

"We had to be eligible for a commercial license," she said.

"I knew someone in the second class who told me confidentially that she had far, far less than that when she was accepted."

"The requirement dropped right away. She skimmed off the girls who could pass the requirements and that didn't leave anybody much who was eligible."

"By the standards expected of you," I finished.

Jacqueline Cochran gives her report of the school's beginnings in *The Stars at Noon.*

"We started with claptrap equipment consisting of every conceivable sort of primary and basic training planes. The girls housed themselves in nearby motels with free bus service to and from the airport. But the work was launched. The first class embraced women who had considerable air experience. The length of training for subsequent classes was to be variable depending on the capacity of the candidates. While the first class was to last only twenty-three weeks, we soon extended the training period to nine months."

She adds, "The Houston facility was at best a makeshift. The British had a fine training base at Sweetwater, Texas, which they were giving up, so we seized upon it for the women and the second class of trainees was transferred by air to the permanent home."

DRESS REHEARSAL

BACK AT NEWCASTLE on Sunday, November 1, I was surprised when someone down the hall yelled, "Scharrrr! Telephone." It was Cohee, Love's former secretary, who had come back from Dover to visit with us. I liked her. She had a pleasant personality and a great liking for me because, I thought, her sister was also a school teacher. She told me a bit about the new air base being built at Dover and said she was happier living at home, something I could well understand.

After our visit, Gert Meserve and I walked up to the hangar to see the B-17 that Freddy Koupal had brought in on its belly. After hiking about the base for several miles, we both felt better. I said to Gert, "We don't get enough exercise with only an hour of drill every morning. I'm going to start an exercise class for the girls if Nancy will let me.'

"That's okay with me," she replied.

The next morning I knew when I swallowed hard that at last I'd be eligible for a flight as soon as the flight surgeon said my throat was clear. Would I get one through St. Louis? I woke up as fast as turning on a light and was immediately aware that a high wind was wailing overhead and knocking at the barracks walls. I looked out. Outside my bedroom window the telephone poles were obscured by a thick fog. It obliterated the possibility of a mission to the west.

At eight o'clock the flight surgeon put me back on flying status. Then I heard that a bottleneck was choking the output at both the Fairchild and Piper factories. Neither was able to complete the planes already in assembly because subcontracted parts had not arrived. As soon as the parts arrived, we'd all go crazy trying to deliver airplanes as fast as we could.

It was almost two months since I left home. What had I done here? My Ferry Command life thus far had not been very productive. I was again in ground school, where there were only two courses that actively engaged me — Morse code and the Link trainer. But I was also learning to be part of a unit.

That evening Teresa James hobbled into the laundry room saying, "This damn knee! It sure aches like hell."

At last I would be good for something, I thought. "Wait a second," I said. When I returned, I had my hot water bottle and a tube of Ben-Gay. The hot water tap supplied scalding water for the bottle and as I corked it, I said to Teresa, "Get into bed."

She limped across the hall into her room and lay down on the cot. Since the hot water bottle was too hot at first, I wrapped it in a towel and put it on her knee. Then I rubbed in some of the ointment just as others had done for me when my shoulder ached so.

"Thanks, you old bag," said Teresa.

In parting I looked back at her from the doorway and warned, "Stay off your feet and keep warm and you'll feel better tomorrow."

Fortunately, she did.

Back in my room, I wrote Harold another letter. Barbara Towne's husband had visited her and that had triggered another session of homesickness for Harold. I told him, "My mind grows numb and I don't react to people around me when I haven't heard from you for several days. Then your letter arrives and peps me up."

I had told Nancy before the end of October that I must go home soon to take care of some financial family business. Now I renewed my request, asking for a leave of absence.

Nancy had made a promise to me earlier and she kept it. She said I should be gone no more than three days and only that, because as an airline passenger I might get bumped.

St. Louis was the best possible medicine for my soul. Being at home with Harold was wonderful. He had missed me as much as I had missed him. The navy gave him a day's leave for our business and I made all the arrangements while he was at work.

We picked up our old friend Milt Richards and took him to Prange Realty on Grand Avenue. There Prange made up a set of papers which described the sale of my flat to Milton, as a straw party, and his sale of the same property to Harold and me. I didn't follow the technicalities of the procedure too well, but the result was what I had planned.

I then paid the interest which was due and $300 of the principal and signed a new mortgage agreement at five percent interest. After the business was concluded, we returned Milton to his work and went downtown.

We parked in the basement of the Union Market and walked around. On Locust Street an itinerant photographer snapped our picture. When we ordered a copy we realized that neither of us had a good picture of the other — we couldn't afford to have a photograph made when we were married. We stopped at a studio to have individual portraits made for each of us to treasure.

Since we were downtown, it was a good opportunity for Harold to buy some nice things for me. He saw an exceptionally elegant dark brown leather shoulder bag that became mine. Then he bought me two sweaters saying, "Now you wear these and take care of yourself for me."

The visit was too short and on the way back to Wilmington I wondered when I would see Harold again. I got back the morning of November 7 and reported first to Nancy's office at headquarters.

Her great eyes stared at me. "You'll be a flight leader on a mission to Macon, Georgia," she said. "And you'll be leading Esther Nelson."

The honor of being a flight leader on this, my second mission, without having shown my navigational skill was unexpected and like a dash of cold water in my face.

"Moreover," Nancy continued, "I want you to take over the job of teaching Esther how to fly cross-country. She has no self-assurance and lacks experience. Pilotage in California is too simple, and that's all she's done. So you take Esther and tell me when you think she can manage by herself."

I thought the responsibility was a compliment, especially because Nancy had earlier said that my lack of cross-country experience was a disadvantage. From headquarters I walked to group operations where the orders were cut. I found out that on the same orders, Rhonie and Meserve were going to Bainbridge, Georgia, and Helen Mary Clark with Florene Miller were going to Columbus, Mississippi.

A sidewalk photographer made this photo of Harold and Adela Scharr in downtown St. Louis in November 1942.

But operations wasn't sending us via airplane this time. The honeymoon was evidently over. That evening we sat in a truck going to Wilmington and boarded a train for Philadelphia. There we caught a train for a six-hour ride to Lockhaven. Since it was night, we were allowed to have Pullman sleepers. I climbed up to an upper berth, thankful for being agile. I was able to undress and position my clothes so they wouldn't get wrinkled. But as usual in any strange situation, I slept poorly.

When we arrived at the Piper factory, the airplanes were not yet flyable and wouldn't be ready until the following day. We went into Lockhaven and took rooms at the Fallon Hotel. It had a long covered porch lined with a long row of rockers facing the street. In my mind's eye I saw drummers (salesmen) with celluloid collars, striped shirts, suspenders, straw boater atop each head, ogling the passersby and spitting at intervals, sometimes missing the spittoons.

At noon we were hungry and decided to look about the town for a good eating place because we knew we were faced with repeat journeys into Lockhaven for the duration. We could not have had better luck. Nearby was Henry's Dairy Lunch. It looked so clean that we ate there and found the food delicious. We chose the roast turkey and with it the waitress served us oven-hot, freshly baked rolls. The price was geared to our per diem. We knew we'd be back.

What to do that afternoon? The local movie theater had a Sunday matinee of *Bambi,* the Disney movie. We were in uniform and the cashier let us in free. The movie was so sentimental, I could hardly bear it. Sobs stuck in my throat when Bambi, after being unsure that he would ever see his mother again, was reunited with her.

Dinner was at six. When we arrived in the lobby of the hotel, William T. Piper, the founder of the company, his son, and four other officials greeted us. We sat in the private dining room in high-backed, upholstered red seats that matched the ornate window drapes.

Piper appeared to be overwhelmed by being in the presence of women pilots. He treated us to the finest dinner he was able to order. Freshly broiled mushrooms topped thick sirloin steaks. The vegetables and salad accompanying the main course made our dinner a perfect meal.

The men appeared as self-conscious as the WAFS were. Perhaps they were ill-at-ease because, being married, they had been diverted from their families and familiar activities — perhaps a Sunday evening church service or listening to the favorite radio programs or helping children with homework. And if I knew wives, there was at least one who said, "Who does that old Piper think he is? Making you work on a Sunday!" The reply: "There's a war on."

Fortunately dinner was more than hearty and delicious, it gave us chewing time during which conversation was unnecessary and one could think of something to talk about later on. We swapped flying stories, but soon ran out of any that were mutually interesting. Except for the younger Piper, most of the company people were really not dedicated pilots. At about 8:30 we walked out to the lobby and bid our table companions good night. They seemed as relieved as we were to end the evening.

Upstairs my roommate Esther went visiting the others. While she was gone, Rhonie drifted into our room.

"You have a bath?" she asked.

"Yeah," I replied, wondering what else she had expected in a big hotel like the Fallon.

She went in the bathroom to take a look. When she came out seconds later, she said, "I wanted a room with a bath, but we got a shower. Meserve insisted on it."

"So she won't get homesick — it's just like the barracks."

"Of course not. She asked the price of a room without a tub and it's cheaper."

"I didn't know there was a choice," I answered. I wondered how I let that possibility slip past me.

"You know Meserve is from New England and Yankees are always close with their money. So I can't take a bath. I'd never excuse that stinginess in anyone else."

I thought, you evidently don't know that the Scotch, Germans, Swiss, Chinese, and who knows who else, also have reputations for being tight-fisted. Including me, by necessity.

The Piper office had given us the private telephone number of the meteorological office. The following morning we could plainly see that the visibility was only about one mile and the ceiling appeared low. Takeoff was not allowed under those conditions. Each hour we called again, only to learn that the weather was holding us there. At last we became embarrassed and decided we'd better show up at the factory so we'd be ready to go at the first opportunity. We ate lunch at Henry's and then piled into two taxicabs and headed for the Piper plant.

Fortunately Piper officials said our planes were ready. We found them in the tie-down area and checked their condition. That done, we went in to see the airway sequences to determine which route we'd most likely take in the first part of the mission.

At least two Piper employees whispered to me, "Did Mr. Piper take you girls to dinner last night?" At my affirmative reply, each stared dumbfounded, in disbelief. Esther told me, "One guy asked me that and when I told him, he said the old man had never done such a thing before, and he looked at me as if he wondered how we could vamp him into being so generous." Apparently it never happened again. We were the lucky ones.

A small blonde, who said she came from Staten Island to work in the factory to obtain flying time as partial payment for her labor, asked me as many questions as she could about the WAFS. She glanced furtively at her supervisor as we spoke.

"One of our instructors here, Lauretta Beatty, is getting into Jacqueline Cochran's school in Houston. I wish I had more flying time. I'd sure like to go."

"I hope you make it," I replied in parting. "See you around.

By one o'clock we all felt confident that we'd take off directly south. Helen Mary got the latest book of NOTAMs, which is a weekly Notice to Airmen about field conditions, such as runway construction in progress, field closings, or other recent developments which might keep pilots from landing in certain airports. Rhonie and I crowded around her and learned that two of the Pennsylvania airports had recently closed. Chambersburg was not one of them.

We went to operations where a huge table gave us ample room to open our sectional charts and to pencil in our route to Chambersburg. Using a yardstick for a guide, we marked off each ten miles, which was equivalent to a little over an inch. The hop was eighty-nine miles long. After each of us plotted her course, Esther and I got together. I checked on what she'd be doing to find out what course she'd fly.

"What's your true course?" I asked.

"It's 188 degrees," she answered.

"What'll you do with the magnetic deviation?"

"I'll add seven degrees because it's west."

"Okay. Don't mind me doing this nit-picking. You want to make it routine."

"Oh, I'm glad you are," she replied. "When faced with this, I'm scared out of my wits and I can't think."

"Let's make a wind vector," I suggested. "Here's a piece of paper."

Esther worked the problem and when she finished, she said, "I figure the ground speed is fifty-five miles per hour."

"Right. And we know at what angle we'll be crabbing into the wind. But you can't be sure the wind remains the same in direction and velocity. We should be able to make it in an hour and a half, so I'll make out the clearance and we'll get the meteorologist to okay it."

The other two missions were ready when we were. The others packed their B-4 bags onto the front seat of their Cubs and placed the navigation kit and their purses in the small baggage compartment· behind the rear seat, where they sat. I was so used to sitting in the front seat that I switched loads. Before we got in I said, "I'm willing to navigate this if you don't mind."

No one objected. The line boys turned my propeller first, then Esther's. I was poised for takeoff, waiting until I saw that all had started and were taxiing to the takeoff point. Then I led off, feeling that the responsibility of showing Esther the safest way to navigate and to stay on course was more important than looking like a greenhorn to the others. Instead of pointing away from the airport I made a traffic pattern around it until I gained at least 1,000 feet in altitude and headed toward the plotted course.

The town of Lockhaven was on my right and a little triangle made by a stream, the railroad, and my pencil line pointed back to Cubhaven. I made a coordination exercise to look back and line up with the airport to verify that I was being followed. I was. I aimed for a point about two miles to the left of Salona and about a mile to the left of Mackeyville. Not the nose, which was headed toward the right, angling into the direction of the wind. The line on my chart headed out into a spot on my left windshield.

The Cub was very stiff on its controls, just like the Fleet used to be right after its annual inspection. I'm breaking this thing in for the students, I realized.

Pennsylvania is a snap to fly, I thought, with mountain ranges crossing my path at about a twenty-five degree angle from the east. Between them were usually a stream, a road, and maybe a railroad with a town on it.

Helen Mary and Florene were flying at my left; Rhonie and Meserve were on the right. Esther was just to my rear. I kept tabs on them about every five minutes. A Piper Cub doesn't travel very far in five minutes. Cruising speed with a sixty-five horsepower engine was rated at seventy-two miles per hour. Along the way one could contemplate the scenery; anyone would have to be very careless to get lost. But piloting a Cub required patience, for with a headwind, one might wonder if the hop would ever end.

I was reminded of the day at Lambert Field when, in order to get the Kinner Fleet into the traffic pattern, I had to bend the throttle forward and step the airplane down, diving and then leveling, because of the swiftness of the air mass I was going "upstream" in. The best story I heard about the difficulty of flying Cubs against a headwind was told by Oscar Parks, the Lambert Field manager. He said an excited woman telephoned his office one day and in shrill tones informed him, "One of your airplanes is above my house and it hasn't moved in a half hour." Then she demanded, "What are you going to do about it?" Parks commented, "Maybe she thought it was about to fall on her."

We had a strong headwind building up, cross on the nose, and it was gusty, although we were a good, safe distance from the ground near which we could expect bumpiness. With my simple calculator I figured we were making forty-five miles per hour ground speed, three miles every four minutes.

After we crossed the Juniata River, Rhonie began leading Meserve about ninety degrees to the right. They didn't seem to have difficulties and Rhonie hadn't bored ahead to signal to make a change in direction. She was her own flight leader and could make her own judgments. On the chart to our west was Lewistown, and it had an airport not far upstream. Helen Mary elected to remain with me.

I circled Chambersburg Airport, checking it over and getting the wind direction from the sock, as if I weren't aware of it already. The others trailed me. The sun was still high in the sky, so we weren't in any trouble about that. But by the time we landed, a ridge of mountains approximately ten miles to the west cut off the direct rays of the sun and we found ourselves in twilight. Suddenly the place seemed cold and dismal.

Because I landed first, I led the taxiing up to the hangar. No one came out to greet us. We switched off the engines and climbed out. Florene joined me in peeking into a window of the door to the hangar. There were no airplanes inside.

Esther absent-mindedly was still clutching her aeronautical chart. "Let me look at it," I said. On it I saw that the next closest airport was

Waynesboro; Hagerstown was a bit farther. From the gasoline gauge I could judge we didn't have enough fuel for a forty-five minute surplus after we flew to another field. And the sky told us to stay where we were. It appeared to be a hopeless situation.

We were stuck in a deserted field with no way to get our planes into the hangar. We had to RON, to find a place to sleep that night, and to get gasoline in order to continue our mission. Suddenly we heard the sound of an automobile approaching. A sedan appeared and in it was a man of middle years. He got out of the car and came quickly toward us.

"I saw you circling for a landing, so I came right away to tell you. This field is closed."

What we had feared was now a fact.

"Can't we get some gas?" Helen Mary asked.

"No. I'm sorry about this. But we have discontinued all facilities."

"Jeepers!" exclaimed Helen Mary.

"Why wasn't notice of this in NOTAMs?" I asked.

"The field was undesignated only the day before yesterday," he replied.

"What'll we do? We can't fly out of here to any place else tonight," said Esther, looking glum and worried.

A cloud layer had moved in with the wind and it lowered the ceiling, cutting off some of the light we still had.

"I can take you into town," said the stranger. "I was the airport manager here and that's why I felt obligated to come out here to see about you."

"We all thank you," returned Florene.

"Our airplanes can't stay out here," I said.

"Here." The man fished a key from his pocket. "You can put them in the hangar."

With a flourish he unlocked the Yale lock hanging on the hasp. Florene and I helped him push and pull the sliding hangar doors along their top and bottom guide rails. The other two watched. I thought, you can really tell who will pitch in and work in a situation like this.

"This won't end our problems," I stated. "When we get these planes in, someone will have to stay here to guard them." My heart fell. Would it be me? If so, how could I fly the next day, sleepy from doing guard duty all night? Would anyone else volunteer?

Then Helen Mary turned to the man and ventured, "Do you have a Civil Air Patrol squadron here?"

"Yes, we sure do."

"Would it be possible for them to volunteer to take turns guarding our planes until we take off? We aren't supposed to leave them with just anybody."

"I think they'd be glad to do something for the war effort. Make 'em feel important," replied the man.

To myself, I whispered, "Thank God." And to Helen Mary, I said, "Why don't you run into town with him and round up the CAP? While you are there, would you please send in our RON with yours and get us rooms in a hotel?"

In a jiffy, Helen Mary and our savior were gone. Then we made good use of our time by shoving the airplanes in one at a time, swinging them about by their tails and watching that they didn't touch the hangar walls. Before moving each, we took out our pilot's paraphernalia and stacked it in a heap at the corner of the building. My pile was the largest because I had brought my Lear radio. I wanted to check out what Sandy Lerner had told me about using it during flight.

I had already learned that unless a plane were wired specifically for this instrument that it was impossible to get anything on it in the air without an antenna. But the radio could be run on batteries or on AC/DC current. I had batteries in it. Into that strange, godforsaken airport, I brought the Lear when we closed the hangar doors to keep out the cold wind. How dark it was! And no sign of a light bulb. I switched channels on the radio until I found a station on the AM band broadcasting music. I couldn't see the other two, Esther and Florene. They could have been sitting on the floor or in a cockpit. We waited interminably, silently, in the cold and dark, listening to the radio. I danced about in one spot to keep warm. We couldn't even guess the time.

Finally there was the sound of automobiles stopping outside. And voices. Armed with flashlights, the manager and several men in CAP khaki uniforms and insignia had arrived to rescue us. The manager explained that the CAP would guard the planes in four-hour shifts and that they were eager to cooperate.

We couldn't see them very well because of the shifting focuses of the flashlights, but we responded with our gratitude at having them take over. The manager spoke again. "Your other girl is back at the hotel. I'm ready to take you and your baggage in whenever you are."

Were we ready! While we were waiting, I had wondered what was taking Helen Mary so long to bring us help. Now, with our gear stowed in the trunk and the airplanes safe, the warm friendliness of the manager and the coziness of his sedan put our cold ordeal behind us.

Cheerfully Florene chirped, "You don't know how much we appreciate what you-all have done for us."

"You bet," said Esther.

"Yeah," I sighed, as one last shiver went up and down my spine. "How are we going to get the weather report in the morning?"

"You'll have to telephone Hagerstown," replied our driver. "We got no gasoline to get you to the next airport. Do you need any?"

"We'd better get a couple of gallons apiece just to be on the safe side," I replied. From over 1,000 hours of instructing in Cubs, I could be sure that our little planes had consumed gasoline at a faster rate than four gallons per hour. For a fifteen or twenty minute flight to the next airport, two gallons each would be sufficient.

Our rescuer ventured, "There's a filling station down the road a piece. I'll call him to bring his truck up and he'll service your planes when you're ready to take off."

"It's not safe to use automotive fuel in an aviation engine," I said.

"Well, there's nothing much we can do about it," said Esther.

The idea would be a gnawing worry to me, but I was too tired then to lose much sleep over it. At the hotel we unloaded our gear and again thanked our benefactor, who was not through taking care of us.

"I'll give you a call in the morning to see that you get out all right" were his parting words.

The following day, cold rain poured from a dark gray sky. We would go nowhere. The airport manager phoned us and said that the CAP would carry on until we were able to take off.

I told Esther, "I won't be able to stand this weather unless I have more clothes. I'm going to scout around for a man's store and buy some long-handled drawers."

Esther's nose tossed skyward. "It isn't that bad," she said. "I wasn't that cold last night."

I looked at her critically. Sure, she wouldn't feel the bite of the cold as much as I. She carried about thirty more pounds of insulation under her skin. And if she did feel a chill, vanity would keep her out of heavy underwear, which would make her appear even stouter.

"I'll tell you this much," I rose in self-defense. "I flew an open plane in the coldest winter weather back home. I couldn't get into anybody's winter flying suit — I was too tall. So I bought some men's woolen underwear at Sears. The plane had no carburetor heat control, and I usually stayed up no more than a half hour. Even so, I got pleurisy. And I don't want pleurisy again. So I'm getting some underwear." And I left the hotel room.

The former airport manager called us again, saying, "Look. I got hold of a service station owner with a gas truck. As a favor to me, he'll come out to the airport tomorrow and give you enough gas to get to the next airport.''

The next morning we still felt droplets in the air and the ceiling was too low, but Hagerstown meteorologists told us that we'd soon be able to get that far. When we sensed an improvement in flying conditions, we called our manager friend and he took us to the airport. We busied ourselves pushing planes out of the hangar with concise communications to each other, such as ''Hold it!'' ''Over this way!'' ''Bring the tail around,'' and ''Look out for that wing!''

The gasoline truck lumbered in to the outmost plane and stopped. The driver came down from his cab, walked to the rear of his vehicle, and took forth a hose and nozzle.

I wasn't ashamed to be a coward. ''I'm afraid of auto gas,'' I declared.

''It'll be all right. We won't take much,'' soothed Helen Mary.

''But I know a fellow who used some on a cross-country and had a forced landing due to vapor lock,'' I replied.

The truck driver kept unrolling his hose. He unscrewed the gas cap of my plane.

''Do you have a chamois?'' I asked him.

''Yep. What about it?'' he asked.

''I want you to filter the gas through a chamois to keep out water or a stray bit of dirt,'' I said. ''We don't want any accidents.''

He made a face that said, ''Damn woman driver,'' but went back to his cab and brought out a chamois. I stood by to make certain that he used it and that we each got our two gallons to get us to the nearest airport.

Helen Mary made out the form #15 invoice, signed it, and handed the fourth copy to the truck driver. She placed the other three copies in an envelope franked for government business and said to him, ''We'll mail this today so you'll get your money as soon as possible. But if you want to make sure, you can drop it into the mail in town.''

''That's okay with me,'' he replied.

By that time the airport manager had returned. He gave each prop a swing after we'd stowed ourselves and our gear into our planes. After the good-byes and the thank you's, I led out again. Truthfully, I was too worried about the gas we'd taken on to allow anyone else to make the first attempt. My self-confidence mixed with a latent maternal instinct toward the others, I guess.

The magnetic course of about 160 degrees brought us in a straight line to Waynesboro Airport. I'd prepared Esther for this hop by pointing out that we'd pass about a mile east of New Franklin and about a mile and a half south of it we'd almost kiss the railroad that headed eastward. Quincy would be dead ahead and Waynesboro to our right. We made the fourteen-mile trip in fifteen minutes, counting takeoff and circling for a landing.

While we gassed up and made out our flight plan, I asked the airport operator, "Any more airports closed around here besides Chambersburg?"

"Yeh," he replied. "Doersom over near Gettysburg is one. And there's Centerville."

That was information I'd bring back to the barracks. We'd have to pool our knowledge about the problems we might expect. Otherwise the WAFS might not survive their test period.

This time Helen Mary took off first, with Florene flying after. Again I led Esther. We had the added problem of plotting across two sectional charts and having to shift from one to the other during the course. This time we headed 225 degrees paralleling a mountainous uplift for five miles on the east. We flew down a valley, keeping to its eastern half, and aimed between little towns like Leitersburg and Smithburg. A road and a stream on the left were good checkpoints. We could analyze where streams were in the distance by the vegetation lining the banks. And the fine brown lines of the charts showed the topography of the rising land before us to the south of Hagerstown. It was fascinating to compare the chart with the earth beneath us. I zeroed in where the Potomac River shot eastward and met a single track railroad and the road to Sharpsburg. In fifty-five minutes we'd land in Winchester.

The temperature farther south, we found, was a bit warmer, but the atmosphere of Winchester Airport was chilly. We were not welcome. The fixed base operator there let us know that it was hard enough to obtain gasoline for his own activities without sharing it with military transients. As we made out the invoices, I felt guilty because I knew that it might be a few weeks or more before he'd be paid for his precious gasoline. We made a quick exit. Our teamwork paid off. Simultaneously, each member of the group did what was necessary. We were on the ground only a half hour.

The next stop was to be Staunton, Virginia, eighty miles away on a heading of 220 degrees.

"Do you want to try it?" I asked Esther.

She shook her head warily. "No," she replied.

It wasn't a hard course, although the topography was as strange to me as to her. We couldn't possibly get lost using my favorite system of pilotage, which I tried to get her to use also. I held the chart in my left hand with my thumb directly behind the spot where my last known checkpoint was located on the chart. As I moved forward over the ground toward the next checkpoint, I moved my thumb forward along the course line, which was marked in ten-mile sections, toward my destination.

The land abounded with checkpoints. We paralleled the Blue Ridge Mountains to our east and flew smack down the valley made by Passage Creek. By the time we got to Keezletown, southeast of Harrisonburg, a road led into Staunton Airport. The road wandered about from right to left, so I flew a straight course, one that ignored each bend. We had a ground speed of sixty-four miles per hour on that hop, for it took us an hour and fifteen minutes. It was beautiful all the way.

In preparing for the next hop, we found we'd get off the Huntington chart and move on to Winston-Salem. The heading I set for us was 195 degrees, but we were now over rough terrain in a gusty atmosphere. The Carwil compass swung crazily, bobbing left to right and back again. One had to be psychic to maintain a course down the median of the swings. Fortunately, the checkpoints were easy to spot at first. But once we passed over Stuart Draft and got onto the Winston-Salem chart, there was little that man had built to help me until we were in sight of Lynchburg. This interval was an absorbing challenge to my imagination. I used the fine brown lines on the map. Close together, they indicated a steep uplift. When they waved, that told me erosion from water runoff had moved the hillside back at that spot. I matched what I saw on the earth with what was mapped in my left hand.

Wherever there was a little island defined by a brown zero or dot, and especially if a number was printed next to it on the chart, I knew it should be a peak higher than the other peaks in its vicinity.

I saw the beginnings of mountain streams falling to the east and to the west and felt that I was flying over a divide, although not one of much note. A power line crossed our path at a twenty-five-degree angle. I followed its path with my eyes to where it originated on the James River, just northwest of Lynchburg. We were, I was sure, at the fall line of the Piedmont Plateau, the demarcation between the eastern coastal plains and the harder rocks of the mountain ranges of the Appalachians. We crossed the city at 2,500 feet above sea level, but we were so near to its western edge that in case of a forced landing any of us could find a clear area. I let down to 1,940 feet and led the flight in for a landing. We had been airborne for fifty-five minutes, which made our speed sixty-seven miles per hour.

The name of the airport was Preston Glenn. The people there were extremely friendly. Someone even took us into town so we wouldn't have to pay a taxi fare.

On our way into town I turned to Helen Mary. "Wasn't the scenery gorgeous?''

''Except for the brown spots on some of those hills,'' she answered.

''We have a lot of that in California,'' commented Esther. ''Every year forests burn to the ground during the dry season.''

''All we have is a dry season in west Texas,'' said Florene. ''So we don't have those trees to begin with.''

The hotel was not exactly run-down, but it was old and had seen much use. It introduced me to the typical southern hotel in which I would stay many times during my Ferry Command days. These hotels all had a familiar sameness. The carpets were invariably dull. The furniture was cheap but of good design and usually made of dark wood.

We began to form travel habits. We checked the windows to make sure that they would not only lock, but also open. We tested the locks of the doors and tried to remember where the exits were in case of fire.

The following morning, we took a taxi back to Preston Glenn. The fare, divided by four, was nominal.

''Do you want to lead out this time?'' I asked Esther.

''No,'' she replied, ''but I think I'm catching on.''

Good, I thought. I'd rather lead than follow someone who doesn't know what's what. Leading was fun. Would my score be perfect this time? Danville was only fifty-two miles away. The course would be close to 220 degrees.

It was an interesting leg. A stream began just south of the plateau on which Preston Glenn had been built. The stream passed a small town named Lawyer. Why, I wondered. Was it a family name or the place where a lawyer carried on legal business?

Only the angle at which we crossed the stream below gave us any indication we were on course. At times a power line was visible in the west. After we crossed the Roanoke River, we headed for Greensboro. The forty-seven mile hop from Danville took us forty-five minutes with a heading of 225 degrees. We followed a double track railroad from Ruffin to Reidsville.

As Helen Mary and I were making our clearances at Greensboro, we heard, ''Pilot Wilkins from Quantico. Will Greensboro Airport communicate? Mayday. Calling Greensboro. . . .''

We heard no response. As we arranged our charts for easier use in cockpit, a fellow rushed into operations saying excitedly, ''A navy plane, a Grumman F-4F coming into the field, spun in at the edge of the airport!''

Everyone ran out of the building. Just beyond the field a cloud of black smoke rolled high into the air. A pilot could not have survived that blaze. We didn't want to dwell on it.

When I led off, I did not circle the airport where the tragedy had occurred. I just pointed the nose to 225 degrees and watched for High Point, a little city which was due to show up in about five minutes. Then I aimed for two miles west of it. From then on, it was an easy course. Lexington had a spider web of roads radiating from it. Over the dot called Linwood was a power station on the Yadkin River and a dam made a large, long lake to the southeast. Then we saw the roundhouse at Salisbury and a granite quarry south of town. Not far off, about two miles away, we followed the double track railroad and the road to its right until we crossed them just south of Kannapolis. After eighty minutes and eighty-three miles, we landed at Morris Field at Charlotte, North Carolina.

"We-all got a good system working for us," said Florene as we were about to take off again.

"With all these army installations, we don't have to fill out any invoices." Helen Mary's voice was bright.

"And no problems with operators," I said.

Spartanburg was only sixty-one miles away. This leg took us an hour, over a course of 252 degrees. We flew over two fingers of a large lake just to the west of Morris Field. There were good guides — the angle our path made with the transmission line just southeast of Clover. And lots of streams. One could tell from the flow of the streams near Filbert, east or west, what the topography was like, although it was below 1,000 feet, except for one blob sticking out of the plain about five miles to the right of our course as we passed by Clover off its northwest corner. It was Kings Mountain, the scene of fateful battles not only in the Revolutionary War, but also in the Civil War. Seeing places like that, so important to American history, thrilled me.

We circled Spartanburg Airport at 1,750 feet and watched carefully the little training planes circuiting the field. Our next stop, the Greenville Army Air Base in South Carolina, was only about twenty-seven miles away. Like the conscientious beginners we were, we felt we should get in as much flying time each day as we could. "Sure, we can make it," vowed Florene.

But we hadn't counted on a headwind right on the nose at 260 degrees, so it took us thirty minutes. And the sun, falling lower in the west, blinded us as we tried to land. We learned from that experience that landing into the sun should be done only when the sun's rays aren't shining directly into one's eyes. "Next time ask the meteorologist to change the direction of the wind so we might land without that handicap," I said.

The course had been easy to navigate because the two Tiger rivers were at right angles to our course. The Encree River paralleled them farther on. We didn't get an obvious checkpoint until we passed Mauldin and paralleled the road to Conestee. But by that time we were right at the destination.

During that long day of flying, I noticed how much airport construction was going on in the South. And where the earth's thatch had been scraped off to ground level for runways and fields, the earth was red and raw; it looked wounded.

I thought that Lynchburg, Greensboro, Spartanburg, and Greenville were all fine airports. The developments occurring in the South made me ashamed that Missouri, especially St. Louis, was so slow to modernize. What I didn't realize was that federal assistance was helping the other cities because the nation needed year-round, good weather airports for training pilots. And Lambert Field, as a long-established airport, didn't need government assistance.

We tied down our planes, closed our flight plans, saw the line boys fill the tanks, checked our chutes in the operations lockers, and on the way into town, sent out RONs at the telegraph office. The air base driver deposited us at the Greenville Hotel, of the Barringer chain. It was a large building, with 1,200 rooms in the six floors atop the main and mezzanine levels.

Esther and I worked on the next day's flight before we washed up and ate in the hotel dining room. We figured we'd go by way of Winder on the way to deliver the planes at Macon. First she drew her lines and then I drew mine.

During the meal I noticed that Helen Mary ate all of her meat, but skipped most of the vegetables. Not I. With my background of "waste not, want not," I ate everything put on my plate.

Nelson and I always asked for a room with twin beds. Helen Mary and Florene did the same. Esther and I were developing the habit of walking about in the vicinity of the hotel each evening. We were discovering that many towns were look-alikes on the main street. Each had a Lerner Shop with similar merchandise and most of the other chains were represented as well.

At 9 P.M., shortly after we wandered into a Walgreen drugstore to buy some postcards, we were surprised by a thirty-minute blackout. A blanket at the doorway helped to keep the faint, dimmed lights of the store from being seen in the vast darkness without. I was glad that we weren't caught out in the street.

Since we left the base, we hadn't been able to get a shirt washed and pressed. Five days of wearing two shirts was a bit much. We needed to set up a system for doing laundry along the way.

At the airline ticket office in the hotel, I found out what time an airliner was leaving Macon for Washington, D.C., and I said to

Esther, "If we get into Macon too soon tomorrow, we'll have to use our T/R on a train. If we get in later, we'll miss the train and the first public transportation will be an airliner the next morning."

"I don't want to go on a train," she replied.

"We'll have to do whatever comes up as the right thing," I said.

The next morning the army air base sent transportation for us at the hotel at 7:30 A.M. We had already packed and had breakfast in the coffee shop.

Out at the flight line we bid good-bye to Helen Mary and Florene, and soon we were off toward our mission's end. Except for a ten- to twelve-mile-an-hour headwind, the weather was pretty good. It was ninety-one miles to Winder and it took an hour and fifty-five minutes, which meant a ground speed of only fifty miles per hour. I flew a very straight course, helped along by the many streams that we crossed. And then our luck failed.

There was no gasoline at Winder. I guarded the planes and Esther hitched a ride in town with a man at the airport. She came back with a gasoline truck and driver. Once again we went through the procedure with a chamois, but this time we had to fill the tanks, for Macon was eighty-two miles away.

The wind was still moving us back, so we took eighty-five minutes to fly the course of 175 degrees. We finally got to Smart Field and delivered our airplanes to the proper officers. We had missed the train, so we took a RON, and waited for the airliner the next morning. We felt a bit guilty at not being able to start back to base immediately on delivery.

At the Hotel Dempsey in Macon, we made reservations and hoped we wouldn't bump anybody. We ate supper in the elegant, old dining room. On the menu was a lobster dinner for $1.85. I thought I'd try it, far from the sophisticated group at Wilmington. I knew Esther wouldn't mind any awkward incompetence on my part. I was putting up with a lot of hers in flying.

As we waited for dinner, we admired the arches and pillars of the dining room. Then the waiter tied bibs about our necks and offered each of us a huge dinner napkin. He cracked the lobster claws for me and showed me how to take out the meat. After our meal, he brought finger bowls and a slice of lemon on a silver plate.

With all of that put away and feeling much better, we took our little turn about the town. As we came to a street corner, a tiny Negro boy in a sailor suit rounded it. Upon seeing us, he hesitated a second and then saluted us. The action, so unexpected, nonplussed us so that we failed to return his salute until he was already retreating to our rear.

"Oh, boy!" crowed Esther. "That's our first salute."

ON TRIAL

THE NEXT MORNING we flew to Washington. From the airport we took a taxi to the train station. A porter was willing to carry our B-4 bags while we lugged our parachute bags to the coach where we boarded. At Wilmington I telephoned the base for transportation. Fortunately someone was coming into town who would take us back, but it was late afternoon by the time we arrived at the group operations office to turn in our receipts and other flight data. When he read our names, the officer in charge said, "You are already on orders. Be sure to go right away and pick them up."

We stopped next at Nancy's office.

"How did it go?" she asked with no sign of emotion.

"We delivered okay," I answered. "But I want to talk to you about the WAFS having a bulletin board. It could help us prevent delays."

Nancy lowered her long eyelashes as she lit a cigarette. Then she directed a meaningful stare at me, saying, "I'll want to see you about that later." Including Esther in her gaze, she added, "Colonel Baker is sending you out within twelve hours."

"Twelve hours!" Esther's voice rose in protest. She knew when and how to bitch. "Nancy! We just got back here with every shirt, undies and pj's dirty. And just look at my hair! How in the world can we wash our clothes, let me dry and press them, and wash and set our hair and get some sleep in twelve hours?"

My predicament included not only her recital, which had omitted the chore of repacking, but also the sad state of my finances. I was too embarrassed to tell Nancy the finance office wouldn't accept our per diem requests, verify their accuracy, and pay us in a matter of minutes. I had volunteered to serve my country even to death, but how could I carry on government missions if it didn't allow me money for food and lodging along the way? The semi-monthly pay check wasn't due until Monday, November 16. This was November 14. And because I, not the government, was paying for my uniforms, I had no extra dollars to carry me onward. But I remained silent.

My upbringing could explain the restraint that curbed not only in the spending of money, but also in confessing that I had none. It is true that my parents owned their own home before Edward, my oldest brother, was born, but they did so because they were thrifty. Later, during World War I and the early twenties, when shoe workers in St. Louis factories were getting sixteen dollars a day, my father brought home ninety dollars a month as a beat patrolman. He didn't dare switch jobs because he had five children to feed. Feed them he did, by raising a garden and chickens in the backyard and mushrooms in the basement. He installed our steam heating system himself, repaired the house, painted it, and cobbled all our shoes. And my mother sewed all our clothing, baked all the bread, canned and preserved each summer, and cut our hair in the kitchen. On Saturdays she gave me money and I pulled one of the younger children in our coaster wagon to the stores along Easton Avenue from the Mt. Auburn Market in Wellston, the equivalent of twelve city blocks from home, down to Kroger's across the street from the Fairy Theater. I bought whatever was the best and cheapest at each store, and while I went inside, my brother or sister guarded our previous purchases.

Understanding the closeness of my mother's dealings, I never asked her for even as much as a nickel during my dependent years. And I was too proud to join other Soldan High School students of our neighborhood during our mile-long walk home if the group stopped at the bakery on Arlington and Ridge for a nickel sweet roll to sustain them or if they chose a dill pickle from the barrel in a Kosher delicatessen on Easton Avenue.

Nancy handed us our flight orders. We'd start out on a flight with

Helen Richards, led by Pat Rhonie. As Esther and I walked toward the barracks, I faked cheerfulness, saying. "Hey! We're going to do all right, kiddo. It looks like we can repeat some of the hops we just took. We won't have to stay up until midnight plotting courses. We've got most of the lines drawn and our distances are all figured out."

"Yeah?"

"We'll see what the winds aloft will be every time we get gas. I think you'll find that going over the same ground will make it easier for you to navigate this time."

But Esther's mind, already used to leaning on mine, was more concerned with our immediate problems. She said, "I sure don't get Colonel Baker. We come back after knocking ourselves out to do the right thing. So just what is he trying to pull?"

Back in my room in BOQ 14, as I was sorting out the contents of my B-4 bag, I touched the two small packages for Harold that I'd been trying to mail. It appeared that I'd be forced to carry them along again, for the post office was closed and I'd be off again before it opened.

The packages contained inexpensive items to please him: for his dog tags, a chain that would not tarnish; for his new chief's cap, two plastic rain protectors; a pre-Pearl Harbor badge; a package of hard candies; and a pack of fancy-looking cigarettes. He wasn't addicted, so he probably wouldn't smoke them, especially since they were certainly stale by then.

I stood up to place the packages on top of my bureau and noticed for the first time a small stack of letters — from hometown friends and from Harold. As Teresa told me later, "When any one of us older girls go to the post office, we get the mail for everyone in the BOQ and put it in their rooms." So I didn't know whom to thank.

Laundry or not, I couldn't wait. I slit open the envelope with the earliest dated letter and began to read. Engrossed in it, I didn't hear Pat Rhonie come up the stairs and walk over to my doorway. She startled me when she began her recital.

"Colonel Baker has relented," she said. "He now says he'll give us thirty hours between this last mission and the next one so we can do all the things we need to."

From the next room came a shrill "Hallelujah!" as Esther reacted to the news. After a few more words, Rhonie went down the hall. Somehow she managed to give the impression that she was responsible for Baker's change of heart. She always hinted at her close relationship with any authority figure on the base.

We had a busy evening. Almost everyone who had already finished orientation was on orders to go somewhere. The lucky ones had PT-19 assignments out of Hagerstown. But after dinner, Esther and I took the time to listen to a story by one of a small group of young lieutenants seated in a circle at the club.

Supposedly, the story had originated with Nancy the previous evening, perhaps in a similar setting. I visualized Nancy seated on the sofa surrounded by young officers eager to be part of her entourage, sitting cross-legged on the floor and gazing at her with reverence.

The version of the story that we heard was one that sadistic young males enjoy, and I believe the true tale was cut short or altered. It didn't sound like Nancy.

A mission was scheduled to New England, said the lieutenant, and Nancy Love herself took it, accompanied by Cornelia Fort. It ended at an airport with a very strong surface wind. After landing and taxiing to the parking area in front of the hangar, Nancy remained inside her Cub and kept her engine running so that she could control the plane until assistance arrived.

But Cornelia, with less experience and from force of habit, cut back her throttle and turned off the ignition switch. With that the wings began to bob, the Cub began to move, and Cornelia decided she'd have to do something about saving the airplane. She got out of the Cub as quickly as she could and tried to grab a strut as the plane began to ground loop into the wind. Cornelia was not used to tussling with wayward airplanes. The propeller wacked her and she lost her balance and fell to her knees.

With that, a man came from behind the hangar, followed closely by a dog. He helped Cornelia bring her plane back to the line. Nancy beckoned to him and he left Cornelia holding on for dear life.

Nancy discovered that he was the right person to sign the receipts, and she wouldn't cut her switch until he had signed for both planes. Only then did she and all her paraphernalia leave the Cub. Cornelia was ready to leave, too. The last the women saw of the man, he was holding onto a wingtip of each airplane, immobilized, unable to solve the problem of what to do with them in the high wind.

All the young men guffawed at the story. Esther and I exchanged looks and left.

Back at the barracks, the laundry room was a busy place. WAFS were at the washtub, the clothesline, and the ironing board. The showers were getting a good workout, too. Many of the girls, upon going in or coming out, paused at Jamesy's room, where she lay in the comfort of her chaise lounge. We didn't remain there long, for we had much to do. But for a few moments our light, gossipy banter was brought down to earth by the ballast of the problems we had found, faced, and fought with during our recent flights.

Barbara Towne had the distinction of having had a solo mission. Along the way, an airport where she expected to get gasoline had closed, so she went on until, low on fuel, she landed on a country road. She bought gasoline from a filling station and went on to make a safe delivery. After hearing her story, I resolved thereafter to be conscious of roads as possible landing strips. I began to inspect roads along my way and to judge quickly their width, inclines, and the presence of adjacent wires or other hazards.

One group of WAFS had landed at the Indianapolis Municipal Airport and had obtained service with the company owned by the famous racing pilot Roscoe Turner. The girls fretted inwardly as the employees dragged their feet, moving from one airplane to another, putting gas in the tanks as slowly as they could. Then the WAFS were forced to wait a long time as the office force processed the forms to be signed so that Roscoe could get his money from the government.

When one of the pilots, worried about the time and the weather, spoke to him, Roscoe said that he wanted "to use my gasoline on my own civilian operations instead of wasting it on the government's war effort." We listeners realized that we, forever destined to fly tiny military aircraft with short ranges, inefficiently-small gas tanks, and seemingly built-in headwinds, must make a special effort to avoid gassing at Indianapolis.

Once, standing near the center of Jamesy's room, Helen Mary said with remorse, "If the WAFS don't pass their three months probation, it will be my fault."

Her announcement rolled back anything hanging at the edge of anyone's tongue. A wary silence suffused the room.

She went on, "Florene and I delivered those two Cubs where we were supposed to. But the squadron had moved on to another base. We didn't know at first what to do. Then the colonel on the base where we delivered said he wanted those airplanes. So he called our operations for permission to take them and sign for them. After he hung up, he turned to us and said, 'The Second Ferrying Group says it'll be all right for me to take delivery. Now, if you'll hand me the papers, I'll sign for them and you can be on your way.'

"We were glad he was so nice to take care of everything, so we did it. Then, golly! As soon as we got back, operations said Colonel Baker wanted to see us. This time I knew I'd done nothing wrong. We went to his office and he demanded to know why we had let that colonel have those airplanes when they were meant for another squadron."

Helen Mary paused and looked about the floor before raising her eyes to search our faces. Every eye was on her.

She said, "I told him, 'But operations told him he could have them.'

"He said, 'Captain Matz told me he said that.'

"So I felt I could justify myself. I said, 'I can't see that we did anything wrong in giving him the planes.' I was mystified by Colonel Baker's stern expression.

"He said, 'You made a bad mistake. You should have spoken directly to operations yourself on the telephone.'

"I still believed we had acted correctly, so I asked him, 'Can't we even trust an officer and a gentleman?'

"And he finished off with this: 'No, not even if he is a colonel.' "

Following this recital were outbursts and misgivings about the administration of the Ferry Command, crochety Colonel Baker, the whims of operations, and so forth. We felt that these men were justified in testing WAFS, but they weren't about to let us get by with any mistake that men had no doubt made before we did.

Helen Mary went to her room. After she left, guessing began as to the cause of our hazing. The consensus was that Delphine's broken prop at DuPont must have been it. But Barbara Poole said, "She's not the only one who lost a prop."

That statement arrested our conjectures and the silence that ensued gave Barbara the floor. "We couldn't get out of Lockhaven on account of the rain," she began, "and when we did, we avoided it by going to Middletown and Quantico. We thought we'd RON at Charlottesville, Virginia. When we circled the field there, some guys ran out and waved their arms and acted pretty silly. I couldn't figure out what they were doing that for. The field looked all right to me."

Barbara stopped for breath and then emphasized, "We simply had to stop there for gas. I got tired and just went in and landed. The Cub didn't roll very far before it went up on its nose and broke the prop."

"I wasn't going to snitch on you," said Teresa. "But that field was pretty muddy. It must have rained there for days."

"I was leading Towne," continued Barbara, "but she got in all right. She made a good stalled landing and cut her switch. And then Cornelia came on in and when she nosed over, the tip of her prop got it, too."

"The funny one to see was Helen Richards," added Teresa. "She circled the field and dragged it several times and then picked out what she thought was a good, solid spot. Her nose bowed down a couple of times, but she made it. When she got out of the Cub, she sank in mud up to her knees!"

"Gillies and Erickson were with us, too, but they were luckier than we were,'' concluded Barbara.

If we don't anticipate problems better, I thought, we'd soon be landing back in civilian life. Suddenly I remembered my bulletin board idea. Anything, just anything to help save our squadron and avoid disaster. I walked down the hall and dared to intrude on Nancy's off-duty hours by knocking on her door.

''Come in,'' she said, and I did.

My parents had never taught me the little ceremonial polish of leading into a topic after verbalizing nonessential trivia. We didn't have time for such luxuries. So I jumped right in with my idea so I wouldn't waste her time or mine.

''Nancy,'' I offered, ''let's have a bulletin board in the barracks so when we come back from trips we can put on it all the stuff we found out that would help the other WAFS. If we listed the airports we found were closed, it would save someone going in there.

''And I just heard that Roscoe Turner isn't very cooperative about giving service in Indianapolis. We'd avoid such places if we knew about them. Some of the hotels we get into could be listed as 'great' or 'poor,' and if there are nurses' quarters where we could stay at some fields, it would save us the trouble and expense of going into town.''

With all that off my mind, I waited for its effect.

Nancy replied, ''I think that's a good idea. If you want to make up a notice of what you girls have learned, I'll see about getting a bulletin board installed as soon as I can. But I wanted to see you about another matter. How did Esther do?''

''She was too timid about navigating any of the legs. I thought I wouldn't push her. If she feels more relaxed and doesn't have so much to worry about, something might soak in.''

''Isn't Esther gaining any confidence?''

''No, not yet. She's too self-conscious and tense.''

My answers were based on years of observing pupils and flight students when they tried something new on them. I thought that Esther's fear of being judged wanting in navigation skills could possibly stem from a lack of flight experience that didn't coincide with her logbook. I could have been wrong, of course, and I really wanted to help the woman, not hurt her. Besides, she was a challenge to my instructing ability. But I'd never tell Nancy what was going on in my mind.

''When do you think she may be able to lead a flight?'' Nancy persisted.

''I don't know that. I might be able to tell you when we get back,'' I replied. ''I'll try to have her ready this time. You can't tell on what day a student will solo, but things fall into place, you know. And Esther is only a great big kid.''

There was a flash of anger in Nancy's reply as she rose to indicate that the interview was ended. She looked at the door and said, ''Esther is a big fat slob.''

I was speechless. I left and closed the door, closing my lips at the same time. This was something I couldn't share with anyone. To do so would degrade Nancy and humiliate Esther.

By 9 A.M. on Monday, November 16, we were on a C-60 going to Lockhaven. We still didn't have our winter flying suits, but we had our money. Fortunately Cubhaven was running smoothly and the airplanes were ready. At noon we went into town to eat at Henry's Dairy Lunch. Upon our return, the weather report nudged us in the direction of Middletown, a distance of seventy-four miles at a magnetic heading of 160 degrees.

''How about you taking this?'' I asked Esther.

''I don't want to chance it,'' she replied.

We flew mainly at right angles to the mountain ridges. Erosion had cut into much of the rock, leaving many small peaks of harder rock above the terrain. On either side of many of these ridges were roads in the valleys and the beginnings of great rivers, visible as tiny creeks. Runoff water coursed their downward slopes.

What struck me more than anything about Pennsylvania was the ugliness of the little towns beaded at random along the roads and the slag heaps — evidence of mining for underground resources without concern for those above ground. Tears came to my eyes as I saw what had been done to a beautiful country.

We crossed the Susquehanna between Liverpool and Halifax, touched the northeast corner of a tongue of Harrisburg, and came to the area over Middletown. Olmsted Field looked just like another small community until I dropped below 1,000 feet, searching for it, knowing that it must be there. The camouflage was effective to about 600 feet off the deck, and I stayed at that altitude because no other airplanes but ours were in sight. Esther followed me in like a gosling after its mother.

The Penn-Harris in Harrisburg was our choice of hotel. Because we were stopping at an army installation, transportation was arranged for us in the morning, and an employee drove us into town that evening.

For the first time since Esther and I left Macon, I had time to write to Harold. I told him, ''Maybe you'd better ask Kratz's manager how much they'll pay CPTP instructors and what kind of a deal they've got. Three girls have lost props already and if that keeps up, the WAFS are on the way out.''

The next day visibility was poor and the ceiling was low. We hung around the airport, waiting, looking in at the weather bureau every hour as the airway sequences came clacking into the teletype machine. Finally at midday, the ceiling lifted. The sun filtered through the cloud layer to warm the earth and it burned off the bottom of the clouds. Visibility extended to at least three miles.

We four agreed to try for Waynesboro. We figured the hop wouldn't take more than an hour. Rhonie led off and she flew a good leg, but the winds added ten minutes to our time. The air was quite cool.

We thought our luck would hold if we went on to Winchester. I was still leading Esther, but this time Richards navigated for Rhonie. I said before we left, "I don't like the operator there. But we have to get this show on the road." We did, but a strong crosswind added fifteen minutes more than last time to our hop.

At Winchester the weather sequences indicated that the atmosphere ahead wasn't cooperative. We'd have to remain overnight. The atmosphere at the airport warmed up, however. Flight students in the ready room spoke to us pleasantly. We wondered aloud where we should stay that night. One of the fellows said, "If you don't mind not going to a hotel, there's a tourist home near here and it's very nice."

We looked at each other. Rhonie didn't object.

The young man continued, "You won't have to worry about it. Take a look first, and if you don't like it, we'll see that you get into downtown to the hotel."

He drove us to the tourist home, a large white frame house with a matching picket fence. Each of us was shown to a room with a double bed. Mine was next to the common bathroom. It was neat, clean, and comfortable, and cost $1.25.

One of the instructors we'd met telephoned and asked all of us out to dinner, along with several of his students. We accepted gladly. He came by for us and took us to a little restaurant. One of the students was a petite girl, Virginia Alleman, who was so pretty and friendly that she had been chosen as the apple blossom queen of Winchester. She wanted to enter Jacqueline Cochran's school, so we told her what we knew about it. It was an agreeably happy dinner party, made more so when the instructor insisted on picking up the check. Our per diem appeared to be more than adequate for this mission.

Back at the tourist home, we decided that we'd repeat the course laid out last week, at least to Charlotte. That resolved, no paperwork faced us. I slept long and well in my comfortable double bed and wished that I had it back at the barracks.

The next morning at the airport the sequences showed the inclement weather had moved to the east. We thought we'd be able to put in a good day's work, and we were eager to show our efficiency. But the leg from Winchester to Staunton was twenty-five minutes longer than last time. We flew against a crosswind and ground speed averaged only forty-five miles per hour.

As the day wore on, we realized we would be riding gusts all the way. On the leg into Lynchburg, in order to avoid the bumps, we flew at a higher altitude which cut down our ground speed even more, for the headwinds were stronger. The course was familiar, because our previous checkpoints remained visible longer, and the novelty of a strange landscape had already worn off. Navigating was too easy, so I decided to cut out the Danville stop for gas and go directly to Greensboro-High Point, thereby cutting off some mileage and some time spent in traffic patterns.

On this mission we had economical engines. Mine used only 4.1 gallons of gas per hour. There was no reason why we couldn't make the longer hop and still have forty-five minutes' reserve fuel left in our tanks upon landing.

I led off again, trying to follow a bobbing compass by averaging a course of about 210 to 215 degrees. At first there were plenty of things to recognize — the Roanoke River, Altavista with its four bridges, and so forth. But beginning one mile west of Motley, the easy checkpoints were behind us. The roads to Gretna showed up from the west and Gretna itself peeked out from behind a hill as we passed by. Then there was nothing on the chart and no distinguishable features on the ground. All I could do was to look ahead and try to keep several things, a barn for instance, lined up on the same spot on the windshield. Twenty to twenty-five minutes of this procedure made me wonder if I were doing anything wrong.

Some transmission lines appeared, crossing a stream, but the jiggling stream didn't correspond with those angles of a stream crossing my penciled course on my chart. For several minutes I was frightened. I maintained my course until I could orient myself, which was not easy as I tried to look at the chart and not lose track of which scenic features I was using as guides. I was also trying to fly straight ahead, although gusts of wind were throwing the Cub about as if it were a leaf in the sky.

Soon I passed a hill on my right and just beyond it a transmission line came into view. Luckily I found that hill on the chart. The vegetation showed me that a stream had its beginnings there, and I saw a single track railroad, then a highway paralleling the trees. Ahead was a power station at Cascade, and then I was sure of where I was. The wind had begun to die down, and I had drifted three miles off course. I altered my course about five degrees eastward and gradually the distance between me and my intended course disappeared. In the space of twenty miles, I was on course again, near Wentworth. Cautiously I watched for every indication of vegetation along streams. Finally I saw the lumber mill at Summerfield. We got to High Point only five minutes later than we had the week before and this time we had coped with a wilder, stronger headwind.

While we washed our hands in the restroom, Esther said, "It's absolutely uncanny how you can fly a straight line with nothing to go by."

"I got a little off course on that one," I answered.

"But there weren't any checkpoints I could see and we had such poor visibility flying right into the sun."

To change the subject I said, "Winter is coming soon. Did you see the snow in the high places of the mountains in Virginia today?"

"Yes, and I don't like to see it. I don't like cold weather very much," said Esther. We hurried out to catch the next weather sequence just coming in over the teletype.

It took only ten minutes more flying time than the last trip to reach Charlotte's Morris Field. The wind died down as the afternoon wore on. Economy was the reason I wanted to remain in Charlotte that night. Another flight of WAFS had reported they had stayed at the nurses' quarters there. As soon as we got into operations to close our flight plans, I asked about the times meals were served in the officers' mess and maneuvered the four of us into the nurses' quarters. The night nurse allowed me to use her room while she was on duty.

Morris Field was completely paved with a black surface, which made it difficult for a pilot to judge her distance while landing if she was facing the setting sun. But we couldn't complain. The air was springlike in its warmth and felt like balm to our faces after the chill we had been enduring in Pennsylvania and Virginia.

That evening, alone in my assigned room, I wrote again to Harold and confessed that when I was confronted with the choice of being patriotic and leaving him and our home, I was stunned and as unable to decide for myself as if I had been hypnotized. And now that I was doing what I had left him to do, I was so busy that at night all I wanted to do was to go to sleep. On the last mission, my first as a leader, I did paperwork until 1 A.M. This time I made out the forms as we went along, which meant we had to remain a little longer at each stop.

Esther and I separated from Rhonie and Richards the next morning. They were headed south and we were going southwest. I had begun to question Nelson about what she observed on the ground as we flew over it. I felt she should be ready to navigate pretty soon. But I took out first from Charlotte to Greenville. With a tailwind we breezed along and made the eighty-seven miles in sixty-five minutes.

Then we went on to Athens, Georgia, making eighty-three miles in seventy minutes. I could see that if one got off course a bit, it was easy to become confused. A multitude of little streams, twisting and turning, were hard to identify. However they all moved southeasterly.

It was only sixty-seven miles from Athens to Atlanta. The magnetic heading was about 252 degrees. We inspected the chart carefully, looking for landmarks that Esther should be able to identify easily. I had babied her long enough.

Esther led out. We hadn't gone far before she was off course, flying between the Oconee River and the road from Princeton to Watkinsville. I bent my throttle forward and passed her on the right, waving a signal by dipping my wing to the right several times, so she would realize that she should move in that direction. I got us back on course and then led us into Atlanta. I still had a problem, all right!

After we gassed up at Atlanta, we went out to the takeoff area before revving up our engines to check the magnetos. My left mag lost more than 100 rpm. I tried again. The drop in power was too much. I caught Esther's eye and waved my thumb back toward the flight line. We taxied back. A spark plug wasn't functioning correctly. We had to remain overnight while it was changed.

I warned Esther about the danger later. "I tell you, Esther," I said, "I'll never forget the time I was taking Robertson's Cub off Lambert to another field and I couldn't get any altitude. Even to circle the airport, I couldn't make it to a thousand feet. I nursed that thing around and brought it down. All it was was one spark plug. I wouldn't chance taking off, knowing there's a drop in a mag."

Atlanta's Chandler Field was a civilian airport, but the military took up a great part of it. The hangars were chock-full of small airplanes. The field was very busy with a heck of a lot of flying going on. There was a Hotel DeGink there, but no place for us. Someone gave us transportation into town, where we stayed at a hotel on Peachtree Street. As usual, we walked about for several blocks before turning in.

For about ten minutes Esther and I reviewed the last leg of the day. And then we planned tomorrow's trip from Atlanta to Opelika.

"You mustn't feel embarrassed about circling the field after you've gained altitude," I reminded her. "All these fields are strange the first time we take off. Later, when we fly the same legs again, we'll know what to look for in the air and it'll be easier to head out in the right direction. Let's not take any chances."

Using the point of a pencil, we moved down the line she'd drawn on her chart. I pointed out to her how we wouldn't be very far from a single track railroad, beginning in Moreland, then on to St. Charles and Grantville. We wouldn't fly east of that track until we reached the vicinity of Cusseta. If she got south of it, she was to crab to the right a bit. If she lost sight of it, she should edge her plane toward it, even if her flight path wasn't straight. She would never be more than five or six miles past one town before she would be in sight of the next one ahead. It would be a comparatively easy task to navigate.

I could see that Esther didn't trust the compass because it didn't remain steady. So I reviewed with her again how she must not only average the pendulum-like swings of the compass, but also must line up objects ahead in order to stay on her heading.

The next morning Esther flew an acceptable flight to Opelika. Her confidence didn't sprout like an onion in a warm bin, but at least her feelings of inadequacy weren't as firm as they had been before. I thought that ninety minutes of responsibility was enough for her for one day, so I led us into Gunter Field northwest of Montgomery, Alabama. We had been warned that the traffic pattern there was right instead of left turns. It felt a bit strange to follow it, but we fit right in with the students.

Then it was home again from Montgomery's airport. We took the train from Washington, D. C., and arrived at the base late Friday night. Not trusting the administration of our missions, we worked furiously to complete the paperwork for our per diem in order to turn it in on Saturday morning.

"I hope we can stay here until Monday," fretted Esther.

"Me, too," I replied, and then had to go over my column of figures again. The total for days and hours had to be true.

The weather at Wilmington turned colder on Sunday. The ceiling was minimum. I decided we wouldn't get an urgent request from operations for at least an hour and went to church. No one in our group thrilled to the notion of attending church services. I didn't anticipate using my brain cells as I usually did to mentally dispute the preacher. At the base chapel an Episcopalian minister officiated for the Protestant church services. He may or may not have been typical of that denomination's clergy. First he told us what he was going to tell us. Then he told us. He finished by telling us what he had just told us. It was restful because if I missed even two of his go-arounds, I could always pick it up on the third.

I thought Helen Richards might go with me. My strides took me to her room, where she was reading the paper.

"Want to go to church?" I asked.

Without hesitation she answered yes, put on her uniform blouse and cap, and headed for the doorway. On the way I asked her, "How did you and Rhonie get along."

"She was all right," responded Helen.

"You mean you didn't have any problems?"

"No, nothing much. We RON'd at one field that didn't have any tie-down places for us, so we had to use the metal stakes that went with the airplanes."

Richards didn't speak for a dozen paces. Then she added, "It was cold the next morning and I was ready to leave the stakes in the ground when we untied the ropes, but Pat insisted that we unscrew those things out of the ground. It took a long time, but she wouldn't have it otherwise. She said they went with the planes and if we didn't deliver them, somebody would complain to operations about it."

I began to laugh, imagining the two of them on hands and knees, trying to dig up what resembled an anchor for a dog's exercise chain. Then she began to laugh, too, as we entered the warmth of the chapel.

Back in the BOQ, the second floor telephone rang at 1500. No one else answered it, so I did. It was Nancy.

"Del, we have two flights of PT-19s going to Tennessee. Would you take the girls' names and tell them?"

I got something to write on and she continued, "Gillies, Clark, Meserve, Towne, and James. You, Miller, Richards, Erickson, and Sharp. You and Betty are the flight leaders."

"I'll let them know," I assured her.

"Pick up your orders right away," Nancy warned.

I hung up and started down the hall to the socialite section. Betty and Helen Mary weren't there, but I got hold of the others either in the barracks or at the club next door. Then I called Nancy to tell her about the disappearance of Betty and Helen Mary. She said she would contact them, so I rushed over to pick up everyone's orders.

At 1600, still at operations waiting for a sheaf of about ten orders for each of us, I heard, "WAF Scharr?"

"Yeah?" I answered.

"Phone for you," said a sergeant, laying it on the desk.

I picked it up. "Hello?"

"Del, Nancy Love. I'm glad I caught you. Your flights must be ready to leave the barracks by 1630 or 1645 at the latest."

"I thought we'd leave tomorrow —"

"You told everybody, didn't you?" An edge crept into her smooth voice.

"Yeah. Everybody but Gillies and Clark."

"They'll be there. You simply must catch that train."

"We'll do our best."

I heard the receiver click so I hung up mine. On the counter was the stack of orders. I grabbed them and ran as fast as I could to the barracks.

How we hurried! We tried to remember to bring everything we needed. Masterfully we threw our duds together into our B-4 bags, maps joined ruler, pencil, and plastic navigational aids in the navigation case. Atop our parachutes we stuffed the winter flying suits. In all, we each had about ninety pounds of equipment to carry. Betty Gillies didn't look as if she weighed much more than that.

It was every girl for herself in her struggle to get her burdens down the stairs, across the first floor hall, then down the front steps of BOQ 14, across the lawn, and into the truck taking us to the depot downtown.

The truck lumbered along as fast as the driver could manage it. Nervously I looked at my watch and wondered if we could catch the train. I had no idea how a southbound train could take us to Hagerstown, Pennsylvania; maybe we'd connect with another.

Betty and I were the first ones off. We hurried to the ticket counter and she told me to make my T/R for Baltimore. We scribbled our·requests as if the devil himself were trying to catch us. In retrospect, maybe he was.

"No, the train hasn't arrived yet," said the stationmaster when Betty asked him. "It'll be here any minute."

She and I shepherded the girls and all our baggage as close to the door leading to the boarding platform as the throng of waiting passengers allowed us to. I could see by their expressions that they didn't know our great importance in the nation's war effort. They had their places and wouldn't budge an inch.

The stationmaster announced the arrival of the train. Towne and I squeezed out the door and stood on the platform, listening and looking northward toward Philadelphia. False alarm — no train. We stood there a few moments, mentally urging the train toward us. But a few moments was all we could bear, for our thin woolen uniforms were no barrier to the cold northern wind that smacked against us with every gust. Shivering, we pushed our way back to the others, trying to get warm again.

More than anything, I wanted this mission — my first at leading a group to deliver PT-19s — to be successful. The minutes ticked on.

Somewhere up north a train was dragging its caboose. Impatiently, James and I snaked through the crowd and onto the platform again. Still no train. The raw wind grew more brutal each time we went to look. By now the train was forty minutes late.

Finally we could hear it in the distance. By the time it hissed to a stop, the people in the waiting room had closed ranks to get on board. With what we had to carry, we could not squeeze through or ahead of anyone. The conductor helped lift our baggage to the floor level of the coaches. It was up to each of us to find a place for ourselves. At last we were aboard. We stood, situated in two adjoining coaches, our bags cluttering the aisles.

It was Sunday night and the train was crowded. Soldiers were returning to their posts after a weekend pass and civilians who had been visiting servicemen were returning home. Everyone was tired.

A serviceman offered Florene his seat, which she graciously accepted. There wasn't another soul in our coach who was overcome by the pulchritude of the rest of us. Betty Gillies sat on her parachute bag. The other shorties tried it, too, but they did knee bends every few minutes, as people made their way back and forth down the aisle, bound for the restroom or balancing a paper cup filled with water. When I tried it, my knees found no space to claim for their own. I didn't relish being pushed and shoved as people squeezed by, so I stood all the way to Baltimore, swinging like the north pole of a magnet each time another magnet (passenger) inched by.

Finally, arriving an hour late, the train pulled into Baltimore. Now it was our turn to push and shove, trying to leave the train before the conductor yelled, "All aboard!" By dragging the parachute bags behind us and hoisting the B-4 bags ahead, we escaped the crush of passengers who refused to make way and those trying to board.

With indifferent results we began to hail whatever redcaps were visible. I had not eaten nor had anything to drink since breakfast. A refreshment stand dispensing soft drinks and hot coffee caught my attention. I was tired and ordered a cup of coffee, not realizing that the sanitary conditions might not pass a health inspector's test. Betty was grimly waving at us that she had arranged for taxis.

"Hurry," she said. "We were told to make connections with a bus to take us to Hagerstown and we've kept them waiting long enough already."

We looked at our watches. It was five minutes to nine (2100). As soon as the luggage was stowed, we piled in and were off. But we had missed the bus. When Betty asked why the bus hadn't waited for us, the clerk at the terminal said, "But don't you know there is no government priority on the bus lines? We couldn't hold up the bus for you even if we had known you were coming.''

"When will the next bus leave for Hagerstown?'' asked Betty.

"It leaves here at eleven and gets into Hagerstown at 4:30 tomorrow morning.''

"That must be a milk run,'' I said. We found out the next bus after that left at seven and arrived at ten. I turned over in my mind what would be the sensible thing to do. A five-and-a-half-hour ride versus a three-hour ride. If we took the first, we could eat, but we wouldn't be fit for flying those PTs out of Hagerstown when we got there. If we took the later bus, we might get a quick meal and get some sleep before continuing our journey. I was very tired by then and my throat felt raw and scratchy.

"Betty,'' I said, "let's eat and go to a hotel and get some sleep.'' She agreed.

When we got to the hotel, the clerk quoted his prices to us. Betty gave him a commanding stare and voiced her knowledge that hotels were giving service personnel cheaper rates as their part in the war effort. Since we were in uniform, she bluffed him. We put our things into our rooms and immediately headed for Thompson's Restaurant across the street. It was well known for its oyster stew and chili.

Meserve and I didn't get to bed until midnight, after we had drawn our courses on our charts and noted the mileages. The next morning we were awake at 0530 because we wanted to be certain to have a seat on that bus. I was feeling lousy by this time, but I refused to accept the evidence of illness, hoping that it would go away.

We boarded the bus. As we wound our way across country toward our destination, the weather looked increasingly poor for flying. To make matters worse, the bus made a number of stops and we did not reach Hagerstown until almost eleven o'clock. All our baggage was off before an officer appeared.

Betty greeted him with, "Good morning, Captain Frank.''

He looked worried and ignored her greeting. Sternly he asked, "Where have you been?''

Betty said, "We missed our bus and rather than wait and take a bus at midnight, we RON'd in Baltimore and took this one.''

He replied, "There's nothing in your orders that gives you permission to RON on your way to pick up an airplane.''

"Why is that such a big deal?'' I put in crossly.

"You were supposed to get off that first bus and when you weren't on it, I figured you'd be on the next one. So I was here at 0430 to meet you.''

I didn't dare express my thought, that he was upset because he had been inconvenienced.

Captain Frank continued, "I called NCAAB to find out if they had sent you. Nobody knew where you were."

No one cowed Betty and neither did she kowtow to anyone. Her training and experience led her to managing others deftly, leaving them with no alternative except to obey her. She looked Captain Frank right in the eye, lifting her chin proudly, and calmly stated, "The reason we RON each night on a mission is so that operations knows where every airplane is until it is delivered. We don't have any airplanes yet. I'm sure that except for that, they aren't concerned about us."

Captain Frank changed the subject. He glanced at the sky. "We might as well not go to the factory today," he said.

"How long has the airport been socked in?" asked Betty.

"It was closed early yesterday afternoon," he replied.

"Then why did they rush us over here?" asked Teresa.

No answer.

"It's all my fault," exclaimed Helen Mary, believing that we were being hazed.

Captain Frank had staff cars waiting. The drivers assisted us in loading them with our bulky baggage. Then we were driven to the Hamilton Hotel. My throat was so swollen by now that I could hardly swallow. For lunch I tried soup. And I had nothing to say.

As soon as I got back to the room, I drew warm water for a bath. Betty knocked on my door and I let her in. She looked directly at me and asked, "Are you ill?"

"My throat's a little sore," I admitted.

"Maybe we'd better send for a doctor."

"I don't want a doctor. All I want is to take a bath and lie down and I'll feel better." I spoke crossly.

"Well, you can do that. You'd better go to bed. But your face is gray." She came to me and put her hand on my brow.

"And you have a fever."

"I don't want a doctor!" I repeated, irritation showing in my voice. I immediately felt ashamed. "I want to lead the flight and I'm going to." The crankiness of my voice frightened me, for it was as if another person were saying those things and I had no control over her.

"Do you want me to stay while you take your bath?"

I shook my head no, feeling that if I spoke again I would make matters worse.

"Stay in bed, then" she said and closed the door as she left.

While I was brushing my teeth, I opened my mouth wide in front of the lighted bathroom mirror. It was as I suspected, but I rebelled against my fate. How could I have been so stupid, I thought. Was it the cold north wind on the platform, or the crowd of passengers in the station, or could it have been that questionable cup of coffee? Why hadn't I waited to take a drink?

Once before I had had a strep throat. Thinking it was just a sore throat, I'd gone to Dr. Gundlach who gave me some sulpha tablets and told me to go home immediately. That time, too, I was adamant about having my way. I had told him, "I have to go to Lambert and fly." Students were waiting for me.

He replied, "Of course you do. But just go past your home on the way out there."

I conceded to that much. By the time I got home, I was so ill that I couldn't leave the flat. For me, strep was deadly and cut me down rapidly.

Betty moved my roommate Gertie from my room. Then the army doctor, Colonel Starkes, came to examine me. I shook my head. My face was as gray as death itself. The doctor said nothing as he depressed my tongue, took my temperature, and felt my pulse. He turned to Betty and said, "Temperature is 102." I didn't care what it was. My head ached so much I thought the pressure would split it.

He continued to talk to Betty. "She must remain in bed and drink lots of fluids."

She asked, "What is it, Colonel?"

"The flu," he replied.

Ha! I thought. A lot you know about it.

Colonel Starkes left me some sulphanilamide tablets. Before he left, he told us about his son in the navy who had been in the Battle of Midway and of some of his encounters with enemy fire. I paid little attention, but gathered that he was quite proud of his offspring.

On Monday morning, Betty and the others came to see me, staying their distance — at her urging, no doubt, for her nurses' training made her more aware than they were of the seriousness of my illness. Uppermost in everyone's mind was the question, why had operations ladled out to ten WAFS the unnecessary ordeal we had endured the past two days?

Teresa said, "I sure wish the navy would start a women's ferry group. I'd leave those bastards in Wilmington just like that," and she snapped her fingers.

"I talked to Nancy about that," ventured Betty. "She said I'd have her blessing if I began an outfit like this in the navy. So I got in touch with Bud and we're waiting to see what happens.''

''The navy has a better reputation for getting things done shipshape without so much red tape,'' said Teresa.

Painfully I added, ''I'd like to join the navy.''

Meserve said, ''Helen Mary thinks she's responsible for all this.''

''She may not be the one to blame,'' said Betty. ''I got in touch with Nance. She said Pat was in trouble with operations. She and whoever is with her got to the base where they were supposed to deliver and the squadron had moved 500 miles farther on. Pat called NCAAB and asked, 'Shall we leave the L-4Bs here or take them to where the squadron is?' They told her to go the 500 miles and deliver the Cubs to the proper squadron. So they're flying on and they don't know yet that they're in trouble.''

''Trouble? How can they be in trouble?'' asked Evelyn Sharpe.

''Because they're traveling without orders.''

''Can you beat that?'' sighed Teresa, shaking her head.

''Somebody's a little crazy,'' I whispered.

And then they left me, for Betty shushed them out of the room. She saw how much strain their visit was to me.

About an hour later, Lieutenant Shearer arrived from Camp Ritchie to see how I was. Betty stood in attendance as he examined me.

He addressed her. ''We'll have to put her in a hospital. What is her status. Civilian?''

''Yes,'' replied Betty.

''Then we can't admit her to our hospital. I recommend that she be admitted to the Washington County Hospital here.''

A fine state of affairs! There I was, in the armed services of my country, taken sick while on orders for a mission, and my branch of the service wouldn't even take care of my illness.

The county hospital agreed to admit me that afternoon, when a new billing period began. All my paraphernalia was carted along with me. By that time I didn't care much about anything. The girls watched sadly as I was wheeled past them on a stretcher. My right hand lifted and flapped a limp good-bye. The only stern expression was on B. J. Erickson's face. I had heard she was a Christian Scientist and didn't believe in illness. If she thinks I'm making this up, she's crazy, I thought.

On Tuesday I found out that I had been taken from the orders. Teresa James replaced me as flight leader and another pilot might come from Wilmington to join the team. No one knew for certain. The news dejected me. Since the weather on Monday and Tuesday was just as disagreeable as it had been on Sunday, the WAFS couldn't leave.

Several of them came to see me in the hospital. Teresa asked me to write down my address so she could notify Harold that I was sick and to reassure him that I would get along fine.

Teresa didn't tell me, however, that most of the others had also developed sore throats. They didn't feel very well, but no one ailed for more than a few days. While they were following Betty's prescriptions for recovery, Jamesy was composing a doggerel saga about the tribulations of the WAFS. At the moment, it centered on my problems. Teresa had so much energy that it spilled over into creative efforts. And I found out later that Evelyn Sharp had entertained the others by walking on her hands.

I was in room 365, which had two beds but no other occupant. I was kept busy. Every so often a bright young nurse came in with a salty, hot gargle. With each repetition, it grew more distasteful. They doped me up with sulfa and something else — I was groggy.

Some of the attention I got I didn't ask for. Nurses brought me orange juice and milk at off hours and stayed to talk. They tried on my winter flying equipment and giggled like children. I felt like a celebrity. Now and then a nurse from a different floor looked in to say "Hello, how are you?" and then disappear. I suspected they were curious about a strange creature who flew airplanes.

I heard noises. The children's ward was nearby. For three years I hadn't recalled how many sounds children can make. The noise took away my dejection and the sense of loneliness that I had when I entered the hospital.

And the WAFS helped, too. They had tried to leave on Wednesday but late in the afternoon had to return to the hotel. Before they left, they sent me a beautiful bouquet of yellow and orchid mums. It must have been Teresa's idea. Nancy sent me red roses. Others in Wilmington also sent flowers.

I felt so rich and popular that I longed to share the feeling with others. Most of the hospital was made up of wards, so I asked the nurses to leave me a few roses and mums and to scatter the rest of the flowers among the wards to brighten their Thanksgiving.

No word came from the WAFS that evening, so I knew those birds had flown away. That was something to be thankful for. Being weathered in is a trial to the pilot who would rather fly than do anything else. How I wished I could have gone with them! How I resented the cruel genius who had sent us to the Fairchild factory on Sunday instead of later in the week. Who was it?

Waves of loneliness, sadness, weakness, and frustration rushed into my mind whenever I was alone very long. My heart pounded from the sulfa I was taking. Yet the Washington County Hospital nurses were so friendly and cheerful that my morose thoughts ebbed each time one entered my room. I felt this must be the best hospital in the world.

On Friday the postman brought a card from Teresa. Four telegrams came from the girls waiting at Lockhaven for clear weather. Everyone was trying to make me smile. Dr. Porterfield, who was my physician, told me that he was a cousin of the Porterfield who manufactured planes in Kansas City. I knew about that plane. I had flown it at Lambert Field and watched it fly. The doctor was so proud to be connected with the aviation industry even remotely that I hadn't the heart to tell him that the Porterfield was a clunker, a ground- loving, underpowered aircraft that was too inefficient for the army to use as liaison in battle.

On Saturday a woman of about my age was brought in to the other bed in my room. She began to smoke cigarettes as soon as she arrived, stopping only when a nurse came in to give her a quick stab in the finger for a blood count. Soon she was whisked away to the operating room for an appendectomy. Fortunately for me, she was given a new intravenous anesthetic instead of the usual ether — the smell of ether makes me ill.

On Sunday evening, Dr. Porterfield dropped in to see me and said, ''We're letting you go tomorrow.''

I knew that my temperature had been normal for two days. I swallowed, testing the feel of it. My throat had not yet healed.

''What did I have?'' I asked.

''Streptococcus hemolyticus and staphylococcus albus,'' he answered. Ah, what an impressive mouthful to repeat to display my medical knowledge and the extent of my illness.

I looked out the window at the dribbling snow. It followed the showers we'd been having off and on all during the day.

''Maybe they'll give me an airplane to deliver since I'm here already,'' I said.

''You won't be flying,'' replied Dr. Porterfield. ''I'm sure you'll be grounded for at least a week after you take sulfa. It does something to your blood.''

I would rather have faced flying on a mission than the problem of returning to Wilmington with ninety pounds of baggage to lug around. I felt as weak as an infant.

No one on the hospital staff mentioned a bill before I left. It was sent to NCAAB and forwarded to me at Romulus, Michigan, in early April 1943. I paid it as soon as I received it. My six days of hospital care cost $24, the routine lab fee was $2, the CBC $3.50, and the throat culture was $2. My drug bill was $3.15, making the total $34.65, considerably less than the cost of one lab test today.

On Monday, November 30, at eleven o'clock, a driver sent by Captain Frank picked me up at the hospital and took me to the Fairchild factory airport. Captain Frank greeted me there and said, "You'll board that airplane just coming in. They'll take you back to Wilmington."

The plane, a twin-engine cargo, landed and a group of six men disembarked, each lugging as much as I had to carry. No one knew me. No one offered to help me until I started to struggle toward the plane. Then an enlisted man took my burdens and stowed them in the fuselage for me. I felt terribly weak and my heart pounded in my breast as if it intended to fly away. I was grateful that I had a flight home. I don't think I could have survived on a bus and train.

I overheard the captain who had the manifest talking with Captain Frank and the other operations personnel. He said, ". . . people who goof off and say they are sick." I knew whom he was talking about. But my conscience was clear and I owed him no explanation. He was, I learned later, Captain Matz, the man with the ugly false teeth and popping eyes, in charge of operations in Wilmington. It was he who sent us to Hagerstown, knowing full well the weather was bad.

After taking off from Hagerstown, we landed in Wilmington within forty minutes. Captain Matz taxied to a parking spot at least 300 feet from the entrance to the operations office. Neither he nor the copilot acted as if I were there. No one offered to assist me with my load.

I pulled down my B-4 bag and carried it to the building. Then I rested and went back for the parachute bag. I shoved it from the fuselage feeling hurt and angry. I carried it, too, but had to stop every twenty feet or so and let it drop to the ground. It was all I could do to carry myself. With every step, I thought less and less of the officers in charge of the base. And when I went inside to arrange for transportation to BOQ 14, I overheard Captain Matz tell someone that he "had to bring her back because I was told to do it. I was deadheading back to the base, and there was plenty of room in the fuselage."

What had just taken place was the beginning of what later came to be known as SNAFU Airlines. The need for more rapid transportation of pilots from a base to an airplane factory became more urgent in 1943, 1944, and 1945. Surface transportation and airlines were not efficient. Pilots needing to change planes often had to spend hours in an airport, which wasted not only time, but also per diem expenses. So a military system evolved to take care of this situation. The navy had its own air transportation system known as NATS. The air force named its system, MATS, Military Air Transport Service. It survives today as MAC, the Military Airlift Command.

The pilots at Wilmington, especially the WAFS, were at a disadvantage in getting to and from NCAAB. Our airport wasn't exactly a hub of commercial air transportation. One had to board or depart from an airliner either at Washington, D.C., or at Philadelphia. From there, one connected with an eastern seaboard train via taxicab. The arrangement was costly to us in time, energy, and money. Yet the Ferry Command did not seem concerned that its regulations caused delays.

One of the most cumbersome procedures was moving our baggage in railroad stations. Most often redcaps ignored us — they'd rather carry something small, like a cosmetics case, than our bulky gear. It was always a long distance from the waiting room to the coach car we had to board. And, of course, the flight leader had to fill out a T/R for the trip in order to get tickets, which meant waiting in line. We developed a system. Two girls carried their B-4 bags as far as they could. Then one remained to guard them while the other returned to the starting point. She stood guard over the parachute bags while another one or two WAFS carried their B-4 bags to the relay point. Again one stood guard while the others returned for more gear. By degrees, we made our way to the train.

Sometimes I got impatient and dragged the parachute bag behind me with my right hand while my left carried the B-4 bag. I paid for it with a strain in the small of my back. The small women, like Phyllis Burchfield, looked no larger than their burdens, yet they refused to complain to the men or to each other.

After I got back to the base, I reported to the flight surgeon who declared that I was grounded. On the way back to the barracks, I stopped to see Nancy.

"I can't fly anyhow," I said to her. "Would it be all right for me to go home this week?"

"I don't like to see you go," she answered, "but there's no reason why you can't. Why don't you see our travel people about making travel arrangements to get you home?"

My heart soared. I didn't know that I could do that. I bought airline tickets from Philadelphia with a change at Pittsburgh and was at home with Harold that very night. Of course Harold had to work most of the five days that I was in St. Louis, but while he was gone I rested. By the time I had to go back, I felt much stronger. But for more than a day before I left home, a sense of foreboding hung over me. When I thought of leaving Harold again, tears welled in my eyes.

On the Baltimore & Ohio "parlor car," as it was called in the East, I had seats 39 and 40 to myself because of an error by the reservations clerk. Each chair was topped with a clean white linen doily, and the attendant spent his time making the car spotless. We even had large rest rooms.

As the train sped along, I kept thinking of Harold and home. To keep from it, I opened the old dictionary I'd brought and read it. I can guarantee that reading a dictionary is a good way to keep from bawling one's eyes out.

A doctor and his wife sat across the aisle from me. They were friendly and spoke pleasantly of inconsequential matters. After we had passed Terre Haute, the train suddenly stopped. A railroad employee ran into our coach yelling, "Is there a doctor in the house?"

The doctor jumped to his feet when the man added, "There's a man dying on the train!"

And he did die, poor fellow. We heard that he had just come back from his sister's funeral. She had died of a heart attack. And now he had, too. His wife was frantic with grief. There was no place on the other coaches for the body, so the porters brought him into the men's room on our car.

In Indianapolis police boarded the train. The coroner made out a death certificate. The body was then carried from the train, followed by his mourning widow. Our journey was delayed by this misfortune. As the train again moved forward, we who had witnessed the incident were greatly sobered by it. The unfortunate death drained the uneasiness from my taut nerves; the foreboding disappeared. It was as if the disaster I had anticipated had happened and there was nothing more to fear.

At dinner, a charming elderly man named Hopkins joined the doctor, his wife, and me in the dining car. He was in the phosphate rock business and told us about his travels.

After we returned to our coach seats, a man walking past on his way to the diner halted and looked at me. "I know you," he said. "You're from Lambert Field." Then after a slight pause, he added, "My name is Mabry."

"Aren't you a TWA mechanic?" I asked.

"I was," he replied, "I'm at Dayton now, working on P-47s and B-17s, and a lot of other army airplanes."

"I'm at Wilmington, Delaware," I said.

"Freddie Koupal is at Wilmington, too," Mabry said.

"Yes, I run into him occasionally."

"Would you take a note to him for me?"

"Yes, of course," I replied.

So he wrote it and I tucked it into my purse without looking at it.

Mabry had an excuse for speaking to me, for I was a familiar face from home. But other men did not. I think every soldier and bore on board stopped at my seat and talked to me that night. Wartime conditions plus my uniform gave them the urge to intrude upon me. People wearing uniforms seemed to feel related to anyone else who wore one.

I was just as guilty as they were. In the seats directly in front of me were a chief petty officer and his wife. I leaned forward and said to them, "My husband is a chief petty officer, too. I'm going to tell him that I saw a chief luckier than he, because he married a redhead." Harold's mother had red hair, and he admired it so much that he wished I had it also.

What I said pleased them. The chief smiled at his wife, who was a real carrot-top. Then he looked back at me and asked, "Where is your husband stationed?"

"Lambert Field."

"I've got a friend who was there — Steve Amhrien. I've just been visiting with the Thorntons."

"Oh, I know them both," I replied.

"What's your husband's name?"

"Harold Scharr. The fellows call him 'Mike' because he always works with a micrometer."

"You know, Steve talked a lot about Mike. I'm stationed at Newark and so is Steve. Tell your husband that Steve made chief six months ago."

The woman behind me must have overhead some of our conversation. She said, "My son is a glider pilot."

"Oh?" I said.

"Maybe you remember him," she said shyly and proudly. "He had you for a flight instructor at Lambert."

"Really?" I asked. "What's his name?"

"Kenny Davis."

"No kidding," I mused. "It's a small world."

The lights in the parlor car did not go off until midnight. I was restless. The wheels kept clacking the rhythm of my name over and over. I couldn't get comfortable. At 4 A.M. I walked the aisle to the water cooler for a drink and ate a tangerine I had brought from home. After that, I promptly fell asleep. The lights turned on abruptly at 8 A.M. We were just outside of Baltimore.

With only one suitcase to burden me, transferring to the northbound train was no trouble at all. As soon as I got to the Wilmington depot, I called the base. The motor pool reported that a truck would arrive soon to carry twelve soldiers back to the base. It showed up, but the soldiers didn't, so I got home free.

I reported in at headquarters. Ellie said that everyone was out. Even Nancy was ferrying. When I got to the barracks, Gertie Meserve was the only old hand there. Some newcomers were in orientation and I didn't see them.

"How're you doing, Gert?" I greeted her.

"Not so good," she replied.

Gert's twin brother and some former Tufts College classmates had met in the Coconut Grove nightclub in Boston. Somehow one of the artificial potted plants had caught fire and the whole place had gone up in flames. People tried to get out through the club's revolving doors, but there was a panic and most of the patrons were trapped and died, her brother among them. I gave her my sympathy.

"I can't understand what's the matter with me," she said. "I went to Wilbur's funeral and came back. And I had an attack just like appendicitis, so I have to see the flight surgeon tomorrow."

"I do, too," I said.

Gert went on. "There's a trip waiting for four girls. Maybe if two more come back soon, we'll get out. Even Nancy is out."

"Yeah, I know," I replied. "I'd better fix up my per diem and find out how they'll dock me for my leave." With that, I returned to my room.

Soon I was in the finance office. There I learned that WAFS were allowed two days' sick leave and two days off duty per month. The officer who reviewed my case decided that I would be docked for one day only. If I should ever apply for my yearly leave, that time interval would remain intact. Financially my situation was becoming happier. So was I.

The next day Helen Mary Clark and Esther Nelson returned from a mission and the following day, they, Meserve and I were on orders as one flight. Helen Mary had the position of flight leader. I felt hurt, as if I'd been demoted. But of course I hadn't been flying for two weeks. That evening we went by Pullman to Lockhaven.

Helen Mary told me that some of the pilots had gone to Montana to take some used airplanes, possibly Stearman primary trainers, to Tennessee. That was a trip I wasn't sorry to miss.

At Philadelphia we had to wait for our train connection. We looked outside to check the weather. As we stood on the concrete steps leading to the sidewalk breathing the crisp air, we noticed a black man frantically trying to open one of the heavy plate glass doors. He was also attempting to support a black woman who appeared to be ill.

There are moments in my life that I regret deeply and this was one of them. My impulse was to run up the steps to help him. But I was aware that Helen Mary was my flight leader and I was under her leadership. I looked first to see what she would do, to get a clue as to her reaction. She, too, was watching the drama, but there was no sign on her face nor in her eyes of her wish to be involved. So I just stood there.

Struggling fiercely with his burden and the heavy door, the man succeeded in getting the woman out into the fresh air after several moments. She promptly slipped through his right arm and lay inert upon the concrete platform. He had been too late; she had already fainted. As she lay there, urine slowly trickled from her body and I could see that the man was ashamed. And I, for not having had the courage to do what I wanted to do, was equally embarrassed for myself. None of us said a thing about it, nor even mentioned the incident, so I do not know what my companions thought. We left then to board our train.

At Cubhaven the airplanes weren't ready for us. Esther said, "We broke our necks to do everything before we left. I wish Piper and operations would get things straight once in a while."

We went to Lockhaven and took it easy. There was Henry's Dairy Lunch and the Fallon Hotel. That evening Esther began razzing me. "Scharr hopes to go west instead of south," she said.

Meserve grinned. She said, "She'll spook the weather bureau, all right."

Even Helen Mary, always dignified, put in her bit. "Since I'm the flight leader, I can choose and I'll take the southern route."

There was a choice this time, for we were bound for the slap- happy state of Texas. On December 11, the weather at Cubhaven was better than I'd ever seen it. I prayed and my prayers were answered. The weather to the south was all bad, but toward the west it looked good. And what lay ahead there? St. Louis, of course.

Helen Mary asked me to take the number two position, so if either of the others got off course I could catch up with her and lead her back to the line. The first leg was an easy course to Stultz Field, between Tyrone and Altoona. All we had to do was to follow the valley along the side of Bald Eagle Mountain. Esther was given the assignment of navigator.

The next hop was mine and it was a difficult leg. I no sooner got out of the valley than the flight was over mountainous terrain that looked as if God had slapped it flat with a board. Erosion had cut ridges and valleys throughout, along which tiny streams flowed. It took imagination to figure which of those streams the chart depicted. In one spot the

Black Lick River wound about on its way westward. When I thought we had left it behind, still more came up ahead. After about ten minutes of more winding river twisting beneath us, we eventually crossed another stream that joined it to the north. I suddenly discovered that I was right on course, above the Loyalhanna River.

Looking back, I could see the tiny zigzags in the road between the two streams. I had crossed at the right one. Intuition or some black magic in balancing the swings about the compass heading of 260 degrees gets the credit for that achievement. By now, east of Pittsburgh, the poor visibility was becoming worse because the wind was from the west.

An airliner passed us on our right, bound for the same airport, no doubt. When I saw the Ohio River below (nothing was visible ahead), Helen Mary passed me on the right to lead us into the Pittsburgh-Allegheny Airport. I thought it odd that she should lead us in a circuitous route to the north of the airport. When we were on the ground, she said, "I've been here many times. I'm afraid of collisions with other airplanes coming east on the radio beam, so I led you girls to the right of the beam to avoid any confrontations."

What a place Pittsburgh was! Smoke belched from great stacks. We couldn't even see the city until we looked back after passing it. Much of the downtown area was built in the "Y" of the junction of the Allegheny and Monongahela rivers, which join to form the Ohio. The airport itself was on a plateau and was surfaced entirely by a macadam layer. Numerous navy planes were parked on the ramp.

We got out of there as rapidly as we could because we had no time to waste. Esther's flight had rambled a bit, so it took seventy minutes to go fifty-eight miles. Mine took ninety minutes for eighty-eight miles. Gert had the next leg to Cambridge, Ohio. It wasn't long before she had shifted to about five miles south of the course. I'd tried to remain on course and to motion with my wing-waving, but she didn't take the hint. So long as she held to a course that paralleled our intended one, I made no move to take over the lead. Finally, west of St. Clairsville, she latched onto Highway 40 and for the next thirty miles or so she stayed with it. We closed to a better formation three miles east of the airport.

Later Gert said that for the first part of the leg she had no idea where she was. This was excusable. Many of the railroads and branch lines going out of Pittsburgh were not depicted on our chart.

The airport at Cambridge had had a CPTP, but it had vanished. The field was grassy, part of a farm. The two characters who ran it were the owners of the farm and they looked it, bib overalls and all. The field wasn't situated well, for it sloped downhill toward the south.

The Cambridge, Ohio, municipal airport in 1942, typical of the small fields used by WAFS in their cross-country flying. This grass strip was midway between Pittsburgh and Columbus.

We didn't care to remain there, but it was too late in the day to take off. The men assured us that a watchman would guard our planes. We got gas, tied the planes down, and fastened the stick with the seat belt so the wind couldn't damage the movable surfaces.

We stayed at the New National Hotel at $1.25 a night. At the Modern Cafe, we ate huge T-bone steaks just as moderately priced. Esther was my roommate again. When I opened the window before retiring, I saw a bad omen for December. I turned to Esther and said, "It's raining."

By morning the rain had turned to tiny flakes of snow. We went out to the airport and got the weather report over the telephone. Weather was at or near minimums all around, so we waited for the next sequence. Visibility at Cambridge worsened. The entire Ohio Valley went on instrument flight. Since there was no place inside the hangar for our airplanes, we had to put on propeller covers. The last I saw of the planes, each had a fringe of icicles about three inches long on the trailing edges of the wings and about an inch of snow blanketing the tops.

We went back into town, for there was no sense in remaining outside in that weather. In our room, I knitted several more inches on the second sleeve of the gray sweater I was making for Harold. I wished I'd brought the body with me so I could assemble it. I might as well do something useful — the snow was coming down, down, down, and we were going nowhere.

Later in the day we braved the snow and knocked about the shops in downtown Cambridge. We out-of-doors types couldn't endure being cooped up in a hotel room for very long. I bought my father some London Dock pipe tobacco, which I thought must be very good because it was very expensive.

Each day that we remained at Cambridge we went out to the airport to look at our airplanes. The two elderly bachelor farmers looked at us in turn with fully as great, but, I am sure, a different kind of interest. On December 12, the snow was still coming down at nine o'clock at night.

The weather didn't get above minimums for contact flight until Monday, December 14. We arrived on the field as soon after breakfast as we could. The snow on the ground was three inches deep. We looked at the wings.

"Let's get that snow off!" I said emphatically.

The others were willing to try. We scrounged around and found some rags to use.

"Hey! You have a broom?" I asked one of the incredulous farmers. He'd probably never seen anyone so nutty to fly that they'd work to clean off airplanes like this. He found a broom and I began to brush. Under the snow, we uncovered ice.

We could guess by the weather reports coming from the nearest bureau office that if we didn't get out that day, we might not leave for days. We had to figure out a way to get the ice off the wings without taking the fabric along with it.

"You got some ropes?" I asked our host. He found several large manila ropes such as farmers used. Working on two upper wing surfaces at once, we paired off with the shorter women at the trailing edges and Esther and I at the leading edges. With sawing motions we worked the ropes back and forth, scraping off the ice. Then we slapped the surface, scattering the snow and ice we had dislodged. The task was tiresome and we made slow progress. Footing was slick and the cold air slowed us down considerably.

Worst of all, I had to go to the bathroom and was told by one of the farmers that there was a latrine on the outside of the barn which served as the hangar. I went around the back and there it was, a one-holer, as cold as could be. Alongside the outside was what looked like a frozen amber waterfall and I wondered what it was. Suddenly I realized that the men used that place for urinating. It was a disgusting sight.

All morning we kept at our task. Finally by 1410 (2:10 P.M.) the wings were as clean as we could possibly make them. We inspected everything else and the airplanes checked out okay.

"If the wings are wet, we won't take off as quickly as we should," I said. "The aerodynamics will be spoiled."

"Yes, I know," said Helen Mary. "But you lead off and if you see you can't get off the ground in time, abort the takeoff."

We started the engines. The farmers took their chances swinging those props on the slippery ground. The takeoff into the wind was down an incline and, as luck would have it, toward the hedgerow that lined the field. I stood on the brakes as I revved up the engine and then slowly moved across the field. The plane didn't want to pick up speed. I sensed that I'd get off the ground and be up over the hedge, so I kept on. The controls were slushy, the plane was loggy, but it took to the air and off we flew, heading toward Columbus, Ohio.

It was a cold flight lasting ninety minutes. And when we landed at Columbus, the navy personnel there gave us a reception just as cold. They acted as if they didn't want to bother with us. Ah, but they had to, for by the time we made out our forms and drew lines on our charts to the next stop, it was past 1600 and we'd be running out of daylight if we left.

So it was RON at the Fort Hayes Hotel downtown. And the next day we went to the airport only to discover that the weather to the west was poor for flying. We returned to the hotel room, confident that in a navy hangar there would be no snow or ice to brush off before takeoff.

The following day, December 16, we were able to leave early. Winds were cold and brisk and right on the nose. The straight line course to Dayton, which should have been flown in an hour, took seventy-five minutes. Then we had a short leg to Richmond, Indiana: forty miles in forty-five minutes.

We couldn't avoid Indianapolis or Roscoe Turner's establishment. No one there tried to make us feel at home. The service was slow; the employees were not even civil. They reminded us that we had better turn in our forms as soon as we could so that Roscoe could be paid. We were all angry about how we were treated.

Because we had to cool our heels so long in Indianapolis, we had to stop for the night in Terre Haute, staying at the Hotel Deming. Everything about Terre Haute was a sharp contrast to Roscoe Turner's. In other words, the people were nice.

The next morning Helen Mary led off to St. Elmo, Illinois. The winds were strong and the eighty-three mile flight took 110 minutes, so our ground speed was only forty-five miles per hour. There wasn't anything wrong with the weather but the wind. From there, Helen Mary was unable to decide whether we should take off. She hesitated through several hourly weather reports. I tried to persuade her that the wind was steady and would not be a big problem during landing. We'd simply be flying slower than automobiles moving on the ground. At last she made up her mind — I had nearly lost mine with her indecision by then — and she made out a clearance to Scott Air Field, sixty-two miles away, instead of heading for St. Louis.

"Why not go to Lambert?" I asked. "It's only eighty-three miles away and at forty miles per hour ground speed, we'd still have forty-five minutes extra gas left in the tanks."

Despite my argument, she won. In the air I pouted, flying several miles to the right of the group, turning over in my mind the possibility of leaving the flight and going on to Lambert alone. I thought Helen Mary was being mean, for we got to Scott Field in only eighty minutes.

I was at Scott Field's operations office, ready to take off when the other WAFS were. Self-restrained and without my usual chipper attitude, I had little to say. Instead, I beheld my companions with critical eyes. I saw in Helen Mary's cautiousness, excessive fear and in her noble bearing, a desire to emphasize who was boss. Esther was unashamedly kowtowing to her. Meserve had said to me the day before, "You're insane to want to go home. Why, you'll no sooner get there than you'll have to turn around and come back." I thought, a lot she knows about loving someone. I hoped she'd learn.

For some reason, Helen Mary wanted to refuel at Meramec Airport on Highway 66, only thirty-four miles from Scott Field. Rolla was only 110 miles away, which shouldn't have taken more than two hours at the most. Since she was the boss I indicated no preferences. She assigned to me the small task of leading us into Meramec.

The sight of people I knew at that airport brought me back to my old self. There was John Shifko, one of Harold's oldest naval reserve buddies, now in charge in navy flying there. I introduced everyone all around and we were treated as if we were visiting celebrities.

In my mind I questioned Helen Mary's judgment in giving Esther the job of navigating the next leg to Rolla. Soon after she took off, she started toward Cedar Hill. That heading spelled disaster to me, for one could fly for hours in the Ozarks and never come near an airport in that direction. I pushed the throttle forward. To catch her attention, I overtook her L-4B and waved her toward the right. I led into Rolla, glad to take the responsibility of navigating, for in Missouri there are many small streams, all winding. Once off course, it was easy to get hopelessly lost.

My pride in my contact navigation skills appears insufferable to me now. It was an interesting game of trying to hit each possible checkpoint right on the nose without wandering from the straight line depicted on my chart. We didn't fly high enough to see over ridges. Southwest of St. Louis the land becomes increasingly rugged, but there were no peaks among the hills that were high enough to be given special charting by the cartographers.

I could only imagine where the streams were by the trees I judged were along their banks. And there was little to go by after passing Staunton except my intuition, for I had never flown south of Meramec Airport before. I would never do what some male pilots said they did — follow a railroad track across the country. That was cheating. The wind was pretty frisky over Missouri and the compass swung wildly with every slap and toss. By the time we landed, I was so pleased with my meticulous performance that it made up for my lowered status of the day before. Just see if anybody could top it!

The field at Rolla was sod, not large, and surrounded by trees and brush. There was a slight incline in one direction. A DC-3 had landed just before we did. I was surprised to see such a large airplane in so small a field.

Helen Mary led out to Springfield. She wanted me in the number two position again. I surmised that Missouri topography bewildered her and she was relying on me to help in case she missed a checkpoint. Our compass course paralleled the railroad and a stream a good part of the first ten minutes. With the course established, she easily got into Springfield, taking only ninety minutes to go ninety-eight miles.

Again Helen Mary made me the navigator and we took off for Miami, Oklahoma. On the way we passed a huge building at Mount Vernon, the tuberculosis sanitorium. Visibility had improved, and there were good roads to check on. A few were due east-to-west or north-to-south and the fields between had been surveyed and set out paralleling them. If one kept at the same angle in crossing the fields, one could stay on course with no trouble at all.

There was a CPTP at Miami. One of the instructors was a lad who had been in the program with Brayton, flying out of Lambert and St. Charles. We recognized each other and although he had been shy as a student, he now behaved as my equal in experience.

He celebrated our meeting by taking us to dinner in a cafe such as one finds in small towns. He was already planning his life after the war. He had bought a lot with a good road frontage that backed up to the Neosho River. Here, he thought, he could build a house that would be safe from floods. He intended to buy a boat in which he'd float down the Neosho River to the lake just filling to the south where he would fish. It sounded perfect for a sportsman.

We retired early so that we'd get an early start. Alas, the next morning weather at Tulsa was below contact flight minimums. As soon as one sequence showed that we could take off, Helen Mary cleared us from Miami in a hurry. There was none of the holding back that annoyed me through the Ohio Valley. Esther was as eager as she. They want to arrive at some destination before Christmas, I thought, for it was already December 20.

I wasn't afraid to fly at minimums, but it was risky. The engine's rpms would cut back and I'd put on the carburetor heat. In fact, I had carburetor heat on most of the way. When we landed at Tulsa, each of our engines had a chunk of ice at the carburetor intake. Helen Mary must have realized, finally, that we had at least seven full hours of flying still ahead of us. But the winds were on our tail. We made seventy-six miles in fifty-five minutes. The only noteworthy landmark we passed was Claremore, Will Rogers' hometown. It was three miles to the left of course and we could see it only vaguely as we approached Tulsa.

We had no sooner landed at the airport than I ran into Ben Funk, who was weathered in and waiting for Don Joseph to join him. They flew for an oil company, just as Jimmy Doolittle had, but I remembered Don mostly for his amphibious Duck, which I thought was the slowest gliding airplane of that size to come into Lambert.

The next morning we looked out the windows of the Hotel Alvin and couldn't see the tops of the nearby buildings. Fog. One could almost reach up and touch it. Nothing to do but watch for any change and, if the ceiling lifted, run for the airport.

I had a busy day Christmas shopping. I found a gray knitted petticoat for my mother. I had to curb my buying, for prices there were higher than I expected. To top my successes, I found a nearby post office and sent Harold a huge package with his gifts and those for my friends.

Helen Mary was getting antsy. The sky hung low all day. Then Gert Meserve surprised us. At the American Airlines ticket office, she met a man named Fay whom she had known in Boston. He had married a schoolmate of hers, who, with their baby, had gone back to Massachusetts for the holiday.

Fay was so delighted to see a fellow Bostonian that he invited us WAFS to a steak dinner at his home. He also invited his boss and another male employee to augment the group. We all had a hand in the cooking. After we washed and dried the dishes, we listened to ''The

Messiah'' over the radio as we trimmed his Christmas tree. Then we toasted each other's health with an eggnog.

The boss remarked, ''There should be a men's auxiliary to the USO just for the WAFS.'' And we agreed.

The next day the weather cleared and we got to Oklahoma City, doing 108 miles in eighty-five minutes. The next leg to Wichita Falls had fewer checkpoints. The Canadian River was almost dry. The soil around the muddy water was reddish brown. We passed several oil wells. The Red River Valley was also wide and dry. A power station sat on it. We made 110 miles in seventy-five minutes — those Cubs were really flying.

Our stop was a speedy one, but we took time to eat a sandwich. What intrigued me about the charting of west Texas was that small details ignored in the north and the east were emphasized where the population was scarce. A small town like Megargel showed both its elevator and the mill. In the open country, as we bore down on Abilene, the chart depicted a lone house or cattle pens, even a tank out in the open. There was little else with which one could orient herself. But there were always those dry creek beds known as arroyos to be studied in passing, just to make sure that they coincided with their positions on the chart. In ninety minutes we flew 127 miles, and the long mission was at last completed.

American Airlines took us to Dallas where we changed planes for Nashville. There we had to take another plane to Washington, D.C. And then we repeated the nettling, vexatious problem of transporting our heavy baggage across town to the railroad station, through its lengths, and onto a northbound train.

Two days before Christmas, after washing and ironing and visiting the post office where several packages awaited me, my workday was over, and I was ready for my next assignment.

Betty Gillies stopped by my room, saying, ''Nancy wishes to speak to you.''

Oh, oh, I thought. Helen Mary snitched that I was bullheaded about wanting to go to St. Louis when we had that headwind. Anxiously I bit my lower lip as I followed Betty down the long hall to Nancy Love's room.

''Sit down,'' Nancy ordered. ''I want words with you.''

I sat, wondering what on earth I could say, for I was never prepared to defend myself. I was being sacked. There was no doubt about it.

''The WAFS are being disbursed to three other bases,'' she said. What? No mention of my peevishness with Helen Mary?

''There will be five WAFS stationed at Long Beach. I expect to take

James, Fort, Towne, Sharp, and Erickson. That makes up the cadre of five to be the nucleus for the squadron that'll develop with Cochran's graduates.

"A cadre of five goes to Dallas. I'll start as leader there and I'm taking Batson, Miller, Richards, and Ferguson.

"A group of eleven will remain here at Newcastle Army Air Base under the direction of Betty Gillies and her executive officer, Helen Mary Clark.

"The first group to be stationed elsewhere will go to Detroit by January first. Meserve, Thompson, Poole, Rhonie, and you."

Oh, God, I thought. Rhonie has seniority and she'll be the head of it. How can I stand being bossed by her?

"At this moment," Nancy continued, "I am considering that the leader will be you."

And then I felt even worse. How could I deal with a person like Pat Rhonie? She'd be twisting the base commander or whoever around her finger. My life was going to be hell.

Quizzically, Nancy searched my face. She gave me what she must have thought was the right argument. "You should have flights past St. Louis more often than you can possibly get them here, which I thought you'd like," she said.

"Oh, yes, I'd appreciate getting home more often," I replied. The thought I was having about how terrible it was going to be to contend with Rhonie must have shown on my face.

Nancy elaborated the changes. "The Dallas group will have the best ships to fly right off. Detroit may have Taylorcrafts for a few months, some PT-19As with hatches, AT-6s, and later twin Beech and Cessnas and maybe pursuit."

The promise of other aircraft to fly didn't faze or exult me. I was benumbed by the news of the dissolution of our beloved squadron.

Nancy went on speaking, seemingly unaware that I was dazed. "The girls who remain here at Newcastle, except for Betty and Helen Mary, who have their families nearby and want to remain here for the duration, are weak sisters for the most part. Take Esther Nelson and Phyllis Burchfield. It looks as if they will fly PTs and Cubs for quite a while."

After Nancy dismissed me, I went back to my room, where I opened the packages I had just received. Lucky me! Angela Westermann had sent me a slip. West Presbyterian Church sent writing paper. My mother sent a flannelette nightgown. My sister Ruth's Christmas present was a pair of stockings and a wool dog that her two boys had asked her to make for me.

I sneaked into Jamesy's room, the closest place to find an uncluttered surface large enough to write upon. I wrote to Harold, telling him that the Scout knife I had sent him would be useful when he went hunting or fishing. The straight-edge razor, the type he preferred to use, was the only imported one I could find. It was the best on the market. As I wrote, "The Messiah" was being sung over the radio. The news of my transfer still had not sunk in.

THE BREAKUP BEGINS

AN ARCHAEOLOGIST CONSTRUCTS a whole being from fragments, shards of pottery, remnants of clothing, bones, and religious symbols. He fleshes out the image of a people, even clothes them with customs and attitudes. From a few incidents that I uncovered, I constructed a picture of the events which led up to our dispersal in January 1943. It is conjectural, but likely.

On December 29, 1942, in the 2nd Ferrying Group operations office at NCAAB, Captain Shiner had just returned to his desk after studying the six-hour weather forecast charts. Quickly he glanced through the most recent teletyped hourly sequences. His usually cheerful countenance sagged. He knew that Colonel Baker would chew him out about the airplanes not moving, as if it were all his fault. Shiner felt frustrated. If only he could order the weather as he did the pilots!

The RONs coming in from the west, except for the multi-engine instrument pilots, were from the same places they'd come in from the evening before. Here at NCAAB Shiner knew the pilots were goofing off, trying to avoid ground school, and bitching about not flying. Well, there was no help for it.

Even he was wasting time, but he'd put a stop to that. Business was business. Shiner picked up his telephone and asked the operator to connect him with the operations office at the Fairchild factory at Hagerstown, Maryland.

"Hello. Captain Shiner here. How are things going? . . . Any PTs ready? . . . Good. How many? . . . Are they ready now? You know we can't send over a bunch of pilots and pay 'em per diem while they sit on their cans and wait until . . . Okay. We'll send some WAFS over on Friday. That's the first of the month, about noon. We'll want them to clear out of there right away . . . If the weather remains stinko, we'll keep 'em here 'til it clears . . . You know training command's been screaming its head off for those planes. Light a fire, will you? . . . Roger. Out."

Captain Shiner hung up the telephone and turned toward Corporal Sims. "Lieutenant Taylor says production has slowed down during the holidays. Too many reporting sick."

"Probably hangovers," commented Sims.

"Maybe, maybe not. And Fairchild isn't getting its procurement like it should. The company has too much competition."

Again Captain Shiner picked up the telephone. Whatever he was visualizing in his mind's eye, one couldn't tell except for the blissful expression on his face. He relaxed.

"May I speak to Mrs. Love? . . . Captain Shiner, here. Hello, Nancy. How are you? . . . Nothing much . . . Yes, there's no CAVU any place. Your WAFS are scattered all over the country and weather is SNAFU everywhere you look. . . . Say, who's in right now? Shucks! Just a minute while I get another pencil. . . . Okay. Fairchild will have a slew of them by Friday, we hope. So who have we got for them? . . . No, Nancy, those kids are still at Memphis, but they haven't far to go to deliver. . . . I see. Sure, anything for you. I'll get someone to replace Florene Miller. . . . Yes, I can cut amended orders for her if she's got to be back at the base right away. . . . We'll be sorry to see you go, but there's a lot of that around here these days. . . .Oh, before I forget, Piper has two more L-4Bs. Who's first to take them? . . . To South Carolina. No, we're not sending anyone for PTs until Friday or later. And keep it under your hat. Something is cooking about the Cubs. . . . I can't say. Listen, if Colonel Baker says it's all right, you can tell him that as far as operations is concerned, the WAFS can take a day or two off. . . . Sure. Any time. Good-bye."

After the conversation Nancy Love hied to Colonel Baker's office. She must have talked him into a holiday mood, for she returned to her office and telephoned BOQ 14. I answered the phone.

Nancy said, "Colonel Baker says that any of you who wish may visit with your families *if* you let us know where you will be every minute and it won't take you longer than several hours to get back to the base. . . . Tell everyone, won't you, Sweetie, to be sure they have everything ready to go on a mission Friday morning."

I assured her that I would get in touch with everyone on base and with those who might return. I did so enviously. Those who lived on the East Coast departed as rapidly as they could.

Although I was not present when the following episode occurred, I soon found out what happened and have reconstructed it as it probably was.

As soon as Nancy returned to the barracks that evening, she and Betty Gillies, as was their wont, had cocktails together in Nancy's room. Nancy said, "You'd never guess what Pat Rhonie was up to this afternoon."

Betty fluffed out her upper lip, sipped her rum and Coca Cola, raised her eyebrows and waited.

"She got as far as New York in returning from her mission. She telephoned Colonel Baker *collect* and asked him for an extra day in coming back to the base."

"That's not so bad, Nance. He's letting the others from the East have a little time off."

"But don't you see, Betty, this is different. She'll be paid for her time off because she's still on per diem. There's no way the bookkeeping can be squared away."

"That's true. She should know that. Colonel Baker, too."

"He's must have been taken off guard. It puts him on a spot. The more he thought of it, the angrier he got."

Nancy stretched a bit. She went on, "I'm sure he realizes the rumors she's been spreading about us. He's not the same. Our relationship isn't the same as it was."

"Colonel Baker must realize that we all are aware that Pat can't reconcile herself to the fact that you are the CO."

"Yes, she thinks — but I became the leader because I was working in Baltimore operations for months when there was no hope of starting anything like this."

"Take it easy, Nance. You're sending her to Romulus. There she'll be out of our problems. Out of sight, out of mind. And the airplanes there aren't nearly as great as those in Love Field and Long Beach."

"She'll die of envy. You know how she hates the cold."

"Would that be enough to get her to quit?"

Nancy lifted her shoulders a trifle. "Not Pat. She'll hang on. At least she'll be flying something. Damn! I hate to be tied to a desk so much while the rest of you are out flying."

"Now, Nance, Lieutenant Tracy says you fly the AT-6 as well as anyone he's given transition to."

"Isn't he a sweetie to take me along? Too bad Pat found out about it and drew her own conclusions."

"How else can you stay ahead of Jackie's girls?"

"True. I've got to start in Dallas as soon as possible. From what I understand, they'll be coming out next month and they will have had some BT and AT-6 time, plus instrument and even twin-engine. The WAFS I take with me must be as fully experienced as those grads or we'll all be far behind in transition."

"Wilmington won't have that problem," replied Betty. "The new girls will probably feel downgraded, flying Cubs."

Both women smiled.

Nancy said, "There is no reason why most of the WAFS can't fly advanced types as well or better than those girls. All they need is the opportunity that Jackie has been giving them in Texas. In fact, I don't see any reason why we can't do as well as the majority of the men in the Ferry Command."

Betty reminded her, "That goes beyond our original purpose, doesn't it? We were here only to help out, to help the men to get transition. . . ."

"Yes, but who knows what the new year will bring? We might as well be prepared. I'm only sorry that you and Helen Mary elected to stay here. You should be flying heavier and faster ships."

Teasingly Betty said, "Don't forget Pat."

"She gets her little Taylorcrafts and Stinsons. Oh, I almost forgot. Bob and I had another conference this afternoon and he made some changes. Would you call Del for me, Betty? I want her in on this."

Betty lifted her almost empty glass. "To the new year!" she toasted.

"To Dallas and Long Beach and beyond!" replied Nancy, and they drained their glasses and set them aside.

Again I wondered why I was being summoned to Nancy's room. But this time I felt only curiosity, not guilt. Nancy came to the point immediately.

"Del, you were supposed to leave on Friday for Romulus," she said. "There is a change in plans. Your group will not be the first to leave the base. That gives you one more mission here, an L-4B to South Carolina."

I nodded assent, but puzzlement must have shown on my face.

Nancy continued, "Colonel Baker did not approve of all the transfers. He was adamant that not all our cuties and excellent pilots leave his base. That means that Teresa James will stay here and Bernice Batten goes to Long Beach instead. Nancy Batson won't go to Dallas; Dorothy Scott will go in her place. And Gertie Meserve won't be with you in Detroit. You will have Phyllis Burchfield. Any questions?"

"Yes," I replied. "The weather is bad right now. Will I have time to complete a mission before going away?"

"Why not? I'll gather your bunch together about the fifteenth of January. We're getting the Dallas cadre ready to leave on New Year's Day. Florene has not delivered yet — the girls are stuck in Memphis."

Betty added, "It's taking them forever to deliver."

Nancy defended them. "Operations tells me they are closer to delivering than the men who started when they did from Great Falls. About Long Beach: That cadre is scheduled to go the first of February."

Neither WAF facing me showed any emotion on her face. I can't say the same about mine. Nancy reassured me about what she must have thought I was thinking.

She said, "At Detroit the airport is called Romulus because that's the name of the small town post office nearby. Just like here at Wilmington, you'll be flying trainer type planes for some time. The colonel there is quite amiable and said you would be placed in transition, so you may go on to heavier planes. He was optimistic."

When I returned to my room, I lay on the cot, sorting out the news as it applied to me. I knew little of the other women except for Rhonie and her exalted ego. I had looked forward to being with Meserve. She was a nice kid. It was going to be hard to leave some of the others, too. We had a fine *esprit de corps* these past three months. I felt a close tie with even the ones I had seldom seen. I did not realize then that memories of these women would remain sharp and warm all of my days, and I shed some tears for the prospect of losing contact with them so soon. Then I dried my eyes and set about packing for a trip and moving to Michigan. No time to be maudlin!

On the last day of the year, Nancy and Betty called me into a conference once more. "I'm definitely appointing you as squadron leader at Romulus," Nancy said.

"Doesn't Rhonie have more seniority than I?" It was still hard for me to believe. Either way, Rhonie would be a problem.

"She's not going," Nancy replied.

"But she *is* leaving," said Betty.

"She is clearing the base right now," explained Nancy. The two told me about Pat's collect call which had raised Colonel Baker's ire.

"Not only that —" said Betty.

"Yes," chimed in Nancy. "She didn't show up yesterday after her one day off. She drifted in late at about noon today. The colonel refused to keep her beyond the three-month probation period."

I felt relief. Then the two women put me on the stand. Nancy looked at Betty as if asking her to take the lead. She did. "Have you ever heard Pat say anything derogatory about Nancy?" she asked.

Inwardly I squirmed. How could I avoid answering? I felt as embarrassed as I had when, as a child, my mother wanted to know if my big brother had been smoking in the alley. I couldn't lie and I hated myself for not being able to slither out and off the pin, away from their searching eyes. My thoughts almost overwhelmed me: the cattiness, the guilt about tattling, and the recognition that if I told the truth, it would not be fair to Pat. What Pat had said about Nancy, I thought was true. But I felt that it was a case of the pot calling the kettle black.

After a moment's silence, I replied, "Yes."

"What was it?" Betty wouldn't let go.

"Pat said that she was a heavy drinker."

"We'd like to quote you on that in case she tries to make trouble," replied Betty.

I nodded my head. I had already said too much. Back in my room, I worried that I had withheld something. I had never criticized Nancy to anyone. But my sentiments had been similar to Rhonie's. I had never seen Nancy intoxicated, but at parties at the officers' club, when people like the DuPonts attended as the guests of Baker or Love, they all sat at the long table facing the dance floor and they drank. One evening I watched both Nancy and Pat, at different times, retreat to the ladies' room. Each walked unnaturally stiffly, looking ahead with the typical tunnel vision of the inebriated, fastening their eyes forward as if fearful that they might fall or bump into something if they didn't.

On New Year's Eve, only three WAFS remained in the barracks. Those who had somewhere to go in the East wouldn't be back until morning. Those with dinner and dance dates had already gone.

"You'd think they'd put us on orders by now," ventured tiny Bernice Batten as she peeked into my room. I looked up from the letter I was writing to Harold. To chat with Bernice would be a welcome break, for I liked her and yet didn't see much of her. I lay down my fountain pen and replied, "I wouldn't mind that L-4B if it were going west."

Helen Richards must have overheard me and came from the bathroom across the hall and into my room. She was towel drying her soft, blonde hair.

"Oh, haven't you heard?" she asked. "Cubs aren't being ferried any more. They'll be crated and shipped for the duration."

Bernice and I chorused, "Since when?"

"I don't know. I just heard it at Link trainer this afternoon."

"A good idea!" I replied. "Would you believe from Terre Haute to Scott Field last week, cars on Highway 40 were passing us up? We averaged only forty-two miles per hour."

Batten smiled her usual hesitant smile. She, too, entered my room and half sat on the end of the cot. She added her gossip. "I heard one pilot say it took him six days just to cross Texas."

"He should have taxied it across," laughed Richards.

"The wind shouldn't be too much of a problem," I said. "I've flown students and even soloed them in Cubs when the wind was thirty miles an hour."

Richards disagreed. "A lot of pilots haven't much Cub time like you have. Why, Helen Mary had her own Monocoupe and she says the Cub makes her feel like a leaf in the breeze. She says the darn thing wants to keep floating."

Bernice said, "Betty Gillies has always flown heavier airplanes. She says a Cub is the hardest airplane there is to land three point."

"Maybe so," I conceded. "We're so used to tail wheel airplanes, we don't know any different. I once had a student, Dolores Meurer, who was just great in air work, but she had trouble making a stall landing. When all the secondary PTs were grounded at the auxiliary field, I took her out and showed her how to make a wheel landing. She caught on right away and I soloed her with all the men looking on."

"Wasn't that risky?"

"No. I knew she had it in her."

Bernice said, "Maybe there've been a lot of accidents, like ground loops."

"How would we know? Accidents that men have wouldn't leak out to us," said Richards.

"No, I guess not," replied Batten.

"Why don't we go to the movies?" asked Richards. "My hair's almost dry."

"What's on?" asked Bernice.

"George Washington Slept Here."

"Isn't that with Jack Benny?" I asked.

"Sounds like fun," said Batten.

Richards looked at her watch. "It starts in twenty minutes."

"I'll be ready in a jiffy," I said, and we dispersed.

Anyone who wore government issue clothing, commonly called GIs, could get in to a base movie free. Officers paid only a quarter. WAFS were considered officers, so we wore our uniforms in order to take advantage of the bargain.

We went, we saw, we laughed, and we returned home. Apparently that was all that New Year's Eve offered us. I exchanged my uniform for the hostess gown that Harold had given me for Christmas. I thought he must have paid too much for it, and I cherished it all the more because I felt it was an indication of how much he loved me.

The gown was a soft, pale blue wool serge. The sleeves were long and at the loosely hanging wrist was a white braid trim. The choirboy collar and the front of the double-breasted top were embellished by the same ornamentation.

I went down and across the hall to the bathroom mirror where the light was brighter. I admired the way the gown fit me. Then I presented myself in all my radiance to the others.

Helen Richards exclaimed, "Say! That looks good enough to wear to a party."

I looked down with pleasure. It was a possibility that I hadn't thought of. The gown might really serve as a dinner dress during the winter months.

Richards' eyes twinkled. She challenged me. "I dare you to go over to the officers' club like that."

I had been wondering what was going on next door anyway and the dare wasn't dangerous. "Okay, I'll take it," I replied. "I don't think I'll need a coat. I won't stay long. See you all later."

Outside, on the tiny porch of the club, the noise I heard was unusually loud for a place that was usually quiet. As I entered, the hubbub increased, but my eyes told me that the celebration was restrained.

Balloons and crepe paper streamers were in the air. Staccato poppings caused by lighted cigarettes diminished the colors floating overhead. A long table was set up against one wall so that the formally clothed guests could watch the festivities without encountering the bodies that milled about from table to table. Noisemakers, glasses, bowls of ice, and assorted bottles filled the head table. I recognized Richard DuPont seated there, and several seats away from him, Nancy Love. All the occupants appeared stiff, as if they were on display. A few couples danced in the small space in the middle of the floor. Three enlisted men provided the music.

I snaked through the groups of drinkers, being careful not to touch anyone holding a glass. The bar was in the rear of the room. Officers and ladies crowded two-deep around it. They ignored the bar, for their drinks were only half consumed, but they seemed unwilling to go far from the source of supply.

I ordered a Coke, which cost a dime, because its color fit in and it was not intoxicating. No one seemed to notice at first that I was there or that I was wearing anything unusual. I observed the crowd, my eyes returning to the long table with the glum and silent celebrants. Everyone else seemed to be forcing gaiety, trying too hard at conversing. Suddenly I realized that I, who had never had a hilarious New Year's Eve, was not so deprived after all. The party was disappointing to everyone.

Lieutenant Faso and his wife wound through the throng and headed toward the bar. They greeted me and told me their news. "We'll have to say good-bye, Mrs. Scharr," said Faso. "I cleared the post today."

"We're on our way to California," added Mrs. Faso.

"That's great!" I replied.

"Only temporarily. I'm being sent down under."

Captain Jordan and Lieutenant Haines, both WAFS instructors, joined us. After a few witty sallies, they also said they were leaving Wilmington. They had no idea where they'd be stationed. I surmised that they'd soon be out of the states and off to flying over the Hump into China. There had been such secrecy about the dispersal of the WAFS that I offered no news about us in return.

My friends bid me adieu, so I joined a small group of officers I knew to be friendly. One captain was regaling everyone within earshot about his flights to Merrie England. At the same time, he dispensed foreign coins to the women around him. I knew instinctively that the money had little value. The coin he gave me was Irish and had a harp on it.

The captain was shocking his audience with his tales. "The women in England you wouldn't believe!" he said. "You can't walk anywhere without one coming along and wanting to trade herself for a candy bar or some food."

"Yeah, the morals over there are pretty terrible," another man spoke up.

They apparently didn't realize that the subject was not in good taste for a mixed group. As soon as I could break away, I left.

Back at the BOQ I looked in on Richards.

"How was it?" she asked.

"Nothing much," I replied. "You didn't miss a thing."

It was still before twelve. There was no good reason to go to bed yet, so I finished my letter to Harold, telling him about my evening. I reminded him of the New Year's Eves we had spent together. And then I went to bed, lay awake and thought about them.

On January 2, I wrote a chatty letter to Harold and reported to him that the need for pilots was so great that many were dragged out to combat without the necessary training. Although it was supposed to be a secret, we had heard that the Ferry Command lost thirty-seven men during the previous week on trans-Atlantic crossings and averaged an accident a day.

After mailing the letter — I was practically haunting the post office those days — I came up the back stairs of BOQ 14 and heard noise coming from Teresa James' room. Instead of going back to my room, I went down the hall and peeked into hers.

"You old bag! It's good to see you," cried Teresa.

"Yeah — how long's it been?" I replied.

"The last time I saw you, you were a sad sack in a hospital bed. Come on in," she invited.

I did so. She stopped unpacking and retreated to her chaise, saying, "Talk to me. I'm going to put in some time resting my carcass. I need some good old home comfort. You wouldn't believe the trip we just had."

"How would you like some tea?" I asked. "I'll heat the water and I have cups and everything — Harold sent them to me."

"Yeah? Okay. Maybe that's the ticket. Say, how is the old man?"

"Just fine. I got to see him right before Christmas. I'll be right back."

The water drawn from the faucet was so hot that shortly the teapot was steaming and I re-entered Jamesy's room bearing two cups full of hot tea.

She warned me, "You better look out you don't spill that, sister. I don't want to clean up after you. If I let my head down to the floor, I might not get it back up again."

"Oh, oh — you feel that bad?" I asked.

"That was sure some party last night. Besides, I got the sniffles."

"Well, how did the trip go?"

Jamesy sipped. She said, "What do you think? Operations sends us all the way to Great Falls, Montana, to pick up some beat-up old Stearmans to take to Tennessee. And a whole bunch of fellows were going, so they sent us up on the same train. We yak-yakked all the way."

"That distance? Why didn't they put you on a plane?"

"Who knows why operations does anything? Look what they did to us at Hagerstown." Jamesy's face became more serious. She said, "You know Meserve's brother died in that Coconut Grove fire in

Boston? They caught her in Virginia on her way south, so there were only seven WAFS here to go to Montana. We got orders on December 2 and were up at six the next morning. But at two in the afternoon, Nancy says, "Manana," and we didn't even go the next day. *Look* magazine came and took pictures for eight hours. Then the next day, Nancy can't go with us, she says.

"Then Capt. Ted Thompson of the RAF called and said he had four days' leave. But Kay was supposed to go with us. So they had dinner together in Philadelphia and she had to be at the station at nine that night. He rode on to Pittsburgh with us. In all, twenty-four flying officers were on the train with us."

"I'll bet the girls liked that," I said.

"Yeah. And Florene had a birthday on the sixth, so we all celebrated on the train. When we pulled into Great Falls, man, it was cold!"

"Who went?"

"Oh, there was me — I was flight leader — and Thompson, Florene, Delphine Bohn, Nancy Batson, and Phyllis Burchfield."

"I'll bet it was cold flying those open planes up in those mountains."

"It sure was, but we couldn't get out right away; the weather was socked in. We all hit the Link room. Then we checked out some face masks. I was already having trouble with Burchfield. We wanted to stick together as a group, and when we wanted her to come along, like for a meal, we couldn't find her right away."

We both sipped more tea. Then Teresa's eyes flashed and her animated face became even more alive. She said, "So, one day, it must have been the eleventh, we were in operations haunting the weather bureau, and a Lockheed 13 lands. Out comes a group of brass making an inspection tour. And who do you think gets out with them?" Teresa could hardly restrain her excitement.

"I don't know. Who?"

"Nancy! Nancy Love, that's who. And I said, "Nancy, what are *you* doing here?"

Teresa was pleased, I could tell, by my evident surprise. She continued, "She tells me she's visiting the seven Ferry Command bases, checking on quarters for WAFS. She says Memphis doesn't want any women, but Love Field and Long Beach do, so I ask her confidentially, if it's at all possible, put me in California, and she said she would.

"I rounded up the girls except for Burchie. She's got the idea that 'right now' means much later."

"What else did Nancy have to say?"

"Oh, she was very subtle and suave, you know how she is. She says we'll all probably be wearing ties soon. She had a blister on her right hand. They let her play copilot on the Lockheed and the landing gear kept sticking and she had to knock it to get the gear down. The officers with her treated her royally. There was Colonel Campbell from the War Department and Captain Maxwell and Captain Henry.''

"Getting back to Burchie," I said, for I was interested in her for personal reasons, ''what was the matter with her?''

''I don't know. She worried about the weather a lot. And after we saw Nancy, she seemed worried about commissions. She doesn't come out with what's eating her. Anyway, I finally told her off while we were still in Great Falls. The day we took off, I got her into the flight office at operations and said, 'Now you sit here and don't go wandering out of here.' You couldn't get her to do things like check the weather or the airplanes or anything the rest would do without hesitation. She looked mournful and blank, as if her thoughts were far, far away.

''And then we were ready to get out, at last. I asked Florene to navigate the first leg. We had to start our engines outside in the cold, of course, and it wasn't easy. Those PT-17s use a crank, just like the Fairchilds. First one plane and then another got started and was warming up. Everyone had a face mask on, and the only one you could recognize was Fulton — I'll tell you why in a minute. One plane had nobody in it to turn the switches. Who was missing? I stopped my engine, got out, and went to look. Sure enough, inside the office where I left her with her B-4 and parachute bags, was Burchie, scooched up in a corner. I said, 'Burchie! Why aren't you outside ready to go?' And she looks at me like she has the upper hand and says, 'I'm doing just what you told me to do.'''

My lower jaw dropped. All I could manage to say was, ''More tea?''

''No, kid, I don't want any more.''

''I want another cup,'' I said. ''I'll be right back.''

While I reheated the tea and poured another cup, I questioned the reason for the switch of Meserve for Burchie in the Detroit cadre.

When I returned, Teresa said, ''Say, what's new around here? Anything exciting happen?''

I sat at the foot of her cot and thought a minute. ''Yeah,'' I replied, and a picture of a poignant Cornelia flashed into my mind. I hadn't been on orders during the week between Christmas and New Year's. Every day I expected that my transfer would be written and that I would be on my way to Romulus. An eerie spell was settling over BOQ 14, especially during the evenings. Most of the women were out on missions, and I never knew who would be coming in or going out. There was an air of finality about everything I touched, and the

These WAFS were shown at Wichita Falls, Texas, in December 1942. They had flown these Stearman PT-17s from Great Falls, Montana, and would take them on to Tennessee. From left: Kay Thompson, Phyllis Burchfield, Nancy Batson, Delphine Bohn, Florene Miller, and Teresa James. (Dorothy Fulton also made the flight but is not in the photo.)

suspense of waiting made me tense.

I was unaware that Cornelia was standing at my door, holding onto the door jamb, waiting for me to turn away from the bureau drawer into which I was placing my freshly ironed princess slips. As soon as I saw her, I realized that she was so stupified that it was difficult for her to speak. She said, "I just had a telephone call from home. . . . Fortland just burned to the ground."

The news stunned me. "Oh, Cornelia!" was all I cried out as tears came to my eyes.

"Everything is gone," she went on. "All my diaries are gone. I sent them home rather than take them to Long Beach."

So I learned that from the day she began to fly, Cornelia had fashioned a chronicle of her life in aviation. Of the WAFS, she was certainly the one most qualified to write about us. She was an avid reader, she expressed herself well, and she had the patience to sit alone and write her thoughts while the rest of us either relaxed or ran about socially. No wonder Cornelia had not joined us at our end of the barracks — she had her work to do, a serious task for one so young in years.

Cornelia showed some emotion to me, but she did not break down about her loss in front of the others. She had a certain nobility; she possessed quality and breeding. Now tragedy had threatened her life twice. First she escaped death at Pearl Harbor. Now, because she had not been home, she escaped fire again at Fortland. But the hours and years of her career were only cinders. Pilots are superstitious. They believe that bad luck comes in threes. If there have been two accidents from one airport, for instance, everyone breathes easier once the third has happened.

I didn't look at Teresa as I said, "Cornelia's house burned down. It was built like Mount Vernon."

"Gee, that's sure tough," answered Teresa.

We sat for what seemed an interminable time, but really must have been only a minute before Teresa asked, "Did you ever fly with Fulton?"

I shook my head no as I swallowed more tea. "Why?" I asked.

"Boy! Did she get carried away! She bought herself a ten gallon hat as a souvenir of the great, wild West."

"I'd like to have one, too," I said.

"That's all right," said Teresa, "except we were trying to show off how we fit right in with the boys at the airport and she trots around all over the base at Great Falls with that thing on her head. Even in uniform."

The image of Fulton in uniform with a ten-gallon hat atop her head made me laugh out loud. Teresa rounded out her story. "We were putting our baggage in that side compartment," she said, "all except Burchie, that is, when Delphine goes over to Fulton and says, 'You better not wear that hat when you fly.'

"Fulton says she's going to. Delphine comes from Amarillo and she knows better, so she says, 'You'll lose it. You'll never be able to keep it on your head. It'll even untie a scarf around your neck and whsh! no scarf!'"

I laughed. "That happened to me once in the Kinner Fleet and I sure hated to lose that scarf."

Teresa went on. "Fulton looked pretty stubborn, but Delphine kept at her. She says, 'Why don't you put it with your B-4 bag and wear

Nancy Batson, left, Teresa James, center, and Florene Miller wait out the weather in a hotel in Great Falls, Montana, in December 1942.

your helmet?' And Fulton looks peeved and pays no attention. I could have crowned her. She paid no attention to me, either, and I was the flight leader. That first leg, I looked over at her every once in a while. She scooted way down in the cockpit so she could hardly see out.''

"How in the world did she keep it on her head? Or did she lose it?'' I asked.

"It had chin straps she tied under her chin. You should have been there. With her face mask and goggles and that hat —'' Jamesy laughed with me.

"I guess you'll tell me she finally lost it over Texas where some cowpuncher could find it.''

"Nope. After that leg, she didn't wear it flying. But she wore it around all those western airports. She sure loved that hat.''

"That trip must have been a big adventure for her. Maybe she'd never been west of New Jersey before.''

"All I gotta say is we felt like a bunch of idiots with her acting like a little kid.''

"At least she gave you some excitement along the way,'' I said.

"Excitement? We had everything happen to us. That day Nancy came into Great Falls, Burchie, Florene, and I were sick with colds. I even feel under the weather right now, so you aren't the only one who gets sick, you old bag.

"Florene took off first from Great Falls. And about twenty miles out, she throttles back, so we all throttled back behind her. We go on some more, and she throttles back a little more, and there we were, all of us stalling along behind Florene and no one impolite enough to bust up in front of her. With that snow all over everything, it was pretty hard to tell where those landmarks were. We kept behind her, hanging on our props and wondering what the score is. Finally, she comes to an airport and I come in ahead and land first. The field was Lavina, and it's ten miles off course. Florene comes over to us as soon as she can and says, 'Why didn't any of you jokers get ahead of me and take the lead? The wind took my chart right out of my hand and I throttled back in hopes that one of you would take over.'"

"Oh, no!" I exclaimed. "How awful."

"All she could do was pray and keep headed in the same direction."

"Gosh! We never even thought of a signal like that," I said.

"I had the same thing happen to me getting out of Hagerstown the day before Thanksgiving. But I came back to the airport and my flight followed me, so it turned out all right," said Teresa.

"Delphine's parents had us to dinner at the Herring Hotel when we stopped at her home town. We even made the society page. Wait a sec and I'll show you some of our publicity. They took our pictures and ran a story on us almost every place we RON'd."

Teresa got out her navigation kit, rooted about in it, and came out with some news clippings and glossies, which I looked at avidly.

"You know those Stearmans were used and we had a little trouble with 'em," said Teresa. "Kay had some problems with her motor and it looked like the mechanics couldn't fix it quite right. And the next day, a mechanic stuck his foot through Batson's wing, and the landing gear was acting up on that side — might have been the brakes — so we were held up and everybody was getting antsy. We didn't mind so much when the weather was bad, but then it cleared up and on the sixteenth, Thompson used my name and said she was the flight leader and wanted the airplanes ready in five minutes because we were coming out and wanted to take off right now. Geez! I didn't know about it 'til we got to the field, and was I mad! The head mechanic was having a hard time getting the line boys to work, and anybody who flies knows you have to keep on the good side of them.

"I chewed Thompson out because she impersonated me and all that happened was that we stayed there longer. The other girls were sore at her, too. But she apologized three days later.

"Come to think of it, we saw another group of WAFS at Dallas, flying PTs: Barbara Poole, B. J. Erickson, Esther Manning, and Barbara

Donahue. Getting off, Florene hit a field marker with her prop. There was no damage, but the prop had to be taken off and balanced, just to make sure.

"When we were at Barksdale Field, Burchie had her jacket retailored from a size forty to what would fit her. We were ready to take off from Shreveport and she remembered her jacket. She flew over to get it. Then we flew over to Barksdale and she wasn't there. Where's Burchie? I'll tell you where she was! She was flying overhead, waiting for us. How did she expect us to guess that's what she was doing? By that time, Batson had a pair of sore tonsils and Delphine said she needed a drink."

The recital had me chuckling and shaking my head. But there was more.

"We hit Little Rock the day before Christmas. We went out to eat and everybody was dressed to go except Burchie. We couldn't find her at the airport, so we went to town without her. We still couldn't find Burchie. She called the airport and left the phone number where's she be, but they lost it. After several hours, we found she'd checked into the Hotel Marion.

"Then, believe it or not, the day after Christmas, Burchie was sitting in the lobby, ready to go at 7 A.M."

"Unpredictable?" I asked.

"You're not kidding. By December 29, we were all running out of money and trying like mad to cash checks. Florene gets a call to return in a hurry to Wilmington and Burchie disappears again. In Memphis. . . . Say, I hear Rhonie resigned?"

"Yeah."

"I never did like that dame looking down her aristocratic nose at my hair and griping to Nancy about it."

We heard footsteps on the stairs and said nothing more until Betty Gillies and Helen Mary Clark paused at Jamesy's door just long enough for us to smile at each other and for Betty to say, "The latest word from Captain Matz is that we'll start transition soon." That was good news.

The following day was Sunday, and in spite of protests from the nonexercisers, I asked Betty if we could have sitting-up exercises after breakfast and roll call. She welcomed the idea, so at nine o'clock we went into the second floor hall and I led them in 1-2-3-4, repeat, 1-2-3-4, and so forth, with Jamesy making a face at me and complaining that she hated it. She must have been feeling bad. The next morning when I saw her, I insisted that she go to the flight surgeon. He grounded her for three days and she returned to bed.

Katherine Rawls Thompson models the WAFS uniform. She is pictured at Wilmington, Delaware, in December 1942.

Eight of us got orders to deliver PT-19s to Brady, Texas: Helen Mary Clark, Barbara Erickson, Phyllis Burchfield, Delphine Bohn, Nancy Batson, Bernice Batten, Dorothy Fulton, and I. Helen Mary and I were appointed flight leaders.

The weather kept us from starting off to Hagerstown, but it didn't keep Barbara Donahue, Esther Manning, Barbara Towne, and Evelyn Sharpe from returning from their Texas delivery the next day.

At least some of the WAFS got away, even if they weren't on missions. Kay Thompson went to Fort Lauderdale on a four-day leave to see Ted. Barbara Poole went home for several days, too. Esther Nelson came back from spending a two-week leave with her husband, who was at Long Beach. While we were stalling around waiting to go, Gertie Meserve and Cornelia Fort came back from their latest mission. Cornelia was developing a cold, which gave Betty Gillies another opportunity to demonstrate her nursing skills.

By the time Harold's birthday rolled around on January 5, those of us who hadn't had a mission for a while were so stir-crazy that we'd have tried flying brooms if operations had placed us on orders for them.

I wanted to plan everything about our next mission before we went and in order to decide which maps to take, I went over to operations and mulled over the meteorological trends along the airways that led to

Brady. The northern route appeared to be the better one. The officer in charge of operations was the same old buzzard with thinning hair, watery blue eyes, and horrible false teeth, which he now displayed in a Uriah Heep smile.

"Well, which way are you going?" he asked.

"It looks like we'll take the northern route," I answered.

"What's your first stop?"

I was surprised. It couldn't be anything else, I thought. "Pittsburgh."

"What are you going to Pittsburgh for?" he asked. I thought he must be testing me.

"Because the southern route is socked in with weather stacked up all across the map. And we always stop at Pittsburgh." I'd show him I was no dunce.

"You'll be starting from Hagerstown. Why don't you cut straight across the mountains and fly direct to Columbus? You'll make only one stop instead of doglegging it up to Pittsburgh."

I was taken aback and said sincerely, "I hadn't thought about that." I went over to look at the huge composite chart of sectionals making up the map of airways for the continental United States. I studied it. Then I returned to him and said, "I think it wouldn't leave me enough gas reserve in my tank in case of emergency."

"Aw, the fellows do it all the time," he said. "They eliminate Pittsburgh and they deliver faster that way."

I still wasn't convinced and began to wonder why he was so insistent. I said, "And suppose we got a strong head wind? We might run out of gas. Didn't the men run out of gas?"

The captain grinned so wide he showed his hideous gray false gums. "Well, not quite. One guy's engine quit in the landing pattern, but he made it all right."

I searched his face and intuition turned me as cold as Toledo steel. Very quietly I said, "I'm the flight leader on this mission and I'll be going to Pittsburgh."

But we didn't go that way after all.

Group operations herded eight of us onto SNAFU airline and dropped us at the Fairchild factory on the morning of January 6. We scurried about to find our assigned airplanes and to check them for flyability. Mine, #42-34118, was okay, so I stowed my gear in the baggage compartment and ran in to check the weather sequences.

Weather throughout the Ohio Valley was bad or marginal. The base operations officer said, "This time of year, you'll be more comfortable flying the southern route anyway. You won't find it anything but cold in those open cockpits.''

Helen Mary and I agreed. Besides, if we got out right away, we'd be as far as Charlotte, North Carolina, by evening and we should be able to finish this mission in a hurry. I didn't comprehend the logic of sending me to south Texas when I was soon due to report to Detroit. I just wanted to get the job done in the shortest possible time.

"We have time to eat a little something first," said Helen Mary to her flight — Delphine Bohn, Phyllis Burchfield, and B. J. Erickson.

"I'll make out our clearances to Preston Glenn and join you," I said to mine.

She led them to the factory cafeteria while I filled out two forms and carried them to the meteorologist for his signature. Then I sped with long strides to join the group just finishing coffee. I took milk, thinking it would be better for me.

Back in operations we donned our bulky lambskin-lined two-piece flying suits, helmets and goggles, and gloves. As added protection, we put on thin kidskin face masks. "Which one of you is Lon Chaney?" I asked the others.

"I thought you were," replied Barbara Erickson.

We laughed, seeing each other as weird travesties of female forms and faces.

Nancy Batson, as my navigator, took off first. Helen Mary's flight followed me, our tail-ender and watchdog. Batson proved to be an alert navigator. Her technique for not getting lost was to edge slightly toward each checkpoint about to come into view. I could tell that she was planning where she'd be every minute of the way. A young but sensible kid, I thought, besides being beautiful enough to be chosen for the cover of *Dixie* magazine.

As for me, I was sleepy. It was the milk, I thought. I'd better lay off it before flying. During the entire flight the air was nippy. I soon felt an incipient drip forming and knew I had a problem. From one zippered leg pocket I pulled out a handkerchief. The wind almost jerked it from my gloved left hand as I tried to push open the horizontal slit through which I breathed. It was impossible to do more than touch the lower part of my nose. So at frequent intervals, I dabbed, dabbed, dabbed along.

I landed first at Preston Glenn and as soon as we had taxied up for service, each member of the flight did her assigned job. We joined each other in operations as fast as we could. It was still very cold outside.

"You did a beautiful job of navigating," I told Batson.

She smiled gratefully, and even Helen Mary's flight crew seemed pleased for her. Everybody liked Batson.

But my praise had uncalled-for results. A pace away, her head lowered and eyes askance, Fulton burst forth with, "I'm not staying in this Ferry Command. Nobody appreciates a person, and I don't care about them either."

She turned away from our startled faces and looked squarely at Batten, standing in her way. "What's the matter? Are you jealous?" Batten asked flatly.

Fulton replied, "No, I'm not. I just don't like favoritism all the time." She left abruptly to gaze at the huge aeronautical planning chart.

What was I supposed to do? I wondered. My flight leader assignment was to see that the flight didn't get lost and that each member had an opportunity to prove her navigational skills and her familiarity with being a flight leader. Was I also supposed to help them grow to maturity? I decided to ignore the outburst and feel my way.

If anyone should have been chosen navigator first, it was Batten. Bernice earned her transport license in 1933. She was flying long before I was. Yet she had no illusions of her own importance and was shyly silent, almost a worrywart about abiding by rules and in pleasing those in authority. She was as petite as Betty Gillies, but her serious and almost sad face, with high cheekbones, irregular features, dark eyes, ivory skin, and dark brown hair, was not to Hollywood movie star specifications. She appeared good-looking to me because everything about her went together well. But I saw people with the eye of an amateur sculptor. And, too, I liked her for who she was.

After sandwiches and coffee in the coffee shop, we readied ourselves for flight, this time without the masks. Bernice Batten took the number one position going to Morris Field.

"Well," cried Fulton, "so I'm not good enough . . ."

Calmly Batten addressed her, "You know very well you'll get your turn, so quit crabbing."

Good for Bernice! I hoped she'd be another good navigator and she was. Her ground speed was ninety-two miles per hour and the flight took two hours minus five minutes. As we approached Charlotte, we felt that the air was much warmer. The high cirrus clouds had gradually lowered, as if bowing to greet us, heralding an approaching warm front.

When we landed I complimented Batten and so did Batson. Some of the others did, too. Fulton responded with, "I guess I can't do anything right!"

"We'll see," I said to her. "The next hop is yours." She seemed relieved at last. To make me appreciate her competency, she declared,

"I have been flying since I was ten years old."

Helen Mary and I were already leaving the group, bound for the weather bureau, and when out of earshot, I ventured to her, "I have a prodigy on my hands. She claims to be twenty-four years old and that gives her more years of experience than anyone except Betty."

Helen Mary's face was immobile. She made no reply. I realized that I had said too much and resolved to be more like her, for she never gossiped about anyone.

Upon our return, we overheard Fulton's voice saying, "And besides that, I've had a ground instructor's rating for ten years."

Someone asked, "How could you know all that physics and aerodynamics and meteorology when you were so young?"

Our appearance left the question hanging. The WAFS turned toward us and several pairs of eyes rolled upward, several smiles of disbelief greeted us.

Helen Mary told them, "We probably won't get out of here tomorrow."

"And maybe not for a day or two," I added. "It's already raining in North Carolina and west of here there's icing." To allay any suspicions that we had taken the wrong route, I said, "The bad weather is spread all over. Even St. Louis is socked in tight."

Then Helen Mary sent in both RONs while I telephoned the nurses' quarters. The nurse who answered said, "You'll find the barracks all torn up. Carpenters and painters are coming in tomorrow and they'll be here for the next few days. But you can stay tonight anyway. We have the room."

Welcome news. Our beds would cost only fifty cents apiece. We were wise to hoard our per diem early, for who could tell what tomorrow would bring? Supper at the officers' mess was hot and satisfying. Drop cloths on the floor and ladders in the corridor didn't interfere with our rest that night.

When we woke up the next morning, rain had already begun, but we were eager for breakfast and anxious to learn the weather situation. We packed our bags and got transportation. In the meteorology office, Erickson mourned, "This isn't SNAFU. It's more like TARFU."

"What's that?" asked Batson.

"Things Are Really Fouled Up," replied Erickson.

Our day was shot. Bohn suggested, "Let's see if we can get some Link time."

We left our bags with our parachutes and tiptoed through puddles to the Link room where we signed up for sessions with that ego-destroying gadget. I was scheduled for 9:30 A.M. To while away the time until

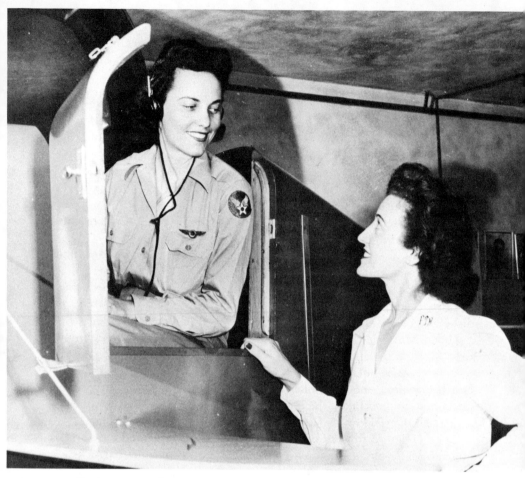

Student Florene Miller in the Link trainer, receives instruction from her mother, Flora Miller. They were both at Love Field, Dallas, early in 1943.

then, I pulled out my Carl Day book on instrument flight training and started again where I'd left off. The room disappeared as I lost myself in the excellent book and the instructor had to tap my shoulder when my time came.

By eleven I was a nervous wreck. I felt dopey enough anyway, having entered that period when I should have been grounded. The Link workouts tired me. The instructor was the best I'd seen, but the controls were stiff and my muscles became sore and stiff, too. I enjoyed working this Link more than the one at NCAAB for it had a stick control for ailerons and elevator instead of a wheel. It also had a gyro instrument.

Instrument flight was foreign to me before I entered the Ferry Command. Practicing it in a Link trainer was difficult at first because it was so palpably phony. One climbed into a stationary model of a cockpit that could be revolved, dipped, and otherwise manipulated by the student inside. The instructor handed the student a radio chart for the nonvisual approach to the airport he had chosen to use for the lesson. The student placed feet on rudders, right hand on the stick, and left hand on the throttle control while still clutching the chart. Then the instructor lowered the hatch.

Inside the light was dim, as if one were flying at night or through thick clouds. The student had to make instrument readings and read the radio station chart by the cockpit lights. The pilot began with putting the "airplane" to rights — checking the instrument panel to see if she had the correct airspeed indicated, the engine rpm at cruising, the gyrocompass set and working, and the earphones ready to hear the first radio signal.

The first signal was usually that of the airport on the chart. The student tried to decide quickly if she were leaving the station or going toward it by the volume changes the operator was making. At the same time she heard either a Morse code signal for N or A and had to figure out which quadrant she was in for that particular radio station. Knowing that, she used the traditional technique of getting herself onto the incoming beam, which sounded like a steady hum, where the N and A signals overlapped each other. That marked the beam on which she was to let down for an instrument landing.

While this was going on in the cockpit, on a large table outside an inked stylus recorded onto a large chart whatever changes in direction the pilot made. When at last she was allowed to leave the torture chamber, she learned what her flight had really accomplished as to proper orientation on instruments. Sometimes the results were embarrassing.

All I got out of my first lesson was that I was stupid, inadequate, and incompetent. I wished that my first instructors had realized how strange it all was to me and that they had explained the airport radio pattern with me before the hatch was shut. At Morris Field, I began to get some "B" grades, which indicated I was making progress. I thought I might go back in the afternoon.

But in the mess hall, the commander of the field, Colonel Gates, singled out Helen Mary and me, as flight leaders, to eat lunch with him and Captain Hill. A self-assured man with a delightful sense of humor, Colonel Gates kept us entertained during lunch. He wasn't about to let such an appreciative audience slip away. As we left the dining room, he said, "You girls aren't going anywhere. Why don't you take a little drive with us and we'll show you the whole post." We did and the tour drove all thoughts of Link from my mind.

"I do this every day," said the colonel. "I believe in keeping the store. It's my job as I see it."

By mid-afternoon, hanging around the field was a waste of time. We went into town, checked into the Barringer Hotel, and had time to do some shopping before the stores closed at five.

Harold was always on my mind, especially because he'd had a birthday the day before we left NCAAB. I'd sent him some small articles, such as a collar stay I'd bought at Carlson's. In public he was always in uniform; the navy did not permit individual interpretations in the wearing of that uniform. Although I always thought of him when I went shopping, probably the greatest gift I could give him was to say from my heart how much he meant to me, which I did, in letter after letter.

While we were stuck in Charlotte that January, Betty Gillies was on her way to ferrying Republic's powerful Thunderbolt, the P-47, affectionately known by its pilots as "the jug." Betty told no one of the interest Colonel Baker and the officer in group control had in allowing her to start training to fly that large pursuit airplane. Therefore, her aristocratic silence aroused no envy, but it also denied her the respect we would have given her if we had known that of her 1,400 flying hours, at least 180 of them were in the twin-engine Grumman Widgeon that she and her husband owned.

We had seen that Widgeon one autumn day when Bud had flown down to see Betty and had been given permission to land at NCAAB. It awed the few who saw it, for it represented a high financial investment which most pilots could not afford. I noticed that Colonel Baker was equally impressed with the Gillies' devotion to aviation.

Nevertheless, the Delaware winter thwarted Betty's progress. Group operations interrupted her study by ordering her to deliver airplanes. As for transition, the male officers stepped in line ahead of her; their priority was directly related to rank.

In the beginning the transition people didn't take Betty seriously. No doubt they eyed her permission to go into AT-6 transition as a feeble gesture by officials meant to show that WAFS at Wilmington were to have opportunities equal to those transferring to Dallas and Long Beach. Etiquette demanded that Betty, as the WAFS leader, would receive training before all others.

She appeared to be destined to failure, however. She was a wisp of a woman, just over five feet tall. The flight instructors knew that during orientation Betty used cushions behind her back or beneath the parachute on which she sat so that she could reach and apply leverage to the controls. How would she ever control an AT-6? The cockpit was designed for more muscular male cadets whose height might reach six feet four inches. Why waste flying time on her?

But they did not reckon with Betty Gillies.

Before volunteering to serve as a WAF, Betty had been a utility pilot (an errand girl, she said) for the Grumman Aircraft Engineering Corporation for which her husband, Bud, a former navy pilot, served as a vice-president. Grumman also employed a test pilot named Vic who was only as tall as Betty. Vic had designed a pair of rudder extenders — two blocks of wood two and a half inches thick with a metal piece that slipped over the top of each pedal. Each extender had a clip on either side where the pilot's heel rested and which held the block firmly in place on the rudder pedal. Each time that Vic or Betty used the the company Widgeon, they slipped these extenders over the rudder pedals.

As soon as Betty learned from Colonel Baker that he was authorizing her transition to larger, heavier aircraft, she telephoned Vic and asked him "to catch the very next navy SNJ [which was the same as an AT-6] that landed at the Grumman factory and to measure its rudders for blocks." Then she asked him to go next door to the Republic factory and sit in a P-47 to find out what block specifications she would need in order to fly it safely. What was right for him would be right for her. Years later she told me about this scheme. She wrote, "Very shortly thereafter a pair of blocks for the AT-6 was dropped off at Wilmington for me by one of the Grumman people en route to Washington. And not long after that I received blocks for the P-47 by the same method. So I was all set."

Betty told me that the AT-6 blocks fit all the other aircraft that the North American Company made, such as the P-51 Mustang. She could even alter the clips so they fit the pedals of a Martin A-30.

So when Betty Gillies climbed into an AT-6 for her first lesson on January 12, 1943, she, like Nancy, began the long, slow climb up the pilot totem pole from the low-man position that WAFS had held from the beginning.

Most of us women military pilots during World War II didn't know how the Big Brass viewed our fate or how that viewpoint changed, depending upon how they and their commands could benefit from us and what stand a rival took. In January 1943 the United States faced crises on many fronts. It was still training troops and gearing up factories toward full production for the war effort. The energies and attention of the armed services and of Congress were bent toward the country's survival. We were a mere two dozen women already ferrying airplanes and one cadet class of women gaining flying experience in

Texas.

Back in September Jacqueline Cochran had responded, by her own admission, rudely, bluntly, and negatively to Colonel Oveta Culp Hobby's suggestion for placing her students under the WAAC command. Lined up against Cochran was ATC's Ferrying Division Chief, Colonel William Tunner, who was still smarting angrily from her ploy to remove the WAFS from his command, a move that then-Col. Luke S. Smith had approved. General Arnold was forced to keep the WAFS where it started, but he appeared to agree with Cochran to keep women pilots out of the WAAC. Since Arnold was the boss of the AAF, that should have been enough, but he was subject to persuasion.

Tunner favored rights for women pilots equal to the male civilians joining the Ferry Command — probation followed by officer rank. In November, the newly-promoted Brig. Gen. Luke S. Smith of Training Command looked like an ally. Smith asked the air judge advocate if, under army regulations AR 35-3500, the aviation training of the WAC in nonfederal schools, such as Cochran's, could be legally and officially authorized.

The judge advocate fired back his answer: No. The ruling meant that if women pilots could enter the service as a branch of the WAAC, they could not legally be schooled in Cochran's establishment. They could instead become cadets in a true military school. Possibly, Cochran would be out of the picture.

During the same week in late November, General Arnold met with Colonel Hobby to smooth out details in problems arising with the incorporation of the WAAC in the AAF, along with the best use of WAAC skills here and abroad. Every WAAC at a desk job or even pumping gasoline on the flight line freed a man for active duty. On the issue of training WAACs to fly, General Arnold passed the buck to subordinates to decide at a conference to be held on November 27.

Col. F. Trubee Davison, Maj. Maxwell Murray, Col. Aubrey L. Moore; and Brig. Gen. Luke S. Smith attended the meeting. Smith urged that the AAF agree to place the WAAC in the AAF as the first legal step in giving them flight training as soon as the WAC was approved by Congress. But General Arnold telephoned the air staff meeting asking the members to abide by his wishes that "all remarks with reference to training of women pilots as WAACs should be withdrawn." Why?

Immediately after the meeting, General Stratemeyer talked to Brigadier General Smith and instructed him to prepare plans for training women pilots so they they would eventually be brought into military status. But Stratemeyer warned Smith, "Do not violate

General Arnold's directive to exclude the WAAC. The WAAC enlist women under the age of twenty-one. This is not for the air force!''

General Arnold's stand was in agreement with that of Colonel Tunner and Nancy Love, who felt that enrolling anyone younger than the legal majority age of twenty-one was too great a responsibility for their organization. As an example, when Mary Lowe of Greenville, Illinois, wrote to Nancy Love in 1942 about joining the newly organized WAFS, she received a curt, disheartening reply that the WAFS was not set up to chaperone or babysit girls younger than age twenty-one.

This stand did not interfere with the training of experienced women pilots for the Air Transport Command. And since the WAAC question was still unsettled, General George of ATC and General Barton K. Yount of TC met with Cochran and exchanged views. They reported to General Arnold on December 3 that they could not agree. Brig. Gen. Luke Smith still believed that women pilots belonged under the WAAC. Cochran and Yount wanted to keep women pilots as civilians at least until the first ones graduated from her training school. Some sharp minds caught the possibility that, after graduation with flying time in true military aircraft, women pilots might be considered as ''AAF cadets'' and might take precedence over the non-militarily trained civilian WAFS, whose probation period would soon end. Cochran had already assured ATC and General Arnold that her graduates would be ready to ferry by then. Exit the WAFS? Perhaps.

General Stratemeyer of TC was anxious to settle the matter. On December 9 he proposed in a memo to the air staff that 2,083 WAACs get flight training in the Training Command and asked that AR 95-60 be amended to permit those WAACs who had the necessary qualifications to have service pilot ratings. In agreement, General Smith sent the memo on the same day to General Arnold and to all others whose views might be expressed on this subject. Cochran sent her views to Col. R. P. Naughton on December 15. Brig. Gen. Walker F. Kraus relayed his position to General Arnold on December 19. Then, memos ceased.

Maybe the reason was Christmas. Maybe not. The subject was dropped for two months while the bill which would create the WAC was pending in Congress. However, General Stratemeyer put Brigadier General Smith to work on December 29. As director of individual training, Smith was asked to pattern two types of school for women pilots. The one already in operation in Houston he called ''Type A.'' It was to be four months in duration and have these characteristics:

One month flying of liaison aircraft — 20 hours

Three months flying of commercial and army types, including cross-country and instrument flight — 90 hours

A new class of sixty-six students would enroll each month, so that a maximum of four classes would be taught simultaneously. Total graduates per year would equal 600 women pilots.

(At least Smith's estimate of the dropout rate was not as great as it had been earlier.)

The "Type B" school would train women with little or no flight experience. They would receive:

Nine weeks of flying of liaison aircraft — 60 hours

Eighteen weeks of flying commercial and army types, including cross-country and instrument flight — 140 hours

New classes would enroll periodically and the school would graduate 250 women each year.

The two schools would turn out about a thousand pilots annually, even though the Ferry Command would accept only 500 in all. There seemed to be no need for a larger number of pilots, and the Ferry Command was then the only possible military employer of civilian pilots.

Like a broken record, the Ferry Command and ATC continued to remind the air staff and the Training Command that they would refuse any graduates with fewer than the compromise of 300 hours of flight experience and would not accept a larger number of pilots than they had originally agreed upon. And General Smith, estimating 854 graduates in 1943 and perhaps 1,600 in 1944, simply told ATC to review once again its future pilot needs.

On February 19, 1943, General Smith again revived the discord between ATC and Cochran. He recommended that members of the WAAC be given flight training and aeronautical ratings. General Yount asked him to put together a plan for placing Cochran's training program into the WAAC. Smith got that job done by March 14 and General Stratemeyer approved it.

While the controversy continued, we ferried airplanes — when we could. For us in North Carolina, the skies were safe again to fly on January 9. This time Fulton navigated and she was consistently all right. Because of the thermals, we decided to fly above 3,000 feet and Fulton stuck to that altitude.

We were still about fifty miles from Atlanta when I saw that the other flight, more than a thousand feet below us, was catching up to us. Then they drew alongside and passed us. Feeling outdone, I went down to their level to see for myself if they had chosen the better flight altitude. I tried to keep the same distance between myself and their tail-ender at a cruising throttle setting. It was impossible. Whoever was leading that hop was bending the throttle forward. I suspected it was Erickson. It had to be someone with a competitive spirit. I went back to my flight's altitude. The others beat us into Atlanta by only a few minutes.

Atlanta was a busy airport. We knew the military had a Hotel DeGink there for men only, so we had to go into town. After RONs, we took taxis to the Brady Hotel, where Esther and I had stayed, and found the accommodations the best.

But it was Saturday. With the night already dark, the reservation clerk reiterated to each inquiry, "No, sorry. We haven't a single vacant room left."

To us he said, "Weekends and holidays are always crowded. If you like, I'll try to get you in someplace else."

"Yes, please," I said, looking worriedly at my charges.

The other four WAFS, talking to each other earnestly, came past us saying, "We're going to eat." They headed for the hotel dining room, leaving their gear in a pile near the desk.

"I wish we had a Hotel DeGink," moaned Batson.

The clerk looked in our direction and we closed in to hear the news. "There isn't an empty hotel room in town," he said, shaking his head for emphasis.

"Do you mind if I use your phone and try?" I asked. He shrugged his shoulders and shoved the phone toward me on the counter. In the yellow pages I found the hotels and began alphabetically with the ones I thought were nearby. At last I connected with the Kimball House. I nodded my head affirmatively to the girls as I asked, "Will you save the reservations for a few minutes until we get there?"

The neighborhood didn't look prosperous. But there were people darting about on the streets and sidewalk, much as a school of fish looking for a nibble, so it couldn't be too bad. The block-long, six-story red brick building was rundown. At the street level was a band of small shops displaying cheap merchandise in spotty, streaked windows. I hesitated going into the lobby, but this was our only port and we'd better take it. I was responsible for my flight's welfare, and they couldn't fly tomorrow without getting some rest.

When we registered, the room clerk told us, "That'll be a dollar apiece." From his tone, although we clearly had baggage with us, we knew he meant at once. It wasn't until we had paid that he gave our two keys to the bellhops, who then lifted the parachute bags and were off across the lobby with each of us stringing along behind, toting her B-4 bag.

The lobby in the Kimball House occupied the entire interior of the first floor. The central square (or rectangle) was guarded by thick wooden pillars. While crossing it, I looked up and saw an open area all the way to the roof, much as in the rotunda of a capitol building. It was hard to keep up with the bellhops in the crowd of people, mostly servicemen, who seemed to be rushing toward some goal.

We followed the bellhops up a broad wooden stairway which led to the mezzanine floor and then took deep breaths as we climbed to the next, where they turned and led us down a wide hall to our assigned rooms. As I walked along the third floor balustrade, I noticed that each floor had a similar wooden barrier to keep people from walking off into inner space. Below, those scurrying about were clearly visible. Anyone on any of the floors was able to watch the activity on the ground floor. Images of a ball downstairs and couples waltzing in formal dress popped into my mind. How many suicides did that lobby know through its many years? I wondered. Or suppose someone got dizzy looking down and fell?

Our bedrooms were high-ceilinged, spacious, and sparsely furnished. We had a lovely mantel above a fireplace that offered no heat. A wash basin hung from an inner wall. "The bathroom is right down on the hall on the right," said our bellhop as I put two quarters into his palm.

Batten and I had never seen such a place before. We gathered the other two and went to inspect the common facilities. The bathroom was huge and floored with marble. A bank of wide doors opened the commode stalls. One opened the door and ascended marble steps, as if to a throne. A lady wearing hoopskirts would have had plenty of room at the sides, fore, and aft to accommodate her entire circumference.

"This place has got to be old," whispered Batten.

"Probably built with Scarlett O'Hara's lumber," I replied, taking a good look around me to be sure no ghosts overheard.

Back in our rooms again, we washed our hands and dried them on the thin, tiny towels provided for us. I could see on the mantel some penny postcards that the hotel had set out to advertise their establishment. I picked up one and read it.

"Hey! I was right," I said. "This place was built in 1870 on the site of the original Atlanta Hotel that Sherman burned in the battle during the Civil War!" I read on and informed Batten, "Rates are $2.50 and down. We really hit bottom. They have 300 rooms and the beds are 'the famous spring air (inner spring) mattresses.' Well, let's try them."

We each chose a bed and pressed on it.

"Mine doesn't have any spring to it," said Batten.

"I want to see how clean it is," I replied. Fears of bedbugs worried me. But in my inspection I found the bed clean. However the cotton blanket meant to keep me warm was short and any nap it may have once had was gone. Would we dare ask for more blankets? Chances are, there were no more.

It was past nine o'clock and we had had no dinner. Out went the four of us looking for any small restaurant still open. Along the way, many a crewcut under a service cap swiveled toward us as its owner hurried along. Our uniforms were the magnets deflecting them; the eyes did not seem to notice the occupants. Once past us, the heads went back to original positions; the eyes were forced to notice the areas ahead so the crewcuts would avoid collisions. Such weaving back and forth I'd seen only in Grand Central Station.

Back in our room, Batten and I unzipped and flattened our flying suits to cover as much of the narrow beds as possible as a supplementary blanket. In retrospect, I think we would have been wiser to have worn them over our pajamas.

The next morning we met the other flight at operations. They looked pretty chipper, so I asked where they spent the night.

"In the Brady," responded Bohn.

"They didn't have any room there," said Fulton.

"We just stayed in the lobby. They couldn't kick us out," replied Bohn.

"Not all night!" said Batson.

"We decided that eventually they'd get tired of looking at us and when anybody checked out, they'd give those rooms to us."

I could only visualize an early call, say, at four or five in the morning. "Then when did you get to bed?" I asked.

"It was about midnight," Erickson tossed in.

I felt like a fool. The only direction my mind had been able to take last evening was to get rooms for us, no matter where. I had not seen the possibility the others had. However, years have passed and I have forgotten many a hotel and its rooms, but not the Kimball House. It was a unique experience, one that I would not have missed. Now, the Kimball House is gone.

On to Birmingham! As soon as we got there, I asked Batson, "Why don't you call your parents?" Fulton was worried about a magneto, so a mechanic checked it out. She was right — it needed to be repaired. So we'd be held up for as long as it took.

Very soon Mr. and Mrs. Batson came by to see their daughter. Upon learning that our flight out would be delayed, those charming and gracious folk insisted that we go with them to their home, which was not very far away. We did, and found the Batson home a well-appointed upper middle-class house where we could really wash our hands and relax with a tall glass of soda.

The Batsons spoke of their other daughter, a tall stunner from the looks of her photograph, who was a student at Stephens College in Columbia, Missouri, where she was studying clothes design and modeling. They also had a son, a flight cadet.

Upon our return to the airport, we found that the other flight had gone on with no problems and we'd have no chance to catch up with them. Since Fulton's plane was now flyable, we said good-bye to the Batsons and took off for Jackson, Mississippi. From there it was a short hop to Monroe, Louisiana. The biggest town on the way was Vicksburg.

I was anxious to get to our destination as fast as possible because Detroit kept gnawing at my mind. If I had known then that Kay Thompson and Barbara Poole had received their travel orders for a change of station the day before and had been busy ever since clearing the base, I would have gone back to chewing my nails, a bad habit discarded before my teens. Soon they would be on their way to Detroit and I still had to deliver this airplane!

On Monday we gassed at Shreveport and headed for Dallas, with hopes of seeing our WAFS there. Only Nancy Love was at operations when we arrived. She told me that my transfer had already been written and that I'd better be in Detroit by Saturday. I felt from her tone of voice that I was being blamed for something I couldn't help. But I held my tongue about being sent on a mission when I should have been sent to Detroit instead, so I could become familiar with the setup before the others got there.

We took off and flew to Brady over wide open spaces dotted with cattle. Vegetation became more sparse the farther west we flew. After we delivered the planes, we took the evening bus to Fort Worth, a three-hour ride, so we could connect with American Airlines. If we were lucky, the flight east wouldn't take any longer than eleven hours. At Washington, we took a taxi to the railroad station, then two hours to Wilmington and a taxi back to the base.

I envied Batson. She could find a bench and lie face down on it and be dead to the world in no time at all. I could not sleep anywhere except in a bed. Getting back to NCAAB was an exhausting ordeal for me.

Back on base at last, January 12 was a day that augured much. However, apprehension over my delayed transfer to Romulus screened the import of omens as I met them. With eyes wide open, I walked into the future blindly.

TO ROMULUS

FOR A MONTH I had felt certain that Betty, seemingly wiser, had persuaded Nancy to put me in charge at Romulus. To myself, I appeared to be the most responsible and reliable workhorse in the group, and my NCAAB BOQ pals were of the same mind. I felt that except for Rhonie's acrid criticisms of practically everyone, Nancy would have chosen her, for they had more in common than the experience of flying.

That cold day when we returned from the Brady, Texas, mission, we invaded the BOQ noisily. It was empty of all souls except for Mrs. Anderson. We clattered up and down the back stairs and through the upstairs hall, tugging, shoving, pushing, and lifting our parachute bags, fattened by winter flying suits, B-4 bags, navigator kits, and purses. Our clear, high voices echoed through the building, emphasizing the cold emptiness of the shell that had once harbored the aggregate of WAFS. To think of the dismemberment of that entity as we dispersed so the buds from Sweetwater could be grafted upon us was a bit frightening. Would we ever be able to meet again as one unit, in body as well as in spirit?

Suddenly the telephone announced the hope of a "looie" that he'd have a date that evening. From then on, it rang every few minutes.

Before unpacking, I gathered and inspected my papers and hurried to base operations with my aircraft receipt and flying time record and then to the finance officer with a request for reimbursement of per diem. That done, I almost ran to the WAFS office at headquarters.

Betty Gillies sat in Nancy Love's chair. I came in smiling and saying "hi!" with my usual alacrity. She glanced up from something she was studying and slipped it into a drawer before picking up a pile of papers that she extended to me.

In a cool, businesslike manner, she said, "Hello. The other girls have already gone to Detroit. You'd better hurry to clear the base right away."

The top sheet, dated January 9, 1943, was my transfer. The second one was my authorized travel form (CP63). Next was a clearance form and extra copies of my orders, enough for anyone who might request a copy.

I stared at the sheaf and asked, "How do I clear the base?"

"You'll have to go to every one of the officers listed on the clearance form and the officer in charge must sign you out. If you have any debts at the club or mess or for the BOQ you must settle them before you leave."

Her manner disengaged her from the common level of membership in the squadron without separating her from it, an art she had mastered better than Nancy. Whatever she did was too foreign to my habits for me to think I could either master the technique or duplicate it. I must observe in order to learn, I thought.

There was a point of equality that I had with the best of the group and I declared it with pride. "I never owe money; I don't run on credit," I said, smiling.

"Make sure you take all your equipment back to the subdepot," Betty ordered as she lighted a cigarette.

"Okay. I'd better order transportation from the motor pool," I replied, turning to look back before I sped away.

Fortunately, nine of the offices on the clearance list were within building #40, headquarters. At one office I stood impatiently waiting until the officer in charge deigned to cooperate. The delay irked me, but I knew the man was wasting my time as a means to elevate himself, to show his importance. Amusing, yes; impressive, no.

Each moment I waited gave me time to question what I could do to ease my predicament. I felt helpless in the circumstances in which I found myself. Getting to Romulus late put me at a disadvantage as a leader. Nancy had been the first WAF at NCAAB. She was acquainted with the principal and most influential personnel and with the entire base atmosphere before any of us arrived on the scene. Even in Dallas, where she was now the leader, she had come first, during her inspection tour of bases.

Betty had been established as the executive officer of the WAFS as soon as we were sworn in, in September. Her takeover could proceed without a hitch because Nancy confided a great deal to her about what went on regarding the squadron. She knew much more than the rest of us, who only went out on missions. At Romulus, I was placed in the awkward position of being tardy, of having to learn from the rest of the cadre who was who, where things were, and how to get them. I worried and hurried through the day without completing all of the clearance forms.

I spent that evening deciding what to put in the footlocker and what to take with me to tide me over until the locker arrived at the 3rd Ferrying Group. I had been happy to learn that the government would pay the expense of sending it by parcel post.

As I packed, I learned that there had been temper tantrums. Not from a disappointed Teresa James, who had had Nancy's promise about going to California, but from Esther Nelson, who couldn't understand why she was not transferred to Long Beach, which neighbored on Ontario, her hometown. And a cross Poole had fretted earlier at being sent to Romulus instead of California as being unfair to her. By now, placating their feelings was beyond the power of Nancy, who was gone, or of Betty, who took a neutral position. And how would an unhappy Poole affect me in Romulus? All night I whacked the metal side of the cot. Two sleepless nights in a row.

At 8 A.M. the following day, a staff car pulled up to the subdepot. I got out, lugging all the materiel I had signed for four months before. The driver assisted a grateful me by carrying the parachute bag.

Inside, at the other end of the long counter, Mrs. Hanum checked each article against a record she took from a file. She said cheerfully, "You may keep all the aeronautical charts. When they get out of date or become too dilapidated, you can get replacements at almost any Air Transport Command base."

When she came to items classified as transferable, Mrs. Hanum said, "You'll need your B-4 bag to carry your clothing en route, so you just keep it, along with the navigator's kit. You will still be charged with them. Anything you've worn, like the summer flying coverall and the goatskin jacket, may be transferred to the Romulus account also."

"I'll keep them," I answered.

She took back her copies with my valid receipts and signed the clearance form. With it she returned my receipt of items returned. "Don't lose it!" she warned. "The army never forgives or forgets."

"I won't," I replied as I headed for the door with my arms full of the items I hadn't been required to return. At the staff car, the driver waited until I arranged my burden on the back seat. Then I went up front to sit with him.

"Where to?" he asked.

"We'll take all these other offices I have to visit before clearing the base as we come to them," I said.

In the same areas as the subdepot were ordnance, chemical warfare, quartermaster, Signal Corps, and the engineering offices. Each one supervised its own personnel, buildings, and equipment as a separate entity.

I thought the whole operation was pretty silly. I'd never been to most of those places before, I'd drawn no supplies from them, and yet they had to approve my transfer. What a waste of motion in the military — ugh!

Back at the barracks, the driver helped me unload and I thanked him at the front stoop, which was as far as he was allowed to go. I toted the equipment back up to my room before marching double-quick to head-quarters.

I handed Betty's secretary my completed clearance form and zipped over to the transportation request office for routing to my new station. From Wilmington I would take a train to Philadelphia. Then an airliner to Pittsburgh and another from there to Detroit — but not until the following morning. "Hurry up and wait!" I muttered to myself as I headed back to BOQ 14 to finish packing the footlocker and loading up the B-4 bag. I arranged for the footlocker to be picked up and sent on. At dinner I looked for people to say good-bye to. And then early to bed.

The next day I alighted from the railroad coach and stood beside my bag that the conductor had set on the platform next to the track. How large the Philadelphia station was! And not a redcap in sight. I started across the huge building, stopping for a brief respite from my heavy burden, feeling hurt and ignored by the several redcaps who avoided looking in my direction. I loathed them for their unwillingness to do their job. I picked up my bag and carried it a dozen paces forward before resting again.

A voice asked, "Can I help you, lady?"

People had told me for years that the residents of the East Coast were always in a hurry, and were rude and unfeeling towards others. Here beside me stood a middle-aged man asking to help me. Somehow I sensed he wanted to do his bit for the war effort, so I said, "I've got to find a cab to get to the airport.''

He picked up the bag and walked with me to the cab stand. It was over forty years ago, yet I remember with gratitude that brief act of kindness by a stranger.

The DC-3 flight to Pittsburgh was short. The last part of the ride was like being bounced up and down on a seesaw, for I had taken the last seat. After leaving the plane, we bent against shifting blasts of wind-driven snow.

As soon as I checked in at the ticket counter, I went upstairs to the weather bureau to scan the hourly sequences contingent to airways to Detroit. The Great Lakes weather was at minimums for instrument flight.

At any other time I would have cancelled and taken a later flight. But the other WAFS were already at Romulus. I'd appear careless of my responsibilities if I delayed my arrival, so I boarded the airplane and chose a seat in the single line on the right side of the cabin.

As was the practice during the war, the stewardess drew the window curtains during takeoff (it was also done during landing), so that passengers might not see anything there that could aid the enemy. As soon as we had taken off and gone a short distance, I pushed aside the curtains and looked out. We were over mountains that disappeared each time the airplane ran through clouds. The air was bumpy and the cabin was cold.

I looked around at the other passengers, who appeared complacent. My misgivings grew about our safety. They don't realize, I thought, what danger we're in. The man across the aisle looked like a minister. A woman nearby smiled gently at the infant in her arms.

Not long afterwards, I noticed that the wings were lower than the mountain tops. My eyes strained to see what lay ahead. We flew past a mountain on my side. Why, we had passed that one before! The pilot was circling. The weather must have closed in at Detroit. Could the pilot make his way back to Pittsburgh? From the number of bankings that the pilot was making, I was sure the pilot was still circling. I wondered what was going on in the cockpit. Could he avoid the mountain tops? To calm myself, I repeated in rosary fashion the Twenty-third Psalm.

At last I felt the aircraft slowing, heard the landing gear clump down and felt its vibrations as it shook the cabin floor. The airplane began its descent. I didn't breathe again until after the momentum slowed once the tires screeched against the runway. We had landed at Pittsburgh.

Now what to do? The airline had no later flights scheduled for that day. The only responsibility it took for our predicament was to send us by bus into downtown Pittsburgh and dump us at the Hotel Pitt. I picked up an outside telephone there and learned that the first train bound for Detroit would leave in the early morning. A dilemma — tomorrow's airline or the train? Before I went to my room, I requested a wakeup call early enough for me to catch the train.

Nothing about the Hotel Pitt pleased me. The dinner meal looked and was unappetizing. What made me even unhappier was the interruptions in my sleep that night. I could feel something bite me, especially on the abdomen and around the waist. How many times did I turn on the light to try to catch whatever it was! I inspected the sheets and mattress for the telltale signs of bedbugs. None. Yet something was biting me. It had to be fleas, and I prayed that they didn't find a home in my B-4 bag.

On checking out I informed the cashier of my ordeal, embarrassed to mention it, but believing that he should know. He acted as if he had not heard what I said. Never again would I enter that hotel.

The train arrived in Detroit in late afternoon. The tedious trip had cut into my patience. How much longer would it take to get to Romulus? I knew that Romulus was twenty-five miles from downtown Detroit. Too far to take a taxi. I telephoned the base for transportation. It would not arrive for another hour.

Walk I thought, and get rid of this tension. See what this town is like. All around the station were old, worn buildings fronted by sidewalks littered with trash. I made up my mind I'd come to town only when I had to.

At last an AAF staff car drove up. I showed the driver my orders. He helped with my gear and opened the rear door for me. Where was my usual liveliness? Instead of cheering up the driver, I sat quietly in the back seat, feeling my fatigue and the cold.

I knew headquarters wouldn't still be open when we arrived, so I'd have to meet the commanding officer tomorrow. I told the driver, "Please take me to where the WAFS are staying."

I'd no sooner got into the barracks than three heads poked out of their rooms to see who had come in. Poole, Donahue, and Thompson gathered about me, their eyes and smiles warm with greeting. Then they showed me the barracks. After NCAAB, our quarters looked very fine.

"How did we rate this?" I asked in disbelief.

"It used to house the civilians working on the base," replied Donahue.

"And civilians aren't allowed to remain or live on the base any more," added Poole.

"You can pick any room you want," offered Thompson. "We've already got ours."

I calculated quickly. A northwest wind blew outside. Leeward to that should avoid the chill of the Michigan winters. We were in a one-story building far from the main buildings. No room near a door would do. Closer to the bathroom, but not too close. The room I chose looked just like the others. The inside walls were finished with drywall plaster-board painted white, as were the two wooden twin beds.

"Where's Burchie?" I asked.

"We don't know where she is. She hasn't shown up yet," said Kay Thompson.

"I'd like to unpack and hang up the clothes I'm wearing to get the wrinkles out," I said.

"We're going to eat pretty soon," warned Poole.

"Where's that?" I asked.

"A half-mile away," said Donahue.

"That's a mighty long walk in the dark," I replied.

"Not walk. Ride, madam!" gloated Donahue.

"We've been calling a staff car to take us," said Thompson.

Poole said, "You'll just love our commanding officer. When will you be ready? He'll be at the officers' club tonight. You'll meet him there."

"I look just terrible," I moaned. "And you look so fresh and neat."

"Don't be silly, Scharr," replied Poole. "You look fine. All you need is to comb your hair."

Poole went to the telephone in the middle of the long hall. She asked for a staff car. I could see how eagerly she wanted to go. She hung up the receiver and declared, "Ten minutes."

I washed my face and hands while the makeup went on around me. Then on with the overcoats and neck scarves. Tilt went the overseas caps to their most attractive angle. Honk went a horn and out we flew.

The WAFS cadre, dressed in white silk shirts and gray-green blouses and skirts, marched into the officers' club and found the commander of the Third Ferrying Group, Col. Carlyle L. Nelson, talking to the base commander, Colonel Wilson, at the bar. After introducing me as their squadron leader, the girls led me to the dining room.

Later, after dinner, Colonel Nelson joined us near the vestibule as we were ready to return to the barracks. He said, "Why don't you ladies join me in an after-dinner drink?"

We looked at each other. We'd better obey. Wasn't the saying, "An officer's wish is his command"? I nodded to the other women and he led the way back into the barroom, where he chose a low, round cocktail table circled by a half-dozen unoccupied captain's chairs. He stood until we were seated. Immediately after Colonel Nelson sat down, the bartender was at his side, unbidden, as though by habit.

"Good evening, Colonel," he said.

"Please bring out my brandy and serve us," said our host.

The enlisted man promptly disappeared behind the bar and soon emerged with a tray on which sat tiny, fat glasses and a bottle of Grand Marnier. With a lionizing flourish, the bartender set the tray and spread of tiny paper napkins before his commanding officer. After half-filling each glass, he retreated to his bar.

I noticed that as the officers entered the room, they glanced sidelong at the colonel's table. They avoided the area where we were seated as if they feared to intrude upon our host's privacy. The situation was strange to me and I sat still while everyone else tasted her drink. Why the segregation? I wondered.

The colonel looked at me and I could see that he knew that I had never drunk brandy before. He said to me softly, "One takes the glass and warms it in one's hand, just like this, until one gets the aroma." He lifted the glass and breathed in deeply. "Then it must be sipped slowly so that one may savor every little drop."

I took up my glass and followed Colonel Nelson's directions. The brandy was hot all the way down. The taste was delicious, like oranges. After several sips, a strange numb vagueness reached my toes. How potent this was! My head felt light. My muscles relaxed and I sat without speaking.

But I didn't have a chance to talk anyway. The two Barbaras, Poole and Donahue, carried on most of the chitchat with the colonel. They were already on the best of terms with him. They knew every joke in the latest issue of *Reader's Digest.* What a pair of raconteurs! I wished I had something bright to say, but instead I soaked up impressions. I was on the outside, just as I'd feared.

Colonel Nelson was a middle-aged man of above average height. His once-blond hair had become sparse and gray. His weathered skin was deeply wrinkled at the corners of his faded blue eyes. They were true pilot's eyes and appeared closer than they were because his fleshy nose spread cheekward below them. On his upper lip, disguising its length, was a narrow moustache as wide as his nose. Because of it, one wasn't likely to notice that his upper lip was a small cupid's bow, not as wide as the lower lip. It gave a sweet look to his face.

Unlike unapproachable Colonel Baker, this man volunteered bits of information about himself. He told us that he had gotten his flight training at Randolph Field near San Antonio. He'd remained in the reserves while employed as an airline captain on TWA. When the air corps found it needed pilots, he was recalled.

Thompson asked him, "How does your wife like Detroit?"

He answered, "My wife cannot stand this Michigan climate in winter, so she isn't with me at present. My wife is a real individual, you see. She attended Stephens College in Columbia, Missouri, and she said they made a real individual of her. We sent our daughter to Stephens, too, but I don't know how much of an individual they made of her."

"Then you stay on the base?" asked Poole.

"Yes. There's an upstairs suite right here on the second floor of the officers' club and I appropriated it."

The chatter went on. I relaxed and remembered a story about Stephens College that a code buster, probably in the OSS, had told me on a train ride. The woman was critical of Stephens as a bona fide institution of higher learning. It introduced innovations that seemed like child's play to an intellectual. Credits were given for drama and for making clothes. An aviation pilot program sponsored by the school was so popular with the daughters of upper class families that its students lived in the large Pennant Hotel across from the airport. Stephens was known as a fun school to attend. In Florida, a similar college curriculum was called "beanbag courses." My seatmate likened Stephens to a scarecrow — all show and no substance.

I thought it wise not to relate this to the colonel, but couldn't think of anything else to say. Then he helped me out. He looked at his watch and said, "I usually join a game of poker just about now, before I retire. So if you will please excuse me . . ."

He stood. We jumped to our feet as if bidden and followed him from the room. He stopped; we stopped. He turned and said, "There's an officers' club dance after dinner tomorrow night. Many of the pilots haven't been able to leave the base because of the weather, so probably you'll meet more people than you usually would. I'll send my staff car around to your barracks to pick you up at about seven-thirty."

"Nineteen-thirty?" Poole smiled impishly at him. His eyes twinkled that she had caught him.

The weather on Saturday was as miserably cold as it had been the day before. There was little one could do except to make oneself and one's clothing presentable.

"What should we wear tonight?" asked Poole, looking in at me as I polished my shoes.

"It's got to be dress uniform. Or else how will people know we are the WAFS?" Donahue, too, appeared at my door, overhearing the

Barbara Donahue, left, and Adela Scharr flank Col. Carlyle Nelson at Romulus Army Air Base. Barbara Poole and Katherine Rawls Thompson stand behind them. The photo was taken January 18, 1943.

reply. "Let's knock them dead," she rumbled huskily.

Down the hall Thompson sang out the memorable refrain of the Montana flight. "Where's Burchie?"

And, of course, no one knew.

Later there was a great scurrying back and forth from bedrooms to showers, into the laundry room, and to mirrors over the wash bowls. We tried to hurry without bumping into each other. Donahue came into the lavatory bearing an enormous bottle of cologne, splashing its contents over her arms, neck, and upper chest.

"Where did you get anything that size?" I asked.

"Her sister-in-law sent it to her for Christmas," answered Poole.

"Huh?" I couldn't believe it.

"Come along. I'll show you all the other booty Donnie got."

Donahue followed us into her room, where Poole took up each huge toiletry with undisguised admiration: dusting powder, face powder, face cream, and an exquisite bottle of perfume. "Mary Chess!" exclaimed Poole. "From her sister-in-law."

I looked at the assortment dumbfounded. It all seemed too pretentious and didn't fit into our way of life at all. Later, forgetting momentarily my resolve to become more like Helen Mary, I found Poole alone and whispered, "Wasn't that unusual for a sister-in-law to give her a gift like that? A boy friend wouldn't spend as much.''

Poole fairly sparkled with her answer. ''Don't you know that Donnie is one of the heirs to the Woolworth millions?''

That night, once inside the comparative warmth of the officers' club vestibule, the WAFS removed their overcoats and caps. From the cloakroom came three laughing lieutenants. They hailed the three WAFS with whom they were already acquainted, who quickly introduced them to me. One said, ''May we hang up your coats and caps?'' Yes, of course.

While we waited until the two looies reappeared from the cloakroom, the third stopped a young captain who was leaving the club with three other officers.

''Girls, I want you to meet Captain McIntyre. He's the head of transition school. Captain McIntyre, these are our new WAFS and you'll get to know them in transition soon. This is Mrs. Scharr, their C.O., Barbara Poole, Barbara Donahue, and Katherine Thompson. Kay is an Olympic swimming and diving star.''

Immediately centering his attention on Kay, Captain McIntyre asked, with adulation showing on his face, ''You were really in the Olympics?''

Thompson's sapphire-blue eyes returned his admiration. I was awed myself. He looked too young for the responsibility of heading transition. He was a tall brunette with an arrogant air. The man who introduced us carried his know-it-all attitude a bit further. ''Maybe you remember when Eleanor Holm was the national swimming champion and got kicked off the Olympic swimming team going to Germany? Kay had to do double duty at Berlin in fancy diving *and* in the swimming competition.''

''Hmmmm,'' responded McIntyre.

We all saw the typical reaction in his eyes at news that someone he met had gained fame or notoriety. I could guess by the expression on her face that Katherine Rawls Thompson felt uneasy, as if she were a rare, small but magnificent specimen on exhibition for all to see.

I was never to meet Captain McIntyre often at Romulus, but when I did he fascinated me. He could turn someone off with an icy gaze or turn on his charm, of which he had plenty. He was on and off like a faucet, depending upon how the outcome of the meeting advanced his interests. The faucet now poured as he looked squarely down at Kay and in dulcet tones he asked her, ''Have you done any flying since you arrived?''

''No,'' answered Thompson wistfully.

Then, not wishing to show his interest too plainly, McIntyre offered, ''You girls come 'round to transition tomorrow and we'll check you out.''

He and his pals put on their billed caps and opened the outside door. ''Aren't you staying for the dance?'' I asked.

''Lord, no!'' replied McIntyre without a backward glance. The door slammed shut behind them. A blast of arctic air occupied the space where the captain had been. I shivered. The way McIntyre had looked at Thompson gnawed at my mind. But soon we were enjoying the evening and for a time McIntyre was forgotten.

After dinner I was introduced to people who introduced me to more people, but I could not assimilate all the names. Romulus was clearly a friendly place. Soon the music began and the WAFS were dancing. Each time a dance number was completed, Colonel Nelson or one of our new acquaintances introduced us to others. And while a number was in progress, out from the stag line came one friendly officer after another to cut in. We felt like belles — something we never had at Wilmington dances.

One man needed no introduction to me. I recognized him as he approached a little group of officers clustered about me during an intermission. He was Cowboy McMahon from Montana, who dressed western style and flew the Mississippi River Fuel pipeline from Louisiana to St. Louis. His airplane was often hangared in Robertson's south hangar on Lambert Field. I knew McMahon came to tease and not to dance.

I had noticed him before on the dance floor with a blonde of uncertain age. One couldn't help noticing her bright red dress. Harold had told me his wife was a brunette, so evidently McMahon was squiring someone else.

''What are *you* doing here?'' was McMahon's greeting.

''I'm stationed here now,'' I said, smiling weakly.

''I'm stationed here myself.'' McMahon turned his head and his gaze down to the captain's bars on his shoulder. My eyes followed. I thought, he's showing off.

''Just wait until I get back to St. Louis,'' Mac said. ''I'm gonna tell Harold all about these Michigan wolves hanging around you. I saw you dancing with all these fellas! Harold's not goin' to like it one bit.''

I knew he wasn't fishing. He knew me of old. I'd tease him right back. I smiled what I hoped was an enigmatic smile and turned toward my next dancing partner. As we waltzed across the floor, I forgot about him.

More than twenty years later, during a one-week Air Force Reserve officers seminar in the Pentagon, I met again one of my dancing partners of that night — Col. James Gillis, by then a lawyer and a state senator from Michigan. When I knew him he was a quiet, somewhat bashful lieutenant.

Gillis said, "I'll never forget how you girls looked that night at the officers' club in Romulus. You were so vital, as if you'd been in the Florida sun. All the other women looked pale by comparison. And we could talk to you and you could talk back because you understood what we were saying. When you're flying like we did, you can't talk about anything else. It was great." Then he added thoughtfully, "You know, the boys didn't see you like other women. Nobody would make a pass at you. You were our sisters in the sky."

His words struck a responsive note in my mind, but I didn't know why at the time. Strangely enough, Gillis, as a young lieutenant, had perceived a kinship that was valid enough to be tested years later.

Especially happy to be with the WAFS that evening was a young couple, Lieutenant and Mrs. Rightman. The pretty, sweet wife was patently pregnant and refused to dance. But she delighted in watching her husband fox-trotting with us. He, still sallow and wan, had just been released from the hospital where he had been isolated with scarlet fever. He was already on orders again and danced with each of us in celebration of his freedom. I hoped he'd dance with us another evening.

Colonel Nelson's party was less active and more dignified than we were. At one point he asked us to come to his table to meet some important people whose businesses contracted to supply the government with war materiel. Ed Price and his wife were introduced to us. He was a tall, dark-complexioned man whose importance was such that even though he was a civilian, SNAFU Airlines carried him now and then to the nation's capital.

All of Colonel Nelson's guests were impressed with our volunteer flying for the military, but what amused me was their evident warming to me more than to the others just because I was the cadre leader. I felt that I didn't belong with these people, whatever it was that they had in mind.

Mr. Price said, "In Michigan, we have only low hills, but we ski anyway. We'd like you to come skate and ski with us some weekend soon."

"I'd love that," I said, "but I'm supposed to deliver airplanes. The chances are that I'd never get away from the base for that sort of thing."

"We'll ask the colonel to excuse you," Price replied.

"Please don't," I responded. "I don't want him thinking I asked for any special favors."

"I'll tell him it was my idea," he said, and with that the matter was closed forever.

How long would they have wooed me if they had known that Donahue was a member of one of America's sixty wealthiest and most influential families, that Thompson was an Olympic star, that Poole had done barnstorming as a parachute jumper? Even Burchie, who still had not shown up, had been an accomplished horsewoman before she took up flying.

A local artist in the party, a Mrs. O'Hara, said she wanted to do my portrait in pastels any time I was free. Nothing came of that offer either, fortunately. I felt foolish enough earlier in the day when Colonel Nelson stopped us after breakfast to tell us to remain in the club until a base photographer arrived. The photographer took a picture of Nelson sitting on a sofa between Donahue and me, with Poole and Thompson standing behind us.

The next day, at Sunday morning brunch, we were surprised to see that photograph in the Detroit *Free Press*. The newspaper related in great detail the purpose of our new assignment. Immediately after brunch, the Barbaras told me they wanted to get into Detroit to try to buy some more papers.

Donahue reasoned, "Detroit is Puddles' [she was calling Poole 'Puddles' now] old stomping ground. She wants to show me around."

"Have a good time and get some papers for the rest of us," I replied. "But wait — don't you want to go to transition?" I called, remembering McIntyre's invitation.

"No, you go," said Poole, already wiser than I about Romulus.

"The weather doesn't look much like flying," added Donahue.

"I spent enough time flying around Detroit City Airport to know how miserable weather can get in a hurry," said Poole. And off the two new buddies went, not to return until nightfall.

Bundled up in our winter flying suits, Thompson and I were halfway to the transition school building when a motor pool sedan stopped beside us and the driver offered, "I'll take you where you want to go."

"We're headed for transition," answered Thompson.

"Isn't that out of your way?" I asked.

"Don't worry. Hop in."

We did and he let us off at the ready room door, the place where pilots wait who are ready when their airplanes and instructors are not. We entered to wait for McIntyre. I glanced at the clock — 1300. Thompson sat rigid, tense. I pulled some stationery from my purse and began to write an answer to Harold's latest letter.

As soon as Captain McIntyre appeared, he said, "You girls will be

WAFS at Love Field, Dallas, flew more advanced trainers than the Romulus cadre. Shown with the Vultee "Vibrator," from left, are Helen Richards, Dorothy Scott, and Florene Miller.

checked out in BT-13s as soon as we can get around to you." He went behind the counter and pulled out some technical orders for the BT-13, then handed them to me as if deferring to my rank. He turned to Thompson and said, "Did you ever fly an AT-6?"

After hesitating, she replied in a low voice, "No."

"I'm flying one now, and I'll take you along," he ordered. He and Thompson disappeared out the door, bound for the flight line.

I didn't like it, but I sat tight. McIntyre knew very well, I thought, that he should have offered the first ride to me. Thompson's pause indicated that she was aware of the correct thing to do, but the poor girl couldn't do anything but obey. If I had objected, it would have been out of character for me and somewhat egotistical. Yet I was worried about how Thompson would perform if he let her handle the controls. I had never flown with her.

I read the BT-13 tech orders intently. Then I stood up and walked to the window to look out. The ceiling had lowered; the atmosphere was opaque. I sat down and started a letter to Helen Krueger. How long would they be up? Well, another letter, this one to Reverend Lampe at West Presbyterian Church. Back to the letter for Harold. At last McIntyre and Thompson returned.

There was the quietness of finality in McIntyre's manner as he nodded coldly to me. He bent and fussed with something under the counter. When he rose again to his full height, he brusquely dismissed us with, "That's all for today. You'll fly tomorrow, Mrs. Scharr." He then turned on his heel and left.

During the long hike to the barracks, Thompson broke the silence. "I did some pretty stupid things out there," she said.

More than the arctic air caused me to shiver. My intuition told me that I would not get transition tomorrow nor at any time in the near future, no matter what the colonel and the transfer orders had stated. What gnawed inside me was the feeling that Nancy or Betty would have handled the afternoon better than I. But how?

Thompson's failure troubled her, too. She explained, "I couldn't see out very well at all. The seat was too low, and visibility was poor. I didn't know where I was and I had to hunt around on the instrument panel before I could find what I was supposed to be looking at there."

Poor girl! What she was really telling me was that Captain McIntyre, the great head of transition, didn't know the first thing about being a teacher. If that's the way the school was handled, I'd do exactly what I'd learned to do at Lambert Field — rely on learning everything by myself.

Back at the barracks, the telephone rang. Thompson's room was closer, so she answered.

"Del," she called. "It's Colonel Nelson. He wants to speak with you."

I ran, dropping my letter on the dresser as I left the room.

"Hello, WAFS Scharr speaking."

"Colonel Nelson. How would you girls like to see the B-19?"

"There's only two of us here. The others went to town."

"That's all right. Colonel Wilson and I were going over to look at it and we thought you'd like to come along."

"Oh, yes, thanks. We'd like that," I replied. I had already overheard that a B-19, an unusual airplane, was parked at the base. Within ten minutes we were seated in a staff car with Colonel Wilson and Colonel Nelson. We went around the field and far to the other side. There, in front of a hangar, was the largest winged contraption I had ever seen. Two wooden buildings, at least two stories high, had been built on either side of the fuselage to protect the engines from the Michigan winter.

As we left the car, Colonel Wilson explained, "It was flown here and put in winter storage." We stared at it in amazement as he added,

"Most people aren't even aware that it is here."

"Wouldn't you like to see what it's like inside?" asked Colonel Nelson.

"You bet!" I said. Thompson was still too cowed and depressed by her bout with the AT-6 to say anything. Led by Colonel Nelson, we clambered into the fuselage. Inside was a maze of passageways. Two led out into the wings to allow a mechanic to work on an engine even in flight. We crawled into one of them behind the engines. It was a bright idea to save the time it would have taken to lift an engine away from a wing via pulleys and employ a derrick in order to bench it.

Colonel Nelson was trying his best to make us feel welcome on his base and Colonel Wilson was equally as thoughtful. I appreciated both their efforts.

When we arrived back at the barracks, we found an unexpected visitor.

"Hello, Sweeties," said Nancy Love, who was washing her hands in the lavatory. "What's been happening?"

"The Barbaras went to town," Thompson put in quickly.

"Burchie hasn't shown up yet," I answered, "and we've just seen the B-19."

"That lug!" retorted Nancy. "If it only flew half-way decently, we could use it. They stashed it away up here for the duration, where the weather will be a perfect excuse for not flying it."

The revelation surprised me, but Thompson and I left the subject without further exploration.

"How did you get in? I mean, how were you able to land here?" I asked.

"I finally sneaked in between some instrument weather. I was lucky. If I'm still lucky, I'll get out of here with an older advanced trainer to take to Louisiana."

"What did you bring in?" I asked.

"An AT-6," Nancy replied.

'Are you hungry?" asked Thompson.

"If the food is good, yes," answered Nancy.

"The officers' club is having a buffet dinner tonight," said Thompson, "and I've heard that it is marvelous."

"How's everyone in Dallas?" I asked.

"Just fine. I got checked out in an AT-6 right away and the girls are getting BT time. The barracks wasn't ready when we arrived, but we have a nice arrangement now."

Neither Kay nor I chose to mention our transition experience of the day. My guess was that Thompson was too embarrassed. I had an

The AT-6, North American's "Texan." Nancy H. Love was the first of the WAFS to ferry this plane, from Dallas' Fifth Ferrying Group.

uneasy feeling that Nancy would have blamed us. Why would she go to bat for us to get basic training if she didn't even consider us important enough to accompany us to Detroit, as she had the group that went to Dallas? The thought quickly fled from my mind, for Nancy's charm was hypnotic. The fault must have been mine as far as Captain McIntyre was concerned. I must work harder to overcome our obstacles by myself, I told myself. And I would have to fail utterly before I confessed our shortcomings to Nancy.

"Do you need anything, like a towel or soap or something?" I asked Nancy.

"I think I can manage with what I brought along," she replied. "But right now, I'm ready for a shower and then some of that wonderful food."

"We've got plenty of rooms. You can take your choice," offered Thompson.

We went our separate ways and regrouped for the ride to the club at 1800. By that time the Barbaras had returned, laden with newspapers. They were delighted to see Nancy.

I had never before seen such a buffet in my life. In the Swedish smorgasbord tradition, arrayed on a long white table was a line of colorful platters. A huge, decorated fish mold, various other molds, and wheels spoked with appetizers. A tremendous roast beef. A boned ham. Black olives, gelatin concoctions, salads, and vegetables. The meal began as a delight to the eye and was consumed as a gift to the palate. I felt a twinge of conscience. This was wartime and food was being rationed. I was partaking of plenty only because I was a member of a group risking their lives for their country. But in truth, I was doing what I loved and what I could do best. I didn't need to be fed like this for doing that.

The buffet was supervised by the mess captain, a man whose family had expertise in fine restaurant cuisine. His appearance was both puzzling and magnetic. With his dark hair, his piercing black eyes, and black brows slanting upward, he looked as if he could have been cast as Lucifer in the story of Dr. Faustus. Yet this tall, imposing officer spent the evening in patient hospitality, carefully supervising and catering to the pleasure of every person in attendance. His wife and small youngsters were present and also were pleasant and gracious to everyone.

We met even more officers and their wives than we had the evening before and enjoyed ourselves immensely. On returning to the barracks, there was a bit of chitchat as we washed our faces and brushed our teeth before we retired to our own rooms.

The third week in January brought new problems to each WAFS leader. Back at Wilmington, Esther Nelson was ill and grounded. Another grounded WAF was Esther Manning Rathfelder, the first to become pregnant. What to do about that? The Army Air Forces had established no tradition for women pilots. She was fortunate to have Betty Gillies as her leader, for Betty could influence Colonel Baker in a positive way. Pregnant Esther was grounded, but was kept on the payroll to do Betty's office work, thereby allowing both Betty and Helen Mary to fly more than a desk.

With Cubs being crated and sent to their destinations, there was a lack of airplanes to fly. Colonel Baker looked to the north, and Helen Mary was soon ordered to lead Gert Meserve, Delphine Bohn, and Nancy Batson to Canada to get PTs manufactured by the Fleet factory, using Fairchild airframes and radial engines.

The Dallas leader, Nancy Love, was weathered in with us at Romulus, so she didn't yet know that Dorothy Scott had been horseback riding over the weekend and had been grounded by a tumble which cracked three ribs and a shoulder.

All of the Third Ferrying Group at Wayne County Airport were grounded. Blustery winds brought us snow from Canada. On all airways leading to Detroit, the ceilings were low and visibility was poor. Crews that could cope with instrument conditions left on missions. Any pilot who was checked out in aircraft at factories outside the weather pattern departed. We WAFS, supposedly in transition, couldn't fly in the soup of our atmosphere and were not supposed to get orders until transition was completed. But how could we be checked out in the airplanes we were to ferry with the weather closed in? It was a week of challenges and I felt I was ill-prepared to meet them. To quote from the old showboat melodrama, I ''had no mother to guide me.''

These lucky WAFS managed to catch airline transportation to or from ferrying assignments. These five, shown with an airline pilot and stewardess (top), are, from left: Esther Nelson, Barbara J. Erickson, Teresa James, Esther Manning, and Bernice L. Batten.

Our barracks, No. 806, was situated one-half mile south of the base intersection of the mess hall to the west and a cluster of drab, two-story barracks buildings, where the other squadrons lived, to the east. Farther west, across the perimeter road enclosing the mile-square airport, was the officers' club. Up along the outer road was the north hangar. Most of the ferrying group business took place at the southwest corner of the airport inside the south hangar, where the transition school had its office, airplanes, hangar and tie-down spaces. It was impossible to reach all these facilities without some means of transportation, so buses driven by volunteer Red Cross workers made regular, scheduled stops along the outer road to the field. We WAFS were quartered eight blocks from the nearest bus stop.

On Monday morning Poole called the motor pool for a ride to the mess hall. The driver told her reluctantly, "Sorry, but we got orders to skip transportation for you ladies here on the field unless you're on orders and have to get somewhere in a hurry."

"We'd just as soon skip breakfast if we have to walk a half mile in weather like this" retorted Poole.

Our short honeymoon with the administration was over. In a few hours, the reunion with Nancy would cool as well. Nancy disappeared after breakfast. We weren't sure what to do, but there was one thing that our three months in Wilmington had taught us. As we walked back to our barracks after breakfast, we saw men pouring from their barracks and lining up in two rows to stand roll call and hear their orders. We did likewise. On the short road south of our new home, we stood shivering in the crisp air just long enough for me to call out our names. Then we broke formation and ran for the door.

Our shoulders were hunched over and we were beating our hands together to improve circulation when the phone rang. It was Nancy.

"Colonel Nelson wishes you to meet with him and me at the south hangar immediately. He is sending his staff car, so be ready when it arrives," she told me.

I broke the news to the others, which stimulated visits to the bathroom and face-fixing at the mirrors.

Colonel Nelson stood at the door of a conference room, which was furnished only with chairs in spartan military style. We preceded him, but waited until he moved to sit down before we took our seats. He smiled broadly at us.

"I've been telling Mrs. Love that we'll check you girls out in airplanes you haven't flown yet," he said.

"They've done a nifty job for us down at Wilmington," Nancy returned. "You'll find them fully capable."

Then the colonel announced, "After due consideration, I have decided to appoint Mrs. Scharr as leader of this cadre. And Mrs. Love concurs."

The other cadre members beamed at me.

"As soon as we have some flying weather," said Colonel Nelson, "you will be flying. We ferry many airplanes from this base and usually we are very busy. Whenever you aren't working in transition or on orders, I expect you to attend the ground school."

It was the same old story, of course. But then he offered something new, which didn't seem quite fair to us. "Until next week," he said, "the new bases employing WAFS may open your squadron to qualified women pilots. The ones accepted here will obtain their orientation here, instead of at Wilmington."

I stared agape at the colonel.

"We have an officer's wife with more than two thousand hours. She's been instructing at Ann Arbor. She felt unwilling to leave her

The first WAFS barracks at Romulus AAB, eight city blocks from other human habitation.

three teen-aged children to go to Wilmington, but now that this cadre is here, she wants to come in.''

"She will have to meet all the requirements necessary," reminded Nancy.

"Everything is in order except for a high school equivalency certificate. It seems that Mrs. McElroy lacked a month of schooling in order to complete her high school graduation. She is working on that now."

Still looking at Nancy, Colonel Nelson said, "Our weekend publicity has brought us a request that you might be kind enough to fill. A radio station has asked for one of the WAFS to address a group of high school students in the interest of patriotism to speak to them about what the WAFS will be doing on this base. It will be broadcast from downtown Detroit."

Nancy flinched. "I never enjoy speaking before a group," she said.

"Oh, it's not bad, Nancy," I intruded. "After you do it several times it gets easier. I get tongue-tied talking to just one person, but speaking to a large group is a snap."

Me and my big mouth! Everyone, especially Nancy, stared at me as coldly as if I had just announced that I was a bastard. My helpful attempt to reassure Nancy hurt me; superiority to a superior is best left unsaid.

"Do you have any questions?" asked Colonel Nelson.

"Do you have a gymnasium?" I asked.

"Yes, we have facilities for the men to exercise and relax, but there are none for women, so physical training will not be a requirement for you girls."

Just as at Wilmington, I thought. Our recreation would be walking to the mess hall and facing the northern gales. Hardly a pleasant prospect or diversion.

"I'll speak to Mrs. Love and Mrs. Scharr about her duties," said the colonel, "so you others are excused to attend transition." They filed out and disappeared. I didn't see them again until the evening meal.

"I think, Mrs. Love, that she" — nodding in my direction — "might gain the most by visiting the 19th Squadron headquarters and seeing how they carry on their operations."

"Very good," replied Nancy, off the hook. "I expect to check the weather conditions and be prepared to return to Love Field by way of Louisiana as soon as possible. I'm on orders, you know."

I figured that the 19th Squadron was located in one of the main buildings of the ferrying group and the only way to get there was via the base bus. I waited at the stop with a few other pilots until an approaching bus lumbered to a stop. The door opened slowly. The driver's arm looked totally incapable of moving the lever, but she managed to. The men, courteous as always, stepped aside to let me enter first.

From the back of the bus I was able to be an amused spectator to the reactions of the male passengers as they boarded and saw the driver. Dressed in a gray uniform with a Red Cross patch delineating her volunteer status, she was a gray-haired lady not more than five feet tall. As each man entered, he hesitated and looked as if he would back out if he could, but trapped by the ones in line behind him and eager to escape the cold, he marched forward, perhaps wishing he had bought more life insurance for his loved ones.

Then, perhaps realizing that the vehicle was not an airplane and

Four Wilmington pilots beat Romulus WAFS to Niagara: Nancy Batson, Delphine Bohn, Gertrude Meserve, and Helen Mary Clark.

would not exceed speeds of fifteen or twenty miles an hour over the ice-covered streets, he reluctantly moved down the aisle and sheepishly sat down. It turned out that the driver was competent and no mishaps occurred. On subsequent passages around the base, I could always pick out the man who had ridden with one of the Gray Ladies by his "devil-may-care" attitude.

A bit of cold wandering about brought me to the 19th Squadron barracks building. I was ill at ease entering this men's world, for that is where they slept, showered, and shaved. I felt as if I were too close to intruding on the intimate scenes in their lives.

The squadron office was on the first floor. The executive officer there gave me the ground rules for running a male squadron because that was all he was familiar with. He went over the details of morning reports that he used for the enlisted personnel. He gave me other unfamiliar forms that left me more befuddled the longer he spent explaining them to me. I knew of no way that WAFS would have enlisted women to supervise unless we became WACs and that wasn't likely.

I hung around the office for a good part of the day until I saw that I couldn't get much more information out of the officers. Certainly they felt relief when I vanished, but no more than I did. I carried my "homework" with me — a burden of pamphlets and organizational charts — and wondered if I'd ever be able to understand this business.

At the dinner table I asked, "What did you get to do today?"

"We read tech orders," replied Donahue.

"Words without end," sighed Poole.

"Amen," added Thompson.

"Gee," I said. "Couldn't you get in a little Link?"

"We tried," replied Thompson grimly.

"We signed up for it," continued Poole with some bitterness. "I was ready to take my turn and some major waltzed in at the last minute and beat me out of my turn."

"Rank has its privileges," commented Donahue archly.

Nancy had been listening and now she spoke. "We must remember that Link trainer time along with instrument training is vital in the war effort for the men who will be using it in ferrying overseas. Let's not lose sight of that."

If her words didn't calm the girls, they shut them up. We ate on in silence.

Afterwards we joined Colonel Nelson at his table in the lounge area and helped him drink his brandy. Somehow he drifted on to the subject of Stephens College again which prompted Nancy to talk about her years at Vassar.

Then Donahue, who had also studied at Vassar, told of a jink she had pulled. Not long before she graduated, she thought it would be stunning to flaunt a streak of white at the temple in her black hair. So she tried to change the color with laundry bleach. It had unusual results. Instead of turning the tress white, it turned it red. Everyone thought the streak was laughable. On the day of graduation, Donahue conceded that the red streak was too bizarre for the ceremony. Frantically she dragged out a bottle of liquid black shoe polish and applied it hastily. She ended her story with a throaty laugh. "I walked down the aisle in that slow promenade and as I passed, the aroma of shoe polish filled the air."

The next day Nancy told me, "The best thing for you to do is to go over to operations to find out how they work."

Because I went alone and was not introduced by Colonel Nelson or by Nancy, the staff did not welcome me. They went about their work and I looked on. No one tried to explain or brief me, although they were fairly friendly. I came away with not much more knowledge than I already had. And I could tell that because there were only four of us — Burchie had not yet arrived — we were the smallest of minorities. Any assignments they passed on to us would be the ones *they* wanted to give us. I would have no voice in the matter and very little status.

I wished I could have seen how Nancy would have responded to them. I was burdened with the traditional feeling that as a woman in a man's world, I must allow them to run the show. I had nothing to offer but hard work and a sincere desire to do well. We WAFS were newcomers and had to take our places, the last in line. Operations would parcel out the mission assignment to pilots who had been on base the longest or who were the most eligible for each task.

We awoke Tuesday morning to a blinding, blowing snowstorm. On our way to the mess hall, as we snaked and slipped across deep drifts, we leaned into the gale-force winds and kept our mouths shut. I swore to myself to remember to wear sunglasses, for I could keep the sharp slivers of ice out of my eyes only by squinting. The sleet smacked our faces with brutal force. The cold enveloping me bore into my cheekbones, accumulating beneath them so that I almost cried out from the pain.

The girls told me later that at the hangars, it was necessary to thaw out the brakes before any airplanes could be started. The mechanics used electric dips to warm the engine oil.

Again the WAFS got no Link time. But at least they found available Morse code equipment — that was not a popular pastime with the pilots. Yet it was a meaningless activity for WAFS. We had not yet ferried anything equipped with a radio and weren't likely to do so in the future. The girls filled their day reluctantly reading technical orders, bulletins, directives, and anything else they could lay their hands on.

Nancy Love was a good sport about the weather although she was anxious to leave. She said at breakfast, "I know what Michigan winters are like. I lived in Houghton, Michigan, and that's much farther north than this is."

"I know what they are, too," muttered Poole, "and I want to go to Long Beach."

At noon we were stunned by the news that Lieutenant Rightman had died in Chicago of spinal meningitis. He had been stricken while on a ferry mission, and the several men who had been in his company were detained in a hospital under observation. Our flight surgeon ordered us to his office where he told us that anyone who had been in close contact with Lieutenant Rightman would have to check in with his office daily for a week because the disease was so contagious.

We had each danced with the lieutenant Saturday night. Very close contact indeed. So we were under suspicion. We held thermometers under our tongues and hoped for the best. Almost as bad, we had to resign ourselves to remaining on base as long as we were under observation. There would be no chance that we could be placed on orders, even if the weather cleared.

As twilight descended, the wind abated. Above the white landscape and across the western horizon, a red sunset spread in a wide fan of glorious color. It was beautiful, raising a sublime hope for the morrow. We were almost transfixed as we watched the colors change as we rode toward the south hangar in the bus. The setting sun left a glow on the snow, and the red of the western sky lingered long after the stars came out and the full moon showed its face in the east. I wished Harold were with me to share the sight.

Once inside the hangar, we each climbed into a BT, where we began to learn the cockpit check. Then we moved about outside the airplane to do a ground check preflight. We resolved to become well enough acquainted with the airplane so that if we got a chance to fly a BT, we would do a perfect job of it.

Friday I had to return to the barracks in the late morning to wait for an officer to bring a receipt form for me to sign for the cot, blankets, and other supplies. Burchie had finally arrived the day before. She was staying temporarily with her husband, George, in the city.

While I was waiting for the housing officer, I wrote to Harold, telling him, "The men pilots are going stir crazy, for they have not been sent to better climes to pick up airplanes for delivery. High above the treetops, the wind hums steadily, dipping again and again, whining in the trees, searching the barracks for entry, clutching and tearing, endeavoring to loosen something to carry away as a souvenir. All of us feel closed in, and Poole especially would like to get out of here."

Yet there had been a bright spot in transition. I saw a short film produced by Bell Corporation on how to fly the P-39, the Airacobra. It made me feel like taking one of them up some day, despite their reputation as a difficult and dangerous plane to fly.

As I continued to wait for the housing officer, I thought of how little we had accomplished since Sunday. A string of dragging, futile days, relieved for me only by two hours of Link trainer, some Morse code, and the daily inspection for meningitis symptoms — stiff neck, fever, and extraordinary pulse rate. Fortunately for us, the symptoms never appeared.

I still didn't know how I could guide the WAFS operations here. The men in group operations decided our assignments. We were too small a unit to be important. I didn't wish to be obnoxious in a Cochran way, nor had I an influential husband or beauty as did Nancy, to give my position any weight.

During the days we didn't see Nancy. Some evenings she must have had dates with the society people she knew in the Detroit area. We also didn't see our newest member, Lenore McElroy, except in the mornings, for she was busy with orientation. We never knew that it was Nancy Love and not Captain McIntyre who gave McElroy her flight check and a "thumbs-up" verdict.

The opportunity for McElroy's test came when a flash of clearing weather thrust aside the cloud cover long enough to allow a flight to include advanced coordinated turns. Following the short interval of sunshine, the clouds closed in again as swiftly as they had parted, and winter attacked with renewed fury, a demon on the rampage, tearing at man-made structures, and piling snow against the window panes. However, the insulation provided by the snow barred the fierce wind, so inside the barracks we remained comparatively warm and comfortable.

We knew by this time that Happy Hour was celebrated on Fridays after work until dinner at the officers' club. The drinks were half price. Burchie had disappeared again, bound for Detroit and George. Our foursome decided to check our makeup and comb our hair in the ladies room at the club rather than walk the mile to the barracks and back in the cold. We were too early for dinner, but already the club was busy.

Romulus was too far from Detroit to have regularly scheduled public bus service. Most men on the base had no cars to drive, for gasoline rationing was so rigorous that only enough fuel for one trip to the city per week was allowed. Besides that, most of the lonely, unmarried officers had little money and nowhere to spend their evenings except at the club. There, at least, were Ping Pong and billiards in the game room. The young men met few women on base, so they welcomed the WAFS as females to talk to, delighting to find women who knew the lingo they spoke. And on Fridays, until six o'clock, they could drown their frustrations in two drinks for the price of one — a quarter each instead of the usual fifty cents. The Coke I ordered cost a nickel. The bar was crowded and people greeted each other like long lost friends.

After dinner, at Colonel Nelson's bidding, we settled ourselves in the armchairs that ringed his chosen cocktail table and watched as he nodded to the bartender to bring his after-dinner brandy and glasses. He beamed, for he had cornered the only aviation-talking women. At other tables, officers cast sidelong glances in our direction. None of them would have dared to join us or to interrupt whatever we were talking about.

A lull in the story-telling and *Readers' Digest* jokes gave me an opportunity I'd been waiting for. My words rushed eagerly to nail Colonel Nelson while his mood was mellow. I said, "I tried to see you today, Colonel, but you were too busy. I wanted to talk to you about the WAFS flying — "

Abruptly Colonel Nelson held up his hand to stop me. Lips parted, I waited. He spoke. "I make it a rule never to speak about business once I leave my office in the afternoon. Never try to talk to me about military problems outside business hours."

The brush-off wasn't meant to be cruel, but I felt as if I had my face slapped. There was nothing more for me to do. I'd bide my time until Monday. To me his attitude was unfair to the men waging war, unable to drop everything when the sun went down. Did men in battle stop at 1700 every afternoon? Did the pilots ferrying planes across the ocean suddenly quit? I wondered where Colonel Nelson got his ideas. He'd been an airline captain — maybe the pilots' union demanded no more than specified hours of duty before a rest. I knew that as a teacher, no matter how tired I was, if a pupil came to me after school hours for help, I would take the time to make a problem clear to him. And that wasn't as important as winning the war! So I had little to say until the colonel looked at his watch.

He said, "It's time for my game of cards. When I've lost my five dollars that I allot myself for amusement, I'll quit."

As Donahue and Poole followed the CO into the card room, Donahue explained, "One of the fellows wants to play some gin rummy."

Pilot reunions sometimes reveal what one didn't or shouldn't have known during the war. In 1985 I learned that even at Wilmington during our probationary period, the two Barbaras had become a gambling duo, eager for high-stakes games with the officers.

With their departure, two lieutenants came over to join Thompson and me. Another lieutenant bounced into the lounge and hovered about our shoulders. He rubbed his hands and happily declared, "Am I glad you girls came here!"

One of our companions said, "That's Schwartz."

Schwartz gloated. "I just had a mission in an enclosed cockpit. We started out here by taking all those open cockpit jobs from Canada. Well, we won't be doing that any more. They say you girls are going to take them instead."

We tried to ignore him. He was needling us, but at least he was honest.

"How about a game of Ping Pong?" he asked, looking at us as if we were prey.

No one stirred.

"Hey how about you, Scharr? Want to try? I'll beat you."

Somewhat tense, I replied, "Okay. I need the exercise."

I followed him out of the lounge and into the game room, where I'd never been. Two lieutenants were in the midst of a game. While we waited, Schwartz kibitzed the players and I went over to the pool table where Cowboy McMahon and his blonde date were knocking balls into pockets with such masterful skill they amazed me. The woman was as good as he. Their game didn't last long.

Cowboy looked at me calculatingly and said, "I'll play you a game."

"I don't know how," I begged off.

"How come you don't know how to play billiards?" he asked.

I noticed out of the corner of my eye that the two looies had quit and that Schwartz held both paddles and balls. As I left McMahon to join Schwartz, I replied "Because I didn't have a misspent youth."

The game with Schwartz didn't last long. As he scored points against my zero, one onlooker put balm on my feelings. "Don't worry that he's winning," he said. "Schwartz always wins. That's why he suckered you into this game. None of the fellows will play with him any more."

"That's all right," I replied. "I don't mind if I lose at this. It's not important."

After I laid down the paddle and ball, another officer said, "I don't know too much about pool, but I'll show you some pointers about the game."

He taught me how to hold the cue and to sight from the cue and cue ball in lining up with the ball to be hit into a side pocket. "It's a matter of science," he said. "This is the only game in which the element of luck is lacking."

Tiring soon of that meticulous sighting, I thanked my instructor for the information and went out to find Thompson ready to go to the barracks. We both picked up Poole and Donahue, who were laughing and swapping jokes at the bar.

Poole lifted her glass as if in a toast and swung it to her lips. I was glad that she seemed happy. I wondered what had been eating her that morning. Perhaps it was because she hadn't yet had her morning cup of coffee. At any rate, she had seen that I was trying to get us up and away once more, even though my attempt was unsuccessful.

As we buttoned up our overcoats, the high, whistling notes of a discordant wind song outside sirened a warning to bundle up our faces and necks as well. As courageously as we could, we moved out into the gale. Fortunately the wind was at our backs and hurried us along to the barracks over the treacherous ice. Once there and in bed, with my spine still paralyzed by the cold — the temperature was twelve degrees below zero even without a wind chill factor — I lay sheltered but shivering and taut with a primeval fear for the enemy raging without.

My body gave off no heat of its own, and of course we had no electric blankets, so my cold feet and superactive mind usually kept me sleepless for hours. I had joked that my too few corpuscles played tag throughout my circulatory system and never touched each other long enough to get warm. It was an exaggerated truth.

As I lay awake I reflected on the beastly week behind us. Added to our sorrow for Mrs. Rightman was our apprehension about our own vulnerability. No one wanted to die just yet.

Staying on the base was straining everyone's patience, but Poole was having a harder time than the others. Somehow I had to do something to ease the strain.

Saturday morning, on leaving the breakfast mess, we watched officers and enlisted men scurrying from their barracks to their appointed places for squadron roll calls.

I pushed up my cuff to see my wristwatch and immediately quickened my pace. I looked back over my shoulder and urged, "Let's go. Roll call's supposed to be at eight."

Burchie had joined us for breakfast, coming all the way from Detroit to do what she knew she must. Her short legs were stepping rapidly to keep up with the others. I wanted the group to maintain the appearance of a unit, so I shortened my strides and tried to pace at their measure. Inwardly I strained to beat the passage of time, but to no avail. We arrived five minutes late and I thought, "We'll have to get an alarm clock from somewhere."

At the far side of the barracks by the entrance, I halted and said, "Let's get in line for roll call."

"Why? Who's going to see us?" was Poole's tart reply.

I answered, "We're supposed to have a roll call."

"It's preposterous to stand roll call outside," she rejoined.

"And it's cold out here," added Thompson, making no move to comply as she stood shivering and rubbing her gloved hands together. Our breath rose in small clouds of vapor from our faces.

"Let's go in then," I conceded, feeling the chill as keenly as any, and I led the way. I held the door open for them as they passed me and added, "We must have a roll call every day."

"You know we're here, so what's the difference?" asked Poole.

With that I closed the door tightly against the bitter cold and we dispersed to our rooms. I was in a situation for which I had no facile answers. I felt dull and stupid and wondered how Nancy or Betty would handle this show of insubordination. I drew back from antagonizing the cadre, for they appeared happy that I had been chosen as their leader.

Yet, what was so awful about having roll call? We could save ourselves much ongoing irritation if we accepted the regulations of the masculine military world. We had no right to ignore their customs. How could I ease my cadre's feelings?

I never thought that the need for roll call would be disputed. It was a way of life in any organized service accountable to citizens because it was run by taxpayers' money. My father had stood roll call for more than thirty years before retiring from the St. Louis police department. Harold had stood it for thirteen years at the U. S. Naval Reserve station at Lambert Field. I, as a public school teacher, followed the rule that I be in my classroom fifteen minutes before the bell rang for children to enter the building. Why, even businesses had time clocks that employees were required to punch upon entering and leaving. Thomas Edison punched one and he was the boss. We had had our instruction at Wilmington. Why didn't it stick with Poole?

Soon after I'd hung my coat, cap, and gloves in my closet, I came out into the hall and spoke loudly. "Okay, gals, let's have a little squadron meeting out here."

They came out of their rooms and made an informal group around me. I began, "We're in Rome — or Romulus — and while here we'll have to do what the Romans do. We don't expect favors because we are women. We showed that in Wilmington. So we'll have roll call at eight.

"Sure it's different here. But there are times when you can ignore it," I went on quietly and as evenly as I could. "If you are ill, you report at eight to your flight surgeon's office instead. But you must report somewhere. If you are on orders and here on the base, you don't have to show up for parades and inspections. Every male pilot follows the same rules."

"If we can't get transition here like the men do and like the girls at the other bases," burst out Poole, "I'm going to quit ATC!"

Her large blue eyes flashed icy fire as she tossed her chin forward and up.

I made no reply. Donahue's loud throaty laughter shook the silence that engulfed us after Poole's declaration. In her deep voice, Donahue said, "You looked so funny when you said that."

Poole mulled over that remark. When she smiled back at Donahue, we took it that she had decided her pal meant to be comic and not unkind. As if on cue, the others smiled, too. But I felt that Poole's pettish moods outweighed the charm she displayed when life went her way. If she was determined to be antagonistic, I hoped she'd make good her threat. But I'd rather she made a go of it. I'd do what I could to help.

"Back to roll call," I said. "Remember that when you are back from a mission, you get time to rest. Until you recuperate with at least eight hours' sleep, you don't stand roll call."

There was no response, for they already knew what the rules were. I took a different tack, speaking directly and kindly in Poole's direction. "The weather has been lousy this past week. Not even the instructors were flying in transition. Of course we couldn't fly. Nobody could help it."

With all eyes on her, a mollified Poole said, "What'll we do today?"

"For one thing, the flight surgeon wants to see us again. It looks as if none of us has developed spinal meningitis, so we'll probably be put back on orders. Why don't we do what we have to around here and go up there just before noon, so we won't have to return before lunch. After lunch, we'll try Link. I'll call the Link room and see what we can get from them. Okay?"

Everyone smiled at the prospect, so I went down the hall to the telephone and asked the operator for the number of the facility. When I finished my conversation, I hung up and declared loudly, "It's okay for Link this afternoon."

The girls' faces showed at their doorways.

I added, "Not many takers at Link this afternoon."

Poole replied, "The wolves are all getting ready to howl in Detroit tonight, that's why."

"I'd like to go into Detroit myself and see the town," Thompson said wistfully.

Burchfield broke her customary silence with, "There's no bus from here that goes there. George and I found that out."

"There's nothing to do here," said Poole.

"Ground school?" I suggested.

"Phooey! Dear old Morse code. It makes me feel like a Boy Scout," retorted Poole.

"One would never guess that by looking at you," said Donahue.

"Have hope," I ventured. "Maybe they'll have a spy movie or a movie about survival in the Arctic, or even about lice.''

"Yeah, we could use survival right now," said Thompson, "but I'll try to get Link if I can."

"Unless some brass comes along and beats you out." Poole was still bitter about her experience.

"At least if we circulate where people see us, instead of staying way out here, they won't forget us," I added.

"This can't last forever," said Burchie.

"It only seems like forever," retorted Donahue. Poole smiled in agreement.

While washing and hanging up my socks and underwear, I returned to the problems before me. We simply must get some flying or we'd all go batty. If we couldn't fly, I wanted to go home to Harold. The inactivity on the base, the unfulfilled promises, the brutal weather — no wonder nerves were on edge. If we were busy, roll call and the other demands from the army would not matter.

We had no alert room in public view that might display our conformity with the rules. Somehow I'd ask for one, for without that show, remaining hidden from view, the temptation was to fall into civilian carelessness and slipshod behavior. I could visualize a morning when a phone call would announce a mission and someone would still be in bed, others would be without breakfast or unpacked and not ready to go. I felt that the success of the WAFS here would reflect on all of the WAFS. On the other hand, the cadre could quickly be reduced to a shambles of a squadron. How could I get that across? The dilemma that I faced would not have existed if we had been militarized. We should have been from the start, as Colonel Tunner intended.

One factor I overlooked. Popularity is a fleeting fancy, as colorful as a balloon. The first prick of adversity or criticism by a sharp tongue can collapse it. I shouldn't have counted on being liked.

The telephone rang. It was Colonel Nelson, saying that all WAFS were to be excused from military duties Saturday afternoon and Sunday morning. And he confided in me that a Mr. O'Hara had donated one of his automobiles, a seven-passenger Lincoln limousine, to the officers' club as soon as gasoline rationing took effect. "Last night," continued the colonel, "I got the idea that the Lincoln should be turned over to the WAFS for your own transportation about the base and for trips into town. When the officers who direct the club get together, I'll try to persuade them to allow you to use it. So, depending upon the vote taken, it should become effective in a day or so."

"How will we get gas?" I asked.

"From our supply here at the base. It's for official business," replied the colonel. If we got the use of a car, it would certainly help us endure the frigid weather better.

With the prospect of time off, we made for the flight surgeon's office as swiftly as we could. But I took time to caution my companions. "We don't like it that we aren't flying," I said. "But who knows? The weather could get suddenly better."

"It'll turn suddenly worse, but better? Never! Forget it," grumped Poole. "This is January in Detroit."

"You've got to look for the bright side," said Kay Thompson.

"What bright side? Nancy's still trying to get away from here, just as she's done every day she's been here." Poole was drooping with despair.

We didn't disagree with her. Nancy had been aloof in Wilmington; here her ties with us were already loosening. Poole's disillusionment was apparent.

"About good weather," I said, "'When if ever come perfect days,' — just suppose a call came at 8:10 this morning and we were told we had to take off right away on a mission. Suppose some of us were still in bed with curlers in our hair? And we hadn't showered or had breakfast and there wasn't time to dress, besides getting our flight gear and the charts together. What then?"

No one answered me.

"We've got to be ready for work when we're supposed to report for duty. Roll call only insures that we are. Now let's go."

I held the barracks door open for the others. As Thompson passed me, she chirped, "My momma done tole me we'd have days like this."

Later, the WAFS' exodus to Detroit left me alone in the barracks. I had a slight cold, so decided to take life easy and felt much better for it. Nancy came back early from wherever she'd been.

"The weather is impossible," she declared. "There is simply no airway I can take out of here."

When we got to the club for dinner, arrangements were already under way for a big bingo night. Many officers had their families in tow, which meant more introductions. Like me, Nancy didn't care for bingo, but I put up with the game just to be with the group. She found officers to talk to. With so many families around, I felt the game was like one at Wellston Masonic Lodge in St. Louis with Rob Morris' OES Sunshine Sewing Circle officiating. As usual, I did not win any prizes, but I felt I was no longer a stranger.

The girls were back by noon on Sunday. Then operations told us that because the weather was zero-zero, we'd get the rest of the day off. Lt. Colonel Wilson came by the barracks to take me to his house, where he was picking up his wife and baby Joyce to take to the buffet supper. I appreciated the friendliness of the Wilsons and the chance to be inside a home again. Joyce at age two was one of the prettiest blonde tots I'd ever seen.

The buffet again was sumptuous. The chef had prepared vegetable appetizers, several kinds of salad, baked ham, summer sausage, meat loaf, chicken liver pate, and a variety of eclairs for dessert. The price was sixty cents.

With the promise of a dance the next Saturday, several officers asked me if they could take me as their date. I refused, but said I'd save a dance. Nancy Love said to me, "You are a darn fool to be so cautious." I replied that I was doing what I thought Harold would want me to do. Again we didn't see eye to eye.

THE DEEP FREEZE

THE MICHIGAN WEATHER finally cleared on Tuesday. I wanted to get Poole into the air before she quit as she had threatened to do. I telephoned Captain Stoddard of group operations as soon after 8:00 A.M. as I thought polite, giving him time for such official duties as swallowing another cup of coffee.

"Good morning, Captain Stoddard, WAFS Scharr. How are things? I see the weather man raised the roof . . . a welcome change and the WAFS are crazy to deliver. . . . You really mean it? . . . I'm standing by. Thanks."

I put down the receiver and waltzed a few steps. Then, in keeping with my status, I changed to a stately pace and paused outside Donahue's door. Inside Donahue was at the mirror of her dresser, tucking some windblown strands of hair into her huge pompadour. Poole lay on the bed, arms lifted upward, with one hand over her mouth stifling a yawn.

Emphatically I announced, "Cross your fingers. We will probably fly today."

Hearing that, Burchie darted from her room and Thompson came from the lavatory to join us, their eager faces turned toward mine. Even Poole sat up in bed, galvanized by the news.

But it wasn't until 1030 that the telephone rang again. I sped to the middle of the hall.

"WAFS alert room," I answered, creating it with my words. "Yes, this is Scharr speaking. . . . Thank you. . . . Yes, I understand. We'll be off and running!"

There was no need to call a meeting. The WAFS had been drawn together as by a magnet.

"Operations has L-5s for us to ferry as soon as we get checked out in them. So they told transition to check us out today. Let's hurry before they change their minds."

Because our business was official, I called the motor pool for transportation to the south hangar.

"Hurry!" I called as I ran to my room to do what all of us were doing — zipping on our winter flying suits.

"Yeah, hurry up and wait!" Poole commented sarcastically.

Within twenty minutes we were in the students' ready room at transition. The question was, who was to be checked out first?

"I have a hunch I'd better stick close to the phone in case Captain Stoddard wants to contact me again today," I said. "Shall we do as we did in Delaware? The first ones sworn in come first — Poole, Donahue, Thompson, and Burchfield."

Just then Lieutenant Gillis walked in. His flight cap was off and his light blond kinky hair stood at attention. He looked at us and then at the flight board.

He said, "When the two instructors out there come back, they'll want to eat lunch. So why don't you knock off and get back here about 1300. Who's going first?"

At last, after one o'clock, Poole and Donahue went upstairs into the blue. Thompson, Burchie and I sat in the ready room earnestly studying the technical orders on the Stinson L-5. We discovered that it was a tandem liaison type trainer with wing flaps. It had high wings, like a Cub, but a 190-horsepower inline Lycoming engine. What's more, it contained an interplane communications system in a box, which held both receiver and broadcaster. This was usable at 300 feet above the terrain. In order to make it effective, the pilot had to unwind the aerial by hand and rewind it above 300 feet before landing.

"Hey!" Thompson pointed at her tech orders. "We'll be able to talk to each other in flight!"

That would be better than our wing-waving and nose-dipping signals we'd devised at Wilmington.

"Nobody'll be able to hear us. We have no radio," I replied.

The telephone rang. "WAFS Scharr," said the corporal at the desk, holding up the receiver for me.

"Scharr speaking," I said. I listened for at least a minute, my facial expression changing from pleasure to dismay to worry. All I said before putting down the receiver was, "Poole and Donahue are being checked out now. I'll come by as soon as I can."

I looked at the wall clock and then at the girls, who were eyeing me closely.

"Operations wants me to pick up our orders as soon as I can. I sure hope the others get down soon."

"Where are we going?" asked Thompson.

"Canada, for five PT-23Fe's."

"What's that?" from a worried Burchie.

"A lil ole Fairchild with a two-twenty-horsepower radial Continental in its nose."

"Canada! Where in Canada?" Thompson must have had hopes of seeing Ted.

"I don't know where it is. We have to catch a train at 1600. I think he said Fort Erie."

Just then Donahue breezed in, with her parachute slung over her right shoulder. She set it down, looking questioningly as if to say, "Who's next?"

Burchie looked relieved about missing the checkout, but Thompson, elated, stepped toward Donahue saying, "We've got a mission!"

"Where's Poole?" I asked.

"She was landing when we taxied in. She'll be right here."

As I was calling motor pool, in walked the second flight instructor alone, carrying two chutes.

"Where's Poole?" I asked him.

"She hailed a jeep out there. She said she wanted to see the flight surgeon about a nasty cold." He caught the eye of the other instructor, raised his eyebrows just perceptibly, and shrugged his shoulders. The corners of his mouth grimaced downward.

I felt the back of my neck tighten. Frantically I searched the base telephone directory and dialed the flight surgeon's office.

"Mrs. Scharr speaking. Has WAF Poole come in there yet? . . . Please put her on." I breathed hard. "Poole, we have planes waiting for us in Canada. We have to catch a train at 1600. Will you be okay to go or not?"

Poole had committed herself to being ill. Now she strove to get ungrounded. The doctor had already taken her temperature and pulse

Dallas WAFS Dorothy Scott, Opal ("Betsy") Ferguson, and Florene Miller walking to their Vultee BT-13s on the flight line. These aircraft were faster, heavier, and more prestigious than the old PT's still being flown by the Romulus cadre.

rate and examined her ears and throat.

"I think I can do it," she said.

The doctor later told me that he warned Poole to take plenty of rest and aspirins every four hours. He had said to his assistant after her departure, "They'll probably get weathered in some place and she'll get over it. They can't fly very high, anyway. Look at the clouds."

Meanwhile, one of the transition instructors hailed a jeep for us. We rushed into our barracks rooms and packed our B-4 bags. Inside my parachute bag I stuffed fur-lined mittens, overshoes, the two-piece flying suit, and the brown leather face mask. I was a bit worried about that chute. I'd asked the parachute riggers to loosen the body straps so I could wear a winter flying suit and they had forgotten to do so when they repacked it. It was too late now to borrow another one.

I got out the pile of sectional charts and ran to the middle of the hall to dial operations, fully realizing that the success of this mission rested wholly on my shoulders. As I sped past Donahue's room, I saw that Donahue was dragging her B-4 bag and a lumpy parachute bag and starting for the door. Good girl, Donahue. She was fast.

"Don't forget your face mask!" I warned.

"Got it!" said Donahue.

I turned to the phone. "Hello, Scharr here. You didn't tell me where we are taking those PTs," I said and waited for the answer.

"Montgomery, Alabama? . . . Oh, *you* decide our route? Can you give it to me so we can fish out the correct sectionals to take?" I thought to myself, they don't trust us. What do they think we are?

After listening to the list, I said, "Okay, I've got it. . . . We haven't much time. May Donahue pick up the orders? . . . Then I'll have to come by on the way out of the base. . . . Would you ask motor pool to send transportation for us? We're running sort of close."

As I put the receiver on the hook, I yelled, "The sectionals we need are Detroit, Cleveland, Cincinnati, Huntington, Nashville, Chattanooga, and Birmingham. Where's Poole?"

As if on cue, Poole walked into the barracks with much dignity.

"Poole!" My voice had an edge to it. "We're running out of time. We're ferrying open planes and you'd better take all your winter flying equipment, even the face mask."

"Ugh! Open planes?" She halted as if vacillating over the idea while Thompson tried to pull her parachute bag around our laggard. Then, resolving her dilemma, she went on to her room, as Thompson overtook her, rushing to her own room for the rest of her paraphernalia.

Donahue went immediately to Poole's rescue. She sorted through Poole's pile of sectionals, flipping the chosen ones onto the floor. Scooping them up with a dramatic wave of her large hands, she stashed them into the navigation kit. She threw and stuffed the winter flying outfit into the parachute bag, but Poole packed her own B-4 bag, slowly and carefully.

I had finished my preparations and already had on my overcoat, ready to go, when I decided to make a rapid inspection of the barracks, just to be sure that things weren't in too bad shape in case there was a quarters inspection while we were gone. Thompson was standing vigil at the door, opening it every few seconds to see if our transportation had arrived.

When I got to the washroom, I remembered I'd had panties and socks drying on the line. Only the socks remained. I took them down, folding them as I went down the hall, and yelled, "Where's my panties

I had hanging on the line? Anyone pick them up by mistake?''

Donahue thrust her head from Poole's room. She replied, ''I took some off the line. But I have enough clean ones. They're on my bunk.''

They were. I put them in my dresser drawer, vowing to think about the incident when I had more time. What to do about Leonore McElroy? I wrote her a note to explain our absence. She always reported to me on time. I told her to carry on as usual in her orientation class and placed the message on the hall floor so she wouldn't miss it.

Finally our vehicle arrived and each piece of baggage was relayed through the door, with each of us struggling with our own equipment. Donahue had already jumped up onto the truck and was pushing the bags toward the front, shoving them into a row, leaving a space clear for us, who had to sit on benches along the sides.

The driver came to assist us and said, ''One of the men told me he didn't see how the Ferry Command could expect those little bitty girls to throw a parachute bag up on a truck. Girls like that should stay at home and leave us men to fight the war. But I says to him, 'Yeah? And how many GIs know how to fly an airplane?' That shut him up.''

We climbed in, anticipating a long, uncomfortable ride. We stopped at the operations office, where I ran in, picked up the orders for flight 6282, C.P. 37, ten copies for each one of us stapled together plus a T/R for the train ride. I ran back to the truck, jumped in, and the driver took off.

I looked at my watch. We were already twenty minutes past 1600. The train was due to leave Michigan Central Station at 1700. Only forty minutes left to get there and Detroit was twenty-five miles away!

I urged the truck forward. My spirit, leaping ahead, pulled on the lumbering vehicle. The strain made my head ache. What could I say to Captain Stoddard if we missed that train? I spoke as loudly as I could to make the driver hear. ''The train leaves at five o'clock.'' He nodded his head and the truck gained momentum.

Now then, how to organize so there'd be no hitches at the station? I looked at the T/R. Unbelievable. It was for Pullman accommodations. I said to Thompson, ''When we get there, if the train hasn't left, will you run over to the ticket office and get our tickets?''

Thompson nodded and put the T/R in her purse without looking at it. I was praying hard. I hated every stop sign for putting us farther behind in our meeting with the train. And as we stopped for each red light, we slid and leaned forward. When the driver started off in first gear, we slid and leaned backwards. Every time he shifted gears, we waved back and forth in unison.

At last we saw the station ahead and prepared for a rushed departure. Fortunately the train was twenty minutes late. But there was an obstacle I had overlooked. Because we were going to Canada, we had to go through customs. Before we could leave the station, we had to tell officials where we were born and to declare what luggage we carried. As soon as she had cleared, Thompson disappeared and came rushing backing, "We got Pullmans!"

In a flurry of excitement and with the help of two redcaps, we boarded the right car. Then we settled down and waited for the conductor to take our fares. The sight of our uniforms prompted the conductor to say, "My car isn't full tonight. Would you like a stateroom?" He unlocked one for us. It even had its own private washroom. I'd never traveled in such style before. It made operations at NCAAB look stingy.

We relaxed in comfort and privacy until six o'clock when we trouped to the dining car where waiters in white, starched jackets served us. The side windows of the car reflected the inside lights and mirrored the spotless tablecloths and shining silverware, which seemed to brighten the room even more.

The dinner was not grand, but was palatable and sufficient and we enjoyed it and the coffee afterward. We could afford such a dinner now because we were back on per diem. Our orders stated that since we were in Canada, we could spend a dollar more each day.

At 2130 we arrived at the Fort Erie, Ontario, railroad station. I'd been studying a sectional chart, so I had learned that Fort Erie was across the Niagara River from Buffalo, New York. We got off with our baggage and the train clattered off into the dark night. We lugged our stuff into the small provincial station and guessed that the town was neither affluent nor large.

"Where is this hotel?" I asked the station manager, handing him the note that Captain Stoddard had given me.

"Mather Arms? That's about two miles away."

"Where might we call a cab?"

"Oh, you won't get a cab. All gasoline sales have stopped. Rationing, you know. There's no way I know you can get there."

"Oh, for God's sake!" Poole began. Her voice trailed off.

"I'll run outside and try to flag somebody down," volunteered Donahue.

"No!" I warned. "I'll call the Fleet Aircraft Company."

When I did, the man who answered the telephone turned to someone else and said, "Five girls who say they are WAFS are at the station." I got no further response from him, so I telephoned the Mather Arms.

"Are there reservations for five women pilots for tonight?" I asked.

There were. "Who made the reservations for us?"

"Mr. Pate. He's the control officer at Fleet."

"Well, we're at the railroad station and have no way of getting to the hotel."

"Mr. Pate said his office boy was to meet you. I guess the kid had a date and just forgot."

I called the Fleet factory again, explaining our predicament. I could hear Poole's voice complaining in the background. I thought, I'm doing the best that I can.

At last, perhaps to keep the office boy out of trouble, the guard (for that's what he must have been) resolved our difficulties. He arranged for a Mr. Wright to pick us up and take us to the hotel. A truck would pick up the parachutes and other gear and take them directly to the factory so we wouldn't be bothered with transporting them in the morning.

Time dragged on. As we waited, shivering in the cold station, we felt deserted and forlorn. Several young boys wandered in for a drink of water. We knew they were curious about us and were too shy to ask.

Eventually Mr. Wright arrived. We helped the two men load our parachute bags onto the truck and got into Mr. Wright's sedan. At last we were cozily crowded in, three in the front seat and three in the rear. The ice on the road was about six inches thick and deeply rutted with uneven ridges between. The automobile skidded each time the driver changed directions and was forced to follow new grooves. Fortunately no other vehicle was traveling that dark and lonely road.

When we arrived, I simply couldn't believe that the Mather Arms was a hotel. There was no outside sign. But Mr. Wright acted as if it were and helped us unload our B-4 bags and navigation kits from the trunk. Then he left us to our fate, saying "I'll send someone for you in the morning."

"This looks just like a little country store," I said. We entered the front door, supposing it opened onto the lobby. The interior was in disarray, with plaster broken off and lathes uncovered, lumber strewn about, and white dust over everything. We picked our way across the vacant room, exploring, until we were in a hallway at the rear where we found a clerk on duty. He told us he would give us his three best rooms, the newer ones. There were no other guests, and these rooms were the only ones currently presentable.

As the clerk led us to our rooms, I said, "Barbara needs all the rest she can get, so let her have a room to herself." I could have added what was in my mind and perhaps in the minds of the others — no one wanted to catch Poole's bad cold.

Our rooms had so-called modern furniture, ugly, without style, and each contained a skimpy full-sized bed, too small to be shared by two tall persons. The middle room was the only warm one; it had heat piped to it.

"You take this one, Barbara," I said to Poole, and in she went.

To her right was another room with heat connected. The clerk said, "The room farthest from the office isn't connected yet to the heating system."

My sentiments were that a flight leader must look after her flight, just as an officer should look after his troops. I said, "I'll take the one without heat."

Donahue, good sport that she was, said, "I'll go with you, Del," so Burchie and Thompson shared their luck.

As usual on a mission, we unpacked only necessities from our B-4 bags — toothpaste and brush, soap, comb, pajamas, and whatever else that each individual was addicted to. We'd gotten no further than that when Poole first knocked and then opened our door, saying, "Let's go down to the tavern — they call it a pub up here — and get some Canadian ale. I could use a nightcap and I think it would do my cold good."

I agreed and said, "I may need something to get me to sleep." Already I regretted having sent my winter flight suit along with my parachute by truck to the airport. If the blankets weren't warm enough, I'd be awake, shivering, all night long.

We all went to the pub, which was in the basement and filled with the artisans responsible for the untidiness upstairs. Most were still in their workclothes, although their faces were rosy and clean. At several tables were townspeople who had ventured through the cold to partake of their nips.

Somewhat self-conscious because we were the only women present, we ordered one ale apiece. We didn't speak to each other as we waited; we were too tired. The waiter brought us tall, foaming glasses and almost empty bottles. We drank. When we had finished, we asked the waiter for the tab. He said, "You can't pay for it. Someone else has already taken care of it."

Surprised, we looked at each other, speechless. Then he returned in a twinkling and placed another bottle of ale beside each glass.

"We didn't order these," protested Thompson.

"That's all right," answered the jolly fellow. "Somebody's treating you."

"May we have the check for what we ordered?" I asked. I felt uncomfortable, for these saloon customers were strangers and I wondered if they thought we were barflies.

"Sorry, ma'am, but that's already paid for. Another of your admirers."

"But why?"

"Oh, it's the custom around here. You'll get a half-dozen before the night is out."

With that prospect facing us, we filled our glasses and drank what we could. Then we departed hurriedly before someone else followed the local custom.

I was glad when Donahue jumped into her pajamas and into bed like a flash. The outside temperature hovered at zero, I opened the window enough for fresh air, but not enough for a draft. The blankets we pulled over us were new, fluffy, and warm.

The next morning, before we ate our Canadian breakfast of tea, rolls, and hot oatmeal, we had already packed our B-4 bags and checked out. So when Mr. Pate and his assistant, the fellow who had forgotten to meet us the night before, arrived, there was no hitch in the proceedings. They took us to the Fleet factory in a company station wagon.

Eager to fly, for the air was beautiful, crisp, and clear, we inspected our airplanes and signed for them with haste. But although the weather was CAVU (ceiling and visibility unlimited), we were not allowed to take off. The Niagara Airport was closed because the Carborundum Company's factory smoke kept visibility below contact flight minimums over there. I knew that in St. Louis winds always picked up speed after 0930. The same happened in New York. However, the smoke blew westward and right toward the Fleet factory at Fort Erie.

As we waited for a wind shift, Mr. Pate told us, "Don't forget, you must land at Niagara because of customs. You can't skip it."

"Not again!" wailed Poole. She looked better this morning. Her eyes weren't watering and her nose had lost its pink. "We didn't even have a chance to buy anything."

"Not even a bottle of ale," I cracked. As we waited, we drew our first several courses on the huge planning table in the pilot's lounge. Donahue, always the individual, laid her charts out on the floor and kneeled above them.

Mr. Pate was apologetic. "We can't send you to Buffalo Genessee. Niagara Falls is a temporary port of entry. But you'll like it. Bell Aircraft has a factory there and the people are always nice to pilots. They're bound to take your pictures, too."

"Nothing doing. Not the way I look with this cold," retorted Poole. And to us she said, "Let's look at the falls."

The course from Fort Erie to the Niagara Falls Airport would take a compass heading of due north. From there we would fly due east to the airport. It would be a matter of only seven miles and less than five minutes in order for us to the see this attraction from the air, which would be a first for each of us.

Most of my experience as a flight leader had been with Nelson, so I felt cautious about my flight. The WAFS with the least military cross-country experience were Donahue, Thompson, and Burchfield. But the flight was short and I would lead it myself, for the rule was that the flight leader should come up from behind and be the first to land at the destination.

When visibility appeared to be a minimum outside the airport, although it was extremely poor at Fort Erie, I said, "I'll circle the airport until you have had time to take off. That'll give me more time to line up a proper heading with the landmarks."

We donned our flight suits. Then I tried to slip on my brand- new parachute. I was in trouble. It would not fit easily over my suit. It took all my strength to attach the leg straps. In order to fasten the catch at the center of my chest, I exhaled as much breath as I could and, bending forward, with much difficulty I joined the straps.

Each WAF climbed into her airplane, taking the forward cockpit, just as an instructor would. A line boy jumped on the left wing root of my plane, inserted an engine crank, and rotated it with as much force as he could, for the engine oil was cold. At last the flywheel was spinning fast enough to start the engine. It was my job to keep it going. Seeing his success, the line boy pulled out the crank, jumped off the wing, and placed the crank in the baggage compartment before taking on the next airplane.

I watched to see that he fastened the baggage door securely and then, as I waited for the others to get their engines started, I checked my instruments. The Continental engine was a radial without any cowling to give it streamlining and a classy appearance. I thought, these will be gas burners, I bet, and they'll be much slower than the PT-19s we'd been used to.

When all five engines were running, I released my parking brake, revved the engine a bit and turned out toward the takeoff point, where I checked the magnetos and the carburetor heater. All okay.

Upstairs I made two circuits of the field, waiting for the others. The smoke had become thicker below, but visibility wasn't too bad once one got on top of it. At last out of the haze came one airplane followed by another. I was still circling, waiting for the entire flight, when the two airplanes made a turn and lost altitude. The haze swallowed them up.

Adela Scharr measures a course in the Bell Aircraft Corporation's pilots' lounge in Buffalo. Other pilots, from left, are: Kay Thompson, Barbara Poole, Phyllis Burchfield, and Barbara Donahue.

What was going on? I was annoyed at not being followed as we had agreed. I continued to circle until two other airplanes emerged from the haze. I thought that more than enough time had elapsed. The group must be together now. I led to the north, edging a prohibited area that bordered the Niagara River. I looked back. Only two airplanes were following me! Where were the others? I signaled that I was turning back to Fort Erie and I expected the two to follow me. But instead of staying with their leader, as we had been trained to do at Wilmington, the two went on.

Now what can I do? I asked myself. I was not yet frantic, but was puzzled by this peculiar reaction. I had committed myself to finding out what was wrong and when I returned to Fort Erie, I saw that one airplane had not taken off yet. Should I go down? No, I'd continue to circle until this one took off, so she, at least, would be following me. Who was down there? Burchie? I worried about her; the others seemed to have more self-confidence. And too, when we made our plans, Burchie never changed her facial expression. She always seemed to be dreaming about something else. I wondered if what was being said really soaked in.

Aha! The WAF had taken off and after gaining altitude followed me. I stuck to my previous course toward the falls. The WAF trailing me came close to my airplane and then dropped back. Her flying was so erratic that I thought she was crazy. I couldn't understand what she was doing, yet I felt an empathy for her and worried about what was going on.

I tried to shrug it off. "Heck, kiddo!" I said, glancing back at my aerial companion, "I'm here this far. I'm going to see those falls." And I did. They really looked small from the air.

I turned to the east to go over the city of Niagara Falls. At the airport I counted the PTs on the ground. We were missing one. Where was she? My lone wingman went on ahead and landed. At last, when I saw a PT coming from the south, I landed, too, and the final member of the flight came in after me.

I was exasperated. This was our very first mission and it was the worst flight I had ever seen or expected to see in my career. Each WAF had been given a position to fly in loose formation and each knew the WAFS rules. Why didn't they follow what they'd learned at NCAAB?

I can count on one hand the number of times I have felt true anger in my life. This was not one of them. I did not even simulate anger, a trick I had used in the classroom once in a while to impress a second-grader. But I was worried, disappointed, bewildered, and — especially — cold. All this must have shown in my face as we tried to unscramble the mystery of the vanished flight formation. The others appeared to have thought their actions were perfectly normal, or at least that is how I interpreted their expressions.

The explanation that emerged was understandable, but not satisfying. Poole took off right after I did, followed by Thompson. Poole's motor sputtered, and frightened, she turned back to Fort Erie. Thompson turned back with her, saw Poole land, and decided to go on alone. The second two were Donahue and Burchie. When I signaled them to turn back, Donahue didn't follow me and Burchie stuck with her. The airplane that I saw remaining at Fort Erie was Poole's and she flew it so crazily because she was afraid her engine would quit. She was almost frantic when I led her over the city of Niagara Falls, but we were high enough to glide to a clear landing outside the city — the correct procedure in flying over towns or rivers — and when Poole saw the airport she couldn't get down fast enough.

I didn't blame her for trying to go on living. But Thompson was another story. She had gone on too far and when she spotted Lake Ontario ahead of her, she tried to retrace her flight. She must have been confused until she recognized from her chart that she was at the east half of the Niagara River close to Grand Island. She was too far south and headed for the airport from there, the last one in.

With this beginning, this bungling of procedures, our teamwork boded nothing but disaster. I was worried. I had been handed a can of worms and when I opened it, they had wiggled out in all directions at once. Would I ever get the lid back on? I had no time to think about it then. But I marked it on the calendar.

We went through customs, which wasn't a problem, and then came refueling. I'd been flying forty-five minutes in all. Therefore my calculations should be comparable to a valid cross-country test of fuel consumption. My PT would be using sixteen gallons per hour instead of the twelve and a half that the Ranger used. That cut into our radius of flight, but was not the reason we had to stop so often on that mission. Weather was the culprit.

We felt like celebrities when the operations officer at the huge brick complex of Bell Aircraft said, "I'm calling the photographer. You're getting your pictures taken."

I demurred, knowing how Nancy felt about publicity for us, but he insisted, saying, "Some Wilmington girls came through here and we took *their* pictures." And he displayed large glossies of Delphine Bohn, Helen Mary Clark, Gertrude Meserve, and Nancy Batson.

We thought *we* were. the first WAFS to get Canadian PTs. So: NCAAB was muscling into Romulus territory. The picture of our friends was such a good one that the officer gave each of us a copy. Then the photographer arrived to take our picture.

We had to wait until a mechanic could check Poole's engine, so we went to the Bell cafeteria for lunch. The repair still had not been made when we returned to operations. An inspection showed that nothing was wrong. Her difficulty with the engine was due to her unnecessary use of carburetor heat. After all, ground temperatures were below zero. So her engine ran rough.

We planned the next hop. A straight course from Niagara Falls to Erie, Pennsylvania, would cross the lake and be only ninety-six miles long. But it was too far from land and therefore unwise to take. I urged the girls to keep their positions in the formation I chose for them. Our course would go due south, skirting the city of Buffalo on its western edge and following the radio range leg to Dunkirk. From there we'd skirt the lake approximating the northeast radio range into Erie. We penciled the segments of the course in blue, so they'd be easy to see. Since our planes carried no radios, we had to rely on pilotage or get lost. And it was terribly cold.

"If we don't wear our face masks," I warned, "this wind will either chap our faces or frost our skins.''

I led the way this time and I didn't want any of the foolishness we had had before. The lake looked forbidding. The flight was seventy brutal minutes of bitter cold. We couldn't have gone on farther, both because sundown would have caught us and because we were stiff, almost frozen from the cold.

At Erie, I asked the proprietor, Herman Steimer, "Can I call our RON here? Or is the telegraph office in town open?''

''You can call it from here,'' replied Herman as he and his line boys helped us to tie our airplanes down securely. How fiercely the wind blew! And how glad we were to get to the hotel in town. But the blankets were insufficient to warm even the toastiest of persons and we passed the night in fits of wakefulness.

The next morning we took a taxi in order to get to the airport by 0800, glad that we weren't too far away and that we could split the fare five ways. On arrival I checked the weather maps and sequences while the others preflighted their planes. Too bad. Cleveland had visibility zero — smoke. Now what? We'd been given the course to follow and weren't to devise alternates. So we had to wait.

I went outside with the bad news and began my own preflight. No one lingered outside on a day like that was! We stashed our B-4 bags and our navigation kits, keeping out the maps we intended to use. Then into Herman's pilots' planning room we ran to wait out the weather. Every hour we checked the weather room to see if Cleveland was on contact flight yet. But the smoke hung in there. As we already knew, there's nothing quite so wearing as hoping for good weather that simply won't show up.

Herman Steimer was very Pennsylvania Dutch, a large man who resembled Wallace Beery. What a kind person he was! At eleven o'clock he treated us to hamburgers and coffee, then he topped that off with a slice of delicious apple pie.

An hour later, Cleveland was still smoking and I was chomping at the bit. So I telephoned Romulus operations office to get permission to go south via Akron to Columbus. They said okay. Then immediately thereafter a wind from the east began backing the snow-laden atmosphere onto the line I'd laid out as our intended route. It became too risky. At the same time, Cleveland finally opened up. At 1330 we made ready to take off. Herman cranked until he was red in the face. All by himself he started each one of our planes.

''God bless you, Herman,'' I prayed.

Poole was the navigator and I brought up the rear. As I watched the others fly, I could see the little differences in the way they handled their crafts. Learning to recognize how my companions flew would make it easier for me to identify them in the future. Burchie, for instance, held one wing just a bit lower than the other. I settled down to watching how well Poole navigated, being distracted every so often by endeavoring to wipe my drippy nose.

I had counted eleven airports close by or almost directly on our course. If Poole had any more engine trouble, she could land somewhere. If she got off course to the north, the big lake was no more than seven miles away. If she lost sight of the water by drifting to the south, she could fly parallel to the highways and the railroad leading into Cleveland. But Poole had no trouble. When we reached the eastern edge of the city, we flew its perimeter on the south past Mather to the large airport situated on the southwest pendant sticking out from Cleveland proper.

By the time we closed our flight plan, gotten the planes gassed, and checked the weather — which at that time was very unsettled throughout Ohio — we decided that it was too late and too risky to attempt a ninety-minute flight to Columbus. After completing that one-hour-and-ten-minute flight in zero temperature from Erie and being brunted by a relative ninety-five mile-per-hour gale, we were relieved to park the parachutes overnight.

I sent the RON, the Cleveland Hotel reserved rooms for us, and operations gave us transportation. In the staff car and out of the beastly weather, we soon warmed up. When Donahue told us it was Poole's birthday, we decided to splurge.

I'd never seen a downtown complex like that in Cleveland. A huge railway station was the center of numerous shops, and the hotel was right there for the rail traveler's convenience. Union Station in St. Louis also housed an elegant hotel, but the shops in its vicinity on Market Street were pawnshops and vendors of cheap and shoddy merchandise. Both railroads centers had Fred Harvey restaurants.

Before we went upstairs to our rooms, we headed for the Fred Harvey's Tropical Room, where we each drank a cocktail and toasted our birthday girl. Quiet Burchie ventured into our casual chitchat. She said, "George is stationed at Lockbourne in Columbus."

"Oh, he is?" I replied. "You've got to be sure to see him. Maybe if you're lucky, we'll RON there."

We were interrupted by a drunken man who swayed across the room, no doubt drawn by curiosity about our uniforms. We tightened up, annoyed, as he spoke incoherently and haltingly. He was so close we were afraid that he might topple over on us. But the proprietor soon came to our rescue and booted Mr. Inebriated out of that refined establishment. We finished our liquid salutes to Poole's health and left to relax in our rooms, to bathe, and then to return to uniform dress, this time in skirts, so that we might dine in the Bronze Room of our hotel.

I hoped that all that we had endured since leaving Romulus was binding us into a unit, helping us to face any new difficulties as one cadre. Our closeness showed in our relaxed repartee in aviation jargon — we had borne common inconveniences and we needed each other. But how long would that closeness last?

At dinner we enjoyed ample and well-prepared food served with courtesy and promptness. With the table cleared, we waited for dessert. In came our waiter, bearing a plate with a white cake topped by one flaming candle. In pink icing, "Happy Birthday, Puddles" was inscribed. The fine hand of Donahue was in evidence.

When our meal was finished, Puddles said sweetly, "Thank you, Donnie. I'm going to bed." No more griping.

Burchie begged off, too, saying, "I've got to get my clothes in order. I want to look my best when I see George. And my eye hurts." But she didn't say why.

Down in the hotel complex we had seen a stage-door canteen, a USO that promised to entertain any enlisted servicemen who might feel lonesome and not flush enough to afford commercial recreation facilities. USOs served coffee and snacks, and local girls volunteered to dance or to talk to the homesick heroes about to be shipped overseas. We wouldn't have dared to go in the canteen, except that this one had a sign on the door, "Ferry Pilots Welcome." That meant us, too.

"Suppose they kick us out?" Thompson asked.

"I've been kicked out of better places than this," wisecracked Donnie.

We went in and sat at a table. Three gobs in their navy blue sailor suits joined us. We had not expected that and weren't interested. If they'd have been pilots, we could have had a gabfest, but as it was, there was little we understood about each other. We soon said we were leaving, and the three sailors insisted on walking us to the hotel lobby. They were nice young kids, unduly impressed with our accomplishments. No doubt we were something to tell the other boys about the next day — perhaps even with some embellishment.

When I called the unlisted number of the weather bureau the next morning, the meteorologist said that the day would be bad until mid-morning. So I permitted the girls to visit the hotel beauty parlor to get their hair washed and set. I didn't bother with making myself beautiful and neither did Burchie, who wore her long hair braided around her head like a crown. Instead of being in the beauty parlor, she was in a doctor's office. She had gotten a tiny bit of steel in her eye the day before, had rubbed it, and scratched her eyeball. The doctor was able to remove the metallic grit and gave her soothing drops to heal the sensitive eye. I wished she had told me how bad it was yesterday.

At 1030, the weather bureau told me that instrument conditions still prevailed. I went into the arcade next door to the hotel and bought a huge volume of Audubon prints for Harold. The clerk arranged to have them mailed.

Just before noon, contact flight became possible. Where was everybody? Hurriedly I collected the girls, we got our bags down to the desk, paid our bills, called a cab, and soon were at the airport making out clearances, preflighting, and checking the weather. Donnie was to lead this hop.

Putting my parachute on over my flight suit was akin to shoving a size nine foot into a size seven shoe. I don't know if the pectoral muscle exercises that I did to develop my bust had become effective overnight, but I just couldn't close the straps across my chest that morning. The chest straps guaranteed that the shoulder straps would remain on my body in case I had to jump out in flight. While I struggled with the chute, the line boy was waiting and the girls were in their airplanes. I was holding up the takeoff. It embarrassed me enough to chance further embarrassment.

I said to the young man facing me, "Can you get these straps together?"

Now *he* was embarrassed. He knew that directly underneath that bulky flying jacket and clothing and the straps was where women usually had breasts. He hesitated. He was speechless.

"Oh, come on, don't be afraid," I said, as I half-crouched, placed the straps in his hands, and exhaled as much breath as I could.

With eyes half-closed and praying that he'd fasten the straps soon, I felt one go slack. Then the boy caught it, so he thought, and pulled. But I didn't feel any tightness across my chest. I looked at him. His eyes were closed as if he were afraid to see what he knew he must be doing — to have his hands in such close proximity to my bosom. In his hand he held a handle, not a buckle.

Warily I looked over my left shoulder. On the snow past my heels lay my parachute, folded neatly, but not in its pack. He had pulled the ripcord.

Now what to do? Regulations stated that I should wear a parachute. If mine were packed, how long would that delay our delivery? I was responsible for this one, so how could I borrow another one and leave mine here? I might never come back this way again. Burchie had my sympathy — we could RON in Lockbourne only if we took off right away. We'd go.

The hapless lad stood motionless, still with the ripcord in his right hand. I said cheerfully, "Well, kid, you'll have to help me get it all into the bag."

We placed my life-saving equipment in the baggage compartment, he cranked the starter, and off I went, feeling more free and comfortable than I had been since the beginning of this adventure.

At first, after leaving Cleveland, our course cut Ohio's east- west country roads at about thirty degrees off a ninety degree angle. Donahue was navigating very well. South of Homerville, the roads had no apparent layout. They went every which way. And about that time, haze made our visibility poorer than three miles. Every so often I'd ascend to the bottom of the clouds to ascertain that we still had a ceiling of 1,500 feet over the terrain. Donahue was doing a remarkable job of keeping us on course. At times I couldn't see towns that I thought must be out there. The land was hilly, so not only haze, but also the earth itself obscured our checkpoints.

I came up from behind about ten miles out of Lockbourne and there we joined two flights of P-39s already circling the airport. Each flight had five members, so at least fifteen necks were swiveling at every turn. The tower traffic controller was giving all of us the red light not to land and none of us had radios. But at last everyone landed safely.

Inside the hangar where we closed our flight plan, we got a chance to see who our rivals for landing priority were. They were from our new base, Romulus. Lockbourne appeared more like home, especially since the weather station forecast that we'd be grounded for a few days. Just like Romulus all right.

Burchie's husband, Lt. George Fulton, was on hand to meet her. He said in greeting, "I knew you were coming in, so I was up in the tower when you landed."

She must have sensed that possibility, for when she landed, she made a half-dozen skips before she got her plane down and rolling. In fact, she was so awkward coming in that she got in Poole's way. She couldn't get used to eyes being upon her as she performed — a case of stage fright.

My fleeting impression of George was that he was a cocky little rooster lording it over his meek bantam hen. We didn't see much of them for the next two days.

Fortunately the nurses received us four into their quarters, and they couldn't have been friendlier. The interlude of nasty weather gave me enough time to have my parachute repacked and the harness loosened. The Link trainer operators gave any pilot who asked for it time to practice. I managed to obtain two hours in all and liked it fine, although one day I was given forty-five minutes of rough air right after eating lunch. I felt queasy, but my lunch remained where it was.

On Monday morning, February 1, the cold front that was predicted moved out faster than the forecaster thought it would. We were preflighting, almost ready to leave, when I discovered that I couldn't lift the flap handle in the front cockpit. A bit of line boy muscle and grease fixed that situation. Then, Poole's engine wouldn't start. Off went all our switches and we climbed out to go to lunch, as the line boys pulled Poole's airplane into the hangar. They didn't seem gung-ho enough to suit me. I hoped they'd find out the trouble before we returned.

While we ate, Poole said, "I just don't like that airplane. First it acts as if the engine is quitting. Then at Cleveland the crank broke. Now this. It's just my luck."

"Well, be careful," was all I could reply.

"These engines sure use a lot of gas," said Kay Thompson.

"Yeah," we chorused.

Thinking that Phyllis Burchfield needed her status raised with her husband after her greenhorn landing, I chose her as navigator out of Lockbourne. But I made certain to remind everyone, "Once we're in the air and you are in your assigned position in formation, be sure you keep it and don't ever change. If you have an emergency, use the signals we reviewed. And when we change to echelon positions, coming into an airport, keep your position so I'll land first and then number one, two, three, and four. Let's look as good as the men."

Bound for Cincinnati, we took off into a head wind. Burchie made a darn good straight line of it. She was trying hard. The trip was uneventful. We made fast work of gassing at Lunken Airport, which was very close to the city, but had two drawbacks. It lay in a valley next to the Ohio River and it backed up to a bluff on its north. (My comment to the girls after we landed was, "It wouldn't take much of a flood for Lunken to be dunkin'.")

Thompson was the navigator on the shorter flight to Bowman Field at Louisville, Kentucky. The hop didn't truly test her skill, for the checkpoints were plentiful. Gassing, clearance, and weather — the WAFS zipped through our operational tasks like veterans.

We were ready to go until Burchie's plane began to leak gasoline as her engine was warming up. Off went our switches. Whatever was wrong had to be fixed. The clearance was returned. When we saw how slow the mechanics were, we wondered to each other if they cared at all if the airplanes got delivered. Would we ever win this war? I wondered.

We had to RON at Louisville and that night I slept in the same room with Burchie. Poole's cold had returned, so she was alone. I couldn't sleep well, for Burchie breathed very loudly. I kept waiting for her to exhale and inhale. And besides, I felt hurt and a bit bewildered. Louisville was as close to home we would get on this mission, so I decided to telephone Harold and surprise him. But when I said "hello" to his "hello," he didn't recognize my voice. He thought I was another woman. Who was she? I wondered. From the CAP? Or the USO? I was sure it wasn't Tess or any Nixies. He was happy that I had called, but even that didn't keep me from feeling low.

The Army Air Force detachment at Bowman was kind enough to send us transportation the following morning. We were waiting for it when it appeared — a truck. We tossed our personal equipment in the middle and sat along the sides.

Again Burchie irritated us. She waited until the last minute to tell us that she had to visit a Western Union telegraph office. She was bashful about confessing that she was low on cash, which I could understand. George, who hadn't been paid until after we had left Lockbourne, promised her that he'd wire money for her to pick up wherever we RON'd. So we ordered the driver to change his course and to go past a Western Union office.

Riding in that truck was not for us and we decided we'd rather pay for a ride in a taxi. As we waited for Burchie to get her money, we got out. I told the driver, "We're going to the base in a cab. Please be sure you bring our bags to the operations office right away."

"Yes ma'am," he replied.

"We're anxious to take off," cautioned Poole, "so get there as soon as you can."

The Western Union clerk called a cab for us, which came immediately, and we congratulated ourselves on getting to the airport without bouncing up and down and swaying back and forth. Once there, we ran through AAF essentials as a team and were ready to go. Or were we? Where were our bags?

Two hours and ten minutes later, with the city police force, state troopers, and MPs looking all over for him, the truck driver arrived at Bowman Field in an advanced state of inebriation.

I was almost ill by then. Thompson said, "Del, you'd better sit down. Your face is so white."

"I think I sprouted a few gray hairs, too," I said.

In a few minutes, five propellers were whirling and I taxied out first to lead the flight to Nashville. For one hour and fifty- five minutes I kept score on myself, with a ninety-two percent rating of passing check-points exactly where I planned. Once in a while I'd be as much as a small field to one side of a bend in a river. I got a lot of practice in figuring just how streams like the Noun, the Green, and the Trammel Fork lay by the trees that bordered them.

"Great navigating!" said Donnie when we were down and rushing through our operational routine.

I murmured "Thanks," but I really didn't need compliments; I was just playing a game with myself.

It was warmer down in Dixie, but we were still jinxed by weather. We had to RON at the Bankhead Hotel. What a blessing to have a room to myself that night! I wanted a chance to think. The personalities of the Romulus WAFS were going to require some differential treatment so I wouldn't rub their fur the wrong way.

There was Burchie — slow, plodding, serious, lovesick, a dreamer almost to the point of balking at reality.

Fearful Poole with her susceptibility to respiratory illnesses. Critical, self-indulgent, jealous, and worried that she would not be treated equally with officers and other WAFS based elsewhere.

Thompson. What made her tick? I didn't know yet.

Donahue. A quick thinker, an eager beaver about flying, uncomplaining, vivacious, witty, a gambler who, when she lost, lost gracefully. She could afford to. Gossip rumored that her father was a big-time lawyer and the family lived on Fifth Avenue in New York City. It was understood that she was an heir to the Woolworth fortune, but I do not believe that any of us realized that either her mother or grandmother owned the Romanoff jewels and that members of the Donahue family were known to drop thousands of dollars in a gambling session during the Depression without a whimper.

Because of her background, some of the WAFS looked upon Barbara Donahue as an interesting character, a good sport who might have remained at home in the lap of luxury, but chose instead to endure our hardships. Perhaps Donahue thought that wealthy people, too, had a stake in their country's fortunes during the war.

I suspect that when the other WAFS evaluated Donahue, they considered themselves fortunate in their genes by comparison. For Donnie was not a beautiful girl. Her figure was a bit exaggerated — her shoulders were broad, her hips very narrow, and she was not as full-bosomed as many of the others. Her hands were large, her feet wide, and her walk odd. She may have affected the latter, for Donnie was dramatic and enjoyed standing out in a crowd. She gave a distinct theatrical impression with her Tallulah Bankhead voice. And she was amazingly self-assured.

I recalled that once at BOQ 14, Donnie threw her woolen uniform coat onto a hot radiator in the hall while she read a letter that someone had handed her. The coat remained there until someone said, ''What's burning?'' Off came the gray coat with several brown streaks where the garment had rested on the tops of the radiator fins. The cleaners could not restore the coat to its former condition. One thing was sure, no one took that coat by mistake.

My mind went back to the washroom in BOQ 14. Whenever Donnie hung up her shirts to dry after washing them, she'd slap them dripping wet over the line, all bunched together, and without clothespins. She might have observed how the rest of us hung up our shirts in order to make pressing them easier, but she did not conform to custom.

The latest incident bothered me, when she had picked up my panties before we left. I was the only one of our group close to her size, but I was too fastidious to share clothing with anyone, even a member of my family. And I did not have the money to replace whatever Donnie might decide to appropriate. If she needed panties, why didn't she buy them while she was in town? And where could I go to a store while on a mission? Or even at the base? The base exchange carried only men's clothing.

The only solution was to get a clothesline from somewhere and rearrange my room so I could string the thing up and dry my clothes in my own room. It would look tacky and make me appear strange, but it would avoid a clash with Donnie.

Finally I considered myself. Inclined to aim at perfection and too serious. I must try not to aggravate anyone with my earnestness. Too much in love with Harold to be carefree. Older than the others, I felt I must get up earlier, keep ahead, study harder, and not waste my time. I must become a capable leader, like Nancy.

The following day, February 3, we thought surely we'd deliver. Birmingham was only about two hours away and Thompson led us. We got an early start, only to find that when we arrived at the Birmingham airport we had no time to waste. The meteorologist warned us that a front would be in the Birmingham area within several hours. How we rushed to leave! As we got back to our airplanes, hoping to take off, a local shower began to sprinkle the airport. Out came the parachutes and we lugged them back to operations.

The rain stopped as quickly as it began. I checked the weather sequences and forecast again and found no change, so we took off with Burchie leading. As we crossed the roads and railroad just west of Irondale, visibility lowered to 1,000 feet above the terrain, which was quite rough north of Coalville, with a ridge running in a southwesterly direction. I could see that Burchie was headed into another shower just ahead, which would cut visibility further. So I pushed my throttle forward, moved to the right and ahead of the flight and headed Burchie off. The closer I got to the weather disturbance, the less I wanted to get into it. I turned 180 degrees to the left, the flight kept its formation and followed me back to Birmingham. It looked as if we were stuck for the day.

To pass the time, I asked for a session in the Link trainer, and after the operator handed me a chart and gave me directions, I hopped into the simulated cockpit. He closed the hatch, activated the machine, and the lesson progressed. I was orienting myself splendidly when, after twenty-five minutes, an officer at operations called and said, "The WAFS had better get out right away. The front is stalled and the forecast is that it won't arrive for another five hours."

With mixed feelings — reluctance to stop and relief that we could go — I left my Link lesson and found the others already aware of the change. I made out another clearance form.

Again Burchie led. She did a beautiful job of navigating until an east wind sprang up about sixty miles out. She didn't notice it or correct her heading. She passed Marbury thinking, I supposed, that it was Wadsworth. As the wind picked up, she drifted farther west until by the time she passed Deatsville, she was about three miles west of it. I gave her a little more time to make the correction herself, but as she kept on toward Prattville, again I bent the throttle forward to catch her. This time I moved ahead on the left and caught her attention, then turned eastward. All four, keeping their formation, turned and followed me. I eased into our desired course, keeping them between Millbrook and Prattville, then hitting the U-bend in the Alabama River where a railroad track met it. Maxwell Army Air Force Base lay ahead, southwest of the river.

Following the traffic pattern, we five PT-23Fe's circled counterclockwise and, after the tower flashed a green light, landed on the runway lined up with the large orange tetrahedron. Once the paperwork was finished, I telephoned an airline for the best and quickest way to return us to Detroit. As we waited for our plane, Poole said with some bitterness, "I put in my two cents worth. On the form I, I wrote, 'junk delivered.' "

Group operations at Romulus gave us time to apply for per diem, to wash our clothes, and to rest after the ten-hour evening and night flight, first to Washington and then, doglegging it via Pittsburgh, to

Detroit. With the curtains drawn as we approached Detroit, I was unaware then of how dangerous that airport could be. It had a huge gas or water tank sitting right beside it, a much larger obstacle than the old grain elevator near Lambert Field.

Colonel Nelson called us all to his office in late afternoon after we got back. He asked, "How did things go?"

We agreed that the weather was our only problem and that we were anxious to go again. The colonel looked as if he had swallowed a canary. He said, "The first graduating class from Miss Cochran's school," and he looked at the paper in his hand, "they call it the Women's Flying Training Detachment, is expected any day now. Mrs. Scharr, it is your job as CO to get the barracks in order for their arrival."

I thought, holy smoke! How much time do I have?

He must have read my mind, for he said, "The class is fifty strong. They graduate on February 15. ATC was given thirty days' notice by Training Command, but you weren't on base, so I couldn't tell you then."

"How many will be coming here?" I asked.

"Between five and ten."

"What must I do?"

"Contact the housing officer and get beds and bedding ready for their arrival."

"Yes, sir," I answered.

"You won't be on orders while you are preparing for the new girls and you must be here to welcome them."

Poole asked, "The rest of us will get our missions, won't we?"

"Plenty of them," replied the colonel. "We have a huge backlog of deliveries to be made."

The other WAFS looked at me with pity. I could see that not a single one wanted the honor of being CO under the circumstances. We already knew it involved a lot of responsibility with no extra pay.

The colonel said briskly, "Operations has you on orders right now, so why don't I excuse you so you can be on your way. Mrs. Scharr, you remain behind."

The girls left and my heart sank. Being CO was worse than I thought it would be.

Colonel Nelson said, "While you're preparing the barracks, you'll have some free time. So I'm turning you over to transition to get whatever time is available to you."

Then he took something from the middle top drawer of his desk and handed it to me. It was a car key. He said, "This is the key to the Lin-

A WAFS flight arrives in Niagara, New York, in February 1943 after a mission in Canada. From left: Dorothy Fulton, ''Sis'' Bernheim, Helen McGilvery, Nancy Batson, and Gertrude Meserve.

coln that Mr. O'Hara donated to us. You can use it to get back and forth from the mess and to help you get about the base. I'm putting the key in your keeping because I consider you very reliable. We'll supply you with gasoline here at the base, but you must pay for it yourselves.''

What a windfall! Or so we thought at first.

I had already missed sixteen days of flying because of a change of station and the horrible Michigan winter. My morale would have dropped like a brick if I could have foreseen that the first false alarm about Jackie Cochran's graduates would delay my next mission twenty-eight days while the other WAFS flew off without me.

A deadline of January 25, 1943, had been set, after which FERD could no longer hire qualified women civilian pilots as they were hiring men. Three well-qualified women — Sis Fine, Helen McGilvery, and Lenore McElroy — slipped in ahead of that date. General Arnold decreed that thereafter any female pilots entering FERD must be graduates of Cochran's school.

Then began an endless exchange of opposing views that marred command relationships in the AAF. FERD would be forced to accept these Cochran graduates although their minimum flight experience was only two-thirds that of civilian male pilots. To FERD the order to accept them was a threat to the safety record that the command had worked hard to maintain. It also signified discrimination against men and against the original WAFS. No wonder Colonel Tunner tried to place hurdles to protect the integrity of his command and himself as commander.

Colonel Tunner's boss, General George of ATC, reminded General Arnold's staff on February 4, 1943, of the numerous accidents FERD had when it hired civilian pilots with 200, rather than 300, flying hours. Demolished airplanes weren't deliverable. FERD had learned a lesson and didn't want to repeat it. Besides, once the women pilots were militarized, cadet graduates would need to have 300 hours before entering the Ferry Command.

Colonel Tunner was busy, too, urging General Craig to militarize the WAFS via the WAC. Inexplicably, his letter was stopped in the air staff, and General Arnold never officially saw it and so could not give it an authoritative answer. Within the Ferry Command, those, like Nancy Love, who knew about Tunner's move, whispered that Cochran had somehow stopped the letter.

Newly promoted to brigadier general, Tunner didn't like incompetent pilots, male or female, and intended to weed out those who weren't capable. He said he'd keep the women cadet graduates "for a reasonable length of time." As each entered FERD, an instructor in her assigned ferrying group would give her a flight test. If she failed, she would be retained for thirty days and then given another flight test. If she failed again, FERD would release her. The Training Command could take her back and give her more training if it chose. Also, if the graduate did not pass the form 64 physical, she would be given two weeks notice and released. Brigadier General Tunner appeared to be insubordinate and stubborn, but evidently his position was firm enough in the military hierarchy to let him remain in command.

The misinformation that Cochran gave to ATC about her school also rankled the Ferry Command. She must have known that her school, supposedly begun in September, was still gathering together its first class in November-December. Yet she told the Ferry Command that graduates would be available in February (after a course that was to last about twenty-two weeks) when she knew that was impossible. Why did she do this? Was she unaware of the status and development of the organization she headed? Was she covering up the temporal deficiencies in the school because she headed it? Was she badgering the Ferry Command to make life harder for it? I do not know. There may be other reasons for the apparent lack of veracity on her part. All I knew about the situation was that because of it I missed ferrying missions and felt lonely and useless. The Ferry Command did not get full benefit of the time for which I was being paid a salary.

While we were waiting for Cochran's graduates in February, Colonel Nelson's "fair-haired boy wonder," Captain McIntyre, who headed the transition school, was the pilot in command of a multi-engine airplane being ferried to Denver. The plane, as usual for such an assignment, carried a pilot, copilot, and an enlisted man as engineer or crew mechanic. The night was clear with no obstruction to visibility. Just west of Denver, the plane smacked into the side of a mountain.

It didn't take much deduction on the part of Romulus pilots to conclude that one pilot took a nap, trusting the other to do the flying. But the second must have placed the airplane on automatic pilot, since there were no weather problems, and perhaps he nodded off, too. The engineer was no doubt in the back of the airplane dozing because he wasn't needed. They reached Denver all right and then continued on west until the mountain got in their way. Without a break for mourning, changes began immediately at transition school at Romulus. Soon the grapevine carried the message that although it would remain where it was for the time being, future classes would be given in a new building. The new classes sounded interesting and helpful to us. The new head was Captain Hennessey, who seemed a good sort. We waited to find out what he could do for us.

It seemed that we were waiting for everything. The other Romulus WAFS discovered that operations had ordered all available men to ferry the newly completed aircraft. There was nothing left to fly. Colonel Nelson had given the WAFS a bum steer.

The morning after we returned to base, several of the fellows left on base asked us in the breakfast line at the mess, "Where's Poole?"

"Oh, she didn't feel like eating breakfast," said Donnie.

It was the first public rift in our solidarity as a group. I hoped that a lack of appetite was the reason and that upon our return to the barracks, Poole would be up and dressed.

She wasn't. If she was ill, I must get the doctor, I thought. I went into her room.

"I'd better call the flight surgeon to send someone over to examine you," I said to her. "If you'd rather go over there, we'll take you in the automobile."

"Whatever you do, don't call him!" Poole was visibly upset. She added, "I'm going to be all right. Give me a little time." And she turned away and closed her eyes.

I couldn't figure out how to help Poole. If she were truly ill, she would be grounded and very unhappy, thereby making us all unhappy.

If she were malingering because she wasn't on orders, she would appear in a bad light with the medics. Maybe she was having a bad period. Another thought crossed my mind, but I dismissed it. I decided to wait it out.

The rest of us went to ground school. At lunchtime, a thoughtful Burchie insisted on buying a lunch and taking the tray to barracks for Poole, who appeared glad to get it.

Would she join us at ground school? No, she preferred to remain in bed. When we returned at 1640, Poole was up and taking a shower. She soon was dressed and ready to leave in time for the opening of the bar at the officers' club. Never before had I met a patient with symptoms to match hers. She left the dirty dishes and tray from lunchtime atop her dresser. I wondered why she didn't take them with her, for Poole was neat in her appearance and in that of her room.

The next morning the tray and its contents were in the hall outside Poole's room. Does she expect room service? I wondered. Again Poole did not go to breakfast with us. The rest of us met at lunchtime and then wheeled over in the Lincoln to the barracks to see how she was. No change.

Poor Burchie. Quite self-consciously, as if ashamed of being an easy mark, she picked up the unsightly tray and returned it to the mess on our way back. I thought, she'll know better next time. I could have laid bets on what Poole would be like when we got off work — and I would have won. She was rarin' to go to the club, where she scintillated among the officers all evening. I began to plan the different approaches I must take to bring Poole back into the fold. It wouldn't be easy.

Nothing was easy. Colonel Nelson had definite ideas about the housing of pilots, which we did not agree with. He wanted to squeeze as many as four pilots to each room. Ford Motor Company was turning out B-24s at nearby Willow Run, and frequently pilots from other bases had to wait at Romulus until a plane or the weather was ready. And P-39s were brought to Romulus for alterations or modifications before being taken northwestward to Alaska, which meant that still more pilots must be housed.

Colonel Nelson intended to treat women equally as far as housing, so not only were beds double-decked to our original single bedstead, but another set was added to each room. I had to take inventory of our supplies to make certain that the WAFS got all the bedding for which the squadron was liable, a task I found very disagreeable.

There were few clement days in February at Romulus. Nevertheless, a painful hunger for flight compelled me to appear at transition school, the only place where local flying was possible if the ceiling lifted. I learned all I could on my own from the AT-6 operation instructions. Many times I sat in an AT-6 in the hangar and went through the procedures, talking to myself and touching the controls as I did so. On February 5 I passed the cockpit check. The next step was to get a ride in one.

The next day I was amused to see at the base exchange that the photograph of Colonel Nelson surrounded by WAFS had been made into postcards which were on sale for a nickel. I sent one to Harold in my next letter. He noticed right away that I, the CO, was the only one who did not have a stripe on my sleeve cuff. It was something I had not noticed, so I asked Thompson about it. She said that when the later WAFS were having their uniforms fitted at Carlson's, Nancy Love was so certain that we'd be militarized that she authorized lieutenant's stripes. But she forgot to tell the earlier WAFS — or maybe I wasn't present at the right cocktail party/bull session. Since I had a personality like "My Last Duchess," trappings meant nothing to me. The stripe was of so little importance that I hadn't noticed either its presence or absence.

On February 8 the ceiling lifted to about 4,000 feet for the first time in a week. As an instructor pilot was signing out AT-6 #899 for one hour of solo, he asked me if I'd care to ride along while he reviewed his maneuvers. Captain Nelson had told me to report to transition, so he must have tacitly approved my riding with an instructor. Nancy couldn't possibly frown on my going along, for she had already ferried AT-6s. I wouldn't be getting ahead of her. So I went.

The pilot sat in the front cockpit. He began by going to a practice area away from the field and choosing two pylons to practice doing eights. On the intercom he asked, "You want to try some?"

Would I? I touched the controls and immediately the plane and I were one, a mind and body with wings. The instructor had done a good maneuver, but he didn't realize that eights on pylons were a favorite of Spike Saladin's and they were one thing I could do with an airplane if I couldn't do anything else. He also didn't know about the more than 1,000 hours I'd put in as a critic of student practice on all commercial flight maneuvers. After four perfect eights, I shook the stick and he went on to S turns along a road. From that he climbed to 3,000 feet for chandelles and lazy-eights and vertical turns. Each time that he felt he'd practiced enough, he allowed me to try.

Back in the ready room, I overheard him tell another instructor, who must have questioned my performance, "She can fly better than I can." He said it without malice or amazement. I felt I had vindicated Kay Thompson's poor performance of a month ago.

The weather was good the following day. As soon as I entered the ready room, another instructor invited me to sandbag for his practice session. I accepted eagerly. The airplane, #898, had slightly different flight characteristics, but a pilot who has flown different types of planes adjusts to the individuality of each. The second instructor wasn't as competent as the first. I have no idea what he reported about me.

Then there was no more flying at Romulus for seven days. Weather conditions were miserable all through the Great Lakes area. The men at operations told me that Donnie and McElroy, trying to ferry PT-23s, weren't making any progress to their delivery destination. At the barracks, as I worked on filing directives and so forth, my thoughts turned again and again to the triumph of landing the AT-6 without a demonstration after only one hour in the plane. During the evenings I thought of Harold and home. Throughout that week without wings, a dread invaded my consciousness of being abandoned forever, tied to a desk in the cold, bleak Michigan post, never to see St. Louis or the sky again. How I prayed for a mission that would take me away from Romulus and toward my home!

Mail gave me some contact with family and friends. One letter dated January 7 from "somewhere in Northwest Africa" came from my friend Pat Ruddy, a St. Louis Ninety-Nine, who had volunteered as a nurse for the 26th General Hospital unit. Billie Gallagher, another Ninety-Nine, had been a dancing instructor and now was a control tower operator at Lambert.

Maybe Colonel Nelson guessed how the unflyable atmosphere at Romulus was affecting us. Maybe he needed to brighten his own life, too. Or maybe Poole, of whom he seemed quite fond, hinted that she might quit ATC (as she did whenever she heard from WAFS stationed elsewhere) and he wanted to mollify her. At any rate, he invited us to dinner at the club one Wednesday evening.

Afterwards, instead of playing his usual poker game with the young men, the colonel wanted to play cards with us. I had always considered cards as a pastime, for fun. No one gambled in my childhood home. When I saw people playing for money in various officers' clubs, they were so serious about the stakes that it was no longer a game. I had made a vow never to turn a hand at cards until the war was won and I was once again with people who believed as I did. I worked hard for my money and there was so little of it that I could not afford to lose any. On the other hand, other people's money belonged to them, and it was dishonest for me to take it without giving them the equivalent value in work. So I didn't play, but I watched.

A middle-aged officer came by and watched with me. He soon tired of it and offered to teach me a few pointers about billiards. I excused myself and accompanied this newfound companion to the pool table. I didn't do very well. Whenever I managed to send a ball into a pocket, its disappearance from view surprised me so that I giggled like a child with a new toy.

Soon Cowboy McMahon appeared with his sophisticated blonde. From casual remarks that I'd overheard, I was aware that the directors of the club were perturbed about officers bringing any casual acquaintances into the base and especially into the club. Some had been known to come only to meet other officers. But frowns in his direction would not have disturbed McMahon. In fact, he enjoyed annoying other people. They suckered us into a game with them. Again I was amazed at how accurately the woman finessed the balls to her advantage. It didn't take those pool sharks long to finish us off and then they had the table to themselves.

The next day Poole and Burchie were sent to Fort Erie to pick up a pair of PTs to take to the southland.

"This one had better not be like the last," grumped Poole without malice, for she was delighted to get away from the base.

That left only Thompson and me to watch the action at the club at the TGIF celebration. A new air force regulation prohibited the selling or dispensing of alcoholic beverages stronger than 3.2 beer on any of its bases. So to get rid of what was on hand at the bar, a dance was scheduled for the following night and drinks would be free for as long as they lasted.

Instead of sticking with me, on Friday Kay went into Detroit to meet her husband, Ted, but they both intended to come to the dance on Saturday. Colonel Nelson invited me to be his dinner guest. Kay said, "The colonel does a combination of the Highland fling and the Charleston. I hope you enjoy the experience."

"You tell Ted to cut in on me if he sees that I'm in trouble," I replied.

"You don't want us to have some fun watching you?" she asked.

That morning the supply officer sent a new typewriter over to our barracks. He refused to send one that was battered and dirty, which was nice, but in dismay I saw that the keys of the new typewriter had not a single mark on them. The alphabet was all blanked out. What was I to do? I had never had a typing lesson in my life. I had practiced with a study book of my sister's and a second-hand, portable Underwood, but I had never learned the touch system. After I explained my predicament to my supply benefactor, he said I'd have to keep this one until a new one came in.

I continued to plow through the details of running the squadron. I took time for another hour in the Link and to read all the tech orders and reports that all pilots at Romulus were ordered to read. During the winter we were told about icing conditions, inadvertent spins, air locks, and similar hazards to one's health.

The Saturday night affair at the club was packed with friendly and sociable people. Mr. and Mrs. Ed Price, the local war contractor we had met before, were the most important civilian guests there. They invited several of us to visit their estate the following afternoon.

Included in the party that went to the Price home was a Major Forester, a most unusual young man. He was handsome and well built, with light brown hair and blue eyes. Since our arrival on the base we had watched him very generously share his talent with the others. He could play either the organ or the piano, not only classical numbers, but also any popular song that someone suggested to him. As soon as he sat at either instrument, officers and WAFS clustered around him.

On our way home in Colonel Nelson's staff car, the colonel led us in singing some old songs. We were relaxed and happy. It was no wonder that "the old man" was viewed with fondness by everyone on his base.

I think he even would have been amused and not reprimanded me had he known that I had allowed the "off limits" rule about our barracks to be broken. I knew that none of the WAFS out on missions would return over the weekend. After the club dance, the Thompsons had two options — to take a cab to a hotel downtown and stay together or to separate and stay on the base.

I said to them, "Don't be silly. If I don't see Ted sneak into our barracks and he is invisible from the hall and I don't catch him in the bathroom, as far as I'm concerned, he will not have been harbored in our barracks."

Kay's room was just across the hall from the bathroom. If Ted was there, I never encountered him. But I'm quite certain that the alternative I offered them was the one they took. It's what I would have done in their place.

Ted's presence on the base had an effect on my morale. I wrote to Harold that if I didn't get a chance to get to St. Louis soon, I'd make myself so obnoxious that they'd kick me out. It was already February 15 and there was no sign of the Cochran graduates. I could have delivered two airplanes in the time I wasted on base waiting for them.

Then operations informed me that I was to get ten new members for the squadron in a few days. All hope of getting on orders now was blasted. In that case, my only recourse to the air was to appear at transition, where the men were warming up to the idea of women pilots.

My first chance at a flight was in a BT-13A. A check pilot was needed for someone going out to practice instrument flying, so I sandbagged as a safety check pilot for fifty minutes and got ten minutes under the hood. Once, as we were approaching the field on the beam and getting ready to simulate an instrument approach to a landing, we had a bird's-eye view of an accident. We circled to watch.

A P-39 carrying a big belly tank came in for a landing. Usually pursuit airplanes carried enough gasoline for a maximum flight of three hours — if one were able to squeeze every drop of gasoline from the tanks. This didn't allow for the forty-five minutes reserve fuel for emergencies. Bell placed a belly tank on the P-39 to give it a longer range, perhaps three more hours, to stretch the usefulness of the plane in combat. That auxiliary fuel was used early in the flight and the combat pilot was supposed to jettison the tank in order to rid his aircraft of the useless drag.

I had heard pilots who were afraid to fly the P-39 say that it never forgave mistakes. This was the first I saw how true that was.

From where we circled, we could not see the bottom of the airplane as it approached the ground. Apparently the pilot forgot or was unable to put the wheels down. He made a good belly landing and in a moment of terror and amazement, I saw sparks hit the pavement behind the tail as the plane ground to a halt. With what was perhaps the fastest exit ever made from an airplane at Wayne County Airport, the pilot left his craft and ran, as the P-39 became engulfed in flames. The fire fighting equipment closed in to foam the wreckage and worked to extinguish the fire as soon as possible.

We waited until the tower operators decided on an alternate landing pattern using another runway so we could get down without interfering with the activity around the P-39. Once down, while we completed our forms, we found out that the pilot was Lieutenant Gold, a dark-haired pilot with a large black mustache, who was invariably smoking or chewing on a cigar. We went out to the field and studied the wreckage. I said, ''By the time the safety board gets through with him, they'll make it so hot for him, he'll wish he'd stayed inside that P-39 — it'd be cooler.'' Ah, I knew so little about safety boards then.

Back at transition, another instrument student asked me to play safety-check for him, but an offer to fly in an AT-6 beckoned me more. Off I went in the same AT-6 I'd flown the week before. Later the men in transition said, ''It's too bad we can't let you fly solo, but you're not allowed.'' An exhilarating cup to taste, but, oh! what bitter dregs.

A chance popped up for me to go for an hour with someone in a twin-engine Cessna, a UC-78. Vain hope. Some majors came into the ready room and they took what they wanted, beating out all captains and looies who wanted to go, too, and, of course, the lowly WAF. I went back to the lonely barracks.

That night three of our cadre returned, the two Barbaras and Lenore. Evidently, Burchie and Poole had gone part of their distance together, but left each other to deliver to two different airfields.

The following evening, like one lone pea in a pod, I again had the barracks to myself. Everyone else was off on a mission. I went to the officers' club at 1800 and left soon after I ate. Many new faces were appearing there, self-conscious, bored young men, in from the Training Command, sporting their shining gold bars on their shoulder straps. They hoped for some companionship. I thought they could find it without me. I went home to write Harold. If his cradling me in his strong arms was an impossibility, as least I could dream about it.

The next evening I arrived at the club at 1730. A Ping Pong game was already in progress in the game room. Lieutenant Schwartz was back and had the table. Anyone who wanted to play had to take him on as an opponent. He clearly enjoyed his advantage. I had worked all day at my filing cabinet in the barracks and needed some activity. I might not have been so lonesome if operations had given me a place to work in its office. I decided I might as well hang around and let Schwartz beat me again.

Captain Mason, an older bush pilot from upper Canada and Alaska, came along to watch. He said, ''I sure wish we could get something else going. I'm tired of Ping Pong and pool and I sure don't want to drink.''

''What might you have in mind?'' I asked.

''I'd like a little more physical exercise.''

There was a pause as we watched Schwartz clobber his opponent. Wistfully, Captain Mason said, ''I know where there's a roller skating rink. It's not far away, but we have no way to get there.''

I answered, ''I'd like that, too.'' I remembered how at Wilmington several of us WAFS spent an evening on rented skates rolling atop a maple floor. I added, ''I have a car that a big mogul gave Colonel Nelson. I think I can drive it if we can get up a party to go. I wouldn't waste the gasoline for only myself.''

With that, Captain Mason went among the Ping Pong spectators. They were young, slim, not very tall, and destined to become pursuit pilots. Then he went into the card room. Returning, Mason said, ''I got five more. Can the car carry that many?''

''Sure. It's a limousine. Let's go.''

The captain nodded to the others, who were waiting expectantly. As he and I left the club, five others followed us. Lieutenant Schwartz looked after us perplexed that anyone should leave instead of watching him trim an opponent.

As I drove at Mason's direction to the edge of a nearby town, the gloomy mood of despair that enveloped my passengers lifted. By the time the fellows had their skates on, they were taller in spirit than the wheels had lifted them. Round and round we went.

I was not an accomplished skater. When I was in the second grade, my teacher had asked us children to bring one of our Christmas gifts to show to the class. I chose to bring my clamp-on roller skates against my parents' wishes. I put them under my desk, but the teacher insisted that I take them to the open wardrobe outside the room, facing the hall. By recess time, the skates had disappeared. Because I had disobeyed my parents, they did not replace the skates or give me a new pair on subsequent Christmases. But even though I had had scant chance to practice skating as a child, my sense of balance was excellent and I was in trouble only when a careless skater brushed me in passing. Or when I went a bit too fast. Every time I felt my equilibrium upset on that night, I also felt the masculine hand of a uniformed skater steady my elbow until I was safely on my own again.

On our way home, Captain Mason said, "I was resting in the stands and overheard a conversation among some of the San Quentin quail. They really raked you over the coals, Del."

"Oh?" I replied.

"Yes. It was funny. They could see you weren't as good on the skates as they were. You're older and they were wondering out loud how it was that you had all those men and nobody was paying any attention to them. So I let them have it with both barrels. I said, 'When that woman was as young as you, she wasn't spending all her free time in a roller skating rink trying to pick up some fellow. She was working and studying and she became an airplane pilot. And Uncle Sam called her to do a man's job during this war. When you can top all she's done, you can start to criticize. Think about it.' And then I got up and joined you."

A soft glow warmed me all over. I hadn't known how the men were taking the WAFS. It was wonderful to be accepted as one of the boys.

"I saw those birds flirting with you," remarked one of the looies. "I wouldn't touch one with a ten-foot pole. They're jail bait."

"Oh, that's why you called them San Quentin quail," I said, feeling like a dumb bunny. I thought to myself how difficult such creatures made the life of lonely young men away from home. If they didn't remind themselves of military regulations and the severity of civilian laws, they might have succumbed to inviting temptations. In 1943 the structure of morality did not coincide with what is in vogue today.

The following morning I had a one-hour lesson in the Link. I was going from the early stages in which I tried to make certain patterns to radio signals. Rough air added to the complexity of the lessons.

As I climbed out of the trainer, my calf muscles complained. It was too bad that I couldn't roller skate regularly. A little physical training in my barracks room might help me stay in better condition. I thought back on the evening before, smiling.

In the chow line at noon, Cowboy McMahon was three people ahead of me, but that didn't stop him from needling me. He leaned back and said, "I'm back. So where's your women pilots?" He had left the base the same time they did.

"Thompson had engine trouble in Nashville. You can't deliver if the thing won't run." He shut up.

After more than two weeks of waiting for Cochran's first graduates, Colonel Nelson called me in to say that there would be a little delay. Maybe a few more weeks. It was time to hit him for a leave and I got it, effective as soon as the others came back. My authorization was to ride as a passenger on a military aircraft of the Army Air Forces departing Romulus on or about February 22.

When the squad returned and finished their paperwork, I got the girls together for an information session. "The new girls aren't due here from Houston or Sweetwater for the rest of this month," I told them.

One of the group replied, "If they think we'll welcome them with open arms . . . they probably think they're better than we are."

"Sure," I said. "They have better planes to fly down there, but they'll start just like we did. And they will be a part of this squadron."

"Not to me they won't." Again, my chronic complainer.

"You'll get over that. The least we can do is to be courteous and friendly and helpful so we can all work together. Life will be more pleasant and we can get the job done. You don't know what good friends you can miss if you close the door on them before they even arrive."

No one made a comment.

"That's all, except I'd like to talk to you, Barbara," I said as I turned to Poole.

When the others had left, I said to her, "Poole, as exec, would you stay on deck while I'm gone for the next three or four days?"

"You know I hate to stay around on the base. I want to fly," she replied, ignoring the tradition that a CO's request should be taken as a command.

Acting according to Nancy Love's precedent, I had appointed Poole as my executive officer because she'd been in the WAFS longer than the others had. I thought the title would make her happy and feel more important, although at first there wasn't anything to do. Now there was, but she was balking.

I said softly, "I'm sorry. I've been tied to this place for over a month. It's only for a few days and then you'll be flying again."

"Hmmm," she grumbled. "You can get somebody else next time."

I went off to St. Louis with a problem simmering in the back of my mind. But once there all I was interested in was being with my darling instead of just writing lovesick notes to him. I returned on the train on Saturday afternoon, February 27.

When I got back to the base, I received a letter from Harold, which mirrored my own feelings. "After I left you at the train," he wrote, "the world looked hostile and lonely to me. I went home, brooded a while and then got the Sunday paper, read same and went to bed not even bothering to get any supper."

I replied, "I am in the dumps since we parted. Am bearing up, chin high and all. We'll be opening a pot of beans together very soon. Watch, will you?"

Another month had begun — March. Outside the meteorology classroom the sky shone whitish-gray and the orchard trees in their rows furled their twig branches like little plumes eastward with the wind. Could spring be at hand? Outside it was bleak and inside the coldness of the room chilled me to the marrow. I remembered that I was in Michigan. Spring would come later than it did in Missouri.

As soon as I got back, the two Barbaras and Kay were put on L-5 orders. Burchie and McElroy were ill, possibly with ptomaine poisoning from eating shrimp. So I was the only one in ground school for a while.

On Sunday the Lincoln had been left at the officers' club because it was low on gas and none was pumpable. That Monday morning I walked to the mess alone in the semi-darkness against a fierce wind far below zero, which carried tiny ice shards that cut my face. The bitter cold penetrated my face and the pain of it reached into my palate. I had put on my flying goggles as a protection for my eyes. Why hadn't I put on my face mask, too? I reprimanded myself and I bent into the wind and pushed myself along.

In contrast to the environment at Romulus, WAFS COs at the other bases found themselves in more benevolent situations. At NCAAB Betty Gillies was flying the Republic Thunderbolt (the P-47) and Helen

Teresa James taxis the 10,000th P-47 Thunderbolt away from the Republic Aviation plant in Farmingdale, New York. The enormous single engine fighter plane, nicknamed "The Jug," was a workhorse combat plane during World War II.

Mary Clark would be next to do so.

In Dallas, every WAF was in basic and advanced trainers. Transition was so open at Long Beach that Nancy Love had requested a permanent change of station to that base from Dallas. On March 5 Nancy Love ferried a C-47 (Douglas DC-3) from Long Beach to Memphis with Barbara J. Erickson as her copilot. According to FERD records, by then Nancy was qualified in C-47s, A-36s, the North American Mustang P-51, and fourteen other types of aircraft, mostly manufactured in the Long Beach area. Those WAFS who got transition on other bases were so chary about their good fortune that I didn't learn about it until after the fact, until they'd been seen ferrying what they had checked out in. Poole found out about it from some source and the rankle of jealousy inflamed her bosom. The rest of us at Romulus were already disciplined to deprivation, to losing some trials in competition, and to showing good sportsmanship, but there was some hurt in our hearts, too.

WHERE'S BURCHIE?

THE RINGING OF THE TELEPHONE broke the quiet in the WAFS barracks on Wednesday, March 3. I ran down the hall to answer it.

"Mrs. Scharr? How many WAFS are available for a mission?" It was an operations officer.

"Phyllis Burchfield and I are the only ones here. The others haven't gotten back yet."

I listened intently for several minutes and then replied with enthusiasm, "Yes, sir! I have it. Thank you, sir."

Galvanized by what I had heard, I hung up the receiver and with brisk strides, hurried to Burchie's door. I looked in. The usually meticulous room looked as if moving day had arrived. Lingerie was folded in neat piles upon the bed. Dresser drawers were open. Burchie stood aloof from the disorder she had created. In a dreamlike state, she was methodically and lovingly braiding the luxuriant cascade of dark brown hair that she refused to cut. Her hair was Burchie's most attractive feature and it compensated for her impassive face, her lack of conversation, and her shy, quiet, and humble manner. The wealth of it must have enchanted George.

I exclaimed joyfully, "Burchie! We just got orders to report to the Stinson factory for a checkout in L-5s. A car is coming by in twenty minutes."

Burchie continued braiding. Her facial expression remained unchanged as she gazed dully at me.

"How far away is that?" she asked.

"I don't know. Somewhere close. We're bringing two airplanes back here for the mechanics to check over. So we'll need our Detroit sectionals."

"Uhh. I haven't pressed my uniform yet."

"There's no need to dress up. You can press when we get back. I'm wearing my winter flying suit."

I started down the hall, changed my mind, stopped, and returned to Burchie's doorway. With loving hands, Burchie was placing a princess slip in her middle dresser drawer.

"Now, Burchie," I stated firmly but kindly. "Drop everything. You have only ten or fifteen minutes to get your duds on in case the driver comes early. Listen. Remember? We're coming back here. You can finish all this when we return."

It didn't take me long before I was back, ready to go, but forced to watch Burchie take from a clothes hanger her winter flying jacket and trousers. As she put them on, I hunted through her pile of charts for the required sectional.

With hesitation Burchie said, "George said he's coming up to Detroit this weekend on a two-day leave."

"Well, you'll have to warn him that you are on orders and he can get leave another time."

"I'm afraid he'll pout and be angry."

"But suppose the mission is routed through Lockbourne?"

The thought of it cheered her and spurred her on so that we were both ready at the door when the motor pool staff car stopped at the WAFS barracks. As we carried our parachutes down the narrow walk, the driver got out to open the trunk. We lifted the chutes in, the driver slammed the lid, and returned to the wheel. We climbed into the back seat.

"Please stop by operations," I requested. From there, where we picked up our orders, we took a ten-minute run across the colorless, drab, and flat Michigan landscape. The Stinson factory was a small, one-story building next to a small sod airfield. The driver took us fieldside, directly to the flight line. He helped us get the chutes from the trunk and off he went while we carried them into the factory's flight operations office. The man in charge said "hello," most cordially.

"Which one of you wants to go first?" he asked.

Burchie's lingual agility surprised me. "She should," blurted out Burchie. "She's the flight leader."

I thought to myself, she'll need time to acclimate herself to a new airplane. If I go first, she can read the tech orders while I'm gone — and probably worry herself sick as she's doing it.

Handing a pamphlet to Burchie, the man said, "Here's the tech orders. Read 'em over." Turning to me, he said, "You can go over the tech orders when we come down. I'll show you enough to keep you out of trouble. Let's go."

I picked my chute from the floor and followed him outside to the first L-5 near the hangar. He was the check pilot in addition to being the official greeter and already had his parachute on the back bucket seat. I placed mine on the forward tandem seat. Together we preflighted the airplane. He saw that I was taking over, so he just followed me around to see if I missed anything. He nodded his head at my thoroughness.

"I want you to know about the radio," he said.

"Radio?" I had almost forgotten that the L-5 had a communications system. It had been so long since we had gotten our orders for our first and my only mission.

Pointing to a box in the cockpit, the man said, "This can't be used to contact the tower and you can't get radio ranges with it. All it's for is communication between flight liaison aircraft maneuvering close to enemy lines. See here?" He pointed to a handle at the right side of the cockpit. "This reels out the antenna after you're airborne. You've got to reel it in again above 300 feet off the ground. Never have it out below 300 feet. You don't want it catching on anything. I really wouldn't bother with it if I were you."

Pointing again, he said, "Over here is the lever that controls the flaps. We use thirty-degree flaps on takeoff for maximum efficiency, and we use forty-five degrees for landing, and that's full flaps. Never try to put your flaps down at a speed of one hundred or you'll tear them off. I'll land first when we come in. Now you take it and we'll see how you do."

The instructor took the observer's station behind me. He saw me hesitate and said, "The step is that part of the strut right next to the fuselage."

"Thanks," I replied. I didn't want to break it up before I had a chance to fly the thing. I lifted myself in and onto the parachute and buckled it and the safety belt.

"The seat adjustment handle is down by the right side of your seat."

I felt around and touched something.

"Yeah, that's it," he said. He continued directing me. "Now set the throttle for starting just about . . . here. Prime the engine about two strokes; it's pretty warm. If it stands quite a while, you have to give it four or five shots of prime. Now lock the primer."

I had already done so.

"Turn the master switch on." He waited until I found it. "Now the battery switch. If it's cold out, get some external source of juice and you'll save your battery. Now press the starter button and if she kicks over, turn ignition to 'both.'"

Like magic, the propeller whirled. Gleefully I thought, imagine having a starter switch again to turn an engine over! No more turning a prop by hand, no pumping a lever like mad while a sad-sack GI balances himself on a wing root and leans toward the engine cowling as he desperately turns a crank and hopes the pilot cooperates. Besides having a starter, the L-5 was enclosed. What luxury! And it was roomier than a Cub.

I acted as if I were alone. I taxied away from the hangar and ran up the engine at 1,000 rpm until the oil reached eighty pounds of pressure and the oil temperature was up to ten degrees centigrade. Putting the brakes on more tightly, I revved the engine to 1,800 to check both magnetos, one at a time. Both okay. On with the carburetor heat. Small drop in rpm. Carb heat off and the engine speed resurged. I throttled back and looked about for the windsock.

"The best part about this liaison aircraft is how it can get in and out of little fields. Put on thirty degree flaps. You'll see." He sounded proud.

I taxied to takeoff position, looking to the air and around on the ground for any obstructions to my path. Then, throttle full forward. The L-5 got off the ground as quickly as a Cub in a headwind. At liftoff I relaxed the nose, picked up the best climbing speed of eighty miles per hour and took off the top revs. Above several hundred feet, I started to milk the flaps gingerly, watching how the airplane reacted. The climb was made with 2,250 rpm to 1,000 feet altitude, where I eased pressure on the stick and set the stabilizer for straight and level flight. Then I climbed, coordinating turns, getting the reaction of the airplane and played around with several level turns at 1,500 feet. I looked all about the area — above, below, and around — to be certain I wouldn't run into anybody. Now came approaches to stalls, with and without using flaps, with and without power. Each time I put the flaps down, I thought, he doesn't have to worry that I'll put 'em down at 100. It's all I can do to get 'em down at eighty-five.

The check pilot made the first approach over the factory roof using full flaps. The descent was as steep as a slip. "You land it," he yelled at me at the last minute. I did, and then he yelled, "Go on around!"

Swiftly I snapped the flaps up to thirty degrees and with throttle pushed full forward, the L-5 leaped from the ground. I made a small Cub pattern about the field and landed.

"Again," called the check pilot.

I repeated the circuit. This time he held the stick and the throttle back, not allowing me to take off again. "Okay, let's taxi in," he said.

After I cut the switch, he told me, "You're checked out."

As I pulled out my parachute, the check pilot went in and brought out Burchie, carrying her chute for her. She handed me the pamphlet. I took it and found my orders in my purse. I was to take #42-14843. Okay. I looked at the airplanes sitting outside the factory until I found it. As I preflighted it, I divided my attention between the airplane and the tech orders. The faster one learned, the safer one would be, I thought.

The L-5 was a step backward from the PT-23. The engine had only six cylinders with 190 horsepower and was made by Lycoming. Fuel capacity and consumption were two big considerations in ferrying, for they not only varied from airplane types of different horsepower, but also from one airplane to another of the same make and engine horsepower. The L-5 had only a normal wing load of twenty-five gallons of fuel and at normal cruise with a throttle setting of 2,230 rpm, it should use about 10.6 gallons per hour. With a forty-five minute fuel reserve, I figured that I'd better keep each hop less than two hours' duration. We'd have to check our engine's efficiency. Hops would be short if we cruised at 105 mph.

After Burchie landed for the last time, I whirlwinded her through a preflight and back we went into the air, with me leading. The Stinson factory was no more than four direct air miles from Wayne County Airport, but the traffic on the field was quite heavy with large aircraft. We made fifteen minutes of circuits before we were green-lighted for a landing.

I said to Burchie when we got back to the barracks, "That darned radio! I don't know why people conclude that every pilot on earth knows so much about any new electronic gadget as soon as they see it for the first time. Why doesn't a check pilot bother to find out how ignorant a person is? I wished we'd had time to reel out that antenna."

The weather closed in again the next morning. At operations, an officer gave me our orders. They read: San Antonio. The L-5s we were to take were the same ones we had brought in from Stinson. I walked over to the huge hangar to see where the enlisted men had placed them.

The L-5s were snuggled under the wings of some huge birds. The head mechanic, a sergeant, seeing me among the airplanes in his charge, headed toward me. He was bigger than I and probably intended to chase me out.

"Hi!" I called even before he came close. "I was just looking to see if these L-5s could come out in a hurry in case the weather lets us fly tomorrow."

Now he was beside me, looking down patronizingly. "Where are you going?" he asked.

"I can't tell you, but if I'm lucky, I'll RON at my home airport, Lambert Field."

"That your home?"

"Yep. St. Louis, the friendliest city in the U.S.A."

The sergeant smiled at my civic loyalty. "How long since you've been back?" he asked.

"My last trip was in the week before Christmas." I didn't feel the need to tell him I'd just had a leave. My answer was truthful, but not in answer to what he'd asked.

He must have felt a little sorry for me, for he offered, "I know how long it takes to fly anything from here to St. Louis. I'll have these airplanes out and ready to go so you'll be sure to RON at home."

This was an unexpected turn for the better. Sis Bernheim told me years later, "We were the darlings of the enlisted men. They'd do anything for us, not like some of those beardless lieutenants who thought we were in the service only to look for husbands."

I opened up to the sergeant. "My husband works at Lambert Field. He's enlisted, too, but he's in the Naval Reserve. He's a chief aviation metalsmith."

"So you're a poor man's Amelia Earhart?" he asked.

I laughed. "Not hardly," I replied. I could never be in her class.

The next day, March 5, there were no signs of precipitation in the forecast to keep us at Romulus. I went to the hangar to ask that our L-5s be placed out on the line.

"I can't get them out quite yet," said the sergeant. "Come around in about an hour." He winked at me.

On my return with Burchie in tow, there they were, ready to go.

The sectional chart of the Detroit area depicted so many railroad lines and highways and so many pink radio ranges and restricted areas to avoid, that I thought Burchie might become confused. It would be embarrassing to her if I took over the lead again. But truthfully, I was anxious for a hard test of my skill. So I led.

After departing the traffic pattern, I crabbed into the wind at a heading of 260 degrees. There were multiple checkpoints to score myself with, such as the transmission line crossing a creek about one mile south of Sabine. Between Raisin Creek (where did they get that name?) and Jerome were many small lakes outlined with their individual signatures or perimeters.

At intervals, light snow showers pelted the L-5s, but visibility remained at least three miles at 2,000 feet above sea level, which was about 1,000 feet above the terrain. We landed at Bendix Airport near South Bend, Indiana, in ninety-five minutes with an average ground speed of 102 mph.

"How about you closing our flight plan?" I asked Burchie. I stayed out in the cold to make certain our fuel tanks were really topped. Ten gallons an hour. It was not as good as I had hoped for.

Later, inside, how cozy the office felt to me. I signed for the gas, we checked the weather report, and made a clearance to Joliet, Illinois.

"Do you want to lead this time?" I asked Burchie.

She shook her head. Burchie looked forlorn. The corners of her mouth turned down as if she smelled something bad. I guessed that her heart lay like a heavy stone in her breast, for this mission was keeping her from George. She needed something to keep her mind off him.

"Come on, you can take it," I said.

Burchie's eyes were pleading. Oh, heck, I thought. I'll do it. I said, "You can take it from Joliet." That would give her enough lead time to get her mind set on it.

Only ninety-nine miles to go. The course was still 260 degrees, but I altered it after crossing the New York Central railroad track. The wind was shifting. When my body was traveling along the line I'd drawn on the chart as I crossed the westbound highway, I yelled in exultation, "Lambert Field, here we come!"

The countryside was bleak and dirty, a gray, drab world in which stark naked trees were silhouetted against a gray sky. Now and then a snow flurry pattered on the windshield. We diverted southward to avoid flying over Gary, Indiana, and the south Chicago suburbs. We landed at Joliet in fifty minutes, making a ground speed of 110 mph at 2,230 rpm. Good cruising speed.

But when I calculated how much gasoline had been consumed, I saw that the engine burned 11.2 gallons per hour. That shortened our radius of flight considerably.

At Joliet we studied the weather again. Nothing in the latest teletype sequence gave us anything to worry about. Still, we'd wait for the next one, due in soon. All the reports were okay, but the report from Rolla, Missouri, was missing. Beyond Rolla, at Springfield, the contact flight

The Stinson L-5 "Sentinel," shown over Okinawa in April 1945, could have been ferried by the WAFS from Romulus.

conditions were above minimums.

I asked the meteorologist, "Do you think we should wait for the next sequence?"

"I don't know why," he answered. Rolla had been okay the hour before.

I said to Burchie, "Let's take off right away. Rolla is far enough from St. Louis. In case we have to, we can land at Bloomington or Springfield, Illinois. They're right on the way."

It was Burchie's turn to lead and I felt I'd have to watch her like a hawk. She reluctantly settled herself in the cockpit and started the engine. I did the same. When I looked over to her, I couldn't see her — she had the sectional chart up and around her face as if she were pouring herself into it. I waited until I thought the delay was ridiculous. I turned off my engine, unbuckled myself, ran to her plane, and tapped on the plastic side of her door.

Burchie lowered the chart and peeked over the edge.

Excitedly I yelled over the noise of the engine, "Let's go, Burchie! We don't have all day."

When I restarted my engine, Burchie released her parking brake and led out for takeoff. We had wasted a valuable ten minutes. The leg was easy enough at the beginning with plenty of checkpoints near the airport. In eleven miles, she was right over Divine as she should have been. But then gusts of wind started to pitch our planes sideways and up and down. Still, it was no worse than the air over the Blue Ridge Mountains in the fall. After passing Mazu, Sunbury, Nevada, and Rowe, I knew Burchie couldn't get lost. The B & O railroad was four miles to the east until we crossed it at Funks Grove south of Bloomington. We passed over the southeast edge of the Springfield Airport. No activity below. Then there wasn't much to go by after Gerard except an abandoned railroad bed. Nice. Burchie had done a good job.

After passing Brighton to the north of Alton, Illinois, I moved forward to lead the flight into Lambert. We were almost home now and I knew the territory. There was gray-stoned Monticello College for girls and nearby, between the railroad tracks, was where Ray Harris had had his little field he'd called Godfrey.

It looked like fog ahead. We flew over the Mississippi River and then over the Missouri, right over the eastern edge of what my folks called Wolf Island. South of the river's edge in St. Louis County, I saw that the fog was actually snow starting to fall. A time for quick decisions. Of course I wanted to get into Lambert. From the looks of the air, it would be on instruments, and I'd have to take my licks for coming in on a contact clearance.

What about Kratz Field or Private Flyers in St. Charles? Burchie would be a problem. She wouldn't be familiar with those small fields. That was out. Go back to Springfield? With a headwind against us, we'd never make it. How about east to Effingham or Vandalia? Still too far and the weather there was unknown.

By now we were down to 500 feet over farmland, still on course, and Lambert only several minutes away. I looked back again. Burchie had moved in closer to my tail.

"Good girl," I said aloud. "I won't lose you."

I knew almost every farmhouse and all the roads in north St. Louis County. I always observed what was beneath us when I instructed flight students. Now I bordered Lindbergh Road, still on course, and scooted along above Highway 140 to where it joined Lindbergh after we passed the little town of Florissant. Lambert was just ahead. I saw the white light atop the tower on the administration building. Lambert was closed to contact flight. I looked back. Burchie was right behind me.

As I flew over the grain elevator and the line of hangars bordering Long Road, where it passed the administration building paralleling Lindbergh, a green light flashed from the tower.

"Good boy, Dobbin," I said, losing speed and altitude. The weather bureau windsock showed number four runway in use. I turned in short, put on the flaps, shoved the nose down, and glided in so short to the fence that I had already turned off the apron and out of Burchie's way in order to leave her the entire 3,500 feet of runway to land in.

I turned my L-5 to the field and the runway so I could watch. Burchie made a good approach. Yet, why did she rev up her engine and go on up again? I watched her fly down the length of the field and turn into the usual traffic pattern. While she was doing that, I looked for any other incoming plane and there being none, I taxied across runway four to the parking area at the side of the old National Guard hangar. The Army Air Forces had appropriated that hangar as a refueling station for its aircraft. In the loft upstairs was one of the chain of Hotel DeGinks where itinerant crews — males, only — could rest.

I was puzzled by Burchie's refusal to land when I'd made the whole runway free for her. But I wasn't worried. I parked my L-5, shut off the engine, filled out the form I, and then saw Burchie making another approach. She was lined up well, but again, at about twenty-five feet off the runway, she pushed on the power and aborted the landing. Up she went.

I got out and was tying down the wings and the tail when Maj. Ralph Page came from the hangar.

"Anything wrong, Del?" he asked.

"Hi, Ralph," I said. "I don't know. I can't understand what could be wrong."

"The snow's coming down faster. She'd better get down next time," commented Major Page, as he looked about and then returned to the hangar.

All sorts of thoughts raced around in my mind. I was unable to see the L-5 now. Where was it? Should I take my L-5 and go up and try to find Burchie in case she had lost sight of the field? If I did that, suppose we ran into each other up there? What if I still couldn't find her?

Then a green light flashed furiously from the tower and there was Burchie approaching runway four again. Once more she went up into the swirling snow and disappeared more quickly than before.

"Oh, poor Frank Dobbin," I said aloud. "He must be out of his mind by now." The tower operator was my friend and I knew that he was pulling for Burchie to land as hard as she was. And I was, too.

Where was Burchie? She was gone. Only the snow was out there and all around us, falling thicker and faster every passing minute. Sad and crushed by the guilt of having brought Burchie to this predicament, I felt myself age ten years at least.

Then, to the east, I spied an airplane. It was above the end of the wide runway a mile long that had been built the previous spring and summer. It almost paralleled number four. It was called runway six because, according to the compass rose, one landed on it in a sixty degree, or northeasterly, direction. It was where the flight of five P-39s had ended so disastrously the summer before.

"Please, God, let it be Burchie, but no more going up. Let her land that thing," I prayed.

The approach was visible even where I stood and Burchie was making it a long one. The airplane made several stepdowns in its gliding path. And then, finally, she was down.

I felt bad about bringing my wingman into conditions with which she could not cope. Yet weren't all the WAFS supposed to be technically as proficient as each other?

Now that Burchie was safely on the ground, busily taxiing until she found the National Guard hangar in the snowstorm, I found no reason why I should remain outside to wait for her to appear. I was exhausted and took refuge in the hangar. Major Page asked when I entered, "How about a cup of coffee, Del?"

"I can sure use one," I replied.

Not long after, Burchie entered, seemingly calm and dignified. She never showed much emotion. I walked across the room to meet her. I didn't want the men to hear, but I was dying to find out.

"What in God's name was the matter?" I whispered.

In a no-nonsense, matter-of-fact manner, Burchie said slowly and loudly, "I couldn't get my flaps down."

With that, my bright, rosy bubble of WAFS equality, which had been pinched again and again by missions with Nelson and the first hop of the Romulus squadron, burst and was gone forever. Burchie didn't even need to use flaps at that airport.

Harold picked us up at the airport as soon as he was free. We didn't have room at our flat to put Burchie up for the night, and we wanted to be alone anyway, just as she did when she was with George, so we took her to a good, moderately priced hotel on Natural Bridge Road not far from our home.

The next day it was still snowing and we couldn't leave. I'm sure that Burchie was as glad as I was to have a rest, for we both had coughs and my throat was quite sore.

When we left on the seventh, Harold came over to the National Guard hangar to see us off. I'd flown over Missouri on this route only in a Cub. Now, in an L-5, we could bypass Rolla. We were in Springfield in less than two hours. From there we went to Tulsa for gasoline and RON'd at Tinker Field near Oklahoma City.

The next day we gassed at Meacham Field at Fort Worth and then at

Waco before delivering at San Antonio. After the delivery was complete, we were driven to the airline office to get a return flight. I asked Burchie to make out the T/R for us so a clerk would issue our tickets. When she got back, I asked her, "You didn't let the clerks see our orders, did you?"

"Yes. They wanted a copy, so I gave it to them."

" Oh, you shouldn't have done that!" I cried. "They are a military secret. You'd better get them back."

Burchie said nothing and shook her head no. Then she retired to the ladies' room to pout. There was nothing for me to do but to go to the counter and get the copy back myself. I was put out with her. I thought to myself that when we got back to base, I would not be eager to let her go to Lockbourne Air Base at Columbus right away.

We boarded the plane. Because we were bumping two other passengers, we didn't sit together, so I was unable to speak to her while I was still annoyed about her attitude. We had to change planes in Chicago. On the plane to Detroit we had adjoining seats and Burchie confided something to me that further nonplussed me. She had left her navigation case in the ladies' room at Midway Airport. In it were all her important papers, most of them secret, including the receipt for the aircraft she had ferried to San Antonio and her book of T/Rs. That was like leaving signed checks for travel expenses for anyone to cash in. I was alarmed at Burchie's lack of responsibility and her disregard of government trust. I must make her more aware of it, even if it meant punishing her.

I said to her, "Of course you know you can't go to Columbus until I give my consent. Certainly you must finish the paperwork for this mission and hand it in first."

When we landed at Detroit City Airport, she sent a telegram to American Airlines in Chicago. We learned the next day that American clerks had found the case and that it would be on the 1440 plane. Burchie went to the airport to retrieve it. She didn't return. Instead she went AWOL to Columbus.

I asked McElroy, "Do you think she might have made up her mind to leave and go live with George?"

Lenore answered, "The only way to cure a love affair with George would be a steady diet of him."

"He's pulled the wool over Burchie's eyes quite thoroughly," I commented. "I tell you, Mac, I had the very devil of a time with her poking along. She simply didn't want to go."

"Was she always like that or is this a new development?" Lenore asked. I told her about the problems Teresa James had had with her in

Montana.

Only at hearing that did McElroy confide what else she knew. She said, "While you were away in St. Louis, Burchie wanted some time off. Barbara Poole told her she could take a day off since we're allowed one off for every six on duty, but not to leave the city."

"Why didn't Barbara tell me?" I asked.

"I guess she didn't want to cause Burchie any trouble, because Burchie did leave the city."

Oh, Lord, I thought, I don't want to be there when Burchie, living in her own little dream world, finds herself in a jam in an airplane and can't react until it's too late.

On our way back to the base, both airline flights lost altitude entirely too fast in landing. I had already developed a cough and cold before I left St. Louis. The air pressure during the airliner landing drove the infection into my ears. When I got to Romulus I was deaf.

I went to see the flight surgeon, Doc (Lee) Wahl, as soon as I could, although I knew he would ground me until my ears were better. And I took advantage of the occasion to bring up my biggest problem: Burchie.

Lee Wahl replied, "I've been meaning to bring up that subject myself. You know, it's my business to observe all pilots on this base — sometimes surreptitiously — watching for any peculiar behavior."

I hadn't known, but he continued, "I've noticed Phyllis Burchfield. She isn't open and alert to her environment like the rest of you. She appears to be brooding over something."

"Very introverted," I said. "She doesn't confide in anyone."

"My advice is this: Let her go to Columbus in the hope of getting her out of the spell she is in."

So her foot dragging and daydreaming were evident to others. I had nothing against Burchie, I just thought she'd be happier elsewhere.

The next day Kay sat at the same table with Lee Wahl at breakfast and told him that I was too sick to come to breakfast. He knew there was usually nothing wrong with my appetite, so he decided to come to the barracks to check me over. Once there, he listened to the wheezing in my chest. My temperature was 101 degrees.

"How do you like my accordion music?" I asked as he told me to take deep breaths.

"You'll never make it to Broadway," he answered. "I'm sending over some pills. Just remain in bed."

Fifteen minutes later, the telephone rang and Kay answered. It was Lee Wahl, who said that since there were no facilities for taking care of me on base, he was sending an ambulance to take me to the Marine

Hospital in Detroit.

When the ambulance arrived, Kay said she'd go with me since she wasn't on orders. It was such a rough ride that it made *her* ill. For me, it was cold, torturous, and interminable. The converted truck had nary a recollection of ever having had springs. I was so weak when I got out that I bumped my head.

I didn't have enough strength to climb to the top of the long flight of concrete steps leading to the hospital lobby. Halfway up I sat down and wept in anger at my own weakness. One of the two attendants who had brought me was quite concerned and patted my shoulder, knowing nothing else to do. I was too large a burden to carry. After a few sobs I was rested enough — and angry enough for showing my weakness — that I pulled myself up the rest of the way. A wheelchair was waiting at the top.

I was wheeled into an office where I was asked all sorts of questions relating to the pain in my chest, such as, "What was your mother's maiden name?" and "Where was your father born?"

It was considerate of Lee Wahl to worry about my health, but he had never been to Marine Hospital and he couldn't have know what conditions were like there. I was put in a room with a WAVE officer who also had a bad cold. The room had a tremendously high ceiling and was freezing.

Someone took my temperature. Then they took away my clothes and made me put on one of those short hospital gowns that open in the back. When the meal trays came, the WAVE's tray was placed on her bedside table. Since I didn't have a table, my tray was put on the cold radiator at the other side of the room. If I wanted to eat what was on it — which I didn't because it looked terrible — I had to walk over to the radiator on the cold floor in my bare feet and stand with my behind showing. No one bothered to check on me nor to give me any medicine. Darn Lee Wahl anyhow, I thought. Every four hours someone brought the WAVE some orange-colored liquid to drink.

"It's cough medicine," she informed me.

"Ugh!" I said.

"It's not bad," she said. "It tastes just like Cointreau."

"What's that?"

"A liqueur. I'll get a bigger dose next time and let you taste it."

She did. It was great. Thereafter we both drank her cough medicine as an after-dinner drink. It was the best thing I put into my stomach there. I lost five pounds on their diet.

The second day I thought I'd oblige the hospital by telling them I felt fine and wanted out. There was no response. On the third day, I was put in a wheelchair and sent to the lab for a chest x-ray. When I returned, I had a new bed and bed table. My temperature was back to normal.

The WAVE had several books to read. Thoughtful Kay had brought one along for me to enjoy, Cornelia Otis Skinner's *Our Hearts Were Young and Gay.* It was so funny that I went into spasms of laughter and wept as I read it.

Kay sent me a letter about the talk she had had with Captain Hennessey of transition.

"I asked about school," she wrote, "and he replied that he had not forgotten us, but that he had been up to his neck in getting the new transition school organized, and that very shortly now he hoped to put us all in transition at once in one whole AT-6 flyin' machine. Of course we've heard this same line of applesauce before, but it did sound good to hear it again. I'm sure that one of these days one of those promises will amaze us speechless by holding water. He also added that there might be a batch of AT-6s to deliver soon 'n' also that after we got checked out on those we would go to AT-9s."

Kay also asked what to do about Burchie.

Lenore spelled out the problems more clearly in her letter. "Burchie came back, but hasn't been around here," she wrote. "Guess she went to the doctor. She told Poole something about having a spot on the lungs, but when I took the sick book up to be signed for you, he put Burchie's name on it as having been examined, but put her on duty status. We don't know what to do about her and trips. Guess just let her go, unless we hear from you. Poole asked me to stay here in WAFS operations until she came back, but I stick around anyway except when I'm in class because I think I understood you to say you wanted me to. However I don't say anything, only I told Group Operations what you said, for me to stay unless it's necessary to make a trip. Righto? If I am mistaken, give me a ring at home. . . . I tried to call you there, but they refuse to let you come to the phone."

Good old Lenore McElroy. She'd take a task and carry on without a grumble. Lord knows who I'd be able to rely on. Certainly not Burchie. I knew from Thompson that Ted was pressing her to be home ready for him whenever he came back from an ocean hop. He wanted his wife to jump through his hoop when he barked his commands. I didn't trust Donnie to be reliable, although she was quick and bright. Poole didn't want to be bothered with the thankless task of extra office work that meant no freedom and no per diem. That's why I had cautioned Lenore to stick around, for Poole might leave the office unattended and the paperwork and details in the reports would not be correct. I had been right about that hunch, for Poole was off on a mission, leaving her onerous executive duty to McElroy. Signs pointed to a change in squadron officers.

On Thursday the WAVE, now dressed in her dark blue uniform, looked back from the door as she was leaving.

"I want to get out of here, too," I said.

Then she was gone, leaving me lying quietly alone in the room. I began to notice more keenly than before the noises of a hospital — the brisk footsteps past my closed door, the murmurs of doctors and nurses going their rounds, and the rolling of carts through the corridors. One sound, repeated at irregular intervals, grated upon my ears. Sometimes I would not hear it for several hours; then it would persist, seemingly forever. I didn't know how long I'd be able to endure the weak but raucous shouting of the man in the next room.

I tried to analyze the annoyance. I guessed my tormentor was elderly. An old marine, perhaps? What he was yelling was indistinguishable at first. Then I picked out a recurring theme. Another patient might call "Nurse! Nurse!" or "Help me!" I finally understood that this old man was calling, "Go back!" After a pause, he would command again, "Go on, go on back." He repeated this until, I believed, his consciousness ebbed. Then there was silence until he began again hoarsely shouting, "Go on, go on home!" Over and over and over.

I imagined myself as the old man and was struck by the drama he was portraying. I whispered to myself, "Why, he's going somewhere and he's leaving home. His dog wants to come, but he doesn't want the dog to follow him. He must love that dog very much." Thereafter the old man's pleadings no longer irritated my nerves. I knew.

The following morning I awakened to quiet. Not long afterwards, a nurse entered my room with a thermometer in her hand.

I said to her, "The old man next door died during the night, didn't he?"

Startled, the nurse quickly recovered her professional poise. She stuck the thermometer under my tongue and grasped my wrist while concentrating on the face of her wristwatch. When she completed the pulse count, she said acidly, "We do not make a practice of discussing cases with the other patients."

"That's fine," I agreed. "But without being a medic, I knew he was dying yesterday. There'd be no harm done now. He's gone. He did die, didn't he?"

"Yes," spit out the nurse as she closed the door behind her.

Only then did tears come to me. Poor fellow! He had left with no family or friends to see him off and to give him love and comfort at the end. And he, knowing where he was going, was determined to journey on without his faithful dog at his side.

Late that Friday afternoon an intern entered and said, "We are discharging you from the hospital tomorrow morning."

"What time should I be ready?"

"You must be out before eleven. When do you want to go?"

"Maybe nine o'clock? May I use the telephone to call my base for transportation?"

"Yes," he said and left.

"At last," I spoke out loud. "Whoopee!"

The staff car driver stopped at Preston-Sweet on the way back to Romulus. He waited in the reception room, for the weather was still bitter cold. In an interior room the photographer showed me the first prints from the negatives of pictures that I'd had taken there. The *St. Louis Post-Dispatch* had requested a good photo for the story they were going to run. The man showed me which one the *Post* would take.

I looked at it in silent disapproval. It wasn't at all like the picture and articles about me that the *Post* had had in its morgue since 1936. The pose was too autocratic and military. From the bulky gray overcoat that hid my uniform to the white scarf and flight cap, the three-quarters view of my face, with chin held high, I was the image of what an ordinary civilian might believe that women in the military looked like. But it wasn't Del Scharr.

The photographer's voice intruded upon my musings. "We have our own color process, which I think is superior to Kodak. It requires more painstaking work, but it is well worth the cost and effort. Now, which portrait would you like?"

I studied the prints laid out before me, being careful not to touch them. I said, "I think this one looks more like me and that's what I want. I don't like flattery."

"Very good choice. That one, in color, in an eight by ten will be forty-five dollars."

I was shocked. Hastily and recklessly, I chose two copies in the cheaper black and white, one for Harold and one for Mom and Pop. These three on all the earth were the ones who surely loved me. The money wouldn't be wasted.

Back at the base, the first stop was at the flight surgeon's office. He alone decided if I could fly again. Lee Wahl had news for me. He said, "You're the only WAF left on base."

"Huh?"

"We got a message from the flight surgeon at Lockbourne. Burchie came down with a respiratory ailment, too, and he said he grounded

Adela Scharr had this portrait made in Detroit in April 1943. The St. Louis Post-Dispatch *used a similar photo in a feature section, in full color.*

her there for at least a week.''

''She was on a mission?''

''Yes, we let her go.''

''Where are the others?''

''Kay and Lenore McElroy are on a mission together. The two Barbaras contracted colds at Wilmington. Donahue had walking pneumonia, so they say, and is resting at her home in New York. Maybe Poole is at her home, too, since she's from New Jersey and that's close to Newcastle.''

''Oh, gee — that means I'll have to stay on the base. I'm not still grounded, am I?''

''You're okay now. You're back on flying status and eligible for transition. I'm recommending that you not be given a mission until it's in the right direction.''

''Thanks, Lieutenant Wahl,'' I said. He had become a good friend to all of us, as well as the flight surgeon.

I walked into my room to find an iced layer cake with a note beside it telling us to eat it to get my strength back. It was from Lenore.

I wailed, ''I can't eat all this!'' There was no one left to share it with. How lonely the barracks was without the others. I was uneasy about the silence, which was broken only by the sound of the periodic shoveling of coal by someone tending the furnace from an outside opening in the furnace room. I concentrated on doing the administrative work — record keeping, sorting out directives, bulletins, and other red tape that had accumulated in my absence. It was imperative for me to know what was going on.

It was the middle of March. New faces were appearing in the mess and at dinner. FERD was gaining some cadet graduates from the Training Command schools near San Antonio. Most of the graduates, I learned from Lee Wahl, went to fighter and bomber assignments in tactical groups. Those who were good pilots but considered inept as fighter pilots were being relegated to the Air Transport Command and began ferrying the aircraft needed by their more daring or accomplished classmates.

As I soon found out, a number of these youngsters did not have as much flying time as seasoned civilian pilots who later became officers in the Ferry Command. They did not see the WAFS as their sisters in the sky, but as new female acquaintances, more accessible and interesting than any women they could pick up in bars downtown or in small towns on their missions. On base, the lack of transportation and their slim base pay gave them little to do in the ''boondocks,'' as they called Romulus, except to go to the officers' club. It was their meeting place, akin to the corner drugstores where the young blades could chat. And chat these cadets did, mainly about airplanes and how to fly them.

Ordinarily these fresh, newly-winged creatures paid little attention to me, for one look at my left hand discouraged them. However, this group, seeing no other WAFS around that weekend must have thought there was no harm in trying. One fellow in line behind me at lunch asked for a date. Another spoke to me and wondered if he could take me to the movies. And one Southern lad appeared to me to be a little too forward in trying to get to know me.

Only the unmarried second looies monopolized the club. A number of married officers had found quarters for their families outside the base. When they left the field in the evenings, they weren't seen until eight o'clock the next morning. Like Lenore and her husband, they paid their fifteen dollars per month barracks bill and used it only when necessary; for instance, if they were named officer of the day or if they had to be on ready call for a mission with an uncertain takeoff time.

The WAFS barracks seemed lonelier than ever when evening came. I realized how alone I was, a half-mile from any habitation, and instinct warned me that wolves were prowling close by. Fearful that knowledge of my defenseless isolation might invite an intruder, I warily walked the hall from one end to the other, making certain I was alone. Before retiring, I leaned the back of a chair so its top was under the doorknob. It would resist the opening of the door.

The next morning, although it was Sunday, I requested in writing to Colonel Wilson that a lock be placed on my door for my personal safety. Upon my return from brunch, it was there with a key inserted.

Again I studied the cake atop the dresser. It was delicious. It would be stale before the others got back. We had no kitchen nook with a refrigerator. Since I was supposed to be in transition, I reasoned that one or two pilots there would be glad to have some cake. Over to the school I went. There were only two pilots around.

"Do you fellows like cake?" I asked.

"Sure we do," replied Captain Owens. He was a stocky fellow of less than medium height. His sun-reddened face was rather large for his head. He looked like a wholesome, hard-working farmer, despite his extensive background in aviation.

"It's here for you guys in transition," I announced. "The WAFS are all away except me and I can't bear to see good food go to waste. And I don't want it going to my waist," I added, pointing to my middle. I put the cake on the counter and left.

At lunchtime on Tuesday, a magnanimous young man approached me and asked, "How about doing some instrument flying in a BT-13 tonight?''

"I'm sorry. I don't think I'll have time for that."

"You girls want transition, don't you? Come on, I'll even let you fly it a little bit."

"No, thanks." I ended the encounter, thinking, that darned masculine superiority, rubbing it in that I can't fly because I'm a WAF. Why should I take a ride in a BT-13 at night, a comparatively strange airplane with a stranger, not even an instructor. Suppose he were a wild and woolly flyer, wanting to show off? After that morning I couldn't get excited about a little BT anyway.

At transition that morning, Captain Stoddard came in and made out a clearance. He glanced at me as I was studying a tech order and said casually, "I'm checking a guy out on a B-25. How would you like to ride along?"

I always weighed any proposal to be certain that I'd be doing what was right according to Nancy Love. This presented no problem. Stoddard was one of the regular instructors and I was supposed to be in transitional training. It was considerate of him to invite me. I needed as much vicarious experience as I could get in those unfamiliar airplanes.

"You bet!" was my reply.

"Okay, take a chute and come along."

I followed him out to the airplane and climbed up into the interior after him. It was the first time I'd even been near a Mitchell. Inside it looked like a construction of gray steel framework. No nonsense; a businesslike and masculine war machine.

"Why don't you stand behind the left-hand seat and watch what he's doing?" said Stoddard.

What they were doing was too fast for me to follow. I had not seen so many gauges and switches before in my life. Words flew back and forth between them. It was all I could do to pick out the tachometer in the upper right part of the instrument panel.

Somebody was doing something on the ground down there. Stoddard yelled, "Switch off!" and repeated what the man in fatigues yelled up at him. The propellers began to turn.

Brakes were on. There was an adjusting of the altimeter reading after the pilot talked to the tower over the radio. The tower gave us information about the runway in use and the wind velocity. Much flicking of switches and adjusting went on in response. Then the brakes were off and we were rolling.

I watched how the pilot used the throttles during taxiing. There was more to the ground test before takeoff than in an L-5, more than magnetos and carburetor heat. As the pilot was being checked out, I kept my eyes glued on the show right in front of my eyes with the same concentration as a child choosing what he'd like to eat in a bakery window.

"Hey, look!" Captain Stoddard pointed to a two o'clock position in the windshield. "Turn right and let's take a look," he added.

A white house was burning. The wind blew the blaze high and wide. We were fascinated by the horror of it. Nevertheless, the crew went back to the business of checking out a pilot so he could ferry a B-25. The wind gusts were as high as seventy miles per hour that day. We learned later that in an unrelated incident, one of the Romulus pilots in transition bailed out of a P-40. He was reported to be not feeling well about the head and chest.

Captain Stoddard was fully satisfied that his student had passed the test. He must have taken pity on me, because he spoke confidentially to the pilot, who nodded his head, unbuckled the seat belt, and climbed out of the left-hand seat. I pressed myself back into the cannoneers compartment to allow him to exit.

"Want to try it?" Stoddard asked me.

"Yeah!" Surprised and happy, I lifted my feet over the pedestal between the pilot and copilot seats, let myself down into the pilot's seat, buckled the safety belt, and took the wheel, while I positioned my feet on the rudders. No seat adjustments were necessary. I was as tall as the man who'd left.

Now I had to concentrate on a number of instruments and gauges at once. I was allowed to make climbing turns and level turns. I always strove for perfection in the attitude of the airplane and not by using pressures that felt right for the last airplane I had been flying. So I did not realize that anything was amiss, although I had to reset the stabilizer and throttle, and my leg pressures were uneven. The airplane did not even waver. I was concentrating on keeping the B-25 straight and level and maintaining the altitude and course I was supposed to fly.

"Do you know what happened?" asked Stoddard.

I looked at him blankly, shaking my head no. I didn't know that anything had happened.

"Look out the right side," he ordered.

He leaned backward so I could see. The propeller wasn't turning and the blades were feathered at an odd angle, front to back.

"I just gave you a single-engine procedure," he said.

I didn't care to have the propeller not revolving out there, but what he did had no meaning to me. I just kept the plane straight and level, on altitude and on course.

"Watch," he said. He played around with some switches and before I knew it, the propeller was revolving again. The men were acting as if I had done something remarkable. It took no effort at all on my part. And later that day, a motor corps driver told me that Stoddard had remarked to her that he was surprised at my strength.

I wrote to Harold that night, "The B-25 is a he-man's airplane in a wind. In rough air it takes two hands on the wheel. Makes me happy to get my hands on something like that ship."

Captain Stoddard allowed me to enter the landing pattern and to land the thing, although on the ground the wind was strong enough to pick a person off her feet. I landed, taxied it, and got to take it around again. The men in the B-25, both instructors and students, said nothing about how I flew it.

When we were back in the office, Captain Stoddard said, "We didn't fool you. You fooled us."

And Captain Owens said in front of everyone, "Why don't you come along with us tomorrow?"

I was not feeling up to par again. This time it was an attack of diarrhea. It could have been an aftermath of my bad cold. It would not have seemed logical then that it could have stemmed from Colonel Nelson's order for me to remain on base to greet the Sweetwater graduates.

The next time I went up in a B-25, there were many students learning to handle the controls. When I got a chance, I crowded behind a pilot and watched eagerly.

One of the students said with malice, "Your Jackie Cochran tried flying a B-25. When she landed, she dropped it in so hard that the struts went up through the wings."

I had heard criticism of Jackie Cochran before, but until then, I had heard nothing about her flying that I was willing to believe. I retorted, "You're just saying that. I don't believe it."

"It's the truth," he insisted. "The plane was damaged, out of commission, and we couldn't use it."

Another student, not busy with the controls, said bitterly, "Yeah. She gets what she wants. How many times did she sit on Arnold's lap to get her way?"

I took umbrage at his casting aspersions upon any woman who had accomplished a great deal in aviation, as much as I was once piqued by Spike's remark, "Del, what you need is a sugar daddy." So I replied, "You don't know what she does in the War Department. You weren't there. That isn't fair."

"Aw, can it! She's a lot of hot air."

"Then prove it," I replied.

"Sure I will. I got a friend from home in the Canadian Royal Air Force Transport Command, and he was in Montreal when this happened. Jackie flunked the regular copilot test in a Harvard trainer and they turned her down for ferrying across the ocean for them. They figured she was in it for all the publicity she could get. Well, the pilots were told that anyone who wanted to take her across as a passenger could. She had big-shot connections, you see. One pilot got $1,000 from her to let her go along. Weather was bad all the way and she never touched the controls, the pilot said. And she couldn't have been a copilot. The Hudson has a yolk control. It has no duals."

That stupefied me. What could I say? Jackie Cochran intrigued me. But would I take an apparently jealous person's evaluation of her as the truth? I'd wait and see. Maybe she had been given flight time in a B-25 and this young man resented it because he had not gotten checked out yet. I questioned in my mind if these pilots resented me.

When I got my chance to fly the B-25 that day, I felt as if we were made for each other. The only part that was strange was sitting in the left-hand seat. As an instructor, I was used to sitting in the copilot seat as I checked out students in side-by-side cockpit airplanes. Owens did the radio work, talking to the tower.

"He'd have a panic if he heard a woman's voice," said one of the students behind me and everyone laughed. I made a perfect landing.

The next day I came to transition again, for more time had been promised me. I was worming my way in by the only means I considered square and legitimate — my performance.

However, Captain Owen had something to tell me. "I talked to the Big Brass about you and the B-25. I said I could check you out right now. And they said they weren't allowing any WAFS to fly multiengine. They don't want a woman pilot in command. You'd have to fly with a flight engineer and he'd be an enlisted man. It's something to do with your not being an officer, I think. Anyway, I told them I'd check you out right now if I could."

The revelation surprised me. All I thought about my two hops in a B-25 was that I welcomed the chance to be aboard and I wanted to show that McIntyre had been wrong. The WAFS did know how to fly. That Harold Owens' fairness had been met with age-old traditional prejudice saddened me. And when the men went out to fly this time, I was left to sit and read about the planes that I wouldn't be allowed to fly. Sister? A step-sister, perhaps. A Cinderella without a prince in high places.

At the time, Captain Owens' news was not a disappointment to me. I was inured to prejudice against women. But in the back of my mind, I remained mystified by what WAFS on other bases were experiencing compared with the chances we got at Romulus. To me, there was something missing, something we were not informed about.

According to FERD records, the WAFS in March ferried thirty-nine UC-61As and two C-47s (Nancy Love and B. J. Erickson). I soon began to wonder about Nancy Love's priorities. Maybe she did not expect us at Romulus to get the breaks she was getting. Was that the reason she sent the ones she did — including me — to Romulus? Maybe the fact that she had not checked out yet in the B-25 had something to do with my not getting transition in it. What I didn't realize was that I was a class I pilot and the B-25 was a class IV plane, a category higher than AT-6, C-47, or pursuit.

To authenticate the miscarriage of my transitional training, one may refer to the March 16 staff meeting notes at FERD headquarters. The following day, Major Teague used them to draw up a directive in order to limit the use of WAFS. It emphasized that we could not become copilots on bombers. Captain Owens must have been warned that very day to cut the WAFS from any multi-engine transitional training.

To make matters worse for me and the Romulus cadre, our own Colonel Nelson took his cue from that directive and in a letter dated March 25 from the Third Ferrying Group to all operations personnel entitled "Assignments of WAFS," he repeated the original directive under which we entered the command — that we were "to fly light trainer aircraft only." He went further by stating we must not be given transition on twin-engine aircraft nor any training toward flying pursuit. Moreover, operations was to assign the WAFS to missions on days when they didn't assign male pilots along the same airways. "No mixed flight assignments or crew assignments will be tolerated."

At the same time at Long Beach, the Sixth Ferrying Group commander allowed WAFS and male pilots delivering the same types of aircraft from a factory to be placed on the same flight mission orders.

Of course Nancy Love read the Romulus directive and Colonel Campbell, the FERD director of operations, made a note that she objected to it.

On the same day of the WAFS directive, Colonel Nelson told me that our ferrying group was destined to become a foreign wing. Men receiving instructions for foreign deliveries would have so much priority over the WAFS that only one hour of Link trainer time would be spread among the six of us. One lesson every six weeks! Colonel Nelson said that all the men, hundreds of them, were to be classified as

The Long Beach cadre shown with a BT-13, from left: Barbara Towne, Cornelia Fort, Evelyn Sharp, Barbara Erickson, and Bernice Batten.

to their ability before we'd get a chance to fly an AT-6, an AT-16, or an AT-19.

I wrote to Nancy Love, ''Because of the way things are panning out, Barbara Poole has informed the colonel that she and Barbara Donahue wish to transfer. He refuses to transfer anyone who wishes to do so in order to get out of the cul-de-sac of ferrying light airplanes. He is against anyone trying to further her own ambitions or to be on the same plane (meaning level) as WAFS of other groups. Barbara spoke too emphatically (I was away on a mission) about her desires. This didn't help her situation very much. If Barbara is denied a transfer, she threatens to quit and she wants to know if she could apply at another ferrying group after she resigned here. What are your recommendations as to this action? . . .

''Another thing I think you should know — our colonel told me that he told Colonel Tunner that all of us should stay on the same level, that no WAFS should have more opportunities simply because they happen to be at a base that can provide them. I do not agree to this premise and hope that it does not carry any weight. In this case I would say that any talent should be developed if at all possible.

"We have also heard that commissions are close at our heels. Katherine has promised Ted that she would not take one. Will she be forced to do so in order to stay in the WAFS?

"We hear all about the wonderful things you girls are doing. No man comes into the base without advertising how all of the other WAFS are progressing. Cheers from us. Keep it up!

"The girls here have made an excellent record thus far in plane deliveries. Colonel Nelson is proud of the women and says that he would like some more. No wonder! With L-2Bs and L-5s scattered all over the country by the boys (in accidents). I would suggest in line with this that girls be sent here whose capabilities show that they are restricted to flying the types of airplanes mentioned above. That doesn't mean that I wouldn't appreciate talent up here. I detest waste in any form, and I'd feel guilty about any really "hot" pilot vegetating where she would not be doing the most good for all of us.

"The other girls feel low about the ultimatum given us. All except McElroy want a chance to fly bigger and better aircraft. They'd like to be of as much service as anyone. McElroy will not leave Detroit. . . . I doubt that Phyllis can move fast enough to fly anything larger than what we have here. Lately, she has perked up and shows a more alert attitude, so I may be wrong about her. I've not talked to Barbara Donahue as she is ill with virus-pneumonia, still in the hospital. . . .

"I shall do anything in my power to carry out your orders and I want to do whatever possible to make our organization one to be admired, efficient in the war effort."

In retrospect, what I wrote after a show of grief over remaining the lowest category was a mistake. "There is one thing I'll have, though, the memory of taking off and landing a B-25 from the left side and doing everything that a first pilot does. It was easy enough, I can assure you. But with copilot trips out, that avenue also is blocked up here." I realized later it would have been even worse if I had bragged that Captain Owens had told me that he'd have checked me out in a couple of hours.

Having an undetermined military position, the WAFS were low women on the totem pole of officer status, and what was happening way up there didn't always filter down to us. We didn't know whether we could get opportunities to fly faster aircraft, for Nancy did not keep us informed about her wishes for our future or of how she was busy being checked out in larger aircraft. FERD records supplied the information many years later.

I religiously followed the rules about getting official sanctions for WAFS publicity. We found out that *Look* magazine of February 8,

1943, an article in *This Week,* and a fictional serial in *Liberty,* "Lady with Wings," had all given the impression that WAFS were forced to fly through bad weather and were greatly overworked at NCAAB. Both impressions were untrue. One result of the publicity was that Captain Ryan of the office of individual training in the FTC was listed as liaison for the WAFS. All telephone inquiries about us were to go to him, although he had no connection with us. FERD must have had inquiries about getting into Miss Cochran's program, for the public believed that if a girl was accepted at Sweetwater, she had joined the WAFS.

Once again, in the spring of 1943, there was talk about our joining with the WAAC, who were expecting to drop "Auxiliary" any day. Brigadier General Smith's plan to put Cochran's training program in the WAAC was submitted on March 14. Now Cochran seemed agreeable, but Tunner and Nancy Love did not. They looked for "between the lines" possibilities that Cochran might obtain an advantage.

From FERD records, I judge that Nancy could not sway Tunner to change the ruling on transition for any of us except Nancy and Betty Gillies. Nancy went to see General George of ATC in order to influence him, and she made a favorable impression on him.

Between January 12 and March 8, Betty Gillies went up the transition ladder to a P-47. In a letter to me dated August 25, 1976, she wrote, "It was mid-winter when I started and lots of time went by between flights. In between snowstorms and ferrying missions I got in about ten-plus hours in the AT-6. Transition consisted of about four hours, forty minutes of dual landings and takeoffs. The rest, solo practice. While I was getting the required time in the AT-6, I also checked out in the AT-9 (which had two 295-hp Lycoming engines in it) but I don't think that was the usual procedure. The AT-9 was used more for transition to the Martin A-30.

"After my first solo flight in a P-47 on March 8th, I put in about fourteen hours practicing landings at Newcastle and made a required cross-country with landings at two other airports. It was quite difficult getting those fourteen hours in as it was not very often that Transition School had a P-47 on the line and operating. Besides which I was off on ferrying missions a good deal of the time. So it was May 4th before I made my first P-47 delivery."

Petite Betty also told me, "It really was no problem fitting myself to the airplanes. I sat on a cushion which, with the parachute, put me up plenty high. And the only real long-legged airplanes were those for which I had the blocks. I could use a cushion behind me quite well in all but the P-38, the 47, and the 51. In those cockpits the gunsights were too close to my face if I used a cushion behind me. The blocks Grumman made up gave my legs the length I needed.

"I don't know why I happened to fly the 47 before Nancy. It just worked out that way. I don't suppose they had any 47s where she was. The 2nd Ferrying Group at Wilmington was responsible for the deliveries from Republic at Farmingdale, so I guess it was only a natural sequence of events that led to my getting the transition. (Am sure that if Nancy had been at NCAAB she would have been the guinea pig!)"

Helen Mary Clark was also progressing in transition at NCAAB, but Teresa James was given the most glamorous assignment of any WAF. A PT-19 had to be delivered to Hollywood for an AAF movie with the famous stuntman and aerial acrobatic star Paul Mantz. Teresa said she was next on the duty roster to get a mission and that's why she was chosen. I would have believed her then, but now I think it was because she had more time in as a flight leader and was more experienced in FERD cross-country than the rest of the Wilmington squadron. I wonder if Colonel Baker was as eager for the rest of the WAFS to obtain transition to a P-47 once Betty and Helen Mary had it. If so, was this assignment given to Teresa to lessen the blow to her ego when she discovered that the P-47 was not to be for her?

At any rate, Teresa was ecstatic as she gathered together all she would need for such a long mission, coast to coast. She included more than twenty-four sectional charts to cover her route which, in case of bad weather, could be changed. With good weather, the mission in a PT-19 might take more than a week at 105 mph without a headwind. She needed to bring enough clothing in order to be neat and clean upon delivering.

With the sanction of her home base, Teresa got VIP treatment after she arrived in Hollywood. This was before the advent of television, but she was a guest on a radio program and met Bob Hope and Ginny Sims as well as other movie celebrities. While staying at the best hotel for several days, she visited the movie studios and was wined and dined as a celebrity herself. It was heady stuff.

Life was not so glamorous for me. I was in my room ironing clothes when a telephone operator called to tell me that I had a telegram. I had to dress and rush to the closest pay telephone, which was at the officers' club, before I could get my message. It was from Harold in Indianapolis and read, "WEATHER BAD LEAVING FOR ST LOUIS BY TRAIN LOVE HAROLD."

What a disappointment. He had telephoned me the day before that he was going to Indianapolis and hoped to get an airliner to Detroit. I

Teresa James dressed in winter flying gear ready to take off in a PT-19 from Hagerstown, Md. for trip to Burbank, Ca. Delivery was to Paul Mantz for the WAFS film Ladies Courageous.

asked a captain who taught instrument flying at night if there were any chance his flight could go in that direction, but the weather was too bad for instrument instruction.

Harold was scheduled on a flight to Detroit, but another man with a prior claim showed up. Not only had he passed up other flights to get this one, but his home was in Detroit. Harold stepped aside. Then the flight was canceled anyway. I wrote Harold in reply to his wire, "The dripping of freezing rain broke my heart this morning for I knew then we'd not see each other today. Why, I couldn't even eat breakfast!" He never was able to visit me at Romulus.

Teresa James won attention from Hollywood stars after her ferrying mission to the West Coast. She is shown with comedian Bob Hope at Hollywood's Brown Derby restaurant.

The graduates of Cochran's school had not yet appeared. Why was I on base? Certainly not for transition. At last operations relented and placed me on orders to pick up L-5 #42-14835 and take it to the 77th Observation Squadron at Alamo Field, San Antonio, Texas.

I thought I was to go by myself and was surprised when I picked up my orders to find that I would fly with a young 2nd lieutenant. Operations evidently decided that I'd make a good aerial babysitter for this newly-graduated cadet.

We took off the next day as soon as the weather was at or above minimums. The sergeant had our little puddle-jumpers ready at the hangar door.

I led to South Bend; he led to Joliet. I chided him for not following a straight course according to the compass. He was wont to follow roads and railroads. "You can get lost that way," I said.

Before we took off for St. Louis, I said, "We'll fly right over my parents' home before we reach Lambert." I showed him where that would be on the chart. "I'll get down to 500 feet and cut out my engine a couple of times to attract their attention and then we'll go on and land." I didn't invite him to do anything but to circle and wait for me.

When we reached my parents' house south of the Missouri River, I let down a bit, pulled back the throttle and then pushed it forward again several times. The old folks came out, I dipped my wing and started on up.

But I had not reckoned with Mr. Smart Alec. When I went down to 500 feet, he decided to follow, but he went down to the treetops and buzzed the neighborhood again and again. I had to fly around upstairs, waiting for him to stop. That I was angry with him for that silly demonstration was evident to him when we got down. I blistered his ears.

When I closed my flight plan over the phone, Paul Dobbins said, "Someone up by the river called us and said you were buzzing dangerously low. I told them I knew you and I was sure you wouldn't do anything like that."

I told him what happened. He said he wouldn't report it.

Harold took me to Mom and Pop's for supper. They said at once, "The Houlihans got sore about that low flying airplane. They said it must have been you, but we just laughed at them."

"They reported it at the field," I replied, "but it didn't get them any satisfaction."

All evening we chattered. Mom had heard Teresa James on the Philip Morris radio program. And I told them about being such a dumbbell in Link. The instructor left out a lesson on mechanical beam bracketing and put me on advanced before he told me what he wanted me to do. I was completely lost.

I related our adventures with the Lincoln. A week ago I had parked it on the road beside our barracks and the road gave way beneath it. A truck with a derrick had to pull it out. The man who swung it out of the muck suggested that I park it on a parking lot built for automobiles which was next to the barracks. I started to turn the Lincoln into that small lot and the car went umph! and sank right in the middle of the road, which was so narrow that no cars could get around it. Fortunately, traffic near our barracks was nonexistent. I took out the keys from force of habit and went in to bed, leaving the vehicle mired just as it was. The Michigan roads were in awful condition. Water couldn't drain off because the terrain was so flat. As the frost thawed, the roads turned to mush.

I talked to my folks only about those things which were not military secrets. What I flew and where I went was kept from them, but I'm sure my mother remembered the gossip so she could relate it over the telephone to her cronies.

The next morning, after saying good-bye to Harold, I preflighted my L-5 and then decided to go up the flight line to Lambert weather bureau to see for myself what flying would be like that day. I might run into someone I knew. At the Robertson south hangar, I stuck my nose in and said "Hi!" to Clem Bacon, the bookkeeper. No one else was around, even in the lobby or at Schneidhorst's restaurant. Upon entering the weather bureau on the second floor of the administration building, I saw Bob Coverdale, one of the flight instructors at St. Louis Flying Service.

"Hello," he said tentatively. He'd never been very friendly. I'd never hired his Cub for any of my students. I'd flown once with Julia Gallagher in it and advised her not to continue flying in it until it had been rigged right — it was out of rig from being flown acrobatically. I also knew Coverdale was not keen about women flying.

"Hi," I replied, smiling from force of habit, for Coverdale meant little to me. I beelined to the teletype machine, which was busily clacking off the latest airway sequences.

Coverdale followed me. "I hear you got in trouble with the CAA."

"Yes, I did," I answered, remembering the last flight to Lambert when Burchie refused to land.

"Have to make a written report. An airliner had to wait in order to take off," he offered.

I thought, I'll bet that puffs up his ego. Aloud I answered, "Maybe. I haven't heard yet. I didn't do much wrong." I read a sequence avidly. Coverdale was still there, very tall, stout, his cigar in his mouth.

I added defensively, "I was the flight leader and have to take the blame."

I continued to study the sequences prior to the one pertinent to a flight to Springfield, Missouri. I sneaked a sideways glance at Coverdale. He came from Pennsylvania. Maybe he knew Burchie.

Without taking my eyes from the lengthening yellow paper, I said carefully, "Tell me, Coverdale, did you ever know a woman pilot in Pennsylvania named Phyllis Burchfield?"

"I sure did," he replied and he took his cigar from his lips.

With that, I turned to study his face. "Can you tell me anything about her — how was she as a pilot?"

Coverdale waved his cigar to his mouth, drew on it, and lowered his arm as he smiled broadly. "Yeah, I knew Phyllis Burchfield," he began. "I was at the field when she took her flight test for her license. In Pennsylvania, the CAA inspectors always go the rounds of small fields to test the students. They set up a date at ours, and she was one of 'em to test that day. So she had to spin before the inspector rode with her.

"Before he sent her up, he told her, 'Climb up to 3,000 feet. Make a two-turn spin to the left and come out right on the button. Then climb up again to 3,000 feet and make a two-turn spin to the right. But remember, don't lose any more than 500 feet of altitude in your spin.

You come back over the spot, cut your throttle, make two 360 degree gliding turns to the left, keep the pattern, and land on the spot. Don't undershoot or overshoot, and no slips or fish-tails to get in.'''

Coverdale was obviously enjoying his recitation. He went on. "Phyllis went on up and did her first spin. It was okay. And she climbed up and did her right turn spin." Coverdale paused before going on.

"The airplane went on spinning down. We saw it go down behind the mountain range. Boy, we were stunned. Then we began walking to our cars — to go see what we had to do. And then a plane comes in over the hill. It came on in and landed. It was Phyllis.

"The inspector yelled at her. 'What was the matter with you?'

"And she looked at him like she was accusing him. She says, 'You told me not to lose any more than 500 feet, so I watched the altimeter and when I lost 500 feet, I pulled out.'''

"You aren't making that up?" I asked. "Is that true?"

"You bet your life it's true," replied Coverdale. "I was there. I saw it."

"Now you know why I'm in trouble with the CAA," I answered. "My wingman was Phyllis Burchfield."

(An altimeter is really an aneroid barometer which registers the air pressure. Ordinarily the higher one goes, the less the pressure. This measurement is converted into feet above sea level. When one descends rapidly, as in a spin, by the time a difference in 500 feet of altitude is shown, the airplane is much lower than it appears to be, for there is a lag in the instrument. Burchie should have known this and ignored the inspector's comment about how much altitude to lose.)

After I left Lambert, I found a wonderful surprise at Springfield, Missouri. Four of the Wilmington cadre — Teresa James, Esther Nelson, Helen McGilvery, and Sis Bernheim — were there. They had heard from the operations officer that a pilot Scharr was due in soon, so they decided to wait for me. We immediately planned a rendezvous in Tulsa.

At Tulsa, after whizzing through servicing as quickly as possible, it was jabber, jabber, jabber, as we ate lunch. I had little to say, for they were full of their experiences. They had RON'd at Scott Field and stayed at the WAAC barracks. What struck them as horrible were the cotton khaki GI drawers that the enlisted WAACs wore. The following night there was a fire in their hotel in Springfield. Two of them got excited and wanted to save what was important, so they threw their clothes, purses, and mission papers out of the window. It wasn't necessary. Except for loss of sleep, the girls were none the worse for the wear on their nerves.

We parted at Tulsa. Their PT-19s were bound for the West and we were heading to Fort Worth via Tinker Air Force Base. When we landed at Meacham Field in Fort Worth, we were told to get gasoline at the newly constructed Tarrant Army Air Field. In five minutes we were there.

At Tarrant operations, the young lieutenant was whisked away to Hotel DeGink and I was placed in a staff car and delivered to the nurses' quarters for the night. The previous evening, my parents had handed me all the latest mail from relatives around the country. My Uncle Charlie Leuenberger from Denver had written that his son Harold was at Tarrant Field as a statistician. He had a Ph.D. and had been teaching at San Francisco University, so I believed him to be a civilian employed there.

While I was telephoning to learn about transportation, especially to find an evening meal, into the nurses' parlor came two first lieutenants bearing some tree blossoms. They sat down and waited for their dates. I stared at one of them. He certainly resembled the cousin I had seen only once on an evening thirteen years ago. If he had been a civilian, I would have asked his name. Since the man was an officer, I knew it could not be he.

When I finished telephoning, I was bold enough to enter the parlor where the two men were chatting. The one said, looking intently at my left sleeve, "I have a cousin —" and I didn't allow him to finish.

"You're Harold!" I cried. And he was. Uncle Charlie had written him only days before that I was in the WAFS and that we might meet accidentally someday. I joined their party and with their dates, we all had a great time eating, gambling (my cousin staked me and I refused to take the ill-gotten gains), and even drinking. I drank two daiquiris and when I got back to my bed, the room kept going 'round and 'round.

WE LOSE ONE

THE NEXT DAY the lieutenant and I gassed up at Waco AAFB and went on to deliver the planes to the 77th Observation Group at Alamo Field, San Antonio. Then we got a quick ride to the airline ticket office, where we sat in a row of some six or seven wooden chairs waiting for counter service to book our transportation home.

One of the women clerks glanced at my uniform and asked, "Did you know Cornelia Fort?"

The way she said it made my heart miss a beat. The muscles at the back of my neck and those across my shoulders tightened.

"Yes," I answered with a terrible premonition, for none of us should have been known so easily by name.

"She got killed here in Texas," replied the clerk. "Here's the newspaper."

I got up from my chair and went to the counter, took the newspaper from the woman and, immobilized, read the headlines and story beneath. When I returned to the counter to hand back the newspaper, I felt dizzy. I sat down again, speechless, and lost in thought.

I didn't want to believe it, but it must be Cornelia. What had been the last I had heard about her? That she was disappointed that Nancy had not named her the flight leader of the Long Beach cadre, although Nancy was still there. That she had been seeing a young major and it appeared to be a serious attachment, more than a friendship, and I was so glad for her.

The newspaper stated that another airplane had struck Cornelia's about twelve miles from Merkel, Texas, on March 21. The propeller had torn into her airplane and she had spun in. Evidently she had been killed instantly. She did not have a chance to survive.

What really happened took a long time in seeping out through AAF records and the grapevine. The flight started innocently enough. Cornelia was on the same orders as a flight of young male pilots from Long Beach. They had decided to fly in a loose formation, but some of them began teasing her and then they began to pretend that they were fighter pilots. She was easy game for them, for she had never had any evasive training in military maneuvering. By the time they got to Texas, a few of the men had become too bold and were flying too close. A joke had become harassment.

Lt. Frank W. Stamme, Jr., came close enough to frighten Cornelia, so she tried to evade him, but she zigged when he guessed she would have zagged and he snagged her.

They picked up what they could find of her. "Only about sixty pounds," said my informant, "and the string of cultured pearls she wore hidden under her shirt."

As for Stamme, a court-martial board found him at fault and put no blame on Cornelia. Yet he went on flying, because he was able to land his airplane, and — as the excuse went — the Ferry Command was short on pilots and needed him.

A notice of Cornelia's funeral was sent to our CO at Romulus:
CORNELIA FORT FUNERAL 1500 OCLOCK CWT CHRIST CHURCH BROAD NASHVILLE THIS DATE PERIOD HOME ADDRESS MRS. E. FORT, MOTHER, JACKSON BLVD NASHVILLE END LAND END. It was signed HERNDON.

They shipped her home to Nashville with a Civil Service grant of $250 toward funeral expenses and a flag for the funeral service, the emblem for which she had given her young life.

During the next few days, I brooded over Cornelia's death as the culmination of a tragedy. The Japanese had almost gotten her at Pearl Harbor, then Fortland had burned and with it Cornelia's precious diaries, her account of her life. Now there was nothing left.

Cornelia Fort, WAFS.

Other WAFS, no doubt sobered by Cornelia's fate, dealt with the problem of being buzzed more successfully. Helen Mary Clark told me that when a pilot flew at her wingtip when she was flying pursuit she dropped down and back and came up to sit at the edge of his wing. The maneuver made the pilot very nervous because he knew that she had not been taught tight formation flying. He quickly buzzed off and she had no more trouble with the men.

I thought long about Cornelia. Maybe she hadn't had as rough and tumble a childhood as I had had, playing with my three brothers. Maybe she enjoyed the attention the pilots gave her. Maybe she thought of them as graduate cadets and more highly skilled than they were. Again, maybe she was such a lady she didn't know how to tell them to quit.

Even yet when I think of Cornelia, the muscles about my mouth tighten, my eyes pinch shut, and I find it difficult to stifle the convulsive spasms of grief. She was only twenty-four years old, so intelligent, a lady who walked with me and talked about books and music and drama. She should have lived to tell the story of the WAFS.

Two days later, back at Romulus, we six WAFS went together to the dispensary. The flight surgeon had ordered us to begin the same immunization program that the Ferry Command demanded of its male pilots. Only Poole vocalized her dread with "I don't like to take shots!" but we ignored her.

The clerk typed up cards for each of us which included name, I.D. number (our commercial license numbers since we had no military assignment), age, and race. From our dog tags he took our blood type.

The first immunization on our list was for smallpox. I'd had a severe reaction to my first and third vaccinations. This would be my fifth and I expected another bad reaction. Next was triple typhoid.

The U.S. Army had been using a culture made from a human typhoid carrier since the Boer War and it had become less effective as years went by. A colonel stationed in the Panama Canal Zone during the Depression was intrigued by the problem of using the blood of a West Indian in the area who was a carrier of the disease. The Panama Health Department gave him a job and kept him under observation to keep him from transmitting the disease. After being transferred to Washington, D.C., the colonel developed a vaccine from the carrier's blood, which was twice as effective in giving immunity as the older vaccine. From 1938 the army obtained contributions of the man's blood to revitalize their stock of vaccine. It was potent stuff. We were told that the first and second shots would make a fever in the arm where injected. The third shot might make us quite ill.

We treated the visit to the dispensary lightly, joking about it. As soon as we were finished there, we got the word that we were on orders. The two Barbaras were flying together again and I was to lead the others to Plainview, Texas.

We four were driven to the Stinson factory to pick up four L-5s and we left them overnight in Romulus' big hangar to be checked by the mechanics. The only way south the next morning was by way of Patterson Field at Dayton, Ohio. The Ohio Valley had good weather, so we headed for Terre Haute, gassed, and RON'd at Lambert Field, putting in five hours of flying and about eight hours of duty time.

From St. Louis the usual route went past Springfield, Missouri, to Tulsa, Oklahoma. By the time we reached Tinker Field outside Oklahoma City, Thompson had a backache. She told us it was a weakness from an incident during her high diving days. If we had thoughts that something else might be the cause, we made no comments. Amarillo was too far away, so we quit for the day to give Thompson a rest. Riding the gusts was like being atop a bucking bronco.

The following morning, Thompson's back still ached, but she assured us she could stand the pain. I led to Amarillo. Occasionally a checkpoint showed up on the chart, such as "building," "ranch," "tank," or even a dry creek bed. We faced a stiff and bumpy crosswind. How I loved the challenge!

I wrote to Harold, "We flew low. You never saw such country. For the most part, it's all one big airport. One can land anywhere. Saw many good cattle in nice, green pastures. There's a lot of dry land, too. We got to see yucca and junipers as we went farther into the Panhandle. It was a long hop of two hours and forty minutes and I used only twenty-four gallons of gas."

At Amarillo the wind picked up to twenty-seven miles per hour with gusts by the time we landed at noon. While we ate lunch, the winds were clocked at thirty-five plus. Plainview had no weather station and Lubbock, fifty miles south of it, was reporting only fifteen-mile-per-hour winds. I didn't trust the forecast.

"When can we catch the first plane out of here?" I asked at the TWA ticket counter in the Amarillo airport.

"None 'til 0821 tomorrow morning," was the response.

"Looks like we'll have to RON here anyhow," I said as I turned to the others. "How about getting a room in town?"

They agreed and we checked into the Herring Hotel. Nothing to do but go shopping. Thompson and I bought Indian rugs. And every hour I checked with the meteorologist so we could find out how the winds were blowing. At 1630 the wind slowed, so we returned to the airport, read the 1730 sequence, and were in the air by 1800. I was in the lead so we wouldn't waste any time. We flew low over the open, deserted land to avoid the fiercer headwind higher up.

I reported to Harold, "The ground below us fell away abruptly and I looked down into a chasm that, for all the world, resembled the Grand Canyon of the Colorado River, but on a smaller scale. It was part of Palo Duro Canyon."

We landed an hour before sundown at Plainview where the wind was so strong and frisky that the airport manager had to help us tie down our L-5s. I held onto my right wing and Thompson's left as she tied down her right wing and tail. Then she helped me. We made sure the elevators and ailerons didn't move by tying the stick back securely, using the seat belts.

The field operator called the bus line and the bus made a special stop at the field for us. Luckily, we got seats and were traveling light, since we'd already checked into the Amarillo hotel. Once back at the hotel, McElroy, Thompson and I had champagne to celebrate and it made me dizzy. The next morning flying back to Detroit, Kay got sick on the airliner. I sat beside her and held her head, even though it made me a little nauseated.

While we succeeded in bucking the wind to deliver L-5s to Texas, FERD was bucking the pressure of the press to exploit the news value of the WAFS. Cornelia Fort had written an account of her experience at Pearl Harbor and her views on the importance of WAFS as the first women pilots in the AAF. Both the *American Magazine* and the *Ladies Home Journal* clamored for opportunities to ghostwrite our exploits. But FERD already knew what a hindrance to work publicity could be and did not want our work glamorized. Jealousy might develop if a story were written about only one or two WAFS, and there was already enough jealousy because of the inequity in the kinds of aircraft flown. We were in the Ferry Command to fly its missions, not to develop our careers after the war. A letter from FERD to the War Department bureau of public relations entitled "Ghost Writing on WAFS" hammered the lid shut on news of our activities.

On March 31 Burchie and I were directed to go to the Howard Aircraft factory at St. Charles, Illinois, and from there to Maxwell Field, Alabama with two PT-23s. We had heard about St. Charles. Every male pilot who had been assigned to get a PT-23 from Howard was anxious to repeat the experience. Eagerly we picked up the orders at operations just before noon.

At the lunch mess, Lieutenant Schwartz, in line behind us, noticed that we had official papers.

"Where are you going?" he asked.

"To the Howard factory," I answered.

"Boy, are you lucky," he said. "When you get there, be sure to RON at the Baker Hotel." He sat down with us to tell us more about it.

"It was built by a millionaire who is nuts about horses. He had a lot of race horses. You'll see pictures of horses all over the place."

Burchie's eyes lost their faraway look.

An enrapt Schwartz continued, "But the remarkable thing is the old man liked to travel and on his trips he would buy all sorts of nice furniture. Every bedroom in his hotel is furnished to show a certain country. It's authentic all the way through and the furniture is the best in taste you'll ever see."

"Competing with the Waldorf," I said.

"The Waldorf isn't in it. And just wait until you get in the coffee shop in the morning. Don't miss it. The entire counter is of inlaid wood from all over the world. It's really beautiful. And you've got to eat in their dining room. And whatever you do, be sure to walk outside because the hotel is built on an old millrace on the Fox River. You stand on a kind of balcony and you can watch the water go over the dam right down below where you are. When you eat, every day there's someone playing organ music. And the floor of the dining room has a space made of glass blocks with lights set in them and that's where you can dance later on.''

Whew! Schwartz could hog more than a Ping Pong game, I thought. We all knew he was a big kidder. We'd have to be foolish to believe what he said.

We were on a hurry call to get on this mission, so we didn't stay around to learn any more about the Baker Hotel. I almost broke my neck and unraveled my nerves getting us off the base and to St. Charles, making the right connections.

After an airline trip from Detroit to Midway, we had to find the intercity rapid commuter transit system that ran a special train past St. Charles. Lugging our equipment was never easy, but this time the ride was swift, lasting only an hour, and the coach was cleaner than those along the Atlantic seaboard. After all our paraphernalia was deposited on the station platform, Burchie waited with it while I telephoned the Howard factory. They sent an automobile for us. We found our airplanes, inspected them, and signed acceptance papers.

"Hey, Burchie," I said as we looked for defects. "These aren't like what comes out of the Fleet factory."

She walked over to me and said quietly, "This is better quality."

I picked up the starter crank, rubbing my right palm over its well-tooled and finished surface. "A work of art," I sighed.

We indeed went to the Baker Hotel and that evening I gratefully (if silently) apologized to Lieutenant Schwartz for doubting him. Everything he had said was true. Moreover, the formally landscaped grounds along the riverbank even included a boathouse. I had never been in such an elegant setting before. Of all the hotels in which I have been a guest since, the Baker continues to rank *numero uno.*

Not surprisingly, the RON stop after the gas stop at Springfield, Illinois, was Lambert Field. The next day, before we left the old National Guard hangar, we chatted over coffee with Maj. Ralph Page and happened to mention that it was the day for our second typhoid shot.

Major Page said, "You mustn't take a chance on missing this one. Do you want to start a series all over again?"

"No," we said in unison.

"You can get the shot at the Naval Air Station. I'm going to call 'em and see if they won't give it to you." And he went directly to his phone to talk with the pharmacist mate. He returned and said, "I'll give you transportation and you can get it right away."

We did, and then we took off. I led the hop. I knew Harold watched until we were out of sight, so I wrote to him two days later, "From Burchie's behavior on takeoff, can you see what I mean about her? She went as far as the Missouri River and made a wide circle before she came after me. Did you see me turning, making 360s until she caught up?" I was south-southeast of the local traffic pattern and, of course, watchful for any local traffic. We had taken off on old #1 in a southwesterly direction. Burchie should have made a ninety degree climbing left turn at the edge of the field, for she'd have more than 500 feet by then. Then, still climbing, at 1,000 feet, she certainly knew she should make a forty-five degree level right turn to get away from the local traffic pattern. Burchie was still unpredictable.

I landed first at Sikeston and when I swung the PT around and cut the switch, I saw that Burchie had taxied into a small mud puddle and was stuck there several minutes. Something must be wrong, I thought. The puddle wasn't that large.

As she entered the hangar where I officially ended that hop and was making out a new clearance, I saw that her face was ashen-gray. She was shaking.

"What's the matter?" I was alarmed.

Burchie could hardly speak. "I'm cold and I ache all over," she whispered.

"Have you a place where she can lie down?" I asked the civilian in charge.

"We have a dispensary," he replied.

With one of us at each arm, we walked Burchie over and put her on a cot, piling three blankets on her. There wasn't much we felt we could do except to let her rest.

Sikeston is in "swampeast" Missouri, an agricultural and rural area where cotton was grown. I wondered if the town boasted of a competent doctor. The airfield appeared to be in the middle of nowhere, and I could understand why Jacqueline Cochran refused to consider it as a spot for her training school.

While I was wondering what to do with Burchie, into the airport walked Frank Dunn, a real old-timer pilot from Lambert. We spent some time trading information about where all the pilots we knew were and what they were doing for the war. Parks Air College had hired him along with many others in the St. Louis area and they were based at three locations.

At intervals I peeked in at Burchie to see how she was doing. After about ninety minutes had elapsed, she came into operations. She seemed embarrassed to have caused us concern.

"Let's go on," she said.

I touched her forehead and then mine. Hers was a mite hotter than mine, but she looked normal. Memphis was only an hour away, for we'd have a good tailwind. We decided to try it.

At Memphis we rested a while in the canteen, waiting to see if Burchie would have another spell. No more chills, she said. While we were there, Carl Hempel from Lambert, who was now stationed with the 4th Ferrying Group there, came in and "shot the breeze."

Then, in operations, we drew our lines on our charts to Muscle Shoals. It appeared okay according to the NOTAMs and the facilities pamphlets we carried for field information. But when we landed there, no gasoline was available. The men at the airport didn't know how to use a crank to start a PT, so I gave a little demonstration lesson in winding up the starter by rotating the crank.

I felt proud of Burchie that she had volunteered to navigate from Memphis to Muscle Shoals and that we had both made beautiful cross-wind landings in strong, gusty winds. We took off again and about twenty miles farther along our route we stopped at Courtland, where we got gasoline at an army basic training school.

I took the lead off toward Birmingham, feeling a bit queasy and thinking that the sensation would pass. We had wasted too much time on the ground already. Very soon, I felt so ill that I could hardly hold up my head. We flew over a wilderness area and I was sick all the way. Surrounding the muscle where I'd had the shot, my left arm was sore and hot. I could almost hear the violent pumping of my blood through that arm. It was all I could do to focus on the map and on where I was going.

We reached Birmingham two miles to the left of where I should have been. Because we were making such good ground speed, I led on to Montgomery, where we both made beautiful landings in a wind just as cross as I was sick. During that long, agonizing day, because we had gusty winds to contend with on top of our typhoid reactions, I prayed frequently, especially as we landed. And I was heard.

We wanted to get back to base and rest, but our luck was bad. The airliner we had to take out of Maxwell was not on time. We left there at 0300 the following morning and got back to Detroit in early afternoon, both us of trying to sleep most of the way back.

Lee Wahl grounded both of us because of our severe reactions. I rested most of what was left of April 3 and tried to get in condition to make a trip to Detroit the next day in order to buy a pair of shoes to wear with my uniform. Finding the time, the place, and the object of any purchase was a problem for all WAFS in the Ferry Command. At Romulus it was next to impossible.

On the qt I told Burchie, "You can take two days off. You have your week's day off for two weeks that you've missed, so take it now."

Burchie began to show an interest. Her head lifted like a sunflower toward the sun — and in the direction of Lockbourne.

"I'll just say you're in town," I continued. "We won't mention which town, will we?"

Burchie flashed me a rare smile. This time she was predictable. She moved like lightning getting out of the barracks.

By this time, operations was beginning to realize that WAFS differed from male pilots in matters other than their sex. We made record time in delivering and did so without even scratching an airplane. And operations began to look at me differently, having made three deliveries in eight days of flying, despite adverse wind conditions. If only Colonel Nelson wouldn't keep me stuck on the base! All my life I had learned that there was no argument greater than performance to earn success. I had no other way to go. I was sure that operations would eventually reward WAFS if we kept up the good work.

I was worried when McElroy was sent alone on a mission the next morning and had to contend with high, gusty winds all along her route. But Mac got safely from Romulus to Birmingham with an L-5 in one day. For a plane like that, that was speedy. Good old Mac.

While Mac was bouncing up and down, I got as far as Detroit where I was unable to find a comfortable pair of oxfords with low heels. I telephoned my friend Louise Hildebrand Ciochetti and tentatively promised to visit with her if and when I got into town again. Before heading back to Romulus, I passed by the photographer's studio to pick up the photographs I had ordered.

It wasn't until late summer in 1962, when the Ninety-Nines convened at Wilmington for the twentieth anniversary of the formation of the WAFS, that I learned what had happened at NCAAB the day Burchie and I flew our PT-23s away from St. Charles, Illinois.

Said Helen Mary Clark, "Base operations yelled for a flight of WAFS to take three PTs out to Pocatello, Idaho. The next in line for orders were Nancy Batson, Helen McGilvery, and Sis Bernheim."

The call caught Nancy Batson in her favorite prone position, seemingly dozing and stretched full length on a wooden bench in the WAFS alert room. She had skipped ground school that day in hope of being placed on orders. The exciting news of a mission brought her to upright, wide-awake alertness.

Helen Mary said, "I told them to be ready as soon as they possibly could."

What a flurry the trio got into, with Sis gesturing and raising her voice, calling "What are we going to do?" And McGilvery making nasty comments about their having prematurely turned their winter flying gear back to the supply depot. The hubbub subsided quickly as soon as Batson commandeered a jeep to take the three to the subdepot.

Then back came the prospective flyers, lugging their B-4 bags and navigators kits with all those charts they'd need for their epic adventure. They huffed and puffed and hurried, feeling very lucky to be the ones chosen to go.

They struggled up the hill and reached the level of the flight line where they placed their burdens on the concrete and paused for breath. Several pilots stuck their heads out of the male pilots' alert room and called, "What's the matter, girls? Going somewhere?"

"You're darn tootin'," called back Sis.

They hied to the office at the rear of their alert room, eager to lay hands on those orders.

Helen Mary said, "Then I told them what day it was."

"April Fool," somebody chimed in.

Helen Mary went on. "Batson just blew her top. In a huff, back they went to the subdepot and returned their stuff and then they retreated to BOQ. After a while they drifted back and all was sunny again. That night we were late for dinner. We hurried from work to freshen up."

"We felt serene and beautifully dressed for dinner," said Sis. "We primped at the wash basins and waited. When the first wails echoed through the hall, we stood at the top of the stairs and called to them, 'What's the matter, girls? Going somewhere?' And we left 'em."

"Our clothes were knotted, brassieres and all, and all sorts of personal belongings had to be ferreted out of strange places. Our shoes laces were tied in knots. Slips and pjs sewed in every conceivable manner, and the beds were shortsheeted. Jeepers! It was awful," said Helen Mary, shaking her head.

"We got even with them," laughed Sis. "But we never could get ahead of that foxy little Betty Gillies. We ate dinner and hung around the officers' club and when we came back, there was the most god-awful odor in our rooms. They'd rubbed it on our sheets and anything we might grab onto, so we had to be careful. We cleaned it as best we could, but that smell lingered in my room and I thought it would never wear off."

"What was it? Limburger?" I asked.

"No. Neet," she yelled.

During the FERD orientation program for civilian pilots, we did not get an explanation of how Civil Service regulated its employees. The men, for whom the orientation program was designed, were slated to become officers and enter the military after three months or, if they washed out, become subject to the draft. At first WAFS were to be treated just as men pilots were. But it seemed less and less likely that we would become officers, and we could be sacked without fear of the draft.

All we knew about Civil Service was that we drew our salaries from it. We had no written regulations or guidelines to follow, and I had nothing to back any position I might have to take. I felt very much alone as CO.

When I asked Poole, as exec, to take my place on base if I should get a mission before the Cochran graduates appeared, she retorted, "I'm not going to do it!"

I thought she couldn't be as selfish as she sounded. Maybe she really didn't understand that a title carries responsibilities as well as an honor. Perhaps she didn't deserve the title.

"Barbara," I replied slowly. "I need an exec who is willing to be on deck when I ask her. It isn't for all the time."

Now, looking back, I realize that she felt strongly about doing something she thought I'd prevent her from doing, such as taking a leave or being on missions with Donnie, for whom she had an affinity. But she didn't confide in me about that. Her response was an angry, negative shake of her head, a lift of her chin, and a stubborn, non-compliant set to her mouth.

"No." She walked toward the door of my room. "I came into the Ferry Command to fly and I won't get stuck on this miserable base." And she flounced out of the room.

I thought long and hard about our disagreement. I realized that although Poole could be charming, her recalcitrant behavior stemmed from some hidden resentments against authority, perhaps from her childhood. Still in all, I could not let the organization or myself suffer. Finally I resolved to make up a special order relieving Barbara Poole from the job she found too onerous to do and appointing Lenore McElroy as executive officer of our squadron. I looked for reasons for the clash in my own personality. At that time I thought I was readily friendly, approachable, and seemingly popular with everyone. This incident caused a tiny crack in my self-image. How would anyone else — Nancy or Betty — handle this situation? I was afraid to ask.

Unfortunately, I was unable to tell Poole before anyone else learned of my decision. Without informing me, which was insubordination, she took a leave. One of the girls said Barbara might have gone to Wilmington to see a boy friend. My doubts about replacing her vanished. I thought, yes, I'm doing the right thing. Mac is open with me, and that's how the relationship should be.

As civilian employees, we did not get guidance from the army on handling personnel, and we did not get any other assistance. In order to get compensation, we had to be disabled in the line of duty. Illness was our own problem as I had found out at Hagerstown and at the Marine Hospital. Yet we were regulated in ways that we found inexplicable. A directive was issued on March 29 that ordered us not to fly for a period of eight days or thereabouts each month during the menstrual cycle — one day before, during, and two days following. If we happened to be on a mission during that time, we were to lose our per diem, although we would still receive base pay.

Exclamations burst like fireworks. "What!" "Who thought that one up?" "Are they trying to get rid of us?" "I'm not going to stay on base all that time!" "How are they going to know?" "They just couldn't make us stand inspection." "That's my own personal business."

I followed through after a fashion. I said, "I'm supposed to find out from you when your next period is coming up and inform the flight surgeon."

Blank stares. Mouths closed. And then each confessed that she had no idea when her period would begin. Such an irregular group one might never see again. But no one in operations, nor Lee Wahl, was indelicate enough to interview me about this matter, so at Romulus nothing was done about grounding the WAFS.

In Dallas, however, Florene Miller cooperated with operations and they devised a system. She brought a pack of cards, one card for each member of her squadron, to the operations office daily. All those who were out on missions, on leave, or grounded because of illness or whatever were dealt out face down. These blank cards were passed over when assignments were given out. In that group were those not allowed to fly because of the March 29 directive.

What the other two bases did, I do not know. Each ferrying group had its own system. But where did the Ferrying Division get the idea that a menstrual period was such a great stress for a woman? It took as its model for this directive the CAA rulings against which Betty Gillies had fought and lost when she was president of the Ninety-Nines. Its handbook stated that many women fainted during a menstrual period and it was thought that this had once led to a fatal accident.

Why had I not been told of this danger by the doctors who gave me the qualifying tests for my licenses? I was in the middle of my menstrual period when I passed my private flight test, my commercial flight test, and when I got my flight instructor's rating. The fatal accident that the CAA cited could have been due to pilot error. Maybe the woman casualty had had insufficient instruction. Mechanical trouble, bad weather, and the terrain could also be blamed.

The Ferrying Division's surgeon's directive was sent to the Air Transport Command surgeon. On April 23, he released his opinion. He agreed with the first part of the directive, that pregnancy should disqualify a WAF from flying, but he disagreed that women should be grounded during a menstrual period because it would be too difficult to enforce. He suggested that the senior WAF in charge was to refer a menstruating female (as if she were ill) to the flight surgeon who would relieve her from flight duties for as long as he thought necessary. The grounded WAF had to spend her nonflying time attending ground school.

But that wasn't the end of the matter. The ATC surgeon's regulation was evaluated by the air surgeon of the AAF, who asked the FTC surgeon how the WFTD cadets at Sweetwater were handled. He reported that the FTC did not restrict women pilots whatever. So the AAF surgeon made a ruling that took precedence over the ATC and FERD rulings. He said that pregnancy would disqualify a pilot, but menstrual cycles should be handled individually and locally. If it were necessary for a WAF to be grounded while on a mission and as a result the delivery of an airplane was delayed, she should not be censured. It is interesting to note that when WAFS were given a bona fide opportunity to goldbrick by claiming menstrual distress, they refused to take it.

As the weather began to warm up, I thought about getting a bicycle. It would give me exercise and freedom in getting around the base. At last, after three weeks, I was given time in the Link trainer. It had been so long since I'd been in, I felt that my bracketing was not very neat as I tried to maintain airspeed while I completed two ninety degree orientation problems.

I received two letters at this time that discouraged me. What I read between the lines was that Nancy and Betty were expecting to become the first women in the AAF to fly faster and heavier types of airplanes and that after they did so, a line would be drawn and the rest of the WAFS could expect to remain pilots of smaller and slower aircraft. I wished I had never told Nancy about getting a little time in the B-25.

The first letter, from Nancy Love, read:

March 30, 1943
6th Ferrying Group
Army Air Base
Long Beach, Calif.

Mrs. Adele R. Scharr, W.A.F.S.
3rd Ferrying Group
Romulus Army Air Base
Romulus, Michigan

Dear Adele:

I'm sorry to be so late in answering your important letter of March 25th. I have been on a trip and have just returned.

Your problems in Detroit are great, I know, and I am trying my best to do something about them. However, I want first to emphasize that inequalities and apparent injustices are inevitable in this stage of the development of the WAFS, and that protests and loud feminine wails at this stage of the game will do us all immeasurable harm. This is not directed at you, but is a sort of negative statement of policy.

The fact that I have checked out in a C-47 and P-51, and Betty in the P-47 should encourage all the girls, rather than precipitate bitter complaints. I have tried hard to avoid any appearance of being privileged above any girl in the group, because I don't feel that I should be. However, I was appointed Director of the WAFS, and Betty is, in effect, second in command. We should logically, therefore, be the "guinea pigs" for any new ideas, and that is what we have been.

There are several things pending about which I cannot write you, since they are still in the category of hopes rather than accomplished facts. They have, however, a good chance of working. Until then I can only ask that you keep the girls quiet and ask them, as patriotic citizens to do a good job with the material at hand. They aren't any worse off actually, than hundreds of Flight Officers and Second Lieutenants in all of the Ferrying Groups.

There is no reason for us to expect special privileges. I quite agree with your statement that talent should not be restrained, and I honestly feel that a fairly large percentage of the first WAFS can and will, eventually, fly ships right up to the limits of their capabilities, but they should not expect to be handed everything on a silver platter any more than the men. They must realize that women pilots are still not accepted, and if one group seems to be getting better breaks than the others, please make them realize that all is not lost forever.

If Barbara Poole wants to resign, I should leave it up to her, with no persuasion either way. I have received several urgent and bitter letters from her. She has, I'm afraid done a lot of harm by her impulsiveness, and if her attitude is unchanged, perhaps she would be happier out of the WAFS. I like her, and would be sorry to have her go but I am very much afraid that she doesn't realize the situation. I wrote her once asking her to be patient — I can't do much more. It's come to the point where "Survival of the Fittest" must be our motto, and the WAFS is too important to let personalities, wounded feelings, etc. to enter into the picture.

In closing, Del, I can only reiterate that I am doing all I can and hope you'll all sit tight up there and do the job until things develop. There are plans afoot, and I am hopeful for all of us who have the ability to fly bet-

The Douglas C-47 (DC-3), although already an old plane, was a workhorse during World War II.

ter ships. I hope to get to Cincinnati within the next two weeks, and then on into Detroit.

Please let me know the developments.

Regards,

Nancy

C.C. Betty Gillies

The second was from Betty Gillies:

April 3, 1943

Dear Nance,

A thousand thanks for the copy of your letter to Del, and your swell long letter which arrived today. I would have written you long long ago, except that I was waiting for just such, so that I could fit my train of thought into yours, rather than launch forth on a long dissertation of my own without knowing how you felt about things, and what was in the offing.

Del sent me a copy of the letter she wrote you, and it was the first indication I had had that things weren't running so smoothly in Detroit. I reacted to it in very much the same way that you did. I feel sorry for Del because I am sure she is doing everything possible to keep the girls happy, — and I feel very much out of sympathy with any girl who is dissatisfied with the type of equipment she is flying be it L-2s, PTs or BTs! After all, damn it, we all came into this organization with the full understanding that we were going to ferry Primary Trainers and Liaison types, — not for a moment were we led to believe that we would fly anything bigger or better, — at any rate, not until there was such a terrific pilot shortage that we were *needed* to fly larger equipment. No one has let us down at all, and the girls are doing just exactly what they expected to do when they came in here.

The morale down here is 100 percent excellent, — and gosh, I could hug each one of them for the swell attitude they all have. There hasn't been a word of complaints, — which is as it should be, — and they all seem to have retained the same pep and enthusiasm they had when we started out on our first L-4 trips. At this point I don't think a single one of them would transfer to another base if she could, — and that is saying a lot! Nance, this is a swell group and by that I mean everybody in it! Life is just a bowl of cherries, — I don't think I have ever laughed as much as I have this past two weeks during which we have all been together. Each one of the girls gets along beautifully with every other one, — and well, it's almost a miracle. Last week we had 40 C-61's to move, — a regular shuttle system, — and we had more darned fun. The ships have swell little Bendix radios, so we were able to get most of the girls checked out on radio procedure. We gave all those who hadn't used radio before a good pre-flight drill in the hall at BOQ, — my room was LG field, and the Coco Cola machine was WA — en route were NK, PG, and BO. With map in hand, each girl went down the line, changing frequencies, calling Range stations, reporting position etc. Sounds silly, but the result was that each girl did a swell job on the radio when it was the real McCoy. They really sounded like old timers, and there wasn't a slip. (which is more than I can say for myself when I first used a radio!)

I talked to Esther Nelson today and apparently she has no idea of resigning. She really has improved 100 per cent and I haven't heard a complaint from her since her letter came back from Col. Spake refusing her transfer to Long Beach. In fact, she hasn't said a word about it and has seemed to resign herself very well to being content with things as they are. As for her flying, — as far as I can see it is perfectly satisfactory. She had never flown a Fairchild 24 before we went to get those C 61's and she checked out in them without any trouble at all, delivering in good shape. She is very cooperative, — and well, I just have no fault to find with the job she is doing.

As for Dorothy Fulton, — Dorothy is a darned good pilot and an exceptionally good navigator. She desires earnestly with all her heart to make friends and, possibly because she tried too hard, she fails. Her only trouble is that she talks too much, but it is not dangerous talk, or critical talk, it's usually just talk about Dorothy. She is getting over that though and has improved no end during the past month. As for her husband, — he's just plain nuts, but that is none of my business and, as long as he doesn't interfere with the successful completion of her missions, I sure don't intend to make it mine! I truthfully have no fault to find with Dorothy, — she does a good job.

Lord Harry, — we can't be so damn particular about personalities. What we have now, whatever they may be, are angels compared to what we are going have in the near future. And gee, I certainly wouldn't think of asking a girl to resign just because she didn't have in her whatever it takes to be a "hot ship pilot." There are always going to be PT's and BT's and L something-or-others, and they are going to need pilots to ferry them, — and it is just as important to ferry them as it is any other airplane. After all, we came in here to relieve man-power, — not to take their jobs away from them.

Nance, I frankly think we are all putting a little too much *emphasis* on "transition." Sure we all want to fly fast ships, but in constantly promoting that ambition we are all losing sight of the job we came in here to do. The girls are becoming dissatisfied because the opportunities are not equal. This is leading to pure feminine jealousy, — which is understandable under the circumstances. I believe the less said about "transition" the better, and, because you cant keep a good man (or girl) down, progress is *bound* to take its course. The girls who have "what it takes" will get ahead no matter where they are stationed, — as individuals, not in groups. It has ever been thus! As you remember, there was very little talk of transition up until the time the three new bases came into existence. Everybody was 100 percent satisfied. Since then it seems that the tendency has been for the girls to forget that they are trying to serve their country in the war effort and instead they are centering their thoughts on their own personal ambitions, — they want to fly big ships purely for their own satisfaction and to "keep up with Mary," not because they think they are needed in that capacity.

All of which is an entirely wrong attitude at a time like this. Thank goodness that feeling has completely disappeared from this base and everyone here stands ready to ferry PT's for the duration if that is what they are needed to do.

You and I have been guinea pigs, — and I think we have proved quite a few points, — but I don't believe that the pilot shortage is acute enough now to expect the powers-that-be to push the girls on ahead. They will have to *need* pilots to really justify giving the girls extensive transition training. Of course I don't know how it is out there, or at Dallas or Romulus, — but here there are plenty of pilots. They cant use them all because they haven't been able to give them the necessary transition as yet, but the transition ships are flying from 7 a.m. to 7:30 p.m. weather permitting.

Col. Baker has been giving us all the breaks possible and I sure do like him for it. He had egged me on with the P47 deal and has started Helen Mary Clark off on the same track (keep this just between us three) I knew of the meeting in Cincinnati, — Capt. Ledbetter told me all that went on but Col. Baker hasn't mentioned it to me and I have the feeling that he is going to continue with his previous plans, whatever they may be, in spite of it. I don't know what his plans are, but anything he wants is OK by me.

Esther Manning is doing a swell job for me here in the office and I am going to miss her like the dickens when she has to go. Col. Baker was so tickled when I told him the news, — I think he would like to be god-father! (incidentally, I'm darned sure that Col. Baker didn't raise hell when he heard that you had checked out in the 51 and the C47. He was honestly as pleased as the dickens, — I was the one who told him about it and he said so.)

Okay on the uniform, — we wont do anything further until we hear from you. Am planning to go up home sometime next week and talk to Bud on this militarization situation. Cant say what I'll do until I have a chance to talk long and lengthily with him, — but personally, I think it is a hell-of-a-note! Helen Mary and I almost got ourselves drunk over it late this aft!

Please forgive all the typographical errors. Esther has me spoiled, — I haven't used the typewriter in weeks and my fingers are all thumbs.

S'all for now. Will drop you a note as soon as there are any further developments. Don't let it get you down, Nance, and keep up the good work. We're all with you 100 percent, and NCAAB WAFS are all healthy and happy.

I felt I wanted some help with my office chores and asked Colonel Nelson after a staff meeting if I could have a clerk once the Cochran graduates came to the base. He said no, explaining that the commanding officers of the squadrons had the extra duties of keeping track of enlisted men in their units and there was a regular military setup in which they worked out their duties. When and if the WAACS came to the base, the WAFS would not be entitled to use one as a clerk because we were only civilians. He emphasized that no directive had been issued that applied to my getting help. Regretfully he said he was only following regulations.

I was silent about the problems Poole caused me for two reasons. He liked her and I did not want to sully his opinion of her. And, Poole had complained to Nancy without my knowledge and Nancy hadn't been able to quiet her. I gathered from Nancy's reply that getting along with Poole's feelings was strictly my problem. I'd have to work out any and all problems by myself as best I could. Most of all, how I wanted to fly! And just as intently how I disliked shuffling papers.

Ambition in a man was a favorable trait. In a woman, it was a defect. Yet the earliest women pilots were very competitive and strove for glory and personal fame. The original WAFS were influenced by the Ninety-Nines and advances in aviation, so we reacted in much the same way. It was difficult for us to be self-effacing or to hide away in an office.

During the week, Col. Charles A. Lindbergh ran a test on the Bell Airacobra, the P-39. From the Ford Motor Company at the nearby Willow Run Airport, he drove to Romulus in Henry Ford's personal, specially-built Mercury, reported to the provost marshal's office for a visitor's badge, and went to the alert room where he studied the technical orders on the P-39 for forty-five minutes. Then he flew it for about two and a half hours, taking off and landing twice.

Lindbergh's advice on flying the airplane, which had caused pilots much trouble, was to raise the gear as soon as the plane was airborne instead of waiting for a safe altitude. He also noted that the left door safety catch might open at 375 miles per hour.

The pilots in the alert room recognized Lindbergh as soon as he entered and promptly pulled out their "Short Snorters Club" cards on him. Lindbergh wasn't caught short. He dug into his pocket and came out with his own "membership card" — a dollar bill that had been autographed by other pilots. If he hadn't had it, he would have had to forfeit one dollar to each person present who did have such proof of membership in the club. Amiably he autographed several P-39 photographs.

After his test runs, Lindbergh was escorted to the officers' club. Captain Hennessey took my arm as soon as I showed up after work and guided me over to Lindbergh to be introduced.

"Colonel Lindbergh," Hennessey got his attention. "I want you to meet a pilot from St. Louis, Del Scharr. She told me that she flew for Robertson Aircraft, too."

Lindbergh acknowledged my presence with a nod of his head. I already knew how socially retiring he was, for many invitations had been sent to him from aviation societies in Missouri, but he never made speeches or showed his face just to please them. I wasn't about to inflict my conversation and presence on that shy man. I murmured a "how-do-you-do" at him.

Hennessey tried to get Lindbergh's interest aroused by saying, "When the WAFS are ready to fly the Airacobra, Del will be the first woman to take 'er up."

Lindbergh looked a bit more interested, so I went back to the St. Louis idea.

"Have you been back to St. Louis lately?" I asked.

He shook his head and barely whispered, "No."

"I didn't work for Robertson long," I said. "Major Bill had only one Cub and just a few students. I free-lanced most of my time."

Lindbergh wasn't good at small talk. I relieved him of any discomfort he might feel at being pressed to continue. With a "I am very happy to have met you," I left the room and went into dinner, worrying and dreaming at the same time.

What Captain Hennessey had said bothered me. I couldn't be the first woman to fly the P-39. It would have to be Nancy, for that was how I interpreted her letter — that she wanted me to know that as the one in command, she must be the first to fly all military airplanes. Only because she was not at Wilmington did Colonel Baker venture to place Betty in a P-47. Once done, it couldn't be undone.

Involuntarily my thoughts returned to my B-25 episode. Someone had not allowed me to continue flying it. Who had cut me out of the B-25 transition? Was it anyone on the base? I thought not. Was it Nancy? I would never have believed that until I received her letter. I could never ask her directly, for doing so would embarrass her. She kept a wall of reserve between herself and most of the other WAFS. I couldn't intrude into that reserve, even to ask for a chance to fly better planes. The worst thing about the questions being raised in my mind was that I had no one nearby in whom I might confide.

I was loyal to Nancy. She knew so much about military matters and worked according to protocol and regulations. I would not show any public dissent. We WAFS had to present a united front and at our base I must lead the other women in keeping it that way.

It was evident that our behavior at all ferrying bases was of interest to military and civilian personnel. If we did not get along with each other, men considered it proof that women were inferior. They readily pointed out that men weren't catty, that they did not gossip, and that they were always good sports if someone played a trick on them or if they didn't get the assignment they wanted. When I heard such statements, I wondered silently how it was that men fought wars, engaged in questionable diplomacy, and broke treaties. Women were such a small minority in governments that they couldn't be blamed for the great ills of the world. But I kept my mouth shut and locked my arguments in my mind. If I noticed any tension building around me, I opened my mouth only to break it, to make someone laugh, or to change the subject.

Perhaps it seems that I had no courage. I felt that I had, but I was boxed in by the combined result of parental and scholastic training, which differed from what traditional society gave to girls in those days. Most parents tried to make their daughters as ornamental as possible so they would be able to make a "good" marriage with someone who could support a family financially. Daughters were allowed or even encouraged to beg or wheedle in order to obtain what they couldn't achieve otherwise.

In my home, it was different. Each of us very early became aware that we must support ourselves. Much was demanded of us. My parents had little extra money and I learned as a toddler that I must never ask for so much as a penny. I never learned to beg. Rather than borrow, I did without. It was a strict upbringing, with an emphasis on self-denial. I did not indulge whims. It was easy for me to adjust to military life. And suppose that I wished I could fly a B-25 again? Or that I cherished the hope of doing something of value in aviation? I had learned well to do without!

At a squadron meeting, I told the others that we should not become objectionable in trying to press for flying in transition. We'd fly our missions efficiently and safely and let our work speak for us. I spoke no more of transition to anyone, and the only time I contacted group operations was to inform the officers there of what they already knew — that certain WAFS had returned to base and were ready for another mission. I knew how to obey and I did it.

Most of the WAFS were on base the morning of April 8 when we went as a group to the flight surgeon's office to take the third typhoid shot.

On the way, Poole complained, "I don't want any more of this!" In a few minutes, she added, "I don't like shots." We made no comments. Soon she said, "I'm not going to take it."

But she continued walking with us into the building and into the office. We took off our uniform blouses and rolled up the left sleeve of our shirts. Poole was not talking any longer. Her face gave no indication of what she was thinking. I was first in line and was rolling down my sleeve after the shot when all of a sudden Poole bolted from the line. She left the office as fast as she could without any explanation.

We were awaiting orders that day and attending ground school. All day long we had listened to her complaints about the army making us take shots. Donahue was sympathetic, but treated her rebellion as a joke.

That evening Lee Wahl questioned me at the officers' club. "She doesn't appear to be a very stable person," he said. "How is she in her flying?"

"She flies all right." I defended Poole.

"I just wondered. Some men faint when they get a shot or vaccinated. But she didn't faint. She probably has a very active imagination," he concluded.

The same day, operations cut orders for McElroy, Poole, and me, but weather kept us on the base until April 11 when we flew L-5s to South Bend and then on to Rantoul, Illinois. The weather forecast was favorable as I led off to Lambert, where Lenore's husband was stuck and waiting to get out. She wanted to see him and of course I wanted to see Harold.

It was only mid-afternoon and our flight was within twenty miles of Lambert Field when the atmosphere became hazy. The closer we got, the more the visibility deteriorated. As we crossed the rivers north of St. Louis, it became impossible to see ahead. I knew that if Lambert Field were open to contact flight, we'd run into traffic. The navy's "yellow perils" were making their circuits and bumps close to the field, spelling danger with the possibility of a collision. If the field were closed and on instruments, I'd have to answer to the CAA if we landed. How inspector Cooper would love that!

As much as I disliked turning away, not only because of Lenore, but also for myself, I turned left in the direction of Scott Air Force Base near Belleville, Illinois. I didn't know the exact direction from where I was in the air, but I knew I'd manage to get there.

Suddenly I saw a crescent-shaped lake beneath me. I had never been there, nor had I seen it from the air, but I knew in a flash that it was Horseshoe Lake. Lakeside Airport must be below. A small airport east of East St. Louis and northwest of Collinsville, Illinois, it would do. We descended to 500 feet above the terrain in order to see better. At that altitude I started to circle the field to look it over before landing. But McElroy was a nervous type and she cut me off, landing first. Then I landed and Poole came in right after me.

Omar Midgett was still the proprietor of the field. He knew me although we had never met. The closest contact I had had with him was the day that Gus Philips called him from Lambert while I was in his office. Gus was writing down what Omar was telling him, when suddenly Omar cried out, "Help! Help!" and there was silence. Gus was so perplexed that he hung up the phone and did nothing more. The newspapers carried the news the following day that men had entered Midgett's office and beat him up. We never found out why.

"I'd like to call Lambert Field," I told Omar.

"Go right ahead. It's over there," he said, pointing to the phone.

Paul Dobbins answered my call to the tower. When he found out where I was, he said, "Come on in, Del. The navy is still flying here. We haven't closed the field yet."

"No, thanks, I'm staying right here. Do me a favor, though, and close our flight plan for me?"

Then I called the navy hangar and asked to speak to Chief Scharr. When Harold answered, I told him, "It's not safe to try to get into Lambert. Listen — Captain McElroy is over at the National Guard hangar. His wife and Barbara Poole are here at Lakeside with me. Would you pick him up and the two of you come downtown to the Mayfair Hotel to meet us?''

His reply was a delighted, ''Yes!''

I knew Omar couldn't afford to pay everyone's toll calls, so I paid him a quarter for each. Someone at Lakeside took us to the Mayfair in downtown St. Louis where our husbands were already waiting. They checked in and Harold and I headed for home in the blue Ford sedan.

''I'm taking you to the Chase,'' Harold informed me.

We ate dinner in that elegant restaurant and Harold, who never liked the spotlight, got up the nerve to dance with me (just once) for he knew I was dying to do so.

The next morning I took the Marcus and Natural Bridge buses downtown, lugging my B-4 bag and navigation kit, making myself a cheerful nuisance to the regular bus riders who had to step around them.

Lenore, Poole, and I left the Mayfair in a taxi. Split three ways, it wasn't very expensive to ride to Lakeside Airport. Then we flew to Lambert for gas at the old National Guard hangar. Our next stop was Springfield, Missouri, where I met Don Joseph, flying the pipeline, and a civilian pilot named Morse who was also delivering an L-5 to Abilene.

Morse thought we were a bunch of ninnies for drawing lines on our charts in order to keep on course. He said, ''I never draw a line. I take one of the red lines bordering the airway and fly it.''

''But then you have to fly in to hit the airport,'' I replied. ''Besides, the red line is too thick and hides some of the checkpoints.''

Morse went his way and we went ours, but we met at refueling stops and I didn't see that our way had any advantage over his. But I didn't change. Morse told us that he had been a bush pilot in the northernmost states and Canada and had flown over much more rugged terrain than the Ozarks. He was a nice sort, much older than the youngsters coming into Romulus from the cadet schools in the South.

With a refueling stop at Wichita Falls, Texas, we spent less than three hours from Tulsa to Abilene. We landed at the municipal airport, the only place where our outdated 1942 aeronautical chart showed the army to be. It wasn't there.

A strange thing had been happening at Abilene since Helen Mary, Gertie Meserve, and I delivered Cubs before Christmas. We were to find it happening with recurring frequency on our flights across the South. The army was constructing a military airport only five minutes via L-5s away from the civilian field. On either side of the white Band-

Aid runways laid down the middle, the bare earth lay exposed like a wound, for machines had ripped off its grassy covering and leveled its contours. We landed on a Band-Aid and delivered our airplanes to a field not yet on a map.

We returned to Romulus on April 14 and were at the Stinson factory the next day to ferry more L-5s to Romulus where the mechanics checked them over. That same evening we three landed our L-5s to RON at Lambert.

What luck for me! Not only did I see Harold twice in one week, but bad weather forced us to lay over another day. Group operations had entrusted me with the task of going to every large airport along the way to Abilene to find out firsthand what gasoline service and other facilities were available to the Ferry Command. I told Harold with enthusiasm, "It's about time operations learned what's going on — those guys don't know half of what the ferry pilots have to contend with!"

Since the weather was bad, there was no sense in my running out to Lambert on the 16th. Instead I went downtown to spend some time with Lenore and Poole, who had stayed again at the Mayfair. We walked on Eighth Street to Olive Street to do some window shopping. Within the space of five city blocks, I was stopped by or greeted by as many pedestrians, all of whom knew me well.

Poole said, "That's remarkable. It's amazing to me that in a city as large as St. Louis, so many people know you."

"St. Louis is the friendliest city in the country," I explained. "And they're interested in aviation here."

"It's more than that," she replied. "I flew up at Detroit City Airport and I could go downtown and not see anyone I knew all day."

The next day we made up for the weather delay by delivering in Abilene. We were back at the base during the night. There was no reason why I should not have had another L-5 mission right away, but I was left behind while the other WAFS took off again.

Nancy Love came by Romulus briefly. I felt that she really didn't understand our situation and misinterpreted it. She indicated that some changes would be made soon, but I decided I'd "wait and see." After all, I was from Missouri.

Changes for the male pilots were in process all spring. One St. Louisan whom Harold and I knew from Lambert, Col. Harry Johannsen, was transferred to Long Beach. I thought he'd probably wind up as executive officer. He'd joined the Royal Canadian Air Force as soon as he could, so he had had ferry experience long before Pearl Harbor. His family owned Johannsen Bros. Shoe Company, which manufactured elegant shoes for stylish women. The Johannsen name hit the society columns with regularity.

The men who had completed transition to instrument flying and to fighters, cargo, and bomber types were disappearing from the base. Their replacements were usually new to the Ferrying Division. They were mostly cadets out of the Training Command who thought that because they now had earned wings they were great pilots. The Training Command had given them advanced training so they were placed in either pursuit or multi-engine transition. Many of them were soon flying the P-39 Airacobra. Overall, they were unproved or weak in cross-country navigation, so usually an experienced pilot herded them to their destination, just as I had done with Nelson.

The accomplished pilots had gone into FERD's parent organization, the Air Transport Command headed by General George. They were additions to or replacements for the pilots completing their tours of duty overseas as ferry pilots. They were sent to North Africa, to the Hump on the way to China, or to refueling posts all over the world. Simply and fairly, each man was supposed to go where he was qualified to fill a position. Anyone as naive as I believed that happened in every case. I still had a head full of ideals and a belief in fair play.

The pilots returning from their tours of duty overseas may have been assigned by happenstance, but no matter. Those who returned to fly ''easy'' missions away from war zones were happy even to be based in Michigan. Anywhere in the United States was heaven to them. Some confessed that they kissed the ground at the first place they landed in the States.

One such pilot was Captain Russell B. Miller, whose father had been a World War I pilot and had taught ''Dusty'' to fly. Before he was of age, Dusty had been an instructor at Hicks Field in Texas. Then for a year he'd been the youngest and smallest pilot ferrying bombers in ATC. For three years he hadn't had much time with his wife and son. The past Christmas he'd spent as a patient in a small field hospital in an African jungle. He had lost weight, but not his nerve, his sense of humor, or his popularity with his buddies. He was a boy-wonder at twenty-four — and handsome, with dark hair and eyes and a Ronald Coleman mustache.

BOYS WILL BE BOYS

BURCHIE, MAC, AND I were the only WAFS on the base the day before Easter.

"Is Mac home?" I asked Lenore. "If he is, why don't we all go to the dance tonight at the officers' club?"

"Sure," she said. "How about you, Burchie?"

"Yes," said Burchie.

It was agreed and they went to ground school while I stayed to work on records for the squadron. In the middle of the afternoon, group operations phoned our barracks and said that a C-60 was leaving soon and that we were to be on it. Would I come over right away to pick up the orders? I ran over.

As he handed me the orders, the officer said, "The other two WAFS will fly together as a flight for most of their trip, but we are sending you alone in a different direction." Lenore was taking the L-2B Taylorcraft to the First Fighter Command, Mitchel Field, New York. Burchie was taking her plane to the 441st Base Headquarters at Milleville, New Jersey, and I was bound for the 301st Subdepot at Moody Field, Georgia.

Back at the barracks we hurried like mad so we wouldn't keep the pilot waiting. We knew how men hate to wait for women to get ready. For a while I didn't think about the dance. I had been looking forward to it, for Romulus was a friendly base and I loved to dance. The mission was going to spoil Easter eve for me.

The other two WAFS were so certain that we would attend the dance that they had ordered a corsage as a surprise gift for me to wear. I could see the pained expression on their faces, such as happens when plans go awry, as they handed me a florist's box after we boarded our plane. The corsage was lovely, red roses and a white gardenia and as fragrant as it was beautiful.

Burchie said shyly, "We didn't know if you'd get to St. Louis or if you'd stay on the base, but it's our Easter present to you."

How could I tell Burchie and Mac how touched I was? I looked down at the corsage in my hand. It wasn't right to put it back in its box. "I'll put it on right now and wear it on the flight," I said. "The flowers are too pretty to be wasted." I pinned it carefully below my shoulder strap.

The pilot on that flight was Captain Pusey. Every bucket seat held a parachute and atop each sat a ferry pilot. It was a congenial group and the greatest wise-cracker of all was Dusty Miller.

We hadn't been flying very long when the copilot came back to me and said, "The pilot wants you to fly copilot."

It wasn't fair to the junior officer and made me feel uncomfortable to take his place. He was supposed to be getting experience and I would never need it. But Pusey was a man not to be thwarted. He was too formidable to confront. There was no one like him in the ferry command.

A major had told me about his first encounter with Pusey. "In walks this fellow," he said. "He must have been at least six foot four and built like a brick outhouse. He looks around and hangs up his B-4 bag just where I wanted to put my clothes. Then he plunks himself down on my bed and says, 'I'll take this one.'"

I replied, "You outrank him. Why didn't you tell him you saw it first?"

"Oh, no!" laughed the major, who had entered the military with that rank because he was a lawyer and lawyers were in short supply. "I soon found out that he'd been a Golden Gloves champion and a medalist in the national swimming championships and he'd been a first captain on TWA. I wouldn't mix with him. The fellows who've been with him howling in the downtown bars in Detroit say he's some fast operator. Yeah, Pusey is quite a guy."

But somehow Ralph Pusey made an entirely different impression on me. He had told me once that he and his wife lived in Kansas City, headquarters for TWA, and that he wished he could be stationed closer to home. "My wife is as tall as you," he had said. "When we have a dance sometime on base, I hope you'll dance with me. I don't like to dance with short girls." He treated me as a friend and an equal and was never condescending, as many men were.

Captain Pusey appeared quite jovial as I seated myself in the right-hand seat. I looked over the instrument panel as soon as I was safety-belted and had hands and feet on the controls. He began explaining to me the intricacies of the C-60, which I was unable to understand, for he was giving me a lot of double-talk, the rage that year at Romulus. I never learned how to do it and no one could possibly understand it. Kay Thompson was good at it, and I had heard that Helen McGilvery dished out pseudo-aviation jargon so convincingly that eavesdropping civilians listened to her avidly, hoping vainly to understand what she was saying.

Pusey hadn't gone very far with his chatter before I caught on, but he didn't stop. I was surprised when I recognized something he said. I thought he was still kidding when he asked me, "Did you ever fly over Rabbit Hatch, Kentucky?"

When I said I hadn't, he continued, "When you fly for an airline, you have to know the route better than the back of your hand. You have to know how long it takes from one town to the next and keep your ETA for each checkpoint on schedule in spite of the wind and the weather. That's how I know there's a Rabbit Hatch, Kentucky." Then he listed a number of other towns with strange names he'd flown over.

Pusey was distracting, but I was determined to fly that C-60 the best that I could. I got the two throttles at the proper rpm and the plane trimmed just right to get the best speed "on the step" and maintain altitude. Then I relaxed.

Dusty Miller joined us, his slender body completely filling the passageway between the cabin and the pilot compartment. He and Pusey were conversing in double-talk, which both found hilarious. Dusty, the imp, was smiling so broadly, he showed most of his even, white teeth.

The wheel felt a bit heavy in my hands. I took hands off. The nose slowly dipped. I'd thought I'd done a perfect job of stabilizing the airplane. I tried again, for the C-60 was unfamiliar to me. I wound the stabilizer back, barely touching the wheel, and the C-60 was balanced once more. Then I looked at the altimeter. I hadn't kept the plane at 4,000 feet. It was climbing. So I started to wind the stabilizer the other way.

Dusty said, laughing, "Can't you fly this airplane?"

I became suspicious as he spoke; then I became sure. "Get out of the way," I said to Dusty. "I want to see what's going on back there."

The game was over. Dusty had been standing as wide and as tall as he could so that I would not able to look back into the cabin. He had also been waving the other passenger-pilots forward. As soon as I adjusted the stabilizer, he motioned them to tiptoe to the rear. Because an airplane in flight is balanced just as a seesaw is, placing the weight farther forward or backward made the weighted side go down. I laughed as wholeheartedly as the others at the trick.

I flew the airplane the rest of the way to Dayton, but Pusey landed it and helped me to taxi the thing as close to the hangar as we could. As we cut the engines, the line boys looked up to see in the copilot's seat a woman wearing a corsage pinned at her left shoulder. We figured that shook them up. They probably thought, "What's this man's army coming to?"

Pusey discharged most of his passengers at Wright-Patterson Air Base. We stayed on board and he and his copilot flew us to Akron. There we got off. Pusey told us a bus went to Alliance, our destination. A taxi took us to the Akron-Alliance Transit Company. But there were no more buses into Alliance that day, so we had to wait until the next, which was Easter Sunday. There was nothing to do but to find out when the bus left the next morning and to spend a quiet Easter eve at the Portage Hotel, each with her own thoughts of loved ones far away.

We were going to be smart and allow at least a half hour at the bus terminal the next morning to get us and our baggage on board. But when we got there, there was already a long line of people ahead of us. We inched our way forward in the queue. Each time we moved, we dragged our paraphernalia along beside us. Some of the passengers made ill-mannered comments about the room we took. We pretended to be deaf.

But our parachute and B-4 bags were an old story to the energetic bus driver. With practiced motions and in rhythm, he piled all of them under or atop the first seat. I was able to slide into a seat over the wheel near the rear of the bus, an objectionable seat that no one had deigned to use. Mac sat beside me and Burchie was across the aisle. She was quiet and I figured she was lost in thoughts about George.

Mac and I chattered like birds about the farms we were passing. We were interested in the spring sowing, the houses, the buds on the trees. We razzed each other about our demotion from 190 horsepower to Continental 65s. In the distance, Alliance loomed larger and larger as

we approached it. We were disappointed when we arrived. It wasn't
what we had expected.

The bus terminal was dirty. Soot was piled up along the foundations
of the buildings bordering the sidewalks. Captive in the dirty stuff were
scraps of paper and other refuse. A soldier from Wayne County Airport was standing in line to board as we got off. He recognized us and
spoke.

Inside the bus terminal I found a phone booth, an evil smelling cubi-
cle with an invisible floor — it was covered with discarded candy wrappers, cigarette butts and pack wrappers, and a dried apple core. I
telephoned the Taylorcraft factory. A guard answered. He asked me to
remain where I was. Lieutenant Fairfield would come to the bus station as soon as he could.

We waited outside in the street. The wind sometimes carried the feel
of fresh air along with it. We gazed about us. Never had I seen any
town, except the isolated coal mining communities in Pennsylvania,
that compared with the filth and grime in Alliance, Ohio. Yet the shab-
by neglect on Main Street where we stood contrasted sharply with the
neatly dressed women on their way to church. Almost every one of
them wore a corsage.

By the time Lieutenant Fairfield came for us, we had grown tired of
standing and had shoved our equipment into the waiting room, where
we had sat for twenty minutes. We pushed and shoved our gear into
the car. It didn't take us long to reach the factory. Even though it was
Easter, a secretary was on duty. Inside the factory we looked in horror
at all the L-2Bs in various stages of completion.

"Don't tell me we'll have to ferry more of these?" asked Mac.

I couldn't speak. I could only follow Lieutenant Fairfield to the large
table where we could figure out our routes. He, being an officer and
having a chance to be in charge, took it into his head to assign us the
routes we were to follow. He was flustered, as if handling three women
was more than he was capable of.

Soon he and the secretary, Miss Fulton, had the papers ready for us
to sign. The wind had been building up, so we were fortunate that the
airplanes were in the hangar. We checked our L-2Bs inside and out.
They were ready to go.

Unfortunately for me, the lieutenant routed me to Norton, at Columbus, Ohio. I would be flying into a strong headwind. It was unlikely that I could arrive there before the gasoline tank went dry. The hop
was only 120 miles, but my estimated ground speed would be only thirty miles per hour, if I were lucky. The others would have a forty-mile-
per-hour tailwind as they headed east.

With a helper at each wingtip until they were turned into the wind, their L-2Bs zipped off the ground with no forward run whatever and were out of sight in no time.

Lieutenant Fairfield had not decided when I'd take off. If the wind died down, I was to telephone a number he gave me. I left my B- 4 bag in the office when he took me into town and got rid of me. I felt strange about being in Alliance by myself, but it was a strangeness I simply could not analyze.

I saw a restaurant and people inside eating. I tried the door. It was locked. I walked along the main street and everywhere the restaurants were closed. It was uncomfortable walking, for the wind picked up the city's trash and flung it into my eyes and onto my shoes and uniform. I watched a young lad turn the lock on the first restaurant I had tried. He got in! By that time it was 1400 and I was hungry, dirty, and angry almost to the point of tears.

I tried the same door. It opened. I entered and sat at a table. A waitress looked me up and down as I studied the menu. I ordered steak. She left. I went to the washroom to wash my hands. There was no soap and no paper. Cold water and Kleenex did what they could to protect my health. I looked down at my uniform. My wings! Where were my wings? I patted my left breast. They still weren't there. When the waitress came back to my table, I said, "I must have lost my wings. What can I do so they can be returned to me in case someone finds them?"

"You didn't have any wings on when you came in," she said.

Now I was puzzled. I must have lost them on the street. I would have to retrace my steps and look along the streets where I'd walked since noon.

After the steak, which was good, I walked the streets, head down, and found nothing. At a Turner drugstore, I looked for Tabu dusting powder, for Barbara Poole wanted some. I ran into the Wayne County Airport soldier again. Waiting with the bus crowd seemed to be his way of spending time. I found another drugstore and bought some Shanghai sachet for myself, a Yardley sachet as a gift, some Yankee Clover cologne, and a vial each of Lelong Indiscreet and Sirocco. I bought them all, no doubt, in despair.

At ten minute intervals, from 1600 on, I dialed the telephone number that Lieutenant Fairfield had given me. No answer. Finally, at 1700, I called the factory and told the guard that because it was impossible for me to fly away because of the strong wind, I would register at the Lexington Hotel without baggage. He said that he hadn't seen the lieutenant since he took me to town. By that time, I was tired from walking the streets of Alliance and I hated being stared at. I felt naked without my wings. And it was beginning to drizzle. I had to get in somewhere.

I had heard it wasn't "nice" to register at a hotel without luggage, but I signed in anyway. As I was filling out the card, the room clerk answered the telephone and handed it to me.

"This is Mr. Cole at Taylorcraft. I'm sorry, Mrs. Scharr, Lieutenant Fairfield gave you the wrong number to call. He's on his way in and we'll bring your B-4 bag to you."

A likely story, I thought, as the bellhop showed me to my room for the night.

After I did my laundry, festooning the aged ochre shade on a lacquered bridge lamp with my rayon hose and khaki work socks, I thought a warm bath would feel good. Taking the small package of bubble bath crystals, I poured a spoonful into the tub and turned on the water. Then I undressed and turned off the water. I thrust my left foot into the froth that by now almost filled the tub. The water was too warm. Quickly out came my foot, with gobs of bubbles sliding down my ankle and slithering off. In the hole my foot left, I saw greenish-yellow water. Looking at what I'd soon immerse myself in was more than I could bear. By trial and error I obtained a comfortable water temperature and got in. Then I gave myself up to the enjoyment of my Easter Sunday night bath.

The warmth in the tub overcame the chill in the cold, little bedroom. My splashing blocked out the sound of the rain falling outside. I popped a piece of gum in my mouth. Suddenly I felt something hard in the gum. A filling had given way. Now what to do? This Alliance mission was turning into a jinx for me.

I could see the tiny bedroom from where I lay in the tub. A freshly painted white baseboard separated the apple green wall, with its interesting pattern of hairline cracks, from the wine-red broadloom carpet. It wasn't pretty, but it was the cleanest, neatest, and freshest thing I'd seen in Alliance all day. I sat in the water — the nastiest looking water outside a bayou — and reviewed all the events that had taken me away from a dinner dance and brought me here to worry about a hole in a tooth and a missing pair of wings. What had I done to deserve this?

I had bought the *Detroit News* in one of the drugstores and after I got out of the tub I read it lying on the bed. I was almost relaxed, except that my tongue continued to seek the hole left by the filling. It felt like a tremendous cavern. I peered into the mirror to see how large the hole was. It wasn't big at all, and only a portion of the filling was missing.

At last hunger pangs drove me to dress again in my uniform and I left the hotel to hunt down the dairy delicatessen I'd seen during the afternoon. It had been open then, maybe it still was. Once there, I entered and ordered a cheese sandwich.

A thin young woman with very poor teeth, accompanied by a man and several small children, came in and stood waiting at the counter beside me. She looked me over carefully and then stared at my face.

"Are you a flier?" she asked.

"Yes, I am," I replied. I felt like a foolish fraud without my wings, for what proof had I that I was telling the truth? The clerk presented me with the cheese sandwich. I paid for it and carried it to a little table where I sat down. I was ready to begin eating when a young lady who was also standing at the counter came to my table.

"Could you give me your autograph?" she asked.

She fished a piece of paper from her purse and laid it on the table. I found my fountain pen and wrote, "Best wishes! Del Scharr." She thanked me, picked up her paper, and went back to the counter.

The incident embarrassed me and I didn't know why. Maybe I was uncomfortable because I wasn't a great and important person. It could have been that I was critical of the people of Alliance for their lack of civic pride. Yet without any forwardness on my part, people had recognized what I was and what I was doing and they considered both very important.

The next morning Lieutenant Fairfield attacked his duties with such vim that he must have hoped I'd forgotten about the wrong telephone number. Perhaps he was only trying to get rid of me as soon as possible. He ordered a workman to push my L-2B out of the hangar. I blocked the procedure because I was reinspecting the airplane. As I did so, I made a discovery. There on the bottom of the fuselage, shining from among the control wires, was my pair of civilian pilot wings. I was overjoyed, almost to tears of relief.

The flying picture for me had changed because the wind had died down. I could make Columbus, Ohio, in half the time it would have taken me the day before. As soon as I landed, I reached for the packet of forms. Forms I and I-A weren't in it. How come? I thought. Everything had been in order the day before. There was nothing I could do except to use a clearance form to keep track of my flying hours. I'd have to transfer them to the official forms as soon as I could. To do so, I sent Lieutenant Fairfield a collect telegram, requesting him to send all missing papers, especially the forms I needed, to Moody Field immediately. I hoped they would get there when I did.

Off I went to Cincinnati. On the next leg, to Louisville, Kentucky, I had a good tail wind. And then I flew and flew, wondering where my checkpoints were. An L-2B flies no faster than a Piper Cub, so a pilot gets a good, slow look at the countryside. It was a lonesome day with no one in the air but me. It made me feel lost. This was the first step in the training sessions that made it possible for me to go on alone stoically when I had to. The wave of desolation that hit me made me fear that I'd gotten off course. I edged over to the Ohio River to make sure I wouldn't miss Louisville — as if that were possible, flying visually. After what seemed like a very long time (it was only five minutes), I found my checkpoint where it should have been. The wind had shifted and now was directly on my nose. Seeing that I wasn't lost and had been on course all the time perked up my spirits.

I'd flown four hours from Alliance to Louisville. I felt rarin' to go, so I took off for Smith Grove. There were few checkpoints along the way and I went a little off course at Bonneville just to be sure it was the right town. Thank goodness the water tanks close to the railroad stations had the name of each town painted on them. I had to avoid the Fort Knox area, which was restricted, but I picked out the location of Mammoth Cave. Through a thickening haze, I made out the small towns along the way. On the chart, the hills and valleys were all the same color green because the gradient didn't change enough to display elevation differences of less than 1,000 feet. There were no ridges to navigate by, such as there were in Pennsylvania.

It was dreadfully lonesome over the steep slopes of the mountains, but it was beautiful. Redbud trees were blooming, and so were the white dogwood and the wild plum. Scattered through the deciduous trees not yet leafing out were the dark green evergreens, especially the cedars, and outcroppings of rocks. I felt especially blessed to see spring as it took over the Kentucky hills.

Smith Grove brought me down to the ugly realities of ferrying. The only facility on the field was a radio station. No gasoline. No nothing. The radio operator told me he was afraid to leave the radio station and he didn't think he was capable of starting the airplane anyway. He could clear me to Bowling Green, about twenty minutes flying time away, if one counted takeoff, circling, and landing. After landing there, I'd still have an hour's flying time left in the gas tank.

I tied down the wings, put the stick back with the safety belt, turned on the ignition, and cracked the throttle. Then I swung the propeller. The engine kicked over immediately. I untied the wings, loosened the seat belt, swung myself into the front seat, and away I went. It felt good to be able to handle an emergency.

I didn't feel so good soon after. There was no one at all on the airfield at Bowling Green. Everything was under construction except for the finished runways. I needed gasoline. An elderly watchman badly in need of a shave came over to me as I tied the airplane down for the night. He helped me to stake the tail down and then he locked up my parachute bag inside the construction shack. He took me into town to the Helm Hotel on the Dixie Highway.

"I'll pick you up in the morning. What time you want to get out to the field?" my benefactor asked.

"Eight o'clock. Thanks again. Good night," I replied.

I checked into one of the 125 rooms. The price was only $1.50. I ate in the dining room before going to my room, for it was already dark outside. Once in bed I couldn't sleep. Bowling Green was a college town and the hotel was in the main part of town. Students walked along the sidewalk until past midnight, talking loudly and calling to each other. I was nervous and the bed felt itchy, although the next morning I found no evidence of bites. I'd flown more than six hours that day. Maybe that's what made me nervous; maybe I was too tired. I noticed a tiny crack between two toes and worried that it might be the beginning of athlete's foot.

The old watchman picked me up at eight the next morning. I hardly recognized the man. He had cleaned himself up, shaved, and was wearing new overalls. We stopped at a gas station and arranged for the truck to follow us out to the field. A chamois would take care of water or soil in the gas. I wasn't worried.

The watchman wanted my name and address, so I gave it to him. He looked on admiringly as I swung the prop and took myself off to Nashville, where I landed seventy-five minutes later. Then on to Chattanooga and from there to Atlanta, with beautiful scenery throughout the mountains along the way. That night I stayed at the Piedmont Hotel on Peachtree Street, took in a mediocre technicolor movie, *Reap the Wild Wind,* and washed my hair.

The next day, Wednesday, was an easy one with only three and a half hours of flying. Macon was on instruments until 1030, so I couldn't leave Atlanta until then. From Macon I went to Douglass to deliver at Moody Field.

Once in the air, I tried the trick that Donnie had done too successfully in an L-5. She'd taken off her shirt to get a tan and had gotten a raw sunburn instead. But it didn't work for me. The pyrolin on my L-2B wasn't as extensive as that of an L-5 and I didn't get enough sunshine to get tanned.

However, my hops were not disappointing otherwise. Southern Georgia was already into a Midwest June. The vegetation was lush, the atmosphere sultry, and even roses were blooming in the gardens. For the first time I saw Spanish moss hanging from the trees and all sorts of palms. What a treat for me, for back at Romulus winter still returned on a springlike day for a skirmish, just to remind us who is boss in Michigan six months of the year.

Onto the counter at Moody went the paltry packet I'd been carrying with me. "Anything come for Scharr?" I asked a young man behind the counter.

With a British accent he answered, "The factory sent what you are missing. It arrived several hours ago."

He found it on a shelf and placed it on the counter. I smiled gratefully, opened the envelope, and pulled out a sheaf of papers.

"Oh, no!" I cried.

The young man, who had turned his back to me, turned around with some curiosity. "Anything amiss?" he asked.

"Do you know what that guy did?" I asked. "Just look here." And I showed him. The memorandum receipt I held in my hand was labeled Milleville, N. J. It should have been in Burchie's plane.

"Don't worry. We'll sign for the airplane anyway," he said. "We'll make an adjustment by getting in touch with Milleville."

That took me off the hook, except I had to put my flying time record on the form I of an airplane delivered hundreds of miles away. When I finished that, I was ready to go home. Another chap was now busy behind the counter. There was a good deal more traffic to and from the space behind the counter than I had ever seen.

To my query about transportation available to take me back to my base, I received a reply that I simply could not understand. Whatever was the fellow talking about? I asked him again and more slowly he gave me the same gibberish as before. Having cleared that problem to his satisfaction, he went to work at something far down the long counter. I was baffled, but I'd try again. I waved my hand to another gent behind the counter and asked him what was the quickest and best way to get out of there. He not only understood my corn-belt dialogue, I could understand him. His clipped speech was the sort that British actors were known for.

I nodded in the direction of Mr. Gibberish and said, "I'm so sorry, but I simply could not understand him."

My informant laughed and said, "Oh, everybody here has that trouble. He's one of the Lancastershire lads." Then I learned that all the cadets at Moody Field were British youths being trained for the Royal Air Force.

Oh, how I hated to leave that little Taylorcraft. It had an economical engine, averaging exactly four gallons per hour. It used less than a pint of oil in fifteen hours of flying time. My entire operational expenses from Alliance to Moody were only fourteen dollars, or twenty-five cents per gallon. And it was a well-balanced plane, so easy to fly.

The climax to this delivery was that the subdepot provided me with a staff car. I not only had a chauffeur, but another attendant in the front seat as well. They took me on a lovely drive. We stopped at Valdosta, the nearest town to Moody, where I bought a Fostoria bud vase and a dog tag chain. The men said that transportation out of Lakeside was very poor, so they took me all the way to Tallahassee, Florida. At Tallahassee there was no hotel room available, so I was forced to take a night flight to Jacksonville, getting there at midnight. I had a three-hour wait in the terminal before an airplane came along to take me to Detroit via Washington, D.C., and Pittsburgh.

One week prior to my Alliance experience, four WAFS from Wilmington — Betty Gillies, Nancy Batson, Helen McGilvery, and Sis Bernheim — were preflighting and loading their PT-26s at the Fairchild factory at Hagerstown, Maryland, readying to strike out for Calgary in the province of Alberta, Canada.

The PT-26s were really only PT-19s with a transparent hatch. It may seem strange that WAFS flew open cockpit primary trainers during the bitter winter weather and in the spring hatches were put on the planes. But spring was still a long time off in the northern states and Canada.

Closemouthed Betty Gillies made out the clearances for all and looked over the weather situation before departing. She took a calculated look at the synoptic charts showing weather trends across the entire continent and made up her mind without telling the others what she had in mind. The others thought of ferrying as adventuresome and fun, a chance to try to outwit the elements and to arrive at each destination safely and on time.

But this mission started out differently. No sooner had they touched ground and turned off the switches at Akron, than Betty set up tasks for each one, giving no two an opportunity to exchange rumors. In fact, Sis said, "She gave us hardly enough time to pee!"

The pattern was set and copied at Fort Wayne, Indiana, and at Joliet, Illinois, where Betty sent the RON. That was good work for one day, because Joliet was 697 miles from Hagerstown, their airplanes flew only about 100 miles per hour, and the atmosphere they were flying in was moving eastward, which cut down the ground speed. One reason they could fly so long was that when they got into the central time zone, sunset came an hour later.

There was no hangar flying that evening, for Betty said they'd be off the ground as soon as it was safe after the sun came up the next day. The girls were exhausted, but Betty was the boss. Was she testing their stamina? Or proving how formidable she was?

The following day their first stop was at Des Moines, Iowa, and from there they flew to Grand Island, Nebraska, to Kearney, and stopped for the night at North Platte, covering 585 miles. Betty wasn't letting up. The others began to gripe. Betty was adamant, lending no ear to their complaints. Sis said their tongues were hanging out. They didn't take time to dawdle over a hot meal at noon, but wolfed a sandwich, gulped some coffee, and rushed back to their airplanes.

The third day Betty's goal was Great Falls, Montana, so again it was off to bed as soon as possible in order to get an early start in the morning. The first stop the next day was at Scottsbluff, Nebraska. Then they flew into the mountain time zone and landed at Casper, Wyoming, and from there Betty navigated to Billings, Montana.

Sis said she was bringing up the rear, "having a ball" and just relaxed, knowing all the others were great navigators. All of a sudden, Betty turned the lead over to McGilvery. She flew in the lead awhile and then she signaled and turned and that put Batson first. It wasn't long before Batson motioned to me and it was my turn. Yipes! I'd not been paying any attention at all and hadn't the remotest notion where we were, except somewhere west of the Black Hills.

"I just kept the heading I had and tried vainly to find something on the ground down there that somebody might place on a sectional chart as a checkpoint. But no luck. Nobody took over for me and I didn't dare turn it over to Betty. Then, up in front I could make out an airport. Any airport was all right with me at that moment; I was so lost.

"Betty came up from behind and she landed first with us zipping in right after her. It was Billings! They told me what a great job I'd done in navigating. I couldn't convince anyone that I never knew where I was the whole leg. Batson and McGilvery confessed right away that they had been lost, and relinquished the lead as soon as they could. Betty laughs about it now. She says she was lost, too, or she would have led the flight all the way in.

"We wasted no time at Billings. Betty kept egging us on to Great Falls and we made it."

The WAFS flew 846 miles that day. The next day they flew the 275 air miles to Calgary, got their signed receipts and turned around to go back home. Home was a long way off and it took a long time, using public transportation, before they saw Wilmington again.

The painful memory of that rush, rush, rush was already growing dim when each of the four WAFS received a letter of commendation from Colonel Baker for making the delivery in record time. They could look back on what they had done as an accomplishment instead of as an irritating experience. It was above and beyond the call of duty and they deserved the commendation.

Although the WAFS didn't know Betty's plans or moves until after the fact, I don't think that anyone was jealous of her accomplishments. She belonged in the squadron in ways that Nancy never did and was dubbed "the mighty atom," for she seemed to get whatever she went after. She wanted to prove how much endurance WAFS had and that's why she insisted upon squeezing every ounce of energy from her flight members and every minute of available sunlight from the day.

Faced with dissatisfaction from WAFS at Romulus, Colonel Nelson wrote an opinion that Colonel Tunner accepted, that *all* WAFS should be kept from further transition and out of multi-engine aircraft because the crews would be mixed. This was one card that Colonel Nelson played so well I did not find out about it for thirty years. I can guess why he did not disclose his action to us.

Colonel Nelson was a friendly yet lonely man. His wife refused to live in Michigan because of the weather. We WAFS gave him some of the social life he apparently missed on a base twenty-five miles from the city. Whenever we were on the base awaiting orders, he liked us to chat with him during the interval between dinner and his usual session at the poker table.

Nelson was especially fond of Poole. Her moods were fluid and mercurial, changing from sweet to sharp, from tender to stern, from touchy to good humored. Acerbity was usually left behind at the barracks. I suspected, however, that she indicated to Nelson now and then her dissatisfaction with being at Romulus. His letter to Tunner must have been the only way he saw open to him to keep Poole happy with her lot — to cut transition for those at other bases — and he must have had unvoiced prejudices about the capabilities of women as pilots.

All the men in charge could be exceptionally nice to their subordinates, but they wanted to keep them subordinate. Although Colonel Tunner allowed Nancy Love to check out in many airplanes, that's as far as he wanted to go at that time. Nancy needed the prestige of being able to fly more airplanes than Jacqueline Cochran's WFTD graduates, but Tunner saw no reason to allow other WAFS to be similarly upgraded.

When Nancy Love found that her boss was in agreement with Nelson on this issue, she didn't allow the matter to rest. Instead, she went over his head to his boss, General George, whom she had charmed earlier. He agreed with her that the Ferry Command would need women pilots who could ferry any type of airplane when the time came for more men to be in service overseas. The war effort would suffer if men were forced to remain on the North American continent because no one was available to replace them.

Therefore, General George wrote a directive at the end of April 1943 stating that women pilots were to be allowed to go as high as they were capable of going. There would be no limitations on women in the Ferry Command. "It is the desire of the Command," he wrote, "that all pilots, regardless of sex, be privileged to advance to the extent of their ability in keeping with the progress of aircraft development. Will you please ensure that the terms of this policy are carried out insofar as it applies to the ferrying of aircraft within the continental United States."

The Ferrying Division rescinded its previous directives and issued a new letter, "WAFS will be transitioned upon multi-engine aircraft or high-powered single engine aircraft under the same standards of individual experience and ability as apply to any other pilots."

This was in direct opposition to Colonel Nelson's idea. Maybe he considered it a slap in the face. At any rate, he *didn't* advertise the directive and *didn't* tell me about it. I also *didn't* receive word of it by letter, directive, or bulletin from Tunner or Love. Twenty years later I learned about this directive which stated WAFS were to be given transition "when and if available." But any ferrying group's transition school, in cooperation with operations, could keep WAFS so busy ferrying that they would not be on base long enough to progress very far.

I can't say that I blame the instructors in transition for disliking the change they were supposed to make and trying to avoid it. People naturally don't like changes in their routines. And women had the reputation for being hard to handle and subject to fits of hysteria or weeping. Behind their hesitant and reluctant compliance in giving women more transition might also hide the feeling that a superior officer doesn't really know the local situation or doesn't care about the added burdens that change would bring. The military system doesn't lend itself well to explaining to its members all the whys and wherefores of any act.

ON APRIL 14, 1943, the Associated Press reported that the WFTD headed by Jacqueline Cochran at Sweetwater, Texas, would now accept candidates with only thirty-five hours' total flying time. When Colonel Tunner got the message on the same day through military channels, he was not happy.

This wasn't the first lowering of standards that Cochran had achieved since the original 200 solo hours were required of her first class. If she kept the standards to which she had agreed in September — which were much too low to suit Colonel Tunner then — her command would have concluded before the year was out. But she persuaded General Arnold to lower the flight requirements to a minimum of seventy-five hours in December 1942, which allowed her to recruit a second class. This directive was so ambiguously worded that it gave her the power to keep out a pilot with the necessary flight time simply on the strength of her rejection of the candidate's personal traits. At a time when her need for students was so great, what sort of person was she trying to keep out?

Perhaps a leaning toward homosexuality was evident in an early candidate. Cochran never spoke publicly about such an instance. She did mention thirty years later that a Negro girl had applied and that she was dissuaded from entering because of the trouble that her race would bring into the organization. Integration in hotels, restaurants, and rest rooms was far from a reality in those days and the Ferry Command could not protect a pilot from prejudice. Pilots from other minority groups were not excluded — one of Mexican descent and another of Chinese descent were accepted.

Oddly, the same standards in the physical examination were not used for all pilot candidates. Helen Mary Clark had received a waiver for her eyesight and wore goggles with prescription lenses. Yet an excellent private pilot, Laura Sellinger of St. Louis, who had passed the CAA physical examination, wasn't allowed a similar waiver so she could enter the Texas program. On the other hand, many years after the fact an ex-WASP who knew she couldn't pass the rigid army "64" physical confessed to me that she was given the eye test by an army doctor who was a friend of Phyllis Burchfield's. The doctor falsified the record and on the strength of his report and no further examination at Sweetwater, she got into the program. She was not assigned to the Ferry Command on graduation, and the error was never discovered.

The April 14 news release led to a deluge of applications and a clamoring for quick flight instruction by females throughout the United States. It also meant that Colonel Tunner had another fight on his hands to maintain the safety record of his command. Male cadets were coming into his ferrying groups with 250 hours of flight time, supposedly ready for pursuit transition. They were lacking in cross-country experience and further training was necessary before they went overseas. Thus far Tunner was happy with his WAFS. Since the November propeller episodes, WAFS had had no accidents due to their mistakes — Cornelia Fort's accident was not her fault. Furthermore, they delivered promptly and set records that men pilots could envy. Tunner was adamantly against 200-hour wonders coming from Sweetwater. This time he had General George in agreement with him.

On April 24 twenty-three young women of Cochran's 43-W-1 class finally passed the course. The graduation ceremony took place at Ellington Field, Houston, on April 28. Instead of the fifty that Jackie had told FERD were in the class, only twenty-eight had begun the course. The twenty-three graduates looked forward to using the intensive flight training they had received in basic and advanced single-engine trainers and advanced multi-engine trainers. They had had night flying, Link time, and instrument flying. With that experience, they were far ahead of us WAFS in transition and a few WAFS felt cheated. We had received cross-country time in puddle-jumpers in return for our patriotism.

After the first class graduated at Houston, its members had a two-

Cochran's cadets pass in review after their 1943 graduation. They were in school at Ellington Field in Houston.

Jacqueline Cochran and other notables pose for the movie cameras at the graduation of her 43-W class in 1943.

week leave, after which they were to report to their respective stations. Their records of flight time went into their 201 files at their new bases. It was at this time that FERD discovered Cochran had not lived up to the agreement she had made.

She was supposed to recommend that applicants who already had 500 hours of solo flight experience report to Wilmington to test their eligibility for the WAFS. Love, on the other hand, was supposed to recommend to anyone applying to the WAFS who did not meet the requirements to report to Houston and apply for the WFTD.

Of the WFTD April graduates assigned as WAFS to the 6th Ferrying Group at Long Beach, FERD wrote, "It should be borne in mind that the average pilot hours flown by each of these five girls was approximately 400 hours at the time of their assignment . . . and that they do not represent a true cross section of the WAFS to be graduated by the Flying Training Command in the future, who will have only 200 hours total time when they graduate."

The merging of the cadet graduates with the WAFS brought up the problem of leadership of the combined pilots. Logically, Nancy Love should have been the head of all pilots hired by FERD. As time went on and FERD could not or would not assimilate pilots with less training and experience, Cochran's leadership would end. But that wasn't what she had in mind. The woman who was destined to lead all women pilots was slated to be decided by the Army Air Forces. The battle of influence was on. And what would happen to us if we became WACs?

On the last day in April, Captain Hennessey said to me, "We're going to give you girls some transition." I only pretended to believe him. We'd been promised that since the middle of January.

On Saturday, May 1, I received something better than a May basket at my door. Lt. Thomas Oakes telephoned me from group operations, saying, "Mrs. Scharr, are WAFS Poole and Donahue back yet?"

"They came in during the night," I answered.

"If you and those two are able to check out in AT-19s today, we'll put you on orders to fly them tomorrow."

"Does transition know this?" I asked.

"We'll tell 'em. Report as soon as you can."

"Roger, wilco."

"Roger, out."

I went to each Barbara's room. "Good news," I said in lieu of greeting and told them. Donnie bolted from her bed. Poole only turned her head. I ignored her show of disinterest — a cup of hot coffee would flush it away. I knew she was just as anxious for something new as Donnie and I were.

I got to transition ahead of them. They had plenty to do that day, for there was laundry and per diem and the past two weeks salary to pick up.

When the instructor led me to dark gray #42-46673, I knew then that an AT-19 was a Stinson Reliant, the plane that Spike Saladin had gone East to buy for his passenger hops off Lambert Field. Spike had declared it was too hot for me to handle. He had been wrong before, as when he said people wouldn't fly with a woman. I'd prove him wrong again. I had developed an assurance about flying during the last seven months of ferrying that I had not been allowed to develop at Lambert. Spike was a gambler. On his way home with his new Stinson, he tangled with rainy weather and set it down in a soft field. It nosed up and the propeller was damaged. Unfortunately, the truck carrying it on to St. Louis was in a traffic accident and it suffered further damage. My newly acquired experience made me realize now that Spike had been an airport pilot and had been lost going cross-country.

After we preflighted the AT-19, the instructor said, ''Read the tech orders when we get back,'' and allowed me to taxi and take off. I followed my usual procedures when flying any airplane I hadn't flown before. Important to me was the AT-19's reactions when I put down the flaps at 2,000 feet during a glide. When I pretended to abort a landing, I milked up the flaps.

The instructor and I played around with steep turns, climbing and gliding turns, and then he showed me how he would land it. He allowed me to make three complete circuits of taxiing, takeoff, traffic patterns, and landing. Then he said, ''You're checked out.'' It had taken sixty-five minutes.

As we entered the transition office, a corporal told us the other two WAFS were flying. I was about to leave when an instructor making out a clearance for an AT-9 check flight asked if I'd like to ride along in the back seat.

''Sure! I'd like that very much,'' I answered.

It had been six weeks since I had flown in the B-25 and any time transition offered me a chance to learn anything, I'd take it. I knew very little about the AT-9 except that it was made by Curtiss-Wright, had twin engines, and a conventional landing gear that the pilot tucked up and let down in flight. Whenever I saw it landing, one bounce followed another until the pilot got it to remain on the runway. I guessed that the fellows being checked out were landing too fast. Men had spoken of the plane as unpredictable and tricky to handle after the first bounce. Anyone who was considered checked out in the AT-9 acted mighty proud of himself. Some pilots said it was the best training tool they had for separating the men from the boys. If you couldn't fly the AT-9, you'd never fly pursuit, especially not the P-39 Bell Airacobra. Someone might be able to fly a twin-engine cargo airplane such as the Douglas DC-3 (or C-47) after a length of time as its copilot, but he'd have trouble flying the P-39 unless he had experience in a tricky plane like the AT-9. No one got dual instruction in a pursuit aircraft, and the first time a pilot went up in it, he went up alone. The AT-9 had no other role in the war effort than preparing pilots for pursuit. It climbed at 120 mph, cruised at about 140 mph, glided at 120 mph, and landed at 110.

For forty-five minutes I sat in the back seat and imagined myself at the controls. After we landed, the instructor turned his head and said, "I want you to change seats and try it."

He took off and then I did fifteen minutes of air work. He landed it. Afterwards, he allowed me to taxi it. I concluded that the AT-9 was harder to fly than was the B-25. I was worried that I might never check out in it.

The next day was Sunday, but that made no difference to the Ferry Command. I went over to group operations early to pick up our orders for the AT-19s.

As Lt. Oakes handed me the orders, he said, "We've had some trouble lately with some independent airport operations, especially Roscoe Turner at Indianapolis and Robertson in St. Louis. There's been a gas shortage in a few military bases, too, so we are routing you to Fort Knox and Memphis and you'll deliver in Dallas. If you have to get into any other airport, be sure it is an army base."

I nodded my agreement. I understood the Robertson situation at Lambert. Major Bill survived by hanging on to a shoestring. His financial position was very precarious and unless he were paid for services immediately, he'd be broke and out of business.

"Do me a favor," I asked Oakes. "Don't send Lenore McElroy on a mission while I'm gone. Somebody's got to mind the store." He agreed.

The weather was too bad for us to leave at once. My mood was just as drippy, for once again I wouldn't be able to see Harold. Would I see him before the navy sent him overseas?

On Monday we were at the flight line at nine o'clock. A front was still hanging on in the area and we'd not be allowed to push off until the weather sequences showed its movement farther to the east. We took off after lunch and I asked Donnie to lead. We had checkpoints galore. We passed close by Toledo, Lima, Dayton, Cincinnati, and Louisville before we landed at Godman Field three and a half hours later. The itinerary afforded us a chance to practice radio procedures. I tuned in a station ahead of us, bracketed the beam on a leg going toward it, and bracketed a beam leaving it. Except for the few Link trainer lessons we had had, we had no previous experience flying "by ear" cross-country.

When we approached the field, I had to lead them around a large danger area designated on the chart where no flying was allowed. It was Fort Knox. Anti-aircraft guns stood ready to prevent anyone from making off with our nation's gold supply. At Godman, the operations people were gracious. They allowed us to remain overnight in a guest house reserved for officers' visitors to the base.

I hadn't been with the Barbaras since March, and they had had many flights together since we moved to Romulus. Since they returned from missions at the same time, operations placed them on the next delivery order together. They were obviously congenial and had formed a buddy arrangement. I felt like the odd man who was not needed in their routine.

On our second morning out. Poole said me, "When we get to Memphis, we're supposed to look up Colonel Nelson."

Surprise slacked my jaw and opened my eyes.

"He's at a meeting with Colonel Tunner and all the group commanders," she explained.

I thought it was strange he had not told me. A weight lay momentarily on my heart. But of course she reinforced his ego and made him laugh with her jokes and pert remarks. He must have dropped the information in a conversation when I wasn't around. Still . . .

I turned my concentration to the AT-19. It had a 285 Lycoming engine and was furnished with an extra gas tank to be used on long hops. When one wanted to use the gasoline from the extra tank, a wobble pump at ceiling height pushed the gasoline into the main tank. The only problem was that there was no gauge to indicate how much to pump.

No one had been designated as flight leader on our flight order. Instead, we were listed in alphabetical order. I decided when we left Godman, the next leg of the flight would be mine. There were far fewer checkpoints than on the hop from Romulus. The rugged terrain over Kentucky and Tennessee made us fear a forced landing. And there were few airports in the area. We'd be trying to fly the radio beams.

I headed due south and the iron beam (railroad) of the Illinois Central coincided until past Cecilia, where I tuned in Smith Grove radio on the 368 frequency, following the southwest leg at approximately 200 degrees. The north edge of the red beam depicted on the chart made a nice straight line to follow. We soon passed Glendale, one of the three

CAA auxiliary fields along the airway to Nashville.

I noticed checkpoints on the ground that I would not have guessed were there from looking at the chart. Although the hills weren't above 1,000 feet and so were not marked with tan lines on the chart, I could easily distinguish the lay of the terrain, seeing by the gullies the path of streams down the hills when heavy rain washed soil and rock away. At one high point just to the north of Gallatin, the third CAA field, streams ran from it to the northwest, southwest, and southeast. The scenery was spectacular. Groups of evergreens dotted the landscape. The streams ran clear and where they leaped over obstructions, the water was white. Dogwoods were in bloom and deciduous trees were just leafing out.

In rounding the turn toward the west at Nashville, I stayed north of Berry Field and picked up the north side of the 246-degree leg on the range frequency of 304. We knew Morse code, but that wasn't a necessity for the aeronautical charts gave each range station's signal in dots and dashes. Nashville's was —. .—. and we could hear it every twenty-nine seconds so we could identify it.

I played around with the wobble pump for a few minutes, even though the flight wasn't long enough to deplete the main tank. Poole, who was flying my right wing 500 feet away, came around from behind and got between me and Donahue. She was maybe a hundred or so feet away and looked as if she were saying something while she waved her wings at me. I quit pumping gasoline. There must be something wrong, I decided. I throttled back, wondering what it could be. I rechecked my instruments. The oil temperature was too hot, so I went into a slower cruise.

Abruptly the two Barbaras flew on ahead and left me. I could not understand why they should do such a thing.

I turned back to the oil temperature. I had had only one similar experience. I had preflighted the Kinner Fleet right after it had had a regular check by Spike's certified mechanic, Franky. The oil level was very low. I told Franky about it, saying, "You must have drained the oil and forgot to put any more in."

He gave me a queer look, went to get a few more quarts, and filled it to my satisfaction. Then I went out to pilot a sight-seeing flight.

The first ride I was hired to pilot on a sight-seeing flight was taken by two unsuspecting little ladies. The ticket seller placed them in the wide front seat of the Fleet, fastened the safety belt, handed them helmet and goggles and made certain that they were secure. Then I started the engine and took them for their ride. They wanted to fly west of Lambert toward St. Charles and the Missouri River.

I was so conscientious that I was not only looking at my watch so we wouldn't cheat Spike out of his profit, but also at other traffic for safety's sake, the terrain for a field to land in if necessary, and the instrument panel to keep an eye on the condition of the airplane. I was headed back to Lambert over small, rough fields when I saw the oil temperature go up and the oil pressure head down!

All I could think to do was to throttle back in hopes of keeping the engine running. At the same time I called Frank Dobbin in the airport tower, "Lambert tower . . . Fleet 69V to Lambert tower. Coming in short. Not in regular traffic pattern."

As we approached the field, letting down with throttle set at putting us into the airport, I thought, those poor, dear old ladies! They trust me and I might not even make it.

But I did. I just made it over the fence at runway #4. The taxiing distance to the Fleet's assigned area along the ramp was short enough that the engine didn't quit until I cut the switch.

I left the plane and whispered to the ticket seller, "No more passengers."

Bob Luce, who was operating Spike's business while he was out of town, said, "What's the matter? We've got customers waiting."

"I'm not flying that airplane until it gets an overall engine check," I told him.

"You're chicken," he answered.

"If you're so brave, you go out and fly it," I said. "But remember what I said." Intuitively, I knew he would not, although he'd have been willing for me to do it.

The Fleet was pulled off the line and checked during the following week. The culprit was discovered — a cracked crankshaft. The old ladies and I had been lucky. The propeller could have fallen off.

Now here I was again, this time all alone, for my wingmen were too far ahead for me to see them, and over treacherous terrain. I throttled back to the slowest cruising speed. The next forty-five minutes were the longest and most apprehensive period I had ever spent in the air.

It was a time for thinking. I had painful, confused thoughts. Didn't the Barbaras realize that I throttled back because I was in trouble? Did they realize it and fly ahead anyway? If I ended my hop at Memphis, how should I treat this incident? A flight was supposed to stick together and RON together. Should I show that my feelings had been hurt? I had learned in childhood to try not to show if I had been hurt.

At last I landed safely. In the operations office I approached Poole and said and as calmly as I could, "What were you signaling about back there?"

She replied, "Your gasoline was flying out the vent on the top of the wing. It looked like it was siphoning out."

My emotions were too strong for speech. A memory popped into my mind of a trip a Lambert acquaintance had made in a Cub. Somewhere in Pennsylvania he was forced to land on a highway because he ran out of fuel. The gas cap had been screwed on wrong and the wind had siphoned the gasoline from the fuel tank, depleting it in a hurry. An experienced pilot like Poole should have realized my danger.

Upon my form I, I wrote that the oil temperature was excessive in the plane. To make sure the problem would get attention, I found the head mechanic and told him what had happened.

He replied, "Don't worry. I'll have the mechanics look it over tonight and if it is flyable, we'll have it ready tomorrow morning."

Operations sent in our RONs, and we made reservations at the nearby Alamo Courts. In the ladies' room at the officers' club, we changed into skirts for dinner. We ran into Lt. Lee Wahl in the lounge. We didn't know he'd be there, too. He told us about the retirement party for Colonel Stevens.

He pleaded, "Take pity on a homesick old buddy from Romulus and let me take you to Colonel Stevens' farewell dinner. There's dancing afterwards, too." Donnie and I accepted the invitation readily.

The dinner was quite a festive affair in spite of the fact that the colonel almost wept when he made his speech. He was going to Great Falls, Montana. I guessed he was the outdoors type because the base personnel gave him fishing equipment as a farewell gift. We heard that Colonel Nelson would be leaving Romulus soon and that we'd be getting a dapper-Dan type named Colonel De Arce.

When Colonel Nelson appeared, he beamed at us and announced, "If you girls get back here by tomorrow evening, we'll have a B-17 here. We'll take you back to Romulus with us and save T/R expenses."

The next day Poole led to Dallas, a five-hour hop. It was the longest I ever sat in one spot without moving and it pained my hip sockets. How did Amelia Earhart manage to sit seventeen and a half hours from Hawaii to California?

The Dallas tower told us that a crosswind of thirty-five miles per hour with gusts up to fifty would greet us on the ground. Yet each of our landings was a perfect three-point, wheels and tail. As I followed the "follow me" jeep to the parking spot, I tusseled with the AT-19, for it was like a stubborn and willful creature that balked at turning out of the wind.

If the others felt as I did, they also must have had a comfortable satisfaction that in a comparatively strange airplane we had whipped the aircraft's tendency to turn into the wind, that we had used the radio range for the first time, and that we were somewhat acquainted with a manifold pressure gauge and a constant speed propeller. It had been a period of transition for us, small as it was, and I prayed that it would continue.

The line boys helped us secure our airplanes and then we loaded our equipment into the back seats of two jeeps, hopped in, and headed for operations. We saw that Love Field was alive with activity and loaded with airplanes.

An officer accepted our AT-19s and while he was processing the papers, Donnie asked him, "What are you going to do with these airplanes?"

He answered readily, "We'll ferry them down to South America. They'll be used for submarine patrol duty because they have such a long cruising range."

At that point a sergeant hurried over and whispered into the lieutenant's ear. His eyes found mine and he said, "There's a long distance call for you. Would you step inside the counter and take it?"

He lifted a hinged section of the counter for me to pass through. I went to the telephone and picked the receiver off the desk. On the other end was a captain in Memphis who said, "Colonel Nelson is ordering you WAFS to fly back only as far as Memphis instead of returning directly to Detroit."

"Yes, I get the message," I replied. "Thank you," and hung up. After the group commanders' meeting in Memphis was over, we'd take a B-17 back to Romulus with Colonel Nelson.

Operations gave us transportation to the civilian section of Love Field, where I exchanged a T/R for our airline tickets. In doing so, I bumped three passengers, who would be forced to wait for the next available flight, regardless of how imperative their needs to be someplace else.

Our baggage was checked and we had time to waste, so we strolled about the terminal building. In a candy store I bought boxes for Harold and my mother and a pleasant clerk promised to mail them directly. Poole said she found a good buy in a brand of liquor that she liked. "This is hard to get," she explained as she carried it onto the plane with her.

Our seats on the DC-3 were not together. There was no need to talk to anyone. I sat tensely, mulling over the muddle of impressions in my mind: of Lee Wahl, his affection for Kay Thompson was finally obvious to me; of the Barbaras, whose close companionship appeared to rule out everyone else; of Burchie, who might not make progress in transition; and of Harold, whom I longed to see and to be with.

By the time we got to base headquarters at Memphis, we already had had a long day. We had gotten up two hours before we took off for Dallas. Our flight there had taken five hours, we had spent two hours on the ground there, and four hours flying back to Memphis. We had not rested for thirteen hours.

But the big chiefs had not finished their powwow, so we sat and waited. Finally, since we had no inkling of how much longer we'd have to wait, we went to the Claridge Hotel to rest, asking someone to call us when the meeting broke up. We paid for a night's lodging, but we did not sleep. We lay down on our beds carefully to keep our uniforms as neat as possible.

Long past midnight we boarded the B-17. Major Hennessey (he had been promoted from captain) was first pilot in the left-hand seat. Colonel Nelson was copilot. Another passenger was Colonel Tunner, who was hitching a ride to Cincinnati, his headquarters.

We WAFS went to the rear of the plane where the B-4 bags and parachutes had been dumped. It was dark and the metal floor was cold. We shoved the parachutes together so we could lie down on them during the flight home. In a few minutes the flight engineer came back to us and called into the darkness, "Mrs. Scharr?"

"Yes?" I answered.

"Colonel Nelson wants you in the cockpit."

I got up and groped my way forward toward the light of the cabin. As soon as he saw me, Colonel Nelson climbed out of his seat and said, "You take my place and see what you can do."

Then he and Colonel Tunner stood behind the pilot seats and watched me. I had never been in this type of airplane before. I had to search the instrument panel for the gauges before I could use them. There was a lot of instrument flight equipment on the panel, such as an artificial horizon and gyroscopic compass. I was very tired, but panic must have energized my adrenal glands, for I was able to maintain an altitude within fifty to a hundred feet and to stay exactly on course. I was fearful every moment of making a mistake that would cause the colonels to relegate the Romulus WAFS to primary trainers forever. Night flying is similar to flying in bad weather using only instruments. I was unfamiliar with both. If I hadn't had some Link time, I'd have been totally inadequate.

After what seemed to me to be an inordinately long session, Colonel Nelson asked me to go back and tell one of the others to come forward to fly. Mindful of seniority, I called Poole to be next. "The colonel wants you up front to play copilot," I said.

I settled down on some parachutes near Donnie. Neither of us spoke after Poole left. Perhaps she thought I was asleep or maybe she was impelled by curiosity or by her need to be with Poole. At any rate, Donahue got up and moved out of the dark, cold rear, disappearing forward where the action was. Once more I was alone.

Eventually the two returned and Poole said, "Colonel Nelson wants you back."

When I returned to the cockpit, Colonel Tunner was standing behind the copilot seat in which Colonel Nelson sat contentedly. I took a position behind Major Hennessey, placing my hands on the top of his back rest.

"We'll be coming into Cincinnati soon," said Major Hennessey, with a quick glance back at me.

"You may as well watch the landing," added Colonel Nelson.

The entire procedure fascinated me — the call to the tower and its answer, the pattern around the empty field, the final approach with flaps down and power diminished. As well as I could judge, Major Hennessey was doing a perfect job. His landing was so smooth that I didn't even feel the wheels contact the runway. He really greased them on.

As the airplane rolled down the runway, Major Hennessey ordered Colonel Nelson, "Flaps up."

The field was very dark and I could see the runway ahead indistinctly. Suddenly the plane lurched as if we had rolled into chuck holes or over rubble. Colonel Tunner and I grabbed the backs of the seats in front of us, trying to keep on our feet. We succeeded, but later I discovered a large blood blister on my left thumb.

As soon as he was aware of the thump — almost immediately — Major Hennessey quickly moved his right hand to the space between him and Colonel Nelson, although I couldn't follow exactly what he did. The B-17 stopped its forward motion and the grating noises of metal on metal stopped, too.

Out of the corner of my eye, I could see that Colonel Tunner's face was ashen. His eyes were like ice. Without any adieus or comments, he left the airplane and disappeared into the darkness.

The rest of us got out, too, and stood on the runway. One of the Barbaras spoke. "What happened? We got bumped around back there something awful."

Major Hennessey deferred to Colonel Nelson, saying kindly, "If you wish, sir, I'll call Romulus and ask them to send us an airplane to take us back to the base."

Colonel Nelson only nodded his head. He was speechless.

A jeep drove up and the driver took us and our gear in relays to the operations office. Major Hennessey vanished. Colonel Nelson also disappeared. We three WAFS waited outside the hangar, huddled together, our minds as much in the dark as the field was.

Not long after, Colonel Nelson returned. He broke our chilly silence, saying, "I need a drink. Does anybody have something?"

Our silence continued, discomfitting all of us until Poole replied reluctantly, "I bought a bottle of rye in Dallas. But it hasn't been opened yet."

"Where is it?" asked the colonel.

Poole did not reply, but walked to our B-4 bags in the dark of the ramp. As a body, we moved with her. She searched about until she found the bottle. Then we continued walking, saying nothing, until Colonel Nelson spotted a staff car beside the hangar. He opened the door, got into the back seat with Poole's rye, and shut the door.

We retraced our steps and upon reaching the flight office, in silent agreement entered and sat down to wait for what we knew would be a very long time. At last Major Hennessey reappeared, saying, "Don't worry, girls. We got transportation home."

He went outside again and I followed him. Hearing my footsteps, he turned and waited for me to catch up.

"What was the matter?" I asked.

Nervously he looked about, as if to make certain that no one could overhear his answer. "The colonel mistook the landing gear switch for the flaps and the landing gear began to retract," he said.

"How come it didn't collapse altogether?"

"The B-17 has an electric switch to raise and lower the landing gear. The gear screws up and down. I stopped it before it totally collapsed."

With that, he took off toward the airplane. As I returned to the flight office, my mind flashed back to the time when I had talked to Freddy Koupal after he had gotten into trouble as first pilot when the landing gear on the B-17 he was ferrying collapsed at Wilmington. The first pilot is the one in command and must take the blame for any mishap. Freddy had been bitter. I could see why Hennessey was not. He had witnesses.

I turned the incident over and over again in my mind in the days that followed. Why hadn't Colonel Nelson been ready with his choice of switches before the last minute? Shouldn't he have anticipated the "flaps up" request? Was he too tired to be flying? Had he been drinking? Had concern about his transfer affected his reaction time? I never learned what it was.

Finally we heard an airplane approaching. A C-60 landed and taxied up to the flight office. No one said a word to the crew about why we were stranded in Cincinnati. Poole went around the hangar to inform the colonel that the airplane had arrived. He followed her to where we waited for the clearance to be made out. Poole had her bottle back and stashed it in her B-4 bag. Donnie and I accompanied her.

Poole whispered in awe, "There's hardly any left."

Yet Colonel Nelson showed no outward signs of having consumed almost a fifth of rye in such a short time. My guess was that Poole would not bring up the subject of what our boss owed her for the liquor. He had often invited us to drink a tiny glass of brandy with him after dinner. We all owed him something for his hospitality. Only Poole was able to return the favor.

We were hungry when we got back to Romulus. After saying good night to Colonel Nelson, who climbed the stairs to his apartment, Major Hennessey led us to the officers' snack bar. The breakfast line would form in two hours, but we didn't feel like waiting, so we raided the snack bar refrigerator, returned to our barracks, and went to bed.

That evening we said nothing about the accident. There was enough gossip being circulated about a B-24 that was wrecked at St. Louis. The crew would have to stand court-martial. I wondered what would happen to Colonel Nelson, for it was obvious that Colonel Tunner had a short fuse about anything he considered unforgivable. Already the word was out that Nelson would be replaced by Ponton de Arce. One officer gleefully related that our new boss had been a clown in a flying circus. I couldn't believe it.

Burchie and Thompson were out on missions when we returned, so Lieutenant Wahl escorted Donahue and me to dinner Friday night. Colonel Nelson took Poole as his partner. People passed our table and stopped to say a few words, but the colonel didn't respond well to these salutations. He did respond to our attempts to brighten the meal by telling us to take the next day off.

On our "day off," Mac, Poole, Donahue, and I went into Detroit to get measured for the new uniforms that the WAFS would soon be ordered to wear. While I was in town, I had lunch with Rose Meyers, who wanted more information from me for a feature article on the Detroit WAFS for *Flying* magazine. I had received permission to give her an interview.

Before returning to the base, I browsed in one of the large downtown stores, looking for something to give the colonel before he went away. A half-dozen tall gin rickey glasses caught my eye because they had etched stars scattered over them. I figured I could make a comment on the card I'd enclose with them about anticipating that the stars would soon replace eagles. I wanted to do something for him because he had done so much to make our stay at Romulus pleasant.

That evening the officers had another party. We looked in on it after we had dinner, and I had several dances before I returned to the barracks. I missed Harold and wanted to be alone with my thoughts. Sunday morning at breakfast, I had word of my husband indirectly. A young lieutenant came to my table and said, "I've just been through Lambert Field."

"Yeah?" I ventured.

"Yeah. I met the field manager, Oscar Parks. I asked him if he knew you."

"How is Oscar?"

"Okay, I guess. He said your husband was around the field somewhere and he wondered if I cared to meet him."

"Did you?"

"Heck, no!" the pilot replied. "Why should I be interested in seeing him? He don't wear skirts."

That morning at ground school, I sat in a Link for an hour, solving a problem of letting down safely into the Detroit airport. From there, I went to transition, where I spent thirty minutes under the hood in a Vultee BT-13 with a 450-horsepower Pratt & Whitney engine.

The instructor said, "All acrobatics are forbidden by the instrument school because they damage the instruments," and he winked at me.

He was the boss, so we did chandelles and lazy eights and S turns along a road. To me those were not acrobatics, but the instrument school may have warned against doing them. All I had in mind as we took turns doing those exercises was to try to perform better than the instructor and in that way pierce an opening in transition for the WAFS to fly more than AT-19s.

"Colonel Nelson says the new WAFS are on their way," I told the WAFS that afternoon. "We got here first, so it's up to us to make them feel at home. Let's be friendly and helpful. You'll be their flight leaders, so you'll have to teach them all the things they'll have to know for when they are flight leaders, too. We're all in this army to win the war. They are, too. We've had a perfect record up here and we don't want to spoil it. So give them all the help you can."

I'd heard a little bitching about "Cochran's girls" and I wanted it to be an attitude of the past. Cooperation should be our aim. No one made any comments about the views I stated. I wasn't sure if what I said only drove the resentment underground.

The six new WAFS arrived before dinner time. They were Gertrude

Twenty-three future WAFS graduated from Jacqueline Cochran's school at El-lington Field, Houston, in April 1943. In the center, with the name tag, is Leni Deaton, staff advisor.

Admiral L. O. Colbert of the U.S. Coast and Geodetic Survey pins wings on his daughter Mary Lou during Cochran's first graduation exercise. Cochran is smiling between the two.

C. Brown, Claire Callaghan, Vega Johnson, Marjorie Ketcham, Margaret E. McCormick, and Elizabeth A. McKinley. They were a good looking crowd, but came to us feeling like hot pilots (HP's). I figured that after a number of L-2B trips, they'd be glad to take a PT trip.

"What kind of airplanes do we ferry?" asked Callaghan.

"Mostly liaison and primary trainers," Poole replied.

"We don't want to go back to PTs," said McCormick firmly and with self-assurance.

That statement, uttered at the dinner table, undid my afternoon's attempt to create harmony. Poole said to me later in her room, "Here we've been ferrying and doing the job while they were being paid to get the training that puts them ahead of us."

Poole had a right to be bitter as she realized that we original WAFS might be passed over in transition. We might be forced to watch as the newcomers were given opportunities that were denied us.

"Just wait and see," I whispered. I knew I'd put my back up and fight any injustice if it came.

The next day I escorted the new WAFS to their first lecture on the Ferrying Division. All the WAFS on base went to the flight surgeon for typhus vaccinations. Afterward, I isolated myself in a Link trainer for an hour to work on radio-telephone procedures. The day ended with a warm shower and shampoo. With it I rinsed away all the cares of my job during the day and slept like a top.

But in the morning, my problems were back. Someone in operations telephoned to tell me that the CAA report I had made out covering the incident at Lambert Field when Burchie stayed up in the snowstorm was not made out properly. I had to go over the office and make it out again.

While I was there, I was asked for a pilot to send to Scott Field to pick up an L-2B to ferry elsewhere. My position as a leader got in the way. How I longed to go — Scott was only across the river from St. Louis — but I could not because I had to shepherd the new WAFS. I chose Burchie as the pilot and she left as soon as she could.

On the way back to the barracks I looked into the post office, hoping I'd have a letter from Harold. Instead, there was a brief letter from my friend Helen Krueger telling me that Harold had taken her out to dinner and she had enjoyed the date. And there was a postcard from John Overall from "somewhere in the Pacific."

Back in my office, I telephoned a local dentist and succeeded in getting an appointment for the next day to replace the filling that had broken in Alliance, Ohio. This was a stroke of luck. Ordinarily dentists were so busy that appointments had to be made a month in advance.

Besides riding herd on my new charges and making them feel at home, the day was full of the usual paper reading, paper shuffling, and paper reporting that went with my job. I was able to get away from it all in the evening.

Sometime earlier I had bought tickets for concerts that featured Lily Pons, the celebrated coloratura soprano, and Jose Iturbi, the great pianist. I asked Capt. Harold Owens of transition how he liked classical music. He said he did. So we went to the Pons concert in the WAFS' old car.

Lily was tinier than I expected and she had a tremendous voice. I heard the aria from *The Daughter of the Regiment* for the first time. Of course I told Harold about my evening and escort. It would have been impossible to invite one of the WAFS — it would have appeared like favoritism.

Lt. Col. Sam Dunlap from the transition school at Long Beach arrived on May 12. He lost no time in telling me that he had gotten Nancy checked out on the West Coast in several planes. He was sure there would be more transition for us. I had the feeling he was infatuated with Nancy. I didn't like him.

One of the WAFS at Long Beach told me later that she overheard a conversation between Nancy Love and Barbara (B. J.) Erickson. B. J. had sought out Nancy, asking her, "What am I going to do? The fellow who's checking me out keeps touching me and it seems to me that he's getting a little too fresh. What'll I say to him? What should I do?"

Nancy answered that B. J. should string him along because future favors might be granted. Try to keep him pacified by not fending off every move he made, she counseled. As soon as B. J. was checked out, she could avoid the man and even renege on any implied promises she had made while he had the power to pass or fail her.

My informant was horrified that an older woman had given such advice to a young woman. I agreed at the time, for sexual harassment was almost unknown to me and had certainly never happened to me in aviation. But now I wonder, were we simply not sophisticated enough for the situations in which we found ourselves?

On Thursday and Friday, two lessons in an AT-6 put two hours and fifteen minutes in my log book. My instructor said at last that I was checked out. Now I was almost at the experience level in transition as my new charges.

But none of us was flying AT-6s. Operations cut orders on Friday for two original WAFS and six new ones to take the train to Canton, Ohio,

Cochran's first graduates are shown at the Taylorcraft factory in Alliance, Ohio, with the L2-B's they were to ferry. From left: Claire Callaghan, Elizabeth McKinley, Marjorie Ketcham, Adela Scharr, Lt. Fairfield, Katherine Thompson, Vega Johnson, Margaret McCormick, and Gertrude Brown.

and from there to go by bus to Alliance to pick up eight L-2Bs. The two Barbaras and Burchie were on missions. Mac had to remain on base for transition. So Kay Thompson led Ketcham, McCormick, and McKinley. I led Brown, Callaghan, and Johnson.

The train ride was fun. The girls were enthusiastic about doing something constructive with their skills. The bus trip was more difficult. The driver thought we took too much time carrying on and arranging our eight parachute bags, eight B-4 bags, and as many navigation kits. He was afraid he'd be late in arriving at Alliance.

We couldn't get out of Alliance that day, so I showed the new WAFS how to make out the RON and send it. The weekend weather throughout the Ohio valley was too poor for contact flight, so we spent the time becoming further acquainted.

Gertrude Brown was aptly nicknamed Brownie. Her short, bobbed hair and her eyes were brown. Her skin was lightly tanned by the Texas wind and sun. She was of average height and struck me as being intense and positive, eager to do well.

Claire Callaghan's hair, a bit longer than Brownie's, was also medium brown, but her gray-blue eyes, fairer skin, and cute, turned-up pixie nose made me anticipate her Irish wit even before she showed it. Her parents lived in Chicago, but she had been working in the CAA bureau in Washington, D.C. before she left for Houston. She wasn't afraid to speak her mind frankly, like a true Irishman, but a reticence still lay behind those laughing eyes.

Vega Johnson was also a brunette of average height. She appeared quieter and younger than the others. I thought she was the prettiest of my three attractive wingmen.

Kay's charges included two taller women, Marjorie Ketcham and Margaret McCormick. Ketcham was softer and stouter than McCormick. I wondered if her apparent femininity would hinder her in coping with the hardships I knew she would meet. Each of these girls had graduated from the cadet school, so each must have had some iron in their wills. Ketcham confessed that she had never driven an automobile, certainly a sign of a lack of sophistication.

McCormick was a true blonde, with golden hair and pale blue eyes. She was quite pretty in a delicate British way, but appeared older than the others, for fine lines were already etched about her eyes and at the corners of her mouth. She told us that she had flown a Howard aircraft as a civilian before the war.

Elizabeth McKinley was a petite, quiet, wistful girl with dark blonde hair and blue eyes in a kitten face. One didn't find out what was on her mind.

On Monday the weather appeared to be reaching contact flight conditions, but at the next sequence along our route, it was worse. It was only when I was positive that we could safely go beyond Lockbourne that I made out my clearance and Kay made out hers. We couldn't see the sun through the thick cloud cover. The day remained bleak and the sky dark, but we took off with Kay's flight following mine.

Two hours and ten minutes later I landed first and turned my L-2B on the taxi strip in order to watch the others land. Every L-2B came in at the same distance from the one in front or in back and each made a perfect approach and a three-point landing. These girls are good, I thought, and I bragged on how well they did when we all got settled for the night at the base.

The next day Kay and I appointed one of our members to lead the flight to Patterson Field near Dayton. From there we went on to Richmond, Indiana, and got to Indianapolis before noon, after three hours and twenty-five minutes of flying. We were ready for a short break.

I really didn't relish dealing with Roscoe Turner's establishment again, but in L-2Bs, we couldn't avoid doing so. After we stood around making certain that gasoline was put into each tank and checking that the tanks were indeed full, the paperwork was put in the hands of his office staff. We used the waiting time that Roscoe always gave ferry pilots by doing the only sensible thing — we ate lunch.

We got into Terre Haute seventy minutes after we took off from Indianapolis. By now the girls were displaying some fast teamwork. We got away from there in plenty of time to get into Scott Field an hour before sundown. The weather was turning sour and it began to rain. Two male pilots from Romulus came in after we did. They were also flying puddle-jumpers.

I escorted the girls to the office and saw that each obtained a room in the visiting officers' quarters marked "off limits" to members of the male sex. It was only after I pointed out the officers' club and mess that I left Kay with our fledgling ferriers and returned to the main gate at Scott to board an intercity bus bound for St. Louis. Then I rode two city buses home. My heart had been aching to return for weeks.

The weather did not clear for takeoff until Friday, May 21. The concrete was still wet and the skies dark when we checked the flyability of our planes and discovered that one of the Romulus male pilots had made a chalk drawing with a label on each L-2B. How he knew which plane belonged to whom, I do not know. One was depicted as "Little Petunia." Mine was labeled the "Wabash Cannonball," because that train, according to the song, was also "long and tall."

The navy had opened a brand-new cadet training field at Vichy, Missouri (north of Rolla), because there was no longer enough room in the traffic pattern at Lambert for all of them. I led the run there because I felt that Missouri pilotage was very tricky. So many streams bend and curve back like hairpins around the bases of the Ozark hills and it's easy to get lost. So rather than embarrass the new WAFS, I took on the problem myself. My try for 100 percent accuracy wasn't off more than the width of a small Ozark pasture. I hoped that the others could learn more about pilotage if they weren't under the pressure of leading the flight, feeling the close watch of eagle eyes ready to pounce on a mistake.

We skipped Rolla, the usual liaison stop, and headed for Springfield, Missouri. On the way to Tulsa we noticed a new, large lake filling near the town of Ketchum. At Tulsa, as they had at Vichy, each WAF made such a beautiful landing that I choked with pride.

There was still flying time left in the day, so we pressed on to Tinker Air Force Base near Oklahoma City, totaling six hours and five minutes of flying time. Tinker Field was a huge depository for all sorts of aviation goods from which the AAF could draw. One part of the large warehouse complex was an immense barracks for itinerant pilots. Each of us was assigned her own room along a long corridor. I noticed at this stop that several of the newcomers drank, which was not unusual among pilots of that era. But one odd incident happened that stuck in my mind.

I had undressed and was in my night clothes ready for bed when a knock summoned me to my door. I unlocked it and in came Callaghan, tipsy, it appeared to me. Because of my position as CO, she and Mc-Cormick had jokingly begun to call me "Mommy."

Callaghan made a few inconsequential remarks about the mission thus far. Much that she said was irrelevant and repetitious. I was tired and my lack of response may have led her to ask, "Are you going to bed?"

"Yes," I answered, thinking that I would as soon as she left.

But then Callaghan made herself more comfortable by sitting on my bed and continuing her conversation in which thoughts tumbled out in no logical sequence whatever. I took her to be a highly intelligent person and assumed that liquor had loosened her tongue. I was sure that in the morning she'd regret having bothered me.

Like a weary, willful child, she declared, "Mommy, I want to sleep with you tonight."

"No, you can't do that," I answered. "I never sleep with anybody."

"No, Mommy. I'm going to stay right here and sleep with you."

With no experience handling a situation like this, I did the best I could. "You're supposed to sleep in your own room," I said. "What is the number of your room?"

She told me and stretched out on the bed. I knew she hadn't gone to sleep yet, but was close to passing out. The only solution I could figure out was to go to her room, lock the door after me, and go to bed. My intuition told me to leave.

The next morning I went back to my room to dress and she returned to hers. I never said a word about that visit to anyone else and we two never mentioned it.

The weather bureau forecast spotty showers for that day. We hadn't flown far when showers developed to the east at our left. I maintained my course. A few drops sprinkled on our windshields, but that was all. As we flew farther into Oklahoma, the terrain became rougher. There were large rock outcroppings all along our route. We flew into some rain just north of Ardmore Airfield, but the ceiling did not lower and the visibility was good enough. I could almost feel the alert attitude of the pilots behind me. They were ready for anything.

We landed at noon. Two jeeps came to our rescue. Rain was falling harder now and we would not be leaving Ardmore in a hurry.

"Where can we eat?" I asked the driver nearest my airplane as I tied it down.

"We have a cafeteria," he replied.

We left all of our paraphernalia in the planes except for our purses. The earlier drizzle became a drenching rain during our ride to the cafeteria. When we arrived, we were too damp to be ironed dry.

The cafeteria was a large one-story building, stark plain in decor. The chow line had reached its tail-end when we lined up and filled our trays. At the checkout, the attendant was dispensing drinks. I didn't want milk because it made me sleepy, so I asked for coffee and was handed the most generous amount in the largest cup I had ever seen.

But one sip of that coffee and I was back with it to ask if I could have tea instead. Back to the table I went, knowing coffee might be terrible, but one couldn't go wrong on tea. I tasted the tea. It was as foul as the coffee. Only then did I realize that the water was the culprit. There was too much chlorine in the water system. Once more I traded, this time for milk.

We waited all afternoon as the rain continued and the weather remained below minimums for contact flight. We had to RON at the base. The operations office staff secured a room for each of us in the nurses' quarters. We were lucky to be taken there in sedans instead of open jeeps. The nurses and doctors told us they were having a party that night, since it was Saturday and there was nothing else for them to do. The nearest town was named Gene Autry to honor the cowboy movie balladier. It was, we found out, only a wide place on a nearby road.

With time to spare before the evening meal and since we were terribly thirsty, we got a ride to Gene Autry where some of us got 3.2 beer. I asked for a soft drink, which wasn't very tasty either. Since Oklahoma was a dry state, the party was a big event in the lives of the medical corps at Ardmore. It promised genuine alcohol, so the WAFS appeared interested in attending.

We wanted to be socially acceptable for the event, so we took showers. For several days and several showers afterward, I could still sniff the faint odor of chlorine on my skin.

The party was held in the dayroom of the nurses' barracks. The doctors had easy access to it because it was part of the hospital complex. They drifted in and chatted quietly. The evening was dull until one of the doctors appeared with some liquid he said he had requisitioned.

"What is it?" I asked.

"Grain alcohol," he said.

Drinks were prepared for everyone, but I wouldn't touch the stuff. The imbibers tried awfully hard to be gay and sociable. To me the party was still dull. I thought that Brownie got a little high on the concoction — no wonder. The alcohol content was 100 percent, not cut as it is in commercially sold whiskey. I was afraid it could harm our girls to drink it. The next morning Brownie looked terrible, with dark circles under her eyes and without her usual gaiety.

Regardless of how pilots in the two flights felt that Sunday morning, Kay and I led them to Perrin Field at Sherman, Texas, in a forty-five minute flight. From there I called the airline in Dallas for reservations. We caught the bus to Love Field and returned to Detroit from there.

At Romulus Kay and I showed our charges how to turn in their receipts and other forms and how to obtain per diem. We congratulated each other on doing a fine job.

No sooner were we back than an incident occurred that would have a bearing on our future. Burchie came into my room. Her gnome- like face was serious, colorless, and frowning.

She said, "I think the cleaners have lost my uniform. What shall I do?"

She had returned to the base from her last mission. While receiving her per diem, she saw that there was time to get to the cleaners to pick up the uniform she had left there.

"I asked for my uniform and the attendant looked and said, 'It's not here.' I got the ticket out of my purse and told her the number would show her which was mine. She looked again for a long time through those crowded racks and she still couldn't find it. So she called the proprietor and he came over to the counter and said to me, 'Don't worry. A pilot Donahue came in to have her uniforms cleaned and she said she'd pick up Burchfield's and take it down to the barracks with her. So she took it along."

An unhappy Burchie continued her story. "I thought it was nice of Donnie to bring the uniform back with her, although I hadn't noticed it in my room when I came back on base. So I looked for it in my room again and I even looked in Donnie's room and it's not there either.

My suspicions were aroused, but I feared to mention them. I knew that Burchie would brood over her missing uniform all night long. I had to say something.

"What if you are put on orders again real soon? How dirty is the uniform you have on?"

Burchie replied, "I can wear this for another mission as long as it's not a long one."

She glanced down at what appeared to me to be a perfectly clean uniform. Burchie was always neat and careful. I hoped I was masking the worry I felt for her. She sighed and said, "I guess I'll go back to the cleaners tomorrow. Maybe they made a mistake."

Lenore McElroy in an AT-9, July 1943.

McElroy was about to leave the barracks for her home in Ann Arbor for the night. If Mac knew anything, she'd tell me straight. I searched her out and asked, "Mac, have you any idea where Burchie's uniform could be?"

McElroy knew. She replied, "Donnie has Burchie's uniform. She didn't have a clean one and she took Burchie's from the cleaners and she and Poole went on their mission with Donnie wearing it."

Overhearing this, Burchie looked as if she were ready to faint.

"But Donnie can't fit into Burchie's clothes any more than I can!" I protested.

"Well, they didn't fit very well. The sleeves were up to here." McElroy pointed with her right hand to midway between her left wrist and elbow. "And the pants were really high-water. But she squeezed into it all right."

Burchie said dully, "What if I have a quick call for another mission? And what if Donnie doesn't get back in time?"

"I'll do my best about that," I assured her. Along with my sympathy for the meticulous Burchie was a premonition of disaster.

Burchie was not chosen for a mission for several days. McElroy went off with McCormick and Callaghan. Brown was having a bad reaction to her small pox vaccination, so she stayed put. Kay took all of her group out in L-5s.

Burchie went to ground school transition and I got into an AT-6 again on Tuesday. The instructors must have really liked to fly, for one went with me. I had a feeling that the men couldn't quite believe a woman could fly that hot plane by herself. On the next day, I was able to log another hour and forty-five minutes. I guess I flew with every instructor they had in the school. I was convinced I could fly the AT-6 and could not understand that they weren't, for I had checked out in it May 14.

While I was away last time, Colonel Nelson had left — banished to the Hump, said the gossip, because of his negligence with the B-17. The new colonel, De Arce, had arrived and was beginning to run things his way.

My work load of keeping track of the WAFS and their flying time started to gain momentum, for the weather was flyable almost every day. The base was hopping with activity, and operations had almost too much to do.

As pilots came in from missions all over the country, we pieced together from their bits of information, what was happening to Burchie's uniform. In order to be clothed properly enough to enter any officers' club, Donnie had to be in uniform. If all she had brought on her mission was her pilot coveralls, she would be taboo in every officers' club that we knew about. If she changed at night into a dress, she might be mistaken for a local woman, an officer's pick-up. If she hadn't borrowed Burchie's uniform, the card-playing duo would have missed all the fun of gin rummy after dinner.

The pilots who had seen her joked about Donnie's appearance. One after another of the men would say, "Donahue says to tell Burchie not to worry. She's taking care of her uniform." Then they would laugh like hyenas.

At last the uniform returned. Donnie was smart enough to leave it at the cleaners before Burchie saw it. To Burchie she said, "It'll be ready day after tomorrow." No apologies; no hint of what was to come.

Burchie picked it up herself. It was no longer a uniform she could cherish. It looked several years old and couldn't hold a crease. I guessed that it must have been very badly soiled, for the woolen cloth looked as if it had lost its life. The color was no longer gray-green, but brownish.

My hunch was that Burchie now felt as if she had only one good uniform and shrank from wearing the other. She grew even quieter and more serious. I knew she missed George. She needed someone on whose shoulder she could lean and who might help her recover from the hurt she had received.

Burchie had been the victim of a joke. I soon found out she was not the only one. One evening as Donnie was recounting their adventures, she topped her epic with this story.

"We won every place we stopped and especially in one officers' club. When we picked up the money, I said, 'Don't forget who cleaned you out. My name is Scharr and I'm the head WAF at Romulus. Remember – Scharr!' " Donnie laughed impishly.

She's only trying to vex me, I thought, so I tried not to show my shock and irritation. I even managed a faint smile. Months later her words carried more import than I sensed at the time. In retrospect, I think that I should have told all my WAFS problems to Nancy. At the time, I believed that Nancy would have considered it snitching and would have forgotten that it was she who had burdened me with this responsibility.

In contrast to the 3rd Ferrying Group, which released its new WAFS from their orientation after four days, the 2nd Ferrying Group was more leisurely about placing their newcomers on orders. Colonel Tunner had insisted that the FTC not brief their cadets in the tasks involving ferrying aircraft for ATC. In compliance, Colonel Baker set up a special ground school to acquaint the new WAFS there in the specialized paperwork necessary for ferrying.

Very soon Colonel Baker showed displeasure at his new team because five of the six had family homes close to NCAAB. He grumped that the army policy of assigning male officers away from the home towns should apply to WAFS, ignoring the fact that we weren't militarized and that Civil Service had no objection to its employees living close to their place of employment.

Eleanor Boysen was one of those five. She lived in a guest house at DuPont and entertained her classmates there. She did not see that she must live in BOQ 14 on the base. At Romulus, Capt. Clarence and Lenore McElroy returned to their off-base home at night. They paid their barracks bill like the rest of us. They were as sincere and efficient in their duties as the best.

And how could Baker overlook Capt. Bert Lambert, living at Kent Manor during his off-duty hours? One reason he could — and the reason he could clamp down on Boysen — was that Boysen's interpretation of being in the Civil Service meant that she would work the same hours as all others under that system, an eight-hour day only five and one-half days per week. Her attitude incensed Baker and her ideas about working hours did not conform to the realities of the Ferry Command. She was transferred to Dallas to prove to her that other ferrying groups also worked overtime as needed. The transfer gave her an opportunity to fly heavier and faster aircraft, but her attitude was set and eventually she left Dallas and FERD.

During the last week in May, I flew three times in the AT-6. On Friday, May 28, an honest-to-goodness hotshot pilot, J. D. Brown, who was new to the transition school, asked me to take a hop with him in a B-26. I sat in the copilot seat like a bump on a log while Brown took charge of all controls. The glide to a landing was roller-coaster breathtaking to me. An even greater thrill was the ninety minutes Ralph Parr allowed me in the left-hand seat of an AT-9. I didn't master it, and I feared I might not make the grade.

The following day I felt somewhat better about my chances, for my instructor for eighty minutes was J. D. Brown. When we returned to the flight office, he said with authority, "Let her fly an AT-6 anytime she gets a chance." I was so happy.

Sunday was usually a good day to lasso an airplane in transition. I took out AT-6 #541 for an hour in the morning and #898 for a half hour in the afternoon. The two AT-9s were not flyable; mechanics were giving them twenty-five-hour checks.

I was feeling very lonely because there was no one I could confide in on the base. Lee Wahl, our friend and flight surgeon, had been transferred. I was afraid to mention to instructors or to the men in operations anything that bothered me about the girls. I wrote to Harold. It told him my fears that one new WAF was drinking too much. I thought that if she kept it up, she might be fired. I thought Poole might be, too, but for a different reason.

I obtained transition for Poole on Friday, May 28. It was darned hard to engage any instructor because of the demand for airplanes, which were either in the air or on the ground being worked on by mechanics. The only available time for Poole was right after sunup the next morning, Saturday. We WAFS had learned to take whatever was handed to us and not to grouse about it.

I thought Poole would be delighted with the assignment, since she had been out on missions when chances for transition had come up before. Her face showed no emotion when I told her. Late in the afternoon she said she was unhappy staying at the barracks and was going to go to Detroit and check into a hotel for the night. My authority did not extend into her personal life, but I reminded her of how hard it was to get AT-6 transition and urged her to be back in time for it. It seemed awfully odd to me that a night at the home base would be so distasteful, for she had been off the base much of the time.

The next morning I got a telephone call at the barracks. Poole was on the other end of the line saying, "I don't feel well enough to fly. I'm canceling out."

Kay Thompson shown in a Curtiss-Wright P-40. It was a posed photo — she never flew the plane. The vivacious pilot was a United States olympic champion swimmer, having participated in the 1936 games.

The Curtiss-Wright P-40.

I knew by the hour that even if I could persuade her to change her mind, she'd never get back in time. How would a no-show appear to transition instructors? I simply had to find someone to take Poole's place so the hour would not be wasted. I ran around the barracks to find someone to fly and Ketcham jumped at the chance.

I was puzzled by the ambiguity in Poole's words and behavior. She complained about not being given opportunities to fly faster airplanes. Yet when she had a chance to do so, she put herself into a position so that it was impossible. I decided that I would tell her she was eligible for transitional training, but I would not make another date for her. Only when she showed a true interest in it, we would proceed. I determined not to take her gripes as seriously as I had before.

In the intervening years, I came across the book *Games People Play* by Eric Berne. After studying it, I came to the conclusion that perhaps without being aware of doing so, Poole was playing a game. I think that on one hand she was proud of being a pilot and truly wished to get into larger, faster airplanes. On another hand, subconsciously she feared being washed out and shrank from the stigma. She also may have feared the airplanes themselves. We had heard enough about accidents to make all of us cautious.

Poole said she had made parachute jumps during the barnstorming era. Maybe she had been badly frightened by an incident then. Or perhaps something about the AT-6 test in Montreal, when she was trying to get into Britain's Air Transport Auxiliary, caused her anguish. Poole had not established the patient, plodding stability that tides a person over rough times. Her temperament could not seem to take monotony or hardship as well as the rest of us. She may have been more sensitive than most children or been allowed her own way when she was very young. I recalled that she said she had been sent to a boarding school as a child and didn't like it, so she set a fire. She was forgiven and remained there. After she set the second fire, although it was minor, she was dismissed. That was probably what she wanted. And when she made it impossible to get to transition, that also must have been a wish. The subconscious plays tricks on us all.

The Barbaras may have worked well together because they were both clever. If one suggested a whim, the other caught the significance of the caprice and joined in the fun. We uninspired sticklers to the rules were inhibited by checks that kept us in lines where we believed we must stay. We were each programmed by our individual pasts and only occasionally could we reveal who we really were.

Kay Thompson began her transition into bigger planes on Monday, May 31, with time in an AT-6. Lieutenant Schwarzhoff took three of us pilots to share an hour in an AT-9, and all I got was twenty minutes. I was at a critical stage in transition and would not be placed on orders until I checked out in the AT-9. Flying was keeping me busy, and in the evenings when I was already tired, I recorded how many hours each WAF flew in each type airplane she'd been in that month. The new WAFS were hard to catch and as hard to make understand the importance of keeping records correctly. They often returned from a mission in the middle of the night and before they knew it, they were on orders and gone again.

Supply gave me a large bulletin board, and I made a chart which I put in the middle of the hall, convenient to all, where the WAFS might leave their flight times for me to record. I still had to tail some of them to remind them. There seemed to be a competition going as to who could fly the most hours that month. They didn't want to take any time off, even for legitimate reasons, such as menstruation.

I was becoming alarmed by my own cycle, because I was bleeding in mid-period. The fear of cancer nagged at my mind, but I felt I could do nothing about it. And I didn't know whom to talk to.

I missed Harold very much. I received a letter from him on June 4 telling me how lonesome he was. It brought tears to my eyes. I felt that I hadn't seen him for a very long time. June was a special month for us

— we had three anniversaries, including our wedding anniversary on June 17. To be without him then seemed almost unendurable.

But there was much to keep my mind occupied. One of our problems was the wearing apparel for WAFS on duty. The new women wore civilian clothing, everything from plaid to corduroy, and any type of shoes. The uniforms of the original WAFS were an obvious sign of difference between us and the newcomers. New regulations wiped out that distinction when all of us were informed we could wear the same uniform that the men wore: khaki cotton trousers, shirts, and overseas caps. They could be purchased anywhere in the country, at any department store, and on post or base exchanges. By this time, the weather was much warmer and we could launder the summer cotton uniforms ourselves. We finally returned our winter flying togs to supply.

I was forced to spend a great deal of time at my desk and was very pleased when Mac showed up one morning with a vase full of lilacs, Dutchman's-breeches, iris, tulips, and bridal wreath, so that I had some taste of spring in Michigan.

I attended the colonel's staff meetings when requested and discovered that military staff decisions were arrived at in a much more democratic way than we civilians had believed. Even a WAF or a lieutenant had the right to speak up on a subject pertinent to the ferrying group. The opinion was heard courteously, without any pooh-poohing by all assembled. Of course any expressed idea had to be a serious attempt at solving the problem in question. And no one appeared hurt if his or her solution was not accepted by the colonel, who listened to everyone and then based his resolution on his own judgment of the evidence.

BELL'S BOOBY TRAP

EVERY SO OFTEN SOMEONE would tell me the good news that, as the WAF leader, I was slated to be the first woman in the area to fly the P-39. But before I could, I had to check out in the AT-9. I wasn't at all certain that I would ever get over that hurdle.

On June 1 Lieutenant Parr instructed me for an hour in the AT-9. I began to feel more comfortable with it. A routine was beginning to shape up in the circuit around the field. At takeoff, after engine run-up and magneto check, I made sure that the flaps were up, trim tabs set for takeoff, props full forward, cross feed on, and gas on the desired tank. I rolled forward on the runway at least a ship's length and locked the tail wheel, set the mixture on full rich, and took off on full throttle. As soon as we were airborne, I got the gear up, allowed the nose to dip to get flying speed faster, climbed at 120 mph, and pulled the boost back to twenty-four inches of mercury and set the rpm at 2,000. Then I climbed to 1,000 feet above the airport, drew the boost back to twenty-one inches and the rpm to 1,850. I made an accurate traffic pattern, looking before all turns and staying at altitude. Half-way down the

The Curtiss AT-9 trainer, shown in the spring of 1943.

downwind leg, I dropped the landing gear at no more than 140 mph and boosted the manifold pressure to twenty-two inches and rpm to 2,000. I checked that the indicators and pop-ups showed the gear to be down.

After turning on the final approach, I cut the boost to fifteen inches, cut the speed to 120 mph, and let down the flaps. The props were full forward, in case I had to go around the pattern again. Down to the runway as close as I could, holding off and back with the throttle, I let the wheels roll when I couldn't hold off any longer. I moved the control wheel forward and kept the plane straight on the runway until the tail dropped by itself. I had a bit of trouble with bouncing, for the speed and the plane's attitude needed getting used to. It was busy-busy-busy all around the circuit.

The next day Schwarzhoff took me out for fifty-five minutes. When I came in, I knew. My worry had melted away. As always there were questioning glances and this time I answered them aloud.

I said, "Today I am a man."

Everyone laughed. My instructor half nodded his head and smiled at my using the expression the men used. That afternoon Lieutenant Points took me back to AT-9 #127 and I checked out.

Now I was supposed to be ready for the P-39. Was I? I knew nothing about the airplane except hearsay. Everyone on the base had an opinion about that airplane and wasn't meek about voicing it. Certainly my ears withstood a barrage of opinions, mostly negative. Even E. L. Taylor, the night guard of the Bowling Green field where I had landed in May, had thoughts about the Airacobra. He sent me a letter with news from the airfield.

"There has been two crack-ups here recently," he wrote. "One captain pilot was killed when his P-39 crashed, and two or three days later another captain pilot took off from here for Nashville about 6:30 p.m. and had to bail out. It was also a P-39. So if you ever fly one of those babies be careful."

The number of Romulus pilots who agreed with Taylor's letter grew. They told me the P-39 was a killer. Some of these pilots flew cargo planes, such as the C-47. They were not six-footers, so were not considered as bomber pilot material. The P-39 had a smaller cockpit than other pursuit aircraft and the seat was not adjustable. Anyone taller than seventy inches couldn't fit — and breathed a happy sigh of relief.

Ferrying pursuit aircraft was the mark of a daring and devil- may-care pilot. (Although combat pilots called such airplanes fighters, the Ferrying Division always referred to them as pursuit aircraft.) One such plane was the P-40, made by Curtiss-Wright, which had gained notoriety with the Flying Tigers unit led by Gen. Claire Chennault. This unit attempted to defend China from aerial raids by the Japanese even before the United States entered the war. The planes' noses were painted to look like killer tiger sharks with mammoth teeth.

I was unaware in 1943 that in the pursuit arena the P-40 was considered a step upward in transition to flying the North American P-51 Mustang, the Republic P-47 Thunderbolt, or the Bell P-39 Airacobra. As soon as a pilot survived pursuit training in one kind of aircraft, he was shipped out to do the job for which he had been trained. He might never have seen any other types until he returned to this country. If he lived to come back.

FERD had the task of taking pursuit aircraft to either flying school or to ports of debarkation for overseas. It upgraded its pilots to fly and deliver these ships quickly and safely. This goal differed from the FTC pursuit instruction where students learned the limits of the aircraft they flew and tried to fly one plane exclusively so that they knew it intimately. They took chances; we did not.

There was no way to avoid talk about the P-39. Wherever pilots gathered — to eat, drink, or wait for instruction in the ready room — someone could be heard expressing a sharp criticism of that airplane. Many had heard through the grapevine that Colonel de Arce wanted

The Bell P-39 Airacobra. Its Allison liquid-cooled engine was mounted aft of the cockpit, as was the airscoop — a serious design flaw.

me to fly it and so I received much well-intended advice.

One blond in his late twenties told me, "I just told Major Hennessey I'll be happy to be a copilot in a C-47 for the duration of the war. I don't want to fly pursuit." With a dogged seriousness he added, "They can court-martial me first."

He had good reason to fear the Airacobra. Not only did we see scary happenings at the base, but tales were spread by pilots from other bases where accidents had occurred.

The P-39 had me uneasy. It was an unknown. I would do as I was told and report to transition for ground school to overcome my ignorance. Meanwhile I was able to catch an hour in an AT-6 on June 3 and ninety minutes on June 11. Two days later, a Sunday, I got in two hours and twenty minutes. Monday I flew the AT-9 again for forty-five minutes, but was not allowed to take it alone. I had to have a copilot.

There was much to occupy my time. I had my last shot in the series, this one for cholera, and I had to oversee the immunizations of the other WAFS. I was trying to sort out the new personalities in my care. I was concerned about Elizabeth McKinley's lack of spark and good humor and asked Ketcham if she was normally so withdrawn and aloof. She didn't appear to feel at home.

Ketcham was honest. "She wants to go to Marjorie Kumler's base.

She was good friends with Kumler all through training and the reason she doesn't like it here is because she isn't with Kumler. That's all.''

WAFS came back from a mission with Burchie as leader complaining about her. They said she didn't explain things and didn't help them learn the necessary procedures. To be fair to her, Burchie was not cut out to be a "take charge" person. She didn't impose her personality on anyone. I think she feared doing so. By this time anyway the new girls should have caught on to most of what they needed. Every ferry mission offered new challenges to pilots — that applied to old and new alike.

On the other hand, some flight leader reports indicated that some of the new WAFS did not follow directions. They led the flight away from course and the flight leader had to step in to herd them toward the intended airport. All in all, flight leaders thought leading was a big headache. However, the safety record of the Romulus WAFS was 100 percent accident-free — until Marjorie Ketcham embarrassed us.

Ketcham hit a field marker with the low wing of her PT while on a mission. The flight leader reported that grass at the field was uncut and very high, making the marker's position hard to detect. A slit in the fabric forced the flight to remain overnight while mechanics repaired it and inspected it for further damage. They discovered that a workman had left a large, long-handled screwdriver in the wing. Apparently it slipped down when the fabric was cut, caught on the marker and lengthened the rip. The cost of repair was $24, and Ketcham was ajudged blameless for the accident. We breathed easier after the verdict was reached.

Ferry pilots who had been cadets first and had flown high- powered aircraft in training had difficulty in adjusting to the liaison and primary trainers they were assigned to deliver. The intuition, alertness, and self-control needed to handle a small airplane after flying a large one resulted in too much stress. Or perhaps the small craft offered no challenge. At any rate, pilots were cracking them up. My (kind) opinion was that gliding speed was so slow in small planes that pilots feared they were stalling, so they came in too fast and overshot the runway. As cadets, radios had kept them on course. Without a radio, and without training in the kind of pilotage that I knew so well, they got lost.

The luckier cadets (depending upon the viewpoint) were shifted into transition for the P-39. I watched the takeoffs, landings, and taxiing that went on at the field every chance I could. The young second lieutenants showed their boyishness each time one entered the cockpit of a P-39. Their badge of courage was red — each bought a red baseball cap with a red bill. As soon as a looie was in the plane, he furtively slid off his khaki overseas cap or officer's hat, ducked his head and came up with the red cap, which indicated his accomplishment — soloing the P-39. Then, perky as a rooster and looking just as cocky as a bantam, he'd start his engine. The airplane came to life as no other did. It shivered, almost with anticipation, for all the world like a lively puppy about to jump on its master's lap.

As the P-39 rolled down the runway on takeoff, I thought it was the sexiest airplane I had ever seen. Unlike a puppy, however, it rolled and rolled before the pilot had speed enough to lift the nose wheel off. Then at last the main wheels were off and geared up.

On the same runway, another plane was often also approaching. I watched one come in steep. The pilot didn't round off the bottom until he was almost at the runway. There weren't any bounces, as seen with the AT-9, for the P-39 had an unconventional landing gear. The landing was fast on the main wheels, and the pilot sat hoping he could keep the nose wheel in the air as long as Capt. Lloyd Melichar did. I judged that Melichar was about ten years older than most of the boys because his dark blond hair was already thinning and his build was stocky. Uniforms didn't fit him with the sharp crispness of youth. Any time he brought in a P-39 from the Bell factory, I knew it was he by the landing. No one else could match his performance. Very often he ferried a P-39 carrying the extra large belly tank, which allowed a pilot enough fuel for six hours of flying instead of three. It required a faster glide and landing speed.

Because of the tricycle gear, the pilot could see the runway ahead and keep the takeoff straight. In landing, the tendency to ground loop was supposed to be eliminated by its design.

The P-39 had very clean lines, like a bullet. It was also reputed to be unforgiving if a pilot made a mistake. One instructor who was with me in an AT-6 showed me a high speed stall after gaining 10,000 feet. After the recovery, he pointed out the altimeter and said, "If you fly the P-39, I want you to remember that it has a vicious high speed stall. You saw what altitude we lost in recovery. If you stall out a P-39 near the ground, you won't have a chance."

Gossip that I overheard among pilots taught me more. The tricycle landing gear and the flaps were energized by electric motors. An "up" snap of the switch on each would cause either mechanism to take an "up" position. Woe unto the pilot who got the switches mixed!

The P-39 was used in the African desert forays against the German General Rommel. It had a cannon in its nose which fired through the gear box and the hub of the propeller. Two heavy machine guns of .50

caliber each were synchronized to fire through the propeller. When armed after they'd been ferried, four .30 caliber guns were mounted on the wings. Because of the 20mm cannon in the nose, the engine was placed aft in the fuselage to the rear of the pilot's seat and this caused some complications. The Allison 1200-horsepower engine was in-line and was inadequately cooled, especially while being run up on the ground. This added one more thing for a pilot to remember — to watch the coolant temperature and to check the coolant level before each flight. A ten-foot shaft connected the engine to the propeller. It caused the vibration that made the plane look so lively.

One story that scared prospective P-39 pilots was that if the nose wheel did not lock after landing, the nose would go down and the inertia of the heavy engine behind the pilot's seat could crush the pilot. Another problem was that the Airacobra was heavily armor- plated for the pilot's protection. This added to its weight and took away from the maneuverability that fighter planes needed for success.

A large number of young pilots at Romulus had soloed the P-39, made at least ten landings in ten hours (instead of the three takeoffs and landings required at other bases), made three deliveries from Buffalo or Niagara Falls and were now on longer missions. They delivered the planes as far away as Great Falls, Montana, or Calgary in Canada. Some dreaded a mission to Alaska, where the planes were handed over to the Russians. They were in awe of the high Canadian Rockies and knew that the risks were great if they went down in the wilds of that rugged country. There was only one RON stop on the way, at Fort Nelson in the northwest corner of Alberta. The single barracks there was for males only, so I guessed I would not see Alaska during World War II.

I knew most of the young P-39 pilots by sight but not by name. One was a short chunk of a fellow whom his pals called "Mister Five by Five." He was stolid and never spoke. In contrast, a southerner named Sonny was constantly moving. A favorite mannerism of his was to sneak his hands beneath the rear of his uniform blouse with arms akimbo. As he ran about in a small circle, he flapped the rear of his jacket as if he were rapidly flirting a tail and repeated loudly and flippantly, "Are you nervous in the service?" It always produced the laughing response he anticipated. Another was a quiet and serious gentleman named Showalter. I liked him. He was polite and always spoke of more adult subjects, such as current events and what he would do when the war was over. His flat face, wide-set eyes and thin, hooked nose reminded me of an owl. I couldn't ignore a red-haired southerner named Tom who had a roving eye and decided he had a crush on me.

He could dance well and although he was only about twenty, he often asked me to dance. And he drank too much.

I cannot forget my embarrassment one Saturday evening when the orchestra was playing a popular song, "That Old Black Magic," and Tom stopped short in the middle of the dance floor as we were dancing and headed for the door, emitting a wolf howl before he disappeared. The other dancers and onlookers stared at his retreating back and then turned their eyes in my direction. I was as bewildered as they — I hadn't done a thing.

Tom's pretty wife and small baby soon came to live nearby because his superior officers wanted him to straighten out. I saw no more of him after that, but I heard he got into trouble for being drunk once too often and for unashamedly romancing a woman other than his wife on the grass one night outside the officers' club. I imagine he was busted and placed in the walking army. At least he escaped the vengeance of the P-39.

By mid-June, more disgruntled male pilots were sounding off about their lack of faith in the P-39. Usually the males I had known from childhood on felt it was unmasculine to appear afraid and they certainly would not admit to feeling fear. But at Romulus, rebellion against being forced to fly the "Bell Booby Trap" or the "Flying Coffin" swelled in volume until Colonel de Arce, Major House, and Major Hennessey began to worry.

In one shocking accident, five P-39s were lost. The pilots had grouped themselves in close formation. The lead man, who had some cross-country experience, flew into a cloud (forbidden by both FERD regulations and the CAA) and the others, keeping their formation, followed him. They must have run into each other. One member of the flight was Mr. Five by Five. The accident shook the base badly. I was sure that if Herr Hitler had known about it, he would have bounced up and down, rubbing his hands in glee.

Adding to my feelings of inadequacy as squadron CO and ignorance about the P-39, was a vexing letter from Lee Wahl now in Memphis. I had thought of him as a friend and didn't understand what he was trying to tell me. It read:

> Dear Del,
> You know I'm about to go across. At a time like this, I suppose it's natural for one to think of all his friends and want to wish them well.
> Maybe there's a little going-away present I can give you as a friend and also as a — well — physician in the true sense of the word — in the sense of one who is interested in all the aspects and

ramifications of lives — Please take this in the sincere spirit of friendliness in which I bring it to you.

When you first came to us in Romulus it was like a breath of crisp Autumn air. You had a "set" about you that bespoke leadership determination, a clear-cut purpose and the will and ability to see the job through.

When you are on the job, you doubtless still retain these priceless qualities. But when you were here in Memphis, much as I was glad to see you again, I was a bit saddened too. Something about this F. C. life is softening, rather than mellowing, the attitude you seemed to have at first. Don't let us down, Del. When you're just natural and yourself, everybody loves you. You don't have to step out of character. Just be yourself. And for gosh's sakes, you aren't a rhumba queen. Give it up. It doesn't do you justice. You are the noble type, who needs but to walk quietly into a room, relaxed and poised, to command attention. Jitterbugging isn't becoming to you — and although some may laugh — it makes the observing sad.

This will maybe hurt a mite, but it won't last. If I can save you from being the butt of jokes and laughs, it will have been justified. Was it old man Solomon who said, "Faithful are the wounds of a friend."?

Anyway, I mean well, and there is no gift I'd rather give you than this. Probably no one else is going to get around to tell you, because they don't know how. But I think you are sensible enough to take it straight from the shoulder, so that's it.

Best of everything, Del, and many happy bumps and circuits. I sure have enjoyed working with you and knowing you.

Someday in that mellow-lit tomorrow — when the teeth have been extracted from all the P-shooters, and planes become the couriers of high adventure and the bonds of friendship between all peoples on the earth, you will be looked for at one house, our home, and we'll sit out on the beach, toast hotdogs and talk about these earlier days when the task was new and difficult, and the friendships we made then were beaten at white heat in the fire — and not found wanting.

Lee

I wished I could have talked this over with Lee. I decided that he did not understand that I was the same person reacting to totally different circumstances. When I got to Romulus, the girls were so darn glad I wasn't Rhonie that we got along beautifully at first. I had met with disappointments in not getting to ferry more often than I did. When Lee saw me in Memphis, I had just been deserted by my flying companions when I was in trouble.

Moreover, I enjoyed doing the rhumba. I had given an exhibition at the party that night of what a rhumba should be, as danced in Latin America, and whatever he or anyone else read into the movements of my body certainly was not in my mind, but in theirs. If he thought I should be more regal, he had mistaken me from the beginning. But I would be more observant of my own behavior in the future if I had to please others before I pleased myself.

The first girls from WFTD called the curse "Code X." Mine began on June 13, but I had two sessions in an AT-6 nonetheless. Transitions was once again being reorganized. Only WAFS were allowed in AT-6s. Donahue and McElroy checked out. Kay returned from a mission and began transition in an AT-9.

Kay Thompson deserves some recognition for the trials she had in the AT-6. She was very nearly the same size as Betty Gillies and had the same problems of being small in a huge cockpit that could easily accommodate someone almost seven feet tall. But Kay had no rudder extenders. She should be given credit for courage in trying to overcome an obvious handicap without assistance.

It seemed to me a shame that Ted Thompson was insisting that his wife be at home waiting for him. He was now flying the South Atlantic and was suffering a neurosis about it. Each time he went over that expanse of water, he was not sure that he would survive. He wanted Kay to be with him during the few days he'd be on this side between trips. I considered him an erratic, spoiled boy, and I was certain of losing Kay any day now.

The same applied to Burchie. She went to be with her husband for two weeks. I felt that she might stay longer and that eventually I'd lose her permanently. Donahue was turning out to be the best flier in the lot. I didn't know how far along Poole was in transition. When she checked out in the AT-6, they would tell me.

With Thompson and Burchie going to be with their husbands, I longed to see mine, too. I ached to be at his side. My body ached, too, for I had been sleeping on that narrow, tiny, hard cot so long that my muscles did not relax and I slept poorly. Noises always woke me. The new girls came in from missions at all hours of the night and even if they were considerate and quiet, they woke me.

To keep the noise and bustle as far away as possible, I did not take a roommate in my tiny room. Technically, McElroy had a space allotment in the barracks that she paid for. I decided that her cot would be in my room.

We were expecting eleven new girls soon. I had wanted Colonel de Arce to limit each bedroom to two occupants, but he was adamant that there be four. He must have known more about the expansion of the

WAFS Ruth Franckling.

WAFS than I did and played his cards close to his chest. Double-decker twin cots were installed in each room. By the time the girls came, we were ready for them.

Almost ten years earlier, I had been diagnosed as having a borderline anemic condition. I had had iron shots every week or two which helped me maintain the workloads I habitually carried. The shots stopped when I entered the Ferry Command. At Wilmington, I didn't work as hard or long as at home, so I didn't miss them. But at Romulus, I pushed myself harder and harder. I lacked the energy I had in January and without my realizing it, my pep was slowly ebbing. Poole and Brownie expected me to perform transition miracles for them that I couldn't do in my own behalf. Added to that was the growing accumulation of office work for which I had no love and the deprivation of the love and companionship of my husband, family, and friends. Too many times I was left alone in the barracks while the other WAFS did the real work for which I had left home.

One night while I was alone I heard a jeep pull up next to the barracks and I peeked out to see what was going on. An MP sat there as if he were on guard duty. I realized that the provost marshal must have sent him. I surmised it was for my protection against any impetuous male who might have attempted to relieve my solitude — or himself. To make sure that I would not be disturbed, I always locked my door.

The men were nice to me in a distant sort of way. Several of the looies who were in their early twenties hung around me at transition much as school kids do around a teacher. From conversations that I overheard I learned that many married officers left their wives at home

WAFS pilots, from left, Barbara Poole, Mary Darling, Margaret Ann Hamilton, and (top) Marion Schorr.

with the children while they chased around at night. I drew away from men like that as if they were aliens. I could not force myself to be chummy. We had no common ground except our flying.

The second class of WFTD graduates arrived and I worked to get to know them. By now, however, WFTD was being called WPTP, Women Pilots Training Program. They were: Patricia Chadwick, tall, slender, blonde, enthusiastic; Mary Darling, blonde, not as tall as Chadwick, had great blue eyes that signaled to me an overactive thyroid; Patricia Dickerson, typical Irish good looks, blue eyes and dark hair, an inclination toward chubbiness; Ruth Franckling, a small, brown, noiseless wren; Ellen Gery, a beautiful brunette with slightly bowed legs, of medium height and build; Margaret Hamilton, an even more beautiful brunette, almost petite; Jary Johnson, a nice looking, average sized brunette, who seemed plain and ordinary in the company of the beauties; Margaret Kerr, taller than I with dark hair and blue eyes; Florence Lawler, a red-haired, blue-eyed former nurse with a slight limp; Paula Loop, a beauty with much blonde wavy hair; and Marion Schorr, a medium-sized, pretty brunette, very quiet. The new group was very clannish at first and considered themselves separate from us. I thought that would change.

One Sunday evening Kay Thompson and Ralph Pusey, both champion swimmers, invited me along when they decided to visit a nearby public pool. I could swim any stroke in the book and also dive off a low board, but next to them I was an inept amateur. I could never duplicate their performance. They didn't care and I didn't either.

It was a fun evening. Both of them dived and Kay was spectacular. A boy about ten years old watched Kay make a beautiful complex dive from the high board. Afterward he waded over to us, poked his finger at her chest, and eye-to-eye declared, "You ain't fair to the rest of us people!" Despite the number of years that have passed, I can still sense the warmth of that night, the water, and the regard which those two friends held for me.

All my problems were left behind me on the afternoon of Thursday, June 17, my wedding anniversary, when I boarded the SNAFU airline as copilot. The pilot of the C-60 was Capt. Harold Owens and fourteen pursuit pilots were on the manifest. Our first landing was at Buffalo after one hour and fifteen minutes of flying. Only five deplaned there. A short fifteen minutes later we landed at Niagara Falls and six of the others got off. By this time a lovely moon lit the sky and it was almost dark.

"Would you like to look at the falls?" asked Owens.

"Sure!" I replied.

We saw the falls in the moonlight. This is where honeymooners go, I thought. This was the anniversary, there was the moon, I was with a Harold all right, but he wasn't the right Harold and I felt blue.

We flew from Niagara Falls to Syracuse in an hour and the rest of the pilots left us. The last hop took an hour and a half. I did not take off or land, but Owens wanted me to do quite a bit of flying. On that last leg a strange thing happened to me. The wings of the C-60 began to wave up and down. I tried to keep the airplane doing what I knew it should. After a time, Owens glanced at me and I back to him. I couldn't lie.

I admitted with a touch of awe, "I don't know what's the matter. I can't keep those wings from going up and down."

He laughed and assured me, "I'll take it. What you have is vertigo. Pilots never know when they'll get it, but it can happen when you're on instruments or at night. You sit there and relax and it'll go away."

The vertigo did not vanish immediately. I was thankful to be resting instead of working. But then I did something I shouldn't have. I was feeling well enough to take an interest in the controls and the instrument panel. I touched things and told myself what they were. I touched something and asked, "What's this?"

Owens looked down. Then he looked at me. "Do you know what you just did?" he asked.

I shook my head.

"You just unlocked the tail wheel. When we land I'll have to be extra careful so I don't ground loop this baby."

My rest period was over. I didn't relax until after we had landed and rolled to a stop. By the time I returned post haste to the barracks I was cursed with diarrhea and it took all the next day to get over it. On the following day I was able to fly an AT-9 for an hour around the base. There was still no ground school for the P-39.

I received a letter from my mother that gave me much merriment. She enclosed a clipping that had been in the Huron County *Tribune* of Bad Axe, Michigan. It featured me in a set of four cartoons, each 4″ x 4″, that highlighted my career. The first showed that I married my first flight student (we were already married when I taught him), the second, that I refused to teach psychology instead of celestial navigation at Jefferson College (which I did for one term), and worst of all, that I was still in training to ferry war planes and soon would be a pilot in the WAFS. I wrote back to Mom that if I'd been inclined to have a big head, those cartoons would have deflated it in a hurry.

As Pop used to say, "Never believe half what the papers claim 'is reported.'" Except for two meticulous reporters who'd interviewed me at home, I knew from personal experience that Pop was right. My education in publicity began before I joined the WAFS.

In the complexity of military service, during which my life touched the lives of both the great and the humble, I found that people did not fit into the patterns I learned were correct in my youth. In Wilmington I had been outside the circle of power — a newcomer, a female, and a ferry pilot. I was still naively patriotic, a sentiment I still have not overcome. I thought that my superiors were and ought to be superlative to the rest of us. Wasn't it by their excellence that they rose to the top?

As the cadre leader at Romulus, I tried to be perfect. I aimed for 100 percent accuracy, just as I had as a student. And I suffered regrets each time I gave the wrong answer. What self-abasement I subjected myself to for making Harold Owens worry about a landing, or for having trusted Burchie to use my kind of judgment in a snowstorm, or for taking my wingmen to the Kimball House in Atlanta because I worried that they'd not have a bed that night.

Then, when incidents occurred, such as Donnie usurping my underwear and Burchie's uniform or the two Barbaras deserting me on the leg to Memphis or Poole lying ill during the day only to recover in time for Happy Hour, I wondered what Nancy would do. I didn't know. If I treated grownups like children, I'd make mistakes. The result was that I was stymied and did nothing but wait.

In my own eyes I was not the perfect leader that I wanted to be, but tried to get as close as I possibly could. Perhaps Lee Wahl was right — I had changed. I was trying too hard instead of doing what I could to get someone else to do the work.

As the weeks went by, chinks developed in the images I had of my leaders. Colonel Nelson cracked his image when he cracked up the B-17. Colonel de Arce's image altered in my eyes, too. Word got around very soon after their arrival at Romulus that Colonel de Arce and his Great Falls executive officer, a tall, erect, graying man of offish bearing, were cut-throat and expert bridge players. Officers expressed reluctance to shuffle cards with them. They had had months of playing together as partners and knew the game. Ordinarily officers were more likely to play gin rummy.

Several days after they arrived on base, a couple of the second class of WAFS, Hamilton and Kerr, were in the washroom when I came in to brush my teeth. They were discussing their recent game with the colonel and his exec.

"How much did you lose?" I asked.

A crestfallen Hamilton replied, "Twenty dollars apiece."

That shocked me and my face probably told them that. What an awful price to pay just to be with the CO, I thought. I was shocked mainly that two men with responsible positions, who should have had the welfare of the personnel at heart, had stooped to making these girls pay such a big price for their lesson in gambling. Where was their chivalry? Their compassion?

When next I saw the colonel, I introduced the subject with, "I hear you cleaned out two of the new girls at bridge last night."

The colonel's answer was given with a smirk. "Nobody made them play," he said. "They should have known that when they get into a game, they gotta take their chances on losing."

What could I say? He knew just how to absolve himself.

Later I learned more about Hamilton and Kerr. They had come from Oklahoma where the Kerr family had a glass manufacturing business that competed with Ball of Indiana in selling mason jars and lids to housewives who did their own preserving and canning. Kerr's uncle was then a United States Senator. She told us that when he had been Oklahoma's governor, she walked in the grass of the capitol grounds in blue jeans one day (when only cowboys and farmers wore them) and was accosted by a guard who said, "Who do you think you are?"

She replied that she was the governor's niece, which the guard thought was a likely story. But she proved she was, blue jeans notwithstanding. Kerr added with a carefree air, "That was when I was in my blue jeans stage."

So something new was added to my understanding. All one had to do to slough off misbehavior was to blame it on the stage one was in at the time.

There were moments when I felt I was doing great. One day Pat Chadwick came to me, worried because she didn't have the proper shoes to go with the khaki we were then wearing. It was impossible to get to a store. The other girls told her she'd never get to a store on a mission because there was no time or place to buy anything on the trips they had taken. What was she to do?

I had recently bought two pair of oxfords for flying. I'd worn only one pair, intending to keep the other pair for later. Pat was very close to my height, but slimmer. I judged her feet to be a trifle smaller. I'd chance finding another pair at a later date.

"I have a new pair I haven't worn," I told her. "You can try them on. If they fit, you can buy them from me and pay me when you can."

Pat eagerly put them on and declared that they fit her perfectly. Her sunny outlook on life returned with this transaction and I had made a friend for life.

By Friday, June 18, the transition school was SNAFU once more. The only thing to do was to choose which WAFS should be flight leaders to check on how well the new WAFS could find their way cross-country. I talked to operations. Soon they called me back with the decision that I should lead Donahue on an AT-16 flight from Montreal to California.

"What's an AT-16?" I wanted to know.

Capt. Joe Gurley said, "It's just like an AT-6 except it has 100 less horsepower. We're ferrying them for the British, so they'll have different markings on them."

Shortly he called back saying that McElroy would also make the trip.

The next morning, SNAFU Airlines picked up some men pilots and us at operations and flew us to Montreal. Someone said the men would get Norsemen, a utility plane popular with bush pilots flying cargo into the Canadian wilds. It was a chunky aircraft with bowlegged non-retracting landing gear.

We WAFS had to be checked out at the Noorduyn factory. After thirty minutes of flying and three landings, I was ready to go. But we remained overnight at the Mount Royal Hotel downtown. That evening we toured the quaint section of the city, which was as hilly as San Francisco. I wished we had had time to study the historical sites, but we were there on business.

The factory sent transportation for us in the morning and soon we were off to Toronto, getting there in two hours, twenty-five minutes. In another two hours we were back at Romulus. We traded our interim orders for ones dated June 21. I'd been glad for the change of scenery, but was also glad to be back to relieve Thompson of the desk job before she left.

She told me her back had been bothering her more and more since she had first told me about it. The pain irritated her so much that when she had left her flight members one evening in Nashville to visit Cornelia Fort's grieving mother, she had purchased an orthopedic brace, hoping for relief.

She wore the brace when she flew. As time went on, she knew she wasn't feeling any better. It was an unwieldy contraption, hard to get into, and she was always aware of its constrictions. So in a flight over western Texas, where checkpoints were few, she divested herself of the fiendish thing and threw it out of the airplane. She watched to see where it would land — down by the corral near a ranch house. She wondered how the rancher would explain the garment to his wife, and the possibilities of what would happen helped her to forget the misery she was in.

Because McElroy would be flying, too, I had to commandeer someone for my desk job. I would not have asked Poole even if she had been available. Usually I was unable to anticipate her moods. I knew how much she hated to remain on the base and I avoided crossing her wishes. There must be someone. . . .

Of the several girls still on the base, I chose Paula Loop as the most likely prospect. Her quiet manner and Sunday school face made me feel she was a responsible person. She, too, was from Oklahoma, but didn't reach for a social life.

"Listen, Paula," I said. "I won't be gone long. Don't worry, it'll be easy. All you have to do is be here for a couple of days."

Paula looked uneasily at my desk and replied, "I don't think I can do this —"

"There's nothing to it except you won't be flying while I'm gone. Just take down any messages. There won't be any except from operations. When each girl gets back from her mission, put down the date, the type of airplane, and how many hours she flew. I'll put it in their records when I get back.''

We left Romulus in the afternoon and got to Chanute in a smidgen less than two hours. Seventy minutes later, at Lambert, I telephoned Harold as we gassed at the old National Guard hangar. We'd not make another leg before quitting time.

A few minutes later, Harold came by for us, looking so handsome in his chief's uniform that it thrilled me. The Chase Hotel was the closest one to Lambert Field, so we dropped the girls there on the way home.

The next morning we headed for Tulsa. Ahead of us a huge thunderstorm approached directly on our route. Minute by minute it was building wider and higher. I knew that as a rule those black devils swing toward the northeast in Missouri, so I altered my course to the south, thinking that was the better way to go. But the black ahead continued to spread.

The other AT-16s were following at the proper distance and I started westward after giving myself what I thought was enough distance from the southern edge of the low, dark clouds. Suddenly, for about a second, all was dark around me. Then, just as suddenly, I burst into bright sunlight at the back side of the storm. The storm had moved toward us more quickly than I had anticipated.

I looked back. The others were not behind me. I traipsed back and forth alongside the rear of that thundercloud, wondering and waiting, keeping my position by means of pilotage. Finally out of the north came two flying specks.

At Tulsa they told me that McElroy had bolted and Donnie followed her. She led in a northeasterly direction, keeping ahead of the thunderstorm and finally was able to get around it. We were uncomfortable with each other. I had been greatly concerned about them, for I knew if they flew north it would take a long time to encircle the atmospheric disturbance. I hoped they didn't think I deliberately led them into danger, but I didn't explain the reasons for my course of action.

We ate lunch at Tulsa and the line boys serviced our ships. Then off we flew to Abilene. I thought the airplanes were dreams to fly after all the liaison aircraft we'd been stuck with. I'd been this way to Abilene several times before and anticipated the checkpoints and their appearance before they came into view. By the time I flew a course twice, I was already bored with it as ''old stuff.'' It struck me that TWA had done a good thing in not hiring me, for going over the same route again and again would have been too tedious for me. I always wanted to learn something new.

After servicing at Abilene, off we went to Midland, arriving there in two hours and five minutes. There we took time for a cup of coffee and a snack. We felt like continuing our flight westward, but a stronger urge gave me some embarrassment. I asked the operations officer where the rest room was. There was none for women. Now what to do?

My mind was blank. It could concentrate only on my growing discomfort. Then the young officer had a solution. He called for an MP to go to the small comfort station on the base and order all the men inside "to hurry up and get out on the double." As we arrived, men were rushing out. They stared at us with curiosity and we avoided their gaze out of embarrassment. While we occupied the convenience that had been usurped for us, the MP stood guard at the door, rifle in hand, protecting our privacy.

On the way to El Paso I realized that I did not know the exact time of sundown. What if we broke the rules? When I had been the navigator, I always checked to make sure my wingmen were staying with me. This time neither WAF paid attention to me, for I turned right toward an airfield they had passed and landed. I got more gas and found out the time of sunset. The operations officer telephoned El Paso for me. The tower there said that two ships were just landing. I knew I wouldn't land an hour before sundown, which was the rule, but according to another rule I had to RON with Donnie since we were on the same orders. I hopped over to El Paso and landed just minutes before official sunset.

I'd flown nine and a half hours that day. I didn't feel like pulling rank or superior knowledge about thunderstorms. Our relations were somewhat strained because they had not noticed that I had left the flight — giving them the benefit of a conscience. I guessed that they were so used to being flight leaders that they had forgotten I was the senior WAF.

It was dark by the time we got into El Paso to stay at the Del Norte where operations at Biggs Field said many ferry pilots nested. It was an old home converted to house transients. I did not like it for one reason — there were no locks on our bedroom doors. Things like that keep me awake at night.

While we were in El Paso we walked across the bridge to Juarez, Mexico. We browsed from one *tienda* to another and I got separated from the other two. A rug merchant struck up a conversation with me. He was young and handsome and (I know now) susceptible. He offered me a hand-woven woolen rug, fringed, light tan in color with end stripes and a huge multi-colored diamond insert in the center. The price was only $7.50. I didn't bargain; I bought it. On later visits to

Juarez I found that such a rug was always offered first at more than twice that price. My rug was 4' x 7', so it took up much of the parachute bag, but I looked forward to seeing it on my floor at the barracks.

The next day we were in Phoenix in two and a half hours. We left our planes to head for operations and found Pat Rhonie there on the field instructing in primary trainers. I felt so badly about having been a party to her losing her job at Wilmington that I avoided her. She looked very unhappy. (Rhonie was accepted by Britain's ATA on November 30, 1943, attained the rank of third officer flying class 2 and 3 type aircraft. She left the ATA on November 19, 1944, but for almost a year her skill was used as fully as ours to win the war.)

Donahue remained behind to talk with Rhonie while McElroy and I turned in our clearances and made out new ones. The two were friendly. I should have realized that they had known each other on Long Island when Rhonie was an established pilot and Donnie was still a student. Chances were they belonged to the same aviation country club and ran in overlapping social sets.

Two hours and five minutes of flying brought us to Palm Springs. It didn't look like much of an oasis at the airport. We asked for directions to Hawthorne, California, and the answer was that it was situated in the heart of Los Angeles.

Flying over new territory was a thrill for me. I saw the Salton Sea. Just west of Palm Springs we were forced to fly through a pass between the San Jacinto and the San Bernadino ranges. The course was exciting. Beneath us was the town of Banning with an airstrip alongside the highway and the railroad tracks. Then came Beaumont. All around it trees were laid out in geometrical patterns. Orchards, I thought.

As we flew across the far West, I schemed. Harold and I must plan a trip out here when we could. I wanted to share this with him. And I thought about the pioneers who laid trails to cross this great continent — they were certainly some people!

We were getting closer to Los Angeles. My authority reasserted itself. I got ahead of the girls as we headed toward the ocean, but I dropped to a little below 1,000 feet above the terrain and buildings when I got close to where I expected the airport to be. I squinted and looked at what was down there at an angle instead of straight on. Everything was camouflaged to look like vineyards and trees. When I arrived at the shore, ready to turn and circle until I had solved the puzzle below, I glanced back. Under some curtain-like frames were two yellow airplanes just like ours. I made my turn and went into a downwind leg pattern and landed down a "street" at the Lockheed factory.

The others followed me in.

As soon as we landed, we saw that we were on the site of a great aircraft factory and it was all under cover, even to the outside area where the airplanes were parked. The netting and a village of "city houses" directly above the factory building disguised it.

"How did you know where it was?" they asked me.

I simply raised my two hands palms up, shrugged my shoulders, and wrinkled my forehead. If they're so smart, I thought, let 'em figure it out for themselves.

Before we hustled through the paperwork, I called the airline for reservations to Detroit by way of Chicago. While we were waiting to leave, we found out that our deliveries were bound for New Guinea. At least we didn't have that far to travel. We had to waste some time at Midway Airport and then we were home, back in Romulus exactly seventy-two hours after leaving it. We were worn out.

Our first day home, June 24, didn't allow me a chance to catch up on rest. We heard that Nancy would be coming soon for a visit. Maybe now the uniform question would be settled. The WAACs were definitely being militarized into WACs. Would we be, too? And I was told to report to ground school for the P-39 at last. There was no mention of any other WAFS being included.

And then transition brought out a new rule. Ketcham had been ferrying only liaison aircraft. She was assigned to a PT mission and transition insisted that she be checked out in one before she left. During her last landing roll, an AT-6 going down the runway against the normal direction of traffic taxied head-on into her plane.

Four people, two of whom were instructors, and the tower were involved. Ketcham was cleared, but that didn't help her appearance. Her face had met the edge of the wind deflector in front of the cockpit. Her nose and cheek had been cut. When I learned about the accident, she had just been taken to the base hospital. I wanted to stay out of it. I knew she'd be under sedation for a day or two. But I had to inform her mother.

I was angry with Ketcham. Not because it was a WAFS accident, but because I simply couldn't understand her attitude. Even if she had only been a passenger, she should have been alert to any danger from any direction in the air or on the ground. Taking life easy and trusting someone masculine to protect her was to me a weak and "female" way of life. It didn't belong in the man's world that we lived in. How long would it take for her realize that? And I felt sorry for her, for her lost good looks, and for the pain she must be suffering.

Despite my feelings, I went to see Ketcham as soon as she was able to have visitors. She was bearing her misfortune with a show of stoicism. He face was hidden by a huge swathe of bandages, yet I could see that it was discolored and puffy. She told me that she wouldn't have sinus trouble in the future, for her facial sinuses had been broken and would drain by gravity. I did what I could to make Marjorie's mother's stay pleasant and comfortable while she was there.

I was being kept very busy. There were the usual chores following the end of a mission plus my first lesson on the P-39 — and that was a revelation. Several other would-be pursuit pilots showed up. I was the only woman. We spent the first twenty minutes setting up a movie projector and screen. I had seen the short film of a pilot taking off, flying, and landing a P-39 before. The commentator spoke of how easy it was. That was all. End of first lesson.

A few of us gathered again the following morning. There was no instructor this time, so we had no lesson. Someone promised us a lecture on the type of propeller the P-39 used.

I approached Major House, who was then in charge of the school, and asked him if I might have some material to read about the airplane. He was a short, stout man of ruddy skin and a rather pretty face. His large eyes and his hair were dark. He said there was no material available yet. Without smiling, he told me that when I made a blindfold check of the instruments in the cockpit, I'd get a chance to solo the Airacobra. Well, he had nothing to smile about. There had been thirty accidents for which Romulus pilots were responsible in the last month. Fifteen had been in the P-39 and they all had been fatal.

I went out to where a P-39 was parked nearby the school. I got in and sat down. Might as well start right now, I thought. How was I to find out all the things that could keep me out of trouble? Bell was supposed to have a representative in the office on the other side of the field. That was the place to go.

I asked the first person I saw over there, "Do you have any tech orders or something I can read? I'm slated to fly the P-39 and I want to know something about the plane."

The stout little man in charge broke into energetic bustling about to search for various reading matter that applied to the airplane. As he ladled it out to me, he said, "These are the only tech orders we have here in the office. We'll be glad to help you in any way that we can. If there is anything you need, just let me know."

I looked at the two pocket-sized booklets and the pages of information and said, "I'm going to need some stuff about the propeller before tomorrow."

"We have something, don't we?" he asked the other man in the office, who looked up from his desk.

"Yes, you'll find it right over there," he said as he pointed to a cabinet. In a few minutes I was in possession of another small, fat booklet. I guessed by my benefactor's behavior that I had come as an answer to his prayers. Public relations for the Bell company were not running smooth at the time.

In the privacy of my room I inspected my gifts. There was too much information and it was too complicated. It would require quiet concentration. First, a look at the small handbook on the constant speed prop. I read some of the text. It made no sense to me. I had never seen the inside of a complicated air screw. But a diagram of the structure was a puzzle waiting for me to solve. How to do it? I began again with the text and matched the words to the blueprint of the machinery. The words blurred. I went over them again, saying them aloud. I started to catch on. It was not only making sense, but was fun. I wouldn't disgrace myself the next day. I didn't get much sleep that night, but I knew that propeller forward and backward.

After an early breakfast, I eagerly arrived at the school. Several men and I waited for Captain Melichar to arrive. He started rather unhappily to lecture. It was soon evident that he could not express very well what he knew about the P-39 propeller. I couldn't help myself. Soon I was at the chalkboard explaining what I had taught myself, and Melichar was listening with the others. That was the extent of the instruction I received for P-39 transition. Now I was theoretically prepared to go out and take my chances with that killer plane.

However, I wasn't a man and did not have to pretend a devil- may-care courage that I didn't feel. In my ears rang Lieutenant Tracy's admonition about damaging an airplane. I knew I didn't have the money to pay for mistakes. Concentrate, I thought. Put down on paper the things the tech orders tell you are important. I studied as if my life depended on it. I began to follow in my imagination the procedures mentioned in all those pages. It was impossible. It would never work. Something was terribly wrong. What's more, it was time for lunch and if I didn't get to the mess, there'd be no food until dinner time.

The civilian pilot Morse, who had been warning me every chance he got to stay away from the P-39, was in the chow line. He was limping and had a bandage on his foot.

"What happened to you?" I asked, just to avoid his advice.

"I bailed out and when I landed I sprained my ankle."

"Why? How did that happen?"

"I was in a P-39 somewhere over the Appalachians. The coolant got hotter and hotter and then the engine quit."

I wasn't so ignorant as I once had been. I asked, "Did you check the coolant level or have somebody do it for you before you took off?"

With dismay, he answered, "No."

The one thing he forgot was that the P-39 did not forgive any mistakes. The episode must have been a highly emotional experience, for he wept tears as he said, "Think of your husband. You'll ruin his life if you fly it." He could see no other alternative to certain death than my refusing to fly the P-39. As a civilian I could do so, but I did not promise Morse anything.

My hair was beginning to beg for its Saturday shampoo. I decided to combine study with cleanliness. The sunshine outside was hot, so I took my unusable notes and a towel and sat on the walk by the barracks to let my hair dry, and I began again.

Where the inspiration came from I think only God knows. Suddenly I could see that there was no logical sequence of directions as to what to do with the P-39 for the problems I'd heard the fellows talking about.

They complained that by the time they made their conventional checks at the end of the runway before takeoff on a hot summer day, the coolant had become so hot they had to turn the engine off and sit there until the temperature was again safe for takeoff. After restarting the engine, the tower often heard something like this: "Romulus tower, from P-39xxx, I'm a hot rock, so let me out of here!" Then regulations clamped down on such individuality over the air waves.

I had caught the scent of success. If only I could think it through. Back to my room I went for four slips of paper and I began. Although the Allison engine was a good one, Bell had placed it where it had no chance to be air-cooled, especially at very slow speeds. It wasn't the engine's fault if pilots insisted on dealing with it as if it sat in the nose instead of being covered up in the back of the fuselage. The problem was to eliminate checking the aircraft when it was parked with the engine running or during the taxiing. And never at takeoff!

As my mind roved over the procedures, I'd scratch one and put it somewhere else until the resulting combination of tasks to be done couldn't be rearranged any better. I was confident now that I could fly the Airacobra with finesse.

All ground inspection had to be done before the engine was started. Then the pilot must start taxiing immediately, so off with the brakes. As she taxied, she should check the flaps down and up, instead of waiting for the moment immediately before takeoff. And she should lock the harness while she's rolling.

No dawdling on the engine run-up. Get the motions down pat. Brakes on, auto-rich fuel, throttle forty-three inches of manifold pressure, and check the ammeter. Pull the prop back and forth three times at 2,300 rpm. Check switches and the magnetos. Reduction gear, coolant temperature, oil temperature and pressure? Brakes off and call the tower. Prop full forward?

Take off with forty-three inches' power. Off the ground, flip gear switch up, stabilizer, aware of lights and ammeter, climb at 160 mph with thirty-five inches of boost and 2,600 rpm or twenty-seven inches and 2,100 rpm. Fuel boost off. Switch tank in twenty minutes.

I memorized the landing procedure: Keep an altitude of 1,500 feet. No sloppy pattern. How is oil? Coolant? Booster pump on, check battery and generator, gas on reserve tank. Harness locked. Fuel mixture auto rich. Trim, recheck as she goes along. Throttle back to 170 mph, watch lights. Gear switch down, watch ammeter and lights. Prop forward to 2,800 rpm, throttle forward, check gear visually, trim if necessary. Call tower on downwind leg. Watch for other traffic. On final approach, reduce speed to 145 mph and flaps down. When I see the P-39 will land in the first third of the runway safely, throttle back. As I approach the runway, change attitude. In landing position, chop throttle all the way back.

Even before starting the engine at the beginning, review the procedure for a forced landing on takeoff. If the engine quits, shove the nose down. Gear up, flaps down, fuel tank off, magnetos off, battery, generator, and booster off.

If I have to leave the plane upstairs, make the motions necessary to jettison the hatch and escape.

That was a lot to make my own in a short space of time. Added to what I had read about the P-39, I also studied the Pilot's Information File. On Sunday, June 27, I went to transition to sit in a P-39 and get ready to take the blindfold test. Instead, operations called me to go to the Stinson factory and take an L-5 from there to Romulus. Motor pool gave me transportation. That operations wasn't taking my P-39 transition seriously crossed my mind. I seemed to be the only student in a nonexistent P-39 transition class.

The Stinson people made me shoot three landings, which wasted an hour. The ride back to the base took another ten minutes. Finally I was allowed to take the blindfold test with Major Hennessey. I passed, and he said, "You take P-39 #701 right after lunch tomorrow." It was all settled. I went from 550 hp to 190 hp to 1200 hp, just like that!

That evening I pressed the khaki clothing I had laundered since the return from California and went to bed early. What would tomorrow bring? I was betting everything I had on my own judgment and the knowledge I had dug up by myself. If I were wrong, I stood to lose everything. If I were right, how would Nancy feel? She had promised to visit Romulus. Why hadn't she shown up before this? Something more important must have been going on.

The pulling of strings in the War Department, the manipulations within the top circle of brass around General Arnold to decide the choice for the director of women pilots continued that June without the knowledge of most of us. Except for the first part of January, which she spent in Dallas, Nancy had been in California. Colonel Tunner in Cincinnati was closer in both rank and position to the politicking in Washington. He informed Nancy that it was imperative that she, as WAFS leader, be in Cincinnati instead of at Long Beach. But first she was to ferry a B-25.

On June 28, immediately after the lunch hour, I entered the transition school office lugging my parachute. Where was everyone? Perhaps they hadn't returned from lunch yet, I thought. Or were they out on the flight line waiting for me?

Way out at the edge of the field at the left side of the runway was a small nucleus of men. A transmitter was set up over there and I saw that one man was holding a radio transmitter to his mouth. His body became dramatically active as a P-39 approached the runway. Maybe the next move was mine.

I picked up my chute and walked toward the front door. In a blur of rapid movement, I could make out several persons rounding the corner of the building as if headed for the flight line. The haste of the woman in the trio did not conceal her characteristic step. It was Donahue, accompanied by two of the younger instructors. One was carrying a chute. So intent were they on looking over the outside of the lone P-39 stationed at the edge of the taxi strip closest to the building that they didn't notice my presence until I stopped beside the tail and laid down my chute.

The two men took several steps back, seemingly disconcerted. Donahue's face showed no emotion. My mind caught the scheme: she was bluffing me — the old poker face! She'd not had any official ground school training and she was pretending that it was perfectly natural for her to be preflighting the P-39 that was officially assigned to me. Her parachute was even on the seat.

The situation presented me with an unpleasant dilemma. I was ill equipped to bluff or to push. I knew Donahue was quick and intelligent and these two gin rummy pals of her had no doubt been secretly coaching her. She was a gambler and I was going to see that this gamble would not pay off.

I knew how much went into a successful flight in a P-39 and how important it was for women that a flight be done well. My plight was to halt what they had begun surreptitiously without appearing shrewish, vindictive, or discourteous. If the men were to witness a confrontation between Donahue and me, they would certainly twitter among themselves and exaggerated versions would float around the field forever. But I simply could not stand aside and allow Donahue to preempt not only Nancy's place, but mine, as the leader in charge at Romulus. Donahue wasn't ignorant of military etiquette. This was no uniform she was "borrowing."

With a face as expressionless as I could manage, I said, "Oh! I thought I was next to fly. This is the time and the plane I was scheduled for."

Any flight student, even the dullest, knows that the person who has the appointment has the priority. With feigned generosity, Donahue surrendered the airplane by lifting her chute from the cockpit and saying quite jovially, "Oh, sure. I'll let you take it first," for all the world as if she had a right to it.

She had counted on beating me to the takeoff, I thought, but she had not counted on my determination. The three conspirators left me abruptly to find shade under the wing of a nearby B-25. They sat on the grass and directed their attention to the activity around the airport. It appeared that I no longer existed.

I put my parachute on the bucket seat. Then came the check of all the items on my list for the outside of the Airacobra. Satisfactory. I climbed up on the root of the left wing and lowered myself into the cockpit onto my chute.

The inside got the same treatment. Okay. I closed my eyes and gave myself the blindfold test, reaching out and touching as I named aloud every gauge and control, beginning with the lower left-hand side of the cockpit, up across the instrument panel, and down to the lower right side.

When I opened my eyes, Major Hennessey was standing beside the plane. He smiled and said, "Ready?"

I smiled in return, feeling confident. I nodded my head.

He pointed to the small group at the end of the runway. "They'll be talking to you on the tower frequency when you are landing, so be listening and do what they tell you."

Again I nodded.

"Good luck!"

I waited for an enlisted man to appear with a fire extinguisher. The rest was routine, familiar because I had memorized it well.

"Clear?" I called, seeing easily that it was.

"All clear!" he replied.

"Switch on!" I warned.

The propeller began to whirl. The line man pulled the chocks from in front of the wheels. At last I was taxiing a P-39! But not for me was the delight of a strange new experience. I was busy going through my own taxiing check list.

The outside air temperature was in the eighties, hot for Detroit in summer. How were the gauges? I checked the magnetos and eyed the coolant gauge temperature. It was very close to the red danger zone. Get off quick or not at all, I thought, ending the pre-takeoff check.

As I turned to face the runway in use, I watched an airplane land, hoping it would be off soon. It floated on down past the half-way part of the runway. Why didn't he go around instead? The plane ground looped, tying up the runway.

A siren sounded. Equipment and the crash truck headed for where the plane had spun around. The planes in the traffic pattern went on circling; one on base leg turned for final approach, but remained at altitude and joined the procession around the field.

As for me, the coolant temperature gauge showed red. No need to heat the engine further. I cut the switch and waited alone in the half circle next to the runway, listening to the tower for instructions.

Time passed. The plane had been damaged. The runway was judged not safe to use. The Romulus tower operator began directing traffic to another runway, the shortest one. He cautioned approaching traffic about the wreck on the long runway. The wind was light, the air was hot, and the crosswind was no problem on the new runway.

As soon as the coolant temperature level was safe, I started the engine again without a lineman in attendance and taxied to the new takeoff point, where I cut the switch again. It embarrassed me to have to wait for the coolant to cool, but my reason for doing so was valid.

Once again a takeoff could be safe. No one else had moved up behind me to wait for takeoff. No worry about holding up traffic on the ground. As soon as I saw a clear place for me, a break in the incoming traffic, I hurriedly asked the tower for permission to take off, started the engine again, and moved into the runway. I pushed the throttle forward to forty-three inches of mercury.

The Airacobra lunged forward rapidly. I felt the G's on my torso — my body was pressed back against the rear of the seat with great force. When the speedometer showed that the airplane was reaching ninety miles per hour, I eased the stick back exactly down the middle of my body toward my breastbone. I kept a steady pressure and felt the airplane lighten. The nose wheel had lifted and I was running on two wheels. Ahead was the metal fence at the end of the field, and it was getting closer and closer. Would the plane get off the ground before I reached the fence?

I had flying speed now and I pressed back still more. The P-39 left the runway and immediately I flicked the landing gear switch up. I heard the thump of both gears entering the housing as we flew just a few feet above the fence. As I cleared it, I looked from one wingtip to the other, just checking that I was level. Aloud I said, "Why, this is just another airplane!"

With that assurance, I followed the regular traffic pattern and exited it at 1,000 feet above the airport. I had had more than a thousand hours teaching flying. Now I was both instructor and student. I'd better give myself a good lesson, I thought. As I gained altitude on my way to the practice area over the open countryside, I did coordination exercises first. Then I did climbing turns, some shallow and some steeper, some forty-five and ninety degree turns, keeping my eye peeled for traffic all the while. Every five minutes or so I ran over the entire instrument panel. Then clearing myself at 10,000 feet, I approximated a glide into an imaginary airport with the throttle at 1,500 rpm, just to catch the attitude in a glide. I brought it close to a landing in a stall position to see what it felt like. Then I climbed back up and tried it once more. I'd lost 4,000 feet.

There came to my mind, from somewhere in the ragbag of inconsequential things that reside there, a memory of my brother Hiram and his first automobile, a second-hand Ford touring car. In his youthful exuberance, he had turned the corner at Clara Avenue into Lotus, the street where we lived, without slowing down and found himself on the wrong side of the street, bumper to bumper with another automobile parked next to the curb.

The P-39 was no trainer. Not even an AT-9. With a faster speed, it, like the Ford, would have a larger radius of turn. The traffic pattern I was to take about the airport must be larger and my downwind leg far to the side or I'd disgrace myself by being forced to go around again to head in straight to the runway.

Down we glided. I began a game of make believe. I found a road and made my first pattern, beginning with a downwind leg around an imaginary airport, with the road as the runway. On my first try, I turned into my final approach too far to the right of my intended path. There was not going to be any wrapping that P-39 in a quick, steep turn just to save myself from going around again. I had seen that happen just the day before. A flight had come in from the Bell factory. One pilot made too steep a turn coming into final approach. I had watched his P-39 plunge to the earth near the end of the runway. It had hurled itself to oblivion and the pilot with it for not treating it with respect. No, I would not be too proud to go around again, but I'd like to do it right the first time.

I had kept the tower radio frequency on during the flight just in case someone wanted to call me. I came into the downwind leg at a forty-five degree angle, gave my plane number and began the procedure for landing. I put on the boost, checked the temperature gauge again, turned the gas to the correct tank, the altimeter for the correct altitude, prop full forward, mixture control full rich, landing gear down and locked, flaps full down, stabilizer setting to carry the nose farther down and avoid a stall, and glided in with 1,500 rpm.

As I was about ten feet off the runway, I heard, "Chop the throttle!" It was a voice from another world and for a split second I didn't realize the voice meant me. I was keeping the plane just off the ground and had pulled the throttle back to what I thought was all the way. I pulled it back harder and the wheels rolled along the concrete, moving forward with what seemed to be added impetus, until the nose wheel dropped and I started to touch the brakes lightly. I brought it to a stop just before the intersection. Looking first to make sure, I pressed the electric button that activated the flaps to the up position. The runway had been cleared of the wreck. I taxied around to the men with the transmitter.

That was all there was to it. One solo hop. No mistakes. Congratulations, me. I was still amazed at how fast I was going when I landed. It was breathtaking, just like my first landing as a student which my instructor made in a Wright J-5 Travelair. Somehow I knew that this, too, like the experience in the Travelair, would be the only time I would get this exhilaration in a pursuit airplane. From now on it would be old hat.

After I had written my 1:05 time on the form I, my parachute and I left the plane. The instructors were hovering around Donahue, who would solo next. Then Donnie was off and gone. While she was away, a lineman came by in a jeep. "Gee," he said, awe showing in his face and voice, "you soloed the P-39."

"Look," I replied, "I've never soloed a jeep, much less driven one. So you're ahead of me on that."

"You want to try it?"

"Sure! Why not?"

And out on the grassy area of the airport, away from the runways, I drove the jeep in circles, first one way and then another. I kidded the lineman sitting beside me. "Now I'm making eights around pylons," I

The Bell P-39 Airacobra and the first woman to fly it — Adela Scharr. This photo was made on June 28, 1943.

said. To tell the truth, I got a bigger kick out of the jeep.

Donahue didn't remain in the air as long as I did. She figured out the radius of her last turn pretty well, but she had to maneuver to line up with the runway. She appeared to have too much speed. The men were yelling, "Chop the throttle! Chop the throttle!" until she, like I, came to her senses and did it.

That afternoon as I left the transition school office, Major Hennessey passed me in the doorway. We both paused, close to each other. Confidentially he said, "Now you know what we always knew. I don't know how the fellows are going to like this. They won't be heroes any more."

I looked at him, puzzled.

"You know," he continued softly, "when the boys get into a town and let a girl know that they fly pursuit, they're looked upon as little gods. Now you'll come along and everybody will know they aren't any better than the other pilots. Even a woman can fly 'em."

I didn't know whether that was a compliment or not, but I guessed he was trying to be nice. There was one more thing to do to top off the day — I sent a telegram to Harold. He was one man who would be glad I did it. Then I went to the base exchange, where I wasted no time in trying on red caps for size. One of the young male pilots ambling past stopped to watch me.

He said, "You're really not going to ferry 'em, are you?"

I turned and looked him squarely in the eye. "You bet I am," I said. "What did you think that was? A publicity stunt?" So saying, I took the cap off my head and handed it to the clerk to ring it up.

The day I soloed I became a subject of the realm dominated by gravity. That set me apart from all the earthbound women of the world. With the P-39 I entered a more exclusive circle that set me apart from most of the women who flew. What lay on the road ahead? Gravity would deal more severely with me now if I failed to remember who was king. I must be very careful not to offend the king. Little did I realize that that was not where my danger lay.

In the days that followed, the number of complimentary comments I received from the field personnel made me self-conscious. They considered my flight an act of courage with historic significance. I thought of it as an attempt to solve a problem I had never faced before. I was forced to tackle it in front of God and everybody.

It seems to me that people have a hunger to be identified with greatness, especially with someone whose experiences appear dramatically dangerous. Just by social contact with such a person they feel that the attributes they invest their heroines with will rub off on them. Witness the autograph hunters who long to prove that they spoke to the great person or even touched her. Flattery doesn't make the person they admire any greater. I didn't feel that I was a hot pilot, foolhardy and daring. I was only a careful one. Chances were that the war would give other women pilots besides me opportunities to fly better planes than had Amelia Earhart or Jacqueline Cochran. But we might not get into history — we had no press agents.

The Ferry Command had thus far given me a chance to fly cross-country and to make my own decisions about the weather. It had allowed me to fly airplanes that my old mentors at Lambert Field believed were too hot for a woman. I'd never be a man, if that's what they thought it took, but I had some equipment at my disposal that was superior to what the majority of men had. It could compute all the information I could feed into it, process it, and come up with as perfect a resolution as anyone could get. It was my brain. And with it I was gradually able to solve more complicated problems than when I was on the plateau of liaison and primary trainers.

In the beginning I flew an airplane by feel, "by the seat of my pants." This sense of balance was reliable only in daytime during contact flight conditions. During flight at night or in clouds I needed to rely on instruments and gauges and the radio. It took brains to combine all the visual and auditory stimuli simultaneously. Surprisingly, the bigger the airplane, the easier it was to fly. I knew my limitations, but I made the most of what equipment I had with little or no help from others.

POLITICS

BACK AT WILMINGTON, Betty Gillies wrote a letter dated June 18, to Florene Miller, with copies to Nancy, B. J., and me. She said she felt fortunate with the new WAFS who had arrived on June 14. They had checked out in both PTs and AT-6s and were attending ground school. She expected them to be "all set to go" by June 21.

She continued, "They are apparently not in any too good physical condition when they report here, in spite of the two weeks leave they had for recuperative purposes. One of the girls in the first group had had to go home for a couple of weeks on account of nervous exhaustion. They have all lost weight since their original 64. And in this last group there is considerable dental work that has to be done before they can be released. One of the girls had been granted a waiver because of her teeth . . . [and] she went into training with the understanding that she would have her teeth attended to immediately upon graduation. The result is that we have had to give her three weeks leave without pay.

"At this point, everyone but Teresa and I are out on PT trips, Texas bound. Teresa is just about to check out in the 47. Helen Mary and I have delivered about 20 P-47s to date. . . . Fleetwings has finally gotten into production on the BT-12 and it is expected that the girls will have a lot of those to move before long . . . [it's] actually faster than the AT6. Naturally, the old girls will be given the first crack at them.

"Our new alert room is the nuts. We have the whole what-used- to-be Finance building. It's painted up real pretty, partitioned off for a ping pong room, attractively furnished, and even landscaped! Have my office in the south east corner so everything is nicely centered and convenient.

"Wonder if our little friend, Eleanor Boysen, has arrived at your base as yet. If she has, will you tell her that we have her laundry here and will send it as soon as we know her where-abouts.

"We are still in an utter state of confusion in respect to uniforms. Hope that the powers-that-be are working on the winter uniforms at this point so that next fall wont find us in the same state that we are in now. The new kids are sure good sports about not having uniforms, but they cant help showing some disappointment."

One thing is consistent in wartime military life — nothing stays the same. Although two months earlier he had ordered otherwise, in May Colonel Tunner said he thought women might fly heavier planes than trainers. By the end of June, when one of his staff members asked if women would deliver P-51s, Tunner replied that from now on they would ferry whatever they were capable of flying. (This was not entirely true in practice for everyone at every ferrying group under his command.)

Tunner's change of attitude was dictated by more factors than his supply of pilots and the supply of planes demanded or required by the AAF. In June, through General George of ATC, Tunner conceded that his ferrying division would probably have use for 500 qualified WFTD graduates, a very different figure from the 100 that he said would be enough in September 1942.

Thus far, all his women pilots flew trainers and only a handful were checked out in pursuit. Men still almost monopolized transitional training. Women safely delivered the light planes until the Ferrying Division evaluated the needs of male cadets entering the command. These young men lacked experience in cross-country flying essential to ferry combat planes safely, both here and abroad.

With factories turning out more and more combat and cargo aircraft each month and so many men not yet ready to fly them, what was the sense in keeping women in light aircraft after they had been overly seasoned in the use of pilotage? Wouldn't it be wiser to upgrade the more experienced ones to multi-engine and pursuit and put the cadets of both sexes to the task of delivering trainers?

Only twenty-four women, all original WAFS, including Nancy Love, were ferrying in early May. By the middle of June, women pilots numbered eighty-nine. For July the prospect was a total of 127. And more were expected, month by month. The first ones to get transition would be the original WAFS. The newcomers would get transition when they were ready for it, after more cross-country experience.

It seemed that just as soon as one female problem was solved, another surfaced to keep the AAF Chiefs of Staff and their commands stirred up. The problem of WAAC militarization was still unresolved. WACs would have pay, rank, privileges, and obligations matching those of men in the army. Colonel Tunner and Nancy Love looked seriously again at the possibility of the WAFS being absorbed by the much larger organization.

The commander of the WAAC, Col. Oveta Culp Hobby, had instituted a training school at Des Moines, Iowa. She had made connections with all the army commands with job classifications that her recruits might be able to fill — not only to pound typewriters, but also to service airplanes, repair aircraft instruments, and other technical duties. The WAFS might easily be slipped into that organization, ending the cat slaps that Nancy Love had been receiving from Jacqueline Cochran's office. So Nancy was agreeable to submitting to the command of Colonel Hobby as the lesser of two threats to her autonomy.

But the idea of women pilots being WACS was not agreeable to Cochran. She could either lose her training program or, in order to keep it, have to eat humble pie as a subordinate to another woman. *That* she would attempt to avoid at all costs, as her early moves prove.

Cochran had built a growing institution out of an idea that had few possibilities at first. Her graduates were now adding to Love's strength in the Ferry Command, and her own influence over them ended with their graduation. How could that be changed? And the noise Colonel Tunner continued to make about the standards he considered inviolable to his command were bound to keep the students she was now recruiting, with only thirty-five hours of flying experience, from entering the Ferry Command. They'd have to be placed elsewhere. Who would control them then?

The plan fell into place on June 22. An AAF memorandum intending to unify the command of all women pilots announced that an office of Special Assistant and Director of Women Pilots would be set up in the office of the Assistant Chief of Staff, OC&R (Operations, Commitments and Requirements). The director would become a member of

General Arnold's highest staff and would function on the same level as the other staff members. She was to present ideas about the best uses for women pilots, to decide how many were needed for each duty and to coordinate efforts with other agencies to determine what qualifications the pilots should have, what training they should get, and what health and living conditions were to be maintained. She was to recruit students and train them, advise General Arnold on plans for militarization, make plans for using women pilots in the various commands, make inspection trips, and keep in touch with agencies using the pilots. She was not named.

Also that summer, the Ramspeck Committee of the House of Representatives began questioning the legality of the WFTD or WPTP. There had been no appropriations made for 1943 for a "Table of Organization," the document that any military body must submit in order to qualify for federal funds. And there was no mention of the WFTD in the Military Establishment Appropriations Acts. In fact, the only place it could fit was under Public Law No. 649, 77th Congress or Public Law No. 108, 78th Congress, "for salaries and wages of Civil Employees." The House Committee on Civil Service began looking at the WFTD, too, for the military War Training Program had absorbed it.

When the school had gotten under way with guidance from the CAA, using a collegiate flight curriculum, WFTD was purely civilian in scope. Its airplanes had been scraped up from the bottom of the civilian barrel. My attempts to ferret out answers to questions about the WFTD were unsuccessful. I learned the name of the company that supplied its planes, Aviation Enterprises, but not the state where it was incorporated. At a WASP reunion I asked Cochran where I could obtain information about the founding of the school. She told me that her personal papers and those of her husband, Floyd Odlum, were to be deposited in the Eisenhower Library in Abilene, Kansas, and that she had discarded everything about the WASP. By that time I had heard that Cochran's memory was slipping, so I did not press her further.

What I wanted to find out was where the initial money had come from to make it possible for the aviation company to be accepted in a CAA program. Cochran's school had to be financed somehow. Who were the stockholders? The officers in the company? When did the civilian school assume the status of training cadets for war? When did it become capable of commandeering military-type aircraft and instructors? Those aircraft were diverted from other schools where cadets were being trained for essential war efforts. My aim was to find the truth about Cochran's involvement behind the scene, and by that date I had begun to believe she had built the school for her own aggrandizement.

During the war, a leader like Colonel Tunner could hook into the grapevine and find out what was brewing in the War Department besides coffee. Nancy Love had admirers in Washington who kept the Ferrying Division informed of Cochran's moves. When it appeared that she was moving toward a position of dislodging Love from hers, Cincinnati got wind of it. To anchor Nancy as the WAFS leader within the command, Colonel Tunner wrote an order on June 15, 1943, making her the executive for WAFS in the Ferrying Division. However, he did not make the order public. Instead he waited for the right time to announce it, because Nancy still had a chance at the big job — director of all women pilots.

Harold had written me about his difficulties in finding an instructor to get him ready for a flight test and the time to study for it. He said he felt like a knight of old, jousting against great odds to win his lady's favor. I replied, "I want you to do it for your own satisfaction more than anything. Yes, I know how hard it must be and all the time it takes. . . . And if you should accidentally hit a sour note, it won't mean a darn thing to me except to sympathize. For I hit them, too, and know how it feels.

"Whatever you do in your venture, I want you to know and sense that you have my love. Successful or stumbling, at the top or on the bottom — you are the only person in the world I truly love, for there is no one like you."

I had other news from home. Ray and Jeanette Bratton sent me the birth announcement of their first child, Donna Jean. Laura Sellinger relayed the news that after Bud Klutgen's marriage dissolved, Mark and Mary Raymon's hit rock bottom and now Mary and Bud were becoming a twosome. Both had their commercial licenses and flight instructors ratings, so they joined Stephens College to teach aviation to the students. Tess Swetitch had found a job in Houston, so I guessed she had washed out of the WFTD.

On July 1 and 2, I was able to tally seven and a half hours solo in the P-39. At no time did the officers stationed at the transmitter have to talk to me when I landed. The P-39 and I suited each other beautifully. I understood it and it seemed to know we were partners.

The next day, an inspection team headed by a General Greene came to visit the base. In his entourage were several colonels, other major officers, and Nancy Love. No one had told me she was on the way, so I was still at transition when they arrived. Someone else, probably Donahue or Poole, settled her in.

The staff at Romulus got in touch with the two Detroit newspapers

This photo, printed in the Detroit News *in September 1943, shows Nancy Love flanked by Barbara Donahue, right, and Adela Scharr.*

and invited them to the base to interview Nancy — and broke the news that the base had two brand-new pursuit pilots who were women. The articles appeared in the Sunday, July 4 editions.

Garnet Warfel's feature in the Detroit News was headlined, "Leader of the WAFS Finds Some Aces in Unit Here." Above it was a photograph of us three pursuit pilots seated at a desk. Nancy sat in the middle with a pencil poised above a sheet of paper. I was on the left side, laughing and looking downward at the paper. The camera caught me at an angle that made my face appear long and my nose thin and sharp. But although I didn't like my likeness, there was something else about that picture that I disliked even more. In a prophetic moment, Nancy had turned away from front and center and with a somewhat quizzical smile, was looking into Donahue's eyes. Donahue was laughing with an air of confidence.

In its feature story, the Detroit *Free Press* pictured us standing with Nancy in the middle. Florence Mitchell wrote the article, "Women Ferry Pilots Do Man's Job a la Vogue," in a way to appeal to women.

After the interviews, we attended the formal luncheon held in the general's honor. The protocol I'd picked up told me that the higher the rank, the nearer the officer sat to the general. The WAFS were among those farthest away. I think now that Nancy was miffed that none of the mighty men thought to place her where she belonged as a member of the inspection team. I guided her away from a middle position she took in our lineup so that she would be the closest to him of all of us.

I said, "You belong *there.*" We all moved to accommodate her.

She replied, "It doesn't make any difference where I sit with you girls." Her answer made me feel uncomfortable, as if I had made an issue of rank unnecessarily.

That evening there was a fine banquet, with tables set for small groups. After dinner, the officers and guests changed their seating arrangements during the dancing. Some of the officers at the general's table invited the WAFS to dance, and at the conclusion of several numbers, we ended up sitting at the general's table. He did not dance. He sat and drank. He was an older man with sparse sandy hair. I thought he was a regular army type and, whatever his specialty was, it wasn't flying.

A colonel asked Nancy Love to dance and that was the only occasion that I saw her comply. She looked very prim and stiff and took small, slow steps. The music didn't energize her. We must have gone to different dancing schools, too.

The general's aide was taller than six feet and was a dancer who covered a lot of territory on the floor. He picked on me often and must have liked my style, for he invited me to join him for dinner and dancing at the Statler Hotel in Detroit the next evening.

Once, as we glided across the floor, I asked him, "How hard is your job? What does a general's aide do?"

He replied, "As long as I see to it that he gets his bottle of bourbon every day, I have no problem."

"Not a whole bottle?" I asked in disbelief.

"Of course," he answered. "He can put away that much and never show any signs he's been drinking."

When the dance number was over, we returned to the table to hear General Greene voice his opinion of what types we WAFS were. He started with Poole. "She's the intellectual type," he said. Then he waved his hand at me, saying, "And she's the physical type."

That embarrassed me. I thought he meant sexy and I had tried to avoid giving that impression for years. When Donnie returned with her partner, someone asked, "What is she?"

Boldly he stated, "She's the animal type."

That made me feel a little better, for Donnie at times stalked like a tigress. But I wanted to be sure I understood the general. "What's the difference between physical and animal?" I asked.

He said, "Physical is muscles and doing exercises." That fit well, I thought.

Before the inspection party left the base, Nancy and I were at the transition office. She wished to speak to me privately, so she led out to the grass where we sat down on the ground and watched without speaking as the airplanes took off and landed, getting a little vicarious practice.

Then Nancy turned to the affairs that concerned her. "The bill to militarize the WAAC is in Congress now," she said. "We expect that we shall be militarized along with them. You know what that means."

I was alert and waiting.

"How would you like the rank of captain?" she asked.

In my heart I thought it would be an honor. It would likely make my job easier. But I thought I would remain the same person regardless of what rank I held. My reply was to my inner thoughts rather than to the question. I said, "It's all right with me whatever rank I'd get."

She abruptly changed the subject. "I've had a lot of complaints that the WAFS have been seen ferrying around the country, dirty and unpressed. They make a bad impression of us and it must stop."

She paused for my reply. I hadn't done as much ferrying as the others. First there was the strep throat at Hagerstown and then Colonel Nelson had ordered me to stay on base to welcome the WFTD graduates, who were four months late, and lately I'd stayed on base for transition. But I must have done more ferrying than Nancy and I knew how difficult it was to be as presentable when flying around the country, compared with remaining on base.

"We don't know what we will run into," I said in defense. "The weather can keep us holed up or we might get soaked in the rain. I think sometimes there are extenuating circumstances."

"Whether or not," Nancy retorted, "there must be no more criticism. The worst offenders are the girls from Romulus."

"Romulus?" I couldn't believe it. "They are a swell bunch of girls," I said, "and although I had only one mission with the first group, I haven't seen any who didn't look neat."

"I can't have any more criticism," said Nancy.

I surmised that if there had been criticism, it had been blown up all out of proportion to reality. But I had forgotten about Donnie in Burchie's uniform and who she had said she was.

"I'll speak to the girls," I promised. "They're such eager beavers they don't even take the time off that's allowed them. Did you see on the chart in the hall that some have more than fifty hours already in one month? They ferry to all sorts of out-of-the-way places and have to take buses and trains. Sometimes getting back to base takes a lot of time. Operations says ther're doing a much better job than the men —"

Romulus WAFS, criticized by Nancy Love as being unpressed, shown after ferrying a group of PT-26s. From left: Margaret McCormick, Claire Callaghan, Ellen Gery, Elizabeth McKinley, Florence Lawler, and Mary Darling.

"But they don't look neat and clean on missions," insisted Nancy, "and that has to be stopped before we are militarized."

"I'll talk to them," I repeated. "They'll do better."

Nancy looked down at my feet. I was sitting on the ground with my knees bent and my arms wrapped around them. In that posture the space between my trouser cuffs and my shoes was visible.

"Your socks don't look in uniform," she admonished me.

I looked down at them. I didn't want to wear men's garters and I didn't like my socks draped about my ankles, so I rolled them down in tight rolls that stayed put. Nancy had criticized me as if I had been setting a bad example for my squadron. I unrolled the socks and pulled them up as high as I could.

While Nancy was watching an airplane land, I sneaked a peek at her socks. They had fallen into irregular ridges and folds about her ankles. They didn't look very neat to me. But I heeded what Mama used to say, "Think your share and keep your mouth shut!" Something was making Nancy stew and I didn't think it was the state of dress of the Romulus WAFS. Nothing more was said about neatness and our tete-a-tete ended, the only face-to-face guidance Nancy Love ever gave me.

Before the inspection party left, some of the new WAFS returned to the base and were able to meet Nancy. To them she appeared to be a story-book character, pretty, gracious, and charming — much more so than they had been led to expect at Sweetwater. Margaret Kerr was especially taken with her.

Immediately following Nancy's visit, we noticed that Kerr's hair appeared to be turning gray. Then we caught on to her "prematurely gray hair stage" and chuckled. She had bought a powder that she sprinkled on her hair to imitate the appearance of Nancy Love. Kerr endeared herself to Nancy thereby, for imitation is indeed flattery.

Someone at transition told me that Nancy had also soloed in the P-39. Closemouthed as ever, she did not advertise her accomplishment. The day after she left, the chief mechanic at the huge hangar chatted with me for several minutes. He confirmed that Nancy had soloed and added, "We've got the plane in the shop right now. She did something to the engine and we gotta see if it's flyable or not." Hmmm, I thought, I wonder how my success affected her.

We WAFS didn't know very much about what was happening on the battlefields of the war. We seldom saw a newspaper and letters written from men in the thick of the fighting were so censored that some arrived with peekaboo holes hopscotched all over the message. Because the men pilots flew to Alaska in P-39s or took multi-engine airplanes overseas, they came back with reports about the war situation and we learned of some things that other civilians did not.

One common report came from those who ferried to Alaska. American-built airplanes were ferried to and into all other allied countries except where it was impossible because of enemy occupation and except into Russia. Alaska was as close as our pilots went because Stalin would not allow them to fly over Russian territory. He didn't want them to have aerial maps or knowledge of the best air paths. Russians sent their pilots over to Alaska to pick up the airplanes provided by the United States. In fact, Russian pilots had free access to our country, which made many Romulus pilots irate. The language barrier hindered the Russian pilots from learning how the P-39 should be flown. Our pilots said the Russians knew only two settings of the throttle — full forward or off; there was no in between. Some of Stalin's antagonism may have been based upon the decimation of their air force by the Bell booby trap!

On July 5, the newspapers were given a press release from Colonel Tunner's office announcing that Nancy Love had been appointed executive for the WAFS. That same day, the Associated Press and United Press International learned that Jacqueline Cochran had been appointed the director of all women pilots in the Army Air Forces. The media took the opportunity to exploit the tussle for supremacy between

A national magazine featured the administrative clash between Jacqueline Cochran, left, and Nancy Love.

the two women and to toss off just enough half-truths to make their stories more salable. *Newsweek's* article, which was headlined "Coup for Cochran," began, "Last week came a shake-up." The implication was that Nancy Love had not been a satisfactory executive. There was no mention of Cochran's connection with AAF headquarters because of her school.

Nancy Love would have had to have a thick skin not to be irritated by the criticism of her that followed the announcement. She must have been tempted to inflict her wounded pride on someone who wouldn't or couldn't fight back. Certainly all she had been able to do since September 1942 was to fend off Cochran's probing for weak spots. Thus far, she had played only a defensive game.

Her next move was to start an offensive, and I was in the line of fire.

On July 14 Nancy Love's duties were put down on paper. She was to advise FERD A-3 on the use of WAFS and to plan for training standards within the command itself. (This was already being done by each ferrying group individually.) She was to prepare a program to stimulate interest among the WAFS in qualifying for advanced planes so they could leave the light planes behind.

This directive should have been easy to fulfill, like betting on a fixed race. Everyone I knew wanted to fly up to her capabilities; all she wanted was a chance to do so. The base surgeon of the 2nd Ferrying Group had recently released the data he had collected which showed that women lost fewer days of ferrying for physical reasons than men did. The only disadvantage women had as pilots was that they were smaller.

The rest of the instructions written out for Nancy Love stated that she would work with the command staffs of various departments to assign WAFS to the ferrying groups and to set up rules about conduct, morale, and welfare. She was to make inspection trips and to inform the groups on FERD's policies and the problems affecting WAFS. She was also to review publicity matters and plan solutions to the problem of WAFS housing.

All this was known at FERD headquarters in Cincinnati and probably at the War Department, but we at the squadron level were unaware of any new decisions. Much of what went on was labeled "secret" for about two decades after the war.

In March both General Arnold and Jacqueline Cochran favored women pilots becoming a branch of the WAC. Their objections of the previous autumn had vanished. But because of Cochran's favorable attitude, both Colonel Tunner and Nancy Love were negative about the prospect. Cochran wanted the WAC to admit only those pilots who had been trained in the WFTD. Then Cochran grew cold to the idea, and Tunner embraced it. It seems now that no matter which side Cochran took, Love believed that one of Jackie's goals was to rid herself of the competition that Nancy represented.

During July I continued to solo in the P-39. By July 6 I had flown nine hours and twenty minutes. Then fog and haze kept us out of the air. The weather bureau swarmed with pilots anxious to take off. A big, blond heavy-set fellow named "Doc" Lewis kept everyone laughing. I knew him well — he had taught in CPTP with St. Louis Flying Service and had married my second cousin, Loretta Menetree. He started kidding me about the first time I'd take a P-39 into Lambert Field and branched out into a monologue. He knew I could take the ribbing, even before I laughed with the others.

While I waited for the weather to clear, I had time to write to Harold to give him some comfort as he sweated out his approaching commercial license test. I recalled that the best help I had had when facing the same test came from the Lord's Prayer and the Twenty-third Psalm. I wrote Harold that if he could leave everything up to God, "He'll smooth the rough going and take away the fear."

The next day it was possible to fly, so I got in fifty-five minutes. I wanted to fly the airplane assigned to me later in the afternoon, but I found that Donahue had wheedled an instructor into letting her take the plane out of turn. I felt there could be only one reason for her move to get ahead of me. Bell Corporation was planning to publicize my arrival when I picked up my first P-39 for delivery. Donahue must have wanted some of the glory.

Other WAFS acted as if they were in awe of pilots who could fly pursuit aircraft. Whenever one seemed impressed by my accomplishments, I said, "Listen, you can do it, too. If anyone knows how to fly a Cub as it really should be flown, she can fly pursuit." I meant simply that if you know your airplane you won't get into trouble.

On July 8 I began Code X and felt weak, ill, and depressed. I wasn't in the mood to finish transition in the P-39. For the first time in my flying career I hesitated to fly because of a period. The project was too important to risk disaster. I had to succeed as a pilot to open opportunities for others. Because I felt so low, the fear that I might have cancer popped into my mind again. Be sensible, I thought, leave the field to Donahue.

My spirits rose when I received a telegram from Harold that same day. He had passed his commercial test on the first try. I composed a message for him, but Western Union would not accept it. The operator told me that Western Union would not send congratulatory telegrams because they were superfluous during wartime. So I had to wait until the next day to mail a letter to Harold, telling him how proud I was. "I bet you can fly rings around me now," I wrote.

Still, I knew I wasn't up to par. My reflexes and responses to stimuli felt dull and dead. I was so weary that I didn't even feel the heartache and lump in my throat that I usually felt when I thought of Harold. I went through the motions of preparing for the arrival of ten new WAFS on July 13.

When I reflected on my "old" charges, I thought that Elizabeth McKinley seemed to be getting over her wish to be with her friend Kumler. I knew that Poole would progress in transition as the instructors saw fit. The second group of WAFS were even more eager than the first to fly, fly, fly, and my only worry about them was that I should remind them to keep a neat appearance and to record all their flying time for the 201 files. Burchie and Thompson were still off with their husbands. I wasn't sure they would return.

Brownie had begun nagging me constantly for more transition. She would not take no for an answer and even came into my room after I'd gone to bed to beg me. I didn't know what to do. I knew that even Wilmington was ahead of Romulus in testing the skills of the new WAFS. I must have missed receiving a directive. The only way I could find out if I had was to go to headquarters on my own time and read all the official messages that were filed there. So in the evenings I began making my lonesome way there. The two enlisted men there allowed me to search the files. I felt that if I could find a directive that would allow Romulus WAFS to get transition, I could quote it to back up my request. I had no one to take up the cudgel for me, as Cochran had Hap Arnold and Love had Tunner. I needed some ammunition in the battle of the sexes and an official document would serve well.

One of the mistakes that women made in military service was to go around the chain of command. For instance, if Poole wanted a transfer, she should have written her request to me and I would have given it to the group commander who should have sent it on to the Ferrying Division and then Colonel Tunner would make the decision. Or, it could go through me to Nancy Love. But thus far, no one had requested a transfer through me. If anyone wanted to leave the base, she was sneaky about it, begging favors from the Big Boss on the QT.

Other bases had problems about transfers. On July 10, Brigadier General Tunner (he had just been promoted), sent a letter to Colonel Baker discussing our compliance with military channels. Apparently at Wilmington Betty Gillies was being bypassed by WAFS who wanted a transfer because they knew very well that she'd block it. Since we were not militarized, we had no set procedure to follow.

In mid-July something besides fatigue and a heavy work load kept me from flying. I was watching Donahue land a P-39 from a spot about a hundred feet to the right of the runway. The men with their transmitter were on the left. I could see that she was coming in too fast. The man with mike yelled directions at her. She must have jerked back on the stick, for the nose of the P-39 rose abruptly into the air. Then the plane sank to the runway. I could hear the smack as the tail struck first. Then it was onto its wheels, rolling. But it didn't travel far. I was stunned. What she had done I would have thought impossible. How could a pilot crack a tail that rode so high off the ground?

The accident halted pursuit flying for both of us. I heard from several sources that Donahue pleaded and begged for another chance for several hours after she was told she was being taken out of pursuit, but to no avail. I was also taken out of training because I was a woman. The reasoning prevailed that no woman could fly pursuit. At last someone noticed that there was a difference between Donahue and me. She had about 800 hours of flying time; I had about 1,700. She had more time in ferrying than I did, but I was known for being consistent; she, for being erratic. Therefore it was decided that I would be allowed to continue flying pursuit after all.

When I went back to transition school, Major House asked me what I wanted done with Donahue. The decision to drop her had already been made, yet I could sense that he wanted to palm off some of the responsibility onto me. If she killed herself, he'd like to weasel out of his accountability as head of the school. I should have said nothing, but I answered him that it was his decision, adding, "All I know is that I would feel badly if she got hurt." By the end of the month word got around to me that Major House had taken Donahue out of pursuit because Mrs. Scharr said she didn't want Donnie to break her neck. So he showed his courage by putting the blame on me.

On July 15 I flew almost two hours in Bell P-39 #19030, but that wasn't enough because on the following day, I had more proof that I wasn't considered good enough. An instructor, a male student, and I were sent on a cross-country triangle from Battle Creek, Michigan, to Fort Wayne, Indiana, and back. How badly I wanted to lead on at least one of the hops to prove my ability! But the instructor ignored me and concentrated on the other student. I wondered if he thought I'd show up the other student.

The tower operator at Battle Creek had been alerted that one of the three P-39s landing would be piloted by a woman. We made the standard pattern about the field. The instructor landed first, then the male student, and I took the number three position in the echelon. The instructor asked for landing instructions, but neither I nor the other student did. The people in the tower had to use guesswork to figure out which plane held the woman.

We taxied up to operations, cut our switches, and got out. The tower operators came down to meet us, asking, "Who was the last one in?"

The other two pilots looked at me and I answered, "I was."

"See?" said one operator turning to the other, "I told you the gal was the last one in."

I don't know what the instructor thought as the operator crowed, "The woman made the best landing!" I was sorry that he made an issue of my sex. I wished people would forget about it.

But they didn't. From Deming Army Air Field, New Mexico, I received a letter dated July 14. It was written by a former flight student, now a corporal, who had hoped to become a pilot but lacked the college education and the flying time to become an instructor.

Dear Del,

I was desolated when I learned of your latest achievement. The announcement unerringly emphasized an ever widening chasm between us. Imagine an Airacobra pilot associating with that lowest form of birdman — the Cub pilot! . . .

For you I am ecstatic. At long last your skill with the stick and rudder is gaining the recognition it really deserves, You are truly a hot pilot and a pea-shooter!

What a blow you have given man's impudent tolerance of your sex. Women will follow your shining P-39 as it streaks across the sky, and ask themselves:

"What are we? Women or door-mats?"

While your star is ascending, mine is definitely on the wane. I was on furlough from June seventh to June twenty-second. Shortly after returning, my job was taken over by a WAC! As you know, I'd been working at this task for almost nine months. I felt like the forgotten man.

Afraid of becoming a yard-bird, I sweated out a new assignment. To my relief, I was held on in Section One as a dispatcher. Now the blackboard is my constant companion, and I spend my days dispatching AT-11s. I chalk up the daily flight schedule, assign targets, ships, and pilots.

Life here is a dull, monotonous routine.

Everything indicates an early GI boat ride. WACs are flooding the field, moving into every department. Shipping out is becoming an everyday affair here.

So long,

Herman Haarstick

On July 17 Nancy Love received an order from AAF headquarters listing the names of twenty-three women pilots and a request for two more who were at least sixty-four inches tall. They were to report at the Mayflower Hotel in Washington, D. C., no later than midnight July 19 for two weeks temporary duty with Jacqueline Cochran. The assignment was considered too secret for telephone discussion and Cochran assured Love that the necessary orders would be issued to the various commands. (Each command kept track of its own expenses and none could be incurred without proper official orders.)

The hurry-up order did not give Nancy Love much time to relay the information to the ferrying groups where the chosen women were stationed. Half of the newest class at Romulus was listed and Margaret Kerr of the June group was also included. As soon as word got around, I was bombarded with requests. Anyone who had a friend whose name was on the list and hoped to fly around the country with her asked me to take that name off and substitute another. Margaret Kerr's friends were especially persistent.

Kerr appeared to fit into the Ferry Command very well. She didn't complain about flying small planes and she welcomed every mission she got. I considered her an eager beaver. She apparently did not mind being a WAF. Brownie, on the other hand, had voiced her dislike for being called a WAF. She was discontented about flying small aircraft. I winced at her continual pleadings for transitional training, but I was not rude enough to tell her to shut up and wait her turn. Possibly, if Brownie went on the two-week assignment, she might get some experience that would equal transition. But I thought it would be wrong to substitute Brown for Kerr. I vowed that I wouldn't do it.

I now see that I should have discussed the substitution with Brownie to allow her the choice. That evening after I had gone to bed and dozed off, Brownie came in and knelt at my bed, pleading again for transition. She must have gotten wind of the decision which allowed Donahue, McElroy, and Callaghan to ferry AT-16s. I felt that the choice of Callaghan was wise. She had been eligible for the WAFS even before she entered the Cochran school.

When Brownie continued to badger me, I rolled over and said, "I want to sleep. I'm tired."

She remained kneeling at the side of my cot, looking intently into my face. "Put me in transition," she begged.

My answer was to close my eyes and turn my face toward the wall and remain possum-like until she left the room.

I felt frustrated. Why should I use my influence to please someone who thought only of herself? I wouldn't do it even for myself. No one could accuse me of begging. There would *be* no transitional training at Romulus if we original WAFS had not flown more efficiently and safely than the men. Except for the fact that the number of P-39 accidents had embarrassed the 3rd Ferrying Group, I would not have been asked to fly the Airacobra. I was no miracle worker. Indeed, I was sorely pressed for time to do all the office work required of me and to mediate for the rest of the WAFS, which meant taking part in base staff meetings, besides trying to get in flying time whenever I could.

To my regular chores was added the responsibility for moving the latest graduates into the new barracks and orienting them into the Ferry Command. I had been shorthanded from the beginning. On whom could I rely? Thompson was at her home. Poole balked at helping in any way. Burchie had gone to George, but she was never someone to lean on anyway. Donnie didn't hold still for responsibility; no one could saddle her. Only McElroy had the maturity I could count on, but I hated to impose on her. Was it only last December that I had believed it was an honor to be chosen the commanding officer?

The next day the chosen WAFS shipped out to the Mayflower Hotel in Washington, D.C. With them was Brownie.

"Why me?" she asked.

I had no reply. I was too tired to fight.

Years later one of the WAFS who went to Washington told me that Brownie had thought she would be the leader of the group because of her seniority. Looking back on the incident, I realize that I blundered in not valuing what Brownie stood for. She was forthright instead of furtive. When she wanted something, she came straight to me instead of using stealth or subterfuge.

But I worried about her drinking, which she did not hide as drinkers did in Wilmington. I didn't realize that she wasn't the only one of the WPTP graduates who was a heavy drinker until one morning I went into McCormick's room and found her drinking beer before breakfast.

"Hair of the dog that bit me," she simpered.

She shocked me. But that was a trifle compared to the surprises and shocks that were to come later. Others, too, were not what I had thought them to be. Politics is a craft requiring an avid greed, an ability to plot strategy, and a willingness to twist the truth until it practically disappears. The element of surprise is an important, if devastating, factor in intrigue.

FULL CIRCLE

ALL MY PROBLEMS AT ROMULUS faded temporarily when operations ordered me to board SNAFU Airlines along with twenty-nine new P-39 pilots. We were to go to Bell's Niagara Falls plant. On the way, I was allowed to play copilot for half the time. The radio guided us through the overcast. I became very tired, which caused me some concern.

When we landed, Bell representatives greeted us. The cordiality of the employees was one of the nicest things about being at Niagara. It was 2030 by the time we had checked into the hotel, still early for a Saturday night.

Three of the pilots wanted to see Niagara Falls and I went with them. The immensity of it was more conspicuous from the ground than in the air. On the way back I bought some salt water taffy for Harold.

That night I slept in a big and comfortable bed in a quiet hotel room. The respite made a big difference in how I felt the next morning. The torture of trying to sleep on my small, hard barracks cot and the noisy confusion of so many women in the barracks was beginning to turn me into a nervous wreck. When I returned to Romulus, I slept well again. The change was just what I needed.

Adela Scharr honored each WAFS member, in order of seniority, by lettering her name on the fuselage of each fighter plane she ferried. This is number 1, flown July 18, 1943.

On Sunday morning instead of attending church, we thirty pilots attended Bell's school on the Airacobra. We saw films on the hydromatic propeller and listened to lectures about the Allison engine, the electrical system, emergency operating instructions, and various other items that we should have learned about at the base before we soloed.

Then each of us was given the number of an airplane. Mine was #19902. Before I got a chance to find it, someone from the *Bellringer* interviewed me. I told him I wasn't a star. I had no money, no social position, no important husband, no beauty, and no outstanding ability as a pilot. In fact, why was I being interviewed? Despite my reluctance, my picture was taken with the aircraft and I was informed a write-up would appear in the magazine.

I found my airplane and checked it out before take off. My finger was in the gas tank, making sure that the tank was full in case the gauge was faulty, when I was slapped so hard on the back that I almost lost my balance. I turned around to find 2nd Lt. Walter Starck from St. Louis staring me in the face. He told me he was a test pilot for the army and stationed at Bell.

"I'm real interested in helicopters," he said and added, "What makes you so finicky? You're really scared, testing the tank for gas!"

"I always check my airplane in every way that I can," I replied. His air of superiority didn't intimidate me. I didn't care if he thought I was inferior to him. At any rate, I'm still here and soon after the war he lost his life in a helicopter.

While we were making our clearances before we took off, several of the boys began joshing me, saying that they intended to fly on my wings. I thought they all wanted to gang up on me. But the flight leader looked at the entire lot and said, "None of you guys is going to fly on her wing. I'm flying her wing and the rest of you better leave her alone."

I was on separate orders and took off ahead of the others. Soon the flight leader caught up with me. He stayed on my right wing and two of his fledglings remained some distance back in loose formation. I paid no attention to my neighbor, for I was busy with visual navigation. The "electric" compass happened to be right on course, 260 degrees. We knew we had to fly above 2,500 feet and we remained that high, although small patches of clouds were building up beneath us. I kept track of my time and flew as straight as I could, just to show that I knew what I was doing. The checkpoints were hidden half the time, but I knew I was on course. The compass remained in position, steady as a rock. The air was smooth, the weather was perfect.

We had been flying about twenty minutes when one of the flight leader's wingmen turned in a northwesterly direction into Canada. The flight leader abruptly left my wing and chased after his errant flight member. My plane kept boring through the atmosphere as I watched like a hawk for landmarks.

From my chart I could guess what had happened. Two railroads crossed south of Canfield and it was at that point the pilot turned farther into Canada. He must have taken his eyes off his leader, looked at his map, and decided that the railroad toward Brantford was the one to follow. Young pilots admitted that they had never learned dead reckoning well and followed railroads when they could. Railroads went to big towns and big towns had airports. They'd get down somewhere.

In this instance, the pilot may not have been at fault in changing his course so abruptly. The wind was light and planes were landing toward the north as I approached Romulus. I went through the memorized checklist on the downwind leg. Boost, mixture to auto-rich, trim for level flight, altitude 1,000 feet above the field, gas on proper tank, propeller set so I could go around again and abort the landing if need be, mixture double check, landing gear down, flaps down.

As I turned into the final approach, I glanced at the compass along with other instruments. It did not move! It remained on 260 degrees, as it had all the flight. When I was on the ground and changing my direction while taxiing, it never changed position. That was the first item I jotted on form I, even before I wrote that the hop was one hour, forty-five minutes long. I hoped the wingman didn't get his ear chewed off by his flight leader — maybe his compass didn't work either. As for me, it was the only flight I'd ever made by pilotage without a working compass.

Back in the barracks a pile of papers awaited me to read and initial. Among them were the cipherings of flying times and airplane types. Before I went to sleep that night, I mused on the women I had seen working in the Bell factory at Niagara Falls. They had the important job of laying out the electric wiring through the wings and fuselages of the airplanes as they were assembled. How busy they were and how serious! They were dressed in coveralls. Hairnets or scarves covered their heads.

One of the foremen told me, "We couldn't turn out these airplanes without women. The places where they have to put the wires are sometimes so small that a man can't get his hands in there at all. But a woman has such a small hand and she can use it more like a tool. She ain't clumsy and muscle-bound like most men are. And you know what they say about how a woman can repair anything with a hairpin? Yeah, it sure is true. We need these women in this factory."

The women were small, looking like children allowed to join in a man's world. I saw their hands reach into apertures that mine would not fit into. I wondered, was war the only way that women would ever be allowed to show that they could do more than sweeping, dusting, and cooking? Or all the menial tasks that mankind had delegated to them?

I thought of how war had brought women into military nursing; Florence Nightingale in the Crimean War and Clara Barton in the Civil War. During World War I women began to work in factories doing more than sewing. They also began to fill offices as secretaries, file clerks and typists. By that time, even military forces were using them as nurses, drivers and switchboard operators. From the beginning of World War II, they entered parts of factories hitherto off limits. "Rosie, the Riveter" was more than a song during the war. She was a substantial part of the war effort. And, of course, there were the WAFS, doing their part. Pleased with the thought of our accomplishments, I went to sleep.

This photo, showing Adela Scharr surrounded by male ferry pilots, was introduced in the Congressional Record *in 1978, evidence that the WASPs really were military pilots, flying combat aircraft.*

Late in the afternoon of July 20, SNAFU Airlines put me on its manifest for another flight to Niagara Falls. My orders were to pick up P-39 #20427 and bring it to Romulus for minor changes before it would be ferried away.

Once again I would have a quiet night's rest. I was even assigned the same hotel room. I shared the elevator going up with several male pilots and two elderly ladies. I didn't need a bellhop because all I carried was my navigation kit.

The next morning at breakfast one of the pilots sought me out and said, "I held up for you last night."

Not knowing what to expect, I made no reply.

He continued, "Those two old ladies sure gave you a good going over after you left the elevator. They said what a disgrace it was how women behaved these days. They were shocked at how brazen you were, running around in the same hotel they were in, wearing pants, which shouldn't be allowed. They were giving you the very devil and it made me hot under the collar, so I told them they were all wrong. I said they should be thankful you were doing a man's work and that's a lot more'n most other women can do."

The shock of being found unacceptable by members of my own sex left me unable to comment.

The pilot went on. "I said, you don't know, so I'm telling you. That lady wears pants because her job is flying the most dangerous fighter plane there is and she's here in your hotel because it's made right here in Niagara Falls and the planes weren't ready on time, so we have to wait for 'em. She can't wear a skirt to do what she's doing. There ain't room in it for her to carry a lot of fancy clothes just to please people. She's working for the air corps and we're proud to be seen with her any time just like she is."

He was excited and somewhat breathless from his long recital. I was still speechless and aghast at the hateful prejudice my presence had ignited in what appeared to be two harmless elderly ladies. How could they judge me without learning the facts? What further criticism of me was still ahead? My shock at the unexpected attack on my appearance subsided enough for me to mutter "thanks" as small payment to my defender.

I wondered how many other persons had found me unacceptable by their standards. Maybe I should not have left my room. After I had washed my face and combed my hair, I'd left the hotel to see the movie *Stormy Weather* with Ethel Waters. The title now seemed to symbolize the atmosphere I had unknowingly created.

At the Bell factory an official hurriedly gathered all of us pilots together so that a company photographer could take a quick picture of us before we took off. We assembled before a sunny corner of the buff-brick building. In 1978 this photograph was placed in the *Congressional Record* as evidence that women pilots had led a military life during World War II, even though we were classified as civilians. It helped influence Congress to recognize that we were veterans.

I got off the ground at 1120 and sped my lonesome way toward Romulus. Pursuit airplanes move so rapidly that unless pilots purposely fly in formation, the first pilot off is quickly lost to sight. It's a big, vast sky out there when you are the only being boring through it.

I circled once in close proximity to the Niagara air field and put myself over two tiny islands in the river south of town, which were directly on the course line I'd drawn on my chart. Some pilots confessed to me over the years that the speed of the P-39 and other pursuit aircraft so overwhelmed them that they didn't "come to" until they had attained an altitude of 10,000 feet. But I didn't find the P-39 any harder to fly by pilotage than a Piper Cub. In fact, it was easier because the wind could not drift a pilot off course before the next checkpoint came into view. One didn't need patience in waiting for checkpoints to show up as in a Cub.

Very soon I crossed the Welland Canal, about a half mile north of Port Robinson. The small towns of Fonhill, Fenwick, and Welland Port were right on course. I passed right over the tiny island in the Grand River south of Cayuga. The wind was right on my nose, so the flight took fifteen minutes longer than my earlier one. Visibility was unlimited and this time the compass was working.

I no sooner landed at Romulus and "sold" my airplane to operations than they put me on orders to pick another P-39, #29965. I had to be ready to leave on SNAFU at 1500. I barely had time to run past the barracks for a clean shirt and to pick up mail at the post office.

We found that the paperwork on our aircraft had not been completed at Bell, and we were forced to RON. Again the Hotel Niagara assigned me to the same room I'd occupied before. I think the hotel manager was doing his "duty" by keeping the sexes separated, because on all three occasions there I never saw a male pilot on that floor.

I had enough time while I was waiting to write a letter to Harold. I was very lonesome for him. The pain of separation seemed to be getting worse, almost more than I could bear. I also wrote this letter to Kay Thompson:

> My dear Tommy,
>
> Your long-looked-for letter arrived yesterday and, needless to say, the gang was Johnny-on-the-spot to help me read it.
>
> I take it that you really want to come back, but things at home have not adjusted themselves so that you can at this time. We all know what is best in our own particular cases. So we'll leave the answer up to you. But I can tell you that you are terribly missed and we hope that soon you will be sharing the new barracks with us.
>
> Since you left we have the W-2 and the W-3 classes, all of which are very lovely girls. Five of the last group were taken to Washington on special orders. Also Brownie.
>
> Vega Johnson turned out very well as a flight leader. In fact, all the girls in the second class are just about ready to lead flights. Some are doing it already.
>
> I am completing my last shuttle trip on P-39s (factory to base) and now am among the eligible for LONG trips. Maybe to California.
>
> Nancy will be here to take her instrument training sometime in the near future. Then, the rest of us? . . .

The next day the novelty of a female "peashooter" had already worn off at Bell. Before I took off, I took my lipstick from my purse and wrote CORNELIA FORT along the side of the fuselage. The first P-39 I had ferried, I dedicated to Nancy Love and the second to Betty Gillies. I did so for all the WAFS in the order in which they had appeared at Wilmington.

I learned the following year that B. J. Erickson and Evelyn Sharp also made their marks on the pursuit aircraft they ferried. They scratched their names and addresses on the metal instrument panel, which lasted longer than my lipstick notations. Being young, unmarried, and fancy-free, the Long Beach graffiti artists had different motivations from mine.

Back at Romulus at 1330, I was soon at work in the barracks. Nancy had not replied to my letter asking for information about the status of WAFS in relation to transition. After dinner, I planned to go to headquarters again and try to ferret out the directive that I knew must be there, which allowed WAFS at other bases to get transition. I wanted everyone to join me in flying pursuit planes as soon as possible.

Several girls came to my room after dinner before they departed for a local public swimming pool. Some of them had taken Callaghan's lead and called me "Mommy," but Donahue was more inventive and named me "Madame Peashooter." I sensed no hint of malice or envy in the appellation.

"Why don't you go swimming with us?" asked Kerr.

Did I want to? You bet! I loved to swim, but I felt that I didn't have time to play. I tried to imagine what Nancy Love would do. I remembered how we had gone roller skating once in Wilmington and she had declined to join us. She kept herself apart. I decided to follow her lead and do likewise, even though the tomboy within was fighting hard for expression.

"I can't tonight," I said. "There's something I have to do instead."

Kerr's face showed what I thought was disappointment. Did she think I was snubbing her? At any rate, she left in a huff. I should have gone swimming with them. It is what I wanted to do. Instead I sorted through sheaves of directives and gleaned nothing. I returned to the barracks feeling that again I had failed.

The next morning, Friday, July 23, I was scheduled for SNAFU Airlines at 0900, but Colonel de Arce called a meeting of WAFS to discuss the necessity of going through channels to obtain transfers or other requests. He put me on the spot and I "sirred" him up and down. SNAFU had to wait for us until we got out of the meeting. Five WAFS were going to Fort Erie for PT-26s and I was to go to Niagara for my fourth P-39.

But before I could board, Major Hennessey snagged me because General Tunner and Nancy Love were coming, as well as some other notables. I had to greet them as they landed. I ran back to the barracks, took off my coveralls, got dressed in uniform and joined all the big boys dolled up in their blouses and pinks.

As soon as the general and his staff stepped from the DC-3, guns were fired in his honor and he walked through a military guard. I was surprised that General Tunner remembered me, and so did some of the other officers. It was good to see Nancy, who told me that she would try to get an instrument rating within a week or ten days.

I was included in the lunch. I did not like fanfare, but I felt that WAFS needed the prestige of being included among the leaders at Romulus. Strains of martial music drifted from the grassy plot near the officers' club. All the other WAFS were out on missions, except McElroy — and Poole, who as usual was stewing in her own juices. There weren't enough of us to march in the parade honoring Tunner's promotion to brigadier general.

Nancy outlined the transition set-up. Only pilots with more than fifty hours in AT-16 deliveries and with more than 600 hours of flying time would be eligible to fly pursuit. I also found out that Ketcham would be transferred, along with a few other new WAFS, to a post where she'd tow targets. I was to attend instrument school for two or three weeks before I could accept any more missions. I knew that meant I wouldn't get to St. Louis on a mission, so I began to think about asking for a leave. Certainly others were not shy about asking.

I wanted to see Harold very badly. I felt that he was all I had that I could count on. The uncertainty of life during wartime meant change for all of us, civilians and military alike. Those who fought actively bore more stress than anyone else, yet ferry pilots shared with them much uncertainty in not knowing if an accident would take their lives or a friend's life and in not knowing where they would bed down for the night.

Nancy Love must have felt uncertain about retaining her command of the WAFS now that Jacqueline Cochran had been appointed head of all women pilots of the air forces. She and General Tunner clung to the designation they had given to women ferry pilots — WAFS — since Labor Day 1942. But a new name was emerging — WASP, Women Airforce Service Pilots. Cochran was insisting that it be used as the official designation of every army woman pilot. We didn't know that a tug-of-war existed on this issue until it was settled in August. Then Tunner had to concede defeat and WAFS were absorbed by the WASP.

We were also unaware of Cochran's stand on our militarization. The army, navy, marines, and coast guard had enlisted and commissioned women in their services. But Cochran decided that the WASP must not become a part of the WAC, which left us out of the military altogether. She wrote to General Arnold recommending that militarization be withheld from us "until WASPS absolute worth was proved by performance."

What did that mean for us? The WAFS had done well for the Ferrying Division in the previous nine and a half months. Except for several broken props at the beginning, there had been no accidents attributed to WAFS, no breath of scandal, no bounced checks, and no unseemly conduct. No male squadron did any better in accomplishing missions safely and quickly. I had asked for no special favors for the Romulus cadre and never complained about the hardships we endured.

Already the WAFS had delivered many basic and advanced trainers, a cargo aircraft, a B-25, three P-39s, twenty-eight P-47s, and one P-51. Under their leadership during delivery missions, the women graduates of the first two classes from WFTD had thus far been satisfactory. Cochran slapped us down for some reason of her own or because she wasn't sure of the capabilities of those pilots now being trained by her school. At any rate, we were unaware of the thumbs-down she had given us.

I was too busy with my own problems to sort out what Cochran was doing. I felt that my life was caught in an impasse. Harold was unable to visit me to boost my morale because he was always on duty. I couldn't get home to see him because of my squadron duties and now transition in instrument school loomed ahead. My inability to find a way to get transition for other women irked me. The spotting of blood at the middle of my monthly menstrual cycle was a nagging worry. And I was always tired.

Bleeding is one of the sure signs of cancer. Did I have it? Cancer was then incurable. The time to do something about that problem was now. Yet I backed away from the necessary pelvic exam. I had never had one. Should I turn to the flight surgeon? No! He was a stranger to me and probably knew nothing about gynecology. Would he ground me until he could make a diagnosis? I'd wasted enough time on the ground already.

Modesty was a fetish in my family. It had kept us from evil; now it was keeping me from good. I had to break through my fear of exposure, I thought. The doctor who had performed an emergency appendectomy on me in 1933 must have seen the skin on my abdomen at that time. I reasoned that if he saw it a second time I might not be too embarrassed. He was kind and gentle. He was the doctor I must see as soon as possible.

I couldn't find Nancy to discuss this with her. She was probably getting instrument instruction from Lieutenant Colonel Dunlap, and she had many friends in the Detroit area who kept her evenings busy. I doubted that she would notice that I wasn't on deck. Besides, she wasn't at Romulus to act as my supervisor.

Colonel de Arce gave me several minutes of his time in his office. I told him that I thought I might have cancer and wanted to be checked by my own physician. If I could go to St. Louis on Sunday, I could see him on Monday, and be back by Tuesday.

His eyes twinkled. He might have been imagining where I had the problem I thought was cancer. Or maybe he thought I was being inventive and it was such a good try that he'd give me the time off. He didn't ask me if I had Love's permission; he simply gave me his.

McElroy said she'd keep track of the flight time on those who had returned from missions. She was already in AT-9 transition and making the best landings of any student the school had.

I left for St. Louis. Dr. Gundlach examined me, I had a few hours with Harold, and then I was back again.

"How did it go?" asked McElroy.

"The doctor could find nothing wrong, but he can't explain what causes the bleeding. At least it's not going to ground me yet."

Within the week Major Hennessey asked me for a report on how the new WAFS behaved on missions. I sent him the following:

SUBJECT: NEW WAFS

TO: S-3, Third Ferrying Group, Romulus, Michigan
    Attention: Major Hennessey

1. The graduates of the Training Schools at Sweetwater and Houston who have reported to this station have displayed satisfactory ability in the handling of aircraft. Their aptitude in learning cross-country navigation has been good.

2. All graduates on flying status have flown over 30 hours on missions in the first ⅔ of July. Eight have flown more than 50 hours, which shows efficiency.

3. Most of the girls have a cooperative attitude. The biggest objection by flight leaders has been that a few of W-1 have shown resentment in being called WAFS instead of Women Pilots. The impression they received at Houston was that they would be no part of the Women's Auxiliary Ferrying Squadron. Gertrude Brown, Vega Johnson, and Marjorie Ketcham embarrassed original WAFS on mission in several situations when they were a little odd in behavior about this misunderstanding. On two occasions, the girls were unwilling to return to the 3rd Ferrying Group with their flight leaders and on the missions they disobeyed the request of the flight leader as to the altitude to be flown over the terrain.

4. The squadron leader, Adela R. Scharr, handled the situation so that no further difficulty was evidenced and reported.

In cases like this, I wished that I had had officers' training or some orientation in what was expected of me in official communications.

Nancy had taken up lodging again in Donahue's room across the hall from me. She preferred being there and I made no attempt to try to change her mind. It was a livelier place than my room. Donahue's loud voice could be heard when she was awake. When she slept, she snored. Nancy had a radio with her which she played before falling asleep. It continued to play thereafter. My sensitive ears would not allow me to sleep with noise assaulting my nerves. I said nothing about it, of course, and used my sleepless time writing letters or finishing my paperwork. But it was a disturbance I felt I could do without.

I was working the first night of my return from St. Louis when one of the new arrivals appeared suddenly at my door. Frowning, her large brown eyes searching mine wildly, Mary Ahlstrom was obviously disturbed. Without speaking, my facial expression asked a question.

"I can't get any sleep!" she whispered unhappily.

"What's the matter?" I whispered back.

"Somebody's got a radio going and it bothers me. I can't get to sleep. I can't stand any noise."

I was sympathetic. Her room was at the other end of the long hall and yet I knew she was being disturbed by Nancy's radio. The sound was carried along by the floor and the walls and up to the girl's pillow through the bed itself.

Ahlstrom had to fly the next day. I would never forgive myself if something happened to her. I tiptoed across the hall and peeked into Donahue's room. The radio was blasting away. Nancy looked as if she were sound asleep. There was no longer a need for the noise. I stepped softly inside and watched Nancy's breathing. I turned to Ahlstrom at the door and shook my head affirmatively, reached down and turned the volume knob until it clicked off. Then I tiptoed out. I would not have had the nerve to do it for myself, but I didn't hesitate in doing it for someone else. In a jiffy my light was out and I was wooing the sandman, too.

But my mind was still too active to sleep. I reflected on the addition of Sam Dunlap, the new officer in transition, to the base. Was he General Tunner's solution to the high accident rate of Romulus pilots? My stomach jumped and my rib cage shook with silent laughter at the remembrance of the day when he had ordered those of us in transition to assemble at the takeoff end of the runway. We were the audience to his demonstration of the P-39 as an airplane in which one could make mistakes and still not get hurt.

The day he had chosen for the demonstration was perfect, neither too warm nor too gusty nor clouded by a low ceiling. The men acted like boys who didn't want to watch someone else play the expert. They'd rather be flying themselves. Dunlap took off on the longest runway without using flaps. One fellow grumbled that he should have done it on the short runway and see where he'd end up.

I didn't pay too much attention to what Dunlap did in the air. As for stupid mistakes, I had no intention of making any in the first place. My formulas for safety were already locked in and I'd keep them that way.

After landing, Dunlap acted as if he forgot to put his flaps up. Someone commented that such a lapse wasn't something a guy could break his neck doing. What did it show us?

"Why didn't he wrap it into a tight turn on final?" scoffed another. "I'd like to see him get out of something like that."

More critical witticisms were followed by raucous masculine laughter. The group milled about, not knowing how long to remain there. At last Dunlap approached us in the "Follow Me" jeep and gave us a pep talk. Then we were dismissed.

Dunlap's manner and bearing displayed the high regard he had for himself. I guessed that the show that he put on was in response to his orders. He did the best he could to appear careless without breaking his neck, which he must have considered too precious to snap.

I thought Dunlap would be happy with Nancy on the base. I hadn't seen either him or Nancy around. Maybe he had taken her under his wing, as he had done at Long Beach when he got so much transition for her. But that was no business of mine. I had enough to do without prying into what she was doing with her time. She'd always been aloof from everyone except Betty Gillies, so the situation wasn't new to me.

I was very concerned, on the other hand, about the welfare of a little chick in W-2, Marion Schorr. She was in her early twenties and her enthusiasm for flying shone in her large, dark brown eyes. She seemed impressionable and I was afraid someone would take advantage of her. Captain Brown, the officer in transition who had okayed me for the AT-6, was one of the most exciting men on the base. People looked up to him with awe. Marion was quite taken by his personality. I thought he was married, but I could have been mistaken.

One evening about nine o'clock, I saw Marion tiptoe past my room and leave the barracks. The clandestine way she left led me to guess that she had a date with Brown. Maybe it was just a chance to ride in an airplane, an opportunity to handle the controls, but flying without being chosen for instruction had been strictly forbidden to the original WAFS. I decided to wait and see if Brown were a wolf howling at her before I embarrassed Marion with my admonitions.

(That the attraction between these two pilots was mutual and lasting was evidenced by the fact that after Marion was no longer married to the man she wedded later and Brown was also free, they married each other.)

I was also still uneasy about Brownie. I hoped that she was sitting in a bigger and better airplane than if she had remained at Romulus. Later I found out that she was the leader in charge of the group of women pilots deployed by Cochran from the Ferry Command. That made me feel better.

And I didn't know if Poole would make good on her threats to quit. But I couldn't keep worrying about my squadron all night. Finally I fell asleep.

During the last week in July, Nancy saw me at lunchtime and said, "Del, I want a talk with you."

I nodded my head. No inkling of the subject was given. I thought it was nice that Nancy could spare some of her time to let me know what was going on.

After lunch I joined Nancy and we walked from the mess to our new home, a barracks that men had vacated for us. She was quiet. I was happy in anticipation of our talk, self-confident about my success with the P-39 and looking forward to ferrying it on long missions. I had just learned from operations that I could fly by myself on single orders while all the other pilots must be led cross-country for another fifty hours by a flight leader. It was a boost for the WAFS. The fear of cancer had fled my mind. I welcomed the future.

To break the silence, I said, "This Michigan weather is getting more like Missouri. I'm glad they say it won't get much hotter than the eighties in the summer."

There was no reply. We had reached the barracks and Nancy led the way through the lower floor hall until she reached a room where Lillian Conner was asleep on a cot, face up, seemingly dead to the world.

From that room a doorway had been cut into an adjacent room. Nancy led me in and stopped beside a cot, where she sat down. I took a seat on another cot facing her and waited.

I wondered why Nancy had chosen this room. Our talking might disturb Lillian. She needed the rest. All the Romulus WAFS were making delivery records that month. I would not have thought Nancy would be so thoughtless.

"You realize, Del," Nancy began, "that there's a great deal wrong at this base."

I was glad that at last she knew about how life for us wasn't as pleasant as it was for those at Dallas and Long Beach.

"There's a lot of criticism about the carelessness of the women in this squadron in their dress while out on missions."

I answered, "You told me about that the last time you were here.

Typical "raunchy" appearance of male ferry pilots in hot weather. Cotton khaki wrinkled easily, especially beneath parachute straps and seat harnesses. These pilots were just starting a mission.

Another group of rumpled ferry pilots about to leave the Bell factory in Buffalo.

I've urged the girls to take the time allowed them to get their clothes in order before they go out on another mission. They leave the base looking all right. But you wouldn't believe the crazy places where they've delivered and then all the time it takes getting back here on buses and trains — they're not as clean and fast as the airlines.''

I was proud of the Romulus squadron. To me, the fault of some untidiness was outweighed by the work they'd been doing.

"I've been getting some rough criticism," continued Nancy, "about the appearance of girls on missions all across the country and the worst are from this base." She must have meant from Cochran, I thought.

I saw that I was not getting through to her. I said, "Have you seen our bulletin board? These girls have really been working. Some got in eighty hours this month alone and almost everyone has at least fifty. Then to have to get back to base . . . They fly long hours and the weather is hot. A wrinkled shirt can happen on a long mission. When you think of what they put up with — ''

I could tell that Nancy wasn't accepting my reasoning because of the way she had placed her hand on her hip and stared at me. Abruptly she changed her tack, although maintaining the critical course of her conversation.

"There have got to be changes made in this squadron," she said firmly.

Well, I'd be agreeable to that. What was she leading up to? More transition for the girls? A clerk assigned to the office to help with the load of work? Was Poole going to be let go?

Instead, Nancy stated, "I'll come directly to the point. I have reports on you that as the squadron leader you are totally selfish. I am taking you out of your position."

A hot wave struck my face with a violent slap. The flush overwhelmed me and the sudden blow left me momentarily speechless.

I thought, selfish? Me? How could she say such a thing? And then I worried that our talking had wakened Lillian and I didn't want her to hear the cruel and unjust things Nancy had said to me. Why, since this was official business, hadn't Nancy chosen my office bedroom instead of this room to air her grievance? My muscles tensed as Nancy continued.

"You are very unpopular. None of the girls likes you. I think the best solution is for you to step down."

I began to get my bearings, trying to focus on this new, strange problem. I was still so stunned as to feel almost witless. Me, not the leader any longer? I didn't like the idea at all. Like other strange problems I had had to face, such as soloing the P-39, I began to tackle it rationally.

"If you can tell me in what way I'm disliked, I'll remedy it," I replied.

"I can't tell you without involving personalities," she said. "It would only cause great unpleasantness."

"I still ought to know what's the matter so I can explain my side," I said.

"No, that won't work. Because you can't change yourself. A leopard never changes its spots."

Now I'm a wild beast in her eyes, I thought. She gave me no way to defend myself. I felt miserable.

"Why in the world should you think that the girls don't like me?" I asked.

"Because there are entirely too many requests for transfers out of this base. For instance, where is Phyllis Burchfield?"

"George was going to have an operation and she wanted time off to be with him."

"Then why would she want to be stationed at Long Beach?"

"I don't know, except that I heard he was transferred from Lockbourne and sent to California."

"Where is Katherine Thompson?"

"She had to go home for a while on some business. And Ted was griping about her being so far away in Romulus. She said he wants her there in Florida to see him every time he returns from a ferry mission across the South Atlantic. It has nothing to do with me."

"I simply cannot believe your excuses about either of these WAFS."

I was telling her what the girls had told me and she didn't accept it. I didn't want to snitch on Donahue about what she'd done to Burchie's uniform nor mention that gossip might have gotten to Ted about Kay and Lee Wahl.

"You know that girls have asked for transfer from Romulus without going through proper channels?" Nancy asked.

"I know you wrote me about Poole asking to go where she could fly bigger stuff and Donahue wanting to go with her if she got it. That's okay now, I think. Poole just hated this place in the winter."

"Then there's Elizabeth McKinley." Nancy's voice was icy.

I was surprised. "She never said a word about not liking it here. All I know is when she came she was disappointed that they sent her buddy Marge Kumler to a different base and McKinley wanted to be with her. It sounded to me like two school kids wanting to be in the same class. I thought she'd gotten over it."

"Well, she asked for a transfer to Long Beach."

"I didn't know about that," I said.

"Something has been wrong here at Romulus since the beginning," declared Nancy.

Although no softness or hesitancy appeared in Nancy's manner, I risked saying more because I was curious. I'd seen school principals who certainly were not popular with their teachers, but they were never demoted. Instead, the complaining teacher was transferred. A transfer was what these women wanted. By complaining, perhaps they hoped to be transferred and I would remain at Romulus.

"Getting back to the girls disliking me," I said. "They act as if they are proud of me and admire me for flying the P-39. And I've told them that they would get to do it, too. I've said that anyone who can fly a Piper Cub like it should be flown can fly pursuit."

Nancy only stared at me. Was she the one who was unhappy with me? I wondered why. And why wasn't she chastising the girls who hadn't gone through the proper channels?

"I'd like to know what selfish things I've done as a CO that I shouldn't have done," I said.

Nancy replied, "You haven't spent as much time at your desk as you should. I expect each squadron leader not to leave the base on missions, but to do her administrative work for which she was appointed. There is increasing responsibility as the new girls come in and there'll be more of them as time goes on."

"But, Nancy," I said in defense, "I have had fewer missions than anyone. Except for an AT-16 flight with Donahue and McElroy, I've been at my desk every day since the middle of May. Last week I went to Niagara Falls in the evening and got back by the next afternoon, so I was really gone only overnight."

"I expect every squadron leader to remain at her desk and you are no exception," she replied.

I thought she was being unreasonable. We had all come into the Ferry Command to perform missions. We came to fly airplanes, not desks. Why was she singling me out? What about the other leaders? My hunch was that they had made more missions than I. Betty had sent me a postcard saying that she had a nice one by herself in a new airplane that she was the first to fly. What was the reason for the attack on me? I was bewildered. A sinking feeling nauseated me.

"We shall talk about this some more later," said Nancy. "But my mind is made up. No further discussion is necessary."

She stood up and left me, shattered, disappearing into the room where Lillian Conner still lay asleep. I rose, left the room slowly through the hall entrance, and walked to my room. There I lay on my bed, my mind numb, a blank. Yet thoughts surfaced in a jumble. No matter what tumbled forth, none showed the way back to my happy life as it had been in the morning.

I felt that I had disgraced Harold's name. I never meant to do anything but make him proud and happy that I was his wife. Now I would have to tell him about this. Would he love me less? I'd be dejected forever without him to console me.

Nancy had said that things were wrong at Romulus from the beginning. Yes, for me, too, from the beginning. Why was I put on a mission I couldn't return from in time to arrive at the base with the rest of my squadron? Florene had been ordered to leave the mission so she'd be back in Wilmington in time to accompany Nancy to Dallas. And B. J. went with Nancy to Long Beach. Only I had received no guidance from her. I suspected that Rhonie was Nancy's first choice at Romulus, except for her sharp tongue and chronic envy. Nancy must not have wanted me here. Perhaps Betty Gillies persuaded her to put me in as leader.

Was Nancy interested only in getting to fly more airplanes first? Was she angry because I had flown the P-39 before her? If I hadn't, Donahue surely would have. Was there more I didn't know?

I don't know how long I moped in my room. I put all the latest flying hours on the WASP records, as they were now designated. At last Claire Callaghan rapped at the door jam, looked in, and asked, "Are you going to eat?"

Eat? The word gagged me.

"I'm not eating," I replied, trying to hide the anguish I knew my face disclosed.

"You've got to eat, Mommy," Callaghan declared. "Come on, eat with us." She and Ellen Gery, whom she'd teamed up with, were bound for the officers' club.

Nancy couldn't have meant that all the girls didn't like me, I thought as my mind raced over my dealings with these two. Often one or the other came to me about a point of difference they'd had about aerodynamics or power plants. My opinion would decide the issue for them. Callaghan was invariably right. So I told Callaghan my problem — there had been too many requests for transfers outside the proper channels, Romulus WAFS had been seen dressed carelessly in unclean clothes on missions, and that the girls hated me.

Callaghan took no sides. She said, "Whatever you think the problem is, it's going to hurt *you* if you don't eat. So come with us."

I did, although I had no appetite.

Nancy stopped me for a moment in the hall the next morning. She said, "You won't be placed on orders at this time. I shall speak to Colonel de Arce today.''

I was left in limbo.

Later, from my barracks window, I noticed a group of women pilots crossing a grassy area in the direction of the administration building. Nancy Love? Why was she walking with Barbara Poole, Barbara Donahue, Margaret Kerr, Margaret Ann Hamilton, and who else? I saw that Claire Callaghan was also walking in the same direction. I could see there was discussion in the group and Nancy looked back at her. Immediately the group turned forty-five degrees to right of their original course. Just as promptly, Callaghan changed her course to coincide with theirs. Again Nancy looked back. Then the group assumed its original direction and Callaghan continued to follow them.

Suddenly I understood. Nancy's conference with Colonel de Arce was a kangaroo court. I was watching my accusers, who would also be my jurors and judges. I would have no right to meet them face to face, no right to a self-defense against the charges brought against me, and no justice. The hopelessness of my situation sickened me.

I thought of marching right after them and barging in on their phony trial, demanding fairness. But that behavior would be tactless and undignified. I could not bring myself to be so gauche. So I waited tensely for the guillotine which would end my military flying career and my honor.

Claire Callaghan told me later that she tried to enter the "courtroom" with the others, but was not allowed to do so. She remained outside Colonel de Arce's office until the others had left. Determined, she insisted on speaking with the colonel to tell him how much the women pilots liked me and why.

Colonel de Arce's secretary telephoned me later, asking me to report to his office as soon as I could. I went docilely, like a good soldier, no matter what was in the offing. The colonel was quite pleasant. I brought up the subject of my remaining at Romulus as an instructor in pursuit.

After I presented my side as well as I could, he said, ''I don't know what is wrong. The girls seem to like you and everyone respects your flying. I have nothing against you as a squadron commander. But whatever Mrs. Love wants, she gets. Since this is what she wants, you will step down as commanding officer.''

I wrote to Harold about the interview on July 30, ''Colonel de Arce doesn't want to lose me and said he'd speak to Nancy about my being on the field here instructing in pursuit. I hate to leave, too. But he said that a transfer would be the fairest to me. It's being done every day and the service tries to put people where they are best suited. He's a nice gent. He says if I quit I'd really be doing the wrong thing because it's the bigger airplanes I belong in and I'd not be giving my best if I went back to primary . . . Or is it malarkey they're feeding me?''

The tone of my letter was somewhat aloof. I still wasn't sure of Harold's reaction to my new status. I thought he probably had too many problems of his own to think about mine. Callaghan had called him earlier to tell him — I was afraid I'd weep if I'd talked to him myself and I didn't want to make a fool of myself.

I hated getting rid of the title of leader after carrying it for so long, and I thought I'd even miss the awful burden of responsibility. But I could also see that life would be a little more fun minus the worries. I could spare some time to be sociable again. On the other hand, I wanted to reap the reward of carrying the donkey through the dark days of last winter and spring. Most of all I wanted reassurance that Harold still loved me. I sent my letter to him airmail special delivery. Harold's reply came back at once and set my mind at ease.

Dearest Del,

Just received your letter and am sorry for you for what happened at the base. I had a hunch at the time you came home last week [for the doctor's exam] that you should not have left with Nancy there and you not there to protect yourself. I thought there would be some back-stabbing with the two B's present and you absent. I don't want you to feel that you are saddling me with troubles because you are not and I want you to feel free to tell me your troubles anytime you want to. Aren't we united?

I don't know what to say about your coming home for two weeks, as I want you to, yet don't like to say yes and then receive orders to shove off before you even get here. Some of the orders these men receive call for leaving right away. *However you do what you like* and carry on like a good trooper if I don't see you right away. I love you very much whether you are one pilot or a squadron commander. After all, love is the only thing that counts and Lord knows I love you a whole lot. So, keep your chin up and don't let those back-stabbers get the best of you. . . .

On Sunday Nancy told me quite casually, ''I called Colonel Baker and he said that you will be placed in P-47 transition as soon as you arrive on base.''

I thought, at least now I know where I'm going — back to Wilmington. I considered that base a drag for all its pilots, but perhaps I could be busy there. I wanted to be busy.

''Your orders will be cut tomorrow, so you can clear the base immediately,'' Nancy said.

''I'd like to go home to see Harold before I report,'' I answered.

"You can take a few days for that," she said.

A few days? I couldn't face Wilmington without some recuperation. I was dragging, exhausted from the hard race that I had just lost, and my adrenalin was depleted.

On Monday, August 2, I began the rounds of the base armed with special orders #189, which had an addendum labeled AGV — "Authority is granted to vary itinerary and to proceed to points necessary for performance of this mission."

There was my loophole. A longer rest was necessary for performance of any mission. Immediately I sent a telegram to Colonel Baker asking for the two weeks' leave I knew was coming to me.

At the Romulus supply depot I discovered that I had a problem. When I returned during the winter, I had found the pilot lockers torn up and the enlisted men in the process of moving all belongings from each cubbyhole into a different stashing area. My goatskin jacket had been lost. There was no question that it belonged to me. My surname was on a leather patch which was stitched to the left upper front. Those in charge pretended no responsibility, so I paid for the jacket.

Clearing the base didn't take as long as I thought it would. I took time off to drop by the barracks to put odds and ends into my footlockers and then went back to my official departure regime. While I was in my room packing, one of the W-2 girls, Mary Darling, walked past, looked into my room, came back to watch, and asked, "Where are you going, Del?"

Startled, I looked up at her large, bold, blue eyes and then fastened my gaze on the mass of her blonde hair without knowing what to answer. Certainly she knew what was going on, I thought. Why did she ask? Was she baiting me so I'd show my emotions and then she could relate the incident to my critics? I decided not to give her the satisfaction. Without replying, I retained my deadpan expression, lowered my eyes to my task, and continued packing. Mary left and walked on down the hall. I never learned if she had a part in the unfair trial. At the time, I was taking no chances and putting out no clues for anyone to crow about.

The room was almost as clean as if I had never lived in it. I made sure by double-checking, even under the mattress. All that was left were several handkerchiefs, hanging on my clothes line. I'd get them later. After lunch I went past headquarters to turn in my clearance and to find out what commercial transportation was available. Too long to wait, I thought. Back at the barracks, I took a chance and telephoned operations.

"Is there a delivery going through Lambert Field that I could hitch a ride on?'' I asked.

"Yes,'' was the reply. "Captain Pusey is taking a B-24 to Wichita. He's taking off within an hour, as soon as he's checked the plane."

"May I speak to him?"

After a short wait, Pusey was on the phone.

"Hi," I said. "Can you give me a lift to St. Louis? WAF Scharr."

"I knew it was you by your voice," he said. "Sure thing, Scharr. If you can get right over here. We'll be leaving in a few minutes."

"I've got a B-4 bag and foot locker. Can I take them along?"

"Sure, kid. Make it snappy and I'll put you down on the manifest."

Hastily I hung up and phoned the motor pool for transportation to the flight line. I was told that a jeep would arrive in a few minutes. I dragged one footlocker to the barracks door, then I ran back for the B-4 bag. Lenore heard the noise and came to where I was hurriedly tossing the damp hankies and the clothesline into the other footlocker.

"Listen, Lenore," I said. "Do me a favor and send this locker to Wilmington. I'm going home on a B-24."

McElroy said nervously, "I didn't think you'd leave yet. Wait. I have something for you."

She ran away and returned bearing a small cosmetic case covered in maroon imitation leather. Breathlessly she said, "The girls want you to have this as a going away present."

My stomach made a tight knot. I stared at it coldly.

"I don't want it. I can't accept anything — not now!"

"Oh, Del, but you must," she entreated. "Here. Take it with you. They really want you to have it."

What could I do? There was no time to argue or I'd miss my ride. I didn't know who contributed to the purchase of the case. I believed that there were some at Romulus who liked me. I'd hurt their feelings if I scorned their show of friendship. As for the others — giving me a gift would be in keeping with the hypocrites they were. They would love to rub salt into my wounds.

I had no use for such a case. But at Mac's urging, I took it with me, stuck it in a closet at home, and years later gave it away without ever having used it. I couldn't.

The driver carried the footlocker and put it in the back seat of the jeep. I tossed in the B-4 bag and climbed in to sit with the driver. Mac and I called "good-bye!" to each other, and I turned my back on the Romulus barracks — I hoped forever.

I ran into operations to let Pusey know I had arrived. He added my name to the manifest. An enlisted man put my luggage in the plane and within minutes I was on my way home.

Pusey asked the copilot to give up his seat and allow me to sit in it. "You want to fly it?" Pusey asked me.

Silly boy! Why not!?

"I haven't seen you since we danced together," he said. "I don't know what happened, but they sent me on detached duty to ferry B-25s from Kansas City. Boy! Was I lucky. I got to be home with my wife."

The B-24 was in and out of clouds all along the way. I found that flying the big ship on instruments and then switching to contact flying was a strain. When we arrived at Lambert Field, we found the runway in use was old #3, to the southeast. The grain elevator stood on the approach to the field. Pusey had a sticky time getting around it and back so he could line up with the runway. But he made a good landing and we rolled to just short of the fence outside of the new naval air station.

Our paths crossed months later at another air base, and Pusey told me that when he landed at Wichita that day and taxied to a parking spot, the hydraulic braking system let loose and he had no more brakes. He shuddered to think what might have happened if the fluid pressure had disappeared during his landing at Lambert.

In a matter of minutes, Harold was there. He greeted me by gently enfolding me in his arms and touching his lips lightly to mine. Harold never displayed the depth of his emotions publicly; he always maintained his dignity. From his touch and his eyes searching mine, I knew that he still loved me, no matter what.

"Would you like to go up and see how the old folks are?" he asked.

I nodded my head yes.

He loaded my luggage into the trunk of our dark blue Ford and we drove north on Lindbergh and Old Jamestown Road to where my parents had built their little brick house and planted a line of cedars along the road. We said little on the way, but he reached over and took my hand. In my heart I had already come home.

At the sound of a car stopping in their driveway, my mother came expectantly from the breezeway to greet us.

"Oh, you've come home for the funeral!" she surmised.

I was puzzled. "Funeral? What funeral?" I asked.

She studied my face in disbelief. "You know," she said. "Your boss's funeral. Major Robertson. He died in the glider crash."

And so I learned for the first time of the tragedy that had occurred a few days earlier at Lambert Field. The mayor of St. Louis, the president of the Chamber of Commerce, and several other dignitaries, including Major Robertson, were killed when the glider in which they were riding lost a wing and fell 2,000 feet to the earth before a huge crowd of spectators. It was a disaster that took the city months to

Much of the civic leadership of St. Louis was wiped out in the crash of a glider at Lambert Field on August 1, 1943. Included was Adela Scharr's old boss, Maj. William B. Robertson, third from right.

recover from.

My mother always prepared-a meal as if diners would want second and third helpings. No one left her table hungry. I kept up a good face and did not share my news with them. I wanted to leave unsaid whatever might give them pain.

"I'll be home for a week or so," I said, "and then I'm off to Wilmington to check out in the P-47."

My parents didn't understand military matters; they were satisfied with the explanation. I vowed to keep just as dumb about the matter with anyone I met thereafter. I would stay walled in from everyone — strangers, friends, and those who caused my downfall.

Later, when we were alone, Harold listened gravely and quietly as I told him the details.

"You made a mistake in coming home when Nancy was on the base," he said. "You should have asked her permission first."

"I didn't see it that way. She was busy. We hardly ever saw her. I asked the colonel and he said it was okay."

"You shouldn't have trusted those two Barbaras. I told you that before."

"I hate to say it, but I was afraid Poole might do something underhanded to harm me, so I always locked my door when I was out of the barracks."

"How come?"

"I couldn't forget the story she told about being in boarding school and starting a fire because she didn't like it. She's so moody at times I wasn't taking a chance on getting hurt."

"And didn't Donahue try to beat you out with the P-39?"

"Yes, I know."

"You've had a lot of work and not much fun with the CO job," Harold commented and I agreed. "Then, who would want it?" he mused.

"Nobody." Certainly no one had showed me any ambition in that direction.

"Is there something coming up you haven't told me about? Anything that might make your job attractive to someone else?"

I thought for a while. "Well, Nancy confided in me several weeks ago that we were supposed to be militarized soon and when we were, I'd have a higher rank than the others. I'd be a captain."

"That's it," he said. "That's what somebody is after."

"But getting it this way isn't fair!"

"Who is fair? I've seen stuff pulled off for rank several times. They take a gamble and play to win. Who are your gamblers at Romulus?"

"You know who they are."

"Poole's bitched a lot to Love, hasn't she?"

"Uh huh," I said.

"Burchie and Thompson aren't even on deck. McElroy is out. So unless Love brings in someone from another base —"

"But she's impossible!"

"Wait and see," Harold advised.

I had the time to "wait and see" at last. On August 4 I received a telegram from Colonel Baker giving me two weeks leave. I didn't have to report to Wilmington until August 19. During the days of my recuperation, Harold went to the naval air station daily. I lay in bed, waiting for my adrenalin to activate me. From experience I knew that time and quiet would put me back in commission. Fortunately, Harold understood. So did my parents.

Harold and I talked often about our future. He hoped that the navy would make him an officer since he had his commercial license. We searched our souls for the path I should take. I knew that, no matter what Nancy Love or those at Romulus said, I was a responsible and intelligent pilot who could fly anything if given a chance. Our country needed me. I must go to Wilmington, even though my pride had been injured. I would be reminded of that hurt many times, no doubt, but I would take it because I had to do something for the war effort. I would help bring Harold back from wherever he'd be sent and then we could return to a normal life. And there was always the hope that I'd be vindicated, that there was some fairness in the Ferry Command.

After a few days, the long-awaited blow came, and Harold received orders to report to the naval air station at San Diego. We began to pack at once. As we did so, I wondered, why didn't Nancy allow me to go to Long Beach? Now I'd be going east and he'd be going west. When would we meet again? I tried not to think about it as I washed and pressed the clothes and put some food on the table.

We had to make some quick decisions. Should we rent our flat? Housing was at a premium, but rents had been frozen, so we probably couldn't get much for it. I was leery of trusting strangers to take care of our new furniture and beautiful hardwood floors. Harold suggested we keep it vacant so that my mother could use it when she came in town to the doctor or to go shopping. And I'd drop by now and then to check on it.

Then we had to decide what to do with our Ford. We had had it only a year and it was in excellent condition. As soon as Harold left, I took it to the car dealer who had sold it to us. The manager agreed to give us the money he'd get for it and guaranteed that he'd sell us the first car available after the war. We found out that his word of honor was not nearly as strong as his desire for profit. I did not get delivery of an automobile until Valentine's Day 1948 and then only after informing the local Ford distributor.

I gave the few ration stamps alloted to us for gasoline to my father. My parents lived far from town and markets. They needed gasoline to drive to the doctor or to purchase food.

Reluctantly I began to pack, too. But where was my other footlocker? Hurriedly I wrote to Lenore McElroy asking her to send it on to Wilmington. It was a good thing I did, for the footlocker was still where I had left it. Mac had been very perceptive. She must have sensed that if she sent the locker to Wilmington, I might never see it again. If she sent it to my home, it could serve as an anchor to prevent me from returning to military life. How could she be sure that the patriotism which drew me to Wilmington in the first place was still strong enough to pull me there once more?

My sense of failure overwhelmed me. Again and again my mind

went back to what I had overlooked or handled badly. Was Cochran the one who had criticized the appearance of the Romulus WAFS? Had the malcontents gone directly to her for transfers and ignored military custom? Did Nancy have to show her muscle to Cochran — or her spirit of cooperation? Was I the whipping boy? Or was I, like Burchie, the butt of a joke? Had the newcomers played a political game to divest an incumbent of her office once a prize was in the offing? What a tangle to unravel if only I could!

At Wilmington I'd be flying P-47s. I might learn from Betty Gillies how she was able to keep her squadron happy, if indeed she had.

Although sick at heart and feeling humiliated, I had to go to Wilmington. It was the best way I had to help win the war and bring Harold home. Only eleven months earlier I had gone in the same direction with high hopes and an almost incredible naivete. My innocence had been shattered, but not my spirit, nor my determination. Thus the wheel of fortune came around full circle.

───────   ───────   ───────

Volume II
Sisters in the Sky

The course of the war overseas brought the WAFS into military life. As Allied fortunes changed, the WASP (Women's Airforce Service Pilots) was begun. In the WASP volume, which follows this view of the WAFS history, it is explained how forces developed, pro and con, to determine how far the WASPs matured and advanced as military pilots. Politics in the armed forces and in Congress are factors over which the WASPs had little influence, busy as they were and unimportant numerically. The reader will fly vicariously with them into danger (which most of them survived), share their personal problems, their victories, and their defeats. Although many individuals cited in the first book will continue on in the next, a large number of newcomers will be introduced in volume II.